Roads Through Mwinilunga

Afrika-Studiecentrum Series

VOLUME 38

The titles published in this series are listed at *brill.com/asc*

Roads Through Mwinilunga

A History of Social Change in Northwest Zambia

By

Iva Peša

BRILL

LEIDEN | BOSTON

Cover illustration: A Road in Mwinilunga, 2008, Iva Peša
View from Kabanda in Mwinilunga, 2010, Iva Peša

The Library of Congress Cataloging-in-Publication Data is available online at http://catalog.loc.gov
LC record available at http://lccn.loc.gov/

Typeface for the Latin, Greek, and Cyrillic scripts: "Brill". See and download: brill.com/brill-typeface.

ISSN 1570-9310
ISBN 978-90-04-40790-9 (paperback)
ISBN 978-90-04-40896-8 (e-book)

This book is printed on acid-free paper and produced in a sustainable manner.

Printed by Printforce, the Netherlands

For Gibby Kamuhuza and Julian Chiyezhi

∵

Contents

Acknowledgements   XI
List of illustrations   XIII

Introduction   1
1   Conceptualising Social Change: The Rhodes Livingstone Institute and
     Victor Turner   13
2   Reconceptualising Continuity and Change: Narratives,
     Representations, and Theories   17
3   Continuity and Change in Central African Historiography   21
4   A Local History of Social Change   29
5   Approach, Aims, and Method   32
6   Chapter Outline   38

1   Paths to the Past: Continuity and Change in Mwinilunga,
    c. 1750s–1970s   43
1   Constructing a Region: The Lunda Polity, History, and
     Reproduction   45
2   A Window to the World: Long-Distance Trade and Slavery   54
3   Engaging the *Chindeli*: Colonial Rule and Local Negotiation   64
4   'Cinderella Gets the Ball at her Feet': Food, Labour, and Roads   77
5   The Birth of a Nation? Independence and Beyond   85
6   Conclusion   91

2   Production: Crops, Meat, and Markets   95
1   The Foundations of Production in Mwinilunga   98
     1.1   *On Subsistence and Market Production*   102
2   From Shifting Cultivation to Settled Farming: Policies and
     Practices   108
3   Meal: Markets, State Policies, and Values   114
     3.1   *Cassava: Creating a Land of Plenty*   118
     3.2   *Maize: Faltering Towards Modernity?*   121
     3.3   *The Foundations of Production: Staples, Markets, and the
             State*   123
4   Meat: Hunting, Herding, and Distribution   128
     4.1   *Hunting: Meat, Merit, and Masculinity*   129
     4.2   *Herding: A Source of Meat, a Source of Money*   138
     4.3   *Ideology, Marketing, and Administrative Control: The
             Co-Existence of Hunting and Herding*   142

5   Beeswax   145
6   Pineapples   151
7   The Rationales of Market Production   157
8   Conclusion   161

3 **Mobility**   165
1   Borders, Trade, and Identity   165
    1.1   *Historical Roots of Mobility*   169
    1.2   *Drawing and Crossing Borders: An 'Imaginary Line' on the*
          Map   172
    1.3   *Cross-Border Trade: Calico, Cigarettes, and Cassava*   176
    1.4   *Moving Across Borders: Migration, Identity, and the State*   187
    1.5   *Conclusion*   199
2   Labour Migration: Work, Mobility, and Wealth   201
    2.1   *Constructing the Idea of Work: Discipline, Labour, and*
          Migration   203
    2.2   *Of Modernist Narratives and Life Histories: Patterns of Labour*
          Migration in Mwinilunga   221
    2.3   *Decay or Boom? Labour Migration and Village Life*   236
    2.4   *Conclusion*   252

4 **Consumption: Goods, Wealth, and Meaning**   256
1   From Locally Produced to Store-Bought Goods: Exchange and the
    Creation of Value   258
    1.1   *Production and Exchange: The Foundations of Trade*   260
    1.2   *Goods, Value, and Meaning: Wealth in People and*
          Self-Realisation   266
2   Ironworking: Smelters, Smiths, and Craftsmanship   270
    2.1   *The Practice of Ironworking in Mwinilunga*   271
    2.2   *Mass-Manufactured Iron Tools: Competition or*
          Opportunity?   273
3   Cloth, Clothing, and Culture   280
    3.1   *Bark Cloth and Animal Skins: The Meaning and Value of*
          Clothing   283
    3.2   *From Imported Goods to Objects of Desire: The Spread and*
          Attractions of Manufactured Clothing   285
    3.3   *Clothing, Production, and Social Relationships*   292
    3.4   *Clothing, Culture, and Self-Realisation*   295

4   Grass, Mud, and Bricks: Housing, Community, and
      Permanence   300
      4.1   *Grass, Mud, and the Meaning of Housing*   302
      4.2   *Promoting 'Improved' Housing: Attempts at Housing
            Reform*   306
5   Goods, People, and Wealth: Rationales of Consumption   316
6   Conclusion   326

5 **Settlements and Social Change: Continuity and Change in Village
   Life**   331
   1   Villages and Farms: Settlement Patterns and Social
         Organisation   333
   2   Chiefs, Headmen, and Authority: Governing Village Life   340
         2.1   *Village Leadership in a Historical Perspective*   346
         2.2   *Colonial Adaptation: Authority, Recognition, and Village
               Fission*   348
         2.3   *Village Leadership and the Zambian Nation-State*   353
   3   Continuity and Change in Village Life   355
         3.1   *Accumulation, Wealth, and Personhood*   356
         3.2   *Individualisation, Kinship, and Wealth in People*   361
         3.3   *Social Change in Mwinilunga*   366
   4   Conclusion   367

Conclusion   369

Sources   377
Index   424

Acknowledgements

This book is the culmination of my road through Mwinilunga. It is the result of numerous conversations with people in and on Mwinilunga and I hope it does them justice. This remote corner of the world became vital to my understanding of capitalism, colonialism, and globalisation. By studying its history, I have learnt to challenge historiographical dichotomies between tradition and modernity, subsistence and market production, global and local. This book wishes to show how and why Mwinilunga and its people matter to broader historical processes. My road through Mwinilunga started in 2007 and since then I have incurred countless debts. Let me express long overdue gratitude to the people who helped me along the way.

My first and most important thanks go to the people I met during my stays in Mwinilunga District. In 2008 and 2010, I received warm welcomes in all the places I visited and all the homes I entered. I wish to thank the people I interviewed in Ikelenge, Nyakaseya, Chibwika, Kanongesha, Kanyama, and Ntambu chiefdoms. Your words have profoundly shaped my historical understanding and I hope – despite the language barrier – that you find recognition in the pages that follow. Special thanks go to those families who opened their homes to me and with whom I stayed for weeks at a time: the Chiyezhi family, the Musanda family, the Chinshe family, the Kamuhuza family, the Jinguluka family, the Kalota family, and the Kambidimba family. Sharing *nshima ya makamba* together and talking about proverbs has taught me more than you will ever realise. Indispensable was the research assistance provided by Julian Chiyezhi, Ambrose Musanda, Gibby Kamuhuza, Evans Jinguluka, Kenneth Kalota, and Dennis Ngomi. You introduced me to the people 'who know history', you translated my questions from English to chiLunda, and you taught me about 'deep Lunda culture' along the way. Singular mention should be made of Senior Chief Kanongesha Mulumbi Datuuma II, who went out of his way to facilitate my stay in the district. Every day I spent in Mwinilunga, I learnt something new: from the language, to obscure historical facts, and deeply personal testimonies of historical change. Words cannot express my gratitude for this.

Much of this book is based on archival research and most of this was done in Zambia. Doing research at the National Archives and the United National Independence Party archives in Lusaka and the Zambia Consolidated Copper Mines Archives in Ndola was a delightful experience. Despite my tireless requests for more documents, the staff always answered with a smile, making time for a quick chat about my day. Marja Hinfelaar and the staff at the National Archives of Zambia dispel the myth that African archives are disorganised or difficult to access. The recent efforts at archival preservation and digitisation are nothing short of outstanding. In the United Kingdom, I benefited from the valuable manuscripts at the Rhodes House in Oxford and the correspondence of the Echoes of Service missionaries at the John Rylands library in Manchester.

Academically, this book owes its greatest debt to Robert Ross and Jan-Bart Gewald. As my supervisors, they not only kindled my interest in African history and Mwinilunga in particular, they also gave me the confidence to pursue research independently. Only after submitting my thesis did I realise that their lack of detailed comments on my writings was the biggest compliment they could give. In Leiden, I benefitted immensely from discussions with Mary Davies, Sophie Feyder, Shehu Tijjani Yusuf, Pierre Kalenga, Paul Swanepoel, Mariana Perry, and the many other scholars at the Institute for History and the African Studies Centre. Mary, I could not have wished for a better companion on the writing journey, you taught me about Timothy Chawinga, marmalade, and cheese all at once. Institutionally, this book has benefitted from the NWO funded project 'From Muskets to Nokias' and the informal CART network. I greatly valued the opportunity of presenting my work in Europe and Zambia and receiving comments from Marja Hinfelaar, Giacomo Macola, Miles Larmer, Hugh Macmillan, Walima Kalusa, Bizeck Jube Phiri, and Webby Kalikiti. Marja Hinfelaar always facilitated my trips to Zambia, answered my administrative requests, and made me feel part of SAIPAR. Walima Kalusa encouraged me to work on Mwinilunga, took me dancing, and proved a great source of knowledge.

This book could not have been written without the ceaseless support and encouragement of my parents, Ivo, Bruno, and Mica. Even when the research and writing separated us, you made it worth it. I hope you know how much I appreciate your presence.

Nasakilili nankashi mwani

Illustrations

Photos

1   A muzzle loading gun, 2010   93
2   A village setting in Mwinilunga, 2010   93
3   Chief Kanongesha, 1950s   94
4   A field of cassava, 2010   163
5   Women pounding cassava, 2010   163
6   Hunter with his bow, arrow, and spear, 2008   164
7   Early roads and transport, 1950s   200
8   Mudyanyama Bridge, 1950s   200
9   A porter carrying a load, 1930s   255
10   Returned labour migrants, 1950s   255
11   Chief Ikelenge in his car, 1950s   329
12   *Nkunka*, 1950s   329
13   A trader's Kimberley brick house in Mwinilunga Town, 1950s   330
14   A chief drinking beer in the village, 1950s   368
15   Women welcoming the District Commissioner, 1950s   368

Maps

1   Mwinilunga District   42
2   Trading stores in Mwinilunga District   328

Introduction

Roads and the powerful sense of mobility that they promise carry us back and forth between the sweeping narratives of globalisation, and the specific, tangible materialities of particular times and places.[1]

∴

Roads have figured prominently in the twentieth century history of Mwinilunga, an area in the far northwestern corner of present-day Zambia.[2] Mwinilunga's residents invariably imagined roads as conduits of connectivity, which would link them to distant markets and urban areas, even if most of the time physical infrastructure – in the form of collapsed bridges, potholes, and mud tracks – merely served to underline Mwinilunga's disconnection from economic and political centres of power.[3] Throughout the twentieth century there have been recurrent plans to develop the infrastructure of Mwinilunga in order to boost economic productivity, facilitate the marketing of produce, and ensure more effective integration of this area into the regional and national political economy.[4] As early as the 1910s there were talks about the Benguela railway line connecting Mwinilunga to the Angolan coast. In 1913, Theodore Williams, a colonial officer, wrote to his mother, lamenting that he had 'happened to come exactly to the most elementary place in this elementary country'.[5] Yet by 1914

---

1   Dimitris Dalakoglou and Penny Harvey, 'Roads and Anthropology: Ethnographic Perspectives on Space, Time and (Im)Mobility', *Mobilities* 7, No. 4 (2012): 459. See also Kurt Beck, Gabriel Klaeger, and Michael Stasik, eds., *The Making of the African Road* (Leiden: Brill, 2017).

2   James A. Pritchett, *The Lunda-Ndembu: Style, Change and Social Transformation in South Central Africa* (Madison: University of Wisconsin Press, 2001); Victor W. Turner, *Schism and Continuity in an African Society: A Study of Ndembu Village Life* (Manchester: Manchester University Press, 1957); Dick Jaeger, *Settlement Patterns and Rural Development: A Human Geographical Study of the Kaonde, Kasempa District, Zambia* (Amsterdam: Royal Tropical Institute, 1981).

3   Interview with Julian Chiyezhi, 5 September 2008, Mwinilunga; see the methodology section for more information on interviews. See also James A. Pritchett, *Friends for Life, Friends for Death: Cohorts and Consciousness Among the Lunda-Ndembu* (Charlottesville: University Press of Virginia, 2007).

4   See Chapter 1; also Pritchett, *Lunda-Ndembu*, Chapter 2.

5   Rhodes House Oxford, hereafter (BOD) MSS Afr S 779, Theodore Williams letter to his mother, 21 May 1913.

he was convinced that the area would be transformed through new infrastructure, jubilantly claiming that 'Mwinilunga will become the nearest place in
Rhodesia to England upon completion of the Benguella railway'. He therefore
urged his friends and relatives to 'give up thinking of Mwinilunga as a place of
destitution'.[6] When the Benguela railway line was eventually built, however, it
bypassed Mwinilunga, instead connecting to the Congolese line of rail further
north. Infrastructure in the area expanded extremely slowly, as low population
density and annual heavy rains made the road network expensive to maintain.
At Zambian independence in 1964, the North-Western Province was one of the
least developed of all provinces, whether judged by school attendance rates
or mileage of tarred roads.[7] In the 1960s and 1970s, Mwinilunga became Zambia's largest pineapple producing region, but trucks full of valuable pineapples
regularly failed to reach markets because they would be stuck in the mud roads
for days.[8] Roads, nonetheless, continued to represent aspirations of connectivity to the inhabitants of Mwinilunga District. The commercial exploitation of
high-grade mineral deposits from 2005 onwards allegedly transformed Zambia's North-Western Province from a 'sleeping giant' into a 'place to be'.[9] Apart
from nearby mines such as Kansanshi and Lumwana, there are rumours of rich
mineral reserves within Mwinilunga District, notably a nickel deposit at Jimbe.
This has given rise to the commissioning of new infrastructure, such as hydro-
electricity schemes and roads. Most noteworthy is the planned North-West
Rail line connecting Chingola to Jimbe and onwards to the Atlantic Ocean
port Lobito in Angola. This 'railroad to resources' would 'open up' the area
and 'trigger off massive development'. The project would allow the region's
vast potential, in mineral resources, agricultural production, and forestry, to
be tapped through 'the biggest infrastructural project to be driven by indigenous citizens in the history of Zambia'.[10] Roads, thus, symbolised connectivity,

---

6   (BOD) MSS Afr S 779, Theodore Williams letter to his father, 11 January 1914.
7   See D.S. Johnson, ed., *Handbook to the North-Western Province* (Lusaka: Government
        Printer, 1980), for statistics.
8   Iva Peša, 'Between Sucess and Failure: The Mwinilunga Pineapple Canning Factory in
        the 1960s and 1970s', in *Magnifying Perspectives: Contributions to History, A Festschrift for
        Robert Ross*, eds., Iva Peša and Jan-Bart Gewald (Leiden: African Studies Centre, 2017),
        285–307.
9   Enoch Kavindele, 'Zambia: The Northwest Rail – the Railroad to Resources', *Times of Zam-
        bia* 20 May 2011, http://allafrica.com/stories/201105200535.html; More generally, see Rohit
        Negi, 'Solwezi *mabanga*': Ambivalent Developments on Zambia's New Mining Frontier',
        Journal of Southern African Studies 40, No.5 (2014): 999–1013.
10   Enoch Kavindele, 'Zambia: The Northwest Rail – the Railroad to Resources', *Times of Zam-
        bia* 20 May 2011, http://allafrica.com/stories/201105200535.html.

modernity, and development – from the specific perspective of the locality of Mwinilunga.[11]

By researching various roads through Mwinilunga, this book engages with grand historical narratives of continuity and change, whilst focusing explicitly on local specificity.[12] Aspirations, ideas, and processes of social change can only be understood by grounding historical representations in a particular place and time. Numerous observers have formulated hypotheses about the course of social change in Mwinilunga – including colonial officials, agricultural experts, and a number of renowned anthropologists, notably Victor Turner in the 1950s and James Pritchett in the 1980s.[13] Turner, a path-breaking Rhodes-Livingstone Institute scholar who conducted long-term fieldwork in the area, explicitly focused on the road and its impact on settlement patterns during the twentieth century. Turner linked the movement of settlements towards the roadside to profound social change, through market involvement, labour migration, and changes in kinship relations.[14] Why have infrastructure and settlement been such potent tropes to understand social change in Mwinilunga during the twentieth century?[15]

Historicising settlement changes makes it possible to analyse narratives of social change. Between 1870 and 1970 village layout and settlement patterns in Mwinilunga had changed profoundly. At the close of the nineteenth century villages were defensive, isolated by the deep bush, and some were even surrounded by tall stockades as a reaction to slave raiding.[16] An early colonial

---

11   See Achim von Oppen, *Terms of Trade and Terms of Trust: The History and Contexts of Pre-colonial Market Production Around the Upper Zambezi and Kasai* (Münster: LIT Verlag, 1994).

12   This approach has been inspired by works such as: Henrietta L. Moore and Megan Vaughan, *Cutting Down Trees: Gender, Nutrition, and Agricultural Change in The Northern Province of Zambia 1890–1990* (Portsmouth: Heinemann, 1994); Charles Piot, *Remotely Global: Village Modernity in West Africa* (Chicago: University of Chicago Press, 1999); Jeremy Prestholdt, *Domesticating the World: African Consumerism and the Genealogies of Globalization* (Berkeley: University of California Press, 2008); Landeg White, *Magomero: Portrait of an African Village* (Cambridge: Cambridge University Press, 1987).

13   Turner, *Schism and Continuity*; Pritchett, *Lunda-Ndembu*.

14   Victor W. Turner, *The Drums of Affliction: A Study Of Religious Processes Among the Ndembu of Zambia* (Oxford: Clarendon Press, 1968), 24.

15   For studies of changing settlement patterns in Zambia's North-Western Province, see: Johnson, *Handbook to the North-Western Province*; Jaeger, *Settlement Patterns and Rural Development*; George Kay, *Social Aspects of Village Regrouping in Zambia* (Hull: University of Hull, 1967); Marilyn Silberfein, ed., *Rural Settlement Structure and African Development* (Boulder: Westview Press, 1997).

16   See: Turner, *Schism and Continuity*, 6–7, 41, 228; Pritchett, *Lunda-Ndembu*, 32; David M. Gordon, 'The Abolition of the Slave Trade and the Transformation of the South-Central

official vividly described his approach to such an intractable and remote village:

> With my party in single file I advanced slowly along one of the paths which, owing to the dense bush and matted undergrowth, was more like a tunnel, and presently found myself confronted at a distance of some twenty yards by a stout stockade from ten feet to twelve feet in height, with a narrow gateway closed by a heavy tree trunk swung from a hinge at the top of the gate posts.[17]

The isolated and dispersed character of villages made them difficult to control administratively, especially for the newly incoming colonial administration.[18] Settlements were concentrated in favourable micro-environments (close to water, hunting, and cultivating grounds), yet the fragile nature of resources propelled scattered and frequently shifting residence patterns.[19] Consequently, colonial administrators described settlements as randomly spread over the landscape and attached pejorative valuations to villages and their inhabitants throughout the first half of the twentieth century.[20] Linking settlement patterns to ideas about 'civilisation', the colonial administration set out to change the state of affairs in Mwinilunga:

> For a century or more, they had been harried by slave-raiding parties (...) so only the stronger headmen had been able to form villages – others lived like animals in the bush, eating wild fruits and honey (...) Administration to them means: (i) A decent hut must be built – to take the place of the old grass shelter = "nkunka". (ii) Roads must be made – when a winding track thro' the bush is preferred. (iii) Gardens must be cultivated – whereas they prefer that nature should provide for their wants in the shape of honey & wild fruits.[21]

African Interior During the Nineteenth Century', *The William and Mary Quarterly* 66, No. 4 (2009): 915–38.

17   Edward Arden Copeman, 'The Violence of Kasanza', *The Northern Rhodesia Journal* 1, No. 5 (1952): 65; Description of events in 1906.

18   Jan-Bart Gewald, *Forged in the Great War: People, Transport, and Labour, The Establishment of Colonial Rule in Zambia, 1890–1920* (Leiden: African Studies Centre, 2015).

19   Pritchett, *Lunda-Ndembu*, 49–50, 229–30.

20   National Archives of Zambia, hereafter (NAZ) SEC2/955, R.C. Dening, Mwinilunga District Tour Report, November 1947.

21   (NAZ) KSE4/1, Mwinilunga District Notebooks, F.V. Bruce-Miller, History of the Sub-District, 1918, Folio 29 & 30; (BOD) Richard Cranmer Dening, Land Tenure Report No.7, North-Western Province.

Road construction, infrastructure, and settlement patterns were thus at the heart of colonial control. By concentrating scattered settlements into large orderly villages, which would be loyal to the government and economically productive by generating cash crops and labour, the colonial administration sought to transform villages in Mwinilunga.[22]

The outward appearance of villages had changed dramatically by the 1950s. Following the expansion of infrastructural facilities, most notably the construction of all-weather roads to replace footpaths through the bush, officials remarked that villages in Mwinilunga had started to form 'long almost uninterrupted ribbons' along the roadside and noticed 'a universal movement to the vicinity of the roads'.[23] Colonial observers linked these changing settlement patterns to a myriad of other changes – such as involvement with the cash economy, labour migration, and individualisation – all interpreted as expressions of comprehensive social change.[24] In this ideological context of the 1950s, Turner noted the increasing appearance of 'farms'. He described the 'ribbon development along the road of small settlements, a few hundred yards away from one another, each with its own headman and each containing a small corporate grouping of kin'.[25] Because of factors such as the *Pax Britannica*, the cash economy, and urbanisation, Turner predicted the replacement of large concentric villages by small roadside settlements.[26] He argued that:

> Labour migration to the urban industrial areas is positively emancipating the individual from his obligations to his kinship group (…) If a man wishes to accumulate capital to set up as a petty trader or tailor, or to acquire a higher standard of living for himself and his elementary family, he must break away from his circle of village kin towards whom he has traditional obligations.[27]

Turner interpreted the appearance of 'farms' not only as a change in settlement patterns and village layout, but linked this phenomenon to changes in patterns of production (cash crop agriculture), mobility (labour migration),

---

22   Compare this to other parts of Zambia: Achim von Oppen, 'Bounding Villages: The Enclosure of Locality in Central Africa, 1890s to 1990s' (Habilitationsgeschrift, Humboldt University of Berlin, 2003); Kay, *Social Aspects of Village Regrouping*; Moore and Vaughan, *Cutting Down Trees*.

23   (NAZ) NWP1/2/40, K.J. Forder, Mwinilunga District Tour Report, September 1952.

24   (NAZ) SEC2/963, R.S. Thompson, Mwinilunga District Tour Report, 31 January 1955.

25   Turner, *Schism and Continuity*, 42–43.

26   Turner, *Schism and Continuity*, 220; Turner, *Drums of Affliction*, 24.

27   Turner, *Schism and Continuity*, 43.

consumption (store-bought goods), and social relationships (individualisation and family nucleation). He saw changing settlement patterns as the outcome of a process of comprehensive social change.[28] Did Turner's assumptions and his predictions about the course of social change prove true? Turner assumed that not only were settlement patterns caught up in a process of 'irreversible change' but also that economic relations, interpersonal associations, and ways of life were bound to be affected and transformed.[29] Over the period 1870–1970 village layout in Mwinilunga had changed from dispersed and defensive settlements to concentrated roadside villages, but the question is whether this change in outward appearance also brought about change in other spheres of society. Did changes in settlement patterns necessarily lead to changes in the economic sphere or in interpersonal relationships? Did the appearance of farms radically alter the authority of village headmen? Or did roadside villages produce more cash crops for marketing than villages located at a distance from the road? This book critically engages with such questions. Notwithstanding the changes involved in moving towards the roadside and adapting settlement patterns, there were long-term continuities in livelihood procurement, social conduct, and modes of thought.[30] By focusing on issues of continuity and change, this book highlights the unexpected course of historical practice, which did not always fit into linear narratives and therefore requires an alternative conceptual framework.[31]

How has the process of social change (exemplified by issues of production, mobility, consumption, and social relationships) been negotiated in the area of Mwinilunga between the 1870s and the 1970s? In order to address this central question, it is important to first identify what the standard representation of social change in Mwinilunga District has been.[32] The process of social change in Mwinilunga has – with few exceptions – overwhelmingly been

---

28   Turner, *Drums of Affliction*, 24.

29   Turner, *Schism and Continuity*, 36–37.

30   Compare with: Pritchett, *Lunda-Ndembu*; A case study from an adjacent area is: Kate Crehan, *The Fractured Community: Landscapes of Power and Gender in Rural Zambia* (Berkeley: University of California Press, 1997).

31   For a similar argument, see: James Ferguson, *Expectations of Modernity: Myths and Meanings of Urban Life on the Zambian Copperbelt* (Berkeley: University of California Press, 1999); Thomas T. Spear, *Mountain Farmers: Moral Economies of Land and Agricultural Development in Arusha and Meru* (Berkeley: University of California Press, 1997); Jan Vansina, *Paths in the Rainforests: Toward a History of Political Tradition in Equatorial Africa* (Madison: University of Wisconsin Press, 1990).

32   A similar approach has been adopted by Moore and Vaughan, *Cutting Down Trees*; Kate Crehan, '"Tribes" and the People Who Read Books: Managing History in Colonial Zambia', *Journal of Southern African Studies* 23, No. 2 (1998): 203–18; John L. Comaroff and Jean

interpreted within a metanarrative of linear, comprehensive, and transformative change.[33] Colonial administrators, agricultural experts, post-colonial officials, and anthropologists alike have adopted ideas of transition.[34] This line of thought posited an 'epochal divide' following the impact of exogenous forces, such as colonialism or capitalism. This metanarrative has emphasised external over internal causes of change and has advanced ideas of rupture rather than continuity.[35] Outward expressions of social change that such representations have highlighted are, for example, the replacement of conical grass thatched houses by square brick houses; clothing change from bark cloth and animal skins to imported mass-manufactured clothing; changes in agriculture from 'subsistence' to 'market' production; labour migration to urban areas in search of salaried employment, causing 'detribalisation' and 'individualisation'; or the diminished importance of extended kin-based associations and a focus on nuclear family households. In all these examples, change was interpreted as unidirectional and transformative, rather than as the contingent outcome of contested historical processes. Departing from such views, this book suggests that social change in Mwinilunga was gradual and incremental. Even as numerous changes were variously manifested in outward appearances, the people of Mwinilunga were able to negotiate and appropriate change in accordance with long-established practices and modes of thought.[36] Consequently, new influences were embedded within existing frameworks rather than discarding or transforming these. This tension between continuity and change will be at the heart of this work.

As the example of infrastructure and changing settlement patterns in Mwinilunga suggests, representations of social change did not simply accord with historical practices.[37] Colonial officials, post-colonial experts,

---

Comaroff, *Of Revelation and Revolution: The Dialectics of Modernity on a South African Frontier, Volume Two* (Chicago: University of Chicago Press, 1997).

33   The 'modernisation myth' in Zambia has most eloquently been set out by Ferguson, *Expectations of Modernity*, 14–17, 33; James Ferguson, 'Mobile Workers, Modernist Narratives: A Critique of the Historiography of Transition on the Zambian Copperbelt', *Journal of Southern African Studies* 16, No. 3–4 (1990): 385–412 and 603–21. See parallels in Moore and Vaughan, *Cutting Down Trees*; Pritchett, *Lunda-Ndembu*; Crehan, *The Fractured Community*.

34   See examples in Pritchett, *Lunda-Ndembu*; Moore and Vaughan, *Cutting Down Trees*; Crehan, *The Fractured Community*.

35   See the discussion of the Rhodes-Livingstone Institute below; Spear, *Mountain Farmers*, 8.

36   Pritchett, *Lunda-Ndembu*; see parallels in Spear, *Mountain Farmers*, 238; Vansina, *Paths in the Rainforests*.

37   Issues of discourse, representation, and practice have long been debated in social sciences and historical theory. For the Zambian context, see: Moore and Vaughan, *Cutting*

anthropologists, and even much subsequent historiography have interpreted changing settlement patterns within a narrative of comprehensive social change, or sometimes even within a 'modernist narrative' of transition from 'tradition' to 'modernity'.[38] This book highlights that local historical practice did not fit into such discursive constructs. Moving towards the roadside did not necessarily entail a trend towards individualisation or commercialisation, as contemporary observers expected. Forms of extended kinship and existing patterns of agricultural production retained importance, as people moved towards the road for their own reasons and with their own aims in mind.[39] In the historiography of Mwinilunga, so far linear narratives, which imply ideas of 'development', 'progress', and 'modernity', have been dominant, yet such narratives have obfuscated the non-linear course of historical practice.[40] In order to question established narratives of social change, this book foregrounds the intricacies and contradictions of historical practice.

One illustrative example of the dissonance between representations of social change and historical practice comes from the agricultural history of Mwinilunga.[41] Government officials, agricultural extension officers, and even some scholarly works have proposed a progressive transition from 'subsistence' to 'market' production, yet this has appeared to be far from clear-cut.[42] One of the key contestations of the twentieth century was whether producers in the area would cultivate maize or cassava. During the colonial period as well as after independence, official agricultural propaganda has portrayed maize as a 'modern' cash crop, denouncing cassava as a 'traditional' subsistence crop. Both crops, however, were introduced from America through the long-distance trade during the seventeenth century and are thus distinctly

---

Down Trees; Crehan, The Fractured Community; Ferguson, Expectations of Modernity. More generally, see: Spear, Mountain Farmers; Comaroff and Comaroff, Of Revelation and Revolution; Sara S. Berry, No Condition Is Permanent: The Social Dynamics of Agrarian Change in Sub-Saharan Africa (Madison: University of Wisconsin Press, 1993); Jane I. Guyer, 'Naturalism in Models of African Production', Man 19, No. 3 (1984): 371–88; Jane I. Guyer, 'Wealth in People and Self-Realization in Equatorial Africa', Man 28, No. 2 (1993): 243–65; Piot, Remotely Global; Valentin Y. Mudimbe, The Invention of Africa: Gnosis, Philosophy and the Order of Knowledge (Bloomington: Indiana University Press, 1988).

38   Kay, Social Aspects of Village Regrouping; Von Oppen, 'Bounding Villages.'

39   See examples in Pritchett, Lunda-Ndembu.

40   A similar argument has been made by Ferguson, Expectations of Modernity; Moore and Vaughan, Cutting Down Trees; Berry, No Condition Is Permanent.

41   Iva Peša, 'Cinderella's Cassava: A Historical Study of Agricultural Adaptation in Mwinilunga District from Pre-Colonial Times to Independence' (Mphil thesis, Leiden University, 2009).

42   See Grace Carswell, 'Food Crops as Cash Crops: The Case of Colonial Kigezi, Uganda', Journal of Agrarian Change 3, No. 4 (2003): 521–51; Berry, No Condition Is Permanent.

modern additions to the agricultural repertoire of Mwinilunga. Still, colonial officials and many others have negatively valued cassava. A 1950s agricultural report asserted that 'methods of production of' cassava 'are wasteful and it is preferable that it should be regarded as a subsistence rather than a cash crop'.[43] Yet to this day producers in Mwinilunga overwhelmingly continue to prefer cassava to maize, proudly pronouncing that they are 'cassava eaters'. Moreover, cassava has been marketed on a large scale at different moments, for example in the 1950s to the Copperbelt mines or in the 1990s to Angolan refugees, enabling producers a distinct engagement with the market and generating spells of prosperity in the area. At other moments, however, producers would grow more than enough cassava for their own subsistence, but they might refrain from marketing due to price fluctuations or the inaccessibility of markets. Despite persistent state policies favouring maize as a cash crop, including seed distribution schemes, fertiliser subsidies, and favourable marketing arrangements, cultivators throughout Mwinilunga chose to grow and eat cassava to such an extent that the crop has become an integral part of the region's identity. The large-scale production and marketing of cassava thus complicates representations of social change, which presume a transition from subsistence to market production with an attendant shift from 'traditional' cassava to 'modern' maize.[44] Yet even if concepts of 'subsistence' and 'market' production did not seem to fit the historical reality of Mwinilunga, such concepts continued to be adopted to represent agricultural practices. Representation and practice fed into one another in multiple ways, as 'actions and representations are indissolubly linked'.[45] Colonial representations proved surprisingly influential and persistent, being replicated implicitly and explicitly by government ministries, foreign NGOs, and even being reflected in the language of interviews.[46] Today, farmers in Mwinilunga talk about producing cassava for 'subsistence', as a 'traditional' crop, even if nothing about cassava is actually 'traditional'.

---

43   (NAZ) Department of Agriculture, Annual report, 1953.

44   See: Iva Peša, '"Cassava Is Our Chief": Negotiating Identity, Markets and the State Through Cassava in Mwinilunga, Zambia', in *Transforming Innovations in Africa: Explorative Studies on Appropriation in African Societies,* eds., Jan-Bart Gewald, André Leliveld, and Iva Peša (Leiden: Brill, 2012), 169–90; Catherine C. Fourshey, '"The Remedy for Hunger Is Bending the Back": Maize and British Agricultural Policy in Southwestern Tanzania 1920–1960', *The International Journal of African Historical Studies* 41, No. 2 (2008): 223–61; Achim von Oppen, 'Cassava, "The Lazy Man's Food"? Indigenous Agricultural Innovation and Dietary Change in Northwestern Zambia (ca. 1650–1970)', in *Changing Food Habits: Case Studies from Africa, South America and Europe,* ed. Carola Lentz (London: Routledge, 1999), 43–72.

45   Moore and Vaughan, *Cutting Down Trees,* XXIII.

46   See parallels in Moore and Vaughan, *Cutting Down Trees,* XXI–XXII; Crehan, 'Tribes and the People Who Read Books', 203–18.

A metanarrative of linear social change has been internalised by the population of Mwinilunga who now apply a discourse of 'tradition' and 'modernity'.[47] This book aims to set out, analyse, and question this metanarrative of social change in Mwinilunga, by testing a number of hypotheses arising from the narrative against the contradictory course of historical practice.

Social change in Mwinilunga has been analysed in much detail in the seminal studies of Turner in the 1950s and Pritchett in the 1980s.[48] These anthropologists, however, did not make full use of available historical sources, which are indispensable to an understanding of the process of social change.[49] Both Turner and Pritchett adopted assumptions about the transformative and linear nature of social change, especially as brought about by colonialism and capitalism.[50] One example of this mode of thought is the alleged assertion of colonial hegemony through the introduction of taxation in Mwinilunga District in 1913.[51] The works by Turner and Pritchett have suggested that taxation had a profound effect on society, causing widespread flight, famine, tax evasion, and consequent repressive measures.[52] The British colonial administration, in an attempt to 'demonstrate the overwhelming force at their disposal', 'burned down some Lunda villages, shot some people, and occasionally held wives and children hostage in a calculated display to show the futility of resistance'.[53] Underlining the transformative nature of colonial rule, Pritchett claimed that the British 'discouraged or destroyed most of the traditional means of subsistence, enforcing migrant labor as the only option' to earn tax money.[54] This book pairs a close reading of archival sources with oral history to suggest otherwise. People might have fled into the bush on approach of the tax

---

47   This view is based on numerous interviews: see the methodology section below.
48   Monographs by Victor Witter Turner: *Schism and Continuity; Drums of Affliction; The Ritual Process: Structure and Anti-Structure* (New Brunswick: Transaction Publishers, 1969); *The Forest of Symbols: Aspects of Ndembu Ritual* (Ithaca: Cornell University Press, 1970); *Dramas, Fields, and Metaphors: Symbolic Action in Human Society* (Ithaca: Cornell University Press, 1974); *On the Edge of the Bush: Anthropology As Experience* (Tucson: University of Arizona Press, 1985); works by James Anthony Pritchett viz. *Lunda-Ndembu, Friends for Life.*
49   Jan-Bart Gewald, 'Researching and Writing in the Twilight of an Imagined Conquest: Anthropology in Northern Rhodesia 1930–1960', *History and Anthropology* 18, No. 4 (2007): 471; David M. Gordon, 'Rites of Rebellion: Recent Anthropology from Zambia', *African Studies*, 62, No. 1 (2003): 131–32.
50   Turner, *Schism and Continuity*, 7–10; Pritchett, *Lunda-Ndembu*, 36–37.
51   See Fergus Macpherson, *Anatomy of a Conquest: The British Occupation of Zambia, 1884–1924* (Harlow: Longman, 1981).
52   See Chapter 1; Turner, *Schism and Continuity*, 7–8; Pritchett, *Lunda-Ndembu*, 33–35.
53   Pritchett, *Lunda-Ndembu*, 36.
54   Ibidem, 229.

official, but most returned several days later once the official had passed. The vast terrain of Mwinilunga made temporarily relocating to the bush to avoid paying taxes a viable option. Colonial rule did not necessarily have transformative effects on daily life, as subsequent chapters illustrate, whereas the changes that did occur did not follow a simple linear course.[55] This book pays attention to local negotiation, agency, and gradual change to adjust existing understandings of and explanations for social change in Mwinilunga.[56]

By focusing on one particular area over a prolonged period, this book studies the nature, course, and specificity of social change.[57] Given the availability of detailed anthropological analyses and a variety of historical sources, Mwinilunga District provides a good case to understand processes of social change in twentieth century Central Africa.[58] This allows a testing of the hypotheses about the nature, course, and direction of social change against historical practice. Recent scholarship has fruitfully engaged in questioning the representations through which social change has been understood.[59] Anthropological and historical reconstructions have, for example, challenged the hegemony of colonial rule by asserting cross-cultural dialogue and pointing towards the co-construction of discourse.[60] Others have deconstructed the meaning of allegedly universal concepts such as 'capitalism', by paying attention to processes of appropriation and local diversity.[61] Still others have questioned the usefulness of concepts such as 'modernity' or 'globalisation' outright.[62] Yet despite such nuanced work, assertions of linear transitions from 'tradition' to 'modernity', which overwhelmingly adopt ideas of 'development', persist.[63] This study problematises such narratives, arguing that an effective critique of

55 See Walima T. Kalusa, 'Disease and the Remaking of Missionary Medicine in Colonial Northwestern Zambia: A Case Study of Mwinilunga District, 1902–1964' (Unpublished PhD thesis, Johns Hopkins University, 2003); Spear, *Mountain Farmers.*
56 See Gewald, 'Researching and Writing', 471.
57 Compare with Moore and Vaughan, *Cutting Down Trees*; Crehan, *The Fractured Community.*
58 See the discussion on the Rhodes-Livingstone Institute below; see also Crehan, *The Fractured Community,* 233.
59 For example: Moore and Vaughan, *Cutting Down Trees*; Piot, *Remotely Global.*
60 See for example: Comaroff and Comaroff, *Of Revelation and Revolution*; Spear, *Mountain Farmers.*
61 Crehan, *The Fractured Community*; Berry, *No Condition Is Permanent.*
62 Prestholdt, *Domesticating the World*; Piot, *Remotely Global.*
63 For an overview of recent debates, see: Harri Englund and James Leach, 'Ethnography and the Meta-Narratives of Modernity', *Current Anthropology* 41, No. 2 (2000): 225–48; Ferguson, *Expectations of Modernity*; Lynn M. Thomas, 'Modernity's Failings, Political Claims, and Intermediate Concepts', *The American Historical Review* 116, No. 3 (2011): 727–40.

accepted terms can only be made through a detailed analysis of local history.[64]
Although some of the processes of change described for Mwinilunga have parallels in other areas, it is only by adopting a confined spatial and temporal focus
that meaningful conclusions about the nature of social change can be reached.

This book examines to what extent assumptions underlying standard narratives of social change accurately represent historical reality in places such
as Mwinilunga.[65] Based on a reading of archival sources, coupled with the assumptions about social change proposed by Turner and the Rhodes Livingstone Institute, this study analyses four broad spheres of social change, namely
production, mobility, consumption, and social relationships. In these spheres,
social change has predominantly been represented through narratives of transition, as part of a linear and transformative process.[66] Four hypotheses, which
form the starting point of each thematic chapter, address the assumptions
about the course of social change in these spheres. In the sphere of production, the transition from 'subsistence' to 'market' production of crops will be
questioned; in the sphere of mobility the hypothesis that increased mobility
would bring about transformative change, either positively leading to 'development' or negatively to 'underdevelopment', will be examined; in the sphere
of consumption, the transition from self-sufficiency to market integration
through store-bought goods will be problematised; and lastly in the sphere of
social relationships, the hypothesis that extended kin-based affiliations would
give way to the nuclear family and a process of individualisation will be scrutinised. Each chapter tests one hypothesis against historical sources, assessing
whether existing universalising narratives are indeed valid ways to interpret
social change. To understand the context of this study, an overview of the historiography, starting with the works of the Rhodes Livingstone Institute (RLI),
follows.[67]

---

64   A similar argument is made by: Moore and Vaughan, *Cutting Down Trees*; Crehan, *The
     Fractured Community.*
65   This approach has been inspired by works such as Berry, *No Condition Is Permanent*; Piot,
     Remotely Global.
66   Compare with Ferguson, *Expectations of Modernity*; Frederick Cooper, 'What Is the
     Concept of Globalization Good for? An African Historian's Perspective', *African Affairs*
     100, No. 399 (2001): 189–213.
67   The Rhodes Livingstone Institute is alternatively referred to as the Manchester School.
     See: T. Van Teeffelen, 'The Manchester School in Africa and Israel: A Critique', *Dialecti-
     cal Anthropology* 3, No. 1 (1978): 67–83; J.H. Van Doorne, 'Situational Analysis: Its Poten-
     tial and Limitations for Anthropological Research on Social Change in Africa', *Cahiers
     d'Études Africaines* 21, No. 84 (1981): 479–506; Richard P. Werbner, 'The Manchester School
     in South-Central Africa', *Annual Review of Anthropology* 13 (1984): 157–85; Jan-Kees Van
     Donge, 'Understanding Rural Zambia Today: The Relevance of the Rhodes-Livingstone

1   Conceptualising Social Change: The Rhodes Livingstone Institute
       and Victor Turner

The understanding of Zambia's history has been profoundly shaped by the
pioneering work of the Rhodes Livingstone Institute, a social science research
institute looking at the influence of British colonial rule in Central Africa.[68]
RLI researchers carried out fieldwork in urban and rural locations throughout Northern Rhodesia, from the 1930s to the 1960s.[69] This was the heyday of
colonial rule and socioeconomic change brought about by capitalism, labour
migration, and cash-crop production.[70] This context provided ideal case studies with which the RLI could develop its interest in social change.[71] Significantly,
RLI researchers moved away from the concept of tribes as bounded and ho-
mogenous units, marked by isolation, cohesion or systemic equilibrium.[72]

Institute', *Africa* 55, No. 1 (1985): 60–76; Hugh Macmillan, 'Return to the Malungwana
Drift – Max Gluckman, the Zulu Nation and the Common Society', *African Affairs* 94, No.
374 (1995): 39–65; Lyn Schumaker, *Africanizing Anthropology: Fieldwork, Networks, and the
Making of Cultural Knowledge in Central Africa* (Durham: Duke University Press, 2001);
Gordon, 'Rites of Rebellion', 125–39; Wim M.J. Van Binsbergen, 'Manchester as the Birth
Place of Modern Agency Research: The Manchester School Explained from the Perspec-
tive of Evans-Pritchard's Book "The Nuer"', in *Strength Beyond Structure: Social and His-
torical Trajectories of Agency in Africa*, eds., Mirjam De Bruijn, Rijk Van Dijk, and Jan-Bart
Gewald (Leiden: Brill, 2007), 16–61; Gewald, 'Researching and Writing', 459–87.

68   Gewald, 'Researching and Writing', 461; Crehan, *The Fractured Community*, 55; Schumaker,
      Africanizing Anthropology.
69   Gordon, 'Rites of Rebellion', 126. A small selection of RLI works: Urban – Arnold L. Epstein,
      Politics in an Urban African Community (Manchester: Manchester University Press, 1958);
      J. Clyde Mitchell, ed., *Social Networks in Urban Situations* (Manchester: Manchester Uni-
      versity Press, 1969); Godfrey Wilson, *The Economics of Detribalization in Northern Rho-
      desia I & II,* Rhodes-Livingstone Papers, No. 5–6 (Manchester: Manchester University
      Press, 1942; reprinted 1968); Godfrey Wilson and Monica H. Wilson, *The Analysis of Social
      Change: Based on Observations in Central Africa* (Cambridge: Cambridge University Press,
      1945). Rural – Elizabeth Colson, *Social Organization of the Gwembe Tonga* (Manchester:
      Manchester University Press, 1960); Norman Long, *Social Change and the Individual:
      A Study of the Social and Religious Responses to Innovation in a Zambian Rural Community*
      (Manchester: Manchester University Press, 1968); Max Gluckman, *Politics, Law and Ritual
      in Tribal Society* (Chicago: Aldine Publishers, 1965); Audrey I. Richards, *Land, Labour and
      Diet in Northern Rhodesia* (Oxford: Oxford University Press, 1939); William Watson, *Tribal
      Cohesion in a Money Economy: A Study of the Mambwe People* (Manchester: Manchester
      University Press, 1958).
70   Werbner, 'The Manchester School', 161–63; Macmillan, 'Return to the Malungwana Drift',
      50; Gordon, 'Rites of Rebellion', 126; Gewald, 'Researching and Writing.'
71   Schumaker, *Africanizing Anthropology,* 115; Gordon, 'Rites of Rebellion', 126.
72   Adam Kuper, *Anthropology & Anthropologists: The Modern British School* (3rd edn., Lon-
      don: Routledge, 1996), 1–34, 136; Macmillan, 'Return to the Malungwana Drift', 44–49;

Adopting the materialist approach of diachronic analysis, the RLI instead set out to research social conflicts, schisms, and processes of change.[73]

The RLI sought to identify the processes through which forces such as capitalism and colonialism would bring about social change. Researchers aimed to account for 'the differential effects of labor migration and urbanization on the family and kinship organization, the economic life, the political values, the religious and magical beliefs' of society.[74] RLI researchers innovatively connected issues of industrialisation, labour migration, and colonialism to life histories and micro case studies.[75] They assumed that within the 'total social field' changes in one part would automatically lead to changes in society as a whole.[76] According to Max Gluckman, there were periods of relative stability – or 'repetitive equilibria' – when contradictions, conflict, and change could be contained within the system of society. But there were equally periods in which the equilibrium was disturbed, change could not be controlled, and a radical transformation of society would result.[77] In the case of Northern Rhodesia, capitalism and colonialism seemed to cause just this sort of radical transformation, although it remained difficult to predict the exact timing and nature of the break that would ensue.[78]

In a review article, James Ferguson has claimed that RLI urban research was characterised by a 'modernist narrative' of progressive change through urbanisation and industrialisation, 'a metanarrative of transition in which tribal rural Africans were swiftly becoming modern, urban members of an industrial

---

Binsbergen, 'Manchester as the Birth Place', 18–24, 34–37; Gordon, 'Rites of Rebellion', 128–30.

73   Turner, *Schism and Continuity*; Werbner, 'The Manchester School', 163, 176; Gordon, 'Rites of Rebellion', 131; Macmillan, 'Return to the Malungwana Drift', 47–48.

74   Max Gluckman, 'The Seven Year Research Plan of the Rhodes-Livingstone Institute', *Journal of the Rhodes-Livingstone Institute* 4 (1945): 9; Quoted in Werbner, 'The Manchester School', 163.

75   Werbner, 'The Manchester School', 159–62; Schumaker, *Africanizing Anthropology*; Van Binsbergen, 'Africa as the Birth Place', 39–42.

76   Werbner, 'The Manchester School', 174–75; Macmillan, 'Return to the Malungwana Drift', 50; Schumaker, *Africanizing Anthropology*, 77.

77   Kuper, *Anthropology and Anthropologists*, 139; Macmillan, 'Return to the Malungwana Drift', 52; Paul M. Cocks, 'Applied Anthropology or the Anthropology of Modernity? Max Gluckman's Vision of Southern African Society, 1939–1947', *Journal of Southern African Studies* 38, No. 3 (2012): 649–65; Max Gluckman, *Analysis of a Social Situation in Modern Zululand*, Rhodes-Livingstone Papers, No. 28 (Lusaka: Government Printer, 1958).

78   Macmillan, 'Return to the Malungwana Drift', 52; Gewald, 'Researching and Writing', 470, 476.

society'.[79] Permanent urban settlement, as opposed to temporary labour migration, would mark 'the emergence of Africans into the modern world'.[80] Ferguson has been denounced for misreading the nuances of RLI work and his critics argue that urbanisation has never been portrayed as following a linear path.[81] Nevertheless, RLI work – overwhelmingly concerned with questions of social change – did propose certain assumptions about the nature and direction of change, which Ferguson aptly connected to issues of 'modernity'. In an influential theoretical treatise, RLI researchers Godfrey and Monica Wilson suggested such a linear process of social change, claiming that economic, political, religious, and social changes were all interlinked in a total social field: 'Within living memory men's relations in Central Africa were primitive; now they are being very rapidly civilized'.[82] The RLI applied similar assumptions to rural areas, which were studied through the prism of structural transformations brought about by colonisation, industrialisation, and urbanisation.[83]

Rural RLI studies, exemplified by the work of Audrey Richards, have overwhelmingly described social change in negative terms of breakdown and crisis, brought about by colonialism and capitalism. Especially labour migration, which caused high levels of male absenteeism, would impair agricultural production and strain village organisation.[84] Within this context Turner published his groundbreaking monograph on the socioeconomic organisation of villages in Mwinilunga, focusing on village cohesion and fission.[85] Turner developed the technique of 'situational analysis' within the framework of the 'social drama', which enabled a study of change through specific case studies

---

79   Ferguson, *Expectations of Modernity*, 33; Ferguson, 'Mobile Workers, Modernist Narratives', 385–412 and 603–21.

80   J. Clyde Mitchell, 'A Note on the Urbanization of Africans on the Copperbelt', *Human Problems in British Central Africa* 12 (1951): 20; Quoted in Ferguson, *Expectations of Modernity*, 20.

81   Hugh Macmillan, 'The Historiography of Transition on the Zambian Copperbelt: Another View', *Journal of Southern African Studies* 19, No. 4 (1993): 681–712; Deborah Potts, 'Counter-urbanisation on the Zambian Copperbelt? Interpretations and Implications', *Urban Studies* 42, No. 4 (2005): 583–609.

82   Wilson, *The analysis of social change*, 2 (3–13).

83   Gordon, 'Rites of Rebellion'; Macmillan, 'Return to the Malungwana Drift.'

84   Audrey Richards joined the RLI later, yet her work was formative for rural RLI studies: Richards, *Land, Labour, Diet;* Moore and Vaughan, *Cutting Down Trees.*

85   Monographs by Victor Witter Turner: *Schism and Continuity; Drums of Affliction; The Forest of Symbols.* See also Bennetta Jules-Rosette, 'Decentering Ethnography: Victor Turner's Vision of Anthropology', *Journal of Religion in Africa* 24, No. 2 (1994): 160–81. Turner's ideas about 'liminality', symbol, and ritual have proven to be particularly influential: Turner, *The Ritual Process;* Turner, *Dramas, Fields, and Metaphors.* For a more comprehensive overview of Turner's work, see the sources section.

and manifestations of rituals.[86] He interpreted 'performances of ritual as distinct phases in the social processes whereby groups became adjusted to internal changes and adapted to their external environment'.[87] Even if Turner provided ample evidence of individual variation, agency, and the flexibility with which actors dealt with macro-level influences, he equally pointed to the limits of creative adaptation: 'changes brought about by the growing participation of Ndembu in the Rhodesian cash economy and an increased rate of labour migration, have in some areas (...) drastically reshaped some institutions and destroyed others'.[88]

Turner described the 'breakdown of traditional villages into small units headed by younger men who participate in the encroaching cash economy', heralding crisis within the old order of society.[89] He claimed that 'the old order was doomed' and that 'to become eminent they [individuals] must commit themselves whole-heartedly to the cash economy (...) [which] was breaking down the structure of the village'.[90] Socioeconomic changes led to the disintegration of villages into small units ('farms'), which in turn affected forms of interpersonal association, matrilineal kinship, relationships between generations and genders, as well as forms of political authority and agricultural production.[91] By reconciling conflicting parties and restoring social structure and custom, rituals could slow down the pace of change and temporarily solve contradictions within society, yet the direction of change was irreversible.[92] Despite a veneer of continuity through ritual redress, change was rampant:

> [People] try to slow down the rate of change by many devices, in order that they may carry on their daily lives within a framework of routine. One of the ways in which they attempt to do this is by domesticating the new, and subjectively menacing, forces in the service of the traditional order, so that for a time, for example, cash is accumulated in order to acquire traditional symbols of prestige or build up a clientele of followers to bid for long-established positions of authority. But ultimately the contradiction between the basic assumptions of the new order and those of the traditional order distorts and then disrupts the social structure. The new order smashes the old, and the traditional set of conflicts is supplanted by a different one. During the process of transition, traditional

---

86 Gordon, 'Rites of Rebellion', 131; Kuper, *Anthropology and Anthropologists*, 144–45.
87 Turner, *Forest of Symbols*, 20.
88 Turner, *Schism and Continuity*, 17; Gordon, 'Rites of Rebellion', 131.
89 Turner, *Schism and Continuity*, 10.
90 Ibidem, 136.
91 Ibidem, 138.
92 Turner, *Drums of Affliction*, 90.

kinds of conflict that were formerly not merely controlled by customary machinery of redress, legal and ritual, but were also converted by them into social energy which sustained the system, can no longer be so controlled, for the redressive machinery is breaking down. The result is that such conflicts accelerate the destruction of the traditional order.[93]

Turner's work fits into the general framework of RLI thought on social change.[94] Turner assumed that influences of colonialism, capitalism, and labour migration would lead to changes in patterns of belief, social relationships, and economic organisation. Adhering to a narrative of transformative and linear change, Turner put forward strong hypotheses about the course of social change in Mwinilunga District.

This study tests Turner's hypotheses from the 1950s through an empirical engagement with historical events, processes, and consciousness. With the benefit of hindsight, how can social change in Mwinilunga be understood today? This book is not a restudy of Turner's work, and neither does it attempt to conduct a case study in RLI fashion. Instead, it critically engages with the hypotheses about the course, direction, and pace of social change put forward by Turner.[95] Do narratives of linear change, propounded by RLI scholars, colonial officials, and post-colonial experts, provide the best framework to understand processes of social change, or do alternative interpretations need to be proposed? When viewed within a long-term historical perspective, the changes in settlement patterns that Turner observed as transformative appear contested, gradual, and diffuse.[96] Rather than placing emphasis on ruptures or radical change, this study focuses attention on continuity and local negotiation, contestation, and the appropriation of change. By historicising Turner's observations, a different understanding of social change in Mwinilunga can be obtained.

2   Reconceptualising Continuity and Change: Narratives, Representations, and Theories

Why would it be relevant to study colonial assumptions and RLI thought about social change from the 1950s? After almost seventy years, such ideas may well

---

93   Turner, *Drums of Affliction*, 130.
94   Macmillan, 'Return to the Malungwana Drift', 50–51.
95   This work is significantly different from the work by Moore and Vaughan, *Cutting Down Trees.*
96   Pritchett, *Lunda-Ndembu*, Chapter 3.

be outdated and discredited. Yet RLI conceptions of social change were, in certain respects, very similar to later ideas about the course of historical change.[97] The 'language, metaphors, problems, and solutions' employed in the 1950s have implicitly and explicitly influenced current understandings of social change.[98] To assert a parallel in modes of thought and representations between the 1950s and recent scholarship is in no way to suggest that this work has not moved beyond old debates. It is merely to acknowledge a strong historical legacy, as in Ferguson's words: 'the attachment of anthropologists and others to a linear metanarrative of emergence and progress is clearly an ongoing matter, and not simply an aspect of a now "out of date" historical past'.[99]

Parallel to the RLI interest in social change, 'modernisation' theories dominated academic thought from the 1950s onwards. Such theories provide prime examples of linear conceptualisations of social change.[100] Modernisation theories placed 'tradition' and 'modernity' in stark contrast, suggesting that in a historically progressive process traditional society would move towards modernity.[101] Ideas of modernisation have proven influential and enduring. Even if criticism of modernisation theories has been profound, recent work continues to engage with issues of modernity, its nature, and what it entails.[102] Postmodern studies criticise ideas of modernisation, yet they engage with notions of modernity. Despite all the insecurity about what 'the modern' is, it continues to be a point of departure. Ideas of modernity have become a metanarrative, connoting assumptions that are not always voiced, but are ever present and

---

97   This is evidenced by the academic interest in RLI studies; see for example: Johan Pottier, *Migrants No More: Settlement and Survival in Mambwe Villages, Zambia* (Manchester: Manchester University Press, 1988); Crehan, *The Fractured Community*; Gordon, 'Rites of Rebellion'; Moore and Vaughan, *Cutting Down Trees*; Ferguson, *Expectations of Modernity.*

98   Moore and Vaughan, *Cutting Down Trees,* XXI.

99   Ferguson, *Expectations of Modernity,* 16.

100   These ideas date back to the age of Enlightenment, but their main articulation was after the Second World War by scholars such as Walt W. Rostow, *The Stages of Economic Growth: A Non-Communist Manifesto* (Cambridge: Cambridge University Press, 1960). See: Thomas, 'Modernity's Failings', 727–40; Frederick Cooper, 'Africa's Pasts and Africa's Historians', *Canadian Journal of African Studies* 34, No. 2 (2000): 298–336; Joseph C. Miller, 'History and Africa/Africa and History', *The American Historical Review* 104, No. 1 (1999): 1–32, for a discussion of progressive narratives of history and ideas about modernity and modernisation in African historiography.

101   Shmuel N. Eisenstadt, *Tradition, Change, and Modernity* (New York: John Wiley & Sons, 1972), 10; Cooper, 'What is the Concept of Globalization Good for?', 196–97, 206; Thomas, 'Modernity's Failings', 727.

102   Englund and Leach, 'Ethnography and the Meta-Narratives of Modernity'; Thomas, 'Modernity's Failings'; Ferguson, *Expectations of Modernity.*

inform thought.[103] This book argues that the understanding of social change in Mwinilunga has been heavily influenced by ideas of linear social change, modernisation, and development. These ideas, therefore, have to be taken seriously and examined critically.

By studying a particular historical manifestation of social change, this work highlights 'the persistence of attitudes about modernity (...) that were first initiated by colonial rulers in the 1930s and 1940s but which continued to hold value for development practitioners and national elites until the 1970s' and beyond.[104] Critical development studies have stressed that history is full of 'ideas of linear progress', which cannot simply be avoided.[105] In Cullather's words, even after 'decades of debunking, modernization theory' can come back 'like a bad habit'.[106] The central tenets of such discourses, according to Hodge, 'continue to persist and permeate the minds of policy makers and analysts, seemingly impervious to criticism and meaningful reform'.[107] By putting 'the context, personalities and politics back in', ideas of social change, modernisation, and development can be historicised.[108] By paying attention to diverse, plural, and particular expressions of social change, this book seeks to reveal how the meanings of social change, modernisation, and development have changed over time in Mwinilunga. How did ideas about social change 'emerge, persist, change, succeed, or fail'?[109] This approach enables writing about social change 'without accepting its clichés'.[110] Such a historicist understanding of social change, modernisation, and development has been touted by Unger as 'one of the most productive fields of research in the area of international, global, and transnational history in recent years'.[111] Importantly, ideas of social change, modernisation, and development are not 'an undifferentiated and unvarying hegemonic force'.[112] Rather, their contradictions and complexities – which

---

103   Englund and Leach, 'Ethnography and the Meta-Narratives of Modernity, 226.

104   Joseph M. Hodge, 'Writing the History of Development (Part 2: Longer, Deeper, Wider)', *Humanity: An International Journal of Human Rights, Humanitarianism and Development* 7, No. 1 (2016): 132.

105   Nick Cullather, 'Development? It's History', *Diplomatic History* 24, No. 4 (2000): 647.

106   Ibidem, 646.

107   Joseph M. Hodge, 'Writing the History of Development (Part 1: The First Wave)', *Humanity: An International Journal of Human Rights, Humanitarianism, and Development* 6, No. 3 (2015): 429.

108   Cullather, 'Development?', 648.

109   Hodge, 'Writing the History of Development (Part 2)', 139.

110   Cullather, 'Development?', 642.

111   Corinna R. Unger, 28 April 2016, Humanity Journal Blog: http://humanityjournal.org/blog/comment-on-joseph-hodge-on-the-historiography-of-development-part-i-and-ii/.

112   Hodge, 'Writing the History of Development (Part 1)', 443.

created plural meanings and outcomes – need to be brought out through historical case studies that do not merely analyse discourses, but pay attention to diverse practices and actors. Such practical studies have pointed out that we should 'think of *histories* of development and modernization, with heterogeneous beginnings and divergent paths that regularly intersect, overlap, and are reconfigured along the way'.[113] Ultimately, the global history of ideas about social change 'must be written from the local, by carefully analyzing specific encounters and practices on the ground'.[114] As Engerman and Unger emphasise, 'local studies offer an excellent avenue to the study of global studies of modernization without losing sight of regional, national, and international circumstances'.[115] Adopting a focus on the long-term histories and context of ideas of social change, development, and modernisation as well as the various actors and interests involved and their outcomes on the ground, allows an understanding of social change 'as a dynamic enterprise, not a single unchanging set of ideas'.[116]

The following chapters examine the process of social change in a local setting, as, according to Ferguson, 'the dismantling of linear teleologies of emergence and development remains an unfinished task – indeed a task barely begun – in African studies and elsewhere'.[117] How did 'big forces', such as colonialism and capitalism, influence – but in turn equally become shaped and changed by – actors operating on a small-scale local level?[118] This book asserts that narratives of linear social change did not match the intricacies of historical practice. Change was not all encompassing, as previous practices lingered on and actively shaped responses to change.[119] Rather than stressing linear and transformative social change, people in Mwinilunga tend to emphasise a degree of continuity with the past. Notwithstanding changing appearances and fundamental social change, the Lunda still 'speak of themselves as a people who have successfully maintained their traditions'.[120] Far from being a mark of changelessness, traditions according to Spear, are 'continually transformed

113   Hodge, 'Writing the History of Development (Part 2)', 147.
114   Ibidem, 148–49.
115   David C. Engerman and Corinna R. Unger, 'Introduction: Towards a Global History of Modernization', *Diplomatic History* 33, No. 3 (2009): 377.
116   Ibidem, 380.
117   Ferguson, *Expectations of Modernity*, 17.
118   Crehan, *The Fractured Community*, 9.
119   See: Frank Trentmann, 'The Politics of Everyday Life', in *The Oxford Handbook of the History of Consumption,* ed., Frank Trentmann (Oxford: Oxford University Press, 2012), 521–47; Cooper, 'What is the Concept of Globalization Good for?', 192; Spear, *Mountain Farmers,* 238.
120   Pritchett, *Lunda-Ndembu,* 5; This view has been confirmed by numerous interviews.

as people struggle over social changes and conflicts within their society'.[121] Tradition has enabled people in Mwinilunga to make sense of and deal with change: 'Tradition is thus both persistent and changing, a kind of historical running average, as the lessons of the past are continually reinterpreted in the context of a present that is itself in the process of being assimilated into the past'.[122] Traditions change, but they do so gradually and incrementally, they are 'continually reinterpreted and reconstructed as 'regulated improvisations' subject to their continued intelligibility and legitimacy'.[123] Thus, traditions can be 'critically important in understanding historical processes of social change and representation'.[124] This book asserts that studying the changing role of tradition enables an alternative understanding of the process of social change in Mwinilunga.[125]

3   Continuity and Change in Central African Historiography

In recent years, excellent work has been published on the Central African region and Zambia in particular. Ranging from political histories, to studies of religion and spirituality, consumption and rural-urban connections, this work emphasises the role of individuals in influencing broader societal structures.[126] Through a critical engagement with narratives of social change, this

121   Thomas T. Spear, 'Neo-traditionalism and the Limits of Invention in British Colonial Africa', *Journal of African History* 44, No. 1 (2003): 6.
122   Spear, *Mountain Farmers*, 238.
123   Spear, 'Neo-traditionalism and the Limits of Invention', 26; Neil Kodesh, 'Renovating Tradition: The Discourse of Succession in Colonial Buganda', *The International Journal of African Historical Studies* 34, No. 3 (2001): 511–41.
124   Spear, 'Neo-traditionalism and the Limits of Invention', 5–6.
125   This approach draws inspiration from Vansina, *Paths in the Rainforests*; Corinne A. Kratz, "'We've Always Done It like This ... Except for a Few Details": "Tradition" and "Innovation" in Okiek Ceremonies', *Comparative Studies in Society and History* 35, No. 1 (1993): 30–65; David L. Schoenbrun, 'Conjuring the Modern in Africa: Durability and Rupture in Histories of Public Healing Between the Great Lakes of East Africa', *The American Historical Review* 111, No. 5 (2006): 1403–39; Patrick Harries, 'Imagery, Symbolism and Tradition in a South African Bantustan: Mangosuthu Buthelezi, Inkhata, and Zulu history', *History and Theory* 32, No. 4 (1993): 105–25; Pritchett, *Lunda-Ndembu*.
126   A selection is: Jan-Bart Gewald, Marja Hinfelaar, and Giacomo Macola, eds., *One Zambia, Many Histories: Towards a History of Post-Colonial Zambia* (Leiden: Brill, 2008); Miles Larmer, *Rethinking African Politics: A History of Opposition in Zambia* (Farnham: Ashgate, 2011); Giacomo Macola, *Liberal Nationalism in Central Africa: A Biography of Harry Mwaanga Nkumbula* (New York: Palgrave Macmillan, 2010); David M. Gordon, *Invisible Agents: Spirits in a Central African History* (Athens: Ohio University Press, 2012); Walima

book contributes to such scholarship, thereby reframing some of the long-standing debates within Central African historiography. One of the most fervent and influential discussions in African history concerns the relationship between exogenous forces and local agency.[127] Central African historiography has reflected on the role of colonialism, in conjunction with capitalism, industrialisation, and urbanisation, as propelling an 'epochal divide'.[128] Such work stresses external and transformative change, more than internally generated change or continuity.[129] A prime example within Zambian historiography is Macpherson's work, which asserts that colonial rule was established rapidly and unproblematically, if violently.[130] For Mwinilunga, Pritchett similarly emphasises the rupture caused by the violent imposition of colonial rule. In an attempt to study continuity and change, Pritchett uses history to gain an understanding of the present and to comprehend the 'indigenization of social change'.[131] Due to a reliance on secondary sources to outline the history of Mwinilunga,[132] Pritchett overemphasises historical ruptures, such as the overwhelming influence of long-distance trade, the transformative nature of colonialism, or the impact of post-colonial development schemes. By using a more comprehensive range of archival and oral history sources, this book historicises notions of continuity and change in Mwinilunga, thereby stressing internal over external factors of change and patterns of continuity over

---

T. Kalusa and Megan Vaughan, *Death, Belief and Politics in Central African History* (Lusaka: Lembani Trust, 2013); Patience N. Mususa, 'There Used to Be Order: Life on the Copperbelt After the Privatisation of the Zambia Consolidated Copper Mines', (Unpublished PhD Thesis, University of Cape Town, 2014); Rita Kesselring, 'At an Extractive Pace: Conflicting Temporalities in a Resettlement Process in Solwezi, Zambia', *The Extractive Industries and Society* 5, No. 2 (2018): 237–44; Jessica Achberger, *Negotiating for Development: Zambian Economic Development in the Cold War* (Brill, forthcoming); Duncan J. Money, 'The World of European Labour on the Zambian Copperbelt, 1940–1945', *International Review of Social History* 60, No. 2 (2015): 225–55; Robert Ross, Marja Hinfelaar, and Iva Peša, eds., *The Objects of Life in Central Africa: The History of Consumption and Social Change, 1840–1980* (Leiden: Brill, 2013).

127   See in particular: Comaroff and Comaroff, *Of Revelation and Revolution;* Spear, *Mountain Farmers;* Moore and Vaughan, *Cutting Down Trees.*

128   Stephen Ellis, 'Writing Histories of Contemporary Africa', *Journal of African History* 43, No. 1 (2002): 5; RLI work equally proposed such views.

129   For a critique, see Steven Feierman, 'African Histories and the Dissolution of World History', in *Africa and the Disciplines: The Contributions of Research in Africa to the Social Sciences and Humanities,* eds., Valentin Y. Mudimbe, Jean F. O'Barr, and Robert H. Bates (Chicago: University of Chicago Press, 1993), 167–212.

130   Macpherson, *Anatomy of a Conquest.*

131   Pritchett, *Lunda-Ndembu,* 7.

132   Gewald, 'Researching and Writing', 471; Gordon, 'Rites of Rebellion', 131–32.

rupture.[133] Through a close reading of archival sources, Gewald, for example, has pointed out that 'the incoming colonial administration [in Northern Rhodesia] was far from powerful, and was, instead, dependant on the goodwill of the local population'.[134] Instead of emphasising the transformative nature of social change, as RLI scholars and much of the subsequent historiography has done, this book focuses attention on individual agency, local negotiation, and internally generated processes of change.[135] In this manner, the gradual nature of change and the long-term continuities that shaped consciousness and lived reality in Mwinilunga become apparent.[136] Walima Kalusa, in his meticulous study of medical practitioners in Mwinilunga, paints this kind of more balanced picture. Challenging the transformative, disruptive, and exogenous nature of colonial rule, Kalusa argues that the 'projection of colonizers as an all-powerful entity whose policies turned Africans into hapless victims' obscures 'the ways in which people on the imperial frontier appropriated western (...) knowledge and technologies'.[137] Kalusa proposes studying colonial rule through notions of dialogue and local agency, emphasising that the colonial encounter could produce unintended consequences beyond administrative control. Responses to colonialism should 'be read as part and parcel of a long-established tradition of cultural reinterpretation that preceded and outlived colonialism'.[138] Through a focus on dialogue and local agency, the case study of Mwinilunga informs broader debates about colonialism and social change in Central African historiography.

One way in which this book challenges prevailing analyses of social change in Mwinilunga is through a broad temporal focus (1870s–1970s). The common division of African history into pre-colonial, colonial, and post-colonial periods already indicates that many scholars have viewed colonialism as presenting a fundamental rupture in historical practice, consciousness, and

133   Spear, *Mountain Farmers*, 8.
134   Gewald, 'Researching and Writing', 471.
135   Spear, *Mountain Farmers*, 8: 'Many writers stress the external forces acting on African societies as the main causes of change ... [yet] such a focus is clearly inadequate ... when it comes either to explaining the multitude of changes which have occurred within African societies or to understanding how and why Africans responded to external forces as they did.'
136   Inspiration for this approach was taken from: Spear, *Mountain Farmers*; Vansina, *Paths in the Rainforests*.
137   Kalusa, 'Disease and the Remaking of Missionary Medicine', 9; see also his 'Language, Medical Auxiliaries, and the Re-Interpretation of Missionary Medicine in Colonial Mwinilunga, Zambia, 1922–51', *Journal of Eastern African Studies* 1, No. 1 (2007): 57–78.
138   Kalusa, 'Disease and the Remaking of Missionary Medicine', 221.

representation.[139] Official reports, works by the RLI, and much historiography have suggested that 'colonialism has to be seen as introducing a real
discontinuity'.[140] The break brought about by colonialism has been linked to a
host of transitions, such as those from pre-colonial self-sufficiency to colonial
and post-colonial market integration. Yet such discursive transitions obscure
the long-term trends and continuities that straddle temporal divides.[141] Due to
the availability of written sources, the pre-colonial analysis of this work starts
in 1870, but the historical overview chapter will point out long-term trends
from the 1750s onwards.[142] To question whether political independence in 1964
constituted a rupture or if continuities prevailed, the analysis extends until the
1970s, adding observations from later periods where appropriate.[143] By bridging discursive temporal divides, the focus on the period from the 1870s until
the 1970s contests linear transitions, focusing attention on long-term trends
and continuities instead.

   Mwinilunga shares a number of traits with the surrounding area. A regional
focus that highlights interconnections is therefore indispensable. The empiri-
cally rich work of writers such as Von Oppen, Miller, Schecter, Hoover, Crehan, Kalusa, Chabatama, and Kakoma has facilitated the contextualisation of
Mwinilunga within the long-term historical trends of the broader area.[144] Such
works have pointed out that even global forces that appear at first sight to have

---

139   Ellis, 'Writing Histories of Contemporary Africa', 5; for critiques, see: Schoenbrun, 'Con-
      juring the Modern'; Cooper, 'Africa's Pasts and Africa's Historians', 306, 318; Allen M. How-
      ard, 'Nodes, Networks, Landscapes, and Regions: Reading the Social History of Tropical
      Africa 1700s–1920', in *The Spatial Factor in African History: The Relationship Between the
      Social, Material, and Perceptual*, eds., Allen M. Howard and Richard M. Shain (Leiden:
      Brill, 2005), 103–04.
140   Crehan, *The Fractured Community*, 56.
141   For a critique, see Feierman, 'African Histories and the Dissolution of World History',
      167–212.
142   For pre-colonial trends, see: Von Oppen, *Terms of Trade*; Joseph C. Miller, *Way of Death:
      Merchant Capitalism and the Angolan Slave Trade 1730–1830* (Madison: University of Wis-
      consin Press, 1988); Robert E. Schecter, 'History and Historiography on a Frontier of Lunda
      Expansion: The Origins and Early Development of the Kanongesha' (Unpublished PhD
      Thesis, University of Wisconsin Madison, 1976); Gordon, 'The Abolition of the Slave Trade.'
143   For post-colonial accounts, see: Miles Larmer and Giacomo Macola, 'The Origins, Con-
      text, and Political Significance of the Mushala Rebellion Against the Zambian One-party
      State', *The International Journal of African Historical Studies* 40, No. 3 (2007): 471–96; Ge-
      wald, Hinfelaar, and Macola, *One Zambia, Many Histories*.
144   See above, and Jeffrey J. Hoover, 'The Seduction of Ruwej: Reconstructing Ruund History
      (The Nuclear Lunda: Zaïre, Angola, Zambia)' (Unpublished PhD Thesis, Yale University,
      1978); Chewe M. Chabatama, 'Peasant Farming, the State, and Food Security in the North-
      Western Province of Zambia, 1902–1964' (Unpublished PhD Thesis, University of Toronto,
      1999); Ben C. Kakoma, 'Colonial Administration in Northern Rhodesia: A Case Study of

a universal or homogenising influence are adapted in locally specific ways.[145] The social history of Mwinilunga highlights the specificity, appropriation, and internalisation of change. In this respect, even micro studies of remote localities can advance our understanding of larger forces such as capitalism, as Crehan has pointed out for nearby Kasempa:

> Concern with the small details of people's day-to-day lives in particular times and places allows us to trace out something of what the large abstractions of monetization, commoditization, the state, and so on actually mean on the level of individual lives (...) Precisely because of its narrow focus, the carefully located case study enables us to explore both the creativity of individuals and the structuring of the spaces within which that creativity is exercised.[146]

Studying one locality in depth over a long period illustrates issues of continuity and change, structure and agency, as well as processes of social change.

The history of social change in Mwinilunga contributes to several ongoing debates in Central African historiography. Most notable are the debates on labour migration, capitalism, and kinship. Due to the Copperbelt mines, urban studies and questions of labour migration dominate Zambian historiography.[147] Amin has negatively described Zambia as part of 'Africa of the labour reserves', suggesting that labour migration dominantly marked processes of social change in the country.[148] The effects of labour migration on local communities have received much attention. Most studies have assumed that labour migration would profoundly affect, or even transform, the economic, social, and political organisation of villages, either negatively (leading to

———

Colonial Policy in the Mwinilunga District of Zambia, 1901–1939' (MA Thesis, University of Auckland, 1971).

145 Cooper, 'What is the Concept of Globalization Good for?'; Prestholdt, *Domesticating the World*.

146 Crehan, *The Fractured Community*, 233.

147 See RLI work or recently: Miles Larmer, 'At the Crossroads: Mining and Political Change on the Katangese-Zambian Copperbelt', *Oxford Handbooks Online* (2016); Ferguson, *Expectations of Modernity*; Jane L. Parpart, '"Where is Your Mother?": Gender, Urban Marriage, and Colonial Discourse on the Zambian Copperbelt, 1924–1945', *The International Journal of African Historical Studies* 27, No. 2 (1994): 241–71; For rural studies, see: Moore and Vaughan, *Cutting Down Trees*; Pottier, *Migrants No More*.

148 Samir Amin, 'Underdevelopment and Dependence in Black Africa: Historical Origin', *Journal of Peace Research* 9, No. 105 (1972): 105–19.

proletarianisation, agricultural decline, and family breakdown)[149] or positively
(by creating wealth and agricultural entrepreneurship).[150] Less attention has
been paid to the more gradual and subtle socioeconomic and cultural changes
brought about by labour migration, which were not necessarily transformative. This study sets the case of Mwinilunga within the regional context of mobility, by emphasising the longstanding nature of mobility and the agency of
actors as they participated in urban economies or straddled the rural-urban
divide.[151] Next to economic incentives, labour migrants were motivated by
sociocultural aspirations towards 'self-realisation'.[152] Existing debates have all
too often adopted polarising dichotomies of urban and rural, development and
underdevelopment, or modernity and tradition.[153] The case of Mwinilunga
challenges such dichotomies, by pointing out the variety in migrant labourers'
life histories. Some migrants returned, whereas others stayed in urban areas.
Consequently, clearly defined 'stages' of migration – as suggested by the 'modernist narrative' – do not seem to apply.[154] This book provides an empirical
analysis of life histories, which go against linear narratives of social change and
trajectories of migration, to advance debates on labour migration.

Questions of labour migration are conceptually closely linked to debates on
capitalism.[155] Such works have assumed that labour migration and capitalism,
in conjunction, would profoundly restructure the relationship between rural

149   For rural breakdown, see Richards, *Land, Labour, Diet;* for a critique, Moore and Vaughan,
      Cutting Down Trees.
150   Watson, *Tribal Cohesion in A Money Economy*; Kenneth P. Vickery, *Black and White in
      Southern Zambia: The Tonga Plateau Economy and British Imperialism 1890–1939* (New
      York: Greenwood Publishing, 1986).
151   See Oliver Bakewell, 'Refugees Repatriating or Migrating Villagers: A Study of Movement
      from North West Zambia to Angola' (Unpublished PhD Thesis, University of Bath, 1999);
      Igor Kopytoff, ed., *The African Frontier: The Reproduction of Traditional African Societies*
      (Bloomington: Indiana University Press, 1987); Jens A. Andersson, 'Re-interpreting the
      Rural-Urban Connection: Migration Practices and Socio-cultural Dispositions of Buhera
      Workers in Harare', *Africa* 71, No. 1 (2001): 82–112; Harri Englund, 'The Village in the City,
      the City in the Village: Migrants in Lilongwe', *The Journal of Southern African Studies* 28,
      No. 1 (2002): 137–54.
152   Guyer, 'Wealth in People and Self-Realization'; Andersson, 'Re-Interpreting the Rural-
      Urban Connection'; Englund, 'The Village In the City.'
153   See: Ferguson, *Expectations of Modernity*; Jens A. Andersson, 'Informal Moves, Informal
      Markets: International Migrants and Traders from Mzimba, Malawi', *African Affairs* 105,
      No. 420 (2006): 375–97.
154   See the discussion between Ferguson, 'Mobile Workers, Modernist Narratives' and Mac-
      millan, 'The Historiography of Transition.'
155   See: Amin, 'Underdevelopment and Dependence'; Arjan De Haan, 'Livelihoods and Pov-
      erty: The Role of Migration – A Critical Review of the Migration Literature', *The Journal of
      Development Studies* 36, No. 2 (1999): 1–47.

and urban areas.[156] For rural areas, the role of markets and the influence of global capitalism on spheres of production, consumption, and social relationships have been vehemently discussed.[157] It has long been debated whether Africa's involvement in the world economy led, in Cooper's words, 'along a road toward material and social progress or into a dead end'.[158] The case of Mwinilunga questions linear assumptions about change, such as those suggesting a transition from subsistence to market production, as the example of cassava showed earlier.[159] Capitalism was not a monolithic force, and this is borne out by the variety of reactions to cash crop production throughout Zambia. In the Southern Province, situated along the railway line and well connected to major markets, both small peasants and large-scale farmers emerged who focused on producing maize as a cash crop.[160] The same prosperity did not extend to other parts of the country, though. The Northern Province, quite differently, provides an example of agricultural breakdown under the influence of labour migration.[161] Mwinilunga is different again, for neither did the area experience agricultural collapse, nor did large-scale wealthy farmers emerge. Instead, as Chabatama has shown, 'most of the peasants of North-Western province remained relatively food secure in colonial Zambia, largely due to their resilience, initiative, and industriousness'.[162]

By historicising processes of social change, this book seeks to contribute to debates on the influence of capitalism, markets, and the state in Mwinilunga, and in the Central African region more broadly. Much more than Turner and Pritchett's work, this study focuses on the socioeconomic aspects of daily life.[163] Taking the material basis of society as a vantage point enables a

---

156 Amin, 'Underdevelopment and Dependence.'

157 See: Karl Polanyi, Conrad M. Arensberg and Harry W. Pearson, eds., *Trade and Market in the Early Empires: Economies in History and Theory* (Glencoe: The Free Press, 1957); Paul J. Bohannan and George Dalton, eds., *Markets in Africa* (Evanston: Northwestern University Press, 1962).

158 Frederick Cooper, 'Africa and the World Economy', *African Studies Review* 24, No. 2/3 (1981): 1.

159 Robert H. Bates, 'Some Conventional Orthodoxies in the Study of Agrarian Change', *World Politics* 36, No. 2 (1984): 234–54.

160 Vickery, *Black and White*; Toby Moorsom, '"Black Settlers": Hybridity, Neoliberalism and Ecosystemic Change Among Tonga Farmers of Southern Zambia, 1964–2008' (Unpublished PhD Thesis, Queen's University at Kingston, 2016). See also Andrew Bowman, 'Ecology to Technocracy: Scientists, Surveys and Power in the Agricultural Development of Late-colonial Zambia', *Journal of Southern African Studies* 37, No. 1 (2011): 135–53.

161 Moore and Vaughan, *Cutting Down Trees*, provide a more nuanced view.

162 Chabatama, 'Peasant Farming, the State, and Food Security', 111.

163 Van Binsbergen, 'Manchester as the Birth Place', 36; Van Donge, 'Understanding Rural Zambia Today', argues that the RLI did adopt a specific focus on material aspects of life.

different understanding of processes of social change, highlighting gradual changes rather than ruptures.[164] A socioeconomic approach emphasises issues of livelihood procurement, agricultural production, the consumption of goods, and motives for labour migration.[165] Here are some examples of the questions addressed. How did cash crop production influence social organisation in villages? Was the acquisition of store-bought goods a sign of market integration or did it merely lead to dependency? To answer such questions, a shifting focus on 'large structures' and case studies of daily life are required in order to understand how 'the great surging narrative of contemporary capitalism translates into real power relations among real people in real places'.[166] This work analyses the nature of capitalism in Mwinilunga, whilst remaining attentive to local variations and specificities of production, consumption, and social relationships.

Existing works have suggested that capitalism not only influenced patterns of mobility, production, and consumption but affected social relationships and kinship as well.[167] According to Turner, the effects were negative: 'Everywhere, we see the spectacle of corporate groups of kin disintegrating, and the emergence of smaller residential units based on the elementary family'.[168] Turner predicted that forces of colonialism and capitalism would exacerbate the inherent tension between matrilineal descent and virilocal marriage, causing village conflicts that could only temporarily be resolved through ritual redress.[169] RLI scholars, innovatively laying the foundation for current understandings of kinship, portrayed kinship as one of the mechanisms through which access to land, labour, and material resources could be negotiated, 'the flexible, dependent and contingent result of processes of political manipulation within that group'.[170] Even if the RLI understood kinship association as dynamic and flexible, RLI scholars have equally tended to view the relationship between kinship and socioeconomic and political organisation as causal or unidirectional, assuming that the cash economy would lead to an individualisation of

---

164   For neo-materialism, see Jane Bennett, *Vibrant Matter: A Political Ecology of Things* (Durham: Duke University Press, 2010).

165   For a similar approach, see: Moore and Vaughan, *Cutting Down Trees*; Spear, *Mountain Farmers*.

166   Crehan, *The Fractured Community*, 9.

167   See Robert H. Bates, 'Capital, Kinship, and Conflict: The Structuring Influence of Capital in Kinship Societies', *Canadian Journal of African Studies* 24, No. 2 (1990): 151–64.

168   Turner, *Schism and Continuity*, 43.

169   See: Turner, *Schism and Continuity*; Turner, *Drums of Affliction*; Pritchett, *Lunda-Ndembu*; Van Doorne, 'Situational Analysis', 486–88.

170   Van Binsbergen, 'Manchester as the Birth Place', 37; Van Donge, 'Understanding Rural Zambia Today', 66–68.

society and a disencumbering of extended kinship links.[171] Instead, this study asserts a dialectical relationship between kinship and social change. Socio-economic relations stimulate particular forms of kinship, but in turn, relationships of kinship shape reactions to socioeconomic and political change. Affiliations among extended kin have not simply given way to the nuclear family or to a process of individualisation, as RLI scholars had predicted. Pritchett aptly illustrates the continued importance of relationships of kinship, generation, gender, and class in Mwinilunga.[172] This book builds on Pritchett's examination, asking how relationships of kinship are related to and affected by processes of social change. By looking at the nature, course, and direction of social change in Mwinilunga, this study thus contributes to broader debates on labour migration, capitalism, and kinship in Central Africa.

4   A Local History of Social Change

In order to grasp processes of social change, it is imperative to situate this case study in space as well as time. How is it possible to study broad historical processes, such as colonisation, monetisation, capitalism or nationalism through the lens of a specific locality? Within Zambia, Mwinilunga is regarded as a 'remote' or even 'marginal' area.[173] In Lusaka, some people pejoratively refer to Mwinilunga as 'the end of Zambia', as its border location and bad infrastructure make the area difficult to reach. Crehan asks how we should 'understand the place of "peripheral" rural communities within the overall trajectory of a global capitalist development that would seem to be continually expanding and reaching ever deeper into ever more corners of the world', but which 'at the same time has traced such a grossly skewed and uneven path'.[174] Sometimes locations at the margin can reveal broader processes, such as capitalism or globalisation, with particular clarity, by pointing towards reception, reinterpretation, negotiation, domestication, and local specificity.[175] The conclusions

---

171   Van Donge, 'Understanding Rural Zambia Today', 61. See also: Pritchett, *Lunda-Ndembu*; Crehan, *The Fractured Community*; Moore and Vaughan, *Cutting Down Trees*. Also Berry, *No Condition Is Permanent*; Wyatt MacGaffey, 'Changing Representations in Central African History', *Journal of African History* 46, No. 2 (2005): 189–207.

172   Pritchett, *Lunda-Ndembu*; for a similar view, see Berry, *No Condition Is Permanent*.

173   See: Pritchett, *Lunda-Ndembu*; Von Oppen, 'The Village as Territory: Enclosing Locality in Northwest Zambia, 1950s to 1990s', *Journal of African History* 47, No. 1 (2006): 60–61; Crehan, *The Fractured Community*, 1, 12.

174   Crehan, *The Fractured Community*, 15.

175   Miller, 'History and Africa/Africa and History', 30; Prestholdt, *Domesticating the World*.

reached for Mwinilunga in this book will not necessarily apply to other parts of the region. Nonetheless, studying a specific area illustrates that even processes that appear to be universal do not have a single outcome.[176] Conducting a study of continuity and change in this area provides examples of how broad processes gain local specificity, how social change is mediated through historical practice and local agency. According to Cooper, studying capitalism in African localities is interesting exactly because of its anomalies, which point towards the variability of global trends and outcomes. A study of the locality of Mwinilunga thus illuminates 'large-scale, long-term processes without overlooking specificity, contingency and contestation'.[177]

Mwinilunga is not a bounded unit of study. Prior to the colonial period, Mwinilunga District was not even a unit as such and the inhabitants of the area continue to be characterised by mobility. Labour migration, kinship, and chiefly politics link Mwinilunga to the surrounding region in multiple ways.[178] Most interviewees, for example, had been born in, had lived in or had relatives in Angola and/or the D.R. Congo. Nevertheless, it makes sense to view the social history of Mwinilunga District, which did increasingly become a unit over the course of the twentieth century, through the lens of space and place.[179] A spatial approach, as proposed by Howard, 'draws attention to the places and zones of interaction where people carried out social practices and generated perceptions', about identity, social belonging, and relationships to the wider world.[180] This book analyses how individuals in Mwinilunga constituted social relationships in space, focusing on cohesion as well as contestation between local, regional, national, and global levels.[181] In the 1950s, Turner already pointed towards the importance of space, place and sociality in Mwinilunga by emphasising settlement patterns, village layout and social organisation. He observed that large concentric villages were progressively breaking up into smaller units located along the roadside, a process that influenced both space and sociality.[182] If inhabitants of the area indeed moved towards the roadside,

---

176   Cooper, 'What is the Concept of Globalization Good for?'; Prestholdt, *Domesticating the World*.
177   Cooper, 'What is the Concept of Globalization Good for?', 200.
178   Bakewell, 'Refugees Repatriating', 95–97; Schecter, 'History and Historiography.'
179   For a similar approach in nearby Chavuma, see Von Oppen, 'Bounding Villages.'
180   Allen M. Howard and Richard M. Shain, eds., *The Spatial Factor in African History: The Relationship Between the Social, Material, and Perceptual* (Leiden: Brill, 2005), 21.
181   See: Howard and Shain, *The Spatial Factor in African History*; Cristopher J. Gray, *Colonial Rule and Crisis in Equatorial Africa: Southern Gabon, ca. 1850–1940* (Rochester: University of Rochester Press, 2002).
182   Turner, *Schism and Continuity.*

to what extent did this influence forms of association and daily life? It is ana-
lytically fruitful to view the locality of Mwinilunga as a site where practices
are produced, where social reproduction and contestation takes place, where
meaning and historical consciousness are shaped.[183] These spatial processes,
after all, are the substance of social change.

Studying social change through the notions of space and locality is useful
because a locality is both spatial and social; it connotes not only physical space
but also social connections between inhabitants.[184] Locality can be regarded,
following von Oppen, 'as a particular *mode* of sociality, i.e. as a particular means
of structuring social relations, practices and identities in space and time'.[185]
A locality is not a bounded entity, but is historically constructed. It involves
a continuous process of creation, 'the production of locality', which reveals
power relations and contestations between actors.[186] This book analyses how
the locality of Mwinilunga was shaped and constructed over time. A locality
is inherently relational to a broader context, with which it is in constant dialogue.[187] What has the locality of Mwinilunga been produced 'from, against,
in spite of, and in relation to'?[188] Focusing on the production of locality sheds
light on practices, ideas and values, thereby exemplifying the nature, pace and
outcome of processes of social change. Local neighbourhoods, in Appadurai's
words:

> ... are contexts in the sense that they provide the frame or setting within
> which various kinds of human action (productive, reproductive, inter-
> pretive, performative) can be initiated and conducted meaningfully (...) a
> neighborhood is a context, or a set of contexts, within which meaningful
> social action can be both generated and interpreted.[189]

In this sense, a locality defines its importance and meaning vis-à-vis other
localities, regions and global developments. Such an understanding of locality is inherently contextual, suggesting interactive linkages between different
scales (local-regional-national-global). The production of locality is driven by
this broader context, but also generates its own context, within which local

---

183   Arjun Appadurai, 'The Production of Locality', in *Modernity at Large: Cultural Dimensions
       of Globalization* (Minneapolis: University of Minnesota Press, 2003), 178–99.
184   Appadurai, 'The Production of Locality', 178.
185   Von Oppen, 'Bounding Villages', 17.
186   Appadurai, 'The Production of Locality', 181.
187   Von Oppen, 'Bounding Villages', 14.
188   Appadurai, 'The Production of Locality', 184.
189   Ibidem.

actions, ideas and values become intelligible. This book therefore focuses on
sketching the spatial context of Mwinilunga District, by providing examples of
the connections between Mwinilunga and the Central African region as well as
the specificity of the locality itself. Combining the lenses of space, locality and
history produces a thorough understanding of social change in Mwinilunga.

This study focuses on individual consciousness, motives and agency by approaching social change from the vantage point of everyday history.[190] It seeks
to foreground the experiences, actions and habits of individuals, even if these
appear contradictory, elusive or slowly changing. The everyday is familiar and
can therefore easily escape observation, because it changes so slowly. Yet the
everyday is also the site where 'people find meaning, develop habits, and acquire a sense of themselves and their world'.[191] Moreover, the everyday can be
a platform on 'which people through their actions exercise direct influence on
their condition'.[192] It is in the everyday that practices, habits and beliefs are
reinforced or come under pressure and change. The everyday life of people in
Mwinilunga changed only gradually, thereby refuting narratives of transformative change. Studying everyday life in the locality of Mwinilunga thus contributes to understanding the paradox between continuity and change.

5   Approach, Aims, and Method

This book asserts that historical change in Mwinilunga has dominantly been
understood and represented within a metanarrative of linear and transformative social change. This metanarrative has found expression in three separate,
but interconnected, domains: in official policy, academic debate, and in local
historical consciousness.[193] Representations, be they those of colonial officials, experts, or anthropologists, 'have a foothold in the complexities of the
real world, but more important they have as one of their sets of referents those
practices, meanings, and values' of historical actors themselves.[194] Yet this does
not mean that narratives adequately reflect processes of social change, or
that any single representation provides an indisputable frame to understand

---

190   See John Brewer, 'Microhistory and the Histories of Everyday Life', *Cultural and Social His-
       tory* 7, No. 1 (2010): 89.
191   Frank Trentmann, 'The Politics of Everyday Life', in *The Oxford Handbook of the History of
       Consumption*, ed., Frank Trentmann (Oxford: Oxford University Press, 2012), 522.
192   Ibidem, 529.
193   See Crehan, 'Tribes and the People Who Read Books', for a similar disaggregation.
194   Moore and Vaughan, *Cutting Down Trees*, XIX.

historical practices.[195] This work examines to what extent the metanarrative of social change in Mwinilunga adequately reflected historical practice and processes of social change.

In the chapters of this book, the general metanarrative of social change has been translated into four hypotheses for the spheres of production, mobility, consumption, and social relationships. These hypotheses are as follows: for the sphere of production, a transition from subsistence to market production of cash crops has been proposed; for the sphere of mobility, a mobility transition has been postulated, either positively leading to development or negatively leading to underdevelopment; for the sphere of consumption, a transition from self-sufficiency to a dependency on mass-produced store-bought goods has been proposed; for the sphere of social relationships, a transition from extended kinship affiliation to family nucleation and individualisation has been postulated. These hypotheses, and their attendant predictions about the course of social change, have been adopted by colonial and post-colonial officials, anthropologists, scholars, and to a certain extent even by the population of Mwinilunga.[196] Alleged transitions have been presented as historically progressive in academic work, government policy, and local discourse alike.[197] Due to the passage of time, such predictions can be tested today. Was there indeed a trend towards individualisation? Or did historical practice diverge from the hypotheses formulated within the metanarrative of social change? Such questions will be answered through a detailed reconstruction of historical practices in Mwinilunga from the 1870s until the 1970s. If the hypotheses about the nature and course of social change did not prove true, how can this be explained? Based on historical reconstruction, alternative frameworks for understanding social change in Mwinilunga will be proposed.[198] The account provided in this book is but one interpretation of historical events. Despite careful analysis, there remain inevitable gaps and biases in the narrative. Some notes on the approach, method, and aims of this work will further explain the choices made and point towards the shortcomings.

This study approaches the specificity, nature, and course of social change in Mwinilunga by using a rich body of historical sources. The historical method is particularly suited for studying social change, because history 'is the study of, and explanation for, change'. The historical approach seeks to contextualise

---

195   Ibidem.
196   Turner, *Schism and Continuity*; Pritchett, *Lunda-Ndembu*.
197   Compare with Ferguson, *Expectations of Modernity*.
198   A similar approach has been adopted by Spear, *Mountain Farmers*.

events in order to identify 'the pace, direction, and essence of such change'.[199] Historians make sense of data by collecting, comparing, and integrating information from many types of sources, such as oral, written, and fieldwork materials, into a 'rich, multifaceted reconstruction that cannot be achieved by using any of these sources on its own'.[200] This research has made use of several types of sources, mainly archival material and oral history, combined with oral tradition and fieldwork observations. Because all accounts are 'particular representations embodying whole sets of assumptions', they can never represent 'raw unmediated "reality"'.[201] The historical method, by being attentive to ambiguities and balancing different accounts against each other, is a good tool to reach conclusions about the course of social change.

This research has consulted a wide range of archival sources dealing with Mwinilunga District. At the National Archives of Zambia (NAZ) in Lusaka, broad-ranging material on Mwinilunga District, the North Western Province, and Zambia as a whole is located.[202] The NAZ contain administrative reports, government publications, newspapers, and a collection of historical manuscripts. The Mwinilunga District Reports (tour, monthly, annual reports, and District Notebooks) proved of particular importance. The sources section at the end of this book contains a complete list of consulted documents. Sources for post-colonial history have been drawn mainly from the United National Independence Party archives (UNIPA) in Lusaka. In addition to reports and correspondence of the UNIP government, there is also a collection of material dealing with the African National Congress (ANC) in these archives. Material to contextualise labour migration from the urban end of the spectrum is located in the Zambia Consolidated Copper Mines archives (ZCCM) in Ndola. Additional data were gathered in the United Kingdom, in the Public Records Office (PRO) in Kew, the Rhodes House Library (BOD) in Oxford, and the Echoes of Service missionary collection (EOS) in the John Rylands Library in Manchester. These archives contain manuscripts by colonial officials, as well as diaries, correspondence, and newsletters of the missionaries of the Plymouth Brethren. Even if these documents 'do not constitute coherent reconstructed histories', they provide 'raw materials that make possible the writing of history'.[203]

---

199   David Henige, 'Oral Tradition as a Means of Reconstructing The Past', in *Writing African history,* ed., John E. Philips (Rochester: University of Rochester Press, 2005), 185.

200   Jan Vansina, 'Epilogue: Fieldwork in History', in *In Pursuit of History: Fieldwork in Africa,* eds., Carolyn K. Adenaike and Jan Vansina (Portsmouth: Heinemann, 1996), 135–36.

201   Crehan, *The Fractured Community,* 50.

202   See Marja Hinfelaar and Giacomo Macola, eds., *A First Guide to Non-governmental Archives in Zambia* (Lusaka: National Archives of Zambia, 2004).

203   Toyin Falola, 'Mission and Colonial Documents', in, *Writing African History,* ed., John E. Philips (Rochester: University of Rochester Press, 2005), 274–75.

These writings have been analysed both as representations and as data.[204] Written sources contain information about 'events' and 'facts', but as such they have their shortcomings.[205] Although written sources provide a wealth of information on administrative affairs, law and order, agriculture, medicine, education, and chiefly politics, they remain largely silent on other issues, providing only glimpses of daily life and social change, as Vansina notes:

> The reams of colonial paper express the point of view of outsiders. They do not tell us how events and situations were perceived by colonial or postcolonial subjects and they do not allow us to transcend the interpretations of the official outlook embedded in them (...) Momentous events, which are documented, are rare in the social history of communities, while changing trends often go unnoticed [in the archival record]. Moreover, much of what was going on was simply not visible to outsiders.[206]

To tease out details about social change, documents can be read 'against the grain' or 'in-between the lines'. This approach can recover the ambiguities, power relations, and unspoken issues hidden within archival records.[207] When read carefully, official records can illustrate local historical practice and consciousness even when they have been written by 'outsiders'. On the other hand, archival records can be studied as representations for the discourses they produce. Approaching the archives in this way embraces their shortcomings and biases. Official reports are the foundation upon which anthropologists and later scholars based their narratives of social change and they are thus a good starting point to study the development of discursive practices.[208] Yet archival sources have to be contextualised and, for this, other types of sources are indispensable.

Through oral data, in particular oral history and to a lesser extent oral tradition, this research has sought to supplement, contextualise, and question written sources. The alternative perspective provided by oral sources subordinates:

> ... the official ("elite") record to the recollections of those whose voices seldom appear in this record, and then only in an adversarial way. In

---

204   Moore and Vaughan, *Cutting Down Trees*, XXIII.
205   John Thornton, 'European Documents and African History', in *Writing African History*, ed., John E. Philips (Rochester: University of Rochester Press, 2005), 255.
206   Vansina, 'Epilogue', in *In Pursuit of History*, ed., Adenaike and Vansina, 135.
207   Ann L. Stoler, *Along the Archival Grain: Epistemic Anxieties and Colonial Common Sense* (Princeton: Princeton University Press, 2009), 22, 34. See Moore and Vaughan, *Cutting Down Trees*, XVIII–XXV.
208   Moore and Vaughan, *Cutting Down Trees*, Introduction.

effect these are contributions to the life-history genre, in which individuals great and small testify to their lives, the lives of others as they
saw them, and events from a perspective far different than the canonical
one.[209]

Oral sources facilitate an assessment of different voices and interpretations of
the past.[210] In this study, oral data have been used to question the archival material, to add new perspectives, and to bring out information that had previously remained less visible or even unknown. Yet oral and archival sources cannot
be studied as totally separate, as they influence one another. Oral and archival
sources share discourses and deploy similar frameworks for understanding the
past. Recollections gathered through oral history apply terms such as 'subsistence', 'cash crops', 'tradition', and 'modernity' in a similar manner as written
sources do.[211] A focus on practice sheds further light on local conceptualisations and historical consciousness.

  Studying the dynamic nature of historical practice challenges narratives of
transformative social change.[212] Whereas local voices are only rarely represented in the archival records, actions and practices are discussed, and this provides
insight into aspects of consciousness. When agricultural experts proposed the
cultivation of groundnuts as a cash crop in the 1950s, local cultivators refused
to grow the crop due to ecological incompatibility and labour loads. This was
not a rejection of market production, but should be interpreted as a resilience
of existing practices and modes of thought, an assertion of agency.[213] Tracing
such continuities, contradictions, and acts of resistance in historical practice
can counter linear narratives of social change. If historians do not stress the
'importance of the mutual interpenetration of coexistent practices and representations', Moore and Vaughan urge, they 'are in danger of denying local people a significant domain of action, as well as consistently excluding them from
the texts produced by scholars, officials, and experts on the grounds that they
did not write them themselves'.[214] As much as voices or written accounts are,
practices can be evidence of agency and self-presentation.[215] In Mwinilunga
individuals were able to negotiate continuity within change through practice

---

209   Henige, 'Oral Sources', 187.
210   Vansina, 'Epilogue', 138.
211   Moore and Vaughan, *Cutting Down Trees*, Introduction.
212   See Vansina, *Paths in the Rainforests*.
213   Compare with Spear, *Mountain Farmers*.
214   Moore and Vaughan, *Cutting Down Trees*, XXIII.
215   Ibidem.

and in historical consciousness.[216] Yet historical practices need to be contextualised through oral and written sources. The combination of oral and written sources, and a focus on practice, have enabled an insight into historical consciousness, which is so essential to comprehend processes of social change.[217] Observations from historical fieldwork have strengthened this understanding of historical consciousness, providing local perceptions about the course of social change.

I first conducted research in Zambia for this study from August until December 2008, and then from December 2009 until November 2010. Observations during fieldwork in Mwinilunga not only enabled a practical understanding of issues such as agricultural production, fishing, and house construction but also provided insight into culture and consciousness, gender relations, ideology, and religion. Although observations made in the present cannot simply be extrapolated to earlier periods, they can provide a context within which historical material is placed, as Vansina notes:

> Many threads link present or recent practices to past situations, whether social, political, religious, or economic. While change has indeed affected all these practices (otherwise there would be no history), experiencing the present and doing research on daily life in the recent past illuminates [historical trends].[218]

Historical fieldwork helps balance the biases of other sources. Written records, for example, have a limited field of interest, omitting 'many data about the social details, unmentioned because they are supposed to be well known, and hence the absence of much information about the social reality of the time'.[219] Fieldwork brings forward exactly such data, providing insight into historical consciousness. Another way in which to grasp historical consciousness was by learning the Lunda language. Gaining language proficiency illustrated modes of thought and facilitated social interaction and interviewing.[220] I conducted interviews and historical fieldwork in several localities throughout Mwinilunga (concentrated in Ikelenge, Nyakaseya, Kanongesha, and Ntambu), to gain an understanding of the different villages and forms of socioeconomic

---

216 Pritchett, *Lunda-Ndembu*.
217 Inspiration for this approach has been derived from: Moore and Vaughan, *Cutting Down Trees*; Spear, *Mountain Farmers*.
218 Vansina, 'Epilogue', 136.
219 Ibidem.
220 On the importance of language for historical understanding, see Vansina, *Paths in the Rainforests*.

and political organisation in the area (see Map 1).[221] I conducted informal conversations and semi-structured interviews with a large number of elders (300+), male and female.[222] Based on a reading of the secondary literature and archival sources, I had determined themes of interest beforehand. Yet interviews brought out a variety of new themes and issues, generating a sensitisation to gender relations, property issues, and rituals. Interview questions were open-ended and the conversation would be directed to the topic of interest or expertise of that particular person. For some, this was hunting, for others female initiation, chiefly succession, or a recollection of their personal experiences as labour migrants. Even if not all interviews are quoted in the following chapters, they have fundamentally informed the framework of understanding and the narrative of social change proposed in this book.

By means of such a varied methodological approach, this study attempts to grasp processes of social change in Mwinilunga. To explore 'meanings, mentalities, and perceptions of mind' about the past, local experiences, beliefs, and modes of knowing have been placed at the centre of analysis and juxtaposed to existing narratives of social change in Mwinilunga.[223] This approach has brought out the contradictions, ambiguities, and struggles involved in history, historical consciousness, and processes of social change. In Cooper's words: 'History becomes, then, not the past itself, but struggles over the meaning of the past'.[224] In such a manner, this book seeks to historicise the understanding of social change in Mwinilunga.

6   Chapter Outline

Based on a reading of secondary, archival, and oral sources this study has selected four spheres of social change (production, mobility, consumption, and social relationships). This thematic approach brings out the non-linear

---

221   In 2008, weeklong residences in Ikelenge, Nyakaseya, Chibwika, Kanongesha, Ntambu, and Kanyama were interspersed with stays in Mwinilunga town. In 2010, longer-term residences in Ikelenge (two months), Nyakaseya (one month), Kanongesha (two months), and Ntambu (one month) were again interspersed with stays in Mwinilunga town.

222   A full list of these interviews is provided in the sources section at the end of this book. Together with local research assistants, I contacted these elders, and we paid repeated visits to most.

223   Adenaike and Vansina (eds.), *In Pursuit of History*, XL.

224   Barbara M. Cooper, 'Oral Sources and the Challenge of African History', in *Writing African History*, ed., John E. Philips (Rochester: University of Rochester Press, 2005), 198.

course of history.[225] A thematic approach – much more than a chronological approach – unsettles the linear assumptions that have dominated previous representations of social change in Mwinilunga, highlighting the contradictory and uneven course of change instead.[226] In this manner, long-term continuities appear instead of discursive ruptures.[227] For purposes of historical and spatial contextualisation, Chapter 1 provides an overview of the history of Mwinilunga from approximately 1750 until the 1970s. By placing events in Mwinilunga in a regional and national/international context, interrelationships are highlighted. This overview contextualises subsequent chapters and raises questions about the nature of social change. The chapter problematises continuity and change, points out long-term trends, and questions prevailing periodisation. Were transitions from the pre-colonial to the colonial and post-colonial period indeed sharp ruptures, or did patterns of continuity prevail? Furthermore, it links social change to changes in settlement patterns, a focus that reappears in subsequent chapters.

The following chapters each take one hypothesis about the course of social change as a vantage point. These hypotheses and the attendant narratives of linear social change are then analysed and compared with a study of historical practice. Chapter 2 addresses the sphere of production. This chapter questions whether there was a transition from 'subsistence' to 'market' production in Mwinilunga, by problematising the concepts of subsistence and market production, and by questioning whether these categories were mutually exclusive. Food crops and subsistence production, in fact, constituted the basis for market participation in Mwinilunga. Rather than reflecting agricultural practices, dichotomies between subsistence and market production were part of constructed discourse. By describing the foundations of production in Mwinilunga, this chapter argues that although many producers did partake in market production, this was not universally attractive or beneficial.[228] Considerations of food security, risk minimisation, profit maximisation, and market production are examined in turn. Rather than being a sign of economic rationality or irrationality, the involvement or non-involvement of producers with

---

225   For a discussion, see William Cronon, 'A Place for Stories: Nature, History, and Narrative', *Journal of American History* 78, No. 4 (1992): 1347–76. The narrative approach powerfully shapes the representation of historical events, the causal connections between events, and the understanding of processes of social change.

226   Moore and Vaughan, *Cutting Down Trees,* also adopt a thematic approach.

227   See: Moore and Vaughan, *Cutting Down Trees*; Berry, *No Condition Is Permanent.*

228   Goran Hyden, *Beyond Ujamaa in Tanzania: Underdevelopment and an Uncaptured Peasantry* (Berkeley: University of California Press, 1980).

the market had to do with ideological frameworks and established patterns of production.

Chapter 3 engages with questions of mobility, taking the presumed mobility transition – which posits that individuals in (Central) Africa were relatively sedentary until colonialism, industrialisation, and urbanisation propelled un-precedented mobility – as a starting point.[229] It demonstrates that mobility was always part and parcel of life in Mwinilunga. In certain respects, the colonial and post-colonial state limited mobility through the demarcation of boundar-ies and legislative measures, such as pass laws. Rather than stimulating mobility, the colonial/post-colonial state could act as a constraining force. Notwith-standing restrictions on mobility, individuals were able to circumvent these through cross-border interactions and trade (Chapter 3 Section 1). Mobility proved an effective strategy to minimise risk and maximise profit. Chapter 3 Section 2 separately considers debates on labour migration. The 'modernist narrative' has connected labour migration to issues of 'development', 'prog-ress', and 'modernity'. Others have argued that labour migration would lead to 'underdevelopment', proletarianisation, and rural decay.[230] Through a detailed study of life histories, this chapter explores how mobility influenced the local-ity of Mwinilunga in terms of identity, belonging, and livelihood.

Chapter 4 looks at consumption. This chapter questions the transition from local self-sufficiency in artefacts and goods to a dependency on mass-produced, store-bought goods under capitalist influences. Turner highlighted the role 'of the European-owned stores in stimulating new wants', evident from 'the high percentage of expenditure devoted to store goods'.[231] Yet despite 'new wants' and an apparent 'consumer revolution', changes in the social value, meaning, and use of goods were not necessarily transformed.[232] The consumption of both locally produced and store-bought goods was motivated by a longstand-ing concept of 'wealth in people'.[233] Even as outward appearances changed, the meanings attached to goods remained far more constant. Goods continued to be used in similar ways, to craft and maintain social relationships and alle-giances to kin, neighbours, and dependants.

---

229   See Jan Lucassen and Leo Lucassen, 'The Mobility Transition Revisited, 1500–1900: What the Case of Europe Can Offer to Global History', *Journal of Global History* 4, No. 3 (2009): 347–77.

230   See Ferguson, 'Mobile Workers, Modernist Narratives.'

231   Victor W. Turner and Edith L.B. Turner, 'Money Economy Among the Mwinilunga Ndem-bu: A Study of Some Individual Cash Budgets', *Rhodes-Livingstone Journal* 18 (1955): 31.

232   Ross, Hinfelaar, and Peša, eds., *The Objects of Life in Central Africa*, Introduction.

233   Guyer, 'Wealth in People as Self-Realization.'

Chapter 5 brings the previous chapters together, by assessing whether and how changes in production, mobility, and consumption influenced social relationships. A discussion of social relationships is reserved for the last chapter, because in many ways the context provided by the previous chapters is necessary to enable a grasp of changes in social relationships. Social relationships, after all, are at the core of social change.[234] Did Turner's observations of the disintegration of extended kinship, the emergence of the nuclear family, and trends towards individualisation hold true? Turner posited that the cash economy would destroy ties of kinship within the village, leading to the disintegration of large village units into smaller farms.[235] Nevertheless, social relationships, kinship affiliation, and villages themselves have been flexible enough to accommodate change without breaking down. To what extent did economic and political change also lead to social change?

Colonial officials, anthropologists, and many others have made predictions about the course of social change in Mwinilunga. By testing hypotheses of linear social change, from subsistence to market production, or from kinship to individualisation, this book reaches a different understanding of social change. To better reflect the course of social change, this work proposes alternative concepts such as the foundations of production, culture of mobility, wealth in people, and self-realisation. The central question running through these chapters is how the process of social change has been negotiated in the area of Mwinilunga. How, if ever, can we assess and understand processes of social and historical change? The main argument is that rather than running along a linear path of 'progress', 'development', or 'modernity', change tended to be ambiguous, contested, and gradual.[236] Negating radical transformations of society and defying sharp ruptures between historical periods, this work highlights long-term trends and patterns of continuity in daily life and historical consciousness.[237] In this manner, the question of social change can be viewed in a different light. This book proposes one, hopefully fruitful, lens through which to approach questions of social change and historical consciousness in Mwinilunga.

---

234 See: Moore and Vaughan, *Cutting Down Trees*; Berry, *No Condition Is Permanent*.
235 Turner, *Schism and Continuity*, 43.
236 See: Ferguson, *Expectations of Modernity*; Berry, *No Condition Is Permanent*.
237 See Steven Feierman, *Peasant Intellectuals: Anthropology and History in Tanzania* (Madison: University of Wisconsin Press, 1990); Spear, *Mountain Farmers*.

MAP 1   Mwinilunga District
             MAP DRAWN BY NEL DE VINK

Paths to the Past: Continuity and Change in Mwinilunga, c. 1750s–1970s

The paradox between continuity and change is an enduring feature of the history of Mwinilunga. In the 1950s, when colonial rule and consumer goods had already profoundly altered village life, Turner still identified a strong discourse of continuity throughout Mwinilunga:

> In many parts of Northern Rhodesia the ancient (…) ideas and practices of the Africans are dying out, through contact with the white man and his ways. Employment in the copper mines, on the railway, as domestic servants and shop assistants; the meeting and mingling of tribes in a non-tribal environment; the long absence of men from their homes – all these factors are contributing to the breakdown of (…) the values of kinship ties, respect for the elders and tribal unity (…) But the Lunda (…) in their talk by the village fires still live in the strenuous and heroic past. Whatever time and raids have done to them, 'We are the people of Mwantiyanvwa', they say, and that is that![1]

Ultimately, however, Turner asserted that factors such as labour migration would lead to 'tribal breakdown' and would bring about a radical transformation of society. Nonetheless, up to this day, and despite fundamental social change, the Lunda maintain a notion of continuity with the past through an emphasis on 'tradition'.[2] Some elders might say that tradition has perished (*chisemwa chafwa dehi*). Yet the annual *Chisemwa ChaLunda* ceremony, (re)instated by Senior Chief Kanongesha in 1996, testifies that asserting connections to the past and upholding traditions remains important to individual and collective consciousness.[3] Whereas historical events and processes, such

---

1   Victor W. Turner, 'Lunda Rites and Ceremonies', *The Occasional Papers of the Rhodes-Livingstone Museum* (Livingstone: 1974), 336–37.
2   For a contemporary example of such a focus on 'tradition', see Mulumbi Datuuma II, 'Customs of the Lunda Ndembu, Volume I, The Kanongesha Chieftainship Succession in Zambia' (Unpublished Manuscript, 2010), 5.
3   Debates on 'ethnicity' will be addressed in more detail in Chapter 3 Section 1 & Chapter 3 Section 2 (Leroy Vail, ed., *The Creation of Tribalism in Southern Africa* (Berkeley: University of California Press, 1989), suggests that ethnicity was a construct rather than a fixed category);

as the establishment of colonial rule or gaining independence, undoubtedly propelled change and discontinuity with earlier periods,[4] the effects of these changes have been incorporated within long-term patterns of continuity with the past. Continuity and change went hand in hand, as new influences were embedded within the context of existing practices and modes of thought.[5] Based on an assessment of the long-term socioeconomic and political history of Mwinilunga, this chapter questions the relationship between continuity and change. Has social change been pervasive in the twentieth century or are there foundations for asserting continuity with the past?

In order to provide a framework for the following thematic chapters, this chapter offers a broad historical overview, drawn up around several major themes and landmarks. Only through historical contextualisation can the impact of social change be assessed. The focus is on two aspects. First of all, on the relationships between the inhabitants of Mwinilunga and external actors, whether these were immigrants, traders, or colonial officials. The constant interaction between actors on a local, regional, and global level has influenced events in Mwinilunga in profound ways. Although changes did occur, the population of Mwinilunga was able to appropriate external influences and make sense of events.[6] Secondly, changing settlement patterns are examined as expressions of social change. Settlement patterns were historically flexible and ultimately resilient, going against Turner's hypothesis of 'village breakup' due to colonialism and capitalism.[7] This chapter outlines major trends, examines whether and when change occurred, and provides threads that will be elaborated in subsequent chapters. Rather than asserting linear historical narratives or sharp chronological divisions,[8] this chapter emphasises how people in Mwinilunga negotiated and made sense of change.

---

whereas the recent resurgence of 'tradition' will be addressed in Chapter 5 (Eric Hobsbawm and Terence Ranger, eds., *The Invention of Tradition* (Cambridge: Cambridge University Press, 1983)).

4   Turner, *Drums of Affliction*, 14, asserted that in the 1950s 'great waves of change were sweeping over the lives of the Ndembu', due to labour migration, capitalism, and colonialism. That events, such as the inception of colonial rule, caused drastic ruptures in historical consciousness is argued by Pritchett, *Friends for Life*.

5   Vansina, *Paths in the Rainforests*, 236–37; Monica H. Wilson, 'Zig-zag Change', *Africa* 46, No. 4 (1976): 399–409. For the idea of 'progress' in historical narrative, see Eric Hobsbawm, *The Age of Empire 1875–1914* (London: Abacus, 1987), 26–33.

6   See: Piot, *Remotely Global*; Crehan, *The Fractured Community*.

7   Turner, *Schism and Continuity*.

8   Ferguson, *Expectations of Modernity*, 17. Many RLI scholars adopted ideas about linear social change.

1   Constructing a Region: The Lunda Polity, History, and
      Reproduction

When asked to recount their history, people in Mwinilunga generally start
by saying: 'We the Lunda, we have come from Mwantianvwa'.[9] With this
statement, they refer to the figurehead of the Lunda entity, a polity established
between the beginning of the sixteenth and the beginning of the seventeenth
century.[10] From its heartland surrounding the capital city Musumba, located
along the Bushimaie-Nkalanyi River in present-day Congo, the Lunda polity
gained influence and spread across large parts of the Central African plateau.[11]
Notwithstanding its extensive regional impact, the origins and the political,
social, and economic basis of the Lunda polity consisted of the village. The
village was a territorial as well as a human unit, with a group of matrilineally
related kin at its core. It was governed by a council of elders (ciyul), which
was headed by 'the owner of the land' (mwaantaangaand), a position of ritual
importance through its connection to the founding ancestors of the village.
Individual villages would be grouped together in larger allied units, forming a
vicinage, which paid tribute to the Lunda court through a political representative (cilool).[12] Through such loose patterns of authority – later cemented into
fixed hierarchies of headmen and chiefs by the colonial government – the village, the vicinage, and the central Lunda polity were ultimately interconnected. The Lunda court, which had itself grown from small-scale village origins,
depended on these connections for legitimacy and sought to reciprocate ties
to outlying areas, for instance by sending gifts, endowing rulers with regalia,
or providing protection from outside attacks.[13] The expansion of the Lunda

---

9   All questions about 'early history' or 'origin' would evoke a similar response, providing an
      outline of Lunda dynastic history. For example: Interview with Kasongu Mapulanga, 29
      July 2010, Kanongesha.
10   For a review of the date of origin of the Lunda entity, see Jean-Luc Vellut, 'Notes sur le
      Lunda et la frontière luso-africaine (1700–1900)', Études d'histoire africaine 3 (1972): 65–66.
11   Alternatively referred to as (South-) Central African savannah. For an overview of early
      Lunda history, see especially: Hoover, 'The Seduction of Ruwej'; Jan Vansina, Les anciens
      royaumes de la savane: les états des savanes méridionales de l'afrique central des origines à
      l'occupation coloniale (Kinshasa: Université Lovanium Léopoldville, 1965); Vellut, 'Notes
      sur le Lunda'; Richard Gray and David Birmingham, eds., Pre-colonial African Trade:
      Essays on Trade in Central and Eastern Africa before 1900 (Oxford: Oxford University Press,
      1970).
12   Vansina, Les anciens royaumes; Hoover, 'Seduction of Ruwej'; Schecter, 'History and
      Historiography.'
13   See: Vellut, 'Notes sur le Lunda'; Edouard Bustin, Lunda Under Belgian Rule: The Politics of
      Ethnicity (Lawrence: Harvard University Press, 1975).

polity, achieved by gradually integrating villages on the fringes of its sphere of influence, was greatly aided by the practices of positional succession and perpetual kinship.[14] New subjects could be incorporated into the Lunda political system through the award of political or ritual titles. This linked them directly to the Lunda court and created a hybrid mix of population groups, origin, and authority, blurring the distinction between 'insider' and 'outsider', 'autochthon' and 'immigrant'.[15] Villages had never been isolated or bounded, as even in early history local, regional and trans-regional dynamics, involving a multitude and mingling of actors, had been intertwined.[16]

Today, the subjects of chiefs such as Kazembe in the Luapula Province of Zambia, Chinyama in Angola, and Musokantanda in Congo – encompassing the vast area between the Kasai River in the west and the Lualaba River in the east – all trace common origin through Lunda descent. The prestige, influence, and strength of the original Lunda polity were merely some reasons contributing to the desire of outlying areas to seek association with the capital.[17] At the end of the nineteenth century, Portuguese travellers described Mwantianvwa and his capital in lavish terms:

> The Muata-Ianvo is surrounded by a numerous court, which includes, as principals: the *mutia*, father of Ianvo; the *calala*, chief-executive in charge of transmitting orders to the armed population; the Muene *cutapa*, executor of high justice, generally the uncle of Ianvo; and many highly respected personalities and their *a-cajes* (concubines), who live with them (...) Usually it [his court] is composed of a rectangular palisade, which encloses it completely, and, depending on the magnitude, can be as long as 1500 meters on each side; locked up in the centre is the residence of

---

14   John Iliffe, *Africans: The History of a Continent* (Cambridge: Cambridge University Press, 1995), 104; Giacomo Macola, *The Kingdom of Kazembe: History and Politics in North-Eastern Zambia and Katanga to 1950* (Münster: LIT Verlag, 2002), 39n: 'Through positional succession, the successor to a name or title inherits not only his predecessor's insignia, rights and duties, but also his social and political relationships. Positional succession serves to maintain the form of descent groups and may evolve into perpetual kinship between titles. The perpetual relationship is an expressed kinship relationship between the holders of two names, which does not vary with the actual genealogical relationship of the people who are at any time holding the names. It is a fixed relationship between hereditary names which remains constant through the generation.'
15   Schecter, 'History and Historiography'; Robert J. Papstein, 'The Upper Zambezi: A History of the Luvale People, 1000–1900' (Unpublished PhD Thesis, University of California, 1978).
16   Schoenbrun, 'Conjuring the Modern', 1403–39.
17   Hoover, 'The Seduction of Ruwej', offers a description of this migratory movement and lists the migrating chiefs.

the chief, with two circular walls and a corridor in between, above which is elevated a vast dome (…) [After listing the subordinate chiefs] All these are tributaries to the supreme chief, conform to his laws, and are obliged to send tax through a special committee. Failure of such payment is considered such a grave offence, that only rarely does the head of the tributary remain undamaged in case of repeat. Disposing over the lives of his subordinates (…) he destroys the villages of those who do not contribute to his supremacy.[18]

The goods with which Mwantianvwa surrounded himself added to his grandeur. Items such as lion and leopard skins, ivory, various types of coloured beads, palm oil, game meat, salt, tobacco, a variety of calicoes, gunpowder, and firearms, all attested to his mastery of complex circuits of domestic and foreign exchange, tribute, and trade.[19] By means of these outward manifestations of wealth, prestige, and authority, the Lunda polity was able to strengthen its hold even over previously non-aligned population groups, constructing a region interconnected by the movement of people, ideas, and goods.[20]

Although the level of control from the central Lunda polity rapidly diminished in outlying areas, various social, economic, and political factors tied Musumba, Mwinilunga, and other places of purported Lunda origin together.[21] These included not only the framework of long-distance trade and tribute but also comprised ties of marriage, alliance, friendship, and ritual.[22] Particularly tribute, referred to as the life-blood of the Lunda polity, is illustrative of these links of interdependence.[23] The meaning of the proverb 'kudya kekenyi kusinsishamu' (eating what belongs to a termite one has to replace it), reflects that a chief should be reimbursed through tribute for the benefits his rule bestows on the people, otherwise his rule would be jeopardised and his authority would fade.[24] Because the rule of a chief should provide protection from external threats and redistribute long-distance trade goods to subjects, among other things, the provision of tribute was regarded as an act of moral obligation

---

18   Hermenegildo C.B. Capelo and Roberto Ivens, *De Benguela às terras de Iaca – Descrição de uma viagem na África central e ocidental, 1887–1890, Vol. 1* (Coimbra, 1996), 314–16. My translation.
19   Capelo and Ivens, *De Benguela*, 315 and 317.
20   Bustin, *Lunda Under Belgian Rule.*
21   Vansina, *Les anciens royaumes,* 63.
22   Bustin, *Lunda Under Belgian Rule,* 1–7; Vellut, 'Notes sur le Lunda', 78–84; Turner, *Schism and Continuity,* xx.
23   Bustin, *Lunda Under Belgian Rule,* 5; Vellut, 'Notes sur le Lunda', 78–84.
24   Mulumbi Datuuma II, 'Customs of the Lunda Ndembu', 10.

rather than being exerted by force.[25] For example, a local hunter was expected to offer the chest of his kill as tribute through his headman to Chief Kanongesha. Chief Kanongesha would then send locally prized items such as leopard skins, ivory, or slaves to Mwantianvwa, if not regularly at least on special occasions such as at installation ceremonies. In return, Mwantianvwa would remit valuable trade goods or emblems of chiefly authority, thereby providing subordinate chiefs with legitimacy and prestige.[26] In this way, the various levels of authority were connected to one another, in a hierarchical and centralised, yet loose and reciprocal manner. Although by the end of the nineteenth century Chokwe incursions and slave raids discontinued the regular payment of tribute to Mwantianvwa, and subsequent colonial boundary demarcations cut through existing allegiances, connections within the wider Lunda region continued to be upheld and renewed, remaining significant even at present.[27]

The Lunda-Ndembu – as the inhabitants of Mwinilunga have historically been referred to[28] – trace back their settlement of the present area to a migration from the core Lunda polity.[29] The causes for this migration are to be sought in internal power struggles at the centre and in a desire to extend Lunda influence to outlying areas. Propelled by the penetration of Luba influences from the east, Lunda emissaries set out to secure access to scarce saltpans, hunting grounds, and agricultural land beyond the established boundaries of

---

25 Turner, *Schism and Continuity*, 325: 'The giving of tribute was regarded as a moral obligation rather than as a compulsory matter – ultimately as a recognition of the historical origin and unity of Ndembu in Mwantiyanvwa.'

26 Confirmed by numerous interviews, for example Kasongu Mapulanga, 17 August 2010, Kanongesha, but also (NAZ) SEC2/402, H. Vaux, A Report on the Sailunga Kindred, 1936.

27 Pritchett, *Lunda-Ndembu*; O. Bakewell, 'The Meaning and Use of Identity Papers: Handheld and Heartfelt Nationality in the Borderlands of North-West Zambia', *International Migration Institute Working Paper 5*, University of Oxford (2007).

28 The term 'Lunda-Ndembu' originated in the colonial period, serving to administratively differentiate the Lunda under Senior Chief Sailunga from the Ndembu under Senior Chief Kanongesha. The language currently used in the area is referred to as Lunda, and the term 'Ndembu' seems to have fallen into disuse at present. Throughout this book, I prefer to adopt the generic term 'Lunda' and will use 'Ndembu' only in references to other authors, in quotations from archival sources, or where its use seems specifically warranted.

29 Luc De Heusch, 'What Shall We Do with the Drunken King?', *Africa* 45, No. 4 (1975): 363–72; Thomas Q. Reefe, 'Traditions of Genesis and the Luba Diaspora', *History in Africa* 4 (1977): 183–206; Robert E. Schecter, 'A Propos the Drunken King: Cosmology and History', in *The African Past Speaks: Essays on Oral Tradition and History*, ed., Joseph C. Miller (Hamden: Dawson Publishing, 1980), 108–25; Leon Duysters, 'Histoire des Aluunda', *Problèmes d'Afrique Centrale* 12, No. 40 (1958): 75–98; Victor W. Turner, 'A Lunda Love Story and Its Consequences', *Rhodes Livingstone Journal* 19 (1955): 1–26.

the polity.[30] The departure from Musumba involved many of the current major titleholders in the area, such as Kazembe Mutanda, Ishinde, Musokantanda, and Kanongesha. Nominally, Ndembu refers to the stream along which the migrants sojourned after their departure from Mwantianvwa's court, before dispersing in various directions towards their present locations.[31] Evidence suggests that Chief Kanongesha, one of the main chiefs who came to settle along the Upper Zambezi, reached the present area between 1740 and 1755.[32] According to oral tradition, his following comprised of 12 members of matrilineal kin, some of whose descendants are still important chiefs in Mwinilunga today.[33] These followers were assigned prestigious titles and tasks by Kanongesha, in turn sanctioned by Mwantianvwa. Illustrative are the titles of Mwinimilamba *Ifota*, the pathfinder or the one who led the way in the original migration; Ikelenge *Kalula*, the one who spreads the lion or leopard skin mat on which Kanongesha sits; and Nyakaseya, the one who pours beer for the chiefs, or the ritual wife of Kanongesha.[34] Through movement and the award of political titles Lunda influence was spread, but the establishment of authority in the area of Mwinilunga remained a gradual and intricate process.

Lunda oral traditions describe the settlement of outlying areas, such as Mwinilunga, in terms of epic migrations, involving the swift conquest and forceful subordination of established population groups.[35] This was most probably not the case. Rather, the area of Mwinilunga was occupied as a result of a general and gradual movement of population, from the outset involving mixed population groups located at the southern edge of the Lunda polity rather than constituting a direct thrust from the centre outwards.[36] Intermarriage and the forging of strategic alliances between immigrants and existing population groups were crucial to this process. In the area of Mwinilunga the diverse set of population groups encountered was referred to as Mbwela.[37] Contrary to what some traditions might suggest, the Mbwela were not forcibly subdued or

---

30   Macola, *The Kingdom of Kazembe,* Chapter 2.
31   Schecter, 'History and Historiography'; Confirmed by numerous interviews, for example Ilunga, 16 March 2010, Ikelenge.
32   Schecter, 'History and Historiography', Chapter 4.
33   Vansina, *Les anciens royaumes,* 126; Turner, *Schism and Continuity,* 7.
34   Turner, *Schism and Continuity,* 11; Interview with Wombeki, 27 April and 11 May 2010, Nyakaseya.
35   See Interview with Chief Mukangala, 3 November 2010, Mwinilunga. Turner, *Schism and Continuity,* 2–3, calls the population movement an 'invasion'.
36   This is a summary of the nuanced work by Schecter, 'History and Historiography'.
37   The Mbwela are alternatively referred to as Nkoya or Lukolwe; they are linguistically and culturally diverse, yet constitute a kindred matrilineal group. These groups have commonly been defined by what they are not (a negative contrast), i.e. non-Lunda, rather

chased, but rather were integrated into the newly established Lunda polities in the area.[38] Due to such interaction and mixture of diverse people and influences, cultural hybridity, and the incorporation of change, rather than uniformity of ideas, beliefs, and practices, prevailed in Mwinilunga.

Although Lunda migrants at times derogatorily referred to Mbwela as nomadic or even primitive,[39] they equally acknowledged the importance of Mbwela collaboration in successfully administering the area. Lunda men took Mbwela wives, and Mbwela lineage heads were granted Lunda political titles to bolster ties between the two. Mbwela were acknowledged as 'owners of the land' and given the position of 'ritual installer' of Lunda chiefs (*chivwikankanu*), firmly cemented by practices of perpetual kinship and positional succession.[40] Although the term *'kabeta kaMbwela'* is used to refer to 'the south', denoting the direction in which the Mbwela were chased, Mbwela presence was by no means obliterated.[41] Some Mbwela might have been driven away or killed by Lunda violence, but the fact that even today villages of Mbwela origin persist in the area of Mwinilunga – a marked example being the village of Nsanganyi in ex-chief Mukangala's area – testifies that co-existence was equally possible and was probably common.[42] Nevertheless, Lunda chiefs derive great prestige from claiming to have fought and defeated the Mbwela, as this claim gives them legitimacy to occupy the present land.[43] Because land rights could only be obtained through protracted occupation, cultivation, and connections to ancestral spirits, long-established residents of an area, in this case the Mbwela, enjoyed a privileged position.[44] In order to assert land rights, Lunda chiefs formally had to establish their superiority by subjugating the Mbwela. This gave

---

than by similarity or unity. See Wim M.J. Van Binsbergen, *Tears of Rain: Ethnicity and History in Central Western Zambia* (London: Routledge, 1992).

38   Papstein, 'The Upper Zambezi', suggests that the Mbwela were forcefully subdued. Yet for the area of Mwinilunga, Schecter, 'History and Historiography', has suggested peaceful co-existence and gradual movement of population.

39   Schecter, 'History and Historiography'; Papstein, 'The Upper Zambezi'; Van Binsbergen, *Tears of Rain*. See also archival material and interviews: (BOD) Richard Cranmer Dening, Land Tenure Report No. 7, North Western Province.

40   Schecter, 'History and Historiography'.'

41   Turner, *Schism and Continuity*, 3.

42   Ex-chiefs Pompora and Kangombe, whose areas were transferred from Mwinilunga to Solwezi and Kabompo District in 1948, are reported as Mbwela chiefs.

43   (NAZ) SEC2/222, K.S. Kinross, Ndembo Chiefs on Merger of Courts, July 1944. 'When we Ndembu came from Luunda in early times we found no other Chiefs here but Ambwera whom we conquered ... [Mwinimilamba claims:] Nyakaseya cannot be my senior ... he did not fight with the Ambwera as I did.'

44   Schecter, 'History and Historiography', based on a reading of archival sources (NAZ).

rise to oral traditions of violently battling and chasing the Mbwela, which did not necessarily reflect historical dynamics accurately.

That the Mbwela were by no means powerless, but had to be carefully reckoned with, is tacitly acknowledged by oral traditions. Kanongesha Kabanda, one of the first Lunda chiefs who settled in the area of Mwinilunga, is said to have been severely wounded, whilst fighting the Mbwela in the Mayawu plain, consequently dying from his injuries. This testifies that the outcome of Lunda-Mbwela struggles was by no means predetermined.[45] Rather than being unilaterally imposed, authority had to be brokered between numerous actors. Gradually, Lunda and Mbwela developed relationships of interdependence. Through the award of titles, by means of marriage and ties of kinship, all people in the Upper Zambezi area were eventually linked to the central Lunda court, no matter how tentatively or loosely. Such was the context within which individuals, headmen, and chiefs in the villages throughout Mwinilunga negotiated issues of authority, hierarchy, and power.

Because of their location on the southernmost fringes of the Lunda polity, the communities along the Upper Zambezi enjoyed a relatively high degree of autonomy from the central Lunda court.[46] Notwithstanding important ties to regional or polity-wide developments, village units were the most significant levels of social, economic, and political organisation.[47] The village was the daily stage for social interaction. Agricultural assistance, company in the hunt, or advice and chatter in the light of the nightly fire could all be found within this unit.[48] Livingstone's description from the 1850s offers some insights into the appearance of southern Lunda villages:

> We came to a village every few miles, sometimes passed 10 in a day. These were civil (...) We often entered a village, and when sitting on oxback could only see the tops of the huts in a wilderness of weeds. By & bye the villagers emerged from their lairs, men & women each smoking a long pipe and followed by crowds of children.[49]

---

45 This event is recounted in the official version of the Kanongesha royal history. See Interview with Jesman Sambaulu, 10 August 2010, Kanongesha.

46 Anthony St.H. Gibbons, *Africa from South to North through Marotseland* (John Lane, 1904), 33: 'Since the fall of Muato Yamvo's empire the greater part of this tribe [Lunda] had ... broken up into small independent communities ... owing to want of cohesion the districts more or less remote from the centre have proved a fruitful field for the slave trade.'

47 Vansina, *Les anciens royaumes*.

48 See: Turner, *Schism and Continuity*; Pritchett, *Lunda-Ndembu*.

49 Isaac Schapera, ed., *Livingstone's Missionary Correspondence 1841–1856* (London: Chatto and Windus, 1961), 261–62.

Such villages would consist of small units of matrilineally related kin, accommodating non-kinsmen at will.[50] Although villages appeared to be dotted across the landscape, their location was by no means arbitrary. Settlements would be strategically concentrated along waterways, close to hunting grounds or patches of fertile land.[51] High degrees of spatial mobility prevailed, and villages shifted in intervals ranging from one to twenty years. Movement was motivated by the quest for hunting, fishing, or cultivating grounds, or yet by quarrels and deaths within a village.[52] As a result of these movements, housing structures were of an impermanent nature. Houses would commonly be made of poles and thatching grass, materials that facilitated frequent relocation.[53] Although agricultural production was widely practiced, there was equally a heavy reliance on hunting and foraging to complement supplies of cultivated food.[54]

These highly mobile and impermanent living conditions were described as 'nomadic' or even 'primitive' by European travellers in the area in the nineteenth century. Later, colonial officials referred to Lunda settlements in similar terms: 'They depended a great deal upon wild forest produce in their diet. This was accompanied by a great deal of shifting, and they often lived for long periods in grass or leaf huts'.[55] Yet alternatively, such living conditions could be viewed as ecologically sound and inventive adaptations to a complex and fragile environment.[56] In an attempt to maximise access to resources, individuals sought to diversify their livelihoods by relying on a mixture of hunting, fishing, agriculture, and foraging. Although game appeared to be relatively abundant in the area, it could easily be chased away or depleted. In a similar manner, the fertility of the loose Kalahari sands would rapidly diminish under permanent cultivation.[57] Whereas large, fixed settlements would have strained the fragile resource base heavily, small shifting villages enabled individuals to profit from existing diversity in Mwinilunga.[58]

---

50   Turner, *Schism and Continuity,* XVIII–XIX.
51   (NAZ) SEC2/955, R.C. Dening, Mwinilunga District Tour Report, November 1947.
52   Pritchett, *Lunda-Ndembu,* 91; (NAZ) SEC2/955 R.C. Dening, Mwinilunga District Tour Report, 1947; (NAZ) NWP1/2/17, F.M.N. Heath, Mwinilunga District Travelling Report, 1/1948.
53   Confirmed by numerous interviews, for example Andrew Kambowa, 2 October 2010, Ntambu.
54   Van Binsbergen, *Tears of Rain;* Papstein, 'The Upper Zambezi.'
55   (BOD) Richard Cranmer Dening, Land Tenure Report No.7, North-Western Province.
56   William Beinart, 'African History and Environmental History', *African Affairs* 99, No. 395 (2000): 269–302.
57   See Chapter 2.
58   Turner, *Schism and Continuity,* hints at the influence of ecological factors on the size of village units, but does not recognise their full importance.

The environment influenced not only economic organisation and patterns of livelihood procurement but also village settlements and political authority in the area. Centrifugal political relations, connected to the high degree of spatial mobility, tended to predominate in Mwinilunga. Turner attributed village fissure to the inherent antagonism between matrilineal descent and virilocal marriage. Whereas Lunda descent was reckoned through women, upon marriage women would move away to reside with the kin of their husbands. This caused continual tension, competition, and a high degree of village fissure, as the husband and the brother would both compete for a woman's allegiance and offspring.[59] This 'radical incompatibility' of kinship relations, nevertheless, was not the only factor behind the small size of villages. Small villages equally enabled flexibility in a fragile environment. Because hunting and shifting cultivation formed the economic base of village society, small shifting settlements proved highly compatible and sensible.[60] Possibly, the village breakup into small units or 'farms', which Turner noted in the 1950s, was not new but had parallels with earlier periods. At the end of the nineteenth century, villages and settlements already appeared to be mobile, flexible, and small as an adaptation to ecology. The degree of continuity or change in village layout and organisation will therefore be further explored throughout this book.[61]

Coupled with the geographical mobility and adaptability of villages, political hierarchies remained flexible and open to competition. The distinction between lineage heads, headmen, and chiefs was often ill-defined and success was most clearly demonstrated by the size of the following one could muster.[62] Human labour, far more than land, was a scarce factor. Population densities remained low and did not exceed six persons per square mile even in the late 1960s.[63] The scarcity of population, the abundance of land, the fragile environment and the resulting high degree of spatial mobility, all stimulated political competition among villages. Early colonial administrators pejoratively referred to a lack of 'cohesion', as: 'internecine disputes, and mutual mistrust and feuds between every village and its very neighbour make combination [into large villages] most remote, if not utterly impossible'.[64] In this competitive setting the position of village heads might best be described as that of *primus*

---

59   This is a summary of Turner's more complex argument. See Turner, *Schism and Continuity*, 76 and 302.

60   Vansina, *Paths in the Rainforests*.

61   See Chapter 4 and Chapter 5.

62   (NAZ) SEC2/402, H. Vaux, A report on the Sailunga Kindred, 1936. See Guyer, 'Wealth in People and Self-Realization', 243–65.

63   (NAZ) Ministry of Agriculture, Monthly Economic Bulletin, February 1968.

64   (NAZ) HC1/2/42 BS2/251 Loc.130, G.A. MacGregor, Monthly Report Balunda District, January 1909.

inter pares, holding a position of ritual importance and reigning rather than ruling.[65] A direct correlation between the rule of a village head and the size of a village existed, as one elder emphasised: 'It depends on the rule of a headman how many people there are in a village. A bad headman causes a village to split because of lack of good communication, so people are encouraged to move to their own place'.[66] In the context of these competitive disputes for authority and recognition, a patchwork of ties and connections was created, as population groups continuously shifted and mixed. Yet there were certain tools that could be used to attract a larger, and more stable, following. The effective mastery of flows of trade was one of these.

Through politics, trade, kinship, and mobility, ties of Lunda allegiance have created connections between local and regional actors and influences since the sixteenth century. Although these ties have been continuously adapted as a reaction to historical events, they have retained their significance even in an altered setting. Notwithstanding profound changes within the Lunda polity itself, Lunda connections and allegiances provide a thread of continuity in the history of Mwinilunga.[67] Could the local and regional connections established by the Lunda entity provide a basis for subsequent interactions between Mwinilunga and regional, national, or even global processes, for example influencing reactions to capitalism, colonialism, and patterns of political authority?[68]

2   A Window to the World: Long-Distance Trade and Slavery

Exchange and trade have long played an important role in the Central African region. Occupational specialisation and environmental variation had induced trade, within or between villages, and over long distances. The development of metallurgy, for instance, propelled the exchange of scarce iron tools for a range of available produce, including crops, livestock, and reed mats. In West Central Africa, this exchange dated back to the first millennium A.D. and could cover remarkably long distances, thereby connecting distant communities through extensive networks.[69] Localised trade, involving exchange between neighbouring villages and population groups, complemented regional trade networks. Local exchange was prompted by the differential allocation of scarce natural

---

65   Turner, *Schism and Continuity*, 318–19.
66   Interview with Kasongu Mapulanga, Kanongesha, 17 August 2010.
67   Bustin, *Lunda Under Belgian Rule*; Bakewell, 'Refugees Repatriating.'
68   See especially Chapter 3 Section 1 and Chapter 3 Section 2.
69   Vansina, *Paths in the Rainforests*, 58–61; Jan Vansina, *How Societies Are Born: Governance in West Central Africa Before 1600* (Charlottesville: University of Virginia Press, 2004), 60–67.

resources, as well as by occupational specialisation. The Luvale living on the banks of the Kabompo River, for example, would barter dried fish for grains or game meat with the Lunda living on the other side.[70] Good hunters could barter game meat for supplies of grain crops within their own village or in a neighbouring village. Similarly, for rare supplies of high quality salt people in Mwinilunga depended on Angolan saltpans.[71] Overall, trade served to complement individual and household production, offered people access to a wide range of goods, and enabled the diversification of individual livelihood strategies. Most significantly, trade provided connections between local, regional, and occasionally even global actors. The long-distance caravan trade, constituting an increase in scale and distance covered, built upon and fed into pre-existing forms of local and regional exchange and trade.

Although long-distance trade goods had started trickling into Mwinilunga from the Indian Ocean coast during the first half of the second millennium A.D.,[72] it was especially from the eighteenth century onwards, as a result of the expansion of trade with the Angolan coast, that a wide array of goods from overseas areas became readily available. This exchange provided access to crops (such as maize, cassava, and sweet potatoes), industrially manufactured cloth, firearms, gunpowder, beads, tobacco, and liquor, among other things.[73] After some faltering attempts, stable trade relations were developed between the central Lunda court and the Portuguese, who had reached the Angolan coast by the end of the fifteenth century. Initially relying on indirect trade through African intermediaries, most notably the Ovimbundu, the Portuguese sent their first direct emissaries to the Lunda court around 1800, an act that was soon reciprocated by Lunda dignitaries travelling to the Angolan port Luanda.[74] Under the umbrella of the Lunda polity, trade goods were redirected into channels of tribute, distribution, and hierarchies of power, linking chiefs, headmen, and the village population. Colonial recollections describe that the tribute caravan from Chief Sailunga to his superior Musokantanda, raised through levies from villagers and headmen, carried five large calabashes of honey, six leopard skins, twenty small skins, and ten man-loads of dried fish. In return, Chief Musokantanda sent Sailunga trade goods, consisting of loads

---

70   Papstein, 'The Upper Zambezi.'

71   Hoover, 'The Seduction of Ruwej', 327–56.

72   Roland A. Oliver and John D. Fage, *A Short History of Africa* (London: Penguin Books, 1962), 81–82.

73   Von Oppen, *Terms of Trade*; Miller, *Way of Death*; Jan Vansina, 'Long-distance Trade-routes in Central Africa', *Journal of African History* 3, No. 3 (1962): 375–90; Vellut, 'Notes sur le Lunda.'

74   Bustin, *Lunda Under Belgian Rule.*

of brightly coloured calico, strings of large white and small red beads, as well
as a muzzle-loading gun, which would be distributed further to the villages in
his area.[75] Through these trade networks involving European traders, African
intermediaries and local interests, individuals in the area of Mwinilunga increasingly came to participate in international exchange, both as consumers of
coveted imports and as producers of exportable goods. The significance of international trade should not be downplayed, even if major caravan routes regularly bypassed the area either to the south or to the north and only occasionally
diverged into Mwinilunga.[76] Over time, the effects of the long-distance trade
became increasingly tangible, not only due to its sheer scope but also because
trade goods were incorporated into existing channels of exchange and relationships of power. The long-distance trade connected people in Mwinilunga
to local, regional, and even global networks.

Not only was the growth of the Lunda polity dependent on increasing quantities of trade but the state structure itself also served to encourage trade.[77]
Trade fed into existing patterns of distribution and tribute, circulating goods
through the polity.[78] By means of exchange, tribute, and warfare, the Lunda
amassed large quantities of exportable goods in Musumba.[79] The concentration of population, resources, and wealth in the Lunda capital made it a
uniquely attractive destination for Portuguese traders and African intermediaries, rewarding the long trek to the interior through prospects of high profits.[80] The items attracting traders initially consisted of salt, copper, iron, and a
variety of tropical goods. During the eighteenth and nineteenth centuries these
were increasingly supplemented by slaves, rubber, ivory, and beeswax, all readily exportable from coastal depots.[81] Portuguese traders and local potentates
both attempted to control trajectories of trade. Chiefs and headmen played
a particularly important role as intermediaries or even gatekeepers of trade.
Access to imports bolstered the status and power of village heads, as scarce

---

75   (NAZ) SEC2/402, H. Vaux, Report on the Sailunga Kindred, 1936.
76   Based on Von Oppen, *Terms of Trade;* confirmed by the map drawn in Bustin, *Lunda
     Under Belgian Rule,* and by my own reading of pre-colonial traveller reports. Examples of
     travellers who did pass through the area are: Livingstone (1850), Cameron (1870), Gibbons
     (1890), and Arnot (1890). Frederick S. Arnot, *Garenganze, or, Seven Year's Pioneer Mission
     Work in Central Africa* (London: Paternoster, 1969); Frederick S. Arnot, *Missionary Travels
     in Central Africa* (Bath: Echoes of Service, 1987).
77   For the first view, see Gray and Birmingham, 'Some Economic and Political Consequences
     of Trade', 15; whereas the second view is advanced by Bustin, *Lunda Under Belgian Rule,* 21.
78   Hoover, 'The Seduction of Ruwej,' 340–53; Vellut, 'Notes sur le Lunda', 78–84.
79   Vellut, 'Notes sur le Lunda', 61–166.
80   Pritchett, *Lunda-Ndembu,* 215–28; Bustin, *Lunda Under Belgian Rule.*
81   Bustin, *Lunda Under Belgian Rule,* 1–40; Von Oppen, *Terms of Trade,* 45–99 and 211–35.

goods could be distributed among the village population to create relations of dependency. In the area of Mwinilunga, certain headmen and chiefs, who had managed to manipulate trade relations to their benefit and had obtained a degree of wealth, acted as purveyors of trade or lenders of capital. The role of village heads as mediators of trade had important repercussions for the balance of power in the village, expressed through relationships of indebtedness, pawnship, or even slavery. Colonial court cases were left to deal with the aftermaths of such cycles of debt and dependency:

> Long ago I had a case & to settle this I had to find certain goods. I went to [Chief] Chibwika to borrow these goods & he lent me 1 gun, 1 cloth & 1 load of wax (...) with which to settle my case. Chibwika then came to me later wanting me to discharge my debt. I offered him 3 blankets which he refused saying he wanted a gun on top. I had not a gun so I gave him my daughter Nyatusachi instead as a hostage.[82]

Because indebtedness resulted in dependency on those more successful at controlling flows of trade, access to material wealth could afford headmen and chiefs a greater degree of leverage over village affairs, and could strengthen ties of personal allegiance. Trade goods could function as a store of wealth and, by dispensing scarce commodities, headmen and chiefs could attract a large following.[83] Control over goods and people, mediated through trade, went hand in hand.

The significance of trade goods thus went beyond the sphere of household consumption. Crucially, trade goods penetrated social relationships and hierarchies of power. The settlement of cases, bridewealth negotiations, death penalties, and tribute were all mediated by imported goods, as this early colonial court case testifies:

> I committed adultery with a married woman, Nyailolo; it was sometime after this her child died, and the husband (...) [said that I] had caused the death of his child (...) I paid up to settle the matter, calico & beads.[84]

In the area of Mwinilunga, trade was actively pursued, even over long distances – up to the Lualaba River in Congo and beyond. The goods obtained

---

82   (NAZ) KSE3/1/2/1, Nyansheta of Nyachulu v. Chibwika of Chibwika, 12 February 1919.
83   See: Guyer, 'Wealth in People and Self-Realization'; Miller, *Way of Death*.
84   (NAZ) KSE3/2/2/1, 28 December 1909.

became entangled in social relationships, for example through the settlement of cases. Some of these cases involved slavery:

> Kashali (...) gave Msangi some beads to buy salt with on the Lualaba. Msangi went away to the Lualaba River & bought 6 cakes of salt, & returned with them. Kashali received his salt. At that time he had an affair with Msaila & gave him the salt & some beads (...) He then redeemed Nyamasau with 1 gun, 16 yards [of cloth], & 3 beads.[85]

Furthermore, the long-distance trade profoundly influenced material expectations and patterns of consumption. Social relationships, hierarchies of power, and patterns of consumption were all affected by patterns of trade, and the effects of such trade reverberated well into the twentieth century.[86]

Because imported goods had to be paid for, trade influenced productive relationships as well. Rubber and beeswax could be procured from the forests, and elephants were hunted to provide supplies of ivory with which to acquire imports.[87] A brisk trade in rubber and beeswax to Angola persisted well into the colonial period, as cloth, guns, and liquor could be obtained in return.[88] Food production for trade caravans, which might contain up to 6,000 individuals travelling for months at a time, was equally important.[89] Livingstone described how:

> ... very little exertion is required to procure the staff of life, which in these parts is the manioc (...) Maize, beans, earth nuts, &c, are planted between, and here we have a supply of food for years. The climate is so good, they are either planting or reaping the whole year round. All the different grains, roots, &c, may be seen at one time in every stage of growth.[90]

Not only does this attest that by the 1850s items from overseas, in the form of cassava, maize, and groundnuts, had reached Mwinilunga and had been adopted as mainstays of agricultural production but it also evidences that food production was copious, hinting at the salience of the trade in food. Passing caravans would depend on villages along the route for their supplies of food,

---

85 (NAZ) KSE3/1/2/1, Msangi v. Chingbwambu, 7 July 1912.
86 E.A. Steel, 'Zambezi-Congo Watershed', *The Geographical Journal* 50, No. 3 (1917): 187.
87 Hoover, 'The Seduction of Ruwej'; Vellut, 'Notes sur le Lunda'; Von Oppen, *Terms of Trade*.
88 (NAZ) SEC2/133, N.S. Price, Annual Report Mwinilunga District, 31 December 1937; (NAZ) SEC2/41, Ormeby-Gore Report, 21 May 1937.
89 Vellut, 'Notes sur le Lunda', 139; Von Oppen, *Terms of Trade,* 91.
90 Schapera, *Livingstone's Missionary Correspondence,* 261–62.

and the ensuing demand encouraged the expansion of agricultural production.[91] Cameron, travelling through the area in the 1870s, provides an insight into the provisioning of caravans:

> Being the last station in Ulûnda, we remained (...) a few days to procure corn and make flour for a reported march of five days (...) For a piece of salt I obtained one fowl; but the people would not even look at my remaining beads, being very eager for cloth, of which I had none for trading. My only stores were a few beads and seven or eight viongwa, or shell ornaments from the East Coast.[92]

By means of food, beeswax, or ivory production for trade caravans, the population of Mwinilunga found an outlet for productive activities, thereby firmly linking themselves to international markets and circuits of trade. The long-distance trade with the Angolan coast constituted an increase in scope and intensity compared to previous patterns of trade, but it equally built upon the bases of local and regional exchange. Although the long-distance trade did provide access to new goods and trade networks, the trade was founded on and incorporated into existing patterns of production, consumption, and social relationships in Mwinilunga. Long-distance trade goods were distributed through local and regional sociopolitical networks, thereby influencing and changing the make-up of the village. Looking at slavery further illustrates how the long-distance trade built upon but also altered social relationships and hierarchies of power in the area.

An integral component as well as a spin off to the long-distance trade was the traffic in slaves. Slavery had existed previously within the Lunda polity, as Mwantianvwa possessed large plantations worked by slave labour.[93] Nevertheless, the trade in slaves was greatly propelled by stimuli emanating from the long-distance trade. Slaves were a prized item of exchange, ensuring access to guns, cloth, and beads. In addition, slaves could serve as porters of ivory or beeswax, transporting supplies from the interior to the coast.[94] Although large-scale violent slave raids had severely disruptive effects in the area of Mwinilunga, slavery could equally involve complicity or even active involvement of the

---

91   Von Oppen, *Terms of Trade*, 96, estimated that during the last quarter of the nineteenth century 14,000 tons of foodstuffs would have been required annually to supply the caravans passing through the Upper Zambezi area.
92   Verney L. Cameron, *Across Africa* (New York: Harper & Brothers, 1885), 405–08.
93   Vellut, 'Notes sur le Lunda', 77–78.
94   Gordon, 'The Abolition of the Slave Trade', 915–38; Miller, *Way of Death*.

local population. Elders still recount stories of slave traders visiting villages, where they would buy people in a peaceful and negotiated manner:

> There was a girl who was enslaved, she was called Kabanda. She was en-slaved by the Ayimbundu [Ovimbundu] and sold. Kadata and Chiseki, her grandfather and uncle[95] gave Kabanda a *mubulu* [bracelet]. When the Ayimbundu came, Kadata and Chiseki pointed to the girl with the *mubulu* and sold her as a slave. They told Kabanda to go and chat with the Ayimbundu, who were her relatives, and to come back later. However, when Kabanda arrived where the Ayimbundu were seated, she was taken as a slave. Her uncle and grandfather were given cloth and guns.[96]

Slavery was part of social relationships and hierarchies within the village. Slaves could be demanded as a payment to settle cases, ranging from divorce, theft, and debt to murder. Or slaves might be claimed as compensation after the death of a relative, as this case attests:

> Mapupu himself came to me to claim goods in compensation for his son Chindora's death, saying that since my sister [Nyachianzu] had killed him, being a witch, I her brother must pay. At first he claimed all the goods that Chindora had brought with him from Kambove & given his wife [Nyachianzu], and other goods besides. I paid him 8 yards of calico, one short flintlock gun, one blanket and one string of beads, and he ac-cepted these (…) Mapupu reopened the accusation (…) claiming that (…) he had a right to greater compensation. In fact he claimed goods to the value of Nyachianzu herself & her 2 children, who were given as slaves.[97]

Slaves would either be resold or incorporated into the village and given tasks to do, such as cultivating, building houses, or drawing water. Although it was not uncommon for slave women to marry free men, slaves remained distinguish-able as a separate category up to the 1950s.[98] The motives behind slavery were manifold, and slavery itself was multifaceted, involving violent raids, judicial settlements, and deliberate sale of kin. The practice was not solely an alien

---

95   Usually grandchildren or nephews/nieces (*mwizukulu* and *mwiha* respectively) would be the ones sold into slavery; see Turner, *Schism and Continuity*.

96   Interview with Headman Kachacha, 27 July 2010, Kanongesha.

97   (NAZ) KSE3/2/2/2, N.C. & A.M. Court Mwinilunga Sub-District, Criminal cases, Rex vs. Mapupu, 9 January 1915.

98   Turner, *Schism and Continuity*, makes numerous references to people of slave descent. At present people of slave descent are no longer recognisable as such.

imposition but should rather be understood within existing social relationships and hierarchies of power. The slave trade was actively negotiated and
could even prove beneficial to certain individuals.[99] Authority and concepts
of wealth in people became intertwined, as village heads used the slave trade
to amass a large following and bolster their prestige. The slave and the commodity trade reinforced and fed into each other, creating a vicious circle.[100]
Slavery was connected to the global context of the trans-Atlantic slave trade,
but it equally played into regional and local negotiations, involving internal
African slavery, and the articulation of relationships of debt, dependency, and
authority. Slavery illustrated the complex relationships between goods and
people.[101] Selling kin into slavery might have been an 'accommodation to the
inevitable fact of slaving in the area'.[102] The sale of kin, even if it caused conflicts within the village and region, seemed preferable to being subjected to
slave raids, which were unpredictable, indiscriminate, and difficult to control.
This proposition applies to the case of Mwinilunga, where slave raids caused
insecurity and disruption.

   Although the British formally abolished slavery in 1807 and the Portuguese
outlawed the slave trade (but not slavery itself) in 1834, the practice of slavery
and the trade in slaves continued unabatedly in the interior, probably even
heightening.[103] The 'legitimate trade' in ivory, beeswax, and rubber spurred the
internal demand for slaves as a means of 'production, exchange, and wealth'.[104]
Towards the end of the nineteenth century numerous violent slave raids occurred. In Mwinilunga, these raids were most commonly attributed to Chokwe
and Luvale neighbours. Later reminiscences are revealing, even if stylised:

---

99   Linda M. Heywood, 'Slavery and Forced Labor in the Changing Political Economy of Cen-
      tral Angola, 1850–1949', in *The End of Slavery in Africa*, eds., Suzanne Miers and Richard
      L. Roberts (Madison: University of Wisconsin Press, 1988), 415–35; Martin A. Klein, 'The
      Slave Trade and Decentralized Societies', *Journal of African History* 42 (2001): 49–65; Wyatt
      MacGaffey, 'Kongo Slavery Remembered by Themselves: Texts from 1915', *International
      Journal of African Historical Studies* 41, No. 1 (2008): 55–76; Paul E. Lovejoy, 'The Business
      of Slaving: Pawnship in Western Africa, c. 1600–1810', *Journal of African History* 42 (2001):
      67–89; Charles Piot, 'Of Slaves and the Gift: Kabre Sale of Kin During the Era of the Slave
      Trade', *Journal of African History* 37 (1996): 31–49.
100   Gordon, 'The Abolition of the Slave Trade.'
101   Miller, *Way of Death*, 40–53.
102   Piot, 'Of Slaves and the Gift', 45.
103   Joseph C. Miller, 'Cokwe Trade and Conquest in the Nineteenth Century', in *Pre-colonial
      African Trade: Essays on Trade in Central and Eastern Africa before 1900,* eds., Richard Gray
      and David Birmingham (Oxford: Oxford University Press, 1970), 177–78; Bustin, *Lunda
      Under Belgian Rule,* 25.
104   Gordon, 'The Abolition of the Slave Trade', 925.

> There were (...) cases of slaves being carried off by force, and the roads to
> the west were littered with wooden manacles and the forked neck-sticks,
> as well as with skulls and human bones, showing the extent of this hor-
> rible trade.[105]

Although some Lunda slaves might have been incorporated into Chokwe social relationships through the pawnship system in a relatively orderly manner, others would be sold off or exposed to harsher treatment. The Chokwe
had successfully capitalised on the rising demand for beeswax, ivory, and later
rubber. Displaying exceptional hunting ability, they exchanged forest produce
for cloth and guns (see Photo 1). Guns, in turn, were used to raid for slaves.
Slaves could act as porters for trade caravans or could serve to expand Chokwe
lineages, creating more wealth and power. The Chokwe even managed to raid
Musumba in 1885–88, and for a short period the Lunda polity was overrun by
chaos.[106] These events seriously disrupted the long-distance trade, and the ensuing insecurity proved so severe that changes in settlement patterns resulted.
Whereas slavery could be incorporated into existing Lunda social relationships
and hierarchies, the slave raids at the end of the nineteenth century caused
disruption and propelled profound, but not permanent, change.

The tension caused by slave raiding, still palpable early in the twentieth century, was described by a missionary, as he 'passed several groups of the huts
of these timid, wild-looking people, who have been preyed upon, probably
for centuries, by all the tribes around for supplies of slaves'.[107] Some people
reportedly hid in caves, such as *Kahoshanga* in Nyakaseya and *Nyawunda* in
Sailunga.[108] Others dispersed into the bush and sought security through mobility by shifting around in small bands. Another common response was to build
a stockade (*mpwembu*) around a concentrated settlement:

> The villages of these people are always small but are strongly stockaded.
> Circular earthworks are thrown up around a score of huts, and these are
> surmounted by a substantial palisade, at the base of which bushes and
> creepers are sometimes planted in order to render their fastness still
> more impenetrable. The entrance is through a narrow opening, which is
> firmly bolted by wooden logs on the inside. Usually these gateways are so

---

105   (NAZ) HM6 CO3/4/1, Edward Arden Copeman Memoirs.
106   Miller, 'Cokwe Trade and Conquest'; Bustin, *Lunda Under Belgian Rule;* Hoover, 'The Se-
        duction of Ruwej'; Vellut, 'Notes sur le Lunda'; Vansina, 'Long-distance Trade-routes.'
107   (EOS), Visits to Various Stations, Kaleňe Hill – Extracts from Mr. Arnot's Journal, 36th year
        No. 631 Part 1 October 1907.
108   See interview with Wombeki, 27 April and 24 May 2010, Nyakaseya.

low as to be passable only on hands and knees. At Kanungesa's [Kanon-gesha's] the opening is the shape of a reversed v, only three feet six inches high at the apex.[109]

Although palisades had been built around Musumba since the eighteenth cen-tury at least, outlying villages had remained without stockades.[110] The spread of *mpwembu* during the late nineteenth century, therefore, should be linked to defence mechanisms in reaction to the threats of slave raids. Within stockades, security was sought in numbers, giving rise to villages of 100 individuals or more. To better withstand the looming attacks from slave raiding groups, pop-ulation would amass into concentrated fortified settlements.[111] Slave raiding, thus, did not merely lead to insecurity and chaos but arguably also to greater levels of village cohesion.[112] Within the stockade, village organisation would be cemented, as 'all the functions of defence were laid down and (...) everybody was trained to perform a specific duty when emergency arose'.[113] Containing only a limited number of entrance doors, villages would be safely guarded by strong men, the warriors (*ayilobu*) of a village. The status of the headman or chief of such a large village was exalted. United action upon attack could prove of vital importance and the headman was looked upon to provide guidance. Supernatural protection and witchcraft, mediated through the village head, offered further security. The charm *mujiminu* could be used to make the vil-lage invisible to attackers, whereas an *ilomba* (magic serpent) would guard the village against external attack.[114] Nevertheless, this form of village cohesion proved short-lived. Upon the arrest of violent raids at the outset of the twen-tieth century, colonial administrators complained about village breakup into small units once more.[115] It is questionable whether the emergence of stock-aded villages where centralised forms of authority prevailed propelled struc-tural changes in social and political relationships in Mwinilunga. The leader of a stockaded village would use similar tools to assert political authority as

---

109   Gibbons, *Africa from South to North*, 34.

110   Vellut, 'Notes sur le Lunda'; Bustin, *Lunda Under Belgian Rule*.

111   This view is based on various interviews, for example Kasongu Mapulanga, 29 July 2010, Kanongesha, and a reading of archival sources (NAZ).

112   C.M.N. White, 'Clan, Chieftainship, and Slavery in Luvale Political Organization', *Africa* 27, No. 1 (1957): 72–73: 'The fact that slavery no longer exists as an active element in Luvale life has had the effect of reducing the size of Luvale villages, and the danger of a kinsman being handed over as a slave no longer provides a unifying force in the village.'

113   (NAZ) SEC2/402, H. Vaux, A Report on the Sailunga Kindred, 1936.

114   See interview with Martin Kahangu, 30 September 2010, Ntambu.

115   (NAZ) SEC2/402, H. Vaux, A Report on the Sailunga Kindred, 1936.

previous headmen and chiefs had done. Success in holding people together was due to the threat of attack, and concepts of authority remained embedded in notions of wealth in people. The later reversal to small and dispersed settlements testifies that stockaded villages signalled a temporary change rather than constituting a rupture in sociopolitical relationships.

The long-distance caravan trade, which built upon existing foundations of production, consumption, and social relationships, established remarkably enduring patterns in Mwinilunga. In spite of disruptions caused by slave raids and subsequent colonial boundary demarcations, the long-distance trade lingered on illicitly during the first half of the twentieth century.[116] Furthermore, the long-distance trade established trade networks, patterns of production, expectations of consumption, and ideas about the relationship between goods, people, and power that proved influential during the colonial and postcolonial period. Trade goods provided Mwinilunga with a connection to the world at large. Even if this connection at times remained indirect, and its effects seemed challenging or threatening rather than beneficial, especially in the case of slave raids, local individuals by and large managed to make sense of trade. The familiar and the unfamiliar converged, as new trade goods were appropriated into existing social hierarchies, and settlement patterns were adjusted to ward off threats. Subsequent colonial advances were inevitably understood in the light of the contacts established by the long-distance trade.

3   Engaging the *Chindeli*: Colonial Rule and Local Negotiation

Despite their various backgrounds and intentions, Europeans are invariably referred to as *chindeli* (white person) throughout Mwinilunga. During the nineteenth, and even more so in the twentieth century, engaging the *chindeli* – or disengaging from them – became an important feature of daily life. Whether it was to consolidate and further explore avenues of trade, to prospect for minerals, to preach the gospel, or for other reasons, Europeans gradually sought to intensify and formalise their involvement with the Central African interior, especially after 1880.[117] Building on the foundations of the long-distance trade, new claims to territorial control were advanced towards the end of the nineteenth century, the period retrospectively signifying the dawn of formal colonialism in the area. It would be teleological to claim that Europeans had

---

116   For example: (NAZ) KSE3/2/2/7, Rex vs. Chisele, 24 July 1928.
117   See Jan Vansina, *Being Colonized: The Kuba Experience in Rural Congo, 1880–1960* (Madison: University of Wisconsin Press, 2010).

always negotiated with Africans from a position of strength. Rather, it was initially the other way around, as a handful of Europeans proved heavily dependent on the knowledge, skills, and produce of the local African population.[118] The colonial occupation of Mwinilunga District provides a clear example hereof.

In the sphere of Lunda influence, European presence had increasingly made itself felt through the long-distance trade. From the sixteenth century onwards, European influence had started radiating from the Angolan coast into the hinterland. Initially, this was merely through trade goods, yet traders and other individuals followed in their wake.[119] A clear association between trade goods and the first whites in the area of Mwinilunga permeates present-day recollections, once again underlining the connection between goods, people, and power. Oral accounts hold that early European travellers would leave salt and white cloth as a rapprochement gift at the edge of the village, after unsuccessful attempts had been made to come into contact with local chiefs or headmen. Such narratives suggest that power relations were not necessarily tilted towards Europeans from the outset.[120] From the perspective of the local population, initial encounters with Europeans were rare events, marginal to lived reality.[121]

Towards the end of the nineteenth century, attitudes and relationships started to shift. Spurred by a highly competitive international setting, Europeans made attempts to establish strongholds and direct control over large parts of the African continent.[122] In the light of these developments, the establishment of colonial rule by British authorities in Northern Rhodesia has been presented – most notably in the work of Macpherson – as a swift thrust of a hegemonic 'civilised European power replacing uncivilised African powers'.[123] Despite differing views as to whether colonial domination was established through the deployment of brute force, or by means of relatively peaceful treaties, rarely has scholarship doubted that colonial hegemony was established rapidly and completely.[124] The Berlin Conference of 1884–85 has especially been hailed as

---

118   Gewald, 'Researching and Writing', 459–87; Jaeger, *Settlement Patterns and Rural Development*.

119   See Prestholdt, *Domesticating the World*.

120   Interview with John Kamuhuza, March and April 2010, Ikelenge.

121   Pritchett, *Friends for Life*.

122   Bustin, *Lunda Under Belgian Rule*.

123   Macpherson, *Anatomy of a Conquest*, 2.

124   Whereas Pritchett in *Lunda-Ndembu*, 33–37, and Macpherson in *Anatomy of a Conquest*, argue that colonial rule was established and consolidated by displays of overwhelming force, Peter Slinn, 'Commercial Concessions and Politics During the Colonial Period:

a landmark in the 'scramble for Africa' by European powers who 'carved up the African continent' between themselves.[125] These views, however, grossly over-estimate European power. Likewise, they ignore local responses to colonial advances and present Africans as powerless victims falling prey to all-powerful European administrators. Contrastingly, in Mwinilunga the establishment of colonial rule was gradual rather than sudden, partial, and incomplete – especially in the early stages – rather than hegemonic. Local agency, initiatives, and responses should therefore receive as much attention as colonial interests or European statesmen when examining the establishment and functioning of colonial rule.[126]

The decision to assign the area of Mwinilunga to the British sphere of influence and demarcate international boundaries, which was made at the Berlin Conference and was affirmed by the arbitration by the King of Italy in 1905, did not equal physical occupation on the ground.[127] Only in 1906–7 did reconnaissance of this 'No Man's Land' commence, when a government station was built and an official in charge was appointed.[128] During this initial period, colonial rule was in the hands of isolated 'men on the spot', who had no prior knowledge of the area or language of the districts to which they had been posted.[129] Although on paper and in theory these officials held considerable power over the area and the population, in practice they lacked control over district affairs.[130] British South Africa Company (BSAC) administration of Mwinilunga[131] initially consisted of a Native Commissioner, his assistant, 25 head of Barotse Native Police, and several messengers and porters, who would accompany the administrators, whilst touring the area. Administrative aims remained modest, and no recording of census or levying of taxes took place, to avoid antagonising

———

     The Role of the British South Africa Company in Northern Rhodesia 1890–1964', *African Affairs* 70, No. 281 (1971): 365–84, argues that British rule was established by means of relatively peaceful treaties.

125   Bustin, *Lunda Under Belgian Rule,* 40.

126   See Kalusa, 'A History of Disease.'

127   (NAZ) KDD5/1, Kasempa District Notebooks; Kakoma, 'Colonial Administration.'

128   (NAZ) KSE4/1, Mwinilunga District Notebooks.

129   Macpherson, *Anatomy of a Conquest,* 228.

130   Lewis H. Gann, *The Birth of a Plural Society: The Development of Northern Rhodesia Under the British South Africa Company 1894–1914* (Manchester: Manchester University Press, 1958), 64–65; Bizeck J. Phiri, *A Political History of Zambia: From Colonial Rule to the Third Republic 1890–2001* (Trenton: Africa World Press, 2006), 10–11.

131   Initially referred to as Balunda sub-District, administered within Kasempa District. Mwinilunga became a District in 1926.

the population.[132] Officials openly expressed despair over their lack of control over village affairs:

> The utmost secrecy is observed, and information is very difficult to obtain. Balunda communities mind their own business very surely when dealing with an official – they profess ignorance of their neighbours names or doings; are averse to lead you forward at times, and in many ways show very plainly that they also believe in the shrewd silence that is golden. Beyond the evidence of the man or woman venturing to seek aid or freedom, it is almost impossible to gain any outside information or statements.[133]

In spite of this feeble administrative hold, colonial headquarters ordered the Native Commissioner to 'subdue the wild Ba-Lunda', if necessary by using force.[134] Local non-cooperation with administrative aims evoked harsh treatment. Records of flogging, arrest, destruction of houses, the burning of fields, and other displays of violence by colonial staff were not uncommon.[135] Especially in 1908–9, when George Alexander MacGregor was in charge of the district, much violence was displayed.[136] He raided gardens to obtain food, beat and imprisoned people at random, and even shot a person.[137] Rather than causing submission, MacGregor's approach met with resistance. Whilst touring the district, his party came across countless deserted settlements, which greatly hampered the establishment of orderly colonial rule. People would abandon their villages upon his approach, and only numbers of old men and women would remain in their houses.[138] Some individuals even fled into Angola or Congo, which caused agricultural disruption, as 'no one did any cultivation – they were all running away from Mr. MacGregor and left their land to the pigs'.[139]

---

132 (NAZ) HM6CO3/4/1, Edward Arden Copeman Personal Memoirs.
133 (NAZ) BS2/199 IN2/1/3, J.M. Pound, Monthly Report Balunda District, January 1909.
134 (NAZ) HM6CO3/4/1/, E.A. Copeman Personal Memoirs.
135 For example: (NAZ) HM6CO3/3/1, Edward Arden Copeman Papers.
136 See: Macpherson, *Anatomy of a Conquest,* 124–25; Pritchett, *Lunda-Ndembu,* 33, 228–29; Pritchett, *Friends for Life,* 48–51; Turner, *Schism and Continuity,* 7.
137 (NAZ) A1/1/12 Loc.3975, Slave Trading North Western Rhodesia, 20th January 1910, Crewe to High Commissioner.
138 (NAZ) KSE6/5/1, Secretary of Native Affairs to MacGregor, 26 February 1909.
139 (NAZ) KSE6/5/1, C.H. Bellis, Monthly Report Balunda District, October 1909.

The introduction of taxation in 1913 caused equal, if not greater, disruption.[140] According to some accounts, the tax had propelled two-thirds of the population to flee across the border to Angola and Congo, where taxation was not yet introduced or administrative demands remained less onerous. The distress and resistance caused by the introduction of taxation were described in grim terms by Theodore Williams, a colonial official at the time:

> All the villagers have run, i.e. a population of 8000. All that remains are a few villages in the south. The people here are a wild and primitive lot and quite naturally don't like the idea of spending 10/- on taxes (...) The running last May has caused consequent starvation and the people are getting restless because of this. For these people were not content merely to run and leave their gardens to be eaten by the wild pigs in the bush – but they must also ply the hoe in the hand too and root up even their young cassava, so that they could leave with the feeling of finality and of burnt ships behind them. Now that most of them are back they are starving, and those who did not run are suffering.[141]

Those who refused to cooperate with the policy of taxation were presented with the uninviting alternatives of imprisonment, the burning of their huts, or relocation to Congo or Angola.[142] Violence was not shunned, as colonial official Pound openly proclaimed: 'these folk need a bit of choking off, and I shall not spare the pains to give it to them'.[143] Nevertheless, such examples overstate the violent nature of the early colonial period and equally overemphasise the hold that the administration commanded over the local population. Occasional displays of coercion and violence did occur, yet administrative presence did not have permanently disruptive effects on daily life.[144]

Due to the numerical weakness of the administration, the display of force was neither universal, nor inescapable. After being harassed by MacGregor or upon the introduction of taxation, people did return. Some would return within several days, most would eventually:

---

140   Pritchett, *Lunda-Ndembu*, 33; Macpherson, *Anatomy of a Conquest*, 115–16; Turner, *Schism and Continuity*, 7.

141   (BOD) Mss Afr. S 779, Theodore Williams Correspondences, 8 May 1913 and 16 February 1914.

142   (NAZ) KSE4/1, Mwinilunga District Notebooks.

143   (BOD) Mss Afr. S 777, Theodore Williams Diary, 20 July 1914.

144   It might be argued that it was the other way around, that the colonial administration used violence because of a sense of despair and lack of control. See Piot, *Remotely Global.*

> The Government (...) made certain concessions to encourage the remainder [those who had not fled from taxation] to pay, with some success (...) Favourable reports reaching the deserters, by no means happy in their retreats, slowly village after village returned, so that only a third of those who fled are still absent, and these may come in yet (...) Everything now looks brighter (...) Hundreds of acres of wood have been cut down and burnt, ready for the rains we are daily expecting [to start cultivating].[145]

Shortly after returning from exile, which was more often temporary than long term, villagers would pick up cultivation and daily routines.[146] Moreover, many were apt to deceive officials, merely fleeing temporarily upon their approach. Because administrators travelled with a large entourage of porters and messengers, their arrival would be announced several days in advance. This gave individuals ample time to retreat into the surrounding bush, only to reappear once the touring group had long passed.[147] Consequently, officials would falsely be impressed with images of 'deserted settlements'.[148] Missionaries provided a vivid description of such practices:

> At one village, near where our camp was pitched, the people entirely cleared off at first. By-and-by some little boys crept up, and then, after a time, men came with meal, etc. (...) soon two [women] came with some food for sale. I endeavoured to ensure them that we would neither catch them as slaves, nor eat them, but asked them to come and bring others (...) Quite a number of men came.[149]

These examples suggest that colonial rule could not be established by violent and repressive means. If a harsh attitude was adopted by the administration, this merely caused non-compliance and flight. Therefore, the colonial administration had to rely on collaboration with local intermediaries and had to carefully manoeuvre so as not to alienate the population through oppressive

---

145   (EOS) Walter Fisher, 'A Year of Changes', Echoes of Service, 44th year No. 805 January Part 1 1915.
146   (NAZ) KSE 6/5/1, C.H. Bellis, Balunda District Monthly Report, October 1909.
147   (NAZ) A2/1/4 Loc.3981, BSA2 Tax Evasion No 256, Acting Administrator of North Western Rhodesia, 20 December 1910.
148   (NAZ) KSE 6/1/6, F.V. Bruce-Miller, Mwinilunga Sub-District Annual Report, 1928; W.S. Fisher and J. Hoyte, Ndotolu: The Life Stories of Walter and Anna Fisher of Central Africa (Rev. Ed., Ikelenge: Lunda-Ndembu Publications, 1992), 133.
149   (EOS) Orpah Gertrude Sawyer, 'Visits to Fellow-Workers', Echoes of Service, 42nd year No. 772 August Part 2 1913.

policies.[150] Due to a lack of financial resources, the colonial administration relied on the compliance of the population in order to rule effectively. That is
why generous concessions followed the introduction of taxation.[151] Through
a process of negotiation, the local population was able to exert considerable
influence over the manner in which colonial rule would eventually be established in the area of Mwinilunga.[152]

Taxation can provide an example to understand how relationships of interdependence and hierarchies of power between the colonial administration
and the local population were worked out. Especially in Mwinilunga, an area
that did not seem to hold much potential for mining or agricultural development, taxation was the centrepiece of colonial rule.[153] The dual objectives behind the introduction of taxation were to raise revenue for the cash-strained
BSAC government and to create a cheap labour force.[154] Not only local labour
requirements but equally those of the mines in Southern Rhodesia and South
Africa had to be satisfied. Contrary to encouragements to move south, however, many individuals from Mwinilunga were attracted to the mines in Congo,
encouraged by proximity, favourable working conditions, and the presence of
kin.[155] Officials hoped that by introducing the hut tax individuals would become accustomed to the habit of working, handling money, and moving out of
the village to seek employment: 'The tax does good in making them work a bit,
in learning how profitable work can be, and in taking them abroad to see the
way the more civilised Bakaonde live and thrive'.[156] Taxation, which was connected to notions of 'civilisation', aimed to tie the population to administrative
control, as well as to influence core social values of work and thrift. The colonial administration initially set the height of the tax at 10/-, which coincided
with the average monthly wage of a labourer.[157]

---

150   See Gewald, *Forged in the Great War.*

151   (NAZ) KSE4/1 Mwinilunga District Notebooks.

152   Kalusa, 'A History of Disease'; Bakewell, 'Refugees Repatriating.'

153   Macpherson, *Anatomy of a Conquest,* 105; Slinn, 'Commercial Concessions and Politics',
       365–68; Pritchett, *Lunda-Ndembu*; Crehan, *The Fractured Community.*

154   Gann, *The Birth of a Plural Society,* 76, 113; Richard S. Hall, *Zambia* (London: Pall Mall
       Press, 1965), 87; R.P. Lander, 'The British South Africa Company: An Essay on Its Commer-
       cial History', *Heritage of Zimbabwe* 11 (1992): 1–3; Phiri, *A Political History of Zambia,* 11.

155   (NAZ) KSE 4/1, Mwinilunga District Notebooks; (NAZ) KSE6/1/5, F.V. Bruce-Miller, Mwini-
       lunga Sub-District Annual Report, 1926.

156   (BOD) Mss Afr.S777, Theodore Williams Diary, 16 July 1914.

157   The height of the tax fluctuated over the years. It rose to 12/6 in 1930, but was lowered to
       7/6 in 1934 and 6/- in 1938; (BOD) Mss Afr. S779, Theodore Williams Correspondences, 22
       October 1913.

Taxation could not simply be imposed by the administration, though. For one, collection of taxes was heavily dependent on the cooperation of headmen, not only for compiling a census of village population, but also for forwarding tax money and receipts.[158] To the great frustration of the administration, headmen would frequently protect or hide tax defaulters. Headmen perhaps claimed that defaulters had moved to Congo or were away 'at work', while some had merely gone to the bush to hunt or cultivate.[159] The lack of colonial control over the population was clearly manifested by the aforementioned 'exodus', which followed the introduction of taxation. This 'exodus' exasperated officials to such an extent, that they granted numerous concessions to those who did pay taxes. These concessions included the right to import gunpowder, collect and sell rubber, move to Congo without a pass, and refrain from compulsory road labour.[160] Nevertheless, levels of default remained high throughout the colonial period, lingering around 30% in the late 1930s.[161] Although taxation was a central concern of the colonial enterprise, the imposition and collection of taxes was by no means straightforward. The administration could not demand local cooperation, but rather had to entice people to pay taxes by granting concessions. Dissidence and flight proved effective means to achieve local goals and keep colonial interference at bay, at least temporarily.[162]

Administrative aims went beyond touring the district and collecting taxes. Officials were responsible for hearing legal cases, mapping the district, compiling a vocabulary of the local language, interviewing chiefs and headmen, and much more.[163] The colonial administration introduced a plethora of legislation. To name a few examples, it became necessary to purchase a licence in order to own a gun, the shooting of large species of game was restricted, the cutting down of trees was subjected to limitations to preserve valuable timber species, the upkeep of inter-village paths was made obligatory, and villages were encouraged to concentrate in large settlements along major lines of communication.[164] Even though such regulations could limit pre-existing livelihood strategies, such as hunting or foraging, enforcement of laws was

---

158   (NAZ) KSE6/1/4, F.V. Bruce-Miller, Mwinilunga District Annual Report, 31 March 1922.
159   (NAZ) KSE6/2/1, T.M. Lawman, Lunda District Quarterly Report, 14 October 1912.
160   (NAZ) KSE4/1, Mwinilunga District Notebooks, Folio 29.
161   (NAZ) SEC2/151, Provincial Commissioner Western Province, Annual Report on Native Affairs, 1937.
162   Scott has illustrated numerous instances of such resistance. See James C. Scott, *The Art of Not Being Governed: An Anarchist History of Upland Southeast Asia* (New Haven: Yale University Press, 2009).
163   (BOD) Mss Afr. S779, Theodore Williams Correspondences, 11 February 1913.
164   (NAZ) KSE6/3/2, Mwinilunga Sub-District Reports Indaba, August 1927.

incomplete and could be circumvented.[165] Illustrative was the attempt to regulate, or preferably exterminate, the remnants of the pre-colonial trade in rubber, ivory, slaves, guns, and powder. Colonial officials condemned this trade, carried out by Mambunda, Mambari, Portuguese, and 'undesirable European' traders, who robbed, plundered, and ill-treated the population, whilst illicitly straddling the boundaries between Mwinilunga, Angola, and Congo.[166] Despite restrictive legislation, this trade persisted well into the 1920s, as it offered the local population favourable terms of trade with which the colonial administration could not compete.[167] The establishment of colonial rule and subsequent colonial legislation, thus, did not fundamentally disrupt previous practices or patterns of livelihood procurement. The population could circumvent colonial legislation by exploiting its contradictions or by partial enforcement. Acts of subversion and passive resistance – even if apparently trivial and of limited scope – shaped the contours of colonial rule in Mwinilunga District. Colonial rule was not hegemonic or driven by European interests alone but was negotiated among various actors, who had widely divergent interests.[168] The inhabitants of Mwinilunga sought to further their own interests, struggling to establish a form of colonial rule that would maintain a degree of continuity with past practices, ideas, and modes of life.

Settlement patterns were fervently discussed by the colonial administration.[169] Officials connected living conditions in villages to issues of hygiene, thrift, agricultural production, and, most importantly, amenability to administrative control.[170] Instead of scattered residence in the bush, where the evasion of colonial law and order would be all too easy, villagers were encouraged to gather into more concentrated settlements, containing a minimum of ten taxpaying men.[171] Such concentrated settlements should preferably be located in accessible places along paths or roads, which would facilitate administrative control and compliance. Colonial officials described dispersed living conditions in derogatory terms, particularly condemning *nkunka* (conical grass houses):

---

165   Pritchett, *Lunda-Ndembu*, 228–31.
166   (NAZ) HM6CO3/3/1, Edward Arden Copeman Papers.
167   (NAZ) KSE6/3/1, Mwinilunga Sub-District Report Indaba, October 1916; (NAZ) KSE6/6/2, G. Hughes-Chamberlain, Mwinilunga Sub-District Tour Report, November 1928.
168   Gewald, *Forged in the Great War*; James C. Scott, *Weapons of the Weak: Everyday Forms of Peasant Resistance* (New Haven: Yale University Press, 1985).
169   Sara S. Berry, 'Hegemony on a Shoestring: Indirect Rule and Access to Agricultural Land', *Africa* 62, No. 3 (1992): 327–55; Kay, *Social Aspects of Village Regrouping*, describes colonial settlement patterns in Northern Rhodesia as the outcome of the struggle for colonial administrative control against 'traditional' and shifting residential patterns.
170   Moore and Vaughan, *Cutting Down Trees*, for the Northern Province of Zambia.
171   (NAZ) KSE4/1, Mwinilunga District Notebooks.

The Balunda are a gypsy or nomadic people, for all their old and present huts are but skeleton frameworks, with uprights for walls consisting of poles from one foot to two feet apart with a thatched roof. Plastered walls are the rare exceptions, the usual and almost universal wall being formed by suspending grass mats along the inside of the skeleton wall, forming a break wind only. Sometimes grass is lashed along the wall, so as to completely enclose it. Many communities make no attempt at building decent huts, but live in a collection of beehive shaped, or conical small shelters of about six feet in diameter, and six to eight feet to apex. It is plain that the community building to-day, have vividly before them the possibility of circumstances arising to make them decide to remove again to-morrow.[172]

Inaccessibility and a degree of independence from colonial control, more than anything else, propelled such negative valuations. In order to administer the area, record census, and collect taxes, to make the population controllable and legible, the colonial administration exercised pressure to settle the population in large, stable villages.[173] Nevertheless, efforts to establish large villages were vehemently resisted and the ten-taxpayer rule remained an ideal rather than becoming the norm:

> Before the arrival of Europeans to this corner of the Territory the Lunda were accustomed to live in small family settlements of often only three or four men with their wives and families. The Government however has always encouraged larger villages but they have never been popular here: big villages would lead to factions and quarrelling.[174]

By the end of the 1920s it was recorded that the largest village in Mwinilunga contained 105 people, yet villages with less than 40 people remained more common.[175] Although the colonial administration attempted to make alterations in residential structures and settlement patterns, such efforts did not meet with much success. Changes in settlement patterns were part and parcel of the process of negotiating and appropriating colonialism. Previous settlement patterns were not simply abandoned, but were adjusted to the context of colonial rule.

---

172   (NAZ) BS2/199 IN2/1/3, G.A. MacGregor, Monthly Report Balunda District, January 1909.
173   Scott, *The Art of Not Being Governed.*
174   (NAZ) SEC2/955, H.B. Waugh, Mwinilunga District Tour Report, 11 October 1940.
175   (NAZ) KSE6/3/2, Mwinilunga Sub-District Indaba, 30 August 1927.

Colonial rule envisaged headmen and chiefs as the undisputed leaders of villages in terms of political authority. The colonial administration relied heavily on the mediation of village heads for implementing its policies and laws under 'indirect rule'.[176] In practice, headmen and chiefs occupied a brokering position, shrewdly negotiating with the colonial administration and functioning as the speaking drum for the desires and grievances of village populations. Colonial officials called on village heads to organise the supply of food and labour for administrative requirements and to maintain village paths.[177] Because of their crucial position, the colonial administration sought to encourage the establishment of village heads that would be loyal and cooperative with colonial rule. Correspondence regarding Chief Kanongesha is revealing in this respect (see Photo 3). Due to boundary demarcations, the area of Chief Kanongesha had been bisected between Angola and Northern Rhodesia. Consequently, the British administration tried to tempt and attract this 'intelligent looking man' and 'important Chief' to settle on their side of the international boundary:

> [Kanongesha] has complained that this administration does so little for him (...) He is supported in every way possible by us (...) I shall endeavour to show him that the Government is willing and able to support him in any reasonable demands that he may make.[178]

Because of their own lack of resources and control, the colonial administration was dependent on the performance of headmen and chiefs for successfully administering the area.[179] Village heads could use this dependence to their advantage by negotiating for autonomy and power.[180]

The colonial government could, in some cases, bolster the position of village heads by codifying their rule and assigning them new tasks and responsibilities.[181] Whereas previously village heads had ruled by means of ritual authority, during the colonial period chiefs and headmen became responsible for

---

176 Berry, 'Hegemony on a Shoestring'; Martin L. Chanock, *Law, Custom and Social Order: The Colonial Experience in Malawi and Zambia* (Cambridge: Cambridge University Press, 1985).

177 Pritchett, *Lunda-Ndembu*; Turner, *Schism and Continuity*; (NAZ) KSE4/1, Mwinilunga District Notebooks.

178 (NAZ) KSE6/1/4, F.V. Bruce-Miller, Annual Report Mwinilunga Sub-District, 31 March 1922.

179 Jaeger, *Settlement Patterns and Rural Development*.

180 For a case study of a chief in colonial Malawi, see Mary E. Davies, 'The Locality of Chieftainship: Chiefly Authority in Colonial Malawi, 1932–1974' (Unpublished PhD Thesis, Leiden University, 2014).

181 Hobsbawm and Ranger, *The Invention of Tradition*.

enacting law and order in a more formal manner.[182] Some proved particularly successful brokers with the colonial government:

> Good chiefs will always be respected and good work will make a chief important. All his good work will be considered when his subsidy is paid to him. Chiefs who merely sit down in their villages will on NO ACCOUNT EVER GET BIGGER SUBSIDIES.[183]

Cooperation with the colonial administration provided some chiefs with tangible benefits, such as official recognition and material wealth. The colonial state sought to organise headmen and chiefs into fixed hierarchies, quite different from the shifting, loose relationships of authority that had prevailed during the pre-colonial period.[184] Under colonial rule distinct territorial boundaries and hierarchies of authority between headmen, chiefs, and senior chiefs were drawn up, reserving recognition and government subsidies to a limited number of titleholders.[185] As not all headmen or chiefs were recognised by the colonial administration, colonial rule could threaten as well as benefit village heads. Some titleholders purposefully refused association with the colonial government and as a result the administration tried to delegitimise their claims to authority. An example is ex-Chief Ntambu Sachitolu, who objected to the payment of taxation and subsequently returned his *ndondu*, a sceptre handed out as a symbol of chiefly recognition by colonial officials. Due to non-cooperation, his chiefly title was revoked and he was degraded to the rank of headman.[186] Contrastingly, compliant leaders would be hailed and supported by the colonial administration in case disputes arose:

> Nyakaseya's Chieftainship has always seemed to me to be more important. Economically on account of better land and a large river it is capable of supporting a larger population than Mwinimilamba's. Nyakaseya has taken a Chief's course at Lusaka and the Mission states that he is far

---

182   Pritchett, *Lunda-Ndembu*; Turner, *Schism and Continuity*.

183   (NAZ) KSE1/2/1, G. Hughes Chamberlain to Provincial Commissioner Kasempa, 26 April 1930.

184   (NAZ) H. Vaux, Sailunga Kindred and Dening Reassessment.

185   Pritchett, *Lunda-Ndembu*.

186   Interviews with Headman Kachacha, 27 July 2010, Kanongesha; Ex-Chief Ntambu Lukonkesha, 11 August 2010, Kanongesha; and confirmed by a reading of archival sources (NAZ).

more enlightened and helpful in regard to most matters, and education, than Mwinimilamba.[187]

Association with the colonial administration could thus simultaneously be threatening and prove beneficial. Through negotiation, different parties gradually crafted a balance of authority and power under colonialism.[188] In the process, the local population and the colonial administration became increasingly interdependent.

The colonial government could not boast a base of power or authority in Mwinilunga from the outset. In the initial stages of colonial rule, the administration appeared vulnerable rather than strong. Its feeble hold was still regretted in 1915:

> To visit them once, or in some cases twice, during the year is almost labour in vain. One arrives at a village, collects the inhabitants, talks for an hour or so, and occasionally one thinks a slight impression has been made – that a little of what has been said has penetrated their wooden heads – only to learn in about a month's time that they have drifted back to their old life (...) Some progress has, of course, been made. For example, the great majority are now living in quite respectable huts; small family communities have been collected and built together under one headman; hoed paths are being made between villages; larger gardens are being made, and the natives now are not definitely hostile to the Administration.[189]

Due to the frail command of the colonial state, individuals could default on taxation, flee administrative presence, and maintain trade contacts with Angola and Congo, despite boundary demarcations.[190] Colonial policies could not be violently or unilaterally imposed, but had to be negotiated, leaving the population of Mwinilunga considerable leverage. Officials were dependent on local assistance, collaboration, and approval. Passive resistance, dissidence, and flight were merely some of the tools used to ward off the negative effects

---

187   (NAZ) SEC2/222, Provincial Commissioner Kaonde-Lunda Province to Secretary for Native Affairs, 5 March 1947.

188   See: Piot, *Remotely Global*; Crehan, *The Fractured Community.*

189   (NAZ) KSE6/1/3, F.V. Bruce-Miller, Annual Report Mwinilunga Sub-District, 31 March 1915.

190   Gewald, *Forged in the Great War*; Enid Guene, *Copper, Borders and Nation-Building: The Katangese Factor in Zambian Political and Economic History* (Leiden: African Studies Centre, 2017).

of colonial encroachment.[191] Gradually, however, it became apparent that active involvement with the colonial administration could prove advantageous, most notably to headmen and chiefs whose position could be bolstered.[192] Some, therefore, sought to engage the colonial state on favourable terms, especially from the 1930s onwards. By selling crops to touring officials, seeking employment at the mines, or by establishing large villages under government sanctioned headmen, for instance, the population of Mwinilunga increased its interaction with the colonial administration.[193] The terms of this interdependence were not dictated by administrative aims alone, but were equally shaped by local interests. Colonial rule, thus, did not constitute a complete breach with the past, as important continuities with the pre-colonial period persisted. Yet a balance of power had to be negotiated to accommodate the presence of the colonial government. The outcome of this process of negotiation profoundly influenced social, economic, and political relationships in the area.

4   'Cinderella Gets the Ball at her Feet': Food, Labour, and Roads

The area of Mwinilunga boasts a variety of natural resources, such as game, sylvan produce, and patches of fertile land. These resources have historically been deployed to generate livelihoods, trade opportunities, and to create affluence. Yet, from the perspective of the colonial state Mwinilunga District appeared of only marginal importance to its profit-making interests. The area held potential for neither mining nor large-scale agricultural development. Furthermore, the area was remote from and poorly connected to colonial centres on the Copperbelt and along the line of rail. Mwinilunga was regarded as a periphery, as a labour reserve that might at best be exploited through labour migration and a limited degree of agricultural production.[194] Nonetheless, starting in the

---

191   For the 'exit option', see James C. Scott, *The Moral Economy of the Peasant: Rebellion and Subsistence in Southeast Asia* (New Haven: Yale University Press, 1976); Hyden, *Beyond Ujamaa.*

192   An example of a Zambian chief whose authority was bolstered by colonial presence is the Lozi chief Lewanika of Barotseland: Lawrence S. Flint, 'State Building in Central Southern Africa: Citizenship and Subjectivity in Barotseland and Caprivi', *The International Journal of African Historical Studies* 36, No. 2 (2003): 393–428.

193   Much RLI work has interpreted labour migration, cash crop production, and involvement with the state in terms of 'disruption' and negative 'social change'. See Long, *Social Change and the Individual.*

194   See: Pritchett, *Lunda-Ndembu*; Achim von Oppen, 'Cinderella Province: Discourses of Locality and Nation State in a Zambian Periphery (1950s to 1990s)', *Sociologus* 52 (2002): 11–46.

1930s and increasing in scope and intensity after 1945, colonial involvement with Mwinilunga increased.[195] As a result of metropolitan scarcity and reconstruction after the Second World War and, most importantly, because of the production boom on the Copperbelt, demands for labour and produce from remote rural areas such as Mwinilunga were raised.[196] This affected the productive sphere of society and brought about increased colonial involvement with the area. How did these developments affect the socioeconomic and political organisation of Mwinilunga? Turner argued that capitalism and colonial involvement would lead to village breakup, yet established patterns of production, consumption, and social relationships often proved more resilient.[197]

Because of the ongoing concern to make colonial rule a profitable enterprise, officials and traders made attempts to open up the district and tap the potential of the area. More staff and money was deployed for this purpose from the 1930s onwards, especially for road construction and schemes of 'development'. Agricultural, stock rearing, and fishing schemes were initiated; schools were built and clinics set up.[198] The population of Mwinilunga was encouraged to broaden the base of their livelihood strategies, especially through cash crop production and labour migration, in order to secure access to money to pay taxes and for consumer goods, such as clothing, pots, and bicycles.[199] None of these developments were new as such. Many cash crops, such as cassava or beans, had long been cultivated in the area, and their sale constituted an extension of scale more than anything else. The bartering of cassava to long-distance trade caravans and the sale of meal to the touring District Commissioner had been common practices for years.[200] Similarly, labour migration to the Congolese mines had started in the early 1900s, preceded by the employment of porters in trade caravans heading to the Angolan coast. Likewise, development schemes built on and sought to expand a pre-existing livelihood base rather than initiating schemes from scratch.

---

195   D.A. Low and John Lonsdale, 'Introduction', in *Oxford History of East Africa, Vol. 3,* eds., D.A. Low and Alison Smith (Oxford: Oxford University Press, 1976), 1–63, coined the term 'second colonial occupation' for the period after 1945; Joseph M. Hodge, *Triumph of the Expert: Agrarian Doctrines of Development and the Legacies of British Colonialism* (Athens: Ohio University Press, 2007); Erik Green, 'A Lasting Story: Conservation and Agricultural Extension Services in Colonial Malawi', *Journal of African History* 50, No. 2 (2009): 247–67.
196   Pritchett, *Lunda-Ndembu*; Kenneth P. Vickery, 'Saving Settlers: Maize Control in Northern Rhodesia', *Journal of Southern African Studies* 11, No. 2 (1985): 212–34.
197   Turner, *Schism and Continuity.*
198   Pritchett, *Lunda-Ndembu.*
199   Turner and Turner, 'Money Economy', 19–37.
200   See Chapter 2.

Even if colonial officials considered Mwinilunga District as rather marginal,[201] the area did seem to hold potential, for instance, for cattle ranching, forestry, or for the cultivation of crops such as rice and pineapples. Yet such opportunities were poorly utilised. This was not only due to long transport hauls but also because of a lack of government investment.[202] During the 1950s, nevertheless, the intensification of cash crop production and labour migration enticed the District Commissioner to state that 'the 'Cinderella Province' is at last beginning to get the ball at its feet'.[203] By means of agricultural productivity, marketing, and increased administrative presence, the links between Mwinilunga and the colonial economy were strengthened.

Road construction was especially significant in this respect. One missionary described the changes she witnessed between the 1920s and the 1950s as follows:

> There were no roads then [1920s], only narrow footpaths (...) indeed the term road was only a courtesy title for the rough track through the bush (...) Today motor roads run like great ribbons (white, red or grey, according to the changing soil) through the Central African bush in all directions, and cars can be used to get quickly from place to place.[204]

Access to economic opportunities was profoundly influenced by the transport and communications network.[205] In the area of Mwinilunga, travel by foot and bicycle had been the main modes of transport, as tsetse fly and irregular water flows had limited the possibility of travel by water or animal traction.[206] In 1930 the first motorcar reached Mwinilunga *boma*, and consequently new roads

---

201 Jeffrey I. Herbst, *States and Power in Africa: Comparative Lessons in Authority and Control* (Princeton: Princeton University Press, 2000); Catherine Boone, *Political Topographies of the African State: Territorial Authority and Institutional Choice* (Cambridge: Cambridge University Press, 2003); Jaeger, *Settlement Patterns and Rural Development;* Crehan, *The Fractured Community;* Pritchett, *Lunda-Ndembu.*

202 The term 'Cinderella Province' – holding vast, yet underutilised, potential – has been used to describe Mwinilunga District and the North-Western Province.

203 (NAZ) SEC2/135, W.G. Reeves, North-Western Province Annual Report, 1952.

204 Elsie Burr, *Kalene Memories: Annals of an Old Hill* (London: Pickering & Inglis, 1956), 8, 10, 122.

205 Edward J. Taaffe, Richard L. Morrill, and Peter B. Gould, 'Transport Expansion in Underdeveloped Countries: A Comparative Analysis', *Geographical Review* 53, No. 4 (1963): 503. See Jan-Bart Gewald, 'People, Mines and Cars: Towards a Revision of Zambian History, 1890–1930', in *The Speed of Change: Motor Vehicles and People in Africa 1890–2000,* eds., Jan-Bart Gewald, Sabine Luning, and Klaas Van Walraven (Leiden: Brill, 2009), 21–47.

206 (NAZ) SEC2/41, Native Affairs Development of Mwinilunga: Benguela Railway, March 1937.

were built and existing paths expanded.[207] Previously, headmen and chiefs
had been held responsible by the colonial administration for the construction
and upkeep of inter-village paths. These paths had sufficed for communication
purposes and in order to transport high-value, low-weight goods, such as ivory,
rubber, or cloth in large caravans. However, for quick communication, and for
the transport and marketing of more bulky low-value commodities, including
most agricultural produce, footpaths proved inadequate.[208] During the 1930s
roads suitable for motorised transport were built, one from Solwezi, via the
boma in Mwinilunga to Hillwood Farm in the northwest of the district, one
from Kalene Hill over the Jimbe Bridge to Caianda in Angola, and one from
Hillwood Farm to Mutshatsha in Congo.[209] These connections proved economically salient, as they linked the district to the Benguela railway and the
Congolese railway system, as well as to the Northern Rhodesian Copperbelt.[210]
After 1945 this expansion of the road network continued, linking the *boma* to
the various chiefly capitals in the district.

By facilitating access to markets and providing an outlet for local production, roads had the potential to 'revolutionise' agriculture, as colonial officials
remarked: 'All road extensions and improvements in this district have so far
lead to increased production'.[211] European and African traders, using bicycle
carts or lorries for transport, would tour the district in order to buy up produce
for sale at markets within the district, on the Northern Rhodesian Copperbelt,
or in Congo. In return, these traders would distribute a variety of consumer
goods through the district. The colonial administration welcomed such developments: 'Local people are only beginning to realise that being near a road and
European traders' stores makes it possible for them to have access to a market
where they had none before'.[212] The road acted as a magnetic focus towards
which villages gravitated, in an attempt to take advantage of rising economic
opportunities.[213]

Similarly, the expansion of mining enterprise on the Northern Rhodesian
Copperbelt had a profound impact on the area of Mwinilunga. Although
the mines on the Katangese Copperbelt had attracted labour and crops
from Mwinilunga since the 1900s and continued to do so throughout the

---

207   (NAZ) KSE4/1, Mwinilunga District Notebooks.
208   Von Oppen, *Terms of Trade*.
209   (NAZ) KSE4/1, Mwinilunga District Notebooks.
210   See Piot, *Remotely Global*, on the function of the road as a connective node.
211   (NAZ) SEC2/957, R.N. Lines, Mwinilunga District Tour Report, August 1949.
212   (NAZ) SEC2/958, D.G. Clough, Mwinilunga District Tour Report, November 1950.
213   Jaeger, *Settlement Patterns and Rural Development*.

twentieth century, international boundary demarcations and colonial legislation attempted to limit the Congolese attraction.[214] This goal was only
achieved, to an extent, with the heightened exploitation of mines within
Northern Rhodesia. For the area of Mwinilunga, the Kansanshi mine had provided a labour and food outlet close to home for a brief period after 1908, yet
activity only really took off from the 1930s onwards, when the Northern Rhodesian Copperbelt was developed.[215] The number of African employees on
the mines increased from 5,000 in 1925 to 30,000 in 1930, and rose to 38,000 in
1964.[216] Large numbers of migrant labourers were attracted from Mwinilunga
District, and in the 1960s 50% of the taxable adult male population was reportedly away 'at work'.[217] Next to labour, the mines also needed food for worker
rations. Demand came to outstrip supply, especially in the years 1939–53, and
the call for food resonated as far as Mwinilunga in spite of the distance and ensuing transport costs.[218] Consequently sales of food, not only to the Copperbelt
but also to neighbouring areas of Angola, Congo, and other parts of Northern
Rhodesia, skyrocketed. In 1955, for example, 610 tons of cassava, 104 tons of
beans, 132 tons of rice, 66 tons of sorghum and millet, 57 tons of maize, and
14 tons of groundnuts were marketed from Mwinilunga District.[219] Food sales
brought about prosperity in the area and enabled individuals with cash in their
pockets to buy coveted consumer goods or build brick houses with iron sheet
roofs. High rates of labour migration could go hand in hand with high levels of
agricultural production.[220] During this period, colonial officials described the

---

214   Jean-Luc Vellut, 'Mining in the Belgian Congo', in *History of Central Africa II*, eds., David
       Birmingham and Phyllis M. Martin (Longman, 1998), 126–62.
215   Andrew D. Roberts, 'Notes Towards a Financial History of Copper Mining in Northern
       Rhodesia', *Canadian Journal of African Studies* 16, No. 2 (1982): 347–59. See Johnson, *Hand-
       book to the North-Western Province*, 191–99 for the history of Kansanshi mine.
216   Vickery, 'Saving Settlers', 215; Ferguson, 'Mobile Workers, Modernist Narratives', 395, 604.
217   (NAZ) NWP1/2/101, Loc.4919, E.L. Button, North-Western Province Annual Report on Afri-
       can Affairs, 1960.
218   Jadwiga Lukanty and Adrian P. Wood, 'Agricultural Policy in the Colonial Period', in *The
       Dynamics of Agricultural Policy and Reform in Zambia,* eds., Adrian P. Wood, et al. (Ames:
       Iowa State Press, 1990), 3–18; Vickery, 'Saving Settlers', 231.
219   (NAZ) SEC2/137, P.L.N. Hannaford, Mwinilunga District Annual Report on African Affairs,
       1955. In 1955 the total population of Mwinilunga District was 45,000.
220   According to the RLI, labour migration would lead to 'rural decay' because of the loss of
       male labour force in agricultural production, which would upset village cohesion. See:
       Sara S. Berry, 'The Food Crisis and Agrarian Change in Africa: A Review Essay', *African
       Studies Review* 27, No. 2 (1984): 59–112; J.A. Hellen, *Rural Economic Development in Zam-
       bia, 1890–1964* (München: Weltforum Verlag, 1968), 94–106; Pritchett, *Lunda-Ndembu*,
       184. Amin has argued that 'Africa of the labour reserves' would inevitably become

atmosphere in the area in jubilant terms. 1953 was depicted as 'a year of progress and prosperity', with 'abundant harvests and incentives to be employed'.[221] Through the interaction of local, regional, national, and even global influences, the area of Mwinilunga experienced a bout of prosperity.

Settlement patterns changed in tandem. Whereas villages had previously remained spread out across the landscape, people moved towards the roadside on a large scale during the 1940s and 1950s.[222] This movement was incited by road construction, a desire to access markets and cash-earning opportunities, but equally by colonial prodding and legislation.[223] Villages started to form 'long almost uninterrupted ribbons' along the roadside, and officials noted 'a universal movement to the vicinity of the roads'.[224] The colonial government associated this movement with 'progress', as: 'the best villages were always to be found near a motor road, and the more remote a village the worse it becomes'.[225] Concomitantly, houses were constructed of more permanent materials, and some villages would remain settled in one place for longer periods of time. Reports mentioned cassava gardens that had been under continuous cultivation for 20 years before moving on to new land.[226] Nevertheless, shifting remained common:

> The general tendency to replace pole and dagga houses with Kimberley brick structures which has been noted in the past two years, is becoming increasingly pronounced in all areas (...) It is logical to expect a greater degree of more or less permanent settlement with the advent of more permanent housing (...) [but] even the building of Kimberley brick houses has failed to compete with Lunda instability and one can see whole villages of abandoned Kimberley brick houses whose occupants have split up and moved on (...) I found no land which had been used by the same owner for more than about ten years.[227]

---

impoverished due to exploitation from mining centres: Amin, 'Underdevelopment and Dependence', 105–19.

221   (NAZ) SEC2/136, M. Mitchell-Heggs, North-Western Province Annual Report on African Affairs, 1953.

222   Jaeger, *Settlement Patterns and Rural Development;* Silberfein, *Rural Settlement Structure.*

223   Pritchett, *Lunda-Ndembu;* Turner, *Schism and Continuity.*

224   (NAZ) NWP1/2/40, K.J. Forder, Mwinilunga District Tour Report, September 1952.

225   (NAZ) SEC2/963, R.S. Thompson, Mwinilunga District Tour Report, 31 January 1955.

226   (NAZ) MAG 1/10/1 Loc.76, C.E. Johnson, Agricultural Programme of Work North-Western Province, 29 June 1960.

227   (NAZ) NWP1/2/33, K. Duff-White, Mwinilunga District Tour Report, 5 October 1950; (NAZ) NWP1/2/83 Loc.4914, Land Tenure Report North-Western Province, 1958.

In spite of changes, previous patterns of settlement and residential organisation were not simply discarded. Individuals would move towards the roadside to take advantage of new opportunities, but this did not necessarily involve abandoning existing forms of social organisation, patterns of livelihood procurement, or modes of thought. The movement towards the roadside was not necessarily a step towards government control or capitalist involvement, as colonial observers may have imagined.[228]

During this period the appearance of 'farms' was first noted by officials. These small settlements, generally comprising several houses, would be built at a distance from the main village.[229] The establishment of farms evoked ambiguous responses from the colonial government. Whereas these settlements were viewed as an administrative nuisance, the underlying motives for their establishment could also be judged more positively:

> "Farms" mean that the more enterprising men will bring bits of good new ground under cultivation, bits that would not otherwise be used (...) It is much more easy for good houses to be built in these small settlements as a single family can practice shifting cultivation over a comparatively small area. Consequently the need to move to new lands is absent and the house can be built with the knowledge that it can be in use for a long time (...) Also of course, an enterprising man living by himself is not "sponged on" by his relatives to quite the same extent as would be the case if he were living among them.[230]

Officials linked the establishment of farms to the prosperity brought about by the sale of agricultural produce and to labour migration. Turner equally noted that:

> Most true farms are situated beside the motor roads, for the typical farm-head is a man who has earned money, often on the line-of-rail, and who intends to earn more locally. He may be a petty trader, a tailor with his own sewing-machine, a 'tea-room' proprietor, a 'beer-hall' owner, or a peasant producer raising cash crops. For all these purposes easy access to motor roads is necessary and propinquity to administrative and trading centres advantageous.[231]

---

228 See Chapters 4 and 5.
229 See: Turner, *Schism and Continuity*; Pritchett, *Lunda-Ndembu*.
230 (NAZ) SEC2/957, R.N. Lines, Mwinilunga District Tour Report, 10 January 1949; SEC2/959, K.J. Forder, Mwinilunga District Tour Report, 5 November 1951.
231 Turner, *Schism and Continuity*, 36–37.

Turner predicted that capitalist competition and the desire to earn money would cause a distinct individualism, as well as disrespect for the authority of headmen and chiefs. Generational tensions between wealthy youths and elder figures holding village authority would further give rise to farms.[232] Colonial officials similarly described an impulse: 'which seems to be felt by many of the younger generation to break away from their headmen and village discipline to establish their so-called "farms"'.[233]

Although officials voiced concerns about fading customs and the crumbling of 'tribal authority', these did not appear warranted.[234] The tendency towards village fissure had been long-established, and was already noted in the early years of colonial rule, as an account from 1914 shows:

> Every man wants to be his own headman, and in defiance of instructions often builds a mile or two from his acknowledged headman or chief (...) This alone makes it very difficult to hold a headman responsible for the good behaviour of his people (...) They [chiefs and headmen] frankly admit, however, that they have but little control over the younger members of their tribe.[235]

Rather than being altogether new, the appearance of farms seemed to be part of an established pattern. The following chapters will explore the causes for village fissure in more detail – whether farms resulted from ecological factors, kinship, or from interactions with markets and the state – and will examine the influence of social contestation and power struggles on hierarchies of authority in the village.[236] The local ideal continued to be a large village, headed by a leader who could boast a prestigious genealogy.[237] Nevertheless, small roadside farms appeared as attractive alternatives. Through mobility, farming, or by other means, individuals sought to take advantage of economic opportunities in both familiar and new ways.

---

232 Ibidem, 10, 36, 43, 133–35.
233 (NAZ) NWP1/2/78 Loc.4913, F.R.G. Phillips, North-Western Province Annual Report on African affairs, 1957.
234 Turner, *Schism and Continuity*, 43.
235 (NAZ) KSE6/2/1, Quarterly Report Lunda Sub-District, 31 December 1913 and 31 December 1914.
236 See Chapters 4 and 5.
237 Turner, *Schism and Continuity*; Confirmed by numerous interviews, for example Kadansonu Mukeya, 7 October 2010, Ntambu.

5   The Birth of a Nation? Independence and Beyond

Throughout the colonial period the paramount grievance of the population of
Mwinilunga had been the relative neglect of the area and the lack of government effort in domains such as education, medicine, or agriculture:

> It is a sad thing to us to see that our Province (...) is entirely neglected by
> the Government in many things like education (...) As this Province is
> the only backward area in the colony, the Government should pay great
> attention to it in order that it may develop and be on the same measure
> with other Provinces in the colony.[238]

The marginality of Mwinilunga District, however, created a certain degree of
autonomy, enabling the evasion of unfavourable policies or state influence.[239]
The continuation of illicit cross-border trade with Angola and Congo, un-
deterred hunting in spite of restrictive game and firearm laws, as well as the
cultivation of cassava instead of officially propagated maize, are but some
expressions of this latitude.[240] When political expectations of independence
mounted in Mwinilunga during the 1950s and 1960s, local politicians seized the
opportunity to express lingering grievances and design plans for an alternative
future.

Two political parties, the African National Congress (ANC) under the leadership of Harry Mwaanga Nkumbula and the United National Independence
Party (UNIP) under Kenneth Kaunda, contested for the vote.[241] Throughout
Mwinilunga politicians attempted to attract voters by tangible means, promising schools, hospitals, vehicles, and improved transport, as well as direct material rewards.[242] Next to mundane issues, matters of ideology played a role in
political mobilisation. A balance between local, regional, national, and international factors and interests had to be negotiated, as personal desires were

---

238   (NAZ) SEC2/46, Kaonde-Lunda Native Authorities to the Governor, Lusaka, 3 September
      1946.
239   Herbst, *States and Power*; Boone, *Political Topographies*; Scott, *Moral Economy*; Hyden,
      Beyond Ujamaa.
240   Bakewell, 'Refugees Repatriating'; Pritchett, *Lunda-Ndembu*.
241   Macola, *Liberal Nationalism*; Larmer, *Rethinking African Politics*; Andrew Sardanis,
      Africa, Another Side of the Coin: Northern Rhodesia's Final Years and Zambia's Nationhood
      (London: I.B. Tauris, 2003); William D. Grant, *Zambia Then and Now: Colonial Rulers and
      Their African Successors* (London: Routledge, 2008); Robin Short, *African Sunset* (London:
      Johnson, 1973); Gloria Keverne, *A Man Cannot Cry: The Towering Saga of Passion, Violence
      and Love* (London: Tudor Communications, 1985).
242   (NAZ) and (UNIPA) archives.

adapted to jibe with national policies.[243] The appeal of ANC candidate Rhodes Mangangu was attributed to his distinct ability to manoeuvre between these different levels. He was able to effectively mediate between specific local concerns and the broader setting of national and international politics: 'His influence is due to his powers of oratory, his Europeanised manners and dress, and especially it is due to his visit to England'.[244] Mangangu and other ANC members treated chiefs with particular respect, regarding them as the representatives of local interests. Chiefs, in turn, became enmeshed in the power play of national politics:

> Chief Kanongesha has allowed his political leanings towards ANC to influence his actions in his capacity as Senior Chief, and indeed the strength of this organisation is directly attributable to his "official" support. S. Tepa and John Njapau succeeded by "judicial flattery" of the conceited old man in gaining his ear and today ANC is his main and only source of advice.[245]

In the run up towards independence, local, regional, and national factors became increasingly intertwined, as individuals in Mwinilunga made sense of national and international political struggles through a local lens.

Rather than rally for the dominant UNIP, voters in Mwinilunga overwhelmingly chose to support the underdog ANC.[246] What contributed to this decision was that the ANC enjoyed direct links to the Katangese politician Moïse Tshombe, a relative of the Lunda Paramount Chief Mwantianvwa. This connection caused plans of resurrecting the 'Lunda Empire' to surface.[247] Such ideas were not new, as the District Commissioner noted in the 1950s: 'the Lunda have long cherished a hope that Lundaland, now arbitrarily divided between three European powers, would one day be reunited'.[248] Although but few politicians or other individuals were prepared to actively pursue this goal, the fact that

243 Interview with Peter Matoka, 9 January 2010, Lusaka. Achim von Oppen, 'A Place in the World: Markers of the Local Along the Upper Zambezi', in *Between Resistance and Expansion: Explorations of Local Vitality in Africa,* eds., Peter Probst and Gerd Spittler (Münster: LIT Verlag, 2004), 190, describes 'how local intellectuals and political activists who fight for local self-sufficiency do so by presenting themselves as spokespeople of global ideas and norms ... these struggles may be seen as a form of striving to take part in global modernity.'
244 (NAZ) LGH5/4/5 Loc. 3616, Chiefs Mwinilunga, April 1961.
245 (NAZ) LGH5/4/5 Loc. 3616, Chiefs Mwinilunga, 6 May 1961.
246 Larmer and Macola, 'The Origins', 471–96; Patrick M. Wele, *Kaunda and Mushala Rebellion: The Untold Story* (Lusaka: Multimedia Publications, 1987).
247 Bustin, *Lunda Under Belgian Rule,* Chapter 7.
248 (NAZ) SEC2/961, R.C. Dening, Mwinilunga District Tour Report, 21 November 1952.

allegiances in Mwinilunga were more easily stirred by playing on connections with Angola and Congo, than by reference to a national Zambian state with the remote Copperbelt and line of rail areas as its centre, is significant.[249] The lack of confidence that UNIP would be able, or willing, to alter the marginal future that awaited Mwinilunga District within the Zambian state, caused their candidate Peter Matoka to be defeated by the ANC candidate Ronald John Japau by 9,379 to 6,593 votes during the 1964 elections.[250] Although UNIP booked a national victory, their defeat in Mwinilunga remained a sore spot.[251] UNIP campaigners spread foreboding messages, before as well as after the elections:

> It was apparent that the present aim of UNIP was to spread a feeling of despondency by pursuing the line that UNIP would shortly be assuming control of government and those who opposed or failed to support its cause would suffer reprisals thereafter.[252]

Even though violence was instigated by both ANC and UNIP, causing general feelings of insecurity, serious clashes remained isolated occurrences.[253] A climax was reached when Chief Kanongesha Ndembi, due to recurrent non-cooperation with the UNIP government and blatant ANC support, was deposed from office by government decree in 1966. His subsequent flight across the Angolan border and his mysterious death demonstrated the extent of the ANC-UNIP cleavage.[254] What proved more significant in the long run, however, was that Mwinilunga came to suffer from both latent and outright policies of retribution. Because the area had failed to support UNIP during the elections, agricultural loans, development funds, and political appointments were granted far less copiously in Mwinilunga than in other areas.[255]

---

249 See Erik Kennes and Miles Larmer, *The Katangese Gendarmes and War in Central Africa: Fighting Their Way Home* (Bloomington: Indiana University Press, 2016).

250 Wele, *Kaunda and Mushala Rebellion*, 62.

251 These issues are further explored in Iva Peša, "'We Have Killed This Animal Together, May I Also Have a Share?': Local-National Political Dynamics in Mwinilunga District, Zambia, 1950s–1970s', *Journal of Southern African Studies* 40, No. 5 (2014): 925–41.

252 (NAZ) LGH5/2/2 Loc. 3611, District Commissioners Conference North-Western Province, 8 February 1962.

253 Fights erupted in Ntambu between ANC and UNIP supporters and led to the death of one UNIP youth.

254 Interviews in Kanongesha area, especially with Jesman Sambaulu, 10 August 2010, Kanongesha. This event is also noted in passing by Wele, *Kaunda and Mushala Rebellion*; Larmer and Macola, 'The Origins.'

255 This view is based on a reading of UNIP and ANC archives (UNIPA); see Macola, *Liberal Nationalism*, for similar examples from Zambia's Southern Province.

Kaunda's philosophy of Humanism, executed through five-year national development plans, aimed at reaching ambitious goals such as setting up medical facilities in remote areas, providing universal primary education, developing transport networks, and providing marketing services.[256] A desire was professed to close the gap between the Copperbelt and line of rail areas, on the one hand, and impoverished rural areas such as Mwinilunga, on the other.[257] Various policies attempted to stimulate 'development'. These included government loan schemes, the formation of co-operatives, and the setting-up of national marketing boards, price controls, and eventually the Zambianisation of enterprises.[258] National aims were defined as: 'firstly bridging the gap between urban and rural areas and secondly, trying to gradually achieve a balanced level of development between the Provinces'.[259] In Mwinilunga this development effort found expression in the rapid expansion of medical and educational facilities, as well as the construction of roads and the extension of other services. The First National Development Plan (FNDP 1966–70) provisioned for the opening of schools, the digging of wells, the building of improved housing, and the construction of fishponds.[260] The summit was the pineapple-canning factory, erected under the parastatal G.M. Rucom Industries in 1969. Although the factory processed thousands of pineapples a year, to the benefit of local cultivators, problems soon cropped up and closure followed.[261] Difficulties were equally experienced with agricultural loan schemes, as the meagre funds released in Mwinilunga would be distributed in a biased manner. Loans for seeds, fertiliser, and tractors would be used as political baits, rewarding loyalty to UNIP, as the Credit Organisation of Zambia representative Mr. Chindefu explained:

---

256   (NAZ) A New Strategy for Rural Development in Zambia, 1972; (UNIPA) UNIP5/9/6, Tour Report North-Western Province, 1970.

257   Wood, et al., *The Dynamics of Agricultural Policy*, 21–58.

258   (NAZ) Programme for the Nation – Rural Development Seminar, 19 September 1974; Jeremy Gould, 'On the Genealogy of the Post-colonial state: Lugard and Kaunda on Co-operatives and Authority in Rural Zambia', in *Improved Natural Resource Management: The Role of Formal Organisations and Informal Networks and Institutions*, ed., Henrik S. Marcussen (Roskilde: Roskilde, 1996), 232–57.

259   (UNIPA) UNIP5/3/2/2/8, 1969 Annual Progress Report North-Western Province, 23 February 1970.

260   (UNIPA) First National Development Plan.

261   (NAZ) Rural Development Seminar: Programme for the Nation, 19 September 1974; for a more detailed account of the history of the canning factory, see Peša, 'Between Success and Failure', 285–307.

The way we use for granting loans here is a little bit different from our friends whose districts have only one party. We use our propaganda for one party system in speaking to the people about loans. And indeed we are achieving, we do not get challenges from the people (...) we do not find people losing confidence in Government. All loans so far are given to only UNIP.[262]

Political dissent translated into the paucity of loans, grants, and development effort afforded to Mwinilunga. Similarly, the area only poorly profited from marketing schemes. National marketing boards placed a primacy on maize production and marketing, privileging maize over the locally favoured cassava crop, which was not even accepted at marketing depots.[263] Compared to other parts of the territory, crop sales from Mwinilunga District remained low. Still, some producers did take advantage of marketing opportunities. In the 1969–70 season, the National Agricultural Marketing Board purchased 180 tons of maize, 9.6 tons of groundnuts, 5 tons of beans, 24 tons of rice, 10 tons of vegetables, and 480 tons of pineapples from Mwinilunga District. In addition, unrecorded amounts of produce found their way through individual traders to local markets or crossed the border to Congo and Angola.[264] By pursuing higher education, moving to booming urban centres, or through pineapple cultivation, people in Mwinilunga sought to realise existing opportunities within the shifting national and international context.

In line with colonial policies, the UNIP government advocated the concentration of village settlements:[265]

In the areas which are sparsely populated some re-grouping of the villages will be necessary with intensive development zones, i.e. areas where the natural conditions allow a rapid expansion of economic activities, e.g. good soils, availability of water, roads, etc., and where the density of population warrants the provision of services, and the establishment of non-agricultural enterprises.[266]

---

262 (NAZ) LGH5/2/7 Loc.3612, J. Chindefu to H. Kikombe, 23 February 1966.
263 Wood, *The Dynamics of Agricultural Policy and Reform*.
264 (NAZ) LGH5/5/12, Marketing of Produce North-Western Province, 23 July 1970.
265 Von Oppen, 'The Village as Territory', 57–75.
266 (UNIPA) UNIP5/3/2/2/8, 1969 Annual Progress Report North-Western Province, 23 February 1970.

UNIP officials argued that concentrated settlements, preferably along the roadside, would facilitate the provision of social services, such as schools, hospitals, and water supplies.[267] Permanent roadside villages became the ideal, though never a universal practice. After independence, concentrated clusters of settlement did increasingly develop in the vicinity of social amenities. Close to markets, schools, or hospitals, large and increasingly permanent settlements would spring up.[268] Next to the various chiefly capitals, Mwinilunga *boma* developed into a large township, where government services were centred and individuals would come to trade, access education, or medical care.[269] Yet such large, permanent settlements remained the exception (see Photo 2). Headmen and chiefs feared that labour migration, cash crop production, and other developments would challenge the exercise of their authority and would question established hierarchies: 'Many chiefs feel that they have little part to play in the day to day running of their areas and that they are ignored and unwanted by their own people'.[270] Relationships of power had to be renegotiated as young wealthy men contested the authority of elder lineage heads. Yet overall, the position of headmen and chiefs was not fundamentally threatened. Even at present, some youths aspire to become respected headmen rather than seeking wealth in towns.[271]

In spite of professed intentions and official efforts, the outlook of Mwinilunga at the end of the 1970s did not seem to be much brighter than it had been during most of the colonial period:

> In terms of Agricultural development, North-western Province is one of the least developed in Zambia. This in spite of the fact that the Province has ideal climatic conditions, abundant water resources and suitable soils for all types of cash crops that can be produced such as maize, tobacco, rice and most of the area is free from tsetse fly.[272]

267   (UNIPA) UNIP5/3/2/2/5, Provincial Development Committee North-Western Province, 30 December 1971.
268   Kay, *Social Aspects Of Village Regrouping*; Silberfein, *Rural Settlement Structure*.
269   Johnson, *Handbook to the North-Western Province*.
270   (NAZ) LGH5/2/7 Loc.3612, Mwinilunga Quarterly Newsletter, May 1967.
271   Pritchett, *Lunda-Ndembu;* confirmed by numerous interviews, for example Headman Mwinilunga, 31 October 2010, Mwinilunga.
272   (UNIPA) UNIP1/2/21, Report of the North-Western Province to the National Council, 15 December 1977.

The potential of Mwinilunga District – its soils, rivers, and forests – which had attracted the Lunda immigrants around 1750, still held sway in the 1970s. Nevertheless, obstacles and difficulties prevailed, transport and marketing being but some examples. Within this environment of opportunity and constraint, individuals sought ways to secure their livelihoods, appropriating and domesticating change within existing patterns of thought, action, and ways of life. Although Mwinilunga remained marginal from a national or global perspective, this marginality could be used to the advantage of the area.[273] When the economic crisis of the 1970s hit the national economy, people in Mwinilunga proved distinctly able to cope with economic hardships. Exactly because of the limited national incorporation of the area, individuals could fall back on existing livelihood strategies or patterns of regional exchange and trade.[274] Change was continuously incorporated within a flexible framework of past ideas and practices, modifying the social, economic, and political organisation of Mwinilunga District, whilst leaving foundations intact. By migrating to the mines, trading with relatives in Congo or Angola, or seeking local employment through association with the ruling political party, individuals connected themselves to the world whilst remaining locally grounded.

6   Conclusion

The trends and developments sketched in this chapter straddle rigid divides between pre-colonial, colonial, and post-colonial periods.[275] Although important shifts and changes did occur, long-term continuities have equally been salient. Continuity, nevertheless, should not be equated with changelessness.[276] Continuity was rather a creative adaptation of change – both discursive and practical – within existing practices and modes of thought. The Lunda connection, originating in the sixteenth century yet remaining important to post-colonial political consciousness, is only one such example of continuity. A constant feature throughout the history of Mwinilunga was the interaction between individuals: Lunda migrants, Mbwela, long-distance traders,

---

273   For more about marginality, see Chapter 3 Section 1.
274   See Scott, *Moral Economy;* Hyden, *Beyond Ujamaa;* based on numerous interviews, for example Sokawuta, 22 and 23 April, Ikelenge.
275   Ellis, 'Writing histories of contemporary Africa', 1–26.
276   Schoenbrun, 'Conjuring the modern.'

the colonial administration, and the UNIP government, which created a hybrid mix of people, ideas, and associations. These interactions, encompassing local, regional, and global levels, involved a process of negotiation within shifting constellations of power. Unfamiliar long-distance trade goods were incorporated into existing hierarchies of authority within the village, whereas during the colonial and post-colonial period familiar crops were produced for sale to engage with markets and the state. Settlement patterns were adjusted from small shifting settlements, to stockaded villages, to communities living along the roadside, as a response to changing socioeconomic, political, and ecological circumstances. By means of metaphor, this chapter has explored various paths to the past, assessing long-term threads as well as variations within the history of Mwinilunga. The following chapters, by looking at aspects of production, mobility, consumption, settlements, and social change, will analyse in more detail how people in Mwinilunga negotiated and made sense of historical and social change.

PHOTO 1   A muzzle loading gun, 2010
            IVA PEŠA

PHOTO 2   A village setting in Mwinilunga, 2010
            IVA PEŠA

PHOTO 3
Chief Kanongesha, 1950s
NATIONAL ARCHIVES OF
ZAMBIA, MWINILUNGA DISTRICT
NOTEBOOKS

CHAPTER 2

Production: Crops, Meat, and Markets

During much of the colonial and post-colonial period, government officials, agricultural 'experts', and traders have denounced methods of production and forms of environmental knowledge in the area of Mwinilunga as 'primitive'.[1] Numerous reports would label agricultural, hunting, or fishing practices as exclusively geared towards 'subsistence' or 'self-sufficiency', averse to change, and potentially detrimental to natural resources. Yet triggered by forces such as colonial rule, integration into the monetary economy, and external expertise, these same observers presupposed an imminent transition from 'subsistence' to 'market' production. Turner captured this sense of change eloquently in the late 1950s, when he noted that 'subsistence agriculture is giving way to petty commodity cultivation and hunting is almost extinct'.[2] Rather than simply denoting changes in methods of production or marketing, this alleged transition was highly normative. Government officials, especially from the 1940s onwards, proposed to make production the focal point of various schemes of 'development' and 'progress'.[3] This would involve concerted education, as the 1945 provincial report states: 'The Africans in this province still need educating (...) Much instruction and advice is needed to improve upon the variety as well as the quality and quantity of foodstuffs'.[4] The requisite education would necessarily be initiated by external actors, in particular by agricultural officials propagating 'scientific' innovations.[5] The rationale behind such schemes was that established practices had to be transformed and improved, thereby

---

1 References to Lunda being 'primitive agriculturalists', producing in a crude manner for 'subsistence' reappear continuously in reports from the colonial and post-colonial periods (NAZ).

2 Turner and Turner, 'Money-economy', 36.

3 Hodge, *Triumph of the Expert*; Kate Crehan and Achim von Oppen, eds., *Planners and History: Negotiating 'Development' in Rural Zambia* (Lusaka: Multimedia publications, 1994); Andrew Bowman, 'Mass Production or Production by the Masses? Tractors, Cooperatives, and the Politics of Rural Development in Post-Independence Zambia', *Journal of African History* 52, No. 2 (2011): 201–21.

4 (NAZ) SEC2/193, Kaonde-Lunda Province Newsletter, Second Quarter 1945.

5 John McCracken, 'Experts and Expertise in Colonial Malawi', *African Affairs* 81, No. 322 (1982): 101–16; Helen Tilley, 'African Environments & Environmental Sciences: The African Research Survey, Ecological Paradigms & British Colonial Development, 1920–40', in *Social History & African Environments,* eds. William Beinart and JoAnn McGregor (Athens: Ohio University Press, 2003), 109–30.

substituting the meagre subsistence level of agricultural production by profit-able market production.[6]

Despite apparent examples of high-yielding, market-oriented, and eco-logically sound production throughout Mwinilunga, such as cassava market-ing to caravans in the nineteenth century or beeswax trade at the start of the twentieth century,[7] derogatory discourses of 'subsistence' have been re-hearsed throughout the twentieth century. In 1909, to name but one example, District Commissioner MacGregor complained that 'native agriculture is of the poorest – probably the most primitive to be found' in Northern Rhode-sia.[8] What is more surprising, the binary between 'subsistence' and 'market' production has equally underpinned studies of rural history in Central and Southern Africa to a large extent. Such works suffer from two major shortfalls.[9] Firstly, these studies postulate assumptions about the linear course of history, presupposing a transition from hunting and gathering to herding and settled agriculture. Similarly, the shift from subsistence to cash crop production and marketing is taken for granted. A second problem is the overwhelming focus on external causes of change. Particularly imperialism and colonialism, cou-pled with forces of global capitalism, are considered to have wrought major change in areas such as Mwinilunga. Notwithstanding whether this had result-ed in positive development or negative underdevelopment, the supposition that previously self-contained rural communities had increasingly become incorporated into the market economy and that this, more than any internal factor, constituted the root cause of changes in production permeates much of this work.[10]

---

6   Bates, 'Some Conventional Orthodoxies', 240; for an alternative perspective: Tony Waters, 'The Persistence of Subsistence and the Limits to Development Studies: The Challenge of Tanzania', Africa 70, No. 4 (2000): 614–52.

7   Von Oppen, Terms of Trade.

8   (NAZ) KSE6/1/1, G.A. MacGregor, Balunda District Annual Report, 1909.

9   For reviews of such work, see: Allen Isaacman, 'Peasants and Rural Social Protest in Africa', African Studies Review 33, No. 2 (1990): 1–120; Berry, 'The Food Crisis', 59–112; Ter-ence Ranger, 'Growing from the Roots: Reflections on Peasant Research in Central and Southern Africa', Journal of Southern African Studies 5, No. 1 (1978/79): 99–133; John Tosh, 'The Cash-crop Revolution in Tropical Africa: An Agricultural Reappraisal', African Affairs 79, No. 314 (1980): 79–94; Cooper, 'Africa and the World Economy', 1–86; Gareth Austin, 'Reciprocal Comparison and African History: Tackling Conceptual Eurocentrism in the Study of Africa's Economic Past', African Studies Review 50, No. 3 (2007): 1–28; Anthony G. Hopkins, 'The New Economic History of Africa', Journal of African History 50, No. 2 (2009): 155–77.

10   Emmanuel Kreike, 'De-globalisation and Deforestation in Colonial Africa: Closed Markets, the Cattle Complex, and Environmental Change in North-Central Namibia, 1890–1990', Journal of Southern African Studies 35, No. 1 (2009): 81, 98.

More recently, the premises of these older debates have been challenged. Environmental and local rural histories have looked at the internal dynamics of change in agriculture and related productive activities.[11] Furthermore, local forms of knowledge have been valued in their own right, whereas 'expertise' has been deconstructed and shown to be contested.[12] Nevertheless, assumptions about rural 'development' – and its direction – recur and remain influential. In this respect, areas that do not engage in market production or are 'trapped in decline' are regarded as anomalies.[13] This chapter seeks to complicate narratives of a transition from 'subsistence' to 'market incorporation', by questioning assumptions about the course of change in patterns of production. In doing so, it juxtaposes discursive depictions of productive activities with actual practices, seeking to understand the interaction between the two. Adopting a focus on internal causes of change, several case studies are presented, which suggest that market involvement in Mwinilunga was fluctuating rather than simply intensifying.[14] Repertoires, values, and rationales of production in Mwinilunga will be examined in order to understand the motives behind market involvement, or indeed, non-involvement.

Productive activities in Mwinilunga are based on a multifaceted and adaptive foundation. Production builds upon a mixture of agro-ecological considerations, sociocultural values, as well as economic and political objectives. Although this foundation of production has been subject to continuous adaptation and change, it has consistently revolved around a desire to create a reliable livelihood. In this regard, it is crucial to re-evaluate the concept of 'subsistence', which should not be interpreted in merely negative terms as an absence of surplus.[15] Rather, the daily effort to create a stable basis of subsistence,

---

11 For environmental history, see: Beinart, 'African History and Environmental History', 269–302; James C. McCann, 'Agriculture and African History', *Journal of African History* 32, No. 3 (1991): 507–13. For local rural histories, see: Moore and Vaughan, *Cutting Down Trees*; Spear, *Mountain Farmers*.

12 Paul Richards, *Indigenous Agricultural Revolution: Ecology and Food Production in West Africa* (Boulder: Westview Press, 1985); Hodge, *Triumph of the Expert*; Bowman, 'Ecology to Technocracy', 135–53.

13 Stefano Ponte, 'Trapped in Decline? Reassessing Agrarian Change and Economic Diversification on the Uluguru Mountains, Tanzania', *The Journal of Modern African Studies* 39, No. 1 (2001): 81–100; Shane D. Doyle, *Crisis and Decline in Bunyoro: Population and Environment in Western Uganda 1860–1955* (Athens: Ohio University Press, 2006).

14 See Chabatama, 'Peasant Farming.'

15 See: William Allan, *The African Husbandman* (Münster: LIT Verlag, 1965); Edward P. Thompson, 'The Moral Economy of the English Crowd in the Eighteenth Century', *Past and Present* 50 (1971): 76–136; Scott, *The Moral Economy of the Peasant*; Hyden, *Beyond Ujamaa*.

even in the face of adversity, could constitute a stepping stone for producers
to participate in the market and engage the state on terms suitable to the local
environment and compatible with personal aspirations and priorities. Producers sought to accommodate incentives (price fluctuations, changing state policies, and market opportunities) in ways that were attuned to existing methods
of production and livelihood. Thus, the desire to secure a stable basis of subsistence constitutes a long-term thread underlying productive strategies and
rationales towards market involvement in Mwinilunga. Instead of being mutually exclusive or conflicting, subsistence and market production fed into one
another in multiple ways. Sound subsistence production proved a prerequisite
for market engagement. The examples in this chapter explore the motivations
for engaging with market production, thereby highlighting the rationale behind patterns of production in Mwinilunga. Refuting the discursive transition
from self-sufficiency to market incorporation, this chapter portrays the fluctuating course of productive practices in Mwinilunga District.[16]

1   The Foundations of Production in Mwinilunga

Productive activities in Mwinilunga are intimately linked to the environment.
Geographical, physical and climatic features have influenced agricultural
production, hunting and fishing in the area, yet ultimately, 'people were ca-
pable of manipulating the natural world to their advantage'.[17] Through years
of cultivation, hunting and foraging – based on local knowledge rooted in past
experience – ways have been sought to use Mwinilunga's versatile environment
for productive purposes.[18] Over time, methods of production have undergone
continuous change, for instance by adding new crops to the cultivating repertoire. The foundations of production have thus been adapted to prevailing

---

16   See: Spear, *Mountain Farmers*; Doyle, *Crisis and Decline*; James C. McCann, *People of the Plow: An Agricultural History of Ethiopia, 1800–1900* (Madison: University of Wisconsin Press, 1995); Grace Carswell, *Cultivating Success in Uganda: Kigezi Farmers & Colonial Poli- cies* (Oxford: James Currey, 2007).
17   William Beinart and Peter Coates, *Historical Connections: Environment and History, The Taming of Nature in the USA and South Africa* (London: Routledge, 1995), 4.
18   See: James C. McCann, *Green Land, Brown Land, Black Land: An Environmental History of Africa, 1800–1990* (Portsmouth: Heinemann, 1999); Pritchett, *Lunda-Ndembu*; Marvin P. Miracle, *Agriculture in the Congo Basin Tradition and Change in African Rural Economies* (Madison: University of Wisconsin Press, 1967).

circumstances and requirements, in response to factors such as environment, marketing, trade and politics.[19]

Mwinilunga's environment is the foundation upon which productive activities have been built. This environment is varied, featuring extensive plains, dense forests, high hills, small streams and fast-flowing rivers. Even within a single plot of land microenvironments can differ markedly, a feature which cultivators shrewdly exploit through intercropping. In his memoir, former colonial official Grant provides a vivid portrait of this variety:

> Mwinilunga lay in the Tropics (...) on one of the highest parts of the Rhodesian plateau, some 1,500 metres above sea level at one of the great watersheds of the African continent (...) all rivers and streams ran southwards to join the mighty Zambezi which itself rose in our District (...) The woodlands were largely *brachistygia* woods, with generally low and flat-topped trees. The soils varied from ochre to deep red, not particularly fertile, suited mainly to the cultivation of the staple cassava (...) The trees were that peculiar mixture of evergreen and deciduous (...) [Moreover] one could have (...) the cultivated colours of bougainvillea, wisteria, flame tree, frangipani or canna lily around houses and gardens.[20]

Mwinilunga's environment should not be taken as a static backdrop. Through habitation, cultivation and adaptation, the population has sought to tailor environmental opportunities to changing needs and objectives. The environment enables human action, but equally poses limits to it. Agricultural practices, hunting and fishing are particularly affected by and connected to environmental factors, as rainfall, temperature and soil characteristics influence the flora and fauna of an area. These factors have a bearing on which crops can be grown and which methods of production appear most suitable in a particular setting. On the other hand, human agency can shape and alter the environment for its own purposes. People mould the environment, for example by making use of fire, cutting down trees, fertilising the soil or hunting on game.[21] This intimate connection between people and the environment has created a wealth of knowledge, which provides tools to cope with a challenging, yet potentially promising, surrounding.[22]

---

19   See: Moore and Vaughan, *Cutting Down Trees*; Vickery, *Black and White*; Spear, *Mountain Farmers*.

20   Grant, *Zambia, Then and Now*, 38–40.

21   Beinart, 'African History and Environmental History.'

22   Beinart and Coates, *Historical Connections*.

Mwinilunga forms part of the Central African Plateau, with altitudes ranging from 3,600 to 5,000 feet.[23] The soils of the area (predominantly Kalahari sands) are generally acidic and of low productivity, but specific crops such as cassava and pineapples can thrive on them.[24] Yet soil types and their characteristics vary considerably across the area. Patches of fertile red clay soil, in addition to river floodplains or damboes, provide sites which are more suited to agricultural production, in particular of maize, rice and vegetables. Notwithstanding their moderate fertility, the soils of Mwinilunga have a number of distinct advantages, as they are deep, well drained and can be worked easily. Moreover, the area contains rich forest vegetation (*miombo, chipya, cryptosepalum* and dry evergreen forest) with many different types of trees (*Brachystegia, Julbernardia, Isoberlinia* and *Marquesia* are common species), which provides an attractive setting for game and bees. Tree height and density of growth differ and thick forest (*mavunda*), areas with low stunted trees (*ikuna*), extensive grass plains (*chana*) and riverside damboes exist side by side.[25] In addition, the area is well endowed with water resources, containing numerous streams and rivers in which to fish and from which to draw water. Temperatures average 29°C throughout the year, rising during the hot months of September and October before the rains set in. During the nights, especially in the cold months of June and July, temperatures drop, on occasion causing frosts that can jeopardise the growth of crops. Rainfall is abundant with an average of 55 inches (1,397 mm) per year, yet it is confined to the rainy season from October to April. This limits the potential growth period of crops, as during the dry season from May to September agricultural production is only feasible under irrigation in riverside gardens. Climatic considerations give rise to distinct seasons and a particular division of labour. The complex of village life is closely interrelated to these different seasons – *nvula*, the rainy season from October to April, *chishika*, the cold dry season from May to August, and *nonga*, the hot dry season from August to September. Whilst the main agricultural activities are carried out during the rains, the dry season is a time for hunting, travel to distant relatives,

---

23   District Planning Unit, *Mwinilunga District: District Situation Analysis 2007* (2008), 6.

24   Colonial ecologists Colin Trapnell and Neil Clothier described Mwinilunga's soils as leached soils of low productivity: Colin G. Trapnell and J.N. Clothier, *The Soils, Vegetation, and Agricultural Systems of Northwestern Rhodesia: Report of the Ecological Survey* (2nd edn., Lusaka: Government Printer, 1957), 5–6.

25   This view is based on numerous interviews, for example Zabetha Nkemba, 8 May 2010, Nyakaseya; M.K. Fisher, *Lunda-Ndembu Dictionary* (Rev. ed., Ikelenge: Lunda-Ndembu Publications, 1984).

initiation ceremonies and festivities.[26] There is, thus, a reciprocal interdependence between productive activities and the environment.

This particular confluence of geographical, climatic and environmental features has shaped opportunities for hunting, honey collecting and the cultivation of crops in the area. The environmental diversity of Mwinilunga enables the co-existence of various livelihood strategies: a person can simultaneously cultivate maize in a bush field, catch fish in the river, collect mushrooms from the forest and plant beans along the streamside. The environment can provide many of the necessities of daily life as well as items of trade or ritual importance. Within the vicinity of most villages, food, thatching grass and poles, or even clothing material and iron ore can be obtained. Such an environmental setting of opportunity and constraint has encouraged a degree of fluidity, competition and struggle, which is expressed in the frequent shifting of village locations to access suitable hunting, fishing or cultivating grounds.[27]

A particular expression of the interplay between environmental and human factors is the slash-and-burn type of shifting cultivation, which has developed due to low population densities and the relatively low productivity of the soils in the area.[28] Allan has described this as:

> the felling or lopping each year of a large area of woodland, an area several times greater than that on which crops are actually grown. Felling (...) is done in the early dry season, from May to August (...) Over the area of woodland selected for new gardens the trees are cut with the axe at (...) [knee] height, all but the hardest and toughest trunks, which are left standing, and the branches are lopped from them and spread between the stumps to dry (...) the branches are collected and built into small stacks (...) The brushwood stacks are burned at the end of the dry season, when it is thought that the rains are about to break.[29]

Fields are burnt in this manner to enhance soil fertility, whilst limiting the growth of weeds. After several years of cultivation, when soil fertility is largely

---

26   This account is based on a wide reading of archival sources (NAZ) and observations from
      Mwinilunga. See: Pritchett, *Lunda-Ndembu*; Bakewell, 'Refugees Repatriating'; Chabata-
      ma, 'Peasant Farming'; Johnson, *Handbook to the North-Western Province*; Turner, *Schism
      and Continuity*; Trapnell and Clothier, *Ecological Survey*.
27   Pritchett, *Lunda-Ndembu*, Chapter 2; Turner, *Schism and Continuity*, Chapter 1.
28   (NAZ) The population density in Mwinilunga District was 2.9 people per square mile in
      1943, but rose to 6 people per square mile in 1970.
29   Allan, *African Husbandman*, 66.

depleted, the plot is left fallow to regenerate.[30] Intercropping is another example of environmental adaptation, which agricultural producers practise to spread the risk of crop failure and provide a varied diet. Intercropping involves the growing of different crops, an array of staple and subsidiary crops, on a single plot of land. As staple crops grains (sorghum and millet), cassava and maize are most commonly grown. Subsidiary crops range from pumpkins, beans, sweet potatoes and yams, to leaf vegetables (*wusi, mulengu* and rape), tomatoes, onions and cabbages. Moreover, foraging, hunting, fishing and animal husbandry add variety to the diet and complement the food supply from agricultural production. Although productive activities are generally executed individually, household and village co-operation equally occur (work parties, communal hunts and foraging expeditions are but a few examples).[31] In this manner, through the diversification of livelihood strategies, the spread of risks and an adaptation of humans to their environment, producers in Mwinilunga have attempted to secure their requirements and fulfil objectives of a stable basis of subsistence.[32] Although these strategies vary between individuals, areas and historical periods, they constitute a basic repertoire from which people can tap: the foundations of production.

1.1   *On Subsistence and Market Production*

Throughout the twentieth century, rural producers in Mwinilunga have all too often been portrayed – by colonial officials, agricultural experts or development workers – as eking out a meagre existence from the land. Such views have presented agricultural producers, particularly during the pre-colonial period, as conservative and lacking innovative potential. Early colonial reports blamed rural producers for general 'apathy' and a lack of 'market logic'. In 1909, the District Commissioner complained that 'little indeed beyond manioc [cassava] is grown and but the minimum quantity of that is produced. Travellers find the greatest difficulty in procuring supplies even at exorbitant prices'.[33] Even in reports from the 1950s overtly negative valuations remained commonplace: 'To say that the Lunda (...) do no more than scratch at the earth, is no understatement (...) the overall production of crops (...) would hardly do justice to the Sahara desert'.[34] Officials assumed, however, that this state of agricultural production had started or would soon start to change, influenced by colonial

---

30   See Moore and Vaughan, *Cutting Down Trees.*

31   Pritchett, *Lunda-Ndembu*; Turner, *Schism and Continuity*; Chabatama, 'Peasant Farming.'

32   Compare with: Elias Mandala, *The End of Chidyerano: A History of Food and Everyday Life in Malawi, 1860–2004* (Portsmouth: Heinemann, 2005).

33   (NAZ) KSE6/1/1, G.A. MacGregor, Balunda District Annual Report, 1909.

34   (NAZ) SEC2/958, K. Duff-White, Mwinilunga District Tour Report, March 1950.

rule, capitalism and the propagation of agricultural science.[35] Considering the
region as a whole in the 1960s, Allan suggested that these changes would be
'revolutionary':

> profound changes came with the cash economy (...) the need of every
> man to possess money (...) was something altogether new and revolu-
> tionary (...) It had to be earned by wage labour where work was available,
> or by the sale of the surplus of subsistence food production where mar-
> kets were offered, or by growing industrial cash crops where these were
> introduced by the new masters. These changes did not come easily and
> were at first resisted.[36]

The encounter between African agricultural producers and external forces,
such as trade, markets and European presence, has evoked extensive debate.
Whether seen in a positive light (giving rise to market production and 'development'), or in a negative light (extracting surplus production through brute
domination, causing environmental degradation and leading to 'underdevelopment'), this encounter has unequivocally been interpreted as 'transformative' –
the premise being that external factors had caused change in local methods
of production.[37] Countering such views, the case of Mwinilunga suggests that
change was inherent to agricultural production and was not exclusively driv-
en by external factors. Rather than being initiated by a single push, change in
methods of production was gradual and continuous. Agricultural producers
in Mwinilunga have accommodated factors such as environmental variation,
fluctuating terms of trade or particular state policies into crop repertoires and
methods of production, into a foundation of values, norms, relationships and
practices.[38]

This chapter portrays the dynamic foundations of production in Mwinilunga. At present, officials and producers in Mwinilunga still claim that the main

---

35   Turner and Turner, 'Money Economy.'
36   Allan, *African Husbandman,* 336–37.
37   On underdevelopment, see: Robin H. Palmer and Neil Parsons, eds., *The Roots of Rural
      Poverty in Central and Southern Africa* (Berkeley: University of California Press, 1977);
      Giovanni Arrighi, 'Labour Supplies in Historical Perspective: A Study of the Proletari-
      anization of the African Peasantry in Rhodesia', *Journal of Development Studies* 6, No. 3
      (1969/70): 197–234. On development, see Bates, 'Some Conventional Orthodoxies.' RLI
      scholars believed that labour migration and capitalist penetration would lead to rural
      decline, yet they did acknowledge tendencies towards rural 'development' due to capital-
      ism and marketing.
38   Chabatama, 'Peasant Farming'; Pritchett, *Lunda-Ndembu.*

objective of production is 'food' or 'subsistence' (*yakudya hohu*).[39] For the case of Tanzania, Hyden has contended that 'meeting minimal human needs in a reliable manner forms the central criterion which knits together the peasants' choices of seeds, techniques, timing, rotation, etc.'[40] Generating a stable and sufficient basis of subsistence remains a precarious balance due to environmental constraints, as well as dependency on limited factors of production, such as labour and land.[41] The basic aim of producers in Mwinilunga is, indeed, to feed a household in a dependable manner. Nevertheless, the notion of 'subsistence' production becomes blurred once it is taken into account that production in the area has always been geared towards exchange, ritual and marketing, next to direct consumption.[42] Producers in Mwinilunga have since long been familiar with the exchange, barter and trade of food. Countering colonial portrayals of pre-colonial self-sufficiency, the food transactions between local producers and trading caravans during the nineteenth century should already be interpreted as incipient forms of market production.[43] Subsistence production is evidently more encompassing than meeting the requirements of bare necessity. Being about more than feeding, food production entails social, cultural, political and economic features.[44]

A positive valuation of subsistence could go a long way in explaining productive activities in Mwinilunga in a less dichotomous – *either* subsistence *or* market-oriented – way. In this respect, subsistence can be viewed as the aim to create a stable and dependable basis of production, involving striving for a level of surplus, as a buffer in years of adversity, in case of environmental disaster, to fulfil social obligations or for trade and sale.[45] This stable and abundant basis of production could, subsequently, serve as a starting point to expand levels of production and engage with markets. The idea of 'normal surplus', as proposed by Allan, provides an alternative evaluation of subsistence production:

---

39   Individuals would state that they engaged in agriculture 'just for eating' ('*twatemwanga yakudya hohu*'). Colonial and postcolonial reports are littered with complaints regarding the subsistence – rather than the market – orientation of production in Mwinilunga.

40   Hyden, *Beyond Ujamaa*, 14.

41   Berry, *No Condition Is Permanent*; Gareth Austin, 'Resources, Techniques and Strategies South of the Sahara: Revising the Factor Endowments Perspective on African Economic Development, 1500–2000', *Economic History Review* 61, No. 3 (2008): 587–624.

42   Von Oppen, *Terms of Trade*; Vansina, *How Societies Are Born*.

43   Von Oppen, *Terms of Trade*.

44   Filip De Boeck, '"When Hunger Goes Around The Land": Hunger and Food Among the Aluund of Zaire', *Man* 29, No. 2 (1994): 257–82.

45   Kate Crehan, 'Mukunashi: An Exploration of Some Effects of the Penetration of Capital in North-Western Zambia', *Journal of Southern African Studies* 8, No. 1 (1981/82): 82–93.

It would appear to be a reasonable – if not axiomatic – proposition that subsistence cultivators, dependent entirely or almost entirely on the produce of their gardens, tend to cultivate an area large enough to ensure their food supply in a season of poor yields. Otherwise the community would be exposed to frequent privation and grave risk of extermination or dispersal by famine, more especially in regions of uncertain and fluctuating rainfall. One would, therefore, expect the production of a "normal surplus" of food in the average year.[46]

In Mwinilunga cultivators aimed to produce a surplus at all times, to have sufficient supplies even in years of adversity. This implies that in a year in which no adversity occurs, a surplus would remain which could be bartered, traded or marketed. 'Subsistence' production, then, could serve as the basis for 'market' production.[47] By unpacking notions of 'subsistence' and 'market' production, the progressive transition from one to the other is shown to be futile. On the one hand, 'subsistence' production was often more dynamic than it has been credited for. On the other hand, 'market' production was not so much a linear end-point of historical development. Hyden argues that market production did not have to be a universal attraction to rural producers. On the contrary, it might be 'an ambiguous process, in which the risks of loss are as great as the prospects of gain'.[48]

Examples from Mwinilunga illustrate the interdependency between 'subsistence' and 'market' production, as sound subsistence production often functioned as a stepping-stone for market involvement. Moreover, producers moved in and out of the market, focusing on household production even after years of marketing their crops.[49] In the area of Mwinilunga the repertoire of cultivated crops is highly diverse, making distinctions between subsistence and cash crops anything but clear-cut. Crops grown for 'subsistence' could be – and often were – marketed, whereas crops grown for the market might equally be consumed as food locally.[50] Waters has similarly claimed that subsistence and market production are not necessarily incompatible:

---

46   Allan, *African Husbandman*, 38, 44–45, argues that next to storage, exchange, sale, or working 'beer parties', 'normal surplus' could be used for: 'the fulfilment of social obligations, to acquire prestige by the display of hospitality and generosity, and to honour important people, while in some societies it entered into barter trade and played a part in religious ritual.'
47   Pritchett, *Friends for Life*.
48   Hyden, *Beyond Ujamaa*, 4.
49   See Peša, 'Cassava Is Our Chief.'
50   Carswell, 'Food Crops as Cash Crops', 521–51.

The peasant can 'choose' to have one foot in the traditional moral-based economy and one in the market system (...) The fact that the market economy is of use and interest to peasants does not mean that they have been 'captured'. They do place high values on the goods that markets make available (...) But that is not to say that manufactured items are necessarily 'required', let alone absolutely 'needed'.[51]

Because rural producers possess the factors of production (land and labour) themselves, Hyden has asserted their relative independence. This can be a major asset, making rural producers 'small but powerful', especially vis-à-vis the state and external actors, who struggle to effectively influence, control or 'capture' producers. In this sense, smallholder producers retain a degree of autonomy towards the market and the state, being able to opt out if conditions or policies appear unfavourable.[52] Whereas agricultural officials struggled to promote groundnut cultivation in Mwinilunga, for example, producers eagerly seized the opportunity to market pineapples on their own terms, by combining the household production of cassava with commercial pineapple cultivation throughout the 1960s and 1970s.[53] This chapter explores the motivations for engaging with market production, by foregrounding the rationale behind productive practices and the foundations of production in Mwinilunga. Why, to what extent and on which terms did people in Mwinilunga become involved with the market and the state on a day-to-day basis through their productive activities?[54]

By adopting certain ideas derived from the concept of the 'moral economy', the involvement or non-involvement of producers in Mwinilunga with the market economy can be understood in a different light.[55] The concept 'moral economy' has been popularised in the works of Thompson, Scott and Hyden, in an attempt to counter narratives of expansive capitalism, which suggest linear transitions from subsistence to market production.[56] Although the concept

---

51   Tony Waters, 'A Cultural Analysis of the Economy of Affection and the Uncaptured Peasantry in Tanzania', *The Journal of Modern African Studies* 30, No. 1 (1992): 164, 171.

52   Hyden, *Beyond Ujamaa*; James C. Scott, *Seeing Like a State: How Certain Schemes to Improve The Human Condition Have Failed* (New Haven: Yale University Press, 1998); Scott, *The Art of Not Being Governed.*

53   Peša, 'Between Success and Failure.'

54   Crehan, *The Fractured Community.*

55   Jaime Palomera and Theodora Vetta, 'Moral Economy: Rethinking a Radical Concept', *Anthropological Theory* 16, No. 4 (2016): 413–32. For non-involvement, see Cooper, 'What is the Concept of Globalization Good for?', 189–213.

56   Thompson, 'The Moral Economy of the English Crowd'; Scott, *Moral Economy*; Hyden, *Beyond Ujamaa.*

has been heavily criticised,[57] it can highlight 'the often-contradictory values that guide and sustain livelihood practices' by paying attention to 'norms, meanings and practices' and thereby challenging 'economistic views'.[58] Denounced for being overtly static because of adopting notions such as the 'subsistence ethic', the 'safety-first' principle and conceptions of economic justice (with a focus on patterns of reciprocity, generosity and work-sharing within the village),[59] it should rather be emphasised that all economies are moral economies and 'economic relations are always embedded in institutions of different kinds'.[60] Ideas derived from the moral economy allow a focus on value regimes, meanings, and institutions, thereby explaining why particular forms of economic production, social relationships, values, and norms have persisted next to and in spite of market engagement. Why have rural producers historically made certain choices, seemingly contrary to the economic logic of profit-maximisation?[61] What explains the relative attractions of subsistence or market production in Mwinilunga? Moral economy is 'about understanding the inner workings of capitalism and the qualities of social reproduction at particular historical times and spaces' as well as different regimes of value.[62] More than models of capitalist market integration, the concept of the 'moral economy' can facilitate an understanding of patterns of production, market involvement, and economic trajectories in Mwinilunga.[63]

The remainder of this chapter focuses on explaining the foundations of production in Mwinilunga, which encompass factors of environment, methods of production, modes of co-operation, trade, market involvement, norms, and values. How and why did these foundations of production change and adapt? Seen from a long-term perspective, production in Mwinilunga appeared versatile and dynamic, rather than static. Change could be triggered by numerous factors, including environmental fluctuations, state policies, and marketing opportunities. The foundations of production were flexible, accommodating new crops, techniques, and knowledge, but change was rarely transformative.[64]

---

57   For a review, see William J. Booth, 'On the Idea of the Moral Economy', *The American Political Science Review* 88, No. 3 (1994): 653–67. For a critique, see Samuel L. Popkin, *The Rational Peasant: The Political Economy of Rural Society in Vietnam* (Berkeley: University of California Press, 1979).

58   Palomera and Vetta, 'Moral Economy', 414–15.

59   Scott, *Moral Economy*.

60   Palomera and Vetta, 'Moral Economy', 420.

61   Booth, 'On the Idea of the Moral Economy', 654.

62   Palomera and Vetta, 'Moral Economy', 428.

63   René Lemarchand, 'African Peasantries, Reciprocity and the Market: The Economy of Affection Reconsidered', *Cahiers d'études africaines* 29, No. 113 (1989): 57.

64   Chabatama, 'Peasant Farming.'

Production primarily revolved around generating a stable basis of subsistence. Such a stable basis of production could enable producers to participate in the market economy by producing surplus crops in a relatively risk-free manner. Because of the primacy placed on livelihood and food security, market production mainly involved crops and produce, which were compatible with established patterns of production. In case the market slumped, producers would withdraw from market production and fall back on a stable basis of subsistence, which they were wary of jeopardising unnecessarily. This livelihood basis enabled producers to step into the market by producing surplus crops, yet equally provided a buffer against marketing risks. When it comes to market involvement, producers in Mwinilunga sought to safeguard their autonomy and security of subsistence as much as possible. To understand market involvement, it is thus imperative to understand the subsistence basis of production. Producers sought to negotiate market involvement on their own terms, dealing with factors such as price fluctuations, marketing opportunities, and transport in ingenious manners.[65] How did this foundation of production function and change through day-to-day practice in Mwinilunga?

2   From Shifting Cultivation to Settled Farming: Policies and Practices

Analysing the discourses used by colonial and post-colonial officials to formulate agricultural policies and interventions illustrates their rationale for promoting cash-crop production, marketing schemes, and agricultural 'development'.[66] Even if agricultural practices in Mwinilunga rarely matched these discursive depictions, causing despair among officials, there was a mutual interaction between discourse and practice. In the long run, official denunciations of 'subsistence' production shaped cropping patterns and methods of cultivation, though never exactly in ways envisaged by extension staff. Agricultural policies, and the scientific knowledge at their basis, were attempts at social engineering as much as they were geared towards benevolent agricultural 'improvement'.[67] As Bonneuil has argued, 'the developmentalist state' had ambitions 'to reorganize agricultural production and to hasten African society

---

65   Examples are provided below; see Spear, *Mountain Farmers,* for parallels.
66   Hodge, *Triumph of the Expert,* provides numerous examples.
67   William Beinart, Karen Brown, and Daniel Gilfoyle, 'Experts and Expertise in Colonial Africa Reconsidered: Science and the Interpenetration of Knowledge', *African Affairs* 108, No. 432 (2009): 418.

into modernity'.[68] In Mwinilunga, agricultural policy debates predominantly revolved around settlement patterns, as stable villages instead of shifting homesteads were considered a prerequisite for successful farming.[69] Discourses regarding settlement patterns reflect the rationale of agricultural policies in a particularly clear manner. Official discourse struggled to come to terms with or influence local agricultural practices, though. Exploring the reasons behind the failure of government attempts to fix settlement patterns can further reveal the foundations of production in Mwinilunga.[70]

Throughout the twentieth century, officials in Mwinilunga have wrestled with the issue of settlement patterns, 'both to gain administrative leverage and to prevent deforestation and improve agricultural practices'.[71] The practice of shifting slash-and-burn cultivation, in particular, was considered an administrative nuisance, invariably being labelled 'wasteful' and 'destructive' due to the level of mobility it propelled.[72] Instead, officials proposed forms of fixed farming and settlement, allegedly aiming to 'improve' existing agricultural practices.[73] Colonial policies promised high yields, achieved through scientific methods of production and, ultimately, agricultural 'development'.[74] Post-colonial government schemes went even further, by plotting Intensive Development Zones that would tie farmers to the land through the use of fertiliser, technology and agricultural loans.[75] This transition from shifting cultivation to settled farming, under scientific and improved conditions, runs as a long-term thread through agricultural policies of the twentieth century.[76]

Although settlement patterns in the area of Mwinilunga had been quite dispersed during the nineteenth century, villages would still overwhelmingly concentrate along rivers and streams, close to patches of fertile soil or good hunting grounds.[77] Villages tended to shift their location in intervals of two to twenty years, for example if soils in the area had become depleted, in search of new hunting or fishing grounds, due to deaths, quarrels, or other problems.

---

68   Christophe Bonneuil, 'Development as Experiment: Science and State Building in Late Colonial and Postcolonial Africa, 1930–1970', *Osiris* 2, No. 15 (2000): 267.
69   Kay, *Social Aspects of Village Regrouping*; Crehan and Von Oppen, *Planners and History*.
70   Bowman, 'Ecology to Technocracy', 135–53; Bonneuil, 'Development as Experiment.'
71   Berry, 'Hegemony on a Shoestring', 331; Berry, *No Condition Is Permanent*, 49, 89–94.
72   Moore and Vaughan, *Cutting Down Trees*; Von Oppen, 'The Village as Territory', 57–75.
73   See Von Oppen, 'Bounding Villages.'
74   Hodge, *Triumph of the Expert.*
75   Crehan and Von Oppen, *Planners and History;* Gould, 'On the Genealogy of the Post-Colonial state.'
76   Nick Cullather, 'Miracles of Modernization: The Green Revolution and the Apotheosis of Technology', *Diplomatic History* 28, No. 2 (2004): 229.
77   See Chapter 1.

Upon moving, fields would be abandoned, left to gain fertility and regenerate. Movement could occur over short or long distances, depending on the motives. Due to the low population density and relatively low soil fertility in the area of Mwinilunga, these settlement patterns proved environmentally sound and productive.[78] With the establishment of colonial rule, however, this 'impermanence' was heavily condemned by officials, as it caused a lifestyle 'in the bush' which was mobile and difficult to control.[79] This explains the persistent frustrations with the 'nomadic inclinations' of the Lunda, as reflected in a 1924 tour report:

> With few exceptions all villages were bad, many of the huts appear to be temporary, hastily constructed buildings, while at nearly all villages many residents content themselves with grass makunkas [huts] thrown upon the clearing (...) I have now instructed all headmen that they will be destroyed at once, and replaced by huts properly constructed on an additional cleared space added to the present clearing (...) this country does not want people who are not prepared to build good huts, cultivate properly, and pay their tax.[80]

As this excerpt makes clear, fixed settlements were thought to be beneficial to the administrative aims of order and control. Not only would large stable villages facilitate the enforcement of legislation and the recording of census but they would also aid the collection of taxes and encourage the production of crops for the market.[81] Colonial officials thus propagated that '[people] should have settled homes (...) it is much better to have fair sized villages erect good huts and plant large gardens'.[82] Due to their mobile and intractable nature, officials condemned local patterns of agriculture and settlement as 'crude', no matter how ecologically sound or productive they were.[83] In support of their views, colonial reports would attribute acute food shortages to shifting cultivation of an 'irregular and sporadic nature',[84] which could only be remedied after 'the natives have been taught the value of crop rotation, and more scientific

---

78   This view is based on numerous interviews, for example, Alfonsina Chingangu, 15 October 2008, Ntambu; Pritchett, *Lunda-Ndembu*; Turner, *Schism and Continuity*.

79   Compare with: Moore and Vaughan, *Cutting Down Trees*.

80   (NAZ) KSE6/6/2, C.S. Parsons, Mwinilunga Sub-District Tour Report, 16 May 1924.

81   Bonneuil, 'Development as Experiment', 268–74. Scott, *Seeing Like a State,* on 'legibility'.

82   (NAZ) KSE6/3/1, Mwinilunga Sub-District Report Indaba, 13 October 1916.

83   Compare with: Bonneuil, 'Development as Experiment', 266–68, 276.

84   (NAZ) KSE6/6/2, H.B. Waugh, Mwinilunga Sub-District Tour Report, 9 November 1929.

agricultural methods generally'.[85] As much as for their allegedly higher yields, scientific alternatives to local agricultural practices – shifting cultivation in particular – were presented as 'superior' because they allowed easier and tighter administrative control.[86]

Discourses that denounced shifting cultivation in favour of settled farming along scientific lines fed into agricultural policies and thus affected local productive practices during the colonial and post-colonial period. Even if propaganda for fixed farming in Mwinilunga was based on government misconceptions regarding the environment and agricultural production, policies persistently advocated settled forms of cultivation by 'progressive farmers'.[87] In this vein, agricultural policies from the 1950s – the period of 'high modernism' and the apex of the technocratic developmental state[88] – invariably adopted a discourse of agricultural 'improvement' and 'development'. Policies aimed:

> (1) to raise the level of nutrition (2) to provide a satisfactory income from the sale of suitable cash crops tailored to fit human, ecological conditions and market requirements (3) to stabilise and concentrate the population, with due regard to the protection of natural resources by the introduction of sound methods of agriculture (4) to regulate and wherever possible to rationalise and intensify traditional extensive methods of agriculture (5) to assist in protecting the vital headwater areas.[89]

Officials considered an interventionist policy approach necessary to amend existing agricultural practices in Mwinilunga. Through various schemes, such as school gardens, demonstration plots, irrigation schemes, peasant farming schemes, and livestock distribution, they tried to promote 'improved' methods of production.[90] Such schemes were simultaneously meant to tie farmers to the land, by encouraging investment in fertiliser, input, and farming equipment. Attention was focused on crop rotation, the use of compost and manure,

---

85   (NAZ) KSE6/6/2, F.V. Bruce-Miller, Mwinilunga Sub-District Tour Report, 3 June 1928.

86   'Scientific' knowledge was shaped by the situation encountered on the ground – local and scientific knowledge were co-constructed. See: Bowman, 'Ecology to Technocracy'; Beinart, 'Experts and Expertise.'

87   Moore and Vaughan, *Cutting Down Trees*, 114–16.

88   Beinart, 'Experts and Expertise', 430; Bonneuil, 'Development as Experiment.'

89   (NAZ) NWP1/2/83 Loc.4914, Department of Agriculture North Western Province Annual Report, 1958.

90   This view is based on a broad reading of archival sources (NAZ) and (UNIPA); Moore and Vaughan, *Cutting Down Trees,* provide parallels.

ploughing, anti-erosion measures, and irrigation, among other things.[91] Trans-
lating discourse into practice, these measures attempted to discourage shifting
cultivation.

The peasant farming scheme of the 1940s and 1950s provides a striking
example of how discourse, policy, and practice interacted. This scheme promoted permanent as opposed to shifting cultivation, it advocated the integration of animal husbandry and agriculture (through the use of manure, draught
animals, and fodder cultivation), it suggested various cycles of crop rotation
to improve yields and soil fertility, it propagated methods of soil conservation
and irrigation, but most importantly it encouraged the growth of cash crops for
marketing purposes.[92] 'In order to facilitate future development plans', fixed
and concentrated settlements were promoted, as the District Commissioner
explained in 1955:

> These people should be encouraged to increase the size of their gardens
> and to produce more crops both for the benefit of themselves and of
> others. It can be seen that little progress can be made with stepping up
> the agricultural output of this area until such time as many of the settle-
> ments are re-grouped into more compact and economic units.[93]

Next to having agricultural aims, the peasant farming scheme intended to affect the lifestyle and attitudes of participants, creating 'progressive farmers'
who would market their crops, build 'improved' houses, wear 'decent' clothes,
plant fruit trees, educate their children, and live in nuclear households, thereby
disassociating themselves from the exactions of extended kin.[94] Going much
further than a discursive attempt to alter settlement patterns, policies such as
the peasant farming scheme were meant to change deep-rooted practices and
attitudes, thus influencing the foundations of production in Mwinilunga.

After independence, the humanist rhetoric took rural development even further, basing it in Intensive Development Zones where fixed settlements would
be the norm. As a 1977 report explains: 'The general feeling of the Settlement
Schemes is that plans should be redesigned to settle people in big groups rather than scattered families to facilitate the provision of social amenities (...) like

---

91   (NAZ) SEC2/258, Vol. I, Industries and Trade – Agriculture, General Development and
      Improvement, November 1934.
92   (NAZ) SEC2/336, J.S. Moffat, Peasant Farm Blocks, Experimental Scheme, 1947–48; Pritch-
      ett, *Lunda-Ndembu*.
93   (NAZ) SEC2/963, P.L.N. Hannaford, Mwinilunga District Tour Report, July 1955.
94   (NAZ) NWP1/2/26 Loc.4901, R.N. Lines, Mwinilunga District Tour Report, 6 March 1949;
      Moore and Vaughan, *Cutting Down Trees*, 115; Mandala, *The End of Chidyerano*.

water, schools, clinics etc'.[95] Large, concentrated, and stable villages would facilitate the provision of extension services, farming requisites, marketing, and
social services through state and parastatal actors.[96] But despite rhetoric and
persistent policies, fixed farming did not appear to be catching on in the area
of Mwinilunga. In 1970, it was even lamented that 'the tendency over the last
few years is for more smaller villages to be set up rather than larger ones'.[97] Notwithstanding discourse and policy measures, the foundations of production in
Mwinilunga proved remarkably persistent and subject to internal rather than
external dynamics of change. The case studies in this chapter illustrate why
policy and practice diverged.

Although attempts were made to instigate changes in patterns of production through discourses and policies, producers did not always accept, let
alone welcome these. Villages continued to shift their location, and production continued to be geared towards subsistence as well as market production.
Discourses of agricultural 'improvement' or 'development' tended to overlook
the environmental and labour conditions prevalent in Mwinilunga – the foundations of production – causing a policy mismatch and popular resistance to
proposed agricultural schemes. Even if they were underlain by a benevolent
desire to 'improve' local agriculture, policies in the twentieth century mainly
aimed at bureaucratic control. Yet producers in Mwinilunga were not passive
recipients of policy recommendations. Government schemes designed to
'improve' agricultural practices and stabilise settlement patterns would only
be adopted in so far as they could jibe with existing techniques, methods of
production, and attitudes. Rather than seeing the colonial and post-colonial
states as hegemonic, what should be examined, as Carswell suggests, is 'how
the global discourses of modernity, epitomised by attempts to introduce explicitly 'modern' husbandry practices, were given very different receptions on
the ground', thereby 'highlighting the spatial differences in how modernity
was experienced'.[98] Although settlements in Mwinilunga did increasingly shift
towards the roadside, this did not entail a unidirectional movement towards
market production or stable methods of farming, as officials may have envisaged. Why were some schemes to promote 'improved' methods of farming
resisted? The answer lies in the dissonance between government schemes,

---

95   (UNIPA) UNIP8/1/107, Highlights of the Right Honourable Prime Minister's Tour of the
      North-Western Province from 9th to 19th July 1977.
96   Kay, Social Aspects of Village Regrouping; Crehan and Von Oppen, Planners and History.
97   (NAZ) MAG2/21/86, Brief on Rural Development, North-Western Province, July 1970.
98   Grace Carswell, 'Multiple Historical Geographies: Responses and Resistance to Colonial
      Conservation Schemes in East Africa', Journal of Historical Geography 32 (2006): 399.

environmental conditions, and local methods of production, leading back to the foundations of production in Mwinilunga.

3   Meal: Markets, State Policies, and Values

How was the production of staple foods in Mwinilunga organised, and how and why did it change over time? Was this due to official policy and marketing opportunities, due to historical and ecological considerations, or due to the values and preferences of cultivators? Although official policies throughout the twentieth century were much concerned with promoting the cultivation of cash crops, staple food production was equally a subject of debate. Due to factors of marketing and state control, maize was promoted as the most 'modern' staple crop over the course of the twentieth century, whilst alternatives such as sorghum, millet, and cassava were denounced as 'primitive'.[99] Adopting a binary between 'subsistence' and 'market' production, official discourse presumed an inevitable transition from hunting and foraging to more settled forms of agricultural production based on grain and root crops, presupposing a trend from gathering wild fruits to cultivating sorghum and maize, or from hunting to herding small livestock.[100] Looking at why foraging persisted or why maize was not universally adopted can illustrate market dynamics, state policies, and the foundations of production in Mwinilunga.

The two basic components of a meal in Mwinilunga consist of *nshima* (thick porridge, made by stirring flour into boiling water) and *mafu* (relish, a side dish of vegetables and/or meat, *mbiji*). No meal is complete without these two components. Even if a person has snacked on yams or sweet potatoes, he/she can still claim not to have eaten all day if no *nshima* has been served.[101] The types of flour used for *nshima* have changed over the years, but shifts in preference and use have always been gradual, partial, and contested.[102] Even today, different types of flour are used interchangeably, and occasionally a composite *nshima* is created by mixing two types of flour, whilst cooking. Maize and

99   Pottier, *Migrants No More*; James C. McCann, *Maize and Grace: Africa's Encounter with a New World Crop, 1500–2000* (Cambridge: Harvard University Press, 2005).

100   Kathryn M. De Luna, *Collecting Food, Cultivating People: Subsistence and Society in Central Africa* (New Haven: Yale University Press, 2016).

101   This view has been informed by participant observation and numerous interviews. See: Hoover, 'The Seduction of Ruwej', 331–32; Pritchett, *Friends for Life*, 82–83.

102   Jan Vansina, 'Histoire du manioc en Afrique centrale avant 1850', *Paideuma* 43 (1997): 255–79; Achim von Oppen, '"Endogene agrarrevolution" im vorkolonialen Afrika? Eine fallstudie', *Paideuma* 38 (1992): 269–96.

cassava flour can be combined for making *nshima*, for example, and many regard this as a delicacy.[103] Considered to be 'as old as the Lunda', *nshima* is intimately connected to issues of identity and group cohesion.[104] Some elders recall that, when agricultural production was jeopardised by natural or man-made causes (such as severe droughts or slave raiding), wild roots would be collected from the bush and pounded into flour for *nshima*. In case of severe food shortage this practice might still be reinvigorated, but otherwise wild roots have been replaced by cultivated grain and root crops as the main staple foods.[105] In the area of Mwinilunga, sorghum (*masa*), and millet (*kachai*, finger millet or *mahangu*, bulrush millet) were adopted in the course of the first millennium A.D., whereas from the seventeenth century onwards cassava and maize have increasingly been added to the cultivating repertoire.[106] A gradual historical shift from wild roots, to sorghum and millet, to cassava and more recently maize can thus be discerned. Yet, problematically, officials have presented these transitions as progressions – wild roots, sorghum, and cassava allegedly being more 'primitive' than maize, which has been lauded as the hallmark of 'modernity'.[107] Rather than straightforward, transitions in staple crop cultivation and consumption have been ambiguous, gradual, and contested. Each staple crop has specific advantages and disadvantages in terms of yield, labour requirements, and resilience to disease or drought. People might express a preference for certain crops, but over time preferences could change, and producers overwhelmingly cultivated a variety of crops side by side in order to spread risks, to take advantage of the benefits of each crop, and for reasons of dietary variation.[108] Issues of marketing, state policies, agro-ecological, and labour concerns all influenced the adoption of crops as staples.

Throughout Mwinilunga, foraging has historically played an important role in food provision. Probes into past eating habits evoke responses recalling a time when 'people did not eat *nshima*', but 'subsisted on meat and honey'.[109] Although grain crops had undeniably been adopted on the South Central African plateau by the beginning of the first millennium A.D., grain cultivation did

---

103   Interview with Justin Kambidimba, 22 October 2010, Ntambu.
104   Interview with Wombeki, 11 and 24 May 2010, Nyakaseya; Interview with Solomon Kanswata, 8 September 2008, Mwinilunga; Hoover, 'The Seduction of Ruwej', 331–32.
105   Interview with Kalota, Kanongesha, July–August 2010.
106   Vansina, *How Societies Are Born*; Von Oppen, *Terms of Trade*.
107   Fourshey, 'The Remedy for Hunger', 223–61.
108   See: Jack Goody, *Cooking, Cuisine and Class: A Study in Comparative Sociology* (Cambridge: Cambridge University Press, 1982); James C. McCann, *Stirring the Pot: A History of African Cuisine* (Athens: Ohio University Press, 2009).
109   Interview with Chief Kanongesha's mother, 12 August 2010, Kanongesha.

not necessarily downplay the role of hunting and gathering practices.[110] At the beginning of the twentieth century, colonial officials still remarked that 'the Balunda as a whole seem to be quite contented for a great part of the year to eke out an existence on honey, wild fruits and the products of the bush'.[111] And even today foraging continues to play a role in complementing agricultural practices. The seasonal appearance of mushrooms, wild fruits, and caterpillars, for example, causes general excitement.[112] Nevertheless, restrictive forestry legislation and conservationist policies, coupled with the greater permanence of settlement patterns and fields, have made foraging increasingly problematic over the course of the twentieth century.[113] Honey collectors have to travel long distances from their homes into the bush, creatively circumventing conservation laws, to place their hives and collect honey. Nonetheless, the continued co-existence of agriculture and foraging testifies that there was no inevitable historical transition from foraging to settled agriculture. Contrary to what outside observers might have expected, agriculture and animal husbandry did not displace gathering and hunting. Rather, the 'wild' and the 'domestic' could and did coincide.[114] Foraging activities fitted well into a mobile lifestyle pivoted around hunting, but could equally add variety to the diet of more settled agricultural communities. Within the environmental setting of Mwinilunga, foraging enabled a degree of flexibility, retaining an appeal into the present.[115]

While acknowledging the salience of foraging, traveller accounts from the nineteenth century simultaneously underlined the importance of cultivated foodstuffs.[116] The population of Mwinilunga initially adopted sorghum and millet as their staples. These crops, however, necessitated considerable labour input for land clearing, weeding, and bird-scaring purposes.[117] Due to heavy labour demands, the acreage planted to sorghum and millet remained limited. For a sorghum or millet field of one acre, eight to ten acres of land had to be

110   Van Binsbergen, *Tears of Rain*; Papstein, 'The Upper Zambezi.'
111   (NAZ) KSE6/2/1, A.W. Bonfield, Lunda Division Quarterly Report, 31 December 1916.
112   Widespread excitement prevailed, as the first mushrooms were about to appear in October 2010.
113   Art Hansen and Della E. MacMillan, eds., *Food in Sub-Saharan Africa* (Boulder: Lynne Riener Publishers, 1986).
114   See Tim Ingold, *The Perception of the Environment: Essays on Livelihood, Dwelling and Skill* (London: Routledge, 2000), Chapter 3, for the nature-culture debate.
115   Turner, *Schism and Continuity*; Pritchett, *Lunda-Ndembu*.
116   For example Isaac Schapera, ed., *Livingstone's African Journal 1853–56* (London: Chatto & Windus, 1963).
117   Interview with Muhemba, 4 October 2008, Chibwika; Interview with Headman Kazovu and Kashiku, 12 September 2008, Kanongesha; (NAZ) KSE6/1/5, F.V. Bruce-Miller, Mwinilunga Sub-District Annual Report, 1927.

cleared of trees. Because sorghum and millet require fertile virgin land to yield good crops, whilst the quality of soils in Mwinilunga is in fact relatively poor, the result is that ample burning material is necessary for fertilisation under slash-and-burn cultivation.[118] Apart from being labour intensive, the disadvantage of sorghum and millet is that these crops cause distinct hungry periods. Food shortages usually occur before harvesting, when old stocks are depleted. Colonial officials, for example, lamented that 'there is no doubt but that the natives, who do not cultivate much cassava and depend almost entirely on "kachai" (red millet), are now "hungry" and many are living on fruits and honey'.[119] Moreover, sorghum and millet yields fluctuate heavily from year to year. Because of such disadvantages, sorghum and millet have largely been abandoned as staple food crops.[120] Over the course of the nineteenth and twentieth century, sorghum and millet have increasingly been replaced by cassava and maize cultivation. This gradual trend was recognised by colonial officials in 1935, who noted that cultivators 'are realising the advantages of manioc (...) the more energetic are planting manioc in addition to their old millet, kaffir corn [sorghum] and maize gardens; those less so sometimes abandon their grain crops altogether in favour of manioc'.[121] Still, importantly, there has not been a universal abandonment of sorghum and millet cultivation. After an initial slump, sorghum and millet cultivation expanded significantly when profitable markets arose in the 1950s, incited by the demands of the beer halls on the Copperbelt.[122] Particularly for beer brewing purposes, sorghum and millet remain popular, and at present *kachai* (finger millet) beer is still served during ceremonies as a 'traditional' delicacy.[123] Sorghum and millet continue to be cultivated next to other crops in order to add diversity and to spread risks. Different crops are thus not incompatible and exist side by side, as each crop possesses distinct benefits and is cultivated for different purposes. Whereas some crops serve as hunger reserves, others are used predominantly for beer brewing or are adopted as staple foods.

---

118 (NAZ) SEC2/954, C.M.N. White, Mwinilunga District Tour Report, 13 July 1939; (NAZ) KSE6/6/2, H.B. Waugh, Mwinilunga District Tour Report, 9 November 1929.
119 (NAZ) KSE6/5/1, N.C. Bellis, Lunda District, Report for the Month of October 1910.
120 See Von Oppen, *Terms of Trade*; Pritchett, *Lunda-Ndembu*, 215; Miller, *Way of Death*, 19–20.
121 (NAZ) SEC2/133, N.S. Price, Annual Report Mwinilunga District, 31 December 1935.
122 (NAZ) Mutende, No. 368, 30 January 1951.
123 Interview with Alfonsina Chingangu, 15 October 2008, Ntambu. In 2010 large amounts of *kachai* beer were being brewed in anticipation of the *Chisemwa ChaLunda* ceremony in Chief Kanongesha's area, although *kachai* cultivation was by then very rare.

3.1   *Cassava: Creating a Land of Plenty*

Cassava was introduced to the African continent as part of the 'Columbian exchange' early in the sixteenth century (see Photo 4).[124] From the Angolan coast, the crop gradually spread inland, reaching the area of Mwinilunga by means of the long-distance trade.[125] According to traveller accounts, the crop was well established in the area by the 1850s.[126] Cassava proved a popular foodstuff especially for the provisioning of trade caravans, and its cultivation expanded rapidly over the course of the nineteenth century.[127] During the latter half of the nineteenth century, passing trade caravans made substantial food demands on the producers of the Upper Zambezi area.[128] Caravans were big, slowly moving units, requiring food on a regular basis. Their demands could not be met by regular 'subsistence' production, but instead evoked incipient yet deliberate 'market production'.[129] Some villages made extensive cassava gardens specifically to feed passing trade caravans, as cultivators could obtain cloth, salt, and guns in return for their food.[130] Significantly, Mwinilunga was located directly to the east of the 'hungry country', which was sombrely described by travellers at the end of the nineteenth century:

> [It is] hilly land, known as 'the hungry country', for though there are a few villages at several points off the path, little or no food can be bought there (...) For ten days the road lay through uninhabited sandy plains (...) [and we] had to make forced marches through this in order to reach the villages beyond, where food could be purchased.[131]

After travelling through this 'hungry country' and depleting their supplies, caravans would be eager to obtain food upon reaching Mwinilunga. This

---

124   For an overview of crop introductions to Africa from overseas areas, see: José E. Mendes Ferrão, *The Adventure of Plants and the Portuguese Discoveries* (n.p., 1994); Alfred W. Crosby Jr., *The Columbian Exchange: Biological and Cultural Consequences of 1492* (Westport: Greenwood Publishing, 1972). The Columbian exchange, following Columbus's 'discovery' of America in 1492, marked a wave of exchange between Europe, the America's, Asia, Australia, and Africa, and included various animals, micro-organisms (including diseases), and human population groups. The main focus here will be on crop exchanges.
125   Von Oppen, 'Endogene agrarrevolution', 269–96; Vansina, 'Histoire du manioc', 255–79; William O. Jones, *Manioc in Africa* (Stanford: Stanford University Press, 1959).
126   Schapera, *Livingstone's Missionary Correspondence*, 261–62.
127   Miller, *Way of Death*; Von Oppen, *Terms of Trade*; Pritchett, *Lunda-Ndembu*.
128   See the travel accounts of Livingstone, Cameron, Arnot, and Gibbons; Chapter 1.
129   Von Oppen, *Terms of Trade*, 91–96; Pritchett, *Lunda-Ndembu*, 220–28.
130   Vellut, 'Notes sur le Lunda', 78–93.
131   Fisher and Hoyte, *Ndotolu*, 79, 109.

geographically strategic position made Mwinilunga – at least temporarily – an important provisioning post for passing caravans. Cassava was particularly sought after because the crop was durable and familiar to traders, and it could be easily transported.[132] Von Oppen has estimated that in the 1870s 14,000 tonnes of food were required annually by caravans passing through the Upper Zambezi area.[133] According to Pritchett, this made Mwinilunga 'the breadbasket of the caravan system'.[134] Yet demands would always be erratic. A large caravan requesting food might pass a village one day, but afterwards an entire year might go by before the next caravan would appear. Moreover, the major caravan routes bypassed the area of Mwinilunga either to the north or to the south. Although numerous caravans did frequent the area, Mwinilunga was more often a transit point than the main destination.[135] Cassava cultivation clearly exceeded 'subsistence', but it is doubtful whether marketing had become the driving force behind production. Towards the end of the nineteenth century villages did increasingly adopt cassava cultivation and engaged in trading cassava to caravans, but unpredictable demand made it difficult to expand food production exclusively for this purpose.[136]

Over the course of the nineteenth and twentieth century, cassava has increasingly been adopted as a subsidiary and staple food crop in Mwinilunga. Compared to sorghum and millet, cassava has distinct advantages.[137] The crop is resistant to droughts, pests, and diseases; it is not labour intensive (apart from planting and processing); it provides food all year round (eliminating preharvest hunger periods); and, most importantly, cassava is relatively high yielding.[138] On the acidic Kalahari soils of Mwinilunga, cassava can outperform sorghum, millet, and maize yields.[139] Moreover, cassava fields can be worked continuously for up to twenty years without fertilisation, whereas sorghum and millet fields need to be cleared annually, and can only be worked for three

---

132   Miller, *Way of Death*; Jones, *Manioc in Africa*.

133   Von Oppen, *Terms of Trade*, 96.

134   Pritchett, *Lunda-Ndembu*, 30 – this is probably an overstatement.

135   See the map in Bustin, *Lunda Under Belgian Rule*, 19; Von Oppen, *Terms of Trade*, Appendix on caravan routes.

136   Papstein, 'Upper Zambezi.'

137   Von Oppen, 'Endogene agrarrevolution'; Vansina, 'Histoire du manioc.'

138   See Von Oppen, 'Cassava, the Lazy Man's Food?', 51, for the advantages and disadvantages of cassava cultivation.

139   (NAZ) MAG1/20/4, Director of Agriculture Report, 17 May 1962: In 1962 the yields on Kalahari sands were estimated as follows: Maize – 3 bags per acre, Millet – 4 bags per acre, Cassava – 6.1 bags per acre.

to four years before the soil becomes depleted.[140] Cassava thus diminished the labour requirements of land clearance, but nevertheless a fundamental re-organisation of agricultural techniques was required to accommodate cassava cultivation. Whereas sorghum and millet are planted in rows, cassava requires the construction of mounds. In addition, the processing of cassava can be oner-ous, as the roots have to be dug up, soaked in water to remove their (potential) toxic content, dried, and pounded into flour (see Photo 5).[141] Because cassava only fully matures after two to four years, the crop equally requires a degree of residential stability.[142] The frequent shifting and impermanent settlement conditions propelled by slave raids might therefore have discouraged extensive cassava cultivation at the end of the nineteenth century. Nevertheless, cassava cultivation expanded rapidly once settlements stabilised under the *Pax Britan-nica*.[143] Despite some disadvantages, cassava gradually supplanted other crops as a staple over the course of the twentieth century because it could provide an ample and reliable source of food.[144]

Cassava became so popular in Mwinilunga that the crop was adopted as a marker of identity by Lunda cultivators, who proudly referred to themselves as 'cassava-eaters'.[145] Yet this positive valuation of cassava was by no means uni-versal. Colonial and post-colonial officials always remained sceptical towards cassava cultivation, at times even discouraging production and consumption of the crop altogether.[146] Officials regularly underlined the alleged nutritional deficiencies of cassava, especially the acidity and lack of protein of the tubers. The Lunda were described as a 'weakly tribe' and 'physically inferior' due to their cassava-based diet.[147] Only if locust invasions or droughts had wrought ravages would the colonial administration temporarily resort to promoting the crop, as this example from 1951 shows: 'The cultivation of cassava is encouraged in the native areas throughout the Territory as a famine reserve crop (...) the

---

140   (NAZ) MAG1/10/1 Loc.76, C.E. Johnson, Agricultural Programme of Work, North Western Province, 29 June 1960; Interview with John Kamuhuza, March 2010, Ikelenge.

141   Felix I. Nweke, Dunstan S.C. Spencer, and John K. Lynam, *The Cassava Transformation: Africa's Best-Kept Secret* (East Lansing: Michigan State University Press, 2002); Steven Haggblade and Ballard Zulu, 'The Recent Cassava Surge in Zambia and Malawi', *Successes in African Agriculture*, Conference held in Pretoria, 1–3 December 2003.

142   Von Oppen, 'Cassava, the Lazy Man's Food.'

143   Papstein, 'Upper Zambezi.'

144   Peša, 'Cassava Is Our Chief.'

145   Interview with Solomon Kanswata, 18 October 2008, Mwinilunga; Hoover, 'The Seduction of Ruwej.'

146   Jones, *Manioc in Africa*; Nweke, *The Cassava Transformation*.

147   (NAZ) KSE6/1/1, G.A. MacGregor, Annual Report for the Balunda District, 1909.

crop came into its own during this difficult drought year'.[148] The attitude towards cassava was ambiguous at best, as only two years later negative valuations prevailed once more: 'Methods of production of this crop are wasteful
and it is preferable that it should be regarded as a subsistence rather than a
cash crop'.[149] Because officials regarded cassava as a subsistence crop, the crop
was afforded only minimal marketing opportunities, agronomic support, or
encouragement. Whereas colonial and post-colonial officials propagated rice,
beans, and maize through the distribution of improved seeds, technical support, and favourable marketing conditions, cassava was largely neglected.[150]
Peculiarly perhaps, this official discouragement did not foreclose the local
popularity of cassava cultivation. In fact, cassava cultivation in Mwinilunga
continued unabatedly and even heightened over the course of the twentieth
century. The popularity of cassava will be reassessed after outlining the history
of maize cultivation in Mwinilunga.

3.2   Maize: Faltering Towards Modernity?

Over the course of the twentieth century, government officials in Mwinilunga
overwhelmingly promoted maize as a 'superior' alternative to cassava.[151] Fourshey has eloquently described how in Tanzania 'an image of maize as a model
of modernity' has been advanced.[152] In Zambia, similarly, high-yielding hybrid
maize varieties were acclaimed as 'magic', a 'technological wonder' that would
'feed the nation' and bring about general prosperity.[153] Maize, like cassava,
was introduced through the Columbian exchange to the Angolan coast and
disseminated through the long-distance trade to inland areas such as Mwinilunga by the eighteenth century.[154] During the colonial period, but even more
so after independence, maize was afforded prime official importance. A 1965
agricultural policy document stressed that, 'as the staple food of the people of
Zambia, maize is central in the Zambian agricultural economy'.[155] To support
maize cultivators, government officials made various kinds of input, loans,
and subsidies available. In addition, government-controlled marketing boards

---

148   (NAZ) Department of Agriculture, Annual report, 1951.
149   (NAZ) Department of Agriculture, Annual report, 1953.
150   See Wood, et al., *The Dynamics of Agricultural Policy*; McCann, *Maize and Grace*.
151   Kate Crehan and Achim von Oppen, 'Understandings of 'Development': An Arena of
       Struggle: The Story of a Development Project in Zambia', *Sociologia Ruralis* 28, No. 2
       (1988): 120.
152   Fourshey, 'The Remedy for Hunger', 246.
153   Pottier, *Migrants No More*, 20.
154   McCann, *Maize and Grace*.
155   (NAZ) Review of the Operations of the Agricultural Marketing Committee, 30 June 1965.

arranged highly favourable marketing conditions for the crop, providing secure and profitable outlets.[156] This approach differed markedly from the attitude adopted towards cassava. Cassava was granted minimal attention and could only be marketed through official channels in exceptional circumstances. Differential marketing opportunities and government propaganda may well have discouraged cassava cultivation in favour of maize.[157] Nevertheless, maize cultivation did not succeed in displacing the popularity of cassava in Mwinilunga and this begs further explanation.

Despite its early introduction, cultivators in Mwinilunga only hesitantly adopted maize. By the end of the 1950s the District Commissioner still remarked that 'people are not at present interested in eating maize themselves unless cassava is scarce, they claim indeed it makes them sick'.[158] Notwithstanding protracted propaganda, the 1964 annual agricultural report noted that 'any surplus [of maize] marketed was merely a fortuitous surplus from subsistence cultivators and did not constitute an appreciable amount'.[159] Even if in the 1969–70 season 180 tonnes of maize were marketed from Mwinilunga District, this figure compared unfavourably to other parts of the country.[160] Maize does not grow well in the climate and soils of Mwinilunga, and the quality of the harvested crop is generally poor. In the 1950s, maize marketed from Mwinilunga would invariably arrive on the Copperbelt severely affected by weevils. The quality of the crop would consequently be classified as inferior, which problematised marketing.[161] In addition, the recurrent threat of failed harvests made maize production somewhat of a gamble for cultivators.

In order to obtain maize yields, which can compete on the national and international market, expensive input such as fertiliser, pesticides, and improved seeds are imperative. Yet to access such input, as well as for purposes of provisioning, distribution, credit, and crop sales, individuals are largely dependent on the market and the state.[162] Government-controlled marketing boards, for example, provided input on a loan basis in Mwinilunga in the twentieth century. But in return for this input, a producer would immediately have to repay the debt upon selling the maize harvest. The consequent lack of autonomy caused particular grudges among cultivators, as evidenced by this 1973 excerpt:

---

156   See Wood, et al., *The Dynamics of Agricultural Policy*; McCann, *Maize and Grace*.
157   See Fourshey, 'The Remedy for Hunger', 223–61.
158   (NAZ) SEC2/967, W.D. Grant, Mwinilunga District Tour Report, No. 5, 1959.
159   (NAZ) Annual Report, Ministry of Agriculture, 1964.
160   (NAZ) LGH5/5/12, Marketing of Produce North-Western Province, 23 July 1970.
161   (NAZ) NWP1/2/37 Loc.4903, D. Clough, Mwinilunga District Annual Report, 1950.
162   Crehan and Von Oppen, 'Understandings of Development', 129.

If a farmer sells two bags to Agriculture Rural Marketing Board (ARMB) then the very farmer should be made to repay his loans out of what he has just got from those two bags (...) but how can a farmer live since all his living is taken away from him/her? Now we have a lot of groaning the farmers are murmuring perhaps in future they will stop doing farming because all the money they are getting from their produce is being taken away from them without leaving them some Ngwees to enable them buy clothing, soap, salt, and paying their friends who helped them to do the job [sic].[163]

Numerous producers in Mwinilunga did grow some maize for purposes of marketing or household consumption. In fact, over the course of the 1960s and 1970s, maize was increasingly adopted as a cash crop. Yet although maize might have been a commercially viable option, it left producers vulnerable to the whims of the climate, state subsidies, and marketing boards, creating a dependency on volatile external factors. Because of its numerous drawbacks, maize rarely became the preferred staple crop of producers in Mwinilunga. Despite official propaganda for maize as a symbol of 'progress', individuals did not readily take to maize production and continued to prefer cassava.[164]

3.3   The Foundations of Production: Staples, Markets, and the State

Producer deliberations and preferences in terms of staple crops are firmly rooted in the foundations of production in Mwinilunga. Whereas maize cultivation created a degree of vulnerability to climatic and market fluctuations, as well as dependence on the state for input and subsidies, cassava enabled relative flexibility, autonomy, and security for cultivators.[165] Without expensive input, cassava can generate a dependable source of food and abundant harvests. That is why producers today proudly proclaim that, 'with cassava, we never go hungry!'[166] Cassava might even have enabled an 'exit option', which would allow producers to more easily opt out of, or even evade, involvement

---

163   (UNIPA) UNIP5/3/1/48, J. Chikotola to Administrative Secretary, 1 October 1973.
164   Fourshey, 'The Remedy for Hunger'; Moore and Vaughan, *Cutting Down Trees*.
165   See Peša, 'Cassava Is Our Chief'; Scott, *The Art of Not Being Governed*, 73–74, argues that root crops are relatively more 'illegible' to the state and consequently more difficult to appropriate, control, and tax than grain crops. Cassava cultivators would be considerably better placed to assert autonomy vis-à-vis the state than millet and sorghum cultivators, as these annual crops are much easier to identify, tax, and control than cassava which grows underground and matures slowly.
166   Interview with Justin Kambidimba, 22 October 2010, Ntambu.

with the market and the state.[167] Hyden asserts small rural producers' control of their own means of production and livelihood as a source of strength:

> Much of the power of the small peasants in Africa stems from their control of the means of subsistence. The production of the basic necessities is still controlled by peasants who are difficult to get at, not only because of their numbers but also because they are capable of securing their own subsistence and reproduction without the assistance of other social classes.[168]

If producers can rely on a stable source of livelihood, they are less vulnerable to state sanctions and, as a result, they can afford to be more independent in their interactions with officials. In Mwinilunga, this relative independence of producers, enabled by cassava gardens, did indeed occasionally result in administrative defiance. In 1909, one colonial official noted with exasperation that:

> Little or no food is at present being brought to the Boma for sale (...) [This] is the more annoying when it is remembered how large are the gardens and plentiful the supply of cassava (...) the present position is altogether attributable to the perverseness of a people endowed with so peculiar and erratic a temperament.[169]

Other officials at the time even claimed that 'there may be a determination not to come under our rule (...) to escape from obligations which they fear will be demanded from them'.[170] Even though Hyden argued that the independence of producers could be a source of strength, he equally cautioned that it could block 'development': 'the principal structural constraint to development are the barriers raised against state action by the peasant mode of production'.[171] Examples from Mwinilunga, however, suggest otherwise. Subsistence production by no means posed a barrier to 'development', the production of 'cash crops', or 'market integration'.[172] On the contrary, the strong and stable basis of subsistence that cassava cultivation provided functioned as a source of

---

167   See also Scott, *The Art of Not Being Governed.*
168   Hyden, *Beyond Ujamaa,* 29.
169   (NAZ) KSE6/5/1, J.M. Pound, Monthly Report Balunda District, June 1909.
170   (NAZ) BSA2 A2/1/4 Loc.3981, Acting Administrator North-West Rhodesia to G.A. MacGregor, 20 December 1910.
171   Hyden, *Beyond Ujamaa,* 31.
172   Carswell, 'Food Crops as Cash Crops.'

strength and autonomy. This subsistence basis enabled producers to negotiate with the state and markets on favourable terms suitable to local priorities. The subsistence basis of staple crop production, of cassava in particular, did not preclude market involvement, but rather provided a stepping-stone to expand production of both subsistence and cash crops, whilst maintaining livelihood security.[173]

The cultivation of an array of subsistence crops served as a basis that facilitated the production of cash crops. Subsistence crops provide food and influence the availability of labour for other productive tasks, within or outside agriculture. As argued persuasively by Tosh, the production of food crops for sale is less disruptive of established agricultural practices than the production of non-food cash crops, such as cotton or tobacco.[174] In Mwinilunga, labour is a scarce resource, the allocation of which has to be carefully planned. In this sense, 'if (...) the staple food crop could be marketed', 'the tricky problem of how to distribute labour at times of peak demand was greatly eased'.[175] During periods of peak labour demand, such as planting or harvesting, the possibility of marketing staple food crops indeed alleviated the problem of labour allocation. In order to market staple food crops, output can be expanded by investing additional labour and intensifying existing cultivation methods, rather than by dividing attention between numerous crops or applying unfamiliar cultivation methods to cash crops such as rice or groundnuts.[176] In Mwinilunga, food crops (such as beans, pineapples, maize, but also cassava) have regularly been marketed, blurring the line between subsistence and cash crop production. In this case, subsistence production could function as the basis for market production, as existing methods and levels of production merely had to be expanded to step into the market. Another advantage of marketing food crops is that staple food crops provide a source of livelihood security – they can be held back as a famine reserve in case harvests prove disappointing, or be consumed when markets slump.[177] Because staple crops provide a dependable basis of livelihood, the cultivation and sale of food crops alleviates the impact of market fluctuations and facilitates market involvement. In case marketing opportunities for staple food crops occurred, existing production could – in theory at least – be expanded, as land was generally abundant in Mwinilunga. On the

173   Peša, 'Cassava Is Our Chief'; See Spear, *Mountain Farmers*, who argues that the high and dependable yields of bananas enabled individuals to diversify into cash crop production of coffee.

174   Tosh, 'The Cash-crop Revolution', 79–94; Austin, 'Resources, Techniques and Strategies.'

175   Tosh, 'The Cash-crop Revolution', 89–91.

176   Von Oppen, 'Endogene agrarrevolution', 277.

177   Tosh, 'The Cash-crop Revolution', 89.

other hand, in case of a marketing slump, the unmarketable surplus harvest could be held back for household consumption. Cassava proved to be particularly convenient in this respect, as the crop can remain stored in the ground for several years until marketing opportunities arise and prices become favourable once again.[178] This enabled producers to react to marketing fluctuations rapidly, as they might expand or reduce the size of their fields in reaction to the demand that exists for their crops.[179] In more than one way, therefore, subsistence and market production fed into one another. As the case of cassava in Mwinilunga further illustrates, small-scale agricultural producers were by no means averse to market incentives but reacted to them astutely and eagerly.

Despite being labelled a 'subsistence' crop by colonial/post-colonial officials, cassava simultaneously functioned as a food and as a cash crop. During the 1950s as much as 600 tonnes of cassava flour was marketed annually in Mwinilunga.[180] Surprisingly, these sales figures coincided with labour migration ratios of up to 50%, suggesting that high levels of cassava production could be achieved even when labour resources were scarce.[181] The relatively low labour demands of cassava enabled an expansion of production, either of cassava or of other cash crops. Cassava freed up labour, for instance for labour migration or for the cultivation of pineapples, which became a major cash crop in Mwinilunga in the 1960s and 1970s.[182] If producers could fall back on a stable source of livelihood, in the form of cassava, market involvement posed less of a risk. When the marketing of pineapples proved problematic, for instance, producers could still rely on cassava gardens for purposes of household consumption.[183] Exclusive specialisation in pineapple cultivation was therefore rare, as producers preferred to spread risks by maintaining large cassava gardens. This was the 'safety-first' principle, geared towards risk minimisation rather than profit maximisation, as explained by Scott:

---

178   This view is based on numerous interviews, for example Grace Mulusa, 10 December 2008, Kanyama.
179   Correspondence with Raymond Ngambi, Kanyama, December 2008.
180   (NAZ) NWP1/2/68 Loc.4911, North-Western Province Annual Report for Agriculture, 1955.
181   (NAZ) NWP1/2/102 Loc.4919, E.L. Button, North Western Province Annual Report, 1960.
182   Iva Peša, 'Buying Pineapples, Selling Cloth: Traders and Trading Stores in Mwinilunga District, 1940–1970', in *The Objects of Life in Central Africa: The History of Consumption and Social Change, 1840–1980,* eds., Robert Ross, Marja Hinfelaar, and Iva Peša (Leiden: Brill, 2013).
183   It is significant that pineapple farmers invested their profits into work parties, attracting labour in order to cultivate larger cassava gardens. See interview with Saipilinga Kahongo, 22 March 2010, Ikelenge.

The distinctive economic behavior of the subsistence-oriented peasant family results from the fact that, unlike a capitalist enterprise, it is a unit of consumption as well as a unit of production. The family begins with a more or less irreducible subsistence consumer demand, based on its size, which it must meet in order to continue as a unit. Meeting those minimal human needs in a reliable and stable way is the central criterion which knits together choices of seed, technique, timing, rotation, and so forth. The cost of failure for those near the subsistence margin is such that safety and reliability take precedence over long-run profit.[184]

In Mwinilunga, securing a sufficient and dependable source of food and livelihood indeed underlay the basic choices of crops, cultivation techniques, and market responses.

Cassava enabled such a dependable source of food. The specific agro-ecological characteristics of cassava provided multiple advantages over other crops. Officials did hesitantly recognise this, for example in a tour report from 1940: 'The principle crop in this area is cassava which grows exceptionally well and in great abundance (...) In areas where cassava is the main crop famine seems to be almost unknown'.[185] Cassava yields are higher, more dependable, and less affected by the vagaries of climate, whilst the crop requires less labour input compared to alternatives. In an area where land is abundant, yet labour is scarce, cassava is a particularly suitable crop. Relatively low labour input yielded high returns, enabling producers to diversify into other crops and/or step into the market.[186] The foundation provided by cassava did not prevent, but rather enabled market involvement, by facilitating the investment of time and energy into market production. This explains the persistence of cassava cultivation despite favourable marketing opportunities and official propaganda for maize, and equally sheds light on the ability of labour intensive and volatile crops such as pineapples or rice to flourish. Because producers in Mwinilunga could build on a dependable source of food, in the form of cassava, market involvement was a feasible and relatively low-risk endeavour. As long as food provision could be secured, producers could afford to take (limited) risks.[187] Cassava enabled a degree of enterprise in the area of Mwinilunga, largely cancelling out the shocks of environmental, market, and price fluctuations. That is

---

184   Scott, *Moral Economy*, 13.
185   (NAZ) SEC2/955, C.M.N. White, Mwinilunga District Tour Report, 10 February 1940; and H.B. Waugh, Mwinilunga District Tour Report, 14 December 1940.
186   Jones, *Manioc in Africa*; Von Oppen, 'Cassava, the Lazy Man's Food.'
187   Spear, *Mountain Farmers*; Berry, *No Condition Is Permanent.*

why cassava has become and remains the favoured food in Mwinilunga, in the twentieth century and beyond.

Shifts in preference for staple crops were not straightforward transitions from 'subsistence' to 'market' production or from food crops to cash crops.[188] Up to this day, foraging strategies, sorghum, millet, cassava, and maize cultivation exist side by side in Mwinilunga. Such a combination provides agricultural producers with a wide palette of choices, which generates a reliable supply of food, enables diversity, and facilitates risk-aversion. Values attached to food crops have shifted over the years, influenced by factors such as the environment, markets, and state policies.[189] Although maize has been promoted through favourable marketing policies, it has not become the dominant staple food in the area of Mwinilunga. The dominance and resilience of cassava cultivation evidences that crop choices are underlain by considerations of safety and are aimed at securing dependable food supplies. Yet such aims were not conservative and did not clash with market involvement. The stable basis of cassava production enabled producers to incorporate change more easily by adopting cash crops – either familiar or new – for marketing purposes, whilst retaining a reliable source of food. Although cassava was a foreign introduction to the area, today the crop is described as part of the 'tradition' of the Lunda, which illustrates the ability of producers in Mwinilunga to incorporate change, in the form of a new crop, within long-established practices, modes of thought, and historical consciousness.[190] Apparently, the crop fitted local strategies, goals, and outlooks so well that it was incorporated into existing patterns of production almost seamlessly. Cassava, moreover, enabled producers in Mwinilunga to unleash an inherent potential for agricultural production, turning the area into a 'land of plenty'.[191] Historical transitions, from subsistence to cash crops, or from foraging to sorghum and cassava to hybrid maize, thus appear far more complicated. Examples of hunting and herding in Mwinilunga will further problematise discourses of 'subsistence' and 'market' production.

4   Meat: Hunting, Herding, and Distribution

At each meal the staple *nshima* is accompanied by *mafu*, garnish. The two are indissolubly linked. In Mwinilunga, a variety of vegetable crops are grown,

---

188   Carswell, 'Food Crops as Cash Crops.'
189   Fourshey, 'The Remedy for Hunger.'
190   Peša, 'Cassava Is Our Chief.'
191   Today some people remark that '*makamba mwanta wetu*', Cassava Is Our Chief.

most commonly intercropped with millet, cassava, or maize. Notwithstanding the variety of vegetables, meat is the most valued form of garnish.[192] Meat is obtained through hunting or herding. In a manner similar to that of staple crops, various discourses and valuations have been attached to patterns of meat acquisition. Officials assumed that nomadic hunting would give way to settled forms of animal husbandry, which would be based on scientific knowledge and would be geared towards marketing rather than self-sufficiency.[193] Nevertheless, hunting has remained of paramount importance throughout the twentieth century. Even if hunting has been curtailed by legislation and the scarcity of game, its ideological importance in shaping notions of masculinity and identity remains unparalleled and deserves more attention.

4.1   Hunting: Meat, Merit, and Masculinity

Hunting has figured prominently in the history of the Lunda polity, both as a source of nourishment and ideologically in origin stories, historical narratives, and as a source of pride and power among men.[194] Chibinda Ilunga, the Luba potentate who married the Lunda Chieftainess Lueji and thereby propelled the migration of Lunda emissaries to the Upper Zambezi area, is remembered as an illustrious hunter.[195] Hunting has remained central to Lunda identity, particularly male identity, ever since. A diversity of techniques, such as snaring, trapping, the use of bows, arrows, spears, or firearms are adopted in the hunt (see Photo 6). Despite the co-existence of various techniques, over time hunting with guns has developed as the most prestigious and ritualised form of hunting among Lunda males (*chiyanga* is the praise name of a gun hunter).

---

192   Turner, *Schism and Continuity*; Pritchett, *Lunda-Ndembu*; Hoover, 'The Seduction of Ruwej.'

193   Jeffrey C. Kaufmann, 'The Sediment of Nomadism', *History in Africa* 36 (2009): 235–64; James Ferguson, *The Anti-Politics Machine: 'Development', Depoliticization, and Bureaucratic Power in Lesotho* (Minneapolis: University of Minnesota Press, 1990).

194   Turner, 'Themes in the Symbolism of Ndembu Hunting Ritual', in *The Forest of Symbols*, 38, claims ancient origins for the two hunting cults in the area: '*Wubinda* [a cult for hunters using any technique for killing animals and birds – firearms, bows and arrows, spears, snares, traps, pitfalls, nets, the use of bird-lime, etc.] is the older cult and is said to have come with the forebears of the Ndembu when they migrated from the kingdom of Mwantiyanvwa, the great Lunda chief in Katanga, more than two centuries ago. *Wuyang'a* [a cult for skilled hunters using guns] is believed to have been introduced, along with the first muzzle-loading guns, by Ovimbundu traders who came regularly from Kasanji and Bihe in Western Angola to purchase slaves and beeswax in the mid-nineteenth century. But it shares many features of its symbolism with *Wubinda* on which it must have been speedily grafted.'

195   Reefe, 'Traditions of Genesis', 183–206; Schecter, 'A Propos The Drunken King', 108–25; De Heusch, 'What Shall We Do with the Drunken King?', 363–72.

The Lunda were not slow to obtain firearms,[196] as officials in the opening years of colonial rule remarked: 'the inhabitants of the Kasempa and Lunda Districts have beyond question far more guns than they ought to'.[197]

Hunting has commonly been understood, especially by colonial/post-colonial government officials, within a framework of linear change, which suggests a historical transition from hunting and gathering to more settled forms of agriculture and animal husbandry.[198] Such accounts interpret hunting as 'a survival mechanism, a subsistence fall-back in times of great stress', or even more negatively as 'an inferior form of economic activity'.[199] Throughout the twentieth century, official discourse denounced 'nomadic' hunting in favour of more easily controllable and settled forms of animal husbandry, which would enable the marketing of meat. Yet the case of Mwinilunga demonstrates that hunting was by no means a mere historical phase. In spite of restrictive legislation and the decimation of game populations, hunting has retained its significance and continues to be practised, side by side with more settled forms of agriculture and animal husbandry.[200] Hunting remains a prominent feature of self-identification for the male community, and its importance is reflected in numerous rituals and ceremonies. If purely assessing the meat supplies provided by hunters, it appears as though the status of hunting is unduly exalted above its contribution to livelihood.[201] How can the persistent importance of hunting in Mwinilunga be explained?

The importance of the hunter as a social category is captured by the Lunda saying: 'Whoever kills a hunter has killed the whole village'.[202] Underscoring the prominence of hunting, colonial officials referred to Lunda men as 'inveterate hunters', who decimated game with muzzle-loading guns of Portuguese

---

196   See: Giacomo Macola, 'Reassessing the Significance of Firearms in Central Africa: The Case of North-Western Zambia to the 1920s', *Journal of African History* 51, No. 3 (2010): 301–21; Giacomo Macola, *The Gun in Central Africa: A History of Technology and Politics* (Athens: Ohio University Press, 2016).

197   Macola, 'Reassessing the Significance of Firearms', 318–20; (NAZ) LGH5/1/3 Loc.3604, Lunda-Ndembo Native Authority meeting, 13 April 1961, 'The District Commissioner pointed out that there were 1610 muzzle loading guns in the district and 153 short guns or one gun to approximately 6 resident males, a very high average number.'

198   Creighton Gabel, 'Terminal Food-collectors and Agricultural Initiative in East and Southern Africa', *The International Journal of African Historical Studies* 7, No. 1 (1974): 56–68.

199   John M. MacKenzie, *The Empire of Nature: Hunting, Conservation and British Imperialism* (Manchester: Manchester University Press, 1988), 55; Allan, *African husbandman*, XI.

200   This view is based on numerous interviews, for example Goldwel Mushindi, 3 May 2010, Nyakaseya.

201   Turner, *Schism and Continuity*, 20.

202   Interview with Harrison Zimba, 10 October 2008, Ntambu.

provenance.[203] Turner eloquently depicted the role of hunting in Mwinilunga in the 1950s:

> It may almost be said that the Ndembu social system is pivoted on the importance of hunting. This importance does not derive from the objective contribution to the food supply made by the chase. Hunting owes its high valuation, on the one hand, to an association consistently made among many Central and Western Bantu between hunting and high social status, and on the other, to an identification made among these peoples of hunting with masculinity.[204]

Although hunting indeed was of ideological importance, it equally had a material underpinning. The popularity and high regard of hunting might be attributed, as MacKenzie does, to 'its high productivity in terms of the relative effort involved', as 'success rates were fairly high and yields good, though the time devoted to hunting, in comparison to other economic activities, was relatively low'.[205] Whereas agricultural production required involvement throughout the year, hunting was more flexible, as a hunter could go into the bush with any frequency and for any length of time. Hunting, regardless, was tied to seasonal fluctuations and success depended on the skill of the hunter and on the availability of game. Some skilful hunters enjoyed high success rates. According to recollections, hunters would return from the bush with up to five animals per trip.[206] Yet hunting was a sporadic pastime rather than a fulltime occupation. Because hunting trips were irregular, perhaps occurring once a month, meat supplies generally remained scarce, though highly coveted.[207] Overall, the flexibility of hunting, its high labour returns, and the association of hunting with social status endorsed the persistent popularity of this productive activity in Mwinilunga.

The once plentiful game populations in Mwinilunga drastically declined over the course of the twentieth century, inciting the promulgation of official regulations to restrict hunting.[208] Whilst this precluded game meat as a daily item of diet, the value attached to hunting locally did not diminish. Through hunting, individuals could attain status, or even fame, within the village and

---

203   (NAZ) KSE6/5/1, J.M. Pound, Balunda District Monthly Report, July 1909.
204   Turner, *Schism and Continuity*, 25.
205   MacKenzie, *The Empire of Nature*, 73.
206   This view is based on numerous interviews, for example Windson Mbimbi, 14 August 2010, Kanongesha.
207   Pritchett, *Lunda-Ndembu*, Chapter 2.
208   This view is based on a wide reading of archival sources (NAZ).

beyond. One of the few means for young men to climb the meritocratic ladder was by becoming a distinguished hunter. Marks has argued this for the analogous case of Eastern Zambia: 'Hunting by professionals is more than a subsistence technique. It is a chosen route to manhood involving commitments and goals. It is a social strategy by which hunters compete with other males for positions of leadership among their matrikin'.[209] In Mwinilunga, the high esteem of the hunter even enabled some to challenge the position of the village headman. Nonetheless, Turner saw the personalities of hunter and headman as diametrically opposed:

> Successful gun-hunters are regarded as sorcerers, who acquire their power in hunting from killing people by means of their familiars. That is why great hunters seldom become successful headmen, in the opinion of Ndembu. Their nomadic inclination, their tendency to favour primary rather than classificatory kin in their own villages, and their association with sorcery, disqualify them from performing a role which requires tact, generosity to classificatory kin and strangers, and constant participation in the group life, for its successful functioning.[210]

Turner depicted the hunter as an individual with nomadic inclinations, who uses witchcraft to increase his power and kills, whilst disregarding communal obligations towards kin. Whereas a hunter leaned towards self-centred individualism, a village headman was supposed to keep the needs and desires of the community in mind.

The antagonism between the individual and the collective in hunting should not be overstated, though. Hunters might indeed be wandering, somewhat nomadic individuals. Yet even if hunting could be a path towards masculinity and power, it was not a purely individual pursuit.[211] A hunter would only rarely go into the bush alone; he would be accompanied at least by a junior apprentice. But hunting in larger groups equally occurred. On occasion, communal hunts involving the entire village would be organised.[212] Hunting thus transcended the individual sphere and affected the village community at large. Game meat was the main source of protein in the area, as tsetse fly ruled out the possibility of keeping livestock in large parts of the district. Because game meat was not

---

209   Stuart A. Marks, *Large Mammals and a Brave People: Subsistence Hunters in Zambia* (London: Routledge, 2005), 126.
210   Turner, *Schism and Continuity*, 32, 202.
211   Pritchett, *Lunda-Ndembu*; Bakewell, 'Refugees Repatriating.'
212   W. Singleton Fisher, 'Burning the Bush for Game', *African Studies* 7, No. 1 (1948): 36–38.

available universally or throughout the year, it was considered a special treat, to be indulged in only occasionally.[213] Consequently, its distribution became a bone of contention, which brought the tensions between the individual and the collective to the forefront. Women, children, and men who did not hunt depended on the meat supplies brought home by a hunter.[214] The negative connotations of the term *chibodi*, a man who is not a hunter and therefore is considered an unsuccessful person, clearly illustrate this dependency and subordination.[215] Even if access to meat was unequal – distribution was linked to hierarchies of power, gender, and age – meat would generally be shared within a group of kin. The tension between an individual hunter and the community of kin is aptly captured in the proverb '*Mwisanga nayanga nkawami, ilanga kudya twadyanga amavulu*' – 'I [the hunter] go into the forest alone, but we eat with many people'.[216] The distribution of meat after the hunt was an intricate affair, potentially giving rise to fierce disputes. Selected parts of the kill would be reserved for specific individuals. The hunter would retain the intestines and the head for himself, the chest would go to the headman or chief, the saddle would be distributed among the wives of the hunter, and so on. If a hunter failed to distribute meat fairly, according to the expectations of his kin, grumbling and even accusations of witchcraft would follow.[217] By providing the village with meat, the most valued form of food, a hunter became locally idolised.[218] But this fame would only be upheld for so long as the hunter proved successful in his pursuits, and generous with the provision and distribution of meat. Individual status inevitably entailed relationships with, obligations towards and responsibility for a wider community of kin. Although hunting may have been practised as an individual pursuit, it had collective ramifications, influencing the livelihood of the village and the broader region.

In spite of the continued ideological significance of this productive activity, opportunities for hunting were increasingly curtailed by the diminution of game and consequent protective legislation. Prior to the 1930s, game could

---

213 Turner and Turner, 'Money Economy', 21.

214 Victor W. Turner, 'Themes in the Symbolism of Ndembu Hunting Ritual', *Anthropological Quarterly* 35, No. 2 (1962): 37–57; Turner, *Schism and Continuity*.

215 This view is based on numerous interviews, for example Jonathan Chiyezhi, 2010, Mwinilunga; *Lunda-Ndembu Dictionary*.

216 Interview with Mischek Alfons Maseka, 11 May 2010, Nyakaseya.

217 See Chapter 5.

218 Filip De Boeck, 'Borderland Breccia: The Mutant Hero in the Historical Imagination of a Central-African Diamond Frontier', *Journal of Colonialism and Colonial History* 1, No. 2 (2000); Turner, *Schism and Continuity*; Bakewell, 'Refugees Repatriating'; Pritchett, *Lunda-Ndembu*.

still be found in abundance throughout Mwinilunga, especially in the south of the district, on the river plains and in the stunted bush. Large herds of various species of game were reported at the beginning of the twentieth century, for example by travellers such as Gibbons:

> Two small troops of zebra and about a score of buffalo, as well as the elegant little oribi which rose from time to time from the long grass and bounded lightly away, gave evidence that this open grass veldt was a favourite resort of game.[219]

In the northern part of the district, however, game soon started to become more scattered and only smaller species could still be encountered.[220] By the 1950s, this game situation spread through the district. In 1952, the District Commissioner reported a 'ruthless destruction of game (...) [and] meat hunger', claiming that there was hardly any game left in the district.[221] A complex interplay of factors underlay the diminution of game. Diseases such as rinderpest and sleeping sickness, access to firearms, the disruption of game habitat, local hunting practices, and the presence of European hunters all brought down numbers of game.[222] Colonial officials blamed the Lunda for all the trouble, claiming that ever since they had obtained access to muzzle-loading guns they had killed game indiscriminately.[223] Yet the presence of European hunters, hunters from Barotseland, and poachers from neighbouring areas, who answered the mounting demand for ivory, hides, and skins, equally played a role in diminishing game populations.[224] Local hunters purported to be selective when choosing their prey, enabling the game population to procreate by hunting only the older specimens of a herd.[225] Rather than being disruptive, human presence might even have encouraged game proliferation, by creating an

---

219   Gibbons, *Africa from South to North*, 61.
220   In 1906 a mission station was established in the northwestern part of the district. The mission station attracted a concentration of population, which probably drove away game; see Fisher and Hoyte, *Ndotolu*.
221   (NAZ) SEC2/135, R.C. Dening, Mwinilunga District Annual Report, 1952.
222   MacKenzie, *Empire of Nature*; Marks, *Large Mammals*.
223   (NAZ) KSE6/5/1, J.M. Pound, Balunda District Monthly Report, July 1909.
224   (NAZ) NWP1/2/101 Loc.4919, E.L. Button, North Western Province Annual Report, 1961; (NAZ) SEC2/959, R.C. Dening, Mwinilunga District Tour Report, 1951; (NAZ) KSE6/1/5, F.V. Bruce-Miller, Mwinilunga Sub-District Annual Report, 1926.
225   This view is based on numerous interviews, for example Harrison Zimba, 10 October 2008, Ntambu.

environment with stunted trees and ample undergrowth.[226] Still, colonial officials universally viewed human presence as problematic and harmful to game.

In an attempt to arrest the disappearance of game, various orders and
decrees were put in place to restrict the freedom of the hunter during the twentieth century. A licence became obligatory to hunt larger species of game or to
own a gun, the trapping of game was restricted, and the sale of game meat was
progressively curtailed. Furthermore, Game Reserves and Controlled Hunting
Areas were demarcated in an attempt to limit the indiscriminate shooting of
game.[227] These measures were not merely benevolent government attempts to
protect game. Hunting legislation was closely linked to the control of human
movement and settlement as well. Hunting was associated with 'nomadism',
with mobile individuals who could easily evade administrative control. These
nomadic traits and the notorious autonomy of hunters, in turn, underpinned
administrative criticism of hunting. The pejorative discursive connection between hunting and nomadism, asserted by many officials in the twentieth century, had more to do with issues of control than with the productive activity
of hunting itself.[228] Hunting was no more 'primitive' than settled animal husbandry, and neither was it necessarily geared towards subsistence or averse to
market logic. Similar to debates about fixed farming and shifting cultivation,
officials preferred settled forms of animal husbandry to hunting due to issues
of administrative control. Officials presented animal husbandry as superior to
hunting, even if hunting retained ideological, popular, and practical importance throughout the twentieth century.[229]

Due to the autonomy of hunters and the importance of hunting for livelihood, it is unsurprising that legislation to restrict hunting met with considerable local resistance. Measures of control were fervently debated during
meetings between colonial officials and chiefs, for example.[230] Nevertheless,
legislation was never fully enforced, and there were always ways to circumvent
decrees. Chiefs, on whom the understaffed government relied to enforce game
legislation, were more than willing to turn a blind eye to the 'illegal poaching'
of their subjects as long as they received a portion of the kill themselves. In addition, cross-border movement and trade enabled hunting in neighbouring

---

226 Marks, *Large Mammals*.
227 (NAZ) KSE6/1/5, F.V. Bruce-Miller, Mwinilunga Sub-District Annual Report, 1926; (NAZ)
     NWP1/2/105 Loc.4920, H.T. Bayldon, North Western Province Annual Report, 1963.
228 Kaufmann, 'Sediment of Nomadism'; Scott, *Seeing like a State*.
229 See James Ferguson, 'The Bovine Mystique: Power, Property and Livestock in Rural
     Lesotho', *Man* 20, No. 4 (1985): 647–74.
230 (NAZ) KSE6/3/2, Mwinilunga Sub-District Report Indaba, 30 August 1927.

Angola, where legislation was more lenient.[231] Ingenious methods were devised to bypass restrictive laws, as this example from 1964 attests:

> With regard to the licencing of muzzle loading guns, many owners are acquiring numerous licences from different offices and courts: this enables them to buy extra ammunition permits, normally granting 2 lbs. of gunpowder per half year per licence, and then resell the gunpowder at a handsome profit in the Congo. The traffic is not inconsiderable and must be checked. Insufficient control is exercised in the issue of arms licences by local authority clerks.[232]

Showcasing the inventiveness of hunters, in the 1970s an 'increasing level of poaching in Zambia' was noted, 'even by more responsible people'.[233] Hunting thus continued unabatedly after independence, whilst the autonomy of hunters frustrated attempts at administrative control. Far from being a 'subsistence' activity, hunting was responsive to market incentives, as an example from 1960 shows:

> The exorbitant prices paid for meat in the Congo have encouraged illegal methods of hunting in this area and there is a considerable traffic in dried game meat across the border. Long series of trap lines abound on the plains and snares of great variety and ingenuity were found in the bush.[234]

Still, hunting did become more difficult and prone to risks due to legislation and measures of control, especially from the 1950s onwards. Hunting had always involved risks, though. Gardens were regularly disturbed by wild animals, wild pigs would uproot cassava, and elephants could jeopardise standing crops, but even people could be attacked by game.[235] Because of the risks involved in dealing with wild animals, successful hunters were believed to possess supernatural powers. Elephant hunters, for example, could use the charm *mujiminu* to become invisible, enabling them to more easily approach their targets.[236]

---

231   This view is based on numerous interviews, for example Amon Sawila, 7 September 2010, Kanongesha; Bakewell, 'Refugees Repatriating.'
232   (NAZ) LGH5/2/8 Loc.3613, Mwinilunga, 30 December 1964.
233   (NAZ) LGH5/1/10 Loc.3608, February 1970.
234   (NAZ) SEC2/968, J.T. Michie, Mwinilunga District Tour Report, 1960.
235   This view is based on numerous interviews, for example Kasonda, 1 October 2010, Ntambu, and a wide reading of archival sources (NAZ).
236   Turner, 'Themes in the Symbolism of Ndembu Hunting Ritual'; Fisher, 'Burning the Bush.'

Over the course of the twentieth century, as access to game became increasingly problematic, the prestige of successful hunters merely heightened. Widespread meat hunger (*dikwilu*) elevated the value of meat. Financial resources could facilitate hunting and the access to scarce supplies of meat, as money enabled the purchase of gun and game licences. Yet personal skills and charisma were at least as important in hunting success.[237] Far from being displaced by settled forms of animal husbandry, the importance of hunting persisted throughout the twentieth century in Mwinilunga.

Hunting had gained popularity and prominence because it enabled a degree of mobility, flexibility, and success. Hunting provided meat in a manner compatible with the shifting patterns of settlement prevalent in the area of Mwinilunga.[238] Hunting facilitated the defiance of administrative control and subverted expectations of settled residence. The quest for good hunting grounds was a common reason for villages to shift their location, so that mobility and hunting reinforced each other.[239] As a productive activity, hunting provided a stable source of livelihood. Without meat supplies, quarrels in a village were inevitable. Hunting was more than a means of subsistence, though, as it was loaded with symbolic meaning, providing individuals access to wealth and power within the village and beyond.[240] Meat from the hunt would be marketed once opportunities arose, even if legislation restricted commercialisation and markets had to be sought across the border in Angola and Congo. During the twentieth century hunting was challenged by legislation, game decimation, and sedentarisation.[241] Official policies opposed hunting because the activity was difficult to control. Alternatively, government discourse proposed settled forms of animal husbandry as a 'superior' alternative to hunting.[242] That hunting retained popularity in spite of this, is evidence of the resilience of the foundations of production. The way in which animal husbandry was viewed and adopted in Mwinilunga was greatly influenced by this ideological framework of hunting.

---

237 This view is based on numerous interviews, for example Paul Maseka, 18 May 2010, Nyakaseya; *Lunda-Ndembu Dictionary*.
238 Turner, *Schism and Continuity*.
239 Bakewell, 'Refugees Repatriating.'
240 Turner, *Schism and Continuity;* Turner, 'Themes in the Symbolism of Ndembu Hunting Ritual.'
241 Bakewell, 'Refugees Repatriating.'
242 Kaufmann, 'Sediment of Nomadism.'

4.2   Herding: A Source of Meat, a Source of Money

Even if herding livestock was presented as a 'superior' and more 'market-oriented' alternative to hunting in official discourse and policies,[243] it failed to gain widespread popularity in the area of Mwinilunga. Colonial officials in the 1950s voiced complaints that 'as a tribe the Lunda are not cattle minded',[244] and furthermore 'what stock did exist was of poor grade, due in the main to the people's absolute lack of stock-keeping knowledge and tradition'.[245] The possibility of keeping livestock was restricted by the presence of tsetse fly in the area, especially south of the 12th parallel. Still, most villages possessed a small number of livestock, occasionally as much as one hundred head. Throughout the colonial period, and especially after independence, numbers of livestock increased.[246] Censuses were erratic and of doubtful reliability: 'figures for small stock in the villages are very inaccurate, on account of the commonly held belief that stock, once recorded, become in a sense the property of Government and are liable to be requisitioned',[247] but nevertheless reflected a rise in numbers. Livestock figures ranged from 960 sheep, 1523 goats and 4 pigs in 1928; to 3562 sheep, 3168 goats, 72 pigs and 503 cattle in 1961; mounting to 4000 head of cattle in 1973.[248]

Although local producers did not take to animal husbandry as enthusiastically as government officials had anticipated, a number of expatriate farmers did maintain sizeable herds and appeared to have some success with cattle ranching.[249] Even in their case, however, the viability of livestock enterprises remained doubtful, because of environmental considerations and due to the remoteness of Mwinilunga from major markets.[250] In 1949, the veterinary

243   See Ferguson, *The Anti-Politics Machine.*
244   (NAZ) LGH5/2/1, Mwinilunga District Development Plan, 10 September 1956.
245   (NAZ) NWP1/2/78 Loc.4913, F.R.G. Phillips, North Western Province Annual Report, 1956.
246   This view is based on a wide reading of archival sources (NAZ); Pritchett, *Lunda-Ndembu,* Chapter 2.
247   (NAZ) NWP1/2/40, R.C. Dening, Mwinilunga District Tour Report, 1952.
248   These figures exclude livestock owned by the European population of the area. (NAZ) KSE6/1/6, F.V. Bruce-Miller, Mwinilunga Sub-District Annual Report, 1928; (NAZ) NWP1/2/101 Loc.4919, North Western Province Annual Report, 1961; (NAZ) Tenth Anniversary Yearbook of the Ministry of Rural Development, December 1975. For the postcolonial period, figures are mostly aggregates on a provincial level. These depict a rapid increase: (NAZ) Quarterly Agricultural Statistical Bulletin, September 1975; Annual census of livestock in the traditional sector North Western Province: 1964 10,945 cattle, 2296 pigs, 7995 sheep and goats; 1970 23,508 cattle, 4547 pigs, 13,956 sheep and goats; 1974 30,362 cattle, 7587 pigs, 21,975 sheep and goats.
249   Interview with Paul Fisher, 27 September 2008, Hillwood Farm; Sardanis, *Africa.*
250   These included W.F. Fisher of Hillwood farm, Robinson of Caenby farm, and Paterson of Matonchi farm. Fisher, at the height of his career had a herd of 1,500 cattle: (NAZ)

official judged the potential for animal husbandry in Mwinilunga most unfavourably:

> [Mwinilunga's] great distance from the Copperbelt will, for a long time to come, deter farming people from seeking land within it (...) the drawbacks (...) are the sour veldt, parasites and fly (...) Great damboes, which to look at seem wonderful grazing yet to walk on prove watery death traps to cattle venturing on them, or else the green grass proves so hard and sharp that you cut your fingers if you pull it. Fluke and other internal worms, and ticks galore, flourish and strange cattle must struggle to survive until acclimatised.[251]

Contrary to local individuals, European farmers were able to operate even in the face of adversity. This was due to the large scale of their ranches, along with their managerial and organisational skills, but mostly it was because of profits from side activities such as trade or agriculture.[252] Whilst animal husbandry in Mwinilunga did provide opportunities for market involvement, it faced problems from the outset.

Despite such difficulties, government officials saw potential in local livestock keeping and assigned it prime policy importance, especially after 1945. In the 1950s, officials designated livestock as 'one of the most encouraging avenues of development' and claimed a bright 'future for cattle'.[253] Government schemes promoted livestock ownership by distributing cattle or poultry to chiefs and other 'promising individuals'.[254] Such schemes operated on a loan or repayment basis, an example being the National Beef Scheme initiated in 1967. Officials believed that stock ownership would facilitate 'improved' agricultural methods, by providing manure and enabling ox-drawn ploughing, and would diversify the local diet, through the provision of milk, butter, eggs, and meat.[255] Livestock was ideologically linked to the 'progressive farmer':

LGH5/2/1, Provincial Four Year Development Plan, 1956; (NAZ) NWP1/2/26 Loc.4901, Veterinary Department to Provincial Commissioner, Ndola, 12 September 1949.

251   (NAZ) NWP1/2/26 Loc.4901, Veterinary Department to Provincial Commissioner, Ndola, 12 September 1949; (NAZ) SEC5/136, Murray, Mwinilunga Crown Land Block, 23 December 1958.

252   Interview with Paul Fisher, 27 September 2008, Hillwood Farm; Interview with Andrew Sardanis, 14 December 2009, Lusaka.

253   (NAZ) LGH5/2/1, Provincial Four Year Development Plan, 1956; (NAZ) NWP1/2/78 Loc.4913, E.L. Button, North Western Province Annual Report, 1959.

254   (NAZ) SEC2/185, Kaonde-Lunda Province District Commissioners' Conference, 1956.

255   This view is based on a wide reading of archival sources (NAZ); Crehan and Von Oppen, *Planners and History*; Moore and Vaughan, *Cutting Down Trees*.

Where possible it is obvious that cattle should be part and parcel of mixed farming schemes in order to increase the productivity of the soil, and in any project for the distribution of cattle priority should be given to persons who are engaged in growing cash crops.[256]

A crucial motive behind the promotion of livestock by government officials was that it would 'tend to stabilise the movement of the owners'.[257] Livestock would promote sedentarisation not only through capital investment in stock and land, but also because livestock manure would enhance soil fertility and enable the protracted cultivation of a single plot of land. Animal husbandry would thus encourage fixed as opposed to shifting settlement patterns, by tying producers to the land.[258] In stark opposition to 'nomadic' or 'primitive' methods of hunting, official discourse linked animal husbandry to settled farming, market production, and administrative control.

Why did the ownership of livestock not gain much local popularity, despite official propaganda? Could this be blamed on a lack of market logic or a 'primitive' outlook on the part of producers, as some officials purported, or were there other reasons? For one, although there was 'a desire on the part of local people to own cattle', stock was in short supply.[259] But furthermore, not all stock was equally popular, as the 1956 annual report suggests:

[Sheep, goats and pigs] do not seem to be greatly prised, they are not herded but are left to the mercy of accident and wild animals, and in a Province where there is a chronic meat shortage surprisingly little attention is paid to them (...) Poultry on the other hand are highly esteemed and in great demand everywhere, and there is an insatiable demand for improved cockerels (...) This is partly because the results are quickly visible and partly because the market for poultry on the Copperbelt, in the Congo and locally is an extremely good one.[260]

Preferences for livestock were shaped by ecological, agricultural, economic, cultural, and ritual factors.[261] As the high demand for poultry suggests, producers

---

256   (NAZ) LGH5/5/8, Mwinilunga District Development Plan, 10 September 1956.
257   (NAZ) SEC2/962, P.L.N. Hannaford, Mwinilunga District Tour Report, 28 June 1954.
258   Scott, *Seeing Like a State*; Ferguson, *The Anti-politics Machine*.
259   (NAZ) MAG2/5/91 Loc.144, Minister of Agriculture, North Western Province Tour, 6 January 1968.
260   (NAZ) NWP1/2/78 Loc.4913, F.R.G. Phillips, North Western Province Annual Report, 1956.
261   This view is based on numerous interviews, for example Group interview Kampemba, 30 March 2010, Mwinilunga; Pritchett, *Lunda-Ndembu*, Chapter 2.

were highly responsive to favourable marketing opportunities. For a different reason, sheep and goats were not popular, because they could intrude into unfenced gardens and provoke quarrels with neighbours.[262] Chickens were valued because of their ritual significance. Chickens would be offered to honoured visitors, they would figure in witchcraft ordeals (the 'fowl test'), and they were part of various ceremonies.[263] The rationale behind animal husbandry and the choice of livestock were, thus, informed by multiple considerations.

Amongst these considerations economic factors proved of particular importance. Far from being unresponsive to market logic, the District Commissioner in 1937 remarked how 'the natives regard small stock as a ten shilling note on four legs rather than as a source of meat or milk supply'.[264] In the 1950s, a buoyant livestock trade developed with neighbouring areas of Congo, and 'many people in the District depended on selling chickens, sheep and goats in the Congo for money with which to pay tax and buy clothes'.[265] Although administrative propaganda tried to encourage marketing within Zambia, for example on the Copperbelt, producers obtained higher prices by moving across borders. Even if these international markets were considered illegal, and officials denounced the trade as smuggling, the trade evidences the inventiveness and commercial orientation of producers in Mwinilunga.[266] Instead of bringing about sedentarisation and bureaucratic control, livestock producers defied administrative control and maximised profits through mobility in an attempt to obtain a good price for their meat.

The commercial rearing of livestock contrasted sharply with the domestic uses of stock, as a 1950s report explains: 'In the villages stock are rarely, if ever slaughtered to provide meat, except on important festive occasions such as funerals, weddings, maturity ceremonies, etc.'.[267] Livestock was reserved for consumption on special occasions rather than being slaughtered for meat on a regular basis. Scarcity of supplies contributed to the special ideological status

---

262 This view is based on a wide reading of archival sources (NAZ); Turner, *Schism and Continuity*.
263 This view is based on numerous interviews, for example Mandamu Sapotu, 10 March 2010, Ikelenge; Turner, *Schism and Continuity*; Pritchett, *Lunda-Ndembu*.
264 (NAZ) SEC2/151, Provincial Commissioner Western Province Annual Report, 1937.
265 (NAZ) LGH5/1/3 Loc.3604, Lunda-Ndembo Native Authority Meeting, 5 November 1960; (NAZ) SEC2/965, P.L.N. Hannaford, Mwinilunga District Tour Report, December 1955.
266 Bakewell, 'Refugees Repatriating'; Janet MacGaffey, *The Real Economy of Zaire: The Contribution of Smuggling and Other Unofficial Activities to National Wealth* (Oxford: James Currey, 1991).
267 (NAZ) MAG2/9/11 Loc.171, Department of Agriculture Nutrition Trends, 4 August 1959.

of stock, precluding overt commercial exploitation.[268] Livestock numbers were further kept down because stock was frequently subject to disease and because it could cause quarrels with neighbours, especially if animals strayed into fields unannounced. Still, once commercial opportunities arose, a select number of individuals did capitalise on the trade and sale of livestock. To satisfy the demand for meat in the district, inventive solutions were sought. Martin Kahangu, for example, started transporting cattle form Zambezi District to the *boma* in Mwinilunga after independence. This trade enabled him to open the first abattoir in the district in 1968, which answered the increasing demand for meat among administrative employees and residents of the fledgling town.[269] In spite of the willingness of producers to respond to market incentives, livestock retained more of a domestic use within Mwinilunga. Because markets were confined and competition at existing markets was high, the commercial rearing of stock never took off.

4.3   *Ideology, Marketing, and Administrative Control: The Co-Existence of Hunting and Herding*

Another reason for the relative lack of enthusiasm vis-à-vis livestock was the persistently high valuation of game meat and hunting. Rather than a 'cattle complex' or 'bovine mystique' so well described for other areas, in Mwinilunga a 'hunting ethos' prevailed.[270] This ideological framework – based on environmental and economic principles that had developed and adapted over time – shaped responses to bureaucratic interventions and commercial opportunities. Despite the active propagation of animal husbandry and commercial agriculture, hunting retained importance.[271] The attachment to hunting was driven by factors that went beyond an economic rationale, even though hunting did make a real contribution to livelihood security. Hunting was part of the foundations of production in Mwinilunga.

District Commissioner Short identified hunting as 'the traditional occupation' of the Lunda in 1958 and claimed that 'the poverty of their gardens showed where their real interests lay'.[272] Other officials similarly lamented that the popularity of hunting prevented a more active interest in agriculture and animal husbandry. This strong attachment to hunting begs explanation. Even

---

268   This has been referred to as the 'cattle complex' or the 'bovine mystique' throughout Southern and Eastern Africa; see Ferguson, 'The Bovine Mystique.'
269   Interview with Martin Kahangu, 30 September 2010, Ntambu.
270   Turner, *Schism and Continuity*; Ferguson, 'The Bovine Mystique'; Adam Kuper, *Wives for Cattle: Bridewealth and Marriage in Southern Africa* (London: Routledge, 1982).
271   Bakewell, 'Refugees Repatriating'; Pritchett, *Friends for Life*.
272   (NAZ) SEC2/966, R.J. Short, Mwinilunga District Tour Report, 1958.

though the ownership of livestock had become feasible once the spread of tse-tse fly had been arrested, breeding stock remained in desperately short supply throughout the twentieth century. On top of this, disease regulations and the high price of stock limited the ability of individuals to purchase cattle.[273] Due to its relative scarcity, consequently, livestock was regarded as an inferior alternative to game. Officials in the 1960s remarked that livestock was only considered attractive in case game was difficult to access:

> The Chiefs in this District depend on game meat (...) There is virtually no game in the area and there are very few guns to take advantage of the few remaining animals. As a result, large numbers of sheep, goats and chickens are kept for local consumption.[274]

The ideological framework of hunting remains pertinent today. When consuming a meal, people remark that chicken (*kasumbi*) or goat (*mpembi*) is nice, but it cannot pass for real meat, game. Even if it has become a rare delight, game continues to be regarded as the only real meat.[275] Through hunting, individuals could obtain meat in a manner that facilitated flexibility, mobility, and autonomy. Hunting could easily jibe with a shifting pattern of settlement, administrative defiance, and illicit marketing across international borders where prices were high.[276] Hunting enabled defiance of administrative control and subverted expectations of fixed settlement. Animal husbandry, on the other hand, was associated with sedentarisation, bureaucratic control, and commercial marketing. Herding failed to gain widespread popularity because markets were lacking, far away, or unprofitable.[277] Moreover, there was an aversion to the fixed settlements which herding propagated. In Mwinilunga, soils easily become depleted, even when animal manure is used. Shifting cultivation thus continued to be an environmentally sound solution, which enabled high yields as long as population density remained low.[278] Herding, however, did not necessarily lead to sedentarisation, as the examples of marketing small livestock in Congo and Angola attest.[279] In defiance of official discourse, producers

---

273   (NAZ) NWP1/2/26 Loc.4901, R.N. Lines, Mwinilunga District Tour Report, January 1949.
274   (NAZ) LGH5/2/8 Loc.3613, A.M. Mubita, District Secretary Mwinilunga, 30 August 1967; (NAZ) SEC2/968, J.T. Michie, Mwinilunga District Tour Report, March 1960.
275   This view is based on numerous interviews. See Jonathan Chiyezhi, November 2010, Mwinilunga.
276   Turner, *Schism and Continuity*; Bakewell, 'Refugees Repatriating.'
277   Pritchett, *Lunda-Ndembu*.
278   Ibidem, Chapter 2.
279   Bakewell, 'Refugees Repatriating.'

remained mobile individuals.[280] Yet even more than herding, hunting fitted within preferred patterns of production in the area, enabling flexibility and autonomy. Rather than being averse to market logic, hunting adapted over time.[281] Hunting proved to be a flexible means of livelihood procurement in response to marketing opportunities. Furthermore, hunting held ideological importance, providing individuals with a means to obtain power and respect. Factors of ideology, marketing, and state control all explain the persistent importance of hunting, even as game populations have decreased.

The transition from subsistence hunting techniques to commercial herding practices, as prescribed by official discourse, proved far from straightforward.[282] Hunting enabled high returns for relatively low labour input, making it a popular basis of livelihood. In contrast, livestock herding was labour intensive, required the availability of good grazing lands, and could potentially cause quarrels with neighbours. Furthermore, animal husbandry was not necessarily economically lucrative.[283] Once commercial opportunities opened up in Congo, producers eagerly stepped in, engaging in livestock trade and sale for high profits. Game meat could equally be commercially viable and dried game meat continues to be sold in Angola or on the Zambian Copperbelt.[284] The preference for hunting over herding was thus based on a host of economic, political, ideological, and environmental considerations, grounded in the specific but shifting conditions prevailing in Mwinilunga. Throughout the twentieth century, an ideological framework of game meat valuation predominated, which was left unchallenged by official propaganda for commercial livestock rearing. Turner aptly described this 'hunting ethos' in combination with cassava cultivation as the foundation of production in Mwinilunga in the 1950s.[285] And even after the 1950s, the foundations of production continued to pivot around hunting and cassava cultivation. Such attitudes, which in turn influenced productive practices, should not be seen as unchanging relics of the past, but rather as features constantly adapting to a complex environmental, economic, social, and political setting. Cassava and hunting were both geared towards maximising production, requiring relatively low labour input yet providing a stable source of livelihood. Productive activities constantly adapted to

---

280   Ibidem.
281   Kaufmann, 'Sediment of Nomadism.'
282   Kaufmann, 'Sediment of Nomadism'; David Turkon, 'Modernity, Tradition and the Demystification of Cattle in Lesotho', *African Studies* 62, No. 2 (2003): 147–69.
283   See parallels in Ferguson, *The Anti-Politics Machine*.
284   This view is based on numerous interviews, for example Mamfwela Moris, 28 July 2010, Kanongesha; Pritchett, *Friends for Life*.
285   Turner, *Schism and Continuity*, 32.

existing opportunities, even if this did not directly lead to the commercialisation or market integration that officials envisaged. Producers sought to maximise output from labour returns in a reliable manner without jeopardising
subsistence security.[286] Two examples of market participation – beeswax and
pineapple production – will illustrate the conditions of and reactions to marketing opportunities in Mwinilunga.

5   Beeswax

A 1967 newspaper article described Mwinilunga as an area where 'beekeepers find their land of milk and honey'.[287] Throughout the nineteenth and
twentieth century, notwithstanding some fluctuations, levels of beeswax and
honey production have been consistently high. In 1935, the Provincial Commissioner claimed that Mwinilunga could produce more honey and beeswax 'than the remainder of the Territory combined'.[288] Beeswax in particular
proved a lucrative commodity, firmly embedded in networks of trade, as its
local use-value was practically non-existent. The case of beeswax can reveal
the dynamics of market production over time, highlighting the limitations
posed by transport, price, and market fluctuations.[289] Challenging depictions
of a static pre-colonial period, the case of beeswax illustrates that production
was highly dynamic and market-oriented long before the establishment of
colonial rule.[290] Furthermore, market production did not have to clash with
the production of food crops, as the two could go hand in hand and could even
stimulate one another.

Apiculture is a long-established activity in Mwinilunga. The environmental
setting is particularly suitable to honey production and producer agency has
stimulated a vibrant trade in beeswax.[291] In their ecological survey of the 1930s,
Trapnell and Clothier capture many aspects of beeswax production and trade:

---

286   Turkon, 'Modernity, Tradition and the Demystification', 152.
287   (NAZ) ML1/16/6 Loc.4575, Times of Zambia, 17 April 1967.
288   (NAZ) SEC2/258 Vol.2, Provincial Commissioner Ndola to Chief Secretary Lusaka, 17 Sep-
       tember 1935.
289   See: Michael W. Tuck, 'Woodland Commodities, Global Trade, and Local Struggles: The
       Beeswax Trade in British Tanzania', *Journal of Eastern African Studies* 3, No. 2 (2009):
       259–74; Jean-Luc Vellut, 'Diversification de l'économie de la cueillette: miel et cire dans
       les sociétés de la forêt Claire d'Afrique centrale (c. 1750–1950)', *African Economic History* 7
       (1979): 93–112.
290   See Richard Reid, 'Past and Presentism: The 'Precolonial' and the Foreshortening of Afri-
       can History', *Journal of African History* 52, No. 2 (2011): 135–55, especially 142–44.
291   Von Oppen, *Terms of Trade*.

Beeswax has long been traded by the (...) Lunda, formerly to Angola, and now to traders in Balovale and Mwinilunga. In Mwinilunga the successive flowering of species of Isoberlinia, Marquesia and Brachystegia from early winter to early rains, provides a sequence of supplies in normal years. Bark hives are employed, and methods of preparation of the wax appear usually to be adequate. It is purchased by the trader in 2 ½ or 3 lb. balls at 2 ½ to 3 d. per lb., and finds a ready market either in London or Johannesburg. The current price c.i.f. London is 83 s. to 90 s. per cwt.[292]

A variety of techniques exist to gather honey and produce beeswax. To collect wild honey, trees are cut down, or alternatively bark hives, mostly cylindrical in form, can be constructed. Due to the unique flowering of trees in Mwinilunga, the area attracts numerous bees, which produce a copious honey flow. In the north of the district, the honey season is confined to the months between October and January, whilst in the south of the district a second honey season occurs in May and June. Locally, honey is either processed into a sweet beer (*kasolu*) or used as a dietary supplement to accompany the consumption of cassava roots or meat.[293] Although beeswax is not used locally, it has an international market. Beeswax is used for making candles and seals, or for producing lipstick in the cosmetics industry, for instance.[294]

From the eighteenth century onwards, beeswax became an export product shipped from the Angolan coast.[295] Beeswax initially supplemented exports of ivory and slaves, in return for which consumer goods were obtained.[296] This trade was described by Livingstone in the 1850s:

> The native traders generally carry salt and a few pieces of cloth, a few beads, and cartouches with iron balls (...) The great article of search is beeswax, and from their eagerness to obtain it I suspect it fetches a high price in the market.[297]

Other travellers at the end of the nineteenth century, such as Gibbons, equally underlined the salience of this trade: 'The Malunda cultivate honey more than any other tribe I have met. In addition to wild honey, they procure a very

---

292 (NAZ) Trapnell and Clothier, Report of the Ecological Survey for 1934.
293 This view is based on numerous interviews, for example Bigwan Masondi, 13 October 2010, Ntambu.
294 Tuck, 'Woodland Commodities.'
295 Vellut, 'Diversification de l'économie de la cueilette', 106.
296 Miller, *Way of Death;* Von Oppen, *Terms of Trade.*
297 Schapera, *Livingstone's African Journal*, 121.

plentiful supply from bark hives, which they attach to the branches of trees'.[298] The beeswax trade continued into the colonial period and beyond. Beeswax was shipped from Angolan ports, Benguela in particular, and this trade perpetuated the strong links between Mwinilunga and Angola.[299]

Local traders identified economic incentives, such as profit margins or price differentials, as motivating factors to engage in beeswax trading. Pricing even prompted some traders to try to circumvent prohibitive colonial legislation, as a trader in 1928 explained: 'We decided to take the risk as the traders in Angola give us a lot of money for any beeswax we take to them'.[300] Expatriate traders, most notably Ffolliott Fisher, started buying beeswax in Mwinilunga in 1926. The end product, transported by the Benguela railway to Angola, was destined for export to either Johannesburg or London, where it would be sold for up to £170 per landed ton.[301] Even if colonial legislation denounced beeswax trade as illicit smuggling, local traders were able to effectively compete with expatriates. In a manner that demonstrated knowledge of markets, local traders took advantage of price differentials across international borders and cut transport costs by relying on established networks of trade. The District Commissioner grudgingly acknowledged this in 1937:

> A considerable quantity of wax is taken across the border either by Mwinilunga natives desiring higher prices at Angola or Congo or by natives from Angola or Congo who have journeyed here to buy the wax with English currency in the hope of reselling at a profit across the Border (...) high transport charges and export duties make it impossible for traders in this Territory to pay as much for the commodity as the Portuguese traders [in Angola] can offer.[302]

Favourable marketing opportunities enticed individuals in Mwinilunga to step up beeswax production. In the 1930s, a survey estimated that the average producer owned 20 hives, whilst some possessed up to 100 hives.[303] With prices fluctuating up to a high of 6d. per lb., beeswax production reached levels of 30–40 tonnes per year.[304] Honey collecting became so popular that the District

---

298 Gibbons, *Africa from South to North*, 44–45.
299 Bakewell, 'Refugees Repatriating.'
300 (NAZ) KSE3/2/2/7, Rex vs. Chisele, 24 July 1928.
301 (NAZ) SEC2/133, N.S. Price, Mwinilunga District Annual Report, 31 December 1935.
302 (NAZ) SEC2/133, N.S. Price, Mwinilunga District Annual Report, 31 December 1937; (NAZ) SEC2/41, Ormeby-Gore Report, 21 May 1937.
303 (NAZ) Allan to Director of Agriculture, 11 February 1938.
304 (NAZ) NWP1/2/101 Loc.4919, H.T. Bayldon, North Western Province Annual Report, 1961.

Commissioner in 1955 described it in terms of a 'seasonal exodus', drawing 'the people away from their gardens!'[305] Under favourable conditions, producers in Mwinilunga thus proved particularly eager vis-à-vis market production.

Far from obstructing agricultural production, it was exactly the compatibility between apiculture and agricultural production that made beeswax such a popular commodity. Beeswax production, located in the forests, is spatially segregated from the main agricultural fields. In addition, the placing of hives occurs during the dry season, a period of relative agricultural inactivity. The collection of honey from the hives does coincide with the planting period of crops, when labour demands are at a peak. Nevertheless, honey collection, which can be completed within several days of concerted effort, does not seem to seriously impair agricultural production. Instead, producers regard apiculture as a lucrative, low-risk side activity, which complements agricultural production without conflicting with it.[306] The sale of beeswax provided producers with distinct benefits, and in the 1930s officials reported that 'whole villages sometimes find their tax money by sale of beeswax alone'.[307] The beeswax trade could provide access to scarce commodities, such as clothing, pots, and even bicycles.[308] As a result, producers preferred beeswax over other produce, to the despair of some traders in the 1940s: 'Rubber is not coming in anywhere as well as expected, and this is partly due to the good beeswax harvest, money being easier to get for wax and the work for collecting not so hard'.[309] The popularity of apiculture was virtually unsurpassed, as it required low labour input but provided high monetary returns. Factors such as profitability, marketability, and labour input enticed beeswax production and trade in Mwinilunga throughout the twentieth century.[310]

Various government development schemes sought to stimulate apiculture due to its 'great potentials'. During the 1930s, development schemes mainly focused on instruction and demonstration, promoting methods of wax making in saucers instead of balls and encouraging the construction of hives rather than honey hunting.[311] In the 1960s, marketing was emphasised through the formation of honey and beekeeping co-operative societies. Some bureaucratic proposals could be highly elaborate and ambitious, as this example from 1966 illustrates:

305   (NAZ) SEC2/963, P.L.N. Hannaford, Mwinilunga District Tour Report, September 1955.
306   This view is based on numerous interviews, for example Maladi, 16 May 2010, Nyakaseya.
307   (NAZ) SEC2/133, N.S. Price, Mwinilunga District Annual Report, 31 December 1935.
308   (NAZ) SEC2/41, Note on Resources of Mwinilunga District, February 1937.
309   (NAZ) SEC2/193, Kaonde-Lunda Newsletter, First Quarter 1943.
310   Pritchett, *Lunda-Ndembu*, Chapter 2.
311   (NAZ) SEC2/133, N.S. Price, Mwinilunga District Annual Report, 31 December 1937.

There should be a possibility of having one honey marketing co-operative based initially at Mwinilunga under which a number of producer groups would be formed. Each group would consist of 10 to 20 members who would produce about two to three tons of honey per year and the mother co-operative would provide a honey press, strainers and suitable containers for the honey crop to each group.[312]

Official schemes, at least discursively, sought to 'improve and 'develop' existing apicultural practices in Mwinilunga. Suggestions were only adopted by producers, however, if these did not involve much extra labour or capital input. Methods of producing wax in saucers instead of balls caught on following official propaganda in 1937, because: 'saucers can be made with little extra trouble and require no apparatus that cannot be found in most Native households'.[313] Furthermore, this same report noted: 'It is axiomatic that the success of any scheme to improve the quality of a product depends on securing to the producer a premium for his extra trouble' in the form of good prices.[314] The success of a scheme was premised not on scientific principles advocated by experts but rather on labour, capital input and financial returns. Producers considered whether the requisite extra labour and capital input for apiculture would pay off, but also took into account whether market involvement would not jeopardise agricultural production and livelihood security.[315]

The main problems facing beeswax production and trade related to marketing and transport. Market instability and price fluctuations, in particular, deterred producers. Existing obstacles were aptly summarised in a report from the 1960s:

Lack of buying stations for wax: Beekeepers have to carry their crops 50 miles to the market and some have to carry over 100 miles and even with the good value/weight ratio this long cartage is discouraging. Irregular prices and buying: There have been violent price fluctuations, and stores often stop buying. Fraud by store capitaos: Producers usually know when they are being cheated, but cannot read, so can do little about it except cease production.[316]

312 (NAZ) Ministry of Agriculture, Monthly Economic Bulletin, June 1966.
313 (NAZ) Department of Agriculture, Annual Report, 1937.
314 Ibidem.
315 See Carswell, 'Food Crops as Cash Crops.'
316 (NAZ) ML1/16/6 Loc.4575, Honey and Wax Marketing Policy, 13 May 1966.

Market instability and long transport hauls discouraged some producers and affected sales volumes.[317] During the colonial period prices for beeswax fluctuated between 1/6d. and 6d. per lb., and concomitantly production figures ranged from 10 to 40 tonnes per year. Price incentives could encourage producers, for example when in 1937 Fisher raised the buying price to 4d. per lb. in the villages and 5 ½ d. per lb. at his store, officials 'met many boys taking wax for sale at his store and also two native hawkers with carriers laden with wax'.[318] Nevertheless, even in times of price slumps, producers and traders creatively sought and found ways to sell supplies and overcome transport or marketing difficulties. In 1966, for example: 'with wax valued 2/- a producer can easily carry £5 worth on a cycle'.[319] Producers seemed 'glad to earn their living by collecting beeswax',[320] and government officials in the 1920s noted that, 'if it only helped a hundred elderly men, who are physically unfit to travel a long distance to find work, to get a few shillings each year – then something would have been accomplished'.[321] By adopting flexible strategies of production, trade, and marketing, beeswax producers sought to stabilise their means of livelihood and income, even in the face of adversity.

The case of beeswax production in Mwinilunga provides an example of long-term, yet fluctuating, market involvement. It does not fit any transition from 'subsistence' to 'market' production.[322] Long established in the area of Mwinilunga, beeswax was geared towards marketing from the outset. Over time, the activity continuously adapted to changing incentives and circumstances. Building on existing foundations of production, beeswax production was symbiotic with the agricultural basis of livelihood procurement, aiming to maximise profit from limited labour supplies. Individuals were eager to engage in beeswax production because this was a relatively risk-free form of market participation, compatible with other sources of livelihood procurement.[323] Rather than conflicting with the production of food crops, beeswax production contributed to overall welfare by generating money to buy consumer goods or pay taxes. In case a slump in the beeswax market occurred and alternative sales outlets equally failed, producers would refrain from selling beeswax and consume the honey locally. In this sense, apiculture produced

317   Pritchett, *Lunda-Ndembu*, Chapter 2.
318   (NAZ) NWP1/2/2 Loc.4897, N.S. Price, Mwinilunga District Tour Report, 3 February 1937.
319   (NAZ) ML1/16/6 Loc.4575, Beekeeping Industry Coordinating Committee, 30 April 1966.
320   (NAZ) KSE6/1/4, K.S. Kinross, Mwinilunga District Annual Report, 1925.
321   (NAZ) KSE6/1/4, F.V. Bruce-Miller, Mwinilunga District Annual Report, 1922.
322   Vellut, 'Diversification de l'économie de la cueilette'; Von Oppen, *Terms of Trade*.
323   This view is based on numerous interviews, for example John Kamuhuza, March 2010, Ikelenge.

not only cash crops that could prove unmarketable but contributed to food
security as well. Displaying a high degree of flexibility, producers could step up
beeswax production rapidly when marketing did prove profitable.[324] Producers were sensitive to factors such as prices, market fluctuations, and transport
costs. Yet producers sought to diversify their marketing strategies rather than
being dependent on a single outlet. Although the beeswax trade could be lucrative, producers' livelihoods never depended on it. Agricultural production
and generating a stable basis of subsistence remained the priority of producers. This foundation enabled men to engage in beeswax production and trade
as a subsidiary activity that complemented but did not jeopardise food security. Subsistence and market production thus stimulated one another. When
price fluctuations, unstable markets, or transport problems made beeswax
an unattractive proposition, there was always an 'exit option' in the form of
agricultural production that provided a stable basis of subsistence.[325] Avoiding complete dependence on the market, producers sought to retain a degree
of agency.[326] This autonomy and flexibility eased the effects of market fluctuations and economic slumps on producers, explaining why beeswax was a
decidedly attractive commodity. Pineapple production further illustrates the
rationale behind market engagement in Mwinilunga.

6   Pineapples

Pineapples are so intimately associated with Mwinilunga that the area is referred to as 'pineapple country' in the remainder of Zambia.[327] Even though
the introduction of this fruit dates much further back, pineapples only developed as a major cash crop in Mwinilunga in the 1960s and 1970s.[328] Of
American origin, pineapples spread from the Angolan coast into the interior
through the long-distance trade.[329] By the 1850s the crop was established in the
area, although its exact provenance remained a mystery to travellers. Livingstone remarked, for example, that 'pineapples are reported as existing in the
woods in the Lunda country, and are not eaten by the people. Who introduced

---

324   Pritchett, *Friends for Life*.
325   Hyden, *Beyond Ujamaa*; Scott, *Moral Economy*.
326   Hyden argues that such producers are 'uncaptured' by the market, *Beyond Ujamaa*.
327   In Lusaka and on the Copperbelt, Mwinilunga was immediately associated with pine-
       apples. See Peša, 'Between Success and Failure.'
328   Pritchett, *Lunda-Ndembu*, 60–61.
329   Mendes Ferrão, *The Adventure of Plants*.

them?'[330] Locally, the introduction of the pineapple is attributed to missionary activity and acts of entrepreneurship. Pineapple cultivation spread widely
through Mwinilunga over the course of the twentieth century.[331] Spurred by
colonial and missionary propaganda, as well as local initiative, approximately
30% of all villages cultivated the crop by the 1940s.[332] Still, pineapples did not
become a staple in the diet, and producers initially did not afford the crop
much importance, or even attention. In 1959, a colonial official lamented this
indifference:

> Unfortunately, vegetables, fruit and coffee are not thought of as serious
> cultivation but to be tried as a side-line, or in the case of fruit, to be plant-
> ed around the village and trust to Providence. Providence does not co-
> operate well with pineapples I found when trying to buy some.[333]

In the first half of the twentieth century, pineapples mainly served to diversify
the dietary and marketing repertoires of producers in Mwinilunga. Grown as a
subsidiary crop, pineapples were not assigned agricultural priority.

Upon realising their commercial potential, however, producers eagerly
seized the opportunity to market pineapples. Initially, commercial pineapple
production was concentrated in the village of Samahina, inhabited by a group
of Ovimbundu immigrants from Angola who had settled in Chief Ikelenge's
area.[334] In 1961, the District Commissioner described that pineapple production was: 'confined to comparatively few people who came from Angola where
they had been trained in the art of fruit husbandry and have been practicing
it fairly successfully for a number of years'.[335] The European population of the
nearby mission station, Kalene Hill, provided a steady market for pineapples.
To meet this persistently high demand, propaganda by missionaries and officials aimed to stimulate pineapple production in Samahina through funds,
and technical and marketing assistance. This, in turn, gave the Ovimbundu
an advantage over other producers. Nonetheless, in the 1950s and 1960s, once
it became apparent that pineapple cultivation and marketing could be economically profitable, other producers throughout the district started planting

330   Schapera, *Livingstone's African Journal*, 228.
331   Interview with Headman Larson Samahina, 17 March 2010, Ikelenge; Interview with Paul
      Fisher, 22 September 2008, Hillwood Farm.
332   (BOD) Richard Cranmer Dening, Mwinilunga District Tour Report, 1947.
333   (NAZ) SEC2/967, C.J. Fryer, Mwinilunga District Tour Report, 27 May 1959.
334   Interview with Headman Larson Samahina, 17 March 2010, Ikelenge.
335   (NAZ) NWP1/2/101 Loc.4919, H.T. Bayldon, North-Western Province Annual Report, 1961.

pineapples as well.[336] The pineapple trade mainly focused on the local market, but occasional surpluses would be sold in Solwezi, especially at Kansanshi. Colonial officials heralded bright prospects for pineapples from the outset, for example in 1955: 'there is no doubt that with a little organisation and initiative the production of this fruit could be worked up into a valuable cash crop'.[337] Because pineapples had a good value/weight ratio, which could withstand high transport costs, the marketing of this 'luxury fruit' gradually stepped up. As a result, traders in the 1950s and 1960s started 'buying up the pineapples to fill up back load capacity to the Copperbelt'.[338] The market for the crop among the urban population of the Copperbelt further stimulated production. Due to the acidity of its soils, Mwinilunga proved more suited to pineapple cultivation than any other part of the country.[339]

It was only after independence, however, that the production and sale of pineapples really took off. Whereas in 1965 43 tonnes of pineapples were marketed, by the 1969–70 agricultural season this figure had risen to 480 tonnes, sold at a price of 3 ngwee per lb.[340] This potential for production enticed the UNIP government to erect a pineapple canning factory in 1969, under the direction of the parastatal G.M. Rucom Industries.[341] Calculations pointed out that at prevailing rates of production, the plant could only be kept running for 29.2 hours per year, but construction of the factory continued despite such warning signs.[342] Although large amounts of pineapples were purchased and processed, the viability of the factory further deteriorated over the course of the 1970s:

> The actual growing conditions, the quality of fruit for canning, the high cost of transport, road conditions and high production costs of the cannery alone, have an extremely negative influence on the profitability of the cannery. According to the calculations of Rucom, the loss per case in 1971–72 was K9.45 (...) By increasing production, the average production cost per case may slightly go down, but the total loss will be higher.[343]

---

336 Interview with Aaron Chikewa, 27 April 2010, Nyakaseya.
337 (NAZ) SEC2/963, R.S. Thompson, Mwinilunga District Tour Report, 26 April 1955.
338 Sardanis, *Africa*.
339 Johnson, *Handbook to the North-Western Province*.
340 (NAZ) LGH5/2/2 Loc. 3611, Marketing of Produce North-Western Province, 23 July 1970; (NAZ) MAG2/17/86 Loc. 199, Pineapples, July 1970.
341 For more on this topic, see Peša, 'Between Sucess and Failure', 285–307.
342 (NAZ) MAG2/5/91 Loc.144, Mwinilunga District Tour Report, 14 May 1969.
343 (NAZ) MAG2/17/86 Loc.199, Pineapples, 24 July 1972.

Temporary closures of the factory first occurred in 1974, and as a result 'farmers preferred to sell their pineapples to the Copperbelt where they received high prices rather than at the factory'.[344] The final closure of the canning factory in the 1980s resulted in the disappearance of a major market for pineapples. Although some traders did continue transporting small amounts of pineapples to urban markets, the bright prospects for the future of pineapple production in Mwinilunga had been dashed. Whilst some producers maintained small fields of pineapples, most were discouraged and abandoned the crop.[345]

The remarkably rapid increase of pineapple production in the 1960s cannot be attributed to price incentives and favourable marketing opportunities alone, although these factors did play an irrefutable role. Pineapples generated large amounts of money. In February 1968, for example, the sale of 66,443 lbs. of pineapples raised K1,328.66.[346] Such cash incentives undoubtedly enticed producers in Mwinilunga, who referred to pineapples as 'yellow gold', to expand their fields. Yet pineapple profits were not only ploughed back into agricultural production but equally stimulated the purchase of consumer goods. Saipilinga Kahongo remembers the period when the canning factory was still in operation as a time when people 'started building good houses and wearing nice clothes'.[347] Nanci Kamafumbu, who cultivated a large pineapple field together with her husband, proudly recalls that she 'had cloth of which other women were jealous' and 'could eat lots of meat every day while others were just eating vegetables'.[348] Production and consumption were thus intricately linked, as the prospect of buying consumer goods with the profits from pineapple sales stimulated agricultural production.

Next to and perhaps more than price incentives, environmental factors and labour compatibility informed the popularity of pineapple cultivation in Mwinilunga. Pineapples are mainly harvested between mid-October and the end of February, and to a lesser extent between mid-April and mid-July. Even if the planting, weeding, and harvesting of pineapples takes place during the rainy season, when labour requirements for other crops are highest, pineapple cultivation still proved compatible with other crops and established methods of agricultural production in the area.[349] This is due to the relatively low labour demand of pineapples. A 1972 report remarked that 'little attention is paid to the pineapple plots during the rains when more labour is needed in the

---

344   (NAZ) Rural Development Seminar: Programme for the Nation, 19 September 1974.
345   This view is based on numerous interviews.
346   (NAZ) MAG2/5/91 Loc.144, Minister of Agriculture Tour North-Western Province, March 1968.
347   Interview with Saipilinga Kahongo, 22 March 2010, Ikelenge.
348   Interview with Nanci Kamafumbu, 19 April 2010, Ikelenge.
349   Interview with John Kamuhuza, March 2010, Ikelenge.

cassava and maize gardens'.[350] The labour requirements for land clearing are minimal under pineapples, as one field can be tilled for up to seven consecutive years. Moreover, the most labour intensive tasks of planting and weeding are commonly completed through the collective effort of work parties. In this case, the owner of a pineapple field asks kin, friends, or other individuals to assist with a predefined task. Assistance is remunerated in cash or kind (with beer, meat, and fish in particular). By resorting to work parties labour demands fall less heavily on a single individual, tasks can be completed rapidly, and pineapple profits are distributed among a larger group. Work parties thus enable the maintenance of larger fields than an individual could tend alone.[351] Furthermore, because pineapples are cultivated in separate fields, usually at some distance from the main agricultural fields, pineapple cultivation does not conflict with that of other crops.[352] This compatibility with other crops lends pineapples their distinct appeal. In terms of livelihood, pineapples are not essential, even though pineapple cultivation can be a lucrative side activity. Pineapples have become a popular crop because they complement rather than jeopardise, food production.

Notwithstanding its attractions, pineapple production faced a number of problems that proved difficult to overcome. Although pineapples can grow throughout Mwinilunga District, the soils in the northwest are most suited to the crop. Production is therefore concentrated in the areas of Chief Ikelenge and Nyakaseya, which are 70 to 100 kilometres removed from Mwinilunga town.[353] Because of the decision to establish the canning factory in the administrative centre of the district, to attract produce from all over the district, transport difficulties proved a serious obstacle. Particularly during the rainy season complications were manifold. Trucks could get stuck in the muddy roads for days at a time, causing loads of pineapples to rot. Because pineapples are a highly fragile and perishable crop, such delays resulted in heavy losses for producers and the cannery.[354] Pineapples are not only perishable once harvested, but they also require delicate handling during transport to avoid bruising the fruit. Packaging and transport remained problematic throughout the period of the cannery's operation, whilst marketing difficulties and price

---

350 (NAZ) MAG2/17/86 Loc.199, Pineapples, 24 July 1972.
351 Peter Geschiere, 'Working Groups or Wage Labour? Cash-crops, Reciprocity and Money Among the Maka of Southeastern Cameroon', *Development and Change* 26, No. 3 (1995): 503–23.
352 This view is based on numerous interviews.
353 Interview with the Agricultural Officer Ambrose Musanda, 1 October 2008, Mwinilunga.
354 This view is based on numerous interviews in Mwinilunga, especially Ntanga, 4 March and 27 October 2010.

fluctuations further contributed to the decline of pineapple production over the course of the 1970s and 1980s.[355]

Pineapple cultivation, in spite of these difficulties, was popular among producers. A survey conducted in 1969 counted 251 pineapple producers in Mwinilunga District, who cultivated a total of 288 acres, with individual field sizes ranging from 0.11 to 8.25 acres. The average yield per acre was 1.5 tonnes, and although this figure does not come close to the optimum yield of 18 tonnes per acre under irrigation and close supervision, yields and profits nevertheless proved satisfactory to the cultivator. If cultivated on fertile red soils, irrigated and properly managed, a pineapple field could yield between K26.30 and K700 per acre.[356] Producers engaged in pineapple cultivation with varying degrees of intensity. Whereas some cultivated pineapples as a side activity, others took to pineapple cultivation as a business enterprise, maintaining large fields, engaging pieceworkers, and making arrangements for transport and marketing. A handful of producers purchased motor vehicles with the profits from pineapple sales, and these vehicles enabled them to independently transport harvests to the canning factory or to urban markets. This, in turn, allowed producers to realise high profits and invest in the expansion of their fields and business enterprises.[357]

Within a general environment of constraint in Mwinilunga, pineapple cultivation provided an opportunity. Throughout the 1950s, 1960s, and 1970s, pineapple production was profitable, yet problems of transport and marketing predominated and caused the demise of the canning factory.[358] Although after the closure of the factory some producers continued to market pineapples at urban markets, this trade at best provided a volatile and limited market outlet for the crop. Pineapple cultivation did spur a degree of material wealth in the area, yet it did not amount to the emergence of a distinct class of rural entrepreneurs. Pineapple cultivation often involved communal effort in the form of work parties, as well as the concerted organisation of transport and marketing. Through work parties and social relationships, the earnings of successful pineapple producers circulated through the community. Individuals who pursued profit too blatantly or who failed to consider the well-being of kin and friends risked being ostracised or becoming the target of witchcraft accusations.[359] Pineapple cultivation was attractive to producers because it could be practised

355   Pritchett, *Friends for Life*.
356   (NAZ) MAG2/17/86 Loc.199, Pineapples, 24 July 1972.
357   Interview with Saipilinga Kahongo, 22 March 2010, Ikelenge.
358   Pritchett, *Lunda-Ndembu*, Chapter 2.
359   The man who claims to have introduced the first pineapple to Mwinilunga District has been attacked by an *ilomba*, which explains his short stature. Interview with Aaron Chikewa, 27 April 2010, Nyakaseya.

as a supplementary activity without jeopardising food security, it did not require a reorganisation of existing agricultural practices. In short, pineapple
cultivation built on the foundations of production in Mwinilunga.[360] Nevertheless, pineapple production faced constraints of transport and marketing,
highlighting the structurally marginal position of Mwinilunga within the Zambian economy at large.

7   The Rationales of Market Production

Why did producers choose to engage in the marketing of crops, agricultural
commodities, or meat? And why did some producers actively refrain from
market participation? These questions have to do with agricultural repertoires,
values, and rationales of production. The cases of beeswax and pineapple
production have outlined some of the opportunities of market production in
Mwinilunga, but have equally pointed towards obstacles. Transport, marketing, and price fluctuations posed major and persistent difficulties, which to a
certain extent could be overcome by producing high-value, low-weight commodities in large quantities.[361] Producers expressed a preference for crops and
commodities that could be produced and marketed, whilst only minimally
upsetting food security and established methods of agricultural production.
Producers secured food by relying on the foundations of production, which
revolved around cassava and hunting. Cash crops compatible with these foundations of production were more likely to catch on than those that conflicted
with existing practices.[362] Examining the boom period of agricultural production and marketing in Mwinilunga in the 1950s further illustrates the rationales
behind market production.
    The late 1940s and 1950s were the heyday of marketing of agricultural
produce in Mwinilunga. High demand from the Congolese and Northern Rhodesian Copperbelt, coupled with internal demand from missions and government, drove up prices and levels of agricultural production.[363] As late as 1949,
the District Commissioner had still regretted that 'the distance from Mwinilunga to the Copperbelt markets would appear to rule out all hope of transporting agricultural surpluses to the labour centres. This may be discouraging,
but the economics of the matter cannot be entirely ignored'.[364] Distance and

360   Interview with John Kamuhuza, March 2010, Ikelenge.
361   Pritchett, *Lunda-Ndembu*.
362   Carswell, 'Food Crops as Cash Crops.'
363   Chabatama, 'Peasant Farming'; Pritchett, *Lunda-Ndembu*, Chapter 1.
364   (NAZ) SEC2/957, A. Stockwell-Jones, Mwinilunga District Tour Report, January 1949.

ensuing transport difficulties seemed to preclude the marketing of all but high-value low-weight cash crops. Nevertheless, the high levels of demand during the 1950s made even the marketing of crops such as beans, maize, and cassava possible, at least temporarily. Various types of produce were marketed during the 1940s and 1950s, both high-value labour-intensive cash crops, such as rice and groundnuts, and bulky staple food crops, such as cassava.[365] Yet rather than being separate, subsistence and cash crop production were closely interwoven. Without the basis provided by cassava cultivation, market participation would not have been possible to the same extent.

By the late 1940s, the District Commissioner of Mwinilunga stated that 'the most remarkable feature of the agriculture of the district is the tremendous surplus of cassava meal, which becomes greater year by year'.[366] The overall market production of crops was based on and pivoted around cassava. Although cassava had been denounced by officials as a 'subsistence' crop, in the 1950s it was marketed in large quantities of up to 600 tonnes per year.[367] Furthermore, cassava production enabled the market production of other crops by freeing up labour and providing a stable basis of livelihood. Cassava did not require expensive input, such as fertiliser or pesticides. The major requirement of the crop was labour input. Although the vent-for-surplus model – which posits that land and labour in rural Africa had remained underutilised prior to capitalist penetration and market production – is too simplistic, there were possibilities to deploy labour more efficiently in Mwinilunga.[368] Cassava production was one such method, evidenced by the fact that large surpluses of cassava could be marketed, whilst 50% of males were reportedly absent due to labour migration.[369] Because cassava production provided a stable basis of food, the crop could function as a foundation for market production. Producers aspiring to step into the market could opt to deploy labour to cassava production and market the surplus, or they could invest their time and energy in other (cash) crops. Cultivators could either expand existing cassava holdings, or keep their cassava fields as a stable source of food and deploy labour to cash crops, such as rice or groundnuts. A survey conducted in the 1940s pointed out that all residents of Mwinilunga maintained a cassava field, and thus possessed a stable source of food.[370] By relying on cassava, producers avoided jeopardising food security. Moreover, when engaging in market production cassava was a favourable crop because its labour demands were low relative to other crops

---

365   Pritchett, *Lunda-Ndembu*, Chapter 2.
366   (NAZ) SEC2/156, R.C. Dening, Mwinilunga District Annual Report on African Affairs, 1949.
367   Peša, 'Cassava Is Our Chief.'
368   Tosh, 'The Cash-crop Revolution'; Austin, 'Resources, Techniques and Strategies.'
369   Peša, 'Cassava Is Our Chief.'
370   (NAZ) SEC2/149, A. Stockwell Jones, Mwinilunga District Annual Report, 1942.

and because labour saving techniques (such as infrequent weeding, harvesting in bits and pieces instead of all at once and cultivating on the same plot of land for multiple years) could be adopted.[371] Significantly, cassava could minimise the effects of market fluctuations. If markets collapsed, producers could step out of the market by scaling down the size of their fields, increasing them once more if circumstances proved profitable again. Cassava could be left in the ground for several years before harvesting, providing a store of food as well as an invisible resource for marketing.[372]

Cassava minimised the risks of market production. Crops such as groundnuts or rice, which required large investments of labour and the adoption of new techniques, never gained widespread popularity in the district. Even if such crops could generate high profits, producers were hesitant to adopt them. Groundnuts, for instance, were promoted by the colonial government due to their high calorie and protein content, and because they could be marketed as cash crops in emerging mining centres.[373] Yet for groundnuts to prosper, they need to be planted in separate fields, preferably of freshly burnt virgin forest or fertile red clay soils. Fields have to be shifted every year, because the groundnut crop depletes soil nutrients rapidly. This proved a heavy strain on limited labour resources. Despite official propaganda for groundnut cultivation – by means of seed distribution, agricultural demonstration and price incentives from traders – groundnut cultivation never developed on a large scale in Mwinilunga.[374] Rather than attributing this to a lack of producer initiative or market sense, labour concerns played a decisive role. Groundnut cultivation required a cumbersome reorganisation of labour patterns for the clearing of fields, whereas the prices offered did not justify these additional labour input.[375] Towards the end of the 1950s groundnut production slumped. The trader Sardanis acknowledged that 'at the proposed price and the prevailing yields farmers could no longer make a living out of groundnuts'.[376] Labour, price, marketing, and environmental factors all played a role in producer preferences towards particular crops. The production of groundnuts was enabled by the stable basis of food provided by cassava. Cash crop production, of groundnuts or pineapples for example, posed less of a risk if producers could fall back on

---

371   Von Oppen, 'Cassava, the Lazy Man's Food.'
372   Pritchett, *Friends for Life.*
373   Moore and Vaughan, *Cutting Down Trees;* see J.S. Hogendoorn and K.M. Scott, 'The East African Groundnut Scheme: Lessons of a Large-Scale Agricultural Failure', *African Economic History* 10 (1981): 81–115.
374   This view is based on a wide reading of archival sources (NAZ) and on numerous interviews.
375   See Tosh, 'The Cash-crop Revolution.'
376   Sardanis, *Africa,* 139.

cassava as a source of food and as a labour saving crop.[377] Labour availability
was a major determinant of market production. Labour resources could be negotiated and allocated within the household, as some members might devote
time to cash crops, whilst others produced a reliable source of food. As long as
a subsistence basis in the form of cassava was secured, a household wishing to
engage in market production' could make a conscious decision to engage labour in the production of cash crops or in salaried employment.[378] Food crops
thus enabled and premised market engagement. Rather than being averse to
market logic, subsistence production – to the contrary – enabled producers to
deploy time and energy in market production. Cassava therefore constituted
the foundation of production in Mwinilunga.

By the end of the 1950s, once demand subsided again, it became evident
that transport costs, marketing difficulties, and levels of production indeed
precluded the sale of low-value high-weight crops from Mwinilunga to distant
urban centres.[379] After a period of intense market involvement and sale of
cash crops, producers in Mwinilunga focused on cassava once again. Even if
cassava could no longer be marketed, it provided a stable and abundant source
of food, making the area a land of plenty and affording producers a degree
of autonomy. Cassava and hunting therefore developed as the foundations of
production in Mwinilunga, adapting to changing circumstances and retaining
their importance over time. These livelihood strategies gained such prominence because they enabled flexibility, autonomy, and mobility, whilst ensuring a stable source of food. Rather than being averse to change, cassava and
hunting adjusted over time.[380] The foundations of production 'are not residues
from a traditional past but products of a contemporary social process'.[381] Cassava and hunting enabled a flexible engagement with government and markets, but equally permitted a degree of autonomy and non-involvement. What
officials discursively labelled agricultural 'conservatism' might equally represent an adaptation or even be an expression of change.[382] The foundations
of production in Mwinilunga have an ideological, as well as a material and
practical basis, changing over time and adapting to factors such as marketing, government policies, and producer preferences. Market involvement
was premised on these foundations of production. Alleged transitions from

---

377   Carswell, 'Food Crops as Cash Crops.'
378   Berry, *No Condition Is Permanent;* Austin, 'Resources, Techniques and Strategies'; though
      see Anita Spring and Art Hansen, 'The Underside of Development: Agricultural Develop-
      ment and Women in Zambia', *Agriculture and Human Values* 2, No. 1 (1985): 60–67.
379   Pritchett, *Lunda-Ndembu.*
380   Kaufmann, 'The Sediment of Nomadism', 235.
381   Ferguson, 'The Bovine Mystique', 647.
382   Turkon, 'Modernity, Tradition and the Demystification', 152.

subsistence to market incorporation, therefore, obscure that 'subsistence' and 'market' production could and did feed into each other.

8   Conclusion

Productive activities in Mwinilunga cannot simply be understood in terms of increasing involvement with the market, as many colonial and post-colonial observers discursively proposed. Market production oscillated rather than being a linear process. Producers involved in marketing cassava or beans in the 1950s, or producing pineapples during the heyday of the cannery, in some cases disengaged from market production several years later. Neither was market involvement a new phenomenon introduced by colonialism or prompted by capitalist forces. Already during the pre-colonial period producers engaged in extensive trade of beeswax and cassava with long-distance caravans, for example. Seemingly to the contrary, the introduction of colonial rule coincided with the demise of the caravan trade and established patterns of agricultural trade. The marketing of agricultural produce decreased initially, only to pick up again in the 1940s and 1950s. Rather than an expression of inertia, the situation that early colonial officials denounced as 'primitive' appears to have been a misguided snapshot. Depending on factors such as pricing, markets, environmental considerations, and labour, market involvement fluctuated throughout the twentieth century. Producers were not merely induced to market their crops by official propaganda or price incentives, but relied on a foundation of production, which reflected norms, values, and attitudes, next to economic considerations and environmental concerns.

Market involvement in Mwinilunga was premised on a foundation of production. This foundation proved flexible and adapted over time, though not in the manner supposed by officials or agricultural experts. Preferences for staple crops shifted from sorghum and millet to cassava, whereas maize failed to gain widespread popularity. Hunting retained practical and ideological importance, despite decreasing game herds, prohibitive legislation, and propaganda for animal husbandry. Although these productive practices have discursively been denounced as 'primitive' or 'traditional' by numerous observers throughout the twentieth century, they are nevertheless 'rooted in real economic interests'.[383] Cassava cultivation facilitated and enabled market production and therefore retained popularity into the present. The foundations of production, as Ferguson points out, are 'not a "traditional" relic, gradually melting away in the face of the modern cash economy', they are instead a 'contemporary institution,

---

383   Ferguson, 'The Bovine Mystique', 667.

finding its points of support in diverse places and drawing on a range of power relations which transcends dichotomies such as "traditional/modern" and
"pre-capitalist/capitalist".[384] As one perceptive colonial official remarked in
the 1930s: 'Agricultural practice is, of course, largely determined by tradition,
but tradition itself reflects past environment, and when a tribe has been long
settled in its country its tradition complies with its requirements'.[385] Methods
of production in Mwinilunga are based on such a foundation, which favours
food security, but is not averse to change. If this foundation of production per-
sists, it is actively made to persist, as 'continuity as much as change must be
created and fought for'.[386] Cassava cultivation and hunting in Mwinilunga continually adapted. Far from being a barrier to 'market integration' or 'development', the foundations of production enabled change.

    This chapter has explored the rationale behind patterns of production. The
foundation of production in Mwinilunga enabled flexibility, autonomy, and
mobility, whilst ensuring a stable source of food. Securing adequate means of
subsistence indeed appeared to be one of the main goals of agricultural production. But rather than seeing subsistence production as 'traditional' or as
a barrier to 'development', relying on a strong basis of subsistence in many
cases served as a step into the market. The foundations of production did not
prevent, but enabled market production. This chapter has sought to demonstrate that discourses about production did not match agricultural practices
in Mwinilunga. Discursive binaries of subsistence and market production
do not hold true, as subsistence and market production proved compatible
and interrelated. Producers sought to partake in the market on terms favourable to and compatible with existing patterns of production, social relationships, and ideological frameworks. Rather than focusing on linear change and
market involvement, concepts such as the foundation of production and a
positive evaluation of subsistence might advance understanding of producer
choices and agency. Crop repertoires, agricultural implements, and patterns
of production have undergone continual change and these changes have been
adapted to suit existing practices and ideological frameworks. Change has
thus been incorporated into a foundation of production in Mwinilunga. Next
to discursive attempts to fix settlements and promote sedentarisation, production and mobility could feed into one another in multiple ways.[387] The following chapter explores these in more detail.

---

384   Ibidem, 669.
385   (NAZ) MAG2/9/3 Loc.170, Ecological Methods in the Study of Native Agriculture in North-
       ern Rhodesia, 27 July 1935.
386   Ferguson, 'The Bovine Mystique', 668.
387   Kay, Social Aspects of Village Regrouping, 80–83.

PHOTO 4   A field of cassava, 2010
            IVA PEŠA

PHOTO 5   Women pounding cassava, 2010
            IVA PEŠA

PHOTO 6   Hunter with his bow, arrow, and spear, 2008
           IVA PEŠA

Mobility

1 Borders, Trade, and Identity

Kwenda kumona nzovu – To travel is to see an elephant[1]

Mobility is so central to the socioeconomic and political strategies of people in Mwinilunga that it even functions as a marker of identity.[2] Proverbs and popular representations link movement to the grasping of opportunities, in hunting, trade, or on the labour market.[3] Contrastingly, people who just 'sit around' the village (*kushakama hohu*) are denounced by their peers and are not considered likely to attain wealth, status, or power.[4] Colonial officials have frequently commented on mobility, describing the Lunda as 'naturally migratory'.[5] Even so, Mwinilunga District has simultaneously been portrayed as a quintessentially rural area, remote, isolated, and by implication immobile.[6] This chapter examines various discourses of mobility during the twentieth century. Furthermore, it relates practices of mobility to patterns of social change. How has mobility within and beyond Mwinilunga served to negotiate social change?

Government officials, scholars, and residents of Mwinilunga have had ambiguous attitudes towards mobility during the colonial and post-colonial period.[7] Officials, on the one hand, displayed a sedentary bias and a desire

---

1   Proverb recorded by Gibby Kamuhuza, Ikelenge, April 2010.
2   Bakewell, 'Refugees Repatriating'; Turner, *Schism and Continuity*.
3   De Boeck, 'Borderland Breccia.'
4   Interview with Justin Kambidimba, 22 October 2010, Ntambu.
5   (NAZ) KSE6/2/2, F.V. Bruce-Miller, Mwinilunga Sub-District Half Yearly Report, 30 September 1923. Stereotypes of Africans as 'naturally migratory' or even 'nomadic' have been pervasive among European observers; see Michael Adas, *Machines as the Measure of Men: Science, Technology, and Ideologies of Western Dominance* (Ithaca: Cornell University Press, 1989); Kopytoff, 'The Internal African Frontier', 7.
6   Wim M.J. Van Binsbergen, 'Globalization and Virtuality: Analytical Problems Posed by the Contemporary Transformation of African societies', *Development and Change* 29, No. 4 (1998): 873–903; Jens A. Andersson, 'Administrators' Knowledge and State Control in Colonial Zimbabwe: The Invention of the Rural-Urban Divide in Buhera District, 1912–80', *Journal of African History* 43, No. 1 (2002), 119–43.
7   See general overview works: Mirjam E. de Bruijn, Rijk A. Van Dijk, and Dick Foeken, eds., *Mobile Africa: Changing Patterns of Movement in Africa and Beyond* (Leiden: Brill, 2001); Frederick Cooper, ed., *Struggle for the City: Migrant Labor, Capital, and the State in Urban Africa* (Beverly Hills: Sage, 1983); Howard, 'Nodes, Networks', 103–30; John Urry, *Mobilities*

to regulate mobility through policy formulation.[8] Colonial officials sought to curtail movement through the demarcation of international boundaries, by means of pass laws, and by encouraging fixed settlements.[9] But even in the post-colonial period mobility was designated as a 'problematic' threat to governmentality, because a mobile population is prone to autonomous behaviour that might undermine administrative control.[10] On the other hand, certain government policies actively encouraged mobility over the course of the twentieth century. The *Pax Britannica*, for instance, facilitated long-distance movement, whereas taxation spurred labour migration to thriving mining towns.[11] Despite its elusive nature, mobility has been positively associated with 'development' or even 'modernity' over the course of the twentieth century.[12] Within a 'modernist narrative', RLI scholars linked labour migration to social change, depicting a progressive transition from migrant labourers to permanent urbanites.[13] Local practices of mobility, however, oftentimes disregarded, or rather creatively circumvented, government policies, subverting official discourses and administrative intentions.[14] Mobility proved hard to constrain and provided room for manoeuvre to those who sought to exploit opportunities to their own advantage.[15] The difficulty to adequately police borders and check illicit cross-border trade constituted an administrative nuisance, posing an outright threat to state power and sovereignty.[16] Mobility could have a variety

---

(Cambridge: Polity, 2007). Also Helmuth Heisler, *Urbanisation and the Government of Migration: The Inter-Relation of Urban and Rural Life in Zambia* (New York: St. Martin's Press, 1974), 1–12.

8   Oliver Bakewell, "'Keeping Them in Their Place": The Ambivalent Relationship Between Development and Migration in Africa', *Third World Quarterly* 29, No. 7 (2008): 1341–58, 1345; Urry, *Mobilities*, 31.

9   See Moore and Vaughan, *Cutting Down Trees*.

10   Urry, *Mobilities*, 49–50, discusses the problem of 'governmentality' over mobile populations.

11   Andrew D. Roberts, *A History of Zambia* (New York: Africana Publishing, 1976).

12   Ferguson, *Expectations of Modernity*; Lucassen and Lucassen, 'The Mobility Transition Revisited', 347–77; De Haan, 'Livelihoods and Poverty', 1–47.

13   Ferguson, 'Mobile Workers', 385–412 and 603–21; see also the works by RLI scholars.

14   Stephen J. Rockel, *Carriers of Culture: Labor on the Road in Nineteenth-century East Africa* (Portsmouth: Heinemann, 2006); Patrick Harries, *Work, Culture, and Identity: Migrant Laborers in Mozambique and South Africa, c. 1860–1910* (Portsmouth: Heinemann, 1994); Paul Nugent and A.I. Asiwaju, eds., *African Boundaries: Barriers, Conduits and Opportunities* (New York: Pinter, 1996).

15   Urry, *Mobilities*, 8: Connects mobility to the unruly 'mob'; see also Bakewell, "'Keeping Them in Their Place"'.

16   Nugent and Asiwaju, *African Boundaries*; Eric Allina-Pisano, 'Borderlands, Boundaries, and the Contours of Colonial Rule: African Labor in Manica District, Mozambique, c. 1904–1908', *International Journal of African Historical Studies* 36, No. 1 (2003): 59–82.

of outcomes, which have been fervently debated by social scientists from the 1950s onwards. Although labour migration could provide access to salaried employment and material gain, it has been connected to processes of proletarianisation, detribalisation, and rural impoverishment as well.[17] This brief overview illustrates that mobility has all too often been understood through polarising dichotomies of urban and rural, development and underdevelopment, or even modernity and tradition.[18]

Yet long-standing practices of mobility in Mwinilunga fundamentally challenge such discursive binaries.[19] The dynamics of movement can be better explained by reference to a historical 'culture of mobility', which encompasses economic, political, and sociocultural spheres.[20] This culture of mobility has shaped reactions to and appropriations of colonial/post-colonial discourses and policies, and is key to studying mobility in its own right.[21] If mobility is viewed as a social (rather than a purely geographical) practice, connections and long-term continuities come to light.[22] Physical movement does not necessarily transform or break social relationships, but might instead serve to

---

17 Arrighi, 'Labour Supplies', 197–234; Nii-K Plange, '"Opportunity Cost" and Labour Migration: A Misinterpretation Of Proletarianisation in Northern Ghana', *The Journal of Modern African Studies* 17, No. 4 (1979): 655–76; Amin, 'Underdevelopment and Dependence', 105–19; Bridget O'Laughlin, 'Proletarianisation, Agency and Changing Rural Livelihoods: Forced Labour and Resistance in Colonial Mozambique', *Journal of Southern African Studies* 28, No. 3 (2002): 511–30; see also RLI work: Richards, *Land, Labour and Diet.*

18 See: De Haan, 'Livelihoods and Poverty'; Bakewell, 'Keeping Them in Their Place.'

19 See: Turner, *Schism and Continuity*; Pritchett, *Lunda-Ndembu.*

20 Zolani Ngwane, '"Christmas Time" and the Struggles for the Household in the Countryside: Rethinking The Cultural Geography of Migrant Labour in South Africa', *Journal of Southern African Studies* 29, No. 3 (2003): 683; Hans P. Hahn and Georg Klute, eds., *Cultures Of Migration: African Perspectives* (Münster: LIT Verlag, 2007).

21 The term 'culture of mobility' refers to a sociocultural outlook, shaped by social, economic, and political experiences of movement in history. This outlook shapes future movements. It encompasses the internal logic of whether a person should migrate, and, if so, when and to which destination. Mobility has to do with local valuations, lifecycles, and strategies. This approach places emphasis on the internal (rather than the external) logics of mobility, and focuses on relations between the migrant and society. See Jeffrey H. Cohen and Ibrahim Sirkeci, *Cultures of Migration: The Global Nature of Contemporary Mobility* (Austin, University of Texas Press, 2011), ix: A culture of migration 'acknowledges the various ways in which migration decisions are made and ... demonstrates how individual decisions are rooted in the social practices and cultural beliefs of a population ... Culture – in other words, the social practice, meaning, and symbolic logic of mobility – must be understood along with economics if we are to understand patterns of migration.'

22 This approach has been inspired by: Englund, 'The Village in the City', 137–54; Andersson, 'Reinterpreting the Rural-Urban Connection', 82–112.

create new ties and enhance existing ones.[23] Mobility in Mwinilunga is part of a multifaceted strategy towards self-realisation, revolving around the 'recruitment of skills'.[24] It has to be understood relationally to agricultural production, hunting, trade, and other livelihood strategies. Through mobility a person could become valued, attaining status, wealth, and respect among peers.[25] Mobility is one of 'the varied struggles of people to value themselves in some publicly demonstrable way'.[26] Mobility could serve to diversify and secure livelihoods, maximise opportunities, build personhood, and give shape to the locality. In Mwinilunga, a culture of mobility has motivated, negotiated, and guided movement, mediating processes of social change.

Two forms of mobility, namely cross-border interactions with Angola and Congo (Chapter 3 Section 1), and labour migration to urban areas (Chapter 3 Section 2), will be explored separately. These patterns of mobility have predominantly been understood within dichotomous frameworks. Cross-border trade has been described as an illegal dodging of the authority of the nation-state, or it has been analysed within a profit-maximising logic.[27] Labour migration has been described as part of a transition from rural poverty to urban industry and civilisation. Alternatively, labour migration might have contributed to rural decay itself.[28] By placing mobility within the socioeconomic, political, and cultural context of Mwinilunga, such binaries can be reframed. Rather than disruptive or transformative, mobility might have been constitutive of society.[29] The rural was not necessarily opposed to the urban, whereas trade with Angola and Congo was part of the full repertoire of trade in the area. Patterns of mobility changed constantly, adjusting to shifting geo-political and

---

23   Kopytoff, 'The Internal African Frontier', 22; Andersson, 'Informal Moves', 375–97.

24   Jane I. Guyer and Samuel M. Eno Belinga, 'Wealth in People as Wealth in Knowledge: Accumulation and Composition in Equatorial Africa', *Journal of African History* 36, No. 1 (1995): 115.

25   Guyer, 'Wealth in People and Self-Realization', 243–65; Karin Barber, 'Money, Self-Realization and the Person in Yoruba Texts', in *Money Matters: Instability, Values and Social Payments in the Modern History of West African Communities,* ed., Jane I. Guyer (Portsmouth: Heinemann, 1995), 205–24; Filip de Boeck, 'Domesticating Diamonds and Dollars: Identity, Expenditure and Sharing in Southwestern Zaire (1984–1997)', *Development and Change* 29 (1998): 777–810.

26   Guyer, 'Wealth in People and Self-Realization', 256.

27   See especially: Janet L. Roitman, 'The Politics of Informal Markets in Sub-Saharan Africa', *The Journal of Modern African Studies* 28, No. 4 (1990): 671–96; MacGaffey, *The Real Economy.*

28   Arnold L. Epstein, 'Urbanization and Social Change in Africa', *Current Anthropology* 8, No. 4 (1967): 275–95; J. Clyde Mitchell, 'The Causes of Labour Migration', *Inter-African Labour Institute Bulletin* 6, No. 1 (1959): 12–47.

29   This argument was made early on by: Watson, *Tribal Cohesion.*

socioeconomic settings, building on established trajectories of movement.[30] In order to understand the rationale behind mobility, the local as well as the regional and national/international context have to be explored.[31] By offsetting the limited opportunities within Mwinilunga, mobility could enable access to lucrative markets for agricultural produce or coveted consumer goods. Furthermore, mobility could provide material gain, strengthen kinship ties, or enhance social status. Mobility equally entailed risk, though. Wild animals, customs patrols, and the troubles of settling into another community all added to the difficulty of travel.[32] In this regard, the persistent attractions of mobility, which are related to issues of livelihood, power, and identity, need to be further explored.

1.1   Historical Roots of Mobility

Movement has been a constantly recurring, integral part of social, economic, and political life in Mwinilunga, according to Bakewell 'an intrinsic part of Lunda society and culture'.[33] Mobility, for example, played a fundamental role in the establishment of Lunda settlements in the area. Migrations from the core Lunda polity, situated further north in Congo, allegedly caused the formation of the Kanongesha and other Upper Zambezi chiefdoms (see Chapter 1).[34] Over the course of the eighteenth and nineteenth centuries, furthermore, movement enabled traders to establish ties with the Angolan coast in order to obtain goods that were scarce locally, such as cloth and guns.[35] This long-distance trade has been described in terms of globalisation, or at least proto-globalisation, discharging the myth that pre-colonial African societies were ever immobile, isolated, or self-contained.[36] Trade was crucial, for instance because blacksmiths were few and far between, so some villages had to rely on distant experts for essential provisions of knives, hoes, and axes.[37] Such trade links, in turn, fostered sociocultural ties, cemented political allegiances, and shaped aspects of identity.[38] Individuals and localities constantly pursued

---

30 See Howard and Shain, *The Spatial Factor.*
31 Achille Mbembe, 'At the Edge of the World: Boundaries, Territoriality and Sovereignty in Africa', *Public Culture* 12, No. 1 (2000): 259–84.
32 See Bakewell, 'Refugees Repatriating'; Pritchett, *Lunda-Ndembu.*
33 Bakewell, 'Refugees Repatriating', 94.
34 Schecter, 'History and Historiography.'
35 Miller, *Way of Death*; Von Oppen, *Terms of Trade.*
36 Prestholdt, *Domesticating the World*; Van Binsbergen, 'Globalization and Virtuality', 875.
37 Coleen E. Kriger, *Pride of Men: Ironworking in 19th Century West Central Africa* (Portsmouth: Heinemann, 1999).
38 Kopytoff, 'The Internal African Frontier.'

and developed connections to regional and national and international entities through mobility. Movement facilitated the exchange of marriage partners between neighbouring or more distant villages, thereby solidifying sociopolitical ties and creating an interlinked vicinage.[39] Moreover, environmental conditions propelled movement among those seeking to secure a dependable livelihood in the area. Villages would commonly shift their location at intervals of 1–20 years, to gain access to good hunting, fishing, or cultivating grounds once their former sites had become depleted.[40] But villages could equally shift as a consequence of political quarrels, witchcraft accusations, or death.[41] The movement of individuals across the landscape allowed some to establish a name for themselves, perhaps as good hunters or renowned experts in medicine or healing.[42] In this sense, mobility could be a means of self-realisation, involving 'the realization of one's individual self-identity, autonomy and responsibility, implying volition, intentionality, individual ambition and self-consciousness' as well as a 'gradual body-centred insertion (...) into the lives of other individuals'.[43] Far from being unique, 'everyone has the potential of self-realization, self-creation'.[44] Through mobility, individuals sought to advance broader socioeconomic and political goals. Mobility could be a strategy, a resource to fulfil material needs and achieve immaterial aspirations.[45] Mobility equally played a role in social connectivity, as movement could confirm and expand inter-personal links. The unity of the chiefdom and even the Lunda polity as a whole was continuously redefined, either strengthened or questioned, through contact and movement.[46] Ceremonies such as initiation rites for boys were organised on a regional rather than on a local level, which gave rise to coherent age sets whose members were spread out over the area.[47]

---

39   Turner, *Schism and Continuity*, 47: 'Villages are rarely built in complete isolation from neighbours ... villages tend to be grouped in discrete clusters, of varying numbers and formation. Each cluster is called ... a "vicinage" ... The vicinage has certain jural, economic and ritual functions.'

40   This pattern has been described by Vansina, *Paths in the Rainforests*.

41   Turner, *Schism and Continuity*, 44–48.

42   De Boeck, 'Borderland Breccia.'

43   De Boeck, 'Domesticating Diamonds and Dollars', 794.

44   Barber, 'Money, Self-Realization and the Person', 213.

45   Michael Barrett, 'The Social Significance of Crossing State Borders: Home, Mobility and Life Paths in the Angolan-Zambian Borderland', in *Struggles for Home: Violence, Hope and the Movement of People,* eds., Stef Jansen and Staffan Löfving (New York: Berghahn, 2009), 85–107.

46   Schecter, 'History and Historiography'; Hoover, 'The Seduction of Ruwej.'

47   Turner, *Schism and Continuity,* 187; C.M.N. White, 'Notes on the Circumcision Rites of the Balovale Tribes', *African Studies* 12, No. 2 (1953): 41–56.

Of course there were limits to individual mobility, as travel involved potential hazards and required preparation, capital, and skills. Nevertheless, mobility always remained an opportunity, as formal boundaries were lacking or could be transgressed.[48] These historical roots have shaped a 'culture of mobility' in Mwinilunga, an outlook that mediates attitudes and responses towards movement.[49] Over time mobility has been deployed as a socioeconomic, political, and environmental strategy to make use of opportunities, enhance livelihoods, and shape identities, to connect the local to the regional and global.

Incoming colonial officials did not necessarily comprehend or appreciate these indigenous patterns of mobility, but rather sought to promote mobility regulations that were underlain by aims of administrative control and economic development.[50] Discourses towards mobility were ambiguous as a result. Under colonial rule, the population of Mwinilunga was denounced as leading a 'nomadic existence'.[51] Paradoxically, discourses portraying a remote, isolated, and immobile population simultaneously gained acceptance.[52] Whereas on the one hand colonial officials associated mobility with a lack of control and hence 'primitivity', on the other hand mobility was seen as a route towards and accompaniment to 'modernity'.[53] In this view, colonialism and capitalism would mark a 'mobility transition', lifting the barriers to movement from purportedly self-contained societies, and thereby spurring unprecedented 'development'.[54] Labour migration, in particular, was understood as part of such a transition from rural impoverishment to urban industry and prosperity. During the twentieth century official attitudes towards mobility remained contradictory. By insisting on large, fixed settlements rather than small shifting homesteads, by demarcating boundaries between chiefdoms and international territories, as well as through census records, passes, and other regulations, movement was restrained. Mobility was encouraged in other respects, though. Travelling became easier due to the cessation of slave raids, whereas government policies promoted labour migration, trade and the marketing of produce, all of which incited forms of long-distance mobility.[55] Discourses of mobility were scrutinised, contested, and altered over time. By examining the case of boundary demarcation between Mwinilunga, Angola,

---

48   Rockel, *Carriers of Culture*; Kopytoff, 'The Internal African Frontier.'
49   See Hahn and Klute, *Cultures of Migration*; Ngwane, 'Christmas Time.'
50   Andersson, 'Administrators' Knowledge'; Allina-Pisano, 'Borderlands, Boundaries.'
51   (NAZ) KSE6/1/2, J.M.C. Pound, Lunda Sub-District Annual Report, 1912–13.
52   Van Binsbergen, 'Globalization and Virtuality.'
53   De Haan, 'Livelihoods and Poverty.'
54   Lucassen and Lucassen, 'The Mobility Transition Revisited.'
55   Such policy ambiguity has been described by Bakewell, 'Keeping Them in Their Place.'

and Congo, the relationship between discourses and practices of mobility will be further explored. Even as the boundary was firmly established on the ground, movement, contact, and trade across the border persisted. This example highlights discrepancies between policies and everyday patterns of movement, and underlines the significance of historical roots of mobility.[56]

1.2   Drawing and Crossing Borders: An 'Imaginary Line' on the Map

Despite the demarcation of increasingly rigid international boundaries and attempts at administrative control, movement across borders – connecting Mwinilunga to Angola and Congo – continued because of historical contacts, a culture of mobility, but also in response to new socioeconomic and political circumstances.[57] This protracted cross-border movement, which defied official intentions, begs further explanation.[58] Colonial boundary demarcations went against existing regional forms of mobility, contact, and identity in Mwinilunga.[59] At least from the seventeenth century onwards, the Lunda polity had forged social, economic, political, and cultural ties across the South Central African plateau.[60] These ties had not been territorially bounded, but were rather embodied through connections between people.[61] Social connectivity, in turn, spurred mobility through the exchange of marriage partners and the establishment of long-distance trade links. Although certain rivers might be referred to as the boundaries of the power base of Chief Kanongesha, his influence was not confined to a clearly delineated area.[62] Instead, power was expressed by the following one could effectively muster.[63] The pre-colonial period was marked by fluidity and movement rather than by bounded units.

---

56   A similar argument has been made by: Harries, *Work, Culture, and Identity*.
57   See: Bakewell, 'Refugees Repatriating'; Von Oppen, *Terms of Trade*; Pritchett, *Lunda-Ndembu*.
58   For parallel cases, see Nugent and Asiwaju, *African Boundaries*.
59   'The Barotse Boundary Award', *The Geographical Journal* 26, No. 2 (1905): 201–04.
60   Schecter, 'History and Historiography'; Hoover, 'The Seduction of Ruwej.'
61   For an explanation of this principle, see Robert D. Sack, *Human Territoriality: Its Theory and History* (Cambridge: Cambridge University Press, 1986).
62   (NAZ) KSE4/1, District Notebooks, 26, 53–55: The Lunga River is regarded as the rough boundary between the areas of Chief Kanongesha and Chief Sailunga. However, (NAZ) NWP1/12/23, R.C. Dening Comments on Vaux Report, 31 May 1954: 'There is no proper geographical basis for divisions between Chieftainships in native custom ... The lack of geographical boundaries between Chiefs in the traditional organisation presents administrative difficulties, and this has been recognised and boundaries have been discussed and agreed to in recent years.'
63   Rather than control over land, 'wealth in people' was sought. See Miller, *Way of Death*; Guyer, 'Wealth in People and Self-Realization.' This point is equally made by Bakewell, 'Refugees Repatriating', 94.

Largely unhindered by prohibitive boundaries, the population connected the area through mobility.[64] The colonial state, however, came equipped with different concepts of territorial rule and attempted to fix the boundaries of areas over which it sought to exert hegemony and control.[65] Not only were individuals tied to boundaried and sedentary villages through census and tax registrars but mobility was also further curtailed by the demarcation of international boundaries that directed movement away from regional routes towards new administrative centres.[66]

Colonial officials made attempts to replace existing practices of social connectivity and mobility with forms of rigid territorial rule, based on ideas of sedentarisation.[67] In 1905, by arbitration of the King of Italy, cartography delineated colonial presence in Mwinilunga, even before physical rule was initiated on the ground in 1907.[68] As the twentieth century progressed, international boundaries, with increasing precision and force, came to separate Mwinilunga District, under British rule in Northern Rhodesia, from neighbouring areas of Portuguese West Africa (Angola) and Belgian Congo (Congo).[69] To satisfy static territorial concepts and for purposes of administrative ease, boundary markers such as 'the ideal Congo-Zambezi watershed' or 'the 24th meridian east' were decided on and etched into the landscape.[70] These artificial markers did not correspond to existing allegiances or patterns of mobility, though. When international boundaries were only just being demarcated, their unsound nature was already recognised. District Commissioner Bruce-Miller stated that 'from a purely native point of view this decision was extremely unwise', but 'boundaries tho' are usually fixed up by our "arm-chair" politicians at home'.[71] Even if their attempts were at times ineffective, the colonial administration increasingly sought to fix and control borders and movement.[72] In order to settle

---

64   Kopytoff, 'The Internal African Frontier.'
65   Timothy Raeymakers, 'The Silent Encroachment of the Frontier: A Politics of Transborder Trade in the Semliki Valley (Congo-Uganda)', *Political Geography* 28 (2009): 55–65; De Boeck, 'Borderland Breccia'; Allina-Pisano, 'Borderlands, Boundaries.'
66   Kay, *Social Aspects of Village Regrouping.*
67   Bakewell, 'Keeping Them in Their Place', 1350.
68   (NAZ) KSE4/1, Mwinilunga District Notebooks.
69   See: Garth Abraham, '"Lines upon Maps": Africa and the Sanctity of African Boundaries', *African Journal of International and Comparative Law* 15, No. 1 (2007): 61–84; John W. Donaldson, 'Pillars and Perspective: Demarcation of the Belgian Congo-Northern Rhodesia Boundary', *Journal of Historical Geography* 34 (2008): 471–93; Jean-Luc Vellut, 'Angola-Congo. 'L'invention de la frontière du Lunda (1889–1893)', *Africana Studia* 9 (2006): 159–84.
70   Abraham, 'Lines upon Maps'; Donaldson, 'Pillars and Perspective.'
71   (NAZ) KSE4/1, Mwinilunga District Notebooks, F.V. Bruce-Miller entry.
72   Nugent and Asiwaju, *African Boundaries.*

population groups and exert control, colonial officials 'strongly recommended that villages within 6 miles of the Border be moved outside a 10 mile area, or the practice of this-side-today-and-over-tomorrow will continue'.[73] In connection to this, in 1912, village heads 'were nearly all told by the District Commissioner that they were to move before next harvesting either nearer the station or else right out of the Territory'.[74] Borders came to separate kindred population groups, formerly connected by the Lunda polity, and this process affected ties of tribute, trade, friendship, marriage, and political alliance.[75] Efforts to establish territorial control through boundary demarcation thus profoundly influenced patterns of social connectivity and mobility in the region.

Notwithstanding the demarcation and policing of boundaries on the ground, cross-border mobility was not checked, and regional social ties continued to matter. Even today, people in Mwinilunga say that 'we and the people in Angola and Congo, we are the same people!'[76] At the beginning of the twentieth century, boundaries were still more like 'imaginary lines' that local residents failed to physically distinguish.[77] Borders appeared arbitrary and until the 1920s it remained unclear whether certain villages were located in Northern Rhodesian, Angolan, or Congolese territory.[78] Under the auspices of various boundary commissions, borders continued to be specified and altered until the 1930s.[79] Nevertheless, borders soon gained 'real material significance', if only because population groups could exploit differences of policy and administrative practice on either side of the border.[80] This resulted in movements back and forth across colonial borders, as people aimed to settle under the administration whose demands were least onerous or whose rule appeared most favourable.[81] Borders never became absolute barriers, but

---

73   (NAZ) KSE6/1/2, J.M.C. Pound, Lunda Sub-District Annual Report, 1912–13.
74   (NAZ) KSE6/2/1, T.M. Lawman, Lunda Sub-District Quarterly Report, 14 October 1912.
75   Bakewell, 'Refugees Repatriating'; 'The Barotse Boundary Award', 202: 'Geographers must certainly regret that the old unfortunate system of bounding political spheres by arbitrary lines, without any reference to physical, political, or ethnological facts, has in this case received a new lease of life.'
76   Interview with John J. Chiyuka, 10 September 2008, Kanongesha.
77   Abrahams, 'Lines upon Maps.'
78   (NAZ) KSE6/5/1, Balunda District Correspondence, C.S. Bellis to W. Hazell, 8 August 1910.
79   The various Boundary Commissions active in the area were as follows: The Anglo-Portuguese Boundary Commission (APBC) in 1915 and 1925, the Anglo-Belgian Boundary Commission (ABBC) in 1911–14 and 1926–33.
80   Allina-Pisano, 'Borderlands, Boundaries', 67.
81   Whereas the occasionally violent nature of Portuguese rule and forced labour in Angola, or the Belgian policies of forced cultivation of crops such as groundnuts and cotton in Congo induced many to settle in Northern Rhodesia, the introduction of taxation by the British propelled others to leave. (NAZ) KDD4/1/1, Mwinilunga Sub-District Indaba

remained 'social, political and discursive constructs', gaining significance in the way they are crossed.[82] Apart from being merely restrictive, 'the border is also a place that gives room to considerable creativity and innovation'.[83] Cross-border mobility built on historical ties established by the Lunda polity, recreating social connectivity in new ways under changing economic and political circumstances.[84] Throughout the twentieth century, cross-border movement continued unabatedly, questioning the hegemony of the state, as District Commissioner Price remarked in 1938:

> Considerable numbers of natives are crossing from Angola and Congo [into Mwinilunga] and are making unauthorised settlements, some in inaccessible places (...) In this area there is a phenomenal amount of coming and going between the villages: people are constantly moving their abodes and taking their children with them over the border when they go to work.[85]

Individuals 'built upon long-established historical patterns of independent migration' shaping the border from below.[86] Through mobility and the crossing of borders the population of Mwinilunga could subvert colonial power, challenge official discourse, and create alternative opportunities, by relying on socio-cultural and historical ties.[87]

Borders remained permeable, even as border posts were erected, customs regulations were enforced, or National Registration cards were insisted on. Far from being formal barriers, borders might more usefully be regarded as conduits or corridors of opportunity.[88] As has been remarked for the Benin-Nigeria border, 'interstices are full of power, and (...) border residents are fully aware how they can use their interstitial power – their borderland advantage – to

Chiefs, 5 September 1925. See also Mwelwa C. Musambachime, 'Escape from Tyranny: Flights Across the Rhodesia-Congo Boundary', *Transafrican Journal of History* 18 (1989): 147–59.

82   David Newman and Anssi Paasi, 'Fences and Neighbours in the Postmodern World: Boundary Narratives in Political Geography', *Progress in Human Geography* 22, No. 2 (1998): 187; De Boeck, 'Borderland Breccia.'

83   Raeymakers, 'The Silent Encroachment', 63.

84   Bakewell, 'Refugees Repatriating'; Pritchett, *Lunda-Ndembu*.

85   (NAZ) SEC2/953, N.S. Price, Mwinilunga District Tour Report, 7 November 1938.

86   Andersson, 'Informal Moves', 382; Martin Doevenspeck, 'Constructing the Border from Below: Narratives from the Congolese-Rwandan State Boundary', *Political Geography* 30 (2011): 129–42.

87   Pritchett, *Friends for Life*, especially Chapter 6.

88   Nugent and Asiwaju, *African Boundaries*.

benefit themselves'.[89] In Mwinilunga in 1963, it could still be stated that 'the territorial boundary in this district is merely a line on a map as far as Africans are concerned; they come and go across borders the whole time'.[90] What motivated people to move from one territory to the other and how did cross-border movement influence the exercise of territorial hegemony? The practice of cross-border trade can further illustrate the meaning of the border in Mwinilunga. By crossing borders, the inhabitants of Mwinilunga built on historical connections and patterns of mobility, yet equally responded to new circumstances.

1.3   Cross-Border Trade: Calico, Cigarettes, and Cassava

Throughout the pre-colonial period, regional and long-distance trade have been of paramount importance in Mwinilunga.[91] Links of tribute connected Mwinilunga to the wider Lunda polity, circulating goods such as ivory, cloth, slaves, and salt through the region.[92] Building on these ties of tribute, long-distance trade contacts with the Angolan coast gained significance in the eighteenth and nineteenth centuries. Portuguese traders and African middlemen, such as the Ovimbundu, carried guns, cloth, and liquor, which they would exchange locally for cassava, game meat, ivory, rubber, or even slaves.[93] The colonial administration attempted to check these contacts through the demarcation of international boundaries and restrictive legislation, redirecting trade towards new administrative centres within the territory. Nevertheless, regional trade continued to clandestinely cross borders.[94] Historical trade routes, adapting to changing circumstances, influenced colonial and post-colonial forms of cross-border contact.[95] What explains the ongoing attractions of cross-border trade? How did a culture of mobility in Mwinilunga shape responses to a variety of local, regional, national, and international markets? Apart from economic dynamics, these questions address issues of identity and politics.

Even at present, the representation of borderland areas, such as Mwinilunga, as marginal, fluid, and therefore threatening to the hegemony of the state,

---

89   Donna K. Flynn, '"We Are the Border": Identity, Exchange, and the State Along the Benin-Nigeria Border', *American Ethnologist* 24, No. 2 (1997): 312.
90   (NAZ) LGH5/4/2 Loc.3615, Mwinilunga District Security Scheme, 1963.
91   Vansina, *Paths in the Rainforests*; Miller, *Way of Death*; Von Oppen, *Terms of Trade*.
92   Schecter, 'History and Historiography'; Bustin, *Lunda Under Belgian Rule*.
93   Miller, *Way of Death*; Von Oppen, *Terms of Trade;* Gordon, 'The Abolition of the Slave Trade', 915–38.
94   Bakewell, 'Refugees Repatriating'; Pritchett, *Lunda-Ndembu*.
95   MacGaffey, *The Real Economy*, 21.

retains traction.[96] Until far into the colonial period, border areas remained loosely administered and difficult to control.[97] During the opening decades of the twentieth century villages located along the border formed a refuge for various 'undesirables', smuggling ivory, rubber, guns, and slaves.[98] Although 'control over people's movements (...) was crucial to and even constitutive of the colonial state in southern Africa',[99] individuals could subvert state power through mobility and cross-border trade. Trade was often motivated by economic considerations as 'differences in national economic policies, regional resources, and monetary currencies make borders lucrative zones of exchange and trade, often illicit and clandestine'.[100] Nevertheless, the rationale for trade went beyond economics, encompassing struggles over power and identity.[101] The example of the rubber trade during the first half of the twentieth century illustrates how trade could enable economic gain as well as a degree of political autonomy, by defying borders and questioning administrative control.

1.3.1   Trading Rubber: Borders, Profit, and Autonomy
The rubber trade built on the precedent of the pre-colonial long-distance trade, relying on established trade networks and following similar routes into Angola.[102] Existing trade routes and networks were adapted in order to bypass official controls and maximise profit. In 1912, an official commented on the lucrative rubber trade:

> The prices offered for rubber in Angolaland are very high indeed, and in the face of the law parties are constantly taking rubber where they can (...) The collection of rubber is a particularly easy way of attaining wealth, and natives return with immense loads of calico, powder and guns.[103]

Economic motives played a role, as before 1930 trade goods obtained from the Portuguese were cheaper and more readily available than those at stores in

---

96   De Boeck, 'Borderland Breccia'; Doevenspeck, 'Constructing the Border', 140; Scott, *The Art of Not Being Governed*.
97   See examples in Macpherson, *Anatomy of a Conquest*.
98   See Pritchett, *Lunda-Ndembu*.
99   Allina-Pisano, 'Borderlands, Boundaries', 61; Bakewell, 'Keeping Them in Their Place', 1343–44.
100   Flynn, 'We Are the Border', 313.
101   MacGaffey, *The Real Economy*, 2.
102   Von Oppen, *Terms of Trade*.
103   (NAZ) KSE6/1/2, J.M.C. Pound, Lunda Sub-District Annual Report, 1912–13.

Mwinilunga. Crossing the border to Angola was a constant attraction, induced by price differentials and the availability of markets.[104] In spite of boundary demarcations and official measures of control, such as tariffs and customs, 'devious routes for crossing frontiers came into being and facilitated the development of unrecorded transborder trade'.[105] Because of their marginality, border areas proved difficult to control, as colonial officials grudgingly admitted:

> [People] seem to think how by going to the lower Luizabo [Angola] they are entering no man's land, where they will be left alone by the whiteman (…) Their position between the two borders as well as the rubber trade with all the wealth it begins is the cause of the difficulties they make and their independent ways (…) So long as these border people are so rich in powder and guns, and calico can be obtained so easily for rubber the Wandembo villages within close reach of the border will remain independent in their actions.[106]

In some cases, cross-border trade could be a means of asserting political autonomy, or even expressing resistance to the state.[107] The rubber trade, involving unregulated cross-border movements, and providing access to guns and gunpowder, was thus cause for serious administrative concern. Colonial officials made attempts to limit cross-border contacts, but trade could not simply be checked, especially given the porous nature of the border:

> The areas where most of the indigenous rubber grows are principally situated on the Congo and Portuguese borders, where, on account of the uncertainty of the border line, the country was the last to be occupied, and where the natives are least amenable to control. On the British side of the border they are still rather wild and intractable and the presence of traders not all of whom are scrupulous, tends to keep them so. The fact that such traders used to buy in the Congo and Portuguese West Africa and to smuggle the rubber into British Territory (and encouraged the natives to do the same) tended to create friction and to keep the border in unrest.[108]

---

104   For a more recent example, see De Boeck, 'Borderland Breccia.'
105   MacGaffey, *The Real Economy*, 21.
106   (NAZ) KSE6/2/1. J.M.C. Pound, Lunda Sub-District Quarterly Report, 14 April 1913.
107   MacGaffey, *The Real Economy*, 10.
108   (NAZ) A3/28/2 Loc.3996, L.A. Wallace Report, 4 September 1909.

Rather than being barriers or beacons of government hegemony, borders continued to be corridors of opportunity, enabling trade, profit, and autonomy.[109] Portuguese traders offered high prices for rubber and supplied ample trade goods in return. This enticed numerous individuals to go rubber collecting in Congo, carry the rubber to Angola for sale, and return to Mwinilunga 'staggering under the weight' of trade goods.[110] Trade was not only economically profitable but could be a social and political strategy as well, to evade administrative control and establish, transform, or strengthen cross-border networks of kinship, ethnicity, and trust.[111] Borders provided residents of Mwinilunga with distinct opportunities, District Commissioner MacGregor aptly observed in 1909, as 'in them they see ramparts beyond which we [government officials] may not at present operate, and behind which they are safe and secure'.[112] Building on historical precedents, the rubber trade responded to the new political setting of colonial rule. In its pursuit of profit, the rubber trade sought to evade restrictive administrative policies and assert autonomy. Despite its attractions, the rubber trade gradually died out towards the end of the 1920s. This was due to a combination of factors, including disruptions of the caravan trade, changes in international terms of trade, the establishment of colonial rule, and boundary demarcations.[113] Yet the rubber trade was only one example of a wide variety of cross-border contacts, which continued throughout the twentieth century. Older patterns of long-distance trade were replaced by other forms of triangular trade relations, connecting Mwinilunga, Congo, and Angola.

1.3.2   Circuits of Trade: Enterprise, Legality, and the State

Cross-border trade is, as Roitman has argued, the product 'of historical networks of trade and accumulation which stagnate, thrive, and mutate as new resources are accessed, and as national and global economic factors change'.[114] Indeed, through constant adaptation and reconfiguration, trade with Angola and Congo remained important, if not essential, to Mwinilunga throughout the colonial and post-colonial period.[115] The terms of trade fluctuated

109   Flynn, 'We Are the Border.'
110   (NAZ) KSE6/2/1, J.M.C. Pound, Lunda Sub-District Quarterly Report, 14 April 1913.
111   Roitman, 'The Politics Of Informal Markets', 675.
112   (NAZ) KSE6/5/1, G.A. MacGregor, Balunda District Monthly Report, March 1909.
113   Von Oppen, *Terms of Trade*; Bakewell, 'Refugees Repatriating.'
114   Roitman, 'The Politics Of Informal Markets', 693.
115   Pritchett, *Friends for Life*; Bakewell, 'Refugees Repatriating'; De Boeck, 'Borderland Breccia.'

continuously, according to political and socioeconomic dynamics.[116] It is exactly this constant fluctuation that could be exploited to the benefit of traders and other enterprising agents. Traders would cross and creatively circumvent borders in order to take advantage of higher prices, lower tax rates, or better access to trade goods and resources in other areas. Markets in Angola and Congo competed with, but also stood in relation to, national markets and 'the resulting plurality of markets entails the constituents of a multitude of power bases who are constantly defending and appropriating channels of accumulation'.[117] The extent and variety of trade in the 1950s, described by Mwinilunga's District Commissioner, was notable:

> The markets of the Congo are by far the closest and most profitable for the pedicle area [north-western Mwinilunga], and I am quite prepared to see livestock sold over the border, bringing good prices (...) Angolans (Europeans and Africans alike) come across generally with loads of fish and return with general provisions and cloth (+gunpowder and ammunitions trade). Vehicles from the Congo bring cigarettes (Belga) and other small goods (penknives and the like), and return with either meat or poultry, which fetch a good price on the Congo line of rail only 50 miles away.[118]

The term 'straddling' captures the multiplicity of cross-border trade, which 'involves dispersing risk by balancing alternative types of resources', in a 'struggle for opportunities for accumulation'.[119] The significance of cross-border trade has to be seen in relation to other forms of trade, as well as livelihood strategies such as agriculture, hunting, and salaried employment.

Trade could be enticed to cross borders due to economic opportunities, state policies, and more generally by aspirations of material gain and the desire to secure profitable livelihoods.[120] In case marketing opportunities for certain crops or commodities proved more favourable in Angola, producers in Mwinilunga would be quick to take advantage of the discrepancy. The rubber trade is just one example of this trend, as cross-border trade continued throughout the post-colonial period. Even during the civil war in Angola (1975–2002) consumer

116   Von Oppen, *Terms of Trade*.
117   Roitman, 'The Politics of Informal Markets', 694.
118   (NAZ) SEC2/966, M.A. Hinds, Mwinilunga District Tour Report, 22 September 1958.
119   Roitman, 'The Politics of Informal Markets', 678, 685.
120   MacGaffey, *The Real Economy*, 16.

goods and food supplies were transported from Mwinilunga across the border, realising high profits despite the risks involved.[121] Traders from Mwinilunga also ingeniously exploited price differentials and the ready availability of consumer goods in Congo. The 1948 annual report noted that hawkers 'do a flourishing trade, more especially in the sale of second-hand clothing of excellent quality, which is imported from the Congo in very substantial quantities and retailed at moderate prices'.[122] From the 1930s onwards, livestock made up a large proportion of cross-border trade. Chickens, goats, sheep, and to a lesser extent cattle, were traded from Mwinilunga to the Congolese urban centres, where a fowl would catch up to 25/- in 1960.[123] The local drop in animal figures was blamed directly on 'extravagant selling in the mining areas of the Independent Katanga Province (...) The traffic of fowls to the Congo mining townships had increased and no doubt the developing food shortages will sharpen an already keen market'.[124] Mobility and cross-border trade provided opportunities for material gain as well as a means to exploit disparities in national policies.[125] Trade traversed the boundaries between legal and illegal, regulated and unregulated, European and African, Mwinilunga, Angola, and Congo.

Cross-border trade has to varying extents been designated as illegal by government officials, because it so frequently evades taxation, tariffs, or customs, and thereby deprives the state of revenue.[126] As far as it sought to circumvent border patrols and cumbersome government regulations, trade was problematic from an administrative point of view. Measures of official control, attempting to regulate trade, never proved completely effective.[127] Clandestine trade and smuggling across the border, only rarely intercepted by customs control, flourished and found a lucrative, high-risk, niche throughout the twentieth century, despite restrictive legislation.[128] The extent of transactions and their level of organisation could be considerable, but small-scale tactics were equally common, as the District Commissioner remarked in 1939:

121 Bakewell, 'Refugees Repatriating'; Art Hansen, 'Once the Running Stops: The Social and Economic Incorporation of Angolan Refugees into Zambian Border Villages' (Unpublished PhD Thesis, Cornell University, 1977); Pritchett, *Friends for Life.*
122 (NAZ) SEC2/155, Western Province Annual Report, 1948.
123 (NAZ) MAG2/18/3, North Western Province, Stocktaking Programme of Work, 1960–1.
124 (NAZ) NWP1/2/102 Loc.4919, E.L. Button, North Western Province Annual Report, 1960.
125 See Andersson, 'Informal Moves.'
126 MacGaffey, *The Real Economy,* 12, 19, 31.
127 See: Raeymakers, 'The Silent Encroachment'; Flynn, 'We Are the Border.'
128 De Boeck, 'Domesticating Diamonds and Dollars'; Bakewell, 'Refugees Repatriating.'

There is a large amount of cloth smuggling going on between Belgian Congo and this district. One man was found to have as much as 19 blankets, 174 yards of calico and several coats, trousers, singlets, pullovers, shawls – He was not a hawker but had received practically the whole of two years pay in cloth. The customs amounted to £2.[129]

Opposition between legal and illegal, formal and informal, national and cross-border trade was not absolute. It is only in relation to formal channels of trade that cross-border trade gained significance.[130] As Roitman points out, 'informal spheres are *defined* by the state', whilst binary categories of 'formal' and 'informal' are in fact symbiotic.[131] Examples from Mwinilunga clearly illustrate this, as in the 1960s profits made illicitly through livestock trade with Congo could be deployed to pay government taxes, thereby blurring the divide between formal and informal:

It was well known that many people in the District depended on selling chickens, sheep and goats in the Congo for money with which to pay tax and buy clothes. In view of this the council had last year imposed a levy of 2/6 a head on a person trading with stock across the border, but now many innocent people had been arrested.[132]

Levies and fines imposed to punish traders often failed to effect the desired outcome, as policies to regulate trade were highly ambiguous. Because various circuits of trade were thoroughly intertwined, distinctions between 'legal' and 'illegal' trade proved difficult to make and impossible to enforce.

Even if they did not always fully endorse it, government officials regularly turned a blind eye to cross-border trade.[133] As the example of trade with and through Congo in the 1950s shows, cross-border trade could assume regulated, even officially sanctioned, forms. The profitability of Congolese markets was recognised by the colonial administration, with certain reservations: 'The nearest market for agricultural produce is the Belgian Congo, which is a foreign country and cannot therefore be regarded as an assured market as import controls can, and probably would apply'.[134] In the late 1940s and early 1950s, even low-value high-weight crops such as cassava could find a lucrative market in

---

129   (NAZ) SEC2/953, N.S. Price, Mwinilunga District Tour Report, 21 May 1939.
130   MacGaffey, *The Real Economy*, 2.
131   Roitman, 'The Politics of Informal Markets', 679, 683.
132   (NAZ) LGH5/1/3 Loc.3604, Lunda-Ndembo Native Authority Council, 5 November 1960.
133   For illustrative examples, see Pottier, *Migrants No More*.
134   (NAZ) SEC5/214, Murray, Mwinilunga Crown Land Block, 23 December 1958.

Congo. The eagerness with which producers and traders from Mwinilunga supplied Congolese markets caused a degree of distress, reflected in the 1957 annual report: 'cassava was fetching such a high price in the Congo markets that
growers pulled out mature and immature plants alike and carried them off to
the Congo to make the easy money that was going there'.[135] Yet despite such
concerns, the transport of cassava, maize, and other foodstuffs through the
Congolese railway system gained official approval. When the demand for food
on the Northern Rhodesian Copperbelt peaked, in particular in the 1947–51
period, cassava and maize were transported from Mwinilunga via Mutshatsha
in Congo by rail back into Northern Rhodesia to Ndola.[136] This trade proved
attractive to producers, traders, and the government alike. During this period,
Congolese traders would buy up any surpluses left in Mwinilunga:

> Approximately 1,000 bags of surplus cassava were available, and Mr. Raft-
> opoulos a trader in Belgian Congo, was permitted by the Director of Civil
> Supplies to buy this surplus (for export to the Congo) in the Mwinilunga
> District. The cassava was bought for cash at 9/10th of a penny.[137]

This trade linked African and European traders from Mwinilunga and Congo
together in an intricate network. The District Commissioner Mwinilunga noted in 1955 how he:

> ... met three prosperous Africans whose main source of income accrues
> from buying meal and selling it to a Greek trader at Mutshatsha in the
> Congo at a landed price of 3 ½ d per lb. Transport of the meal is car-
> ried out by W.F. Fisher and Company Limited and paid for by the African
> traders.[138]

Although it proved possible to export foodstuffs from Mwinilunga to Congo
in the 1940s and 1950s, trade could not be sustained at such high levels once
demand in urban centres slumped.[139] Transport costs, customs regulations,
and currency problems all militated against more regularised trade. In the
early 1960s, political upheaval in the Congolese province of Katanga further
disrupted trade relations. In spite of being officially sanctioned during the

---

135   (NAZ) NWP1/2/78 Loc.4913, F.R.G. Phillips, Western Province Annual Report, 1957.
136   See Pritchett, *Lunda-Ndembu.*
137   (NAZ) SEC2/958, K. Duff-White, Mwinilunga District Tour Report, 19 June 1951.
138   (NAZ) SEC2/963, R.S. Thompson, Mwinilunga District Tour Report, 26 April 1955.
139   See: Vickery, 'Saving Settlers', 212–34; Sardanis, *Africa.*

1940s and 1950s, cross-border trade reverted to its illicit status afterwards.[140] This example does illustrate that cross-border trade did not necessarily have to be opposed to government interests, but could in some cases be propelled by official directives.

Differences in currencies highlight the difficulty to effectively control cross-border trade through rules and regulations. Currency differences between Angola, Congo, and Zambia could and often were manipulated to the advantage of traders. At the time of Congolese independence and the secession of Katanga, 'the devaluation of the Katanga franc had rendered trade with Katanga hazardous'.[141] Political upheaval threatened established circuits of trade, which connected Mwinilunga to Congo, as the Native Authority remarked in 1963: 'Hitherto, the district had relied on the traditional trade with Katanga for its wealth. This was now dead. The Congo franc was now worthless and the district must look to other sources of wealth'.[142] Furthermore:

> Tax collection had been retarded as a result of the serious decline of trading with the Congo which used to be the main occupation and source of income for the people (...) Many locals who normally trade and shop in the Congo have ceased to do so and, in doing so, have found themselves burdened with considerable amounts of francs which can now no longer be exchanged at the stores in Mwinilunga nor with passing traders heading for the Congo markets.

Nevertheless, trade was flexible and the severity of the Congolese crisis even proved beneficial in some respects. Deflation of the franc adversely affected exports, but consumer goods became cheaper:

> Export trade across the Border with the people in the Congo has been reduced, but due to deflation of the Congo currency quite a lot of purchases have been made by people on our side as even after customs duty has been paid material is generally much cheaper.[143]

These examples illustrate the futility of separating 'legitimate' from 'illegitimate' trade, as regulated and unregulated trade, legislation, currency, taxation,

---

140   Pritchett, *Lunda-Ndembu*.
141   (NAZ) MCD1/3/29, North Western Province, Provincial Team Meeting, February 1964.
142   (NAZ) LGH5/1/3 Loc.3604, Lunda-Ndembo Native Authority Council, 17 September 1963.
143   (NAZ) NWP1/2/105 Loc.4920, H.T. Bayldon, Mwinilunga District Annual Report, 1963.

enterprise, and personal initiative were all interrelated in various and overlapping circuits of trade.

In spite of official restrictions and political strife, trade with Congo and Angola continued after independence. Zambian relationships with neighbouring countries were profoundly influenced by political upheaval, civil disruption and war in both Congo and Angola.[144] The position of Zambia as a 'frontline state' raised issues of security and border control.[145] The prolonged civil war in Angola influenced economic relationships with Mwinilunga. Regular trade was disrupted and the Benguela railway was shut in 1975, but game meat, foodstuffs, and guns continued to be exchanged across the border clandestinely and some traders even managed to prosper due to such transactions.[146] Trade with Congo was particularly significant during the pineapple boom in Mwinilunga, when large amounts of pineapples were sold in Congolese towns.[147] Even at present such trade continues, as dried fish and game meat are illicitly imported from Angola to Mwinilunga.[148] Trade across the border has remained attractive throughout the twentieth century, both complementing and serving as an alternative to trade networks within Mwinilunga and Zambia.[149] The enduring nature of cross-border trade, even in a context of profound socioeconomic and political change, is striking. Why did trade relationships between Mwinilunga, Angola, and Congo retain such pertinence?

Because the state defines legitimate economic activity, 'illegitimate' cross-border trade has predominantly been understood as an act of opposition to the state, an attempt to avoid its authority and control.[150] Previous examples, however, have shown that legitimate and illegitimate trade cannot be clearly distinguished, as there are many points of intersection. Cross-border trade

---

144 In the case of Congo, events following Congolese independence and the secession of Katanga in 1960–61, after the installation of Mobutu in 1965–67, and again in 1977–78 after Katangese gendarme attacks, influenced security and international trade relationships, and caused population movements into Mwinilunga District. In the case of Angola, there was a prolonged civil war, starting with the struggle for national liberation and continuing with UNITA-MPLA strife throughout the 1960s–1990s. Population flows from Angola into Mwinilunga increased after 1966 and again in 1976, peaking during the 1980s.

145 See Larmer, *Rethinking African Politics*; Sue Onslow, ed., *Cold War in Southern Africa: White Power, Black Liberation* (London: Routledge, 2009).

146 For overviews of the Angolan civil war, see: David Birmingham, *Frontline Nationalism in Angola and Mozambique* (London: Africa Research, 1992); William Minter, *Apartheid's Contras: An Inquiry into the Roots of War in Angola and Mozambique* (London: Zed Books, 1994).

147 See Chapter 2.

148 Bakewell, 'Refugees Repatriating'; Pritchett, *Friends for Life*.

149 Pritchett, *Friends for Life,* Chapters 6 and 8.

150 MacGaffey, *The Real Economy,* 10; Raeymakers, 'The Silent Encroachment', 55.

does not necessarily challenge the state, but rather finds its significance in relation to the state.[151] Crossing the border, as MacGaffey notes, might be 'people's spontaneous and creative response to the state's incapacity to satisfy the[ir] basic needs'.[152] In some cases, cross-border trade could generate higher returns than 'formal' channels of trade, and this might in part explain its dynamics. Nevertheless, cross-border trade cannot simply 'disengage' from the state, as Roitman points out: 'one can hardly disengage from something without engaging in something else – this involves the cultivation of relationships to access resources, and hence confrontation with bases of power and authority which control these assets'.[153] In order to pose an alternative to 'formal' or national trajectories of trade, cross-border trade had to build upon social relationships, bonds of kinship, ethnicity, and trust, which could have historical roots but which were also recreated and reinvigorated to respond to new circumstances.

Ties of kinship and Lunda ethnicity, as well as historical commercial linkages and trade routes, served to enable, encourage, and sustain cross-border trade.[154] The interrelationships between Mwinilunga, Angola, and Congo proved multiple, complex, and enduring. The 1948 Annual Report captured some of the complexity of these relationships:

> The contact maintained by both branches of the Lunda here (Ndembo and Lunda) with their fellow tribesmen in Portuguese and Belgian Territory continues as strong as ever (...) Expanding industries in the Congo attract an increasing number of people from this District, but there is still an appreciable flow of population in the opposite direction (...) The natural areas for trade of this District are Angola and the Congo. Trade with the Congo is two way, consumer goods being brought here from Mutshatsha and other places on the railway line, and native produce being taken there from this district. There appears to be practically no export from here to Angola (...) There is however a good deal of hawking of fish and trinkets from Angola over here.[155]

Ties of kinship, ethnicity, and historical contact functioned as social assets, facilitating access to wealth and power.[156] Cross-border trade and social

---

151   See: Roitman, 'The Politics of Informal Markets'; MacGaffey, *The Real Economy*.
152   MacGaffey, *The Real Economy*, 12.
153   Roitman, 'The Politics of Informal Markets', 691.
154   Bustin, *Lunda Under Belgian Rule*.
155   (NAZ) SEC2/155, R.N. Lines, Mwinilunga District Annual Report, 1948.
156   MacGaffey, *The Real Economy*, 32–33; Roitman, 'The Politics of Informal Markets', 689.

connectivity to Angola and Congo could even function as an alternative to national trade networks. For the case of Congo, MacGaffey has explained that:

> The common cultural background and loyalties of those from the same
> ethnic group, and the mutual obligations and emotional bonds of family
> and kinship, all operate to promote the trust, accountability and sense
> of moral responsibility that is lacking in the official economy and that
> contributes to its irrationality and unpredictability.[157]

In this sense, historical ties of Lunda kinship and cross-border trade could remain functional, even in the changing context of colonial/post-colonial rule.
Within the Zambian nation-state Mwinilunga District is relatively remote
vis-à-vis the Copperbelt, line-of-rail, and Lusaka (see Photo 7).[158] Because the
area is poorly connected by transport networks and far removed from major
markets, alternative avenues of cross-border trade have become attractive. The
historical roots of mobility, connecting the area to Angola and Congo, have
enabled people in Mwinilunga to benefit from regional trade opportunities,
even as circuits of trade have constantly changed to adapt to socioeconomic
and political realities. In the process, ties of identity and affiliation have been
recreated and given new meaning, leading 'to new sources of wealth and power
which are accessed through established channels (i.e. kin- or community-
based relationships) and, in turn, utilised in ways which restructure (but not
eliminate) old institutions and social relations'.[159] Ties of identity and kinship
linking Mwinilunga to Angola and Congo did not just influence cross-border
trade, though. Building on a culture of mobility, notions of identity, belonging
and power were constantly negotiated/renegotiated in this borderland area.
The movement of people, goods and ideas through Mwinilunga thereby served
to shape the locality itself.

1.4   *Moving Across Borders: Migration, Identity, and the State*
Mwinilunga has all too often been referred to as a marginal area – by colonial
observers, UNIP officials, journalists, and scholars alike.[160] In part this has to do
with its geographically remote location, 800 kilometres removed from Lusaka
and more than 400 kilometres removed from the Copperbelt. Whilst Mwinilunga shares an international boundary with Angola and Congo, it is removed

---

157   MacGaffey, *The Real Economy*, 32.
158   See especially: Pritchett, *Lunda-Ndembu*.
159   Roitman, 'The Politics of Informal Markets', 686.
160   Pritchett, *Friends for Life*; Bakewell, 'Refugees Repatriating.'

from the economic and political heartland of Zambia by long transport hauls and poor infrastructure (see Photo 8). But the area's marginality goes beyond physical remoteness and hinges on its relationship to the state. The district does not enjoy favourable resource endowments, possessing neither particularly fertile land nor proven mineral deposits. Consequently, the area has never been central to government or capital interests in the twentieth century.[161] An early colonial official deplored Mwinilunga as 'the most elementary place in this elementary country'.[162] Other officials did occasionally argue that the area held potential, for example having soils suitable for the cultivation of pineapples or for cattle ranching, but this potential remained largely unrealised.[163] The North-Western Province as a whole has been labelled the 'Cinderella Province', holding vast but underutilised potential for development.[164] This marginality of the area, however, did not have to be merely negative. Loose state control and latent economic potential created interstices of opportunity, which could and have been used to the benefit of its residents.[165] In this sense, mobility could challenge and redefine the marginal position of Mwinilunga.[166] According to Tsing, marginality could be 'both the constraining, oppressive quality of cultural exclusion and the creative potential of rearticulating, enlivening, and rearranging the very social categories that peripheralize a group's existence'.[167] In the area of Mwinilunga, mobility constituted a means to cope with marginality, renegotiate its terms, and engage the state and markets on favourable terms.[168] Through mobility the local was recreated and given new vitality.[169] Mobility could be a resource, enabling access to a range of opportunities and allowing strategies of self-realisation. Exactly because of the location of Mwinilunga on the border with Angola and Congo, mobility and trade could provide favourable and lucrative prospects, enabling the alleviation of national marginality by seeking and strengthening regional or international ties. In this respect, issues of identity, mobility, and power interacted.

---

161 Pritchett, *Lunda-Ndembu*; Kakoma, 'Colonial Administration.'
162 (BOD) MSS Afr S 779, Theodore Williams letters, My Dear Mother, Mwinilunga, 21 May 1913.
163 This view is based on a wide reading of archival sources (NAZ).
164 Von Oppen, 'Cinderella Province', 11–46.
165 For a parallel, see Flynn, 'We Are the Border.'
166 See the case studies in De Bruijn, Van Dijk, and Foeken, *Mobile Africa*.
167 Anna L. Tsing, 'From the Margins', *Cultural Anthropology* 9, No. 3 (1994): 279.
168 A similar argument has been made by Bakewell, 'Refugees Repatriating'; Pritchett, *Lunda-Ndembu*.
169 Appadurai, *Modernity at Large*.

Over the course of the twentieth century, mobility has reinvigorated and
given new meaning to regional allegiances, some dating as far back as the
foundation of the Lunda polity itself.[170] Yet ethnic affiliation and notions of
Lunda identity did not remain static.[171] Rather, ethnicity and historic symbolic régimes are continuously 'reinvented in a new setting. New opportunities are appropriated by a system which is itself transformed by the changing
context'.[172] Identity appeared to be situational and fluid, not absolute, fixed or
well defined.[173] This is illustrated by the remarks of a colonial officer in 1963,
dealing with economic ties, political allegiance and population movement in
the area of Mwinilunga:

> The paramount Chief of the Lunda people lives in the Congo and is a
> cousin of Mr. Tshombe. Ethnographically the tribal centre is Katanga;
> economically it is Katanga and the Copperbelt of N. Rhodesia and po-
> litically, whatever the future has to offer. The territorial boundary in this
> district is merely a line on a map as far as Africans are concerned; they
> come and go across the borders the whole time. Therefore there will be
> no such thing as "African refugees" from ANGOLA or CONGO. It will
> merely be a case of living with one lot of relatives instead of another, and
> it is going on all the time.[174]

Patterns of mobility and aspects of identity thus appeared to be thoroughly intertwined, as the movement of people, goods, and ideas continued to go back
and forth across the border.[175] Through mobility, people could take advantage
of favourable conditions and policies on either side of the border. Thereby, the

---

170   See especially: Bustin, *Lunda Under Belgian Rule*; Pritchett, *Friends for Life*.
171   Ethnicity is understood here as a flexible form of allegiance and identity, in accordance
      with John Comaroff and Jean Comaroff, *Ethnography and the Historical Imagination*
      (Boulder: Westview Press, 1992), 50: 'Contrary to the tendency, in the Weberian tradition,
      to view it as a function of primordial ties, ethnicity always has its genesis in specific his-
      torical forces, forces which are simultaneously structural and cultural.' 52: 'Not only may
      its character change over time ... but the way in which it is experienced and expressed
      may vary among social groupings according to their positions in a prevailing structure
      of power relations.' 60: 'While ethnicity is the product of specific historical processes, it
      tends to take on the "natural" appearance of an autonomous force, a "principle" capable
      of determining the course of social life.'
172   Roitman, 'The Politics of Informal Markets', 687.
173   See the discussion in Bruce J. Berman and John M. Lonsdale, *Unhappy Valley: Conflict in
      Kenya and Africa* (Athens: Ohio University Press, 1992); see also Max Gluckman, 'Tribal-
      ism in Modern British Central Africa', *Cahiers d'études africaines* 1, No. 1 (1960): 55–70.
174   (NAZ) LGH5/4/2 Loc.3615, Mwinilunga Security Scheme, 1963.
175   De Boeck, 'Borderland Breccia'; Bakewell, 'Refugees Repatriating.'

marginality of Mwinilunga and the lack of government control in the border area could be turned into distinct assets. By moving across the border, individuals could navigate beyond the control of the state, take advantage of economic opportunities, and access markets, whilst redefining notions of identity.[176] Mobility was motivated by prospects of material gain and opportunities towards self-realisation.[177] In the area of Mwinilunga, mobility could be a profitable strategy, evidenced by incessant migratory flows, long-distance trade, and flexible ties of identity and belonging.[178] This gave shape to a historical and adaptive culture of mobility in the area. Moreover, strategies of mobility could question the legitimacy of the national state in favour of alternative regional alliances.[179]

1.4.1   Population Movement, Refugees, and Identity

Historical ties of Lunda identity, connecting Mwinilunga and neighbouring areas of Angola and Congo, remained strong throughout the twentieth century.[180] As the District Officer perceptively remarked in 1958, population movements and issues of identity were closely intertwined: 'the fundamental reason is the tribal and blood relationships and so long as the boundary cuts across the tribal pattern so long the people will come and go'.[181] This constant movement gave rise to administrative concerns, as: 'stabilisation of population in a border area has particular difficulties. But underlying all is the lack of desire to stabilise where people are undecided which side of the border is their true home'.[182] Throughout the colonial and post-colonial period, people in Mwinilunga continued to deploy ties of Lunda identity, in conjunction with mobility, trade, and population movement. For other borderland settings, it has been argued that 'the ambiguities of identities in borderlands can also be strategically played upon to forge, reformulate, and even mobilize ethnic identity to advantage'.[183] When taxation was first introduced in Mwinilunga at the beginning of the twentieth century, for example, numerous individuals, families,

---

176   See: Allina-Pisano, 'Borderlands, Boundaries'; Raeymakers, 'The Silent Encroachment.'
177   Guyer, 'Wealth in People and Self-Realization.'
178   Bakewell, 'Refugees Repatriating.'
179   See especially: Larmer and Macola, 'The Origins', 471–96.
180   Bustin, *Lunda Under Belgian Rule*; Pritchett, *Friends for Life*; Wele, *Kaunda and Mushala Rebellion*.
181   (NAZ) SEC2/966, W.D. Grant, Mwinilunga District Tour Report, 24 October 1958.
182   (NAZ) SEC2/956, J.S. Jones, Mwinilunga District Tour Report, 28 August 1948.
183   Robert R. Alvarez and George A. Collier, 'The Long Haul in Mexican Trucking: Traversing the Borderlands of the North and South', *American Ethnologist* 21 (1994): 607, quoted in Flynn, 'We Are the Border', 314.

and even entire villages changed their place of residence, based on judgments of which territory would offer more favourable terms of settlement.[184] The District Commissioner described such population movement aptly:

> It is plain that the community building to-day, have vividly before them the possibility of circumstances arising to make them decide to again remove to-morrow (...) into Portuguese Territory where, only across the border and within a few miles of this place a Tom Tiddlers ground exists, as yet unvisited by the nearest official (...) Miles and miles of country are available across the border where there is positive immunity from the visits of interfering officials (...) There slave trading prospers; guns, caps and powder are to be had (...) the worrying tax gatherer is unknown, and work, work, work is not the national war cry.[185]

Through mobility, individuals could evade onerous administrative demands, taking advantage of differential policies across the border.[186] Especially to those seeking salaried employment, Congo provided attractions.[187] Congolese towns became known as 'a bourne from where no traveller returns', not only because of the favourable rates of pay and conditions of work in urban areas such as Kolwezi or Élisabethville (Lubumbashi) but moreover because 'Africans are not barred by race or creed from advancing to well paid posts, mostly in the technical and artisan grade'.[188] Depending on prevailing opportunities, government policies, personal preferences, and an assessment of risks, crossing the border could be an attractive alternative to residence within Mwinilunga.[189] On the other hand, there were numerous 'push' factors, driving migration from Congo and Angola into Mwinilunga, as this 1939 example shows:

> The chief reason is the unpopular compulsory cotton growing in the Congo Belge which although now abandoned has given place to equally unpopular compulsory cultivation of groundnuts; the second reason is

---

184 This process has been described in Macpherson, *Anatomy of a Conquest*; Pritchett, *Lunda-Ndembu*.

185 (NAZ) BS2/199 IN2/1/3, G.A. MacGregor, Balunda District Monthly Report, January 1909.

186 See Allina-Pisano, 'Borderlands, Boundaries'; Musambachime, 'Escape from Tyranny.'

187 An overview of mining development in Congo is provided by: John Higginson, *A Working Class in the Making: Belgian Colonial Labour Policy, Private Enterprise, and the African Mineworker, 1907–1951* (Madison: University of Wisconsin Press, 1989).

188 (NAZ) SEC2/962, R.S. Thompson, Mwinilunga District Tour Report, 16 September 1954.

189 Bakewell, 'Refugees Repatriating.'

the alleged unpopular administration in Angola and the third and least important reason is the reduction of tax in this area to 6/-.[190]

Population movement was facilitated by ties of Lunda identity, which were reinvigorated in the process. Lunda identity not only facilitated mobility but also enabled individuals to challenge national policies and ensuing marginality in powerful ways.

Population movements could foster and bolster ties of Lunda identity. Large-scale population movements were set in motion because of political upheaval and civil war in Angola and Congo, especially from the 1960s to the 1990s.[191] Although the international community labelled this as a movement of 'refugees', the flow of population might more usefully be interpreted in the context of long-established practices of cross-border mobility, ties of kinship, and Lunda identity.[192] In 1962, for example, it was noted that 'events in Katanga resulted in an upheaval on our border and an influx of refugees, Cabinet ministers and fleeing elements of the Katangese military forces, including mercenaries (...) The steady flow of immigrants mainly from Angola continues'.[193] This mobility, and the resultant influx of population into Mwinilunga, was seen as problematic by officials. Shelter, food, and other necessities had to be provided, causing administrative and logistical difficulties, whilst straining limited resources.[194] Population movement could equally have more positive consequences, though. Headmen and chiefs welcomed the additional population to their villages as this boasted their prestige and made their villages eligible for government services, since the allocation of schools, hospitals, and other social facilities depended on the number of inhabitants in an area.[195] Furthermore,

---

190   (NAZ) NWP1/2/10 Loc.4898, N.S. Price, Mwinilunga District Tour Report, 1 March 1939.
191   See especially: Art Hansen, 'Once the Running Stops: Assimilation of Angolan Refugees into Zambian Border Villages', *Disasters* 3, No. 4 (1979): 369–74; Art Hansen, 'Refugee Dynamics: Angolans in Zambia 1966 to 1972', *International Migration Review* 15, No. 1/2 (1981): 175–94; Paul J. Freund and Katele Kalumba, 'Spontaneously Settled Refugees in Northwestern Province, Zambia', *International Migration Review* 20, No. 2 (1986): 299–312; Oliver Bakewell, 'Repatriation and Self-settled Refugees in Zambia: Bringing Solutions to the Wrong Problems', *Journal of Refugee Studies* 13, No. 4 (2000): 356–73; Oliver Bakewell, 'Repatriation: Angolan Refugees or Migrating Villagers?', in *Refugees and the Transformation of Society: Agency, Policies, Ethics and Politics*, eds., Philomena Essed, Georg Frerks and Joke Schrijvers (New York: Berghahn, 2004); Bakewell, 'The Meaning and Use of Identity Papers.'
192   Bakewell, 'Refugees Repatriating.'
193   (NAZ) NWP1/2/102 Loc.4919, H.T. Bayldon, North Western Province Annual Summary, 1962.
194   Bakewell, 'Keeping Them in Their Place', explains policy views that depict migration as problematic.
195   Pritchett, *Friends for Life*, Chapter 8; Bakewell, 'Refugees Repatriating.'

migrants and refugee camps formed a market for the sale of foodstuffs.[196] Bartering or selling food for cash, goods, or in exchange for labour services, to visitors, travellers, and migrants, had been a long-established practice.[197] At the beginning of the twentieth century, the District Commissioner remarked that

> Any surplus [of food] they may have is eagerly bought (and usually paid for by labour only) by the continual stream of immigrants from Angola and the Congo. These new arrivals are usually quite content to work for their food or until such time as they can get their own gardens established.[198]

All throughout the post-colonial period food – predominantly maize – was sold to refugee camps across the North-Western Province, in Zambezi and Solwezi Districts, and especially to Meheba refugee camp, which was opened in 1971.[199] On a smaller scale and more informally, migrants who settled outside of refugee camps would buy up the standing crop of cassava or perform work in established gardens throughout Mwinilunga.[200] In a labour and cash strapped environment, this additional income and productive force proved particularly advantageous. A further potential benefit to the economic well-being of the area accrued from the presence of the immigrant population. International donor aid could be redistributed, or even commercially resold, by those dispensing these resources. Consequently, rather than serving as relief for the deprived, food aid, blankets, and cooking utensils proved lucrative items of trade.[201] Although officials regarded refugees as problematic, there were equally beneficial consequences to their presence in Mwinilunga, especially from the perspective of the local population. Issues of identity and belonging among migrants were important in this respect. Through ties of Lunda identity, migrants legitimated their right of settlement and claims to land in Mwinilunga. Numerous migrants, labelled 'self-settled refugees', settled outside of refugee camps, merged in with the local population and refrained from returning to their country of origin upon the cessation of conflicts. Bakewell has questioned whether identity is 'handheld' (the nationality noted on a national registration card) or 'heartfelt', and to what extent the two correspond.[202] Due to incessant mobility, issues of identity and belonging remained uncertain and

196   Hansen, 'Once the Running Stops.'
197   Von Oppen, *Terms of Trade.*
198   (NAZ) KSE6/2/2, F.V. Bruce-Miller, Lunda Sub-District Quarterly Report, 30 June 1922.
199   Hansen, 'Once the Running Stops'; Bakewell, 'Refugees Repatriating.'
200   Pritchett, *Friends for Life.*
201   Ibidem, Chapter 8.
202   Bakewell, 'The Meaning and Use of Identity Papers.'

fluid. This flexibility was already acknowledged by the District Commissioner in the 1920s:

> A large proportion of the new people were not born in this territory, so when Angola is blessed with a more efficient administration it is possible that a number will return to the home of their ancestors: although, if questioned now, one and all would aver that they had shaken the dust of Angola off their feet for ever.[203]

Mobility strengthened ties of Lunda identity among the inhabitants of Congo, Angola, and Mwinilunga. The option of movement – the 'return' of migrants – was always open, as ties of identity and belonging remained negotiable. In the 1950s, the District Commissioner remarked:

> Immigrants from the two neighbouring territories [Angola and Congo] pass through the District on their way to the urban labour markets and sometimes return to settle here [Mwinilunga] but, in many cases, they retain ties and allegiances in their old home areas, which results in protracted visits or removals.[204]

In the 1990s, ties of kinship, allegiance, and ethnicity still appeared to be situational and permeable, rather than fixed or bounded. How did issues of identity and mobility interact? In what ways could ties of Lunda identity serve to question the authority of the Zambian nation-state?

1.4.2   The Politics of Belonging: Crafting and Challenging the Nation-State

In the area of Mwinilunga, the flow of population in various directions created an uncertainty of identity and belonging. This ultimately complicated the issue of national identity, which gained heightened significance immediately before and after independence.[205] The support that voters in Mwinilunga lent to ANC, the relative underdog party, during the run-up towards independence in the 1950s and 1960s, was motivated by resistance to the dominant and exclusionary nationalist discourse of UNIP.[206] Whereas UNIP was seen as a party of 'foreigners' defending a distant national interest, support for ANC

---

203   (NAZ) KSE6/1/4, F.V. Bruce-Miller, Mwinilunga Sub-District Annual Report, 31 March 1921.
204   (NAZ) NWP1/2/37 Loc.4903, D. Clough, Mwinilunga District Annual Report, 1950.
205   See Larmer, *Rethinking African Politics*; Peša, 'We Have Killed This Animal Together.'
206   See: Larmer and Macola, 'The Origins'; Larmer, *Rethinking African Politics*; David C. Mulford, *Zambia: The Politics of Independence, 1957–1964* (Oxford: Oxford University Press, 1967); Macola, *Liberal Nationalism*; Wele, *Kaunda and Mushala Rebellion.*

was locally justified in ethnic terms, referring to the historical Lunda polity and geopolitical linkages fostered through mobility.[207] In this connection chiefs in Mwinilunga in 1962 deplored that:

> They are very sorry and ashamed they are hated by other Chiefs, Government and UNIP because that they are the Chiefs who have made A.N.C. to be strong. Even so they said they can not stop it because they are the people of Mwantiyamvwa not from Nyasaland (...) We dislike Mr. Kaunda. Kaunda is a Nyasalander [*sic*].[208]

At independence, voters in Mwinilunga did not envision a change in their economically and politically marginal position through UNIP's nationalism.[209] On a national level, Lundas were demographically, economically, and politically in an inferior position vis-à-vis Bemba, Nyanja, and Tonga speakers.[210] Consequently, grievances concerning development were mixed with ethnic grudges: 'up to now there are any roads, any buses running your subjects? Any Hospitals? For your information, we your sons here cannot get promoted unless you are Bemba speaking worker [*sic*]'.[211] Poverty and lack of development, which had been the main political rallying points before independence, appeared to change only slightly under the UNIP government.[212] The Credit and Marketing Supervisor in 1964 protested that 'as loans were concerned the district had been forgotten for about ten years'.[213] After independence, popular expectations were not met as development funds lagged behind, planned projects were not completed, or loans were not released: 'The result is that the public is dissatisfied and get the feeling that the government is inefficient'.[214] Local

---

207 Larmer and Macola, 'The Origins'; Pritchett, *Friends for Life*; Bustin, *Lunda Under Belgian Rule*.

208 (UNIPA) ANC2/7, Bernard Mashata, Report of ANC Mwinilunga to National President ANC, 28 June 1962.

209 Pritchett, *Friends for Life*; Larmer and Macola, 'The Origins'; Wele, *Kaunda and Mushala Rebellion*.

210 See Macola, *Liberal Nationalism*; Larmer, *Rethinking African Politics*; and compare to Daniel N. Posner, 'The Political Salience of Cultural Difference: Why Chewas and Tumbukas Are Allies in Zambia and Adversaries in Malawi', *American Political Science Review* 98, No. 4 (2004): 529–45.

211 (UNIPA) UNIP5/3/1/57, Sons on the Copperbelt to all Chiefs North-Western Province, Prior to 1969 Referendum.

212 This opinion has been expressed in numerous interviews, for example John Kapayipi, 17 March 2010, Ikelenge.

213 (NAZ) LGH5/1/3 Loc.3604, Mwinilunga Rural Council, 9 July 1964.

214 (NAZ) LGH5/2/8 Loc.3613, North-Western Province, District Secretaries Conference, 9 September 1965.

grudges were powerful as well as persistent, and in 1967 the North-Western Province development committee even wondered:

> ... why the Colonial Government had hated this Province (...) [and why] this hangover continues today (...) this Province has suffered too long and we expect tremendous changes in this Government (...) The important thing is to fashion the machinery which will respond to the aspirations of the people quickly, otherwise we are running the risk of having Government overthrown because people will not be satisfied with merely having discussions and nothing coming out from it. The effort of building our beloved young nation should in no way fall short of expectations, and so that the livelihood and standard of living of the common man should be improved as fast as possible.[215]

Instead of looking towards the national centre, some sought fortune in regionalism, by strengthening ties to Angola and Congo.[216]

A number of politicians even expressed the desire to 'reunite' the 'Lunda Empire', as the District Commissioner had already remarked in 1952: 'The Lunda have long cherished a hope that Lundaland, now arbitrarily divided between three European powers, would one day be reunited'.[217] By imagining a broader Lunda polity and enhancing linkages to Angola and Congo, in other words by envisaging a different balance of power for the future, the locality of Mwinilunga could subvert its perceived national marginalisation. Whereas UNIP denounced cross-border ties to Congo and Angola, ANC politicians actively fostered links, particularly to Katangese counterparts.[218] Geopolitical linkages fed into local affairs through mobility, as ANC politicians from Mwinilunga travelled to Katanga to raise funds for their campaigns: 'Mr. John Njapau has been delayed by the Katanga President for some valuable goods to help ANC activities'.[219] Although the formal resurrection of the Lunda Empire remained but a vague possibility for most, and was not necessarily actively pursued or aspired, the linkages between ANC and Katanga enhanced the

---

215   (NAZ) CO4/1/3, Development Committee Minutes, North-Western Province, 9 October 1967.
216   This has been described by: Bakewell, 'Refugees Repatriating'; Pritchett, *Friends for Life*; Wele, *Kaunda and Mushala Rebellion;* Kennes and Larmer, *The Katangese Gendarmes.*
217   (NAZ) SEC2/961, R.C. Dening Mwinilunga District Tour Report, 21 November 1952.
218   Macola, *Liberal Nationalism*; Larmer, *Rethinking African Politics*; Larmer and Macola, 'The Origins'; Matthew Hughes, 'Fighting for White Rule in Africa: The Central African Federation, Katanga, and the Congo Crisis, 1958–1965', *The International History Review* 25, No. 3 (2003): 592–615.
219   (UNIPA) ANC2/7, Bernard Mashata, ANC Mwinilunga to National Secretary, 1 August 1961.

popularity of the party locally.[220] Apparently, allegiances in Mwinilunga were more easily stirred by events in Katanga, than by the remote national cause that revolved around the Copperbelt and line-of-rail areas, where UNIP had its strongholds.[221] Ties to neighbouring areas, formerly united through the Lunda polity, seemed to offer more favourable prospects, economically, socially and politically, than connections to the Copperbelt or Lusaka. Through regional and international linkages, the population of Mwinilunga was able to propose an alternative view that offered the prospect of a less marginal future.[222] The demographically, economically and politically weak position of Lundas on a national level strengthened feelings of non-incorporation throughout Mwinilunga, which in turn triggered political opposition, cross-border affiliations and hopes of a 'Lunda Empire'. Through mobility, as well as ties of identity and belonging, inhabitants of Mwinilunga challenged the exclusionary nationalism of UNIP, by means of oppositional affiliation to ANC.[223] Social, economic and political dynamics thus interacted with patterns of mobility, feeding into issues of identity, belonging and ideas of the nation.

This pattern of looking across the international borders for support, rather than towards the national government, continued long after Zambia obtained independence. In Mwinilunga, connections to Angola and Congo remained alive in political thought, but also in population movement and trade.[224] During the Angolan civil war nationalist leaders crossed the border to Mwinilunga, whilst MPLA soldiers had regular contact with chiefs in the area.[225] Cross-border ties could threaten the hegemony of the Zambian nation-state, causing concerns, as expressed by a UNIP official in 1975:

> The behaviour of the freedom fighters in Angola (M.P.L.A.) was discussed as it was revealed that quite many of them come to visit certain chiefs and that one chief has been given a landrover. This behaviour was found dangerous in that it could easily bring division in that area of our country which in the long run would encourage disloyalty towards the state.[226]

---

220 John Japau, 'New Plan for North-Western Rhodesia to Join Lunda with Angola': 'We, of the Lunda Empire, have decided to do away with this government. We are to join together with the people of Angola and Katanga to form up a great force but we don't want fighting we want peace.' Quoted in Patrick M. Wele, *Zambia's Most Famous Dissidents: From Mushala to Luchembe* (Solwezi, 1995), 157.

221 See: Larmer, *Rethinking African Politics*; Macola, *Liberal Nationalism.*

222 Bakewell, 'Refugees Repatriating'; Pritchett, *Friends for Life.*

223 Larmer and Macola, 'The Origins.'

224 Hansen, 'Once the Running Stops'; Bakewell, 'Refugees Repatriating.'

225 (UNIPA) UNIP1/2/13, UNIP Tour of North-Western Province, Addendum, 27 May 1975.

226 (UNIPA) UNIP1/2/35, UNIP National Council Reports, 1975.

The 'Mushala rebellion' during the late 1970s formed a further threat, especially as its leader Adamson Mushala proposed plans to resurrect the 'Lunda
Empire' in defiance of the Zambian nation-state.[227] Although the government
made attempts to forcefully subdue this movement and solidify support for the
ruling party, this was only partially effective, as the 1977 annual report admits:

> The Province has enjoyed peace and calm during the period under re-
> view, in spite of the Mushala terrorist gang which has been terrorising
> the people (...) for the last two years now. However, our fighters from the
> Zambian National Defence Forces have done the best they can to con-
> tain the situation (...) the Party in the Province is enjoying the support of
> the masses though not very many have joined the Party but appreciating
> the efforts of the Party in forging ahead in development.[228]

Because of its geographically remote location and its marginal position within
Zambian politics, opposition to the nation-state in Mwinilunga continued to
be expressed through cross-border movement and ties of Lunda identity. Even
in a changing context, historical ties and notions of identity could be reinvented, given new meaning and instrumentalised through mobility. Being Angolan,
Zambian or Congolese depended on the setting and the accruing benefits, and
consequently issues of identity and political allegiance remained fluid and negotiable. Social connectivity, bolstered by mobility, gave substance to issues of
identity and political allegiance.
    Mobility could be motivated by social relationships, but also by an assess-
ment of economic and political opportunities. Through marriage, trade and
migration individuals established ties beyond their homestead and village.
These ties, at various moments, might serve to strengthen or question existing
power relations, but the socioeconomic and political context in turn equally
influenced mobility and interpersonal ties.[229] Patterns of social connectivity
could be called upon as a safety net in times of difficulty or could be a resource
to take advantage of opportunities. As the examples of cross-border trade, refugee movements and nationalism have shown, 'one can hardly disengage from
something without engaging in something else'.[230] Through mobility the inhabitants of Mwinilunga District could question the authority of the national

227 Larmer and Macola, 'The Origins'; Wele, *Kaunda and Mushala Rebellion*; Pritchett, *Friends
     for Life*.
228 (UNIPA) UNIP1/2/21, Annual Report for the North-Western Province, 31 December 1977.
229 Howard, *The Spatial Factor*.
230 Roitman, 'The Politics of Informal Markets', 691.

state and avert prevailing marginality, by taking advantage of opportunities across the border. They could merely do so, however, by fostering ties of Lunda identity which served as alternative channels of opportunity through cross-border movement.

1.5   *Conclusion*

Mobility has hitherto overwhelmingly been interpreted as a 'transformative' act, either leading to 'development' and 'modernity' or more negatively to 'rural decay'.[231] This chapter has sought to step away from such discursive binaries, adopted by colonial officials, government agents and scholars alike. Instead, it has focused on the 'culture of mobility' in Mwinilunga, illustrating the ways in which mobility is central to Lunda social, economic and political organisation.[232] Through mobility the population of Mwinilunga could subvert state power, challenge official discourse and create alternative opportunities by relying on sociocultural and historical ties. Rather than foregrounding economic or political motives for mobility, this chapter has pointed out the sociocultural dispositions that have informed dynamics of mobility. Mobility could be about social connectivity and self-realisation, as 'migrants are social actors making decisions about their futures'.[233] Rather than transforming society, mobility could serve to constitute it – by building and strengthening villages and connecting them to local and regional networks and allegiances. In this sense, individuals and entire villages might 'move while retaining their structure'.[234]

In Mwinilunga mobility, cross-border movement and issues of identity are thoroughly intertwined. Importantly, mobility has historical roots and builds on existing forms of sociocultural organisation, such as Lunda affiliations with Angola and Congo. Through mobility the local could be recreated and given new vitality. Cross-border movement has, for example, challenged the marginality of Mwinilunga and proposed alternative associations to the Zambian nation-state. In this sense, mobility has been deployed as a resource, an avenue towards wealth and a strategy to gain access to opportunities. Given the limitations of local markets, cross-border trade and mobility provided attractive alternatives. Next to cross-border movement and trade, labour migration has been a prevalent form of mobility and social connectivity in the twentieth century. Labour migration equally built upon the historical culture of mobility in Mwinilunga, by making use of and enhancing existing opportunities.

---

231   Andersson, 'Informal Moves'.
232   Bakewell, 'Refugees Repatriating', 94.
233   Cohen and Sirkeci, *Cultures of Migration*, 14.
234   De Boeck, 'Borderland Breccia.'

PHOTO 7   Early roads and transport, 1950s
NATIONAL ARCHIVES OF ZAMBIA, MWINILUNGA DISTRICT NOTEBOOKS

PHOTO 8   Mudyanyama Bridge, 1950s
NATIONAL ARCHIVES OF ZAMBIA, MWINILUNGA DISTRICT NOTEBOOKS

2   Labour Migration: Work, Mobility, and Wealth

Labour migration, due to its sheer scope, is a form of mobility that has attracted particular attention in the twentieth century.[235] Although it builds upon
and interacts with existing forms of long-distance movement in Mwinilunga,
such as hunting and trade, labour migration has been attributed 'transformative' capacities in the historiographical debate.[236] Labour migration in Southern and Central Africa and its effects on migrants and on rural sending areas
have been fervently debated.[237] Most influentially, the RLI has linked labour
migration to processes of social change.[238] On the one hand, scholars have
interpreted labour migration within a 'modernist narrative', 'a metanarrative
of transition, in which tribal rural Africans were swiftly becoming modern,
urban members of an industrial society'.[239] Such narratives have associated
labour migration with 'modernity', 'development' and 'progress'.[240] Even if
labour migration could provide access to salaried employment and material
gain, it has, on the other hand, been connected to more negative processes of
'proletarianisation', 'detribalisation' and rural decay.[241] In these debates, polarising dichotomies of urban and rural, development and underdevelopment,
modernity and tradition have all too often been applied.[242] Rather than
through such dichotomies, this chapter argues that labour migration can more
usefully be analysed as the outcome of sociocultural dispositions, as a means
towards self-realisation.[243] Labour migration could serve to diversify and secure livelihoods, maximise opportunities, build personhood and give shape to
the locality. By focusing on how labour migration emerged from the culture of
mobility in the area, connections and long-term continuities come to light.[244]

---

235   Turner's work comments elaborately on labour migration; see Turner, *Schism and Conti-
      nuity*. Also, Pritchett, *Lunda-Ndembu*.
236   Ferguson, *Expectations of Modernity*; Andersson, 'Reinterpreting the Rural-Urban
      Connection.'
237   For an influential debate, see: Ferguson, 'Mobile Workers'; Macmillan, 'The Historiogra-
      phy of Transition', 681–712; Potts, 'Counter-urbanization', 583–609.
238   See: Epstein, 'Urbanization and Social Change', 275–95; Mitchell, 'The Causes of Labour
      Migration', 12–47.
239   Ferguson, *Expectations of Modernity*, 33.
240   More generally: Lucassen and Lucassen, 'The Mobility Transition Revisited'; De Haan,
      'Livelihoods and Poverty.'
241   See: Arrighi, 'Labour Supplies in Historical Perspective'; Amin, 'Underdevelopment and
      Dependence'; Richards, *Land, Labour and Diet*.
242   Andersson, 'Administrators' Knowledge'; De Haan, 'Livelihoods and Poverty.'
243   Inspiration for this approach has been taken from: Andersson, 'Re-interpreting the Rural-
      Urban Connection.'
244   Englund, 'The Village in the City.'

This chapter therefore examines the causes, motives and effects of labour migration in and from Mwinilunga.

Whereas in the historiography labour migration has mainly been understood as the outcome of a transformative process of social change, long-term and distinctly local dynamics have shaped the practice in significant ways. At the start of the twentieth century patterns of labour migration were perhaps mainly a response to colonial attempts 'to gain control over the movement of people'.[245] For economic, political and ideological reasons – ranging from the need to secure taxation and revenue, to the 'civilising' influence of wage labour[246] – labour migration was promoted throughout Mwinilunga, as local money-earning opportunities remained limited.[247] Yet 'state and capital did not determine migratory movements', but rather migrants' own initiatives shaped practices of labour migration.[248] Labour migration built on existing patterns of mobility and social connectivity. As de Boeck notes, in line with much older aspirations towards self-realisation, workers sought to 'conquer the city and shape their own moral and social economies in this urban space', and in order to do so they tapped 'into (pre-)colonial sources and routes of rural identity-formation, thereby negotiating and reinventing' urban spaces.[249] Labour migration thus challenges the rural-urban divide, itself an 'invention of tradition'.[250] Movement to town was rooted in distinctly rural realities, as 'the desire to improve the conditions of life in villages frequently leads to periods of residence in town'.[251] Indeed, 'the rural and the urban constitute a single social universe encompassing both rural and urban geographical spheres'.[252] Is it useful to view rural and urban spheres as connected rather than opposed? Could labour migration and urban residence serve to constitute society in Mwinilunga?[253] Recent studies have shown that close ties continue to exist between rural and urban spheres. Migrants maintain connections to their

---

245   Bakewell, 'Keeping Them in Their Place', 1343.
246   See: Andrew Burton, '"The Eye of Authority": "Native" Taxation, Colonial Governance and Resistance in Inter-war Tanganyika', *Journal of Eastern African Studies* 2, No. 1 (2008): 74–94; Ferguson, *Expectations of Modernity*, 3–5; Cooper, *Struggle for the City*, 12.
247   Pritchett, *Lunda-Ndembu*; Macpherson, *Anatomy of a Conquest*.
248   Andersson, 'Informal Moves', 386–87.
249   De Boeck, 'Borderland Breccia.'
250   Andersson, 'Administrators' Knowledge', 122.
251   Englund, 'The Village in the City', 137.
252   Andersson, 'Reinterpreting the Rural-Urban Connection', 84.
253   Watson, *Tribal Cohesion*; Jaap Van Velsen, 'Labour Migration as a Positive Factor in the Continuity of Tonga Tribal Society', in *Social Change in Modern Africa,* ed., Aidan Southall (Oxford: Oxford University Press, 1961), 230–41.

rural 'homelands', send remittances, and move back and forth.[254] In Mwinilunga labour migration fed into a historical culture of mobility, which shaped
responses to employment opportunities and urban residence throughout the
twentieth century. Through aspirations of self-realisation rural and urban areas have been linked in multiple ways, blurring the lines between rural and
urban, continuity and change.[255] In order to understand the origins of and the
rationale behind labour migration, colonial concepts of work, labour and discipline first have to be explored.

2.1   Constructing the Idea of Work: Discipline, Labour, and Migration

At the inception of colonial rule, European and African concepts of 'work' and
'labour' did not necessarily correspond.[256] Colonial discourse, propounded
by officials and employers, often misrepresented local practices of work in
Mwinilunga, in an attempt to control labour, wrest hegemony, and impose
alternative ideological concepts.[257] Yet, as has been argued for the case of
Zimbabwe: 'Africans' participation in the labour market was probably neither
new, nor much controlled by the small, newly-established administration'.[258]
Already in the pre-colonial period people in Mwinilunga had been engaged in
various forms of labour, employment, and long-distance migration in search
of economic opportunities. The village population could be called upon by
the chief to perform communal labour in his garden, hunters might go afar
in search of wildlife, or individuals would hire themselves out as porters with
long-distance trade caravans, to name but a few examples (see Photo 9).[259] Essentially, as Rockel has argued, all these might be seen as examples of 'an indigenous form of labor organization representing a fully fledged *African* response
to the world economic system'.[260] Nevertheless, colonial administrators misunderstood, or rather chose to disregard, such indigenous forms of work. Instead

254   See Peter Geschiere and Josef Gugler, 'The Urban-Rural Connection: Changing Issues of
       Belonging and Identification', *Africa* 68, No. 3 (1998): 309–19. For examples from Zambia,
       see: Crehan, *The Fractured Community*; Moore and Vaughan, *Cutting Down Trees*; Pottier,
       Migrants No More.
255   Englund, 'The Village in the City'; De Boeck, 'Borderland Breccia'; Andersson, 'Reinter-
       preting the Rural-Urban Connection'; John L. Comaroff and Jean Comaroff, 'The Mad-
       man and the Migrant: Work and Labor in the Historical Consciousness of a South African
       People', *American Ethnologist* 14, No. 2 (1987): 191–209.
256   Comaroff and Comaroff, 'The Madman and the Migrant.'
257   Cooper, *Struggle for the City*; Allina-Pisano, 'Borderlands, Boundaries'; Andersson, 'Ad-
       ministrators' Knowledge.'
258   Andersson, 'Administrators' Knowledge', 123.
259   Von Oppen, *Terms of Trade*; Pritchett, *Lunda-Ndembu*.
260   Rockel, *Carriers of Culture*, 7.

of following a fixed schedule, local patterns of work adhered to the rhythms of the sun and the seasons, alternating spurts of intense activity with spells of leisure. Consequently, European missionaries and administrators, who came equipped with different notions of time and work, generally denounced established habits as 'idle'.[261] The Lunda were designated as 'lazy', undisciplined, and antagonistic to work, as a District Official remarked in 1910:[262]

> No demand has ever been made upon them by Europeans to work and, as they have managed to exist so long without having to do so, they are naturally adverse to commencing now (...) They will desert from work apparently almost involuntary, for they can never give a reason except that "their hearts became afraid".[263]

Such discourses have to be carefully scrutinised, especially as they shaped subsequent expectations about work and patterns of labour mobility.

Redefining the notion of labour was crucial to colonial attempts to gain authority and control over the population in Mwinilunga. The administration sought to regulate existing notions of time, rules of discipline, ideas of contract, and rates of pay. Preferably, however, officials sought to impose a wholly new concept of labour, one that was attuned to the European work ethic and the monetised market economy they wished to promote.[264] To this effect, as Cooper has noted, officials and employers sought 'not merely the mobilization of labor power, but the control of human beings, of people living in societies and immersed in cultures'.[265] Exactly because of these social and cultural forms of organisation, however, workers were able to challenge and thwart colonial intentions. Based on historical precedents and concepts of work, men and women continued to shape their working lives according to their own

---

261 Chipasha Luchembe, 'Ethnic Stereotypes, Violence and Labour in Early Colonial Zambia, 1889–1924', in *Guardians in Their Time: Experiences of Zambians Under Colonial Rule 1890–1964*, ed., Samuel N. Chipungu (London: Macmillan, 1992), 30–49.
262 See also Pritchett, *Lunda-Ndembu*; Macpherson, *Anatomy of a Conquest;* J. Clyde Mitchell and Arnold L. Epstein, 'Occupational Prestige and Social Status Among Urban Africans in Northern Rhodesia', *Africa* 29, No. 1 (1959): 22–40.
263 (NAZ) KSE6/1/1, C.S. Bellis, Annual Report Balunda District, 1910.
264 Harries, *Work, Culture, and Identity,* 38–40; Keletso E. Atkins, '"Kafir Time": Preindustrial Temporal Concepts and Labour Discipline in Nineteenth-Century Colonial Natal', *Journal of African History* 29, No. 2 (1988): 229–44; John Higginson, 'Disputing the Machines: Scientific Management and the Transformation of the Work Routine at the Union Minière du Haut-Katanga, 1918–1930', *African Economic History* 17 (1988): 1–21; Rockel, *Carriers of Culture*; Cooper, *Struggle for the City*, 18–23.
265 Cooper, *Struggle for the City*, 8.

insights.[266] A glimpse into this process of negotiation can be gained by looking at the introduction of taxation in Mwinilunga in 1913. Taxation and labour, both central to colonial interests, were closely interrelated.[267] The example of taxation illustrates how the idea of labour was constructed, contested, and adapted in such a way that existing forms of work and discipline retained prominence. The outcome of these negotiations was not a simple imposition of colonial ideas, but rather the fusion of local customs, aspirations, and morals into a hybrid work ethic.[268] By choosing their own place of employment, through desertion or tax evasion, workers in Mwinilunga retained considerable bargaining power vis-à-vis employers and the colonial state.[269] This resulted in a pattern of work that was different from, but compatible with, existing strategies of livelihood procurement. Such historical precedents shaped patterns of labour migration, which 'emerged from within the context of local custom and practice'.[270]

2.1.1   Taxation, Tax Evasion, and Labour Control

Taxation served to further the principal colonial objectives of revenue creation and labour control in Mwinilunga. One of the driving forces behind British imperialism was a quest for material gain and profit, primarily through the exploitation of mineral resources and cash crop farming.[271] Northern Rhodesia, before the development of the copper mines in the late 1920s, seemed to hold little promise for either of these, and consequently the territory came to be regarded as a 'labour reserve'.[272] The chief asset of the territory, so administrators argued, was human labour. This labour could be profitably exported to the farms and mines in Southern Rhodesia, South Africa, or Congo, which

---

266   Allina-Pisano, 'Borderlands, Boundaries'; Andersson, 'Informal Moves.'

267   See especially: Burton, 'The Eye of Authority'; Barbara Bush and Josephine Maltby, 'Taxation in West Africa: Transforming the Colonial Subject into the "Governable Person"', *Critical Perspectives on Accounting* 15 (2004): 5–34; Michael W. Tuck, '"The Rupee Disease": Taxation, Authority, and Social Conditions in Early Colonial Uganda', *International Journal of African Historical Studies* 39, No. 2 (2006): 221–45.

268   Harries, *Work, Culture, and Identity*, 42–43; Rockel, *Carriers of Culture*; but also Thompson, 'The Moral Economy', 76–136.

269   Allina-Pisano, 'Borderlands, Boundaries'; Andersson, 'Administrators' Knowledge'; Burton, 'The Eye of Authority.'

270   Harries, *Work, Culture, and Identity*, 17.

271   Gann, *The Birth of a Plural Society*, 76, 113; Hall, *Zambia*, 87; Lander, 'The British South Africa Company', 1–3; Phiri, *A Political History of Zambia*, 11; Slinn, 'Commcercial Concessions and Politics', 365–84.

272   Ferguson, *Expectations of Modernity*; Heisler, *Urbanisation and the Government*; Amin, 'Underdevelopment and Dependence.'

had started operations towards the end of the nineteenth century.[273] In this
respect, Mwinilunga seemed particularly remote and unattractive, as the area
was connected to major labour centres by long and poor transport hauls.[274]
Even if 'the functioning (and profitability) of the colonial state relied on the
migration of labour', workers did not prove readily forthcoming when prompted by colonial officials or employers.[275] Prospects of creating a reliable labour
force appeared gloomy, resulting in negative stereotypes, as propounded by
the District Commissioner in 1908:

> The Balunda will not work. Porterage is the only work they have yet been
> called upon to perform, and as carriers they are most unwilling and dan-
> gerous, as no Kalunda will hesitate to drop his load, and abandon it to fate
> while he moves off to safety with distant friends.[276]

The dearth of voluntary labour, irregular work habits, high levels of desertion,
and other forms of protest greatly hampered colonial attempts to impose authority and control, thereby jeopardising the profitability of administrative
presence in the area.[277] 'Colonial state policy was unable to channel the movement of local African labourers',[278] who maintained a degree of independence
in their participation in the labour market, Allina-Pisano argues, as 'control
over African labor remained firmly in African hands'.[279]

Apart from raising administrative revenue, the colonial state introduced
taxation in Mwinilunga to stimulate the provision of labour, in an attempt
to create governable and disciplined African subjects.[280] The necessity to
pay taxes was meant to propel engagement with the monetary economy,
either by selling cash crops or by means of salaried labour. As the 1938 Tax
Ordinance aptly shows, taxation was supposed to encourage 'industry' over
'indolence':

273   For examples see: Harries, *Work, Culture, and Identity*; Charles von Onselen, *Chibaro:
      African Mine Labour in Southern Rhodesia, 1900–1933* (London: Pluto Press, 1976); Vellut,
      'Mining in the Belgian Congo', 126–62.
274   Pritchett, *Lunda-Ndembu*; Slinn, 'Commercial Concessions and Politics', 366.
275   Bakewell, 'Keeping Them in Their Place', 1344.
276   (NAZ) KSE6/1/1, G.A. MacGregor, Annual Report Balunda District, 1908–09.
277   See: Allina-Pisano, 'Borderlands, Boundaries'; Andersson, 'Administrators' Knowledge.'
278   Andersson, 'Administrators' Knowledge', 127.
279   Allina-Pisano, 'Borderlands, Boundaries', 65.
280   Burton, 'The Eye of Authority'; Bush and Maltby, 'Taxation in West Africa'; Tuck, 'The
      Rupee Disease.'

The main object of the tax originally, was to raise revenue for the purpose of covering at least a proportion of the expenses connected with native administration. It may have had other objects, such as providing a method whereby some control could be exercised over the natives and it may also have had the object of providing an incentive which would encourage or force a naturally indolent native population to turn out to work.[281]

Nonetheless, indigenous patterns of work continued to be asserted in opposition to the colonial work ethic revolving around salaried labour.[282] The population of Mwinilunga vehemently resisted the introduction of the hut tax in 1913:[283]

> We will not have the TAX, and if the TAX comes then we will all go to Portuguese Territory. If you take our names [census] then the TAX will follow. We cannot pay the TAX until we have money, and we have no money.[284]

Mobility was the main means by which taxation was resisted. Administrative insistence on the payment of taxes caused widespread flight across international borders, which even made officials question the rationale behind their policies.[285] Theodore Williams, a colonial official in Mwinilunga at the time, reflects this sense of ambiguity in his letters:

> The great idea of the tax was that it would make them work for at least one month of the year and bring them into contact with civilisation and money – and so through an oppressive means, would produce a good end. Well, all the tax has done is simply to frighten the people of us, make it harder to make them work for us (for they will work for the Portuguese and others, traders etc. in moderation, and a good many make their money out of expedition for rubber to the Congo – which they sell to the Portuguese), and depopulate the district (...) If getting people to stay and work was the object, the tax was a failure. If driving the people out was the object, then the tax was barbaric – cruel morally and materially a damned foolish thing, for now we have no villages about to bring in food

281   (NAZ) SEC2/346, Native Tax Amendment Ordinance, 1938.
282   See Harries, *Work, Culture, and Identity.*
283   Pritchett, *Lunda-Ndembu*; Macpherson, *Anatomy of a Conquest.*
284   (NAZ) KSE6/1/1, J.M. Pound, Balunda District Tour Report, 30 September 1910.
285   Allina-Pisano, 'Borderlands, Boundaries'; Musambachime, 'Escape from Tyranny.'

[all have fled] (...) The policy here now is to be pretty easy going to re-
gain confidence from the people. Hence the reduced police force, for one
thing. People are not being pressed to pay, but are following each other
and are paying fairly well.[286]

Taxation, thus, could not simply compel the population to go to work. Rather,
established patterns of work and mobility shaped reactions to taxation and
attempts to control labour.[287] In order to evade the payment of taxes, people
would flee on approach of the tax collector. Individuals, family groups, or less
commonly entire villages, might move into neighbouring areas of Congo or
Angola where administrative demands appeared less onerous.[288] Even if only
temporary, this movement caused such panic that the colonial administration
granted notable concessions to taxpayers. In subsequent years, taxation on
plural wives was abolished, road labour was no longer requested, and pressure
to build large concentrated settlements was relaxed.[289] Cross-border mobility
to evade the payment of taxes continued well into the colonial period, as the
District Commissioner remarked in 1928: 'A large number of natives who object to the payment of tax betake themselves to one or the other of the foreign
territories on our border – thereby avoiding both payment and punishment for
neglect thereof'.[290] Through mobility, individuals negotiated the imposition of
taxation, disputing its terms and consequences. Tax evasion was part of 'a
complex range of strategies of resistance, survival and complicity', which prevented the unilateral imposition of colonial power.[291] It proved impossible to
effectively administer default, which posed not only 'a fundamental challenge
to governmental authority and influence', but also 'thwarted the disciplinary
functions of tax'.[292]

The significance of taxation could not be reduced to a binary of payment or
default. Rather, the payment of taxation was part of a process of negotiation,

286   (BOD) MSS Afr S779, Theodore Williams, 23 September 1913, My Dear Father.
287   Allina-Pisano, 'Borderlands, Boundaries'; Burton, 'The Eye of Authority.'
288   Bakewell, 'Refugees Repatriating'; Pritchett, *Lunda-Ndembu*; Macpherson, *Anatomy of a
      Conquest.*
289   (NAZ) KSE4/1 Mwinilunga District Notebooks, 29: F.H. Melland's concessions in 1913 were
      as follows. 1. Taxpayers could import gunpowder for their own use. 2. Taxpayers could visit
      friends in Congo without pass. 3. Taxpayers could collect and sell rubber. 4. Road works
      not to be compulsory. 5. Big villages would not be insisted on. 6. Boma would give 10/- for
      a full load of grain. 7. Second wives would not be taxed.
290   (NAZ) KSE6/1/6, F.V. Bruce-Miller, Mwinilunga District Annual Report, 1928.
291   Bush and Maltby, 'Taxation in West Africa', 7.
292   Burton, 'The Eye of Authority', 85.

involving all kinds of assumptions about work and power.[293] Initially, people did not pay the tax out of an internalised sense of duty, but rather regarded payment as a symbolic ticking of the administrative box.[294] Theodore Williams described that:

> A native is only looked on as a man who has paid his tax or not. Reports mention nothing but tax (...) The people are all keen on paying – will work for a month and go off quite happy with nothing but a scrap of paper. But they show the feeling of "Thank God that's over – now I can go back and live as I want to!"[295]

The ideas behind taxation were contested, in particular by chiefs, many of whom rejected the payment of taxes and discouraged their population from paying. Some chiefs even moved to Angola or Congo, or abdicated rather than concurring with administrative requirements.[296] During the colonial period, the numbers of defaulters in Mwinilunga remained high. The impossibility of enforcing regular tax payment evidenced the feeble nature of colonial control on the ground.[297] Local resistance proved so powerful that the tax rate was lowered from 10 shillings to 7/6 in 1935.[298] The 'civilising mission' of taxation 'failed to instil a "self-disciplinary culture"' among taxpayers in Mwinilunga in any straightforward manner, thereby subverting colonial intentions.[299]

By spurring engagement with the monetary economy, taxation was directly linked to labour migration. Opportunities to earn money within Mwinilunga District were limited and failed to secure sufficient tax money for all.[300]

---

293   Bush and Maltby, 'Taxation in West Africa'; Burton, 'The Eye of Authority'; Berry, 'Hegemony on a Shoestring', 327–55.

294   Pritchett, *Lunda-Ndembu*; Allina-Pisano, 'Borderlands, Boundaries.'

295   (BOD) MSS Afr S779, Theodore Williams, 26 November 1913, My Dear Father; (BOD) MSS Afr S779, Theodore Williams, 11 January 1914, My Dear Father.

296   See: Moore and Vaughan, *Cutting Down Trees*, 11–12, 15–16; Allina-Pisano, 'Borderlands, Boundaries', 79. Chief Ntambu Sachitolu abdicated after the imposition of taxation, returning his government staff of office, *ndondu*. Upon this act, a large part of his population was imprisoned for tax default.

297   Andersson, 'Administrators' Knowledge'; Burton, 'The Eye of Authority.'

298   This reduction did lead to a higher tax collection rate of 87%; see (NAZ) SEC2/133, N.S. Price, Mwinilunga District Annual Report, 1935. During the colonial period, the tax was changed from hut tax to poll tax, and tax rates were adjusted to match prevailing economic circumstances.

299   Burton, 'The Eye of Authority', 75; Bush and Maltby, 'Taxation in West Africa.'

300   Fisher and Hoyte, *Ndotolu*.

Because of this, mobility proved necessary, as government officials frequently remarked.[301] The 1915 annual report provides an example:

> The natives were told that the tax must be paid, and as there was no work in the District they must go farther afield. In the District proper there is practically no opening for employment by which the natives can earn money.[302]

Although the payment of taxes in kind (in grain, flour, livestock, or agricultural implements, such as hoes and axes) was allowed initially, colonial officials discouraged the practice and would only allow it in exceptional circumstances.[303] Instead, the cash payment of taxes was encouraged and soon became a universal requirement, even if at the start of the twentieth century the circulation of British currency was still highly limited in Mwinilunga.[304] To earn tax money, a number of options were available locally. Individuals could sell crops to one of the missions or the administration, trade beeswax or rubber, engage in road construction work, or carry loads.[305] Such local employment was preferred to travelling long distances or engaging in long work contracts, and remained significant in the colonial/post-colonial period.[306] Yet due to a lack of opportunities to earn money locally, numerous taxpayers were propelled to migrate to seek employment in areas where wages were higher or conditions of employment appeared favourable.[307] Men and to a lesser extent women consequently embarked on journeys from Mwinilunga to the mines in Congo, to the Northern Rhodesian Copperbelt, or even to Southern Rhodesia and South Africa.[308] These movements should be interpreted within the context of pre-colonial mobility.[309] In the case of Mozambique, Harries has argued that 'to migrate' for work 'was a common-sense decision that rendered life more secure and predictable, like other economic activities involving travel'.[310]

---

301 (NAZ) NWP1/2/90 Loc.4916, Reports and Returns, Labour in Mwinilunga District, 1961.
302 (NAZ) KSE6/1/3, F.V. Bruce-Miller, Lunda Division Annual Report, 1915–16.
303 See: Moore and Vaughan, *Cutting Down Trees*; Macpherson, *Anatomy of a Conquest*; Andersson, 'Administrators' Knowledge.'
304 Pritchett, *Lunda-Ndembu*; Von Oppen, *Terms of Trade.*
305 Pritchett, *Lunda-Ndembu*; Turner and Turner, 'Money Economy', 19–37.
306 Pritchett, *Lunda-Ndembu*; see: Allina-Pisano, 'Borderlands, Boundaries'; Andersson, 'Administrators' Knowledge'; Harries, *Work, Culture, and Identity.*
307 Pritchett, *Lunda-Ndembu*; Turner, *Schism and Continuity*; Bakewell, 'Refugees Repatriating.'
308 Pritchett, *Friends for Life*; Turner and Turner, 'Money economy.'
309 Rockel, *Carriers of Culture*; De Boeck, 'Borderland Breccia'; Andersson, 'Informal Moves', 382; Von Oppen, *Terms of Trade.*
310 Harries, *Work, Culture, and Identity*, 17.

While the scope of labour migration signified a departure from pre-colonial patterns of mobility, the established culture of mobility in Mwinilunga was still deployed to earn tax money and to make sense of engagements with distant workplaces.[311] Labour and taxation were not only at the heart of colonial politics and power, but affected local livelihood strategies in profound ways as well.[312]

Despite the difficulty of earning money and initial acts of resistance, taxes in Mwinilunga were increasingly paid as a result of administrative urging and more effective measures of control over the course of the twentieth century.[313] Already in 1913 a colonial official remarked that 'there is now a considerable sprinkling of tax-payers everywhere, and they all look upon the tax as a much easier thing than they thought, and this favourable opinion is sowing good seed elsewhere'.[314] To encourage payment, colonial officials provided defaulters with tax relief labour, such as construction work or infrastructural maintenance locally.[315] This proved an attractive alternative to employment outside of the district:

> The tax relief scheme has been in force on a large scale for two years and hundreds of natives have received work for years in default. The natives while disliking the road work recognised its convenience in that they worked off their tax without having to proceed long distances from their homes.[316]

Local employment was often preferred because mobility, though enabling access to lucrative work, could prove disruptive of existing livelihoods.[317] Taxpayers therefore sought to fulfil administrative requirements in ways that would be compatible with agricultural production, for example.[318] At the end of the

---

311 Ngwane, 'Christmas Time'; O'Laughlin, 'Proletarianisation, Agency and Changing Rural Livelihoods.'

312 O'Laughlin, 'Proletarianisation, Agency and Changing Rural Livelihoods'; De Haan, 'Livelihoods and Poverty.'

313 See: Allina-Pisano, 'Borderlands, Boundaries'; Moore and Vaughan, *Cutting Down Trees*; Burton, 'The Eye of Authority.'

314 (NAZ) KSE6/2/1, J.M. Pound, Lunda District Quarterly Report, July 1913.

315 Pritchett, *Lunda-Ndembu*; see: Moore and Vaughan, *Cutting Down Trees*; Harries, *Work, Culture, and Identity.*

316 (NAZ) NWP1/2/7 Loc.4898, Mwinilunga District Travelling Report, 1937.

317 See: Moore and Vaughan, *Cutting Down Trees*, 141–56; De Haan, 'Livelihoods and Poverty.'

318 Allina-Pisano, 'Borderlands, Boundaries', 70; Andersson, 'Administrators' Knowledge'; Moore and Vaughan, *Cutting Down Trees.*

dry season, when men were preparing their fields, labour would be difficult to contract. In 1929, the District Commissioner complained that 'very few of the taxable population were at work – They have duties to perform at home at this time – garden cutting, building and thatching huts, etc'.[319] Taxation could not be imposed on a clean slate, but was rather appropriated within existing social relationships, patterns of work, and ideas about labour. One colonial official sarcastically remarked that kinship ties filtered through even in the formal ob-ligation of the payment of taxation, as workers from Mwinilunga 'will not only earn money for their own tax but also for some of their less robust (or more tired!) friends'.[320] Taxation and ensuing forms of labour migration did not turn patterns of work, labour organisation, or hierarchies of priority upside down. Rather, existing practices and ideologies proved remarkably resilient, guiding workers' entrance into the labour market.[321]

Creating a readily available and disciplined labour force through the intro-duction of taxation did not prove straightforward in Mwinilunga. Resistance, flight, and tax evasion remained powerful tools throughout the colonial pe-riod, which served to drive through local priorities and demands related to the nature of work and labour migration.[322] Forms of everyday resistance succeed-ed in lowering tax rates, shaping labour contracts, and influencing colonial demands.[323] Throughout the twentieth century individuals proved distinctly able to choose their place of employment and negotiate favourable working conditions, laying the basis for their engagement in the labour market through mobility.[324]

2.1.2   Going to Work: Stereotypes, Recruitment, and the Origins of
          Labour Migration
In examining the rise of labour migration in and from Mwinilunga, sociocul-tural dispositions should be considered next to official policies and employ-ers' practices, as mobility was not determined by state and capital interests alone.[325] Notwithstanding colonial attempts to control labour through taxation

---

319   (NAZ) KSE6/6/2, G. Hughes-Chamberlain, Mwinilunga District Tour Report, 8 May 1929.
320   (NAZ) KSE6/1/3, F.V. Bruce-Miller, Lunda Division Kasempa District Annual Report, 1915/16.
321   Harries, *Work, Culture, and Identity*; Andersson, 'Informal Moves.'
322   Harries, *Work, Culture, and Identity*; Andersson, 'Administrators' Knowledge.'
323   See Scott, *Weapons of the Weak.*
324   See: Rockel, *Carriers of Culture*; Harries, *Work, Culture and Identity*; Allina-Pisano, 'Border-lands, Boundaries.'
325   Andersson, 'Informal Moves', 386.

and recruitment, an indigenous work ethic filtered through in work contracts and incipient labour migration. Workers made resolute attempts to negotiate patterns of labour migration to their own advantage. By looking at examples of recruitment and negative stereotyping, it can be illustrated how a culture of mobility, reflecting existing work habits and preferences, shaped reactions to labour migration in Mwinilunga.[326]

Colonial officials, in association with employers, recruiters, and missionaries, formulated persistent 'tribal' or 'ethnic' stereotypes regarding the 'work ethic' of various population groups, such as the Lunda of Mwinilunga.[327] This colonial stereotyping was rooted in an attempt to classify and control the population, in order to more easily tax and extract labour from them.[328] Officials and employers deemed the Lunda suitable only for lower paid, menial types of labour, in particular woodcutting, household work, or farm employment.[329] Frequent complaints concerning the 'lazy' nature of the Lunda, their 'disinclination' to work, and the difficulty to discipline or control workers were voiced.[330] Officials described Lunda messengers as 'not amenable to discipline', prone to desertion, and 'thoroughly antagonistic to work'.[331] Employers, recruiters and officials voiced such stereotypes – reflecting deeply rooted ideas about work, labour, and culture – due to their inability to effectively control local labour. The District Commissioner in Mwinilunga in 1928 viewed the initial rejection of work and subsequent irregular work habits among the Lunda with despair, lamenting that 'references to the "dignity of labour" leave them quite cold'.[332] Paradoxically, negative stereotypes and a defiant attitude enabled workers from Mwinilunga to push through their preferences and exert influence as to

326 Harries, *Work, Culture, and Identity*; Andersson, 'Administrators' Knowledge.'
327 See: Luchembe, 'Ethnic Stereotypes'; Crehan, *The Fractured Community*; Harries, *Work, Culture, and Identity*; Brian Siegel, 'The "Wild" and "Lazy" Lamba as Ethnic Stereotype on the Central African Copperbelt', in *The Creation of Tribalism in Southern Africa*, ed., Leroy Vail (Berkeley: University of California Press, 1989); Robert Papstein, 'Ethnic Identity and Tribalism in the Upper Zambezi Region of Zambia, 1830–1981', in Vail, *The Creation of Tribalism*; Luise White, *Speaking with Vampires: Rumor and History in Colonial Africa* (Berkeley: University of California Press, 2000); Crehan, 'Tribes and the People Who Read Books', 203–18.
328 Crehan, 'Tribes and the People Who Read Books'; Gluckman, 'Tribalism in Modern British Central Africa.'
329 Luchembe, 'Ethnic Stereotypes', 31; Mitchell and Epstein, 'Occupational Prestige'; Pritchett, *Lunda-Ndembu*; Macpherson, *Anatomy of a Conquest.*
330 (NAZ) KSE6/2/1, A.W. Bonfield, Lunda Sub-District Quarterly Report, 30 September 1916.
331 (NAZ) A5/2/1 Loc.4003, G.A. MacGregor, Balunda District Annual Report, 1908–9.
332 (NAZ) KSE6/2/2, F.V. Bruce-Miller, Lunda Sub-District Quarterly Report, 30 September 1928.

the length of service, rate of pay, or type of work they would perform.[333] Even if it greatly frustrated colonial attempts to regularise the provision of labour or accustom workers to fixed contracts, the Lunda sought to uphold a distinctly independent work ethic. In 1909, the District Commissioner complained that:

> A curious system of labour is in vogue with the Balunda of this part. They are willing, apparently, to go to the forest and return at intervals to suit their own tastes with building poles, bundles of thatching grass, etc., for sale on delivery and to engage at other work provided that, when the humour takes a man he be permitted to demand and receive payment for whatever he may have performed – half a day's work, a day's work, or more, or less as the case may be.[334]

The District Commissioner denounced this attitude as 'essentially unsound, disorganised, and unsystematic', yet workers consistently continued to choose their own place of employment.[335] Administrative efforts to promote labour migration to farms and mines, even when mediated by recruitment, went largely unheeded,[336] as this account from 1925 evidences:

> The aLunda do not take kindly to work of any kind (...) I am of the opinion that it is premature to allow a recruiter to operate in this division (...) To send the aLunda away from their homes for a lengthy period would be impolitic until they have thoroughly settled down, made good gardens and villages (...) Mine work is not suited to the local natives; they have not the physique (...) Very few of them have gone down to the farmers (...) Even if the farmers sent a recruiter here the results would be disappointing for years: the local native does not know the work, and also is most averse to binding himself down for more than two months. The work that he knows is wood cutting and he is most sought after by Congo contractors.[337]

---

333   Allina-Pisano, 'Borderlands, Boundaries.'

334   (NAZ) HC1/2/43 BS2/251 Loc.130, G.A. MacGregor, Balunda District Monthly Report, May 1909.

335   Ibidem.

336   For more on labour recruitment, see: Von Onselen, *Chibaro*; Harries, *Work, Culture, and Identity*.

337   (NAZ) KSE6/1/3, F.V. Bruce-Miller, Mwinilunga District Annual Report, 31 March 1915; (NAZ) KSE6/1/4, K.S. Kinross, Mwinilunga Sub-District Annual Report, 31 March 1925.

Exactly because of the negative stereotypes of the Lunda among employers and colonial officials, long-term contracts were not insisted on, coercive labour recruiters were barred from the district, and consequently workers managed to exert influence over their contracts and terms of employment.[338] Negative stereotypes created a space for manoeuvre and enabled the rejection of undesirable, arduous forms of work.[339] Lunda workers voiced distinct preferences as to their place of work and conditions of service, well into the 1930s:

> Agriculture and surface work are most popular with the Natives of this District. Until recently they were somewhat despised as employees (…) But the shortage of labour has given them the chance to enter the labour markets and they are proving that they are not quite so inferior as was imagined.[340]

Stereotypes proved remarkably enduring and could form the basis for 'ethnic' identities.[341] Even today, Bemba workers on the Copperbelt continue to regard the Lunda as 'weak' and suitable for low-rank positions only, referring to them as 'scavengers' and quarrelling with them fiercely in beer-halls.[342] Yet such negative valuations could be used to the advantage of workers, enabling them to negotiate their own work, type of contract, and rate of pay.

Where possible, workers sought terms of employment that would be compatible with their personal aspirations, going to work of their own accord, and using mobility as a negotiating tool rather than acceding to the whims of recruiters.[343] Yet especially during the early period of colonial rule, when labour in Mwinilunga did not prove readily forthcoming, recruitment would be resorted to.[344] In an attempt to engage workers for fixed contracts, usually of six or twelve months, government or employers sent out recruiters to villages.[345] Although labour contracted through recruitment was not necessarily

---

338   Pritchett, *Lunda-Ndembu*; Macpherson, *Anatomy of a Conquest.*

339   See Siegel, 'The Wild and Lazy Lamba.'

340   (NAZ) SEC2/151, Annual Report Western Province, 1937.

341   Crehan, 'Tribes and the People Who Read Books'; Harries, *Work, Culture, and Identity.*

342   Interview with William Ngangu, 26 February 2010, Ndola.

343   See: Harries, *Work, Culture, and Identity*; Moore and Vaughan, *Cutting Down Trees.*

344   See: Pritchett, *Lunda-Ndembu*; Macpherson, *Anatomy of a Conquest*; Michael Barrett, '"Walking Home Majestically": Consumption and the Enactment of Social Status Among Labour Migrants from Barotseland, 1935–1965', in *The Objects of Life in Central Africa: The History of Consumption and Social Change, 1840–1980*, eds., Robert Ross, Marja Hinfelaar, and Iva Peša (Leiden: Brill, 2013), 93–113.

345   Thandekile R.M. Mvusi, 'The "Politics of Trypanosomiasis" Revisited: Labour Mobilization and Labour Migration in Colonial Zambia: The Robert Williams Company in Lubemba, 1901–1911', *Transafrican Journal of History* 23 (1994): 43–68.

strictly coerced, a strong element of pressure often had to be applied to engage adequate numbers of workers.[346] The District Commissioner readily acknowledged this in 1928:

> It is (...) useless to pretend that the recruitment of large numbers of natives by Government uniformed messengers is popular amongst the people. Forced Labour is perhaps too strong a term to use in this connexion; nevertheless, the Native Commissioner would have to wait many months for say two hundred *volunteers* for the Boundary Commission or any other unknown employer of labour.[347]

Yet in Mwinilunga labour was generally not obtained by brute coercion, but would rather be induced by persuasion, by offering high wages or favourable terms of contract.[348] First of all, recruiters, employers, and the state proved heavily reliant on the assistance of conductors, headmen, and chiefs.[349] Such intermediaries could exert considerable influence over the process of recruitment, for example by advising workers to refrain from engaging in a particular contract.[350] Secondly, rather than relying on force, recruiters would frequently resort to material incentives to contract workers. For instance, prospective workers might be seduced by blankets or similar gifts.[351] By weighing employers against one another, by using mobility as a tool, or by refusing long-term contracts, workers continued to assert their own preferences, as the District Commissioner noted in the 1920s:

> The average Alunda is not anxious to give his confidence to any white man that may come along, especially when they are told that if they accept employment it will mean they will be away from their homes for

---

346 O'Laughlin, 'Proletarianisation, Agency and Changing Rural Livelihoods'; E.P. Makambe, 'The Mobilisation of African Labour Across the Zambezi for the Zimbabwean Colonial Market Before the Chibaro Era, 1898–1903', *African Studies* 51, No. 2 (1992): 277–94.

347 (NAZ) KSE6/2/2, F.V. Bruce-Miller, Mwinilunga Sub-District Quarterly Report, 30 June 1928.

348 This observation is based on a reading of archival sources and numerous interviews – it goes against the views proposed by Pritchett, *Lunda-Ndembu*; Macpherson, *Anatomy of a Conquest.*

349 Moore and Vaughan, *Cutting Down Trees*, 141–56; Allina-Pisano, 'Borderlands, Boundaries', 79.

350 See Berry, *No Condition Is Permanent*; Piet J.J. Konings, 'Chieftaincy, Labour Control and Capitalist Development in Cameroon', *Journal of Legal Pluralism and Unofficial Law* 37/8 (1996): 329–46.

351 Barrett, 'Walking Home Majestically.'

over twelve months (...) The majority of the people just walk over the border to the Congo – work for a contractor for a month or two then return to their villages when they have enough money for their tax.[352]

Work preferences were far from uniform in Mwinilunga. Whereas some preferred cash payment, others wanted easy access to consumer goods.[353] In general, flexible contracts were favoured, whilst fixed long-term contracts and long hazardous journeys on foot would be avoided as much as possible. Ultimately, recruitment and colonial policy could not coercively direct labour movement from Mwinilunga, as 'migrants were active participants in the labour market, giving shape to different migration trajectories – differentiated according to wages obtainable, distance from home and length of absence'.[354] The extent of recruited labour is probably exaggerated in Mwinilunga's official records.[355] Instead, workers made use of mobility and an established work ethic to negotiate independent terms of employment and conditions of work. Prospective workers would actively weigh conditions of service, seeking those that appeared most favourable to existing livelihoods. This quest often took them across the border, especially to Congo.

2.1.3   Crossing the Copperbelt: Work and Mobility
In the villages of Mwinilunga, knowledge of urban employment or terms of service remained limited at the beginning of the twentieth century. Communication between villages and urban centres was difficult to establish, whereas the journey to the mines was long and arduous.[356] Although recruiters sometimes provided transport to the workplace, men most commonly sought security in numbers and travelled in large groups. Friends, kin, and individuals from neighbouring villages might gather to decide on a date to embark on the journey to their place of employment. In all, the journey could take several weeks to complete. Migrants would prepare themselves by gathering

---

352   (NAZ) KSE6/1/4, F.V. Bruce-Miller, Mwinilunga Sub-District Annual Report, 31 March 1922.
353   (NAZ) KSE6/2/2, C.H. Anley, Mwinilunga Sub-District Quarterly Report, 31 December 1921.
354   Andersson, 'Administrators' Knowledge', 127.
355   Arguably, the occurrence of recruited labour was overrepresented in the colonial archives because the colonial state played an important role in facilitating recruitment. This point has been raised by Andersson, 'Informal Moves', and Thaddeus Sunseri, 'Labour Migration in Colonial Tanzania and the Hegemony of South African Historiography', African Affairs 95, No. 381 (1996): 581–98.
356   Descriptions of travel are provided in Fisher and Hoyte, Ndotolu; Short, African Sunset.

food, blankets, tools, and trade items to carry on the road.[357] Charms, such as *ndakala*, which would drive away wild animals, snakes, and other threats, were equally taken along. Once the preparations had been completed, travellers would embark in groups of up to twenty people, usually consisting of kin or members of neighbouring villages. Passing through the *boma* first, workers would start dispersing upon arrival in the labour centres, some stopping in Ndola, others continuing to Broken Hill (Kabwe) or even Johannesburg.[358] Not only on the road, but even more so upon arrival, support among friends and kin proved essential. Networks established by previous migrants could facilitate access to shelter, food, and employment, spread news on the latest work openings, or gossip from the home front.[359] Through movement, individuals forged new ties of identity, whilst reinforcing, expanding or questioning existing ones. A culture of mobility, as well as existing social relationships and ideas about work, shaped workers' engagement with the labour market. By the 1930s, colonial officials stated that 'the people are keen to earn money and are willing to work'.[360]

Numerous migrants from Mwinilunga sought employment in mining and railway hubs in Congo. Building on patterns of cross-border mobility and ties of Lunda identity (see Chapter 3 Section 1), mines such as Kambove, Musonoi, and Ruwe, as well as towns such as Élisabethville (Lubumbashi), Kolwezi, and Mutshatsha, proved popular destinations.[361] Employment in Congo was particularly attractive prior to the full development of the Northern Rhodesian Copperbelt in the 1930s, but Congolese towns continued to draw migrants throughout the twentieth century.[362] Workers in Congo would engage in a wide variety of jobs, ranging from woodcutting and household work, to trade and mining. Urban centres in Congo were located relatively close to Mwinilunga and could be reached with less travel than alternatives within Zambian borders.[363] The ease and speed of travel enabled workers to engage in more short-term contracts in Congo. This served to minimise the disruption

357   This account is based on numerous interviews, for example Tepson Kandungu, 11 October 2010, Ntambu, but compare: Pritchett, *Lunda-Ndembu*; Harries, *Work, Culture, and Identity.*
358   Compare with: Barrett, 'Walking Home Majestically.'
359   Cooper, *Struggle for the City*, 38–44; Andersson, 'Reinterpreting the Rural-Urban Connection'; Mitchell, *Social Networks in Urban Situations*; J. Clyde Mitchell, *The Kalela Dance: Aspects of Social Relationships Among Urban Africans in Northern Rhodesia* (Manchester: Manchester University Press, 1956).
360   (NAZ) SEC2/952, K.S. Kinross, Mwinilunga District Tour Report, 20 January 1933.
361   See: Vellut, 'Mining in the Belgian Congo'; Higginson, *A Working Class in the Making.*
362   Bustin, *Lunda Under Belgian Rule.*
363   Bustin, *Lunda Under Belgian Rule*; Pritchett, *Lunda-Ndembu*; Bakewell, 'Refugees Repatriating.'

of village life caused by the absence of male labour, as workers might still engage in agricultural production (cutting down trees and preparing fields) upon completing their two or three month contracts.[364] Due to proximity, the District Commissioner in 1949 noted that 'those who work close by in the Congo seem to come home more often, and to bring more with them, than those employed in the towns of this Territory'.[365] In this manner, labour migration and agricultural production, hunting or animal husbandry did not have to conflict, but could be combined.[366]

Others opted to work in Congo for purposes of tax evasion, to avoid the governmentality of the state, or in an attempt to retain autonomy of contract.[367] Movement to Congo frequently sought to circumvent official channels, frustrating attempts at stricter mobility control:

> Most natives earn their taxes in the Congo (...) Many leave the district without passes, and obtain them at Solwezi, or proceed with friends who have passes already (...) the local native (...) is most averse to binding himself down for more than two months. The work that he knows is woodcutting, and he is most sought after by Congo contractors (...) there have been several attempts at illegal recruiting by capitaos sent by these Congo contractors.[368]

These labour movements caused administrative headaches throughout the twentieth century, yet they did provide workers from Mwinilunga with the opportunity to weigh working conditions on both sides of the border, choosing those that seemed most favourable to their specific aims and aspirations.[369] Congolese employment challenged labour provision to the Northern Rhodesian Copperbelt in the first half of the twentieth century and beyond, as one official remarked in 1949:

> The Congo labour market has always been very popular with these people as it is handy and also, for the main part, they are working with kindred

---

364   This view is based on a wide reading of archival sources and numerous interviews, for example Jackson Samakai, 16 April 2010, Ikelenge.
365   (NAZ) SEC2/957, R.N. Lines, Mwinilunga District Tour Report, 6 March 1949.
366   Andersson, 'Administrators' Knowledge', 127.
367   Musambachime, 'Escape from Tyranny.'
368   (NAZ) KSE6/1/4, K.S. Kinross, Mwinilunga District Annual Report, 31 March 1925.
369   See Luise White, 'Class Struggle and Cannibalism: Storytelling and History Writing on the Copperbelts of Colonial Northern Rhodesia and the Belgian Congo', in *Speaking with Vampires*.

tribes. Whenever the Congo market shrinks, the movement of labour towards the Copperbelt increases greatly in volume, but as soon as new
mines are started inside the Congo Belge the popularity switches back
again to the Congo market.[370]

Social connectivity explains this in part, as in Congolese towns Lunda relatives (even if distant or fictional) might be encountered, whereas on the Zambian Copperbelt Bemba-speaking workers remain dominant even today.[371] As
a consequence, the District Commissioner in the late 1950s could still remark
that within Mwinilunga 'the influence of the Congo is everywhere felt', and 'so
long as the boundary cuts across the tribal pattern so long the people will come
and go'.[372] An added benefit was the paternalistic industrial policy of the *Union
Minière du Haut Katanga*, as 'the Belgians give assistance to labourers families and most of these men had taken their families with them to work'.[373]
Contrastingly, in colonial Northern Rhodesia a policy of encouraging lone
male migrants instead of families predominated, especially before the 1950s.[374]
Workers quickly realised such differences and capitalised on them through
mobility. Even the District Commissioner noted in 1955 that 'labourers and
their families go there where the prospects of employment appear most invit-
ing', and in Congo 'well paid employment and good living conditions are to be
found without difficulty'.[375]

Notwithstanding Congolese attractions, by the late 1920s officials in Mwinilunga contentedly remarked that 'as each year passes the sub-district natives go
of their own accord in ever increasing numbers to seek congenial employment
at N'changa, Kansanshi, Kipushi and other labour centres'.[376] From the 1930s
onwards, work within the territory, particularly on the Copperbelt, gained acceptance due to the availability of employment, which matched established
work patterns and preferences:

---

370   (NAZ) SEC2/956, F.M.N. Heath, Mwinilunga District Tour Report, 21 January 1948.
371   See Larmer and Macola, 'The Origins'; Larmer, *Rethinking African Politics*.
372   (NAZ) SEC2/966, W.D. Grant, Mwinilunga District Tour Report, 24 October 1958.
373   (NAZ) NWP1/2/17, F.M.N. Heath, Mwinilunga District Tour Report, 21 January 1948; Ben-
       jamin Rubbers, *Le paternalisme en question: Les anciens ouvriers de la Gécamines face à la
       libéralisation du secteur minier katangais (RD Congo)* (Paris: L'Harmattan, 2013).
374   See: Parpart, 'Where Is Your Mother?', 241–71; George Chauncey, 'The Locus of Reproduc-
       tion: Women's Labour in the Zambian Copperbelt, 1927–1953', *Journal of Southern African
       Studies* 7, No. 2 (1980–81): 135–64.
375   (NAZ) SEC2/963, R.S. Thompson, Mwinilunga District Tour Report, 26 April 1955.
376   (NAZ) KSE6/2/2, F.V. Bruce-Miller, Mwinilunga Sub-District Quarterly Report, 31 March
       1929.

Nchanga and Kipushi continue to be popular labour centres. The present generation has watched them grow up and the kind of work available so far – building, thatching, timber cutting, road making etc. – appeals to them; moreover they go there voluntarily and independently.[377]

District officials hoped that positive messages spread by returning migrants would attract more workers in future: 'if they return with good reports of their treatment, pay, etc., more of their friends will follow their example and offer their services during the coming year to employers domiciled in this country'.[378] The examples in this section have shown that workers from Mwinilunga could negotiate or even choose employers, conditions of service, and rates of pay, according to their own preferences and by using mobility as a tool.[379] Of course there were certain limits to this freedom, but taxation or recruitment could not simply coerce labour movements. In 1937, after years of employment experience, it was still noted that 'the Mwinilunga native prefers choosing his own type of work and does not relish long term contracts'.[380] What motivated workers to engage in migrant labour and how were ties between the city and the country, between Mwinilunga and urban centres, forged and upheld?

2.2   Of Modernist Narratives and Life Histories: Patterns of Labour Migration in Mwinilunga

Structural explanations for labour migration – foregrounding economic push and pull factors or state coercion – pay insufficient attention to individual life histories, motivations, and aspirations.[381] Examining the rise of labour migration from Mwinilunga (where people went to work, which jobs they performed, how they were contracted, under what conditions, and how this changed over time) sheds light on personalised motives for migration and how these influenced subsequent trajectories of labour migration.[382]

Labour migration ratios from Mwinilunga increased steadily during the colonial period and remained high after independence. Whereas in 1935 7.5% of the taxable male population was reported to be at work outside the district,

---

377   (NAZ) KSE6/1/6, F.V. Bruce-Miller, Mwinilunga Sub-District Annual Report, 31 December 1928.

378   (NAZ) KSE6/1/5, F.V. Bruce-Miller, Mwinilunga Sub-District Annual Report, 31 March 1926.

379   Allina-Pisano, 'Borderlands, Boundaries'; Andersson, 'Administrators' Knowledge.'

380   (NAZ) SEC2/133, N.S. Price, Mwinilunga District Annual Report, 31 December 1937.

381   See: Englund, 'The Village in the City'; Andersson, 'Informal Moves.'

382   See: Mitchell, 'The Causes Of Labour Migration'; Epstein, 'Urbanization and Social Change.'

figures rose to 21% in 1947, 33% in 1952, and 56% in 1960.[383] After independence labour migration ratios were no longer measured as such, but it can be postulated that migration from Mwinilunga to urban areas continued in large numbers.[384] Post-colonial government policies, lifting colonial restrictions on mobility, and relaxing regulations on urban residence, caused Zambia to 'reap the whirlwind', in the words of Peter Matoka. Rural population flocked to the towns, because 'everyone wanted to come to urban areas in search of work, pleasure, or even schooling'.[385] Only after 1980 were there signs of diminishing rural outmigration, or even counter-urbanisation, as the national/international economic downturn caused a slump in urban employment and redirected migration flows away from the Copperbelt to the capital city Lusaka, district centres such as Mwinilunga Township, or to rural areas.[386] The length

383 (NAZ) SEC2/133, R.N. Lines, Mwinilunga District Annual Report, 1935; (NAZ) SEC2/154, F.M.N Heath, Mwinilunga District Annual Report, 1947; (NAZ) SEC2/135, W.G. Reeves, Mwinilunga District Annual Report, 1952; (NAZ) NWP1/2/102 Loc.4919, E.L. Button, North Western Province Annual Report, 1960.

384 For the post-independence period: 'the relatively large population increase for North-Western Province can be partly attributed to the relatively small rate of out-migration in the Province. Whereas the other rural provinces all experienced high rates of net out-migration ... the position in North-Western Province appears to have been rather more stable, though all districts except Solwezi do show some losses due to out-migration, mainly to the Copperbelt ... The loss of population, however, consists almost entirely of males of active working age who are either temporary or semi-permanent/permanent emigrants. What matters is that the Province is losing the most vigorous sector of its population, which cannot but retard the development of the Province', Johnson, *Handbook to the North-Western Province*, 74. The population of Mwinilunga District increased from 45,991 in 1963, to 51,398 in 1969, to 68,845 in 1980, to 81,496 in 1990 – this gives annual growth rates of 2.7% over the period 1969–1980 and 1.7% over the period 1980–1990; see: Patrick O. Ohadike, *Demographic Perspectives in Zambia: Rural-urban Growth and Social Change* (Manchester: Manchester University Press, 1981); Mary E. Jackman, *Recent Population Movements in Zambia: Some Aspects of the 1969 Census* (Manchester: Manchester University Press, 1973). Based on the 1969 census, Ohadike and Jackman both calculated 'expected growth rates', concluding that -2.6% and -3.8% respectively were due to out-migration from Mwinilunga District. Compared to other areas, the North-Western Province is an area of relatively low out-migration; Jackman, 56: 'The general picture of this area between the two censuses was one of slight out-migration ... By far the most important migration link during 1968–69 was with the Copperbelt, but the area is losing population very slowly compared to the other areas with major Copperbelt links, the rate of out-migration being only slightly higher than that of the western area.'

385 (NAZ) HM77/PP/2, P.W. Matoka, A Contribution to the Media Resource Center Freedom Forum, 8 November 1997 – Review of Zambia's 33 Years of Independence.

386 Potts, 'Counter-urbanization on the Zambian Copperbelt?'; Deborah Potts, 'Shall We Go Home? Increasing Urban Poverty in African Cities and Migration Processes', *The Geographical Journal* 161, No. 3 (1995): 245–64; Pottier, *Migrants No More*; Vali Jamal and John Weeks, 'The Vanishing Rural-Urban Gap in Sub-Saharan Africa', *International Labour*

of service showed an increase over time, but fluctuated considerably according to individual cases. Whereas in 1935 a taxable man from Mwinilunga would on average work 0.75 months a year, in the 1950s labour migrants would stay away at their place of employment for an average of four years.[387] Even then, however, some would work for several months, whereas others would remain in town their entire life.[388] The causes, motives, and effects of this persistent trend of labour migration from Mwinilunga thus need to be explained.

Most influentially, the history of labour migration in Zambia has been understood in terms of a 'modernist narrative', as part of 'the progressive, stage-wise emergence of a stable, settled urban working class'.[389] Allegedly, labour migration developed through a number of 'stages', whereby an initial phase of short-term and circulatory migration was replaced by partial stabilisation of labour and eventually by permanent urbanisation.[390] This view proposes that lone male migrants were increasingly supplanted by migrating families, including women and children.[391] Furthermore, this 'modernist narrative' suggests that ties between rural and urban areas were gradually severed, as migrants settled in town for longer periods.[392] Such views present the urban and the rural as two opposing spheres, 'the urban as the site of modernisation, individualisation and change, as opposed to the rural as the locus of tradition, communality and continuity'.[393] In this sense, the movement between rural and urban areas becomes a transformative act of social change.[394] The stage-like progression of the 'modernist narrative' has been fundamentally contested recently.[395] A number of detailed local and regional studies of labour migration have been published which challenge received wisdom.[396] Critics have suggested the

    Review 127, No. 3 (1988): 271–92; Robin H. Palmer, 'Land Tenure Insecurity on the Zambian Copperbelt, 1998: Anyone Going Back to the Land?', *Social Dynamics* 26, No. 2 (2000): 154–70.

387 (NAZ) SEC2/133, N.S. Price, Mwinilunga District Annual Report, 31 December 1935; (NAZ) SEC2/960, K.J. Forder, Mwinilunga District Tour Report, 28 September 1952.

388 This view is based on numerous interviews.

389 Ferguson, 'Mobile Workers', 385; Macmillan, 'The Historiography of Transition'; Moore and Vaughan, *Cutting Down Trees*, 141–56; Crehan, *The Fractured Community*.

390 Ferguson, 'Mobile Workers.'

391 Parpart, 'Where Is Your Mother?'; Chauncey, 'The Locus of Reproduction.'

392 Geschiere and Gugler, 'The Urban-Rural Connection'; Ferguson, *Expectations of Modernity.*

393 Andersson, 'Reinterpreting the Rural-Urban Connection', 89; James Ferguson, 'The Country and the City on the Copperbelt', *Cultural Anthropology* 7, No. 1 (1992): 80–92.

394 Ferguson, *Expectations of Modernity*; Cooper, *Struggle for the City*, 12.

395 Macmillan, 'The Historiography of Transition'; Moore and Vaughan, *Cutting Down Trees*; Potts, 'Counter-Urbanization on the Zambian Copperbelt?'

396 For example: Moore and Vaughan, *Cutting Down Trees*; Crehan, *The Fractured Community*; Pottier, *Migrants No More.*

co-existence of various patterns of migration, thereby questioning the idea of the 'typical migrant'.[397] Furthermore, the enduring ties between rural and urban areas, as well as recent trends of counter-urbanisation, disprove ideas of linear change.[398] By examining labour migration from Mwinilunga, the 'modernist narrative' can be challenged on several points. First of all, migration from Mwinilunga followed a wide range of patterns rather than a linear trajectory from temporary migrant labourer to permanent urbanite. Secondly, ties between rural and urban areas have not been severed. On the contrary, labour migration might be seen in terms of social connectivity, establishing close and enduring links between rural and urban localities. Thirdly, the modernist narrative – as well as much subsequent historiography – places undue emphasis on economic motives for migration. Instead, life histories from Mwinilunga suggest the importance of sociocultural dispositions and aspirations towards self-realisation.[399]

2.2.1   Life Histories of Labour Migrants from Mwinilunga

Life histories of workers from Mwinilunga place the variety of patterns of labour migration into perspective. Even a single individual could combine various patterns of movement within the course of a lifetime.[400] Nyambanza Kaisala, for example, was born in Sailunga Chiefdom in 1905. Over the course of his adult life, Nyambanza had various jobs, which took him far away from his village of birth. After having worked as a cook for four years in Élisabethville (Lubumbashi), Congo, Nyambanza started working as a mine foreman in the same city for eight years. Thereafter, he continued his employment as a foreman, but he moved to Kolwezi, Congo, where he was employed for ten years. Subsequently, he worked at Nkana mine (Kitwe) on the Northern Rhodesian Copperbelt for six years, after which he returned to Mwinilunga to work as a government messenger for six months. Leaving as a single migrant, Nyambanza married after his return from Congo, and he took his wife with him to subsequent places of employment. While he was working, he did visit his home village but not at regular intervals. Moreover, although he did

397   Moore and Vaughan, *Cutting Down Trees*; Englund, 'The Village in the City'; Andersson, 'Reinterpreting the Rural-Urban Connection.'
398   Van Binsbergen, 'Globalization and Virtuality'; Potts, 'Counter-Urbanization on the Zambian Copperbelt?.'
399   Inspiration for this approach has been taken from: Andersson, 'Reinterpreting the Rural-Urban Connection'; De Boeck, 'Borderland Breccia'; De Bruijn, Van Dijk, and Foeken, *Mobile Africa*, 2.
400   These points are equally made by Ferguson, *Expectations of Modernity;* Macmillan, 'The Historiography of Transition'; Moore and Vaughan, *Cutting Down Trees.*

return to Mwinilunga after his retirement from the Copperbelt, he settled in the township rather than in his village of birth.[401] Nyambanza Kaisala's employment history defies the neat categorisations of the 'modernist narrative'. Although Nyambanza was not a short-term 'circular migrant', neither was he 'permanently urbanised', as he continued to move from place to place during his 28.5 years of employment. As a labour migrant, Nyambanza straddled the categories single and married, and due to his loose but significant links to his home area he was neither 'localist' nor 'cosmopolitan'.[402] This life history suggests that it is difficult to fit the intricacies of individual daily lives into smooth narratives of social change.

A different example is provided by Spoon Kapanga, who engaged in his first labour contract at the age of 16, when he left Mwinilunga to work in Nkana (Kitwe) on the Northern Rhodesian Copperbelt.[403] This was in the 1930s and Spoon was employed as a domestic servant for a white man, George. He gained experience in cleaning and cooking (hence his name Spoon), especially of dishes such as roast beef. When his father died, after only one year of employment, Spoon went back to his village in Chief Kanongesha's area to attend the funeral. After several months he decided to return to the Copperbelt, but this time to Chingola, where he was employed as a cook for a mission. Spoon was fired after three years due to excessive drinking, and he went back to Kanongesha. His knowledge of cooking European dishes secured him a job at the Catholic mission at Lwawu, where he worked for the next thirty years.[404] This employment history might be typified as circular labour migration, as Spoon went to town and came back several times during his career. Yet Spoon's story does not fit the purposeful and very short-term back and forth movement.[405] Spoon went back to Kanongesha due to a funeral and because he was fired, not because he wanted to re-engage with the socioeconomic activities (e.g. cultivation, hunting, or politics) in his home village. Spoon's story shows that employment in town and in the village could be related in complex ways, as experience gained in town could secure similar employment in the village. Spoon's trajectory suggests a degree of contingency rather than any purposeful strategy of labour migration or a predetermined career path. In essence, this

401 (BOD) Richard Cranmer Dening Papers: 15 boxes, uncatalogued; notes from 1948.
402 Ferguson, *Expectations of Modernity.*
403 Interview with Spoon Kapanga, 26 July 2010, Kanongesha.
404 See also interview with Brother Joe Weisling, 30 July 2010, Lwawu Mission, Kanongesha.
405 Ferguson, 'Mobile Workers, Modernist Narratives.'

story is a singular one that does not neatly fit the 'modernist narrative' and thus complicates existing accounts of labour migration in the area.[406]

Quite a different trajectory was followed by William Ngangu.[407] In the 1940s, when he was 18, William moved to Ndola to stay with his uncle. William had pursued mission education up to Standard IV at Kalene Hill in Chief Nyakaseya's area, and this secured him a low-level job at the mines in Chingola. He did not like the job, especially because he had a fear of going underground. So he persuaded his uncle to finance further education in Ndola, which qualified him for a job as a clerk. William started as an administrative employee in Ndola and gradually worked his way up within the hierarchy of the mines. He married a woman from Southern Province, who detested his home village in Chief Nyakaseya's area. The couple scarcely visited Ngangu's home, except for special occasions and major ceremonies. Nonetheless, William became one of the founding members of the Lunda cultural association on the Copperbelt, organising meetings and support groups for fellow migrants from Mwinilunga District. When I visited William Ngangu he was very eager to speak about the experiences of fellow Lundas on the Copperbelt, and although he had lived on the Copperbelt almost his entire life he still taught his daughters how to speak 'deep Lunda'. William financed the pineapple transporting business of his brother, and he educated several of his nieces and nephews in Nyakaseya. Whilst permanent urbanisation is presented as a mentality shift,[408] an act of breaking all bonds with 'home', William Ngangu's story seems to be quite different. William maintained close and complex relationships with the people in Chief Nyakaseya's area and with fellow Lundas on the Copperbelt, even whilst carving out a distinctly 'cosmopolitan' lifestyle that involved impeccable English speech, fancy furniture, and fashionable clothing.[409] Although William Ngangu perhaps appeared to be 'permanently urbanised', his life history conveys complex and multiple strategies of identity formation and intricate relationships with his 'home' village.

Mobility is equally central to the life history of Thomas Kasayi, yet his trajectory of labour migration diverges from previous narratives.[410] Thomas' father was a trader in Chief Ntambu's area, and Thomas had decided from a young age that he would take over his father's trading business. He learnt to run the store in Ntambu through practice, but he lacked capital to significantly

---

406   Iva Peša, 'Wealth, Success and Personhood: Trajectories of Labour Migration from Mwinilunga District, 1930s–1970s', *Zambia Social Science Journal* 4, No. 1 (2013).

407   Interview with William Ngangu, 26 February 2010, Ndola.

408   Ferguson, *Expectations of Modernity.*

409   AbdouMaliq Simone and Abdelghani Abouhani, eds., *Urban Africa: Changing Contours of Survival in the City* (London: Zed Books, 2005).

410   Interview with Thomas Kasayi, 29 September 2010, Ntambu.

expand the business. So at the age of 22 in the 1950s Thomas moved to Kolwezi in Congo, where he worked at a woodcutting camp, which involved hard
work but minimal pay. He soon discovered that it would be more profitable to
trade chickens from Ntambu for second-hand clothing from Congo, which he
transported back to his store in Ntambu to sell. Each trading trip would take
him approximately six months to complete and he made at least four such
trips over the next five years. The profit from selling second-hand clothing enabled him to buy cattle, which he transported from Kasempa to Mwinilunga
by foot. Once he had expanded his herd sufficiently, he opened a butcher's
shop in Mwinilunga Township. Thomas Kasayi's trips as a labour migrant and
trader, thus, served the purpose of expanding his business in Mwinilunga. He
strengthened this strategy by building a solid brick house with glass windows
in Mwinilunga Township in the 1960s, which entrenched his image as one of
the most powerful businessmen in the area. Thomas Kasayi's story shows that
rural and urban strategies could be intricately linked. Thomas was neither a
circular labour migrant nor permanently urbanised; in fact his story fits none
of the categories of the 'modernist narrative'. Thomas Kasayi's story suggests
that labour migration could be driven by complex motivations, which straddled the rural-urban divide.[411]

   These examples of labour migrant trajectories are all very different. Together, these stories merely complicate existing narratives of labour migration
and theories of social change, without proposing one coherent alternative to
replace the 'modernist narrative'. What they do suggest, however, is the cen-
trality of personal motivation rather than structural force in explaining labour migrant trajectories.[412] Whereas Spoon Kapanga purposefully sought to
migrate to town to earn wealth, circumstances propelled him to move back
to his village. Even if short-term labour migration had not generated the desired wealth, it had endowed him with the skills to secure lucrative employment locally. Thomas Kasayi's labour migration trajectory followed a similar
short-term pattern, yet his motivations were very different. Thomas' aim was
never to secure urban wealth. Rather, he used urban employment to boost his
rural standing and earn an income with which to expand his trading business.
William Ngangu's career as a labour migrant, contrastingly, involved long-term
urban residence. Yet his motivations might not have been too dissimilar from
those of short-term labour migrants. Even as William earned wealth and status in an urban setting, he simultaneously maintained strong rural linkages.
His urban career, in fact, served to bolster his carefully cultivated status within
Mwinilunga. Structural narratives and rigid categorisations of social change, as

411 Compare with: Englund, 'The Village in the City.'
412 See also Peša, 'Wealth, Success and Personhood.'

proposed by the 'modernist narrative', seem unable to reflect the ambiguities and contradictions of labour migrant trajectories, the messiness of historical change, and the varieties of responses to it.[413] How to do justice to the complexity and individuality of these trajectories, of the motivations, aspirations, and objectives of these men, whilst still arriving at a narrative of labour migration and social change in Mwinilunga?

Labour migration from Mwinilunga followed a variety of patterns from the outset. It was not necessarily a transformative act, but could be constitutive of rural society in Mwinilunga – especially when viewed within the historical 'culture of mobility' in the area.[414] In this sense, labour migration was a strategy to enhance the security and predictability of life.[415] It formed part of a diversity of livelihood options, existing next to, and potentially contributing to, agricultural production, animal husbandry or salaried labour within the district.[416] Labour migration was a strategy, involving an assessment of socioeconomic options, which changed over time.[417] Some individuals might migrate to town, marry there and never move back to Mwinilunga, whereas others would undertake only one trip to work for several months, thereafter investing their earnings in agriculture or trade.[418] These diverse possibilities cannot be reduced to fixed stages. Through life histories, the enduring and complex connections between rural and urban spheres become apparent.

2.2.2 Reconfiguring Locality Through Labour Migration: Economic Motives and the Rural-Urban Divide

As the examples so far have shown, the causes and motives for labour migration were manifold and interrelated. The factors stressed most frequently and forcefully in the historiography, however, pertain to the economic sphere.[419] Labour migration has been understood as the outcome of 'push' and 'pull' factors, being driven by relative poverty and a lack of opportunity in rural areas (push factors), whilst being attracted by a growing demand for labour in industrialised urban areas (pull factors).[420] Economic explanations for migration

413 Lisa A. Lindsay, 'Biography in African History', *History in Africa* 44 (2017): 16.
414 See: Englund, 'The Village in the City'; Andersson, 'Reinterpreting the Rural-Urban Connection.'
415 Harries, *Work, Culture, and Identity*, 17.
416 De Haan, 'Livelihoods and Poverty'; Pritchett, *Lunda-Ndembu*.
417 Moore and Vaughan, *Cutting Down Trees*, 141–42.
418 This view is based on numerous interviews.
419 See: Potts, 'Counter-Urbanization on the Zambian Copperbelt?'; Andersson, 'Informal Moves.'
420 Bakewell, 'Keeping Them in Their Place', 1345; De Haan, 'Livelihoods and Poverty.'

have been proposed at both individual and structural levels.[421] Labour migrants are either seen as acting individually, according to a rationale of economic self-interest and profit maximisation.[422] Or labour migration is seen
as the structural outcome of global capitalism.[423] In this latter view, in sway
among Marxist-inspired scholars, individuals and entire rural communities
have been 'gradually divorced from their means of production and subsistence', propelling the need for labour migration to urban areas where the process of 'primitive capitalist accumulation', effected through taxation and state
coercion, was already underway.[424] This process would result in the formation
of rural 'labour reserves', a 'rural-urban divide', but might in some cases lead to
development.[425] Although other factors should be taken into consideration,
economic factors are indeed important in explaining patterns of labour migration from Mwinilunga. Colonial officials identified the need to earn a monetary income, especially for purposes of taxation, as the driving force behind
migration from Mwinilunga.[426] Some officials judged the Lunda as not very
ambitious in monetary terms or consumptive aspirations, asserting that 'sufficient money to pay their tax, and obtain a few clothes is all they desire'.[427]
Others, however, complained about 'the exodus of the younger generation to
gain what may be termed "easy money" by work on the mines', stating that 'the
earning capacity of the native has increased enormously and must continue to
grow – more money creating fresh wants'.[428]

Migrants viewed opportunities in urban areas in relation to those in rural
areas, as one colonial official in 1958 noted: 'The cost of living is rising rapidly
and we find that many educated men (...) will seek employment in the Copperbelt where more money can be earned [than within Mwinilunga]'.[429] Because
money-earning and employment options within Mwinilunga generally remained limited in the twentieth century,[430] the consequent disparity between
rural and urban income levels propelled some to seek opportunities outside of
their villages:

421   See Urry, *Mobilities*.
422   O'Laughlin, 'Proletarianisation, Agency and Changing Rural Livelihoods' criticises agency
      and livelihoods.
423   Amin, 'Underdevelopment and Dependence.'
424   Plange, 'Opportunity Cost and Labour Migration', 661.
425   See Arrighi, 'Labour Supplies in Historical Perspective.'
426   This view is based on a wide reading of archival sources (NAZ).
427   (NAZ) KSE6/1/4, F.V. Bruce-Miller, Mwinilunga Sub-District Annual Report, 31 March 1924.
428   (NAZ) SEC2/131 Vol.1, D.C. Hughes-Chamberlain, Mwinilunga Sub-District Annual Report,
      31 December 1929.
429   (NAZ) North-Western Province African Provincial Council, April 1958.
430   Turner and Turner, 'Money Economy'; Pritchett, *Lunda-Ndembu*.

Money is very easy to earn and to spend in populated areas and few now
think it worth while to labour on their own for small wages or benefit.
These areas should be the granaries of settled areas. Instead they are becoming backwaters and depopulated areas. The native farmer, with the
cost of transport, cannot possibly compete with wages which are given
on the line [of rail], and the wives of natives now only judge their husbands by what they can provide for them in the way of clothes and a soft
time.[431]

Due to a lack of opportunities to sell crops locally and a general 'discontent
with the prices paid for produce grown at home', some decided 'to give up
agriculture and look for a job' in urban areas where employment appeared
lucrative or easier to obtain.[432] Even in the late 1940s, 1950s, and early 1960s,
when an agricultural boom prevailed and crops could easily be marketed from
Mwinilunga, officials noted that 'the overwhelming majority of males now
look to industry for an assured wage, and will not consider the alternative of
improved farming with its heavy toil and uncertain returns and markets'.[433]

    After independence, migrants continued to judge urban attractions in the
light of rural realities. Government reports from the 1970s lamented that:

    During the six years since Independence (…) we were not able to close
    the gap between urban and rural incomes. In fact, it is even wider to-
    day than it was when we started off on our own. This development does
    not encourage our young people to remain in the rural areas and take up
    farming as a career. The trend to go to the towns is increasing even if the
    people know that the chances of finding a job are very remote indeed.[434]

Although employment proved difficult to obtain in towns, especially from
the late 1970s onwards, urban areas still held relative attractions vis-à-vis rural
areas.[435] These attractions had to do with national income disparities, which
were substantial in certain years. In 1968, for example, Zambian mineworkers
earned K1300 a year, urban wage earners K640, whereas peasant farmers
earned a meagre K145 a year.[436] In connection to this, official reports stated

431   (NAZ) SEC2/955 H.B. Waugh, Mwinilunga District Tour Report, 11 October 1940.
432   (NAZ) SEC2/137, F.R.G Phillips, Mwinilunga District Annual Report, 1954.
433   (NAZ) NWP1/2/102 Loc.4919, E.L. Button, Mwinilunga District Annual Report, 1960.
434   (UNIPA) UNIP5/3/1/52, A New Strategy for Rural Development in Zambia, 1970.
435   Potts, 'Counter-Urbanization on the Zambian Copperbelt?'
436   (NAZ) Report of the Second National Convention on Rural Development: Incomes, Wages
      and Prices in Zambia, 12 December 1969.

that 'rapidly increasing prices for consumer goods and cost of production, on the one hand, and stagnant or even declining producer prices, on the other, make farming not a very attractive proposition'.[437] The contrasts between rural and urban areas were posed in stark terms, of 'stagnation' as opposed to 'dynamism', or even 'tradition' versus 'modernity'.[438] Such a 'dualism' was adopted in discourse and popular consciousness, being reflected in reports from the 1970s:

> On one side we have the monetised side of our economy with all the characteristics of dynamic temporal change based on modern technology. On the other side we have the so-called rural sector characterised by a low level of technology, economic performance and in fact painful poverty, ignorance and disease. The result of the yawning gap between the urban and rural areas in the standards of living is the exodus of able-bodied people from the rural countryside to the line-of-rail urban areas.[439]

Economic understandings of labour migration propose a stark dichotomy between rural and urban areas. Yet residence in urban areas was driven by rural realities, which encompassed more than just economic motivations. Labour migration was often underpinned by a desire to improve village life, functioning as a strategy to enhance the security and predictability of life for the inhabitants of Mwinilunga. Neither viewing rural and urban spheres as dichotomous, nor looking at economic dynamics alone can explain patterns of labour migration satisfactorily. Labour migration formed part of a diversity of livelihood options, existing next to agricultural production, animal husbandry, and salaried labour within the district.[440] Instead of being the outcome of economic push and pull factors, or being determined by state policies, labour migration can be better understood as a strategy towards self-realisation.[441]

2.2.3   Money, Consumption, and Building Wealth

Mobility – and labour migration in particular – was part of a process towards self-realisation. In Mwinilunga a person would become valued within the community through mobility, attaining status, wealth, and respect among peers.

---

437   (NAZ) A New Strategy for Rural Development in Zambia, 23 March 1970.
438   Ferguson, 'The Country and the City', 80–92.
439   (UNIPA) UNIP1/2/12, Chairman of the Rural Development Committee, 22 September 1973.
440   Pritchett, *Lunda-Ndembu*.
441   Andersson, 'Reinterpreting the Rural-Urban Connection'; Englund, 'The Village in the City'; Guyer, 'Wealth in People and Self-Realization'; De Boeck, 'Domesticating Diamonds and Dollars.'

Individuals sought 'the acknowledgement, regard, and attention of other people – which was the basis of reputation and influence, and thus constitutive of social being'.[442] In this connection, 'it was not only the great figures but everyone who seems to have had the possibility of authorship of something, however small', and labour migration was one means of achieving 'reality', 'value', and 'self-realisation'.[443] In Mwinilunga labour migration constituted an integral part of building one's career. Yet labour migration is only one among many strategies towards self-realisation, which include agricultural production, hunting, and trade.[444] That is why labour migration should be analysed in its full societal setting. Work is 'a positive aspect of human activity, and is expressed in the making of self and others in the course of everyday life'.[445] Labour migration did not primarily serve the economic objective of attaining wealth, but was geared towards social standing. Self-realisation, far from being an individual pursuit, proved a thoroughly social undertaking. One could only make a name for oneself in relation to others.[446] For the context of Mwinilunga, Turner explained that 'a man can acquire wealth by working in the White economy as a wage labourer', but 'it seems often (...) to be the aim of returned labour-migrants (...) to obtain influence and subsequently office, in traditional villages'. Turner concluded that most labour migrants 'see the village as their ultimate home, and regard their wage-labour as a means of acquiring the wealth that will give them prestige in the village sphere'.[447] Next to placing emphasis on personal ambitions and social aspirations towards self-realisation, this statement questions the dichotomy between rural and urban areas. Even if labour migration involved physical mobility and (temporary) movement away from the village, it was not necessarily a transformative act. Rather, labour migration could be a means to acquire wealth and influence within the village, by becoming a 'Big Man' and building wealth in people.[448] Gaining the respect of others was the ultimate aim of successful individuals, and this aim could be attained through labour migration.

Labour migration was a 'deliberate strategy to accumulate wealth' rather than being a 'last resort' of impoverished rural producers who sought to generate tax money.[449] Labour migration was not so much rooted in absolute rural

---

442   Barber, 'Money, Self-Realization and the Person', 216.
443   Guyer, 'Wealth in People and Self-Realization', 255.
444   Bakewell, 'Refugees Repatriating'; Turner, *Schism and Continuity*; Pritchett, *Lunda-Ndembu.*
445   Comaroff and Comaroff, 'The Madman and the Migrant', 197.
446   De Boeck, 'Borderland Breccia'; De Boeck, 'Domesticating Diamonds and Dollars.'
447   Turner, *Schism and Continuity*, 135.
448   Guyer, 'Wealth in People and Self-Realization'; Miller, *Way of Death.*
449   Andersson, 'Administrators' Knowledge', 128.

poverty, but was driven by a desire to prosper in rural areas. In this sense, it was part of a process towards self-realisation.[450] In the 1950s, colonial officials in Mwinilunga noted that 'those at work are the younger, more energetic and more educated members of the population'.[451] Indeed, 'it is not the poorest of the poor who migrate – they cannot afford it – but it is those with lower-middle incomes. Mobility is a privilege of the relatively wealthy'.[452] Resources are required to migrate. Not only knowledge, skills, and material wealth but also social capital and personality have to be cultivated.[453] Application letters to the mines on the Zambian Copperbelt suggest that workers from Mwinilunga aspired towards self-realisation. This was viewed as an inherently social achievement, involving family, kin, and ideas of the nation. One applicant declared that 'I would like to develop myself', as she wished to 'be able to look after my family'. She applied to the mines because 'it is one of the largest industries in Zambia which serves both the nation and neighbouring countries'.[454] Another applicant wanted to become 'successful', further wishing his 'career to grow into something which will make me support myself and the relatives who wants support'.[455] A third applicant stated that he wanted to be trained to help the company and the country. He continued: 'I like working very much because I can feed myself. I dislike to stay without working because I can't feed myself'.[456] Educated and skilled individuals, who failed to find lucrative employment locally, would move to urban areas where opportunities were more readily available.[457] Not all mission-educated individuals, for example, could obtain employment as teachers or orderlies within Mwinilunga. Consequently, large numbers would seek their luck on the Copperbelt or in the capital city Lusaka.[458]

The practice of labour migration thus contributed to the process of self-realisation in Mwinilunga. Labour migration was driven not only by economic

---

450 Englund, 'The Village in the City', 151; Andersson, 'Reinterpreting the Rural-Urban Connection'; De Haan, 'Livelihoods and Poverty.'

451 (NAZ) SEC2/966, C.J. Fryer, Mwinilunga District Tour Report, 9 September 1958.

452 Bakewell, 'Keeping Them in Their Place', 1350; De Haan, 'Livelihoods and Poverty', 16–22.

453 See Guyer and Eno Belinga, 'Wealth in People as Wealth in Knowledge.'

454 (ZCCM) Rabby Sameta, Mine No. 76934, Loc. Y4.9A, Born 29.8.1952, Entered Service 21.8.1972, Left Service 1.12.1972.

455 (ZCCM) Moses Kanjanja, Mine No. 82803, Loc. 18.1.5F, Born 18.08.1959, Entered Service 15.05.1979, Left Service 31.10.1992.

456 (ZCCM) G. Sameta, Mine No. 80106, Loc. 16.4.2A, Born 15.2.1956, Entered Service 30.6.1975, Left Service 31.8.1994.

457 Wim H.M.L. Hoppers, *Education in a Rural Society: Primary Pupils and School Leavers in Mwinilunga, Zambia* (The Hague, 1981).

458 Fisher and Hoyte, *Ndotolu*; Kalusa, 'Disease and the Remaking of Missionary Medicine.'

objectives but also encompassed ideology, culture, and aspirations towards a 'good life'.[459] Next to income disparities, differences in the provision of services (health care, education, and leisure) between town and country were pronounced.[460] The 'bright lights' of the city acted as a magnet, and the lifestyle in towns ('town life') propelled labour migration. Colonial officials in Mwinilunga concurred that 'it is only too easy to understand why the young and energetic want to leave the monotony of village life and see the excitements and wealth of the Copperbelt'.[461] The 'beerhalls, tea rooms, and facilities for purchasing European food – all of which appeal to the village African', attracted workers from Mwinilunga to the Copperbelt.[462] Individuals consciously weighed terms of employment, conditions of service, and other factors before taking up urban residence.[463] Urban and rural areas were viewed relationally. In urban areas, wages were higher, whilst employment and leisure opportunities were more available than within Mwinilunga. This opened avenues towards self-Realisation and motivated numerous individuals to migrate. Labour migration, thus, is a 'lifestyle (…) inspired by aspirations that do not simply envisage material accumulation', but are premised on sociocultural dispositions (see Photo 10).[464]

Consumptive aspirations, a motive for mobility that has received relatively little attention in the historiography so far, constituted a powerful incentive to earn money and engage in labour migration from Mwinilunga.[465] One labour migrant, Makajina Kahilu, explained his trip to Johannesburg, largely on foot, as driven by a desire to purchase clothing, to obtain a nice suit contributing to good apparel.[466] Consumptive desires furthermore explain why recruiters offered blankets to prospective workers, and why these were effective inducements to engage in labour contracts.[467] Yet consumption was not a purely economic act, but was connected to social relationships and status.[468] Labour migration provided access to consumer goods, and thereby penetrated social

459   Barrett, 'Walking Home Majestically', 93–113.
460   Hortense Powdermaker, *Copper Town: Changing Africa: The Human Situation on the Rhodesian Copperbelt* (New York: Harper and Row, 1962); Wilson, *The Economics of Detribalization*; Parpart, 'Where Is Your Mother?'
461   (NAZ) SEC2/966, C.J. Fryer, Mwinilunga District Tour Report, 14 November 1958.
462   (NAZ) SEC2/957, A. Stockwell-Jones, Mwinilunga District Tour Report, 30 January 1949.
463   Harries, *Work, Culture, and Identity*; Allina-Pisano, 'Borderlands, Boundaries.'
464   Englund, 'The Village in the City', 152; Andersson, 'Reinterpreting the Rural-Urban Connection.'
465   See: Ross, Hinfelaar, and Peša, *The Objects of Life*, 2–3; Barrett, 'Walking Home Majestically.'
466   Interview with Makajina Kahilu, 8 March 2010, Ikelenge.
467   (NAZ) KSE1/1/1, R.W. Yule, 13 October 1915.
468   See the discussion on 'wealth in people' in Chapter 4. See Wilson, *The Economics of Detribalization*.

relationships, influencing the demands, stakes, and expectations of marriage negotiations, for example.[469] Bridewealth negotiations in a local court in 1917 illustrate this point. When a migrant labourer engaged a girl, he gave her uncle a string of beads as initial bridewealth. When he returned from work in Bulawayo, Zimbabwe, demands were raised, and the man was asked to provide two coats to the girl's uncle and a handkerchief to the girl. After an additional trip to Lubumbashi, Congo, the man was asked for a blanket for the girl's mother, whereas the girl received a four yard piece of calico and a dress.[470] Labour migration thus mediated consumptive aspirations, which could consolidate social relationships. Migrant labourers not only purchased clothing for themselves but would also distribute clothing to their kin in the village, whilst on leave or they would bring back goods after the end of their contracts.[471] Whilst working on the line of rail where consumer goods were cheaper than within Mwinilunga, labour migrants would 'buy what few cloths they require'.[472] Goods functioned as a marker of social relationships but also furthered goals of self-realisation by making wealthy migrants into 'Big Men'. Due to labour migration and the wealth this generated, consumer goods such as clothes, pots, and pans became more widespread in the villages in Mwinilunga and demand for these goods increased.[473] Labour migration raised expectations of consumption and thereby further stimulated the need to earn money and migrate. Once consumer goods came to be regarded as necessities, consumptive aspirations provided an incentive towards labour migration. Migrants' markers of economic success, in the form of clothing, a bicycle, or a sewing machine, enticed others to pursue a migrant career as well.[474] Consumption could act as a self-propelling force behind labour migration, but this was only due to the linkages between consumption, social relationships, and the process of self-realisation.[475]

Urban employment was not motivated by purely economic incentives, but was driven by aspirations of personal and social advancement. Such aspirations resulted in a diversity of strategies and a 'positive appreciation of diversity in life-style and personality type'.[476] Whereas some migrants sought

---

469   See Parpart, 'Where Is Your Mother?'
470   (NAZ) KSE3/1/2/1, Mwaweshya v. Mulambila of Keshi Village, 2 August 1917.
471   Turner, *Schism and Continuity*; Turner and Turner, 'Money Economy.'
472   (NAZ) F.V. Bruce-Miller, Mwinilunga District Annual Report, 1926.
473   (NAZ) SEC2/131 Vol.1, D.C. Hughes-Chamberlain, Mwinilunga Sub-District Annual Report, 31 December 1929; Wilson, *The Economics of Detribalization.*
474   Andersson, 'Informal Moves', 393; Barrett, 'Walking Home Majestically.'
475   Guyer, 'Wealth in People and Self-Realization.'
476   Guyer and Eno Belinga, 'Wealth in People as Wealth in Knowledge', 105.

short contracts so that they could return to their village to cultivate crops, others stayed in town for long periods to accumulate monetary wealth with which to set up a trading enterprise.[477] Strategies towards self-realisation were various, straddling the boundaries between rural and urban spheres. Labour migration was 'shaped by local rural modes, conceptions and categories of wealth, accumulation, expenditure, physical and social reproduction and well-being'.[478] In Mwinilunga labour migration provided a means to build wealth and personhood, but so did pineapple cultivation and hunting. This section has argued that viewing labour migration through the prism of self-realisation enhances understanding of its underlying motives and dynamics. Over the course of the twentieth century in Mwinilunga, a mobile work force was created, which sought opportunities, according to personal preferences, in rural or urban areas. The strategy of labour migration was driven by rural realities and livelihoods, but equally influenced these in turn. It is, therefore, pertinent to ask how labour migration influenced not only the identity and well-being of individual migrants but also society in Mwinilunga.

2.3   Decay or Boom? Labour Migration and Village Life
Even more than the consequences of labour migration on individual trajectories, the historiographical debate has discussed the effects of labour migration on village society and the rural economy.[479] Structuralist economic and political perspectives have suggested that labour migration would lead to either 'development', or 'underdevelopment' and rural decay.[480] On the one hand, urbanisation and industrialisation could generate monetary income and wealth, leading to 'development'.[481] In Mwinilunga this positive association was acknowledged by colonial officials as early as the 1930s: 'Activities have increased in the industrial centres and the prosperity in these areas is reflected in the villages which supply the men who are employed in them'.[482] In connection to this, labour migration generated remittances and an increase in

---

477   Turner, *Schism and Continuity*; Turner and Turner, 'Money Economy'; Pritchett, *Lunda-Ndembu*.
478   De Boeck, 'Domesticating Diamonds and Dollars', 779–80.
479   Richards, *Land, Labour and Diet*; Moore and Vaughan, *Cutting Down Trees*; Palmer and Parsons, *The Roots of Rural Poverty*, are but a few examples.
480   See: Moore and Vaughan, *Cutting Down Trees*; Bakewell, 'Keeping Them in Their Place'; De Haan, 'Livelihoods and Poverty'; Ferguson, *Expectations of Modernity*.
481   Ferguson, *Expectations of Modernity*, 33; Cooper, *Struggle for the City*, 12.
482   (NAZ) SEC2/153, Mwinilunga District Annual Report, 1939.

human capital, benefitting the area of origin by raising standards of living.[483] Nevertheless, the effects of labour migration have remained ambiguous and debated. In a more negative way, labour migration has been connected to issues of underdevelopment and proletarianisation.[484] According to such views widespread rural poverty propelled individuals to earn money through labour migration, yet migration and salaried employment simultaneously divorced workers from an independent means of production in the form of land. This process would make workers increasingly dependent on the capitalist sector and would aggravate the impoverishment of rural 'labour reserves', which had been depleted of the workforce needed to till the land.[485] Scepticism about the negative effects of labour migration on rural society in Mwinilunga has been voiced by colonial and post-colonial officials as well as by RLI scholars.[486] Turner noted that 'changes brought about by the growing participation of Ndembu in the Rhodesian cash economy and an increased rate of labour migration, have in some areas (...) drastically reshaped some institutions and destroyed others'.[487] Discourses of development and underdevelopment, stability and disruption, or boom and decay, need to be further scrutinised. How has labour migration influenced the locality, livelihoods, and sociality of people in Mwinilunga?

Even though colonial policy encouraged labour migration as a means to earn tax money and engage in the monetary economy,[488] concerns were voiced against the practice during the twentieth century. Disconcertedly, colonial officials in Mwinilunga would complain that 'the mines can't "have it both ways", that is have cheap labour and at the same time expect and abundance of cheap food from the villages which they have depopulated'.[489] Because urban employment drained the labour force from rural areas, officials feared that urban and rural wealth could not coincide. Given prevailing labour bottlenecks, wage employment would jeopardise agricultural production. That is why the male absenteeism due to outmigration and the supposedly deleterious effects this had on agricultural production and village make-up were

---

483   De Haan, 'Livelihoods and Poverty', 21.
484   See: Amin, 'Underdevelopment and Dependence'; Arrighi, 'Labour Supplies in Historical Perspective.'
485   Amin, 'Underdevelopment and Dependence.'
486   Richards, *Land, Labour and Diet*, has famously advanced the thesis of 'rural decay'.
487   Turner, *Schism and Continuity*, 17.
488   Bakewell, 'Keeping Them in Their Place'; Ferguson, 'Mobile Workers.'
489   (NAZ) SEC2/131 Vol.2, E. Sharpe, Kasempa Province Mwinilunga District Annual Report, 1930.

cause for such serious distress among officials.[490] In the 1950s, one official lamented that 'there is a lack of men which seriously impairs the village labour force. I frequently met old men and hungry women and children in the same community as possessed miles of good but uncultivated land'.[491] The potentially negative effects of labour migration on agricultural production had been noticed since the 1920s:

> It is becoming more and more evident that the exodus of youths and men from the villages, consequent upon the greatly increased demands for labour, is having a serious effect upon native agriculture (...) It has been reported, from certain districts, that the number of able-bodied men remaining in the villages is so small that the women have been compelled to cultivate old gardens in which the soil had become impoverished. The crops reaped have, naturally, been poor.[492]

In this connection, officials anticipated that labour migration would provoke a 'vicious circle', as 'it is not possible to develop an area if there are no able-bodied people there to do the work, and the people will not stay at home unless there is a means of obtaining a remunerative return for their labours'.[493] As a consequence, 'in the worst affected villages life just stagnates', and 'there is a great tendency for the houses occupied by their [labour migrants'] wives to be allowed to fall into a very dilapidated condition'.[494] Colonial officials in Mwinilunga overwhelmingly regarded the effects of labour migration on village life and agricultural production as detrimental. In the late 1940s, a report stated that:

> The greatest limiting factor is the progressive impoverishment of the villages with the drift to the Towns. It is idle to talk about social welfare and development here unless and until some bold and constructive means can be found and enforced to stop this drift. Over-industrialisation of the Territory, if at the cost of the rural districts, must in the long run prove

---

490 See: Moore and Vaughan, *Cutting Down Trees*, 140–77; Deborah Potts, 'Worker-peasants and Farmer-housewives in Africa: The Debate About 'Committed' Farmers, Access to Land and Agricultural Production', *Journal of Southern African Studies* 26, No. 4 (2000): 807–32.

491 (NAZ) SEC2/959, K.J. Forder, Mwinilunga District Tour Report, November 1951.

492 (NAZ) Northern Rhodesia Department of Agriculture Annual Report, 1929.

493 (NAZ) SEC2/962, R.S. Thompson, Mwinilunga District Tour Report, 16 September 1954.

494 (NAZ) SEC2/967, W.D. Grant, Mwinilunga District Tour Report, 21 April 1959; (NAZ) NWP1/2/2 Loc.4897, C.M.N. White, Mwinilunga District Tour Report, 7 December 1938.

> extremely costly, if not disastrous (...) [Migrants] send no money, no
> clothes home, and the state of the village is most pitiable.[495]

Such rural decay and underdevelopment were attributed to policies of urban
bias, as high wages attracted disproportionate labour force from rural to urban
areas.[496] In order to lessen rural-urban income disparities, especially after independence, government policy rhetorically aimed 'to raise productivity on as
wide a front as is practical in order to (...) make rural life more attractive and
thus curb the drift towards urban employment'.[497]

Nevertheless, these views of rural decay, disruption or even breakdown do
not seem to be in congruence with the rapid increase in agricultural production and the boom in marketing in Mwinilunga in the 1940s, 1950s, and much
of the 1960s.[498] In spite of the drain on the village labour force due to high levels of outmigration, agricultural production flourished and rural life seemed to
prosper. In recent years, some historiography has suggested that migration to
towns did not necessarily result in rural decay.[499] In exceptional cases, rather,
labour migration could prove compatible with high levels of agricultural production and rural prosperity, as the case of Mwinilunga suggests.[500] Whereas
during the opening decades of the twentieth century the marketing of crops
in Mwinilunga District had been confined to administrative and local requirements, from the 1940s onwards as much as 600 tonnes of cassava in addition
to other (cash) crops were marketed each year. Demand from urban areas,
where the copper boom caused heightened food requirements, motivated
this increase in production and marketing, which was possible despite male
labour migration ratios of more than 50%.[501] Whilst some officials in Mwinilunga complained about the lack of 'able bodied men' in the villages, others
noted that notwithstanding high levels of absenteeism there were relatively
few signs of village disruption.[502] How can this paradox be explained? Rather

---

495   (NAZ) SEC2/155, Western Province Annual Report, 1948.

496   Potts, 'Counter-Urbanization on the Zambian Copperbelt?'; Jamal and Weeks, 'The Van-
       ishing Rural-Urban Gap.'

497   (NAZ) Annual Report of the Ministry of Agriculture for the Year 1965.

498   Pritchett, *Lunda-Ndembu*; Turner, *Schism and Continuity*.

499   See: William Beinart, *The Political Economy of Pondoland, 1860–1930* (Cambridge: Cam-
       bridge University Press, 1982); Moore and Vaughan, *Cutting Down Trees*; Pottier, *Migrants
       No More*.

500   Moore and Vaughan, *Cutting Down Trees*, 155.

501   See Peša, 'Cassava Is Our Chief.' In the 1960s, demand slumped again, as long transport
       hauls made marketing bulky produce such as cassava from Mwinilunga unprofitable.

502   (NAZ) SEC2/959, K.J. Forder, Mwinilunga District Tour Report, November 1951.

than understanding rural-urban relations as dichotomous, attention should be
paid to interconnections between rural and urban spheres.

2.3.1   Labour Migration, Agricultural Production, and Village Life
Agricultural production and labour migration have often been interpreted as
conflicting or even mutually exclusive livelihood strategies, especially in terms
of labour input.[503] The case of Mwinilunga suggests, however, that it was not
necessary to choose between agricultural production and labour migration.
Rather, the two strategies could and often have been combined. What is more,
various livelihood patterns positively fed into each other.[504] In workers' de-
cision-making, urban and rural strategies were often profoundly interlinked,
and where possible workers would choose urban employment that proved
compatible with rural livelihood patterns.[505] As Allina-Pisano has argued, labour migrants sought 'to sustain the viability of subsistence agricultural production and to maintain the freedom to enter the labor market on their own
terms'.[506] For the case of Mwinilunga, insofar as possible, workers refused to
engage in long labour contracts that would jeopardise the planting or harvesting of crops. Preferably, they engaged in shorter contracts that enabled a combination of agricultural production and salaried employment.[507] Even if more
money could be earned farther afield, workers preferred to engage close to
home so that they could combine cultivation and wage labour, as the District
Commissioner remarked in 1921:

> The Alunda is still fond of home life, and is usually unwilling to agree to
> work anywhere that will separate him from his family for a long period.
> He much prefers to earn 10/- a month at work near to his home; than
> 20/- a month amongst strangers.[508]

Throughout the colonial period, government-commissioned road construction work within the district provided opportunities for short-term contracts.
Workers would be engaged per 'ticket' of four to six weeks, and they could ter-
minate their employment upon completion of any number of tickets. Road
construction work proved popular for its flexibility. It enabled workers to

503   See: Andersson, 'Administrators' Knowledge', 122; Potts, 'Worker-peasants and Farmer-
       housewives.'
504   See: Turner, *Schism and Continuity*; Moore and Vaughan, *Cutting Down Trees*.
505   Allina-Pisano, 'Borderlands, Boundaries'; Andersson, 'Administrators' Knowledge.'
506   Allina-Pisano, 'Borderlands, Boundaries', 72.
507   See: Harries, *Work, Culture, and Identity*; Allina-Pisano, 'Borderlands, Boundaries.'
508   (NAZ) KSE6/1/4, F.V. Bruce-Miller, Mwinilunga Sub-District Annual Report, 31 March 1921.

return to their village with cash in their pockets, whilst still engaging in key agricultural tasks, such as tree felling.[509] In this manner, salaried employment and agricultural production could go hand in hand.[510]

Labour migration and agricultural production could more easily be combined due to the increasing adoption of cassava as a staple crop (see Chapter 2).[511] Whereas sorghum and millet required the annual clearing of bush fields, which is a labour-intensive and typically male task, cassava could be cultivated on the same plot of land for up to twenty consecutive years (in exceptional circumstances). Cassava cultivation thus substantially reduced the demand for male labour for field preparation, enabling women to manage agricultural production relatively independently.[512] The adoption of cassava thus curbed the negative effects of 'male absenteeism', which colonial officials portrayed as so deleterious to village life and agricultural production.[513] In a sense, cassava facilitated male labour migration, as the annual report of 1947 concurred:

> In areas such as Mwinilunga (...) where a form of "Chitemeni" agricultural is practiced an absence of more than two years on the part of the man has a serious effect upon the food supply of his family since it is the man's work to fell the trees and gather the branches, in the ashes of which the finger millet or kaffir corn is planted (...) where cassava is the staple crop and agriculture is largely stabilised, the presence of the man is unnecessary for the preparation of the gardens.[514]

Cassava cultivation was one of the means by which male labour migration could be combined with agricultural production by women in the villages in Mwinilunga.[515] Yet this picture of male labour migration, leaving wives and children behind in the village, as the 'modernist narrative' has suggested, should itself be reassessed.[516]

Gender and labour relations in agricultural production would indeed be seriously upset if men would migrate to the mines by themselves in large

509 See: Moore and Vaughan, *Cutting Down Trees*, 149–53; Harries, *Work, Culture, and Identity.*
510 See: Allina-Pisano, 'Borderlands, Boundaries'; Andersson, 'Administrators' Knowledge.'
511 Moore and Vaughan, *Cutting Down Trees*, 155–56; Berry, *No Condition Is Permanent*; Pritchett, *Lunda-Ndembu.*
512 Peša, 'Cassava Is Our Chief', 169–90; Chabatama, 'Peasant Farming.'
513 Pritchett, *Lunda-Ndembu.*
514 (NAZ) SEC2/154, F.M.N. Heath, Mwinilunga District Annual Report, 1947.
515 Anita Spring and Art Hansen, *Women's Agricultural Work in Rural Zambia: From Valuation to Subordination* (Waltham, 1979).
516 Ferguson, 'Mobile Workers'; Potts, 'Worker-peasants and Farmer-housewives.'

numbers.[517] Agricultural tasks in Mwinilunga are highly gendered and in the absence of their husbands, women would have to rely on other male relatives to cut down trees and prepare fields for cultivation. Yet self-realisation through labour migration could never be an individual pursuit, but would necessarily involve the household and the village. Men would not make the choice to go to work on their own, in isolation. Rather, their choices would be made relationally, in the context of social connectivity.[518] Although some men did go to work alone – especially younger and unmarried men – many took their families with them.[519] Women and children did move to towns, even though female migration remains poorly documented in the archival sources. During the colonial period and increasingly after independence, women would either accompany their husbands and relatives or move to urban areas of their own accord.[520] Women found ingenious ways to circumvent restrictions on their movement, as this source from 1960 reluctantly admits:

> The Government should inform the drivers of the buses that they should not carry women [to town] without permission from their husbands (...) although police, kapasu and district messenger patrols inspected the buses at Solwezi, Lumwana and Mwinilunga, it was difficult to catch offenders who usually caught the buses outside the town-ship by agreement with the drivers.[521]

Even if women rarely initiated the movement to town themselves, they did not passively follow their husbands either.[522] By the 1950s, it was acknowledged that 'an increasing number of unmarried, divorced and widowed women are leaving the rural areas to escape the drudgery of village life, to seek wealthy husbands in the Copperbelt or in the Belgian Congo'.[523] Those women who accompanied their husbands to town would actively contribute to the family income, although formal employment opportunities for women remained

517   Ferguson, 'Mobile Workers'; Moore and Vaughan, *Cutting Down Trees*; Parpart, 'Where Is Your Mother?'

518   See: Moore and Vaughan, *Cutting Down Trees*; Macmillan, 'The Historiography of Transition.'

519   Parpart, 'Where Is Your Mother?'; Chauncey, 'The Locus of Reproduction'; Ferguson, *Expectations of Modernity.*

520   Andersson, 'Informal Moves'; Parpart, 'Where Is Your Mother?'

521   (NAZ) LGH5/1/3 Loc.3604, Lunda-Ndembo Native Authority Council, 5 November 1960.

522   Parpart, 'Where Is Your Mother?'

523   (NAZ) SEC2/962 R.S. Thompson, Mwinilunga District Tour Report, 20 August 1954.

limited in urban areas.[524] Women would engage in petty trade, of second-hand clothes, or beans for example, or they might find employment as teachers or orderlies.[525] It is therefore more accurate to see labour migration as a household – rather than an individual male – strategy. Young men sometimes made the initial move to labour centres on their own, but they might then return to the village to marry and thereafter take their wives to urban areas to settle there permanently or semi-permanently.[526] Although the percentage of migrating men was probably always higher than that of migrating women, the gender disproportions in the census figures should not be taken at face value.[527] First of all, labour migration was geared towards enhancing rural security. The decision by men to migrate was made within the context of the household, with the interests of women and children in mind. Self-realisation could not be an individual pursuit of men, but was a household strategy. If married men migrated, they did not leave their wives behind. Rather, they sought to enhance their livelihoods and further the wealth of the household. Secondly, aspirations towards self-realisation often resulted in the migration of multiple household members, not single men. This, in turn, could contribute to agricultural viability. If men, women, and children moved to urban areas together, this would not necessarily upset the gender balance in rural areas. Agricultural production in Mwinilunga would, in this sense, only suffer from a loss of labour force and less so from an unequal gender balance. Views of rural breakdown are thus challenged if labour migration is interpreted as a household strategy involving social connectivity.[528] Remittances, the opportunity of schooling relatives in town, or assistance in obtaining employment, all contributed to rural diversification rather than decay.[529]

Census figures should be questioned given the culture of mobility in Mwinilunga.[530] The census figures recording male labour migration ratios exceeding 50% in the 1950s cannot be simply assumed as accurate.[531] Cases of people reported to be 'at work' while they were avoiding tax payment by hiding in the

---

524   This view has been confirmed by numerous interviews, Lucy and Gladys, 6 February 2010, Kalulushi.
525   See Karen T. Hansen, *Keeping House in Lusaka* (New York: Columbia University Press, 1997); Confirmed by interviews.
526   Ferguson, 'Mobile Workers'; Macmillan, 'The Historiography of Transition.'
527   Moore and Vaughan, *Cutting Down Trees*; Andersson, 'Informal Moves.'
528   Potts, 'Worker-peasants and Farmer-housewives.'
529   Andersson, 'Informal Moves'; Andersson, 'Reinterpreting the Rural-Urban Connection.'
530   Bakewell, 'Refugees Repatriating.'
531   (NAZ) Mwinilunga District Annual Reports; Moore and Vaughan, *Cutting Down Trees*; Bruce Fetter, ed., *Demography from Scanty Evidence: Central Africa in the Colonial Era* (Boulder: Lynne Rienner Publishers, 1990).

bush or by visiting relatives are ubiquitous.[532] The population found creative means to deceive the tax registrar, by using false names, claiming to have paid taxes across the border, etc.[533] Furthermore, levels of residential mobility in Mwinilunga remained high throughout the twentieth century. In the 1950s, Turner documented this incessant movement. In one case, a man was born in one village, but he went to live with his maternal uncle in another village. He moved upon marriage, migrated to town, and finally retired in the *boma*.[534] The tax registrar failed to grasp these multiple movements and, therefore, probably overrepresented the percentage of men 'at work'.[535] Furthermore, census figures suggest a steady population increase during the twentieth century. Whereas population estimates for Mwinilunga District were as low as 10,866 in 1920, a total population of 81,496 was recorded in 1990.[536] Apart from natural population increase, this increase might simply reflect revised census methods, as well as immigration from Angola and Congo. These figures suggest, in any case, that population increase may have compensated for high percentages of labour migration. Whereas labour migrants moved away from the district, others came in to alleviate the loss of labour force. Views of rural decay due to labour migration therefore need to be reconsidered.

Labour migration has all too often been viewed as an exit option for impoverished agricultural producers who fail to find market outlets locally.[537] Nonetheless, the assumption that the poorest or the least educated, those deprived of all other opportunities, would be compelled to migrate because of capitalist pressures does not seem to hold. Rather, 'the poorest are generally excluded from migration opportunities. Migration presupposes a measure of relative well-being, which provides the material and ideological conditions for seeking new fortunes through spatial mobility'.[538] Indeed, labour migration ratios from the area around the mission station Kalene Hill have always been relatively high, even though education levels and income-generating opportunities there are favourable when compared to other parts of Mwinilunga.[539] Contrary to what might be expected, areas where crops are difficult to market and

---

532   This view is based on a wide reading of archival sources (NAZ).

533   Allina-Pisano, 'Borderlands, Boundaries.'

534   Turner, *Schism and Continuity.*

535   Moore and Vaughan, *Cutting Down Trees.*

536   See: (NAZ) Mwinilunga District Annual Reports; Central Statistical Office, Zambia, Census 1990.

537   Andersson, 'Administrators' Knowledge'; see Palmer and Parsons, *The Roots of Rural Poverty.*

538   Englund, 'The Village in the City', 139.

539   See: Fisher and Hoyte, *Ndotolu*; Turner, *Schism and Continuity*; Pritchett, *Lunda-Ndembu.*

employment opportunities are poor seem to send fewer migrants to urban areas, whereas more migrants originate from areas with favourable educational and marketing opportunities.[540] Migration is rooted, as Englund notes, 'not so much in the poor rural living conditions as in migrants' desire to prosper in the rural areas'.[541] Agricultural production and labour migration do not have to be seen as conflicting strategies, as they could coincide. Whereas some individuals might focus on marketing pineapples from Mwinilunga, others would seek personal fulfilment by building a career in urban areas, or labour migration could generate the monetary input to invest in pineapple production in the first place.[542] Because labour migration allowed skilled individuals to enhance the scope of their opportunities, this practice contributed to rural sustainability and prosperity rather than leading to breakdown or decay. Labour migrants might invest in agriculture upon return, or they might facilitate the marketing of agricultural produce in urban areas.[543] Rather than causing impoverishment or rural decay, labour migration, in some cases, stimulated rural entrepreneurship and prosperity, thereby constituting the locality of Mwinilunga.[544]

Viewing labour migration as part of the process towards self-realisation can bridge the rural-urban dichotomy at the basis of theories of both development and underdevelopment.[545] If labour migration is interpreted as a social strategy to attain wealth and influence, the focus lies not so much on the disruptive act of geographical mobility, but on the links that migrants create through a complex network of cultural, economic, social, and political relations.[546] Migrants 'often see their stay in town through the prism of their rural aspirations'.[547] Even though labour migration might lead to permanent urban residence, the practice is underpinned by rural realities, resulting in the 'simultaneous and overlapping presence of urban and rural spaces in migrants' lives'.[548] Over time individuals have sought to complement and enhance their existing livelihood strategies within Mwinilunga through labour migration. In an attempt to build one's career and establish personhood, avenues to wealth and success have been sought in either rural or urban localities.[549] Because labour migration

540   See De Haan, 'Livelihoods and Poverty.'
541   Englund, 'The Village in the City', 151.
542   Peša, 'Between Sucess and Failure.'
543   Peša, 'Buying Pineapples, Selling Cloth.'
544   Bakewell, 'Keeping Them in Their Place'; De Haan, 'Livelihoods and Poverty.'
545   Andersson, 'Reinterpreting the Rural-Urban Connection.'
546   Bakewell, 'Keeping Them in Their Place', 1347.
547   Englund, 'The Village in the City', 153.
548   Englund, 'The Village in the City', 142; Andersson, 'Reinterpreting the Rural-Urban Connection', 84.
549   Ibidem.

enhanced opportunities towards self-realisation, by diversifying and securing rural livelihoods, it served to constitute the locality of Mwinilunga.[550]

Going against views of rural decay and underdevelopment, some colonial officials noticed 'comparatively little outward signs of disorganisation', despite high levels of outmigration from Mwinilunga.[551] Labour migration could be an alternative, complementary strategy to agricultural production, aiming to make rural life more secure. Rather than being disruptive, salaried employment contributed to agricultural production through remittances and agricultural investments made by returning labour migrants.[552] In Mwinilunga, markets for agricultural produce were volatile and generally limited. In this setting, labour migration served to cushion the fluctuations of agricultural production and marketing, whilst providing additional income.[553] As colonial officials acknowledged in 1950, the wealth of urban areas spread into rural areas:

> The prosperity in the urban areas was to a lesser degree felt in the rural areas where wages and ration allowances in lieu of rations in kind have shown a steady increase, while the demand for surplus native foodstuffs and fish has brought a considerable sum of money into African pockets in several districts.[554]

Instead of a stark rural-urban dichotomy, rural and urban areas might more usefully be viewed as two sides of the same coin.[555] By straddling the boundaries of both, individuals sought to maximise opportunities and increase livelihood security. There is, thus, a 'mutual dependence between urban and rural fortunes'.[556] Remittances, in particular, contributed to rural diversification and security rather than decay.

2.3.2   Remittances, Social Connectivity, and Self-Realisation

Both government officials and scholars have interpreted remittances in money and goods – judged mainly for their economic importance – as a sign of enduring rural-urban connections.[557] In this connection, colonial officials painted

---

550   De Haan, 'Livelihoods and Poverty'; O'Laughlin, 'Proletarianisation, Agency and Changing Rural Livelihoods.'
551   (NAZ) SEC2/133, N.S. Price, Mwinilunga District Annual Report, 31 December 1937.
552   Moore and Vaughan, *Cutting Down Trees*, 172–77; Pottier, *Migrants No More.*
553   Pritchett, *Lunda-Ndembu.*
554   (NAZ) SEC2/157, Western Province Annual Report, 1950.
555   Englund, 'The Village in the City'; Andersson, 'Reinterpreting the Rural-Urban Connection.'
556   Englund, 'The Village in the City', 149.
557   Geschiere and Gugler, 'The Urban-Rural Connection'; Ebenezer Obadare and Wale Adebanwi, 'Transnational Resource Flow and the Paradoxes of Belonging: Redirecting

a grim picture for Mwinilunga, as migrants did not seem interested in remitting money. While migrants were in employment in urban areas, remittances and contact with kin would generally remain minimal.[558] Long transport hauls and the difficulty of communication with Mwinilunga made that remittances tended to be infrequent and limited, as officials remarked:

> There was no evidence that the migrant workers, speaking generally sent much money home. Taxes were all paid in tikkies and pennies and sixpences, which I took to be the product of local trade, and not of postal orders sent from the towns.[559]

Officials lamented the loose ties between labour migrants and their kin in the villages, as 'they return seldom, and remit money and clothes never'.[560] One official in 1937 remarked that remittances did not seem to be migrants' primary concern, as 'most natives who have savings appear to be more occupied with what use they can make of them on the spot than with safe and cheap methods of remitting money to their relatives'.[561] Rather than remitting on a regular basis, migrants would carry goods or money as gifts or investment capital upon their return. Yet remittances are but one aspect of rural-urban ties, which should be placed in a broader societal context.[562]

Through labour migration and mobility, rural and urban areas have been connected in numerous and enduring ways.[563] This found expression in the economic domain. Some labour migrants contributed to agricultural production in the form of investment in input, such as fertiliser, hoes, and axes.[564] If labour migrants invested their earnings in agricultural production upon return, they might expand production and start marketing crops on a large scale after several years. Some labour migrants invested in cassava production or bought cattle in this manner. Official concerns that labour migration would jeopardise agricultural production, for 'if people are away from their village for six months or more they cannot cultivate proper gardens', appeared

the Debate on Transnationalism, Remittances, State and Citizenship in Africa', *Review of African Political Economy* 36, No. 122 (2009): 499–517.

558   See Turner, *Schism and Continuity.*

559   (NAZ) SEC2/957, R.N. Lines, Mwinilunga District Tour Report, 6 March 1949.

560   (NAZ) NWP1/2/26 Loc.4901, R.N. Lines, Mwinilunga District Tour Report, 10 January 1949.

561   (NAZ) SEC2/151, Western Province Annual Report, 1937.

562   Andersson, 'Informal Moves.'

563   Geschiere and Gugler, 'The Urban-Rural Connection'; Andersson, 'Reinterpreting the Rural-Urban Connection.'

564   Turner, 'Money Economy'; Pritchett, *Lunda-Ndembu.*

unwarranted.[565] Numerous pineapple farmers used their earnings from urban salaried employment as starting capital to buy pineapple suckers or to engage labour to prepare pineapple fields.[566] Migrants earned cash incomes and these were invested in productive enterprises in rural areas. As a result, labour migration could lead to improved rural living standards. In the 1950s, within a time span of five years, the District Commissioner observed a marked 'improvement' in material culture throughout Mwinilunga: 'Dresses, clothes were better, there were more bicycles, more Kimberley brick houses, lamps, suitcases, blankets etc. all seemed to have improved'.[567] Government officials on occasion credited migrant labourers as agents of 'development'.[568] The District Commissioner in 1959 stated that 'returning workers bring with them, as a rule, higher standards of housing and some ideas about gardening for pleasure'.[569] Migrant labour could be a means of self-realisation that straddled rural-urban divides, as Turner acknowledged. Returning labour migrants played a role in diversifying rural livelihoods or creating an environment conducive to enterprise, but this was a social rather than an individual endeavour:

> Remittances of money are sometimes sent home to relatives, but it is more usual for migrants to return with presents and distribute them among kin when they arrive at their villages. Many of the migrants purchase the standing-crop in gardens rather than wait for eighteen months for the cassava crop to mature. Some migrants are beginning to start small 'businesses' with their savings. Some buy sewing machines and set up as tailors, others start 'tea-rooms' on the motor roads, and others again become hawkers and small traders.[570]

What this excerpt evidences is that labour migration should not be interpreted as an individual pursuit leading to personal wealth only. Instead, migrants would distribute earnings among kin upon their return to the village, even if they had not regularly sent remittances whilst in employment. Furthermore, earnings from urban employment were used to support and advance rural livelihoods. Urban wealth was translated into rural farming enterprises, trade, or other businesses. Urban and rural strategies cannot be seen as detached.

---

565   (NAZ) KSE6/3/1, Mwinilunga Sub-District Indaba, 13 October 1916.
566   See Chapter 2; this view is based on numerous interviews, for example Saipilinga Kahongo, 22 March 2010, Ikelenge.
567   (NAZ) SEC2/966, R.J. Short, Mwinilunga District Tour Report, July 1958.
568   See: Ferguson, *Expectations of Modernity*; Moore and Vaughan, *Cutting Down Trees*.
569   (NAZ) SEC2/967, R.J. Short, Mwinilunga District Tour Report, May 1959.
570   Turner and Turner, 'Money Economy', 23.

Rather than acting as individuals, migrants depended on social relationships that straddled the rural-urban divide. Material wealth had to be translated into social success, for only then could a migrant become a 'Big Man', either in rural or urban areas.[571] The realisation of this goal depended on the careful cultivation of skills and relationships, on a personal following, and social connectivity. In this sense, labour migration is motivated by a desire to gain wealth and influence in either rural or urban areas, a desire for self-realisation.[572] Self-realisation should be understood as a process through which individuals enhanced their social standing through connectivity with others. Monetary earnings increased one's social standing, and labour migration provided one avenue to earn wealth.

Still, labour migration did not create a self-propelling dynamic of economic growth or development. Even though labour migration offered prospects of material gain, increased social status, and a return to the village as a respectable 'Big Man', wealth and self-realisation entailed risks as well.[573] Individuals travelling long distances could earn large amounts of money, acquire skills, and bring home copious goods, but they might be struck by adversity along the way. The narrative of *Kabalabala* embodies this sense of opportunity and risk involved in labour migration:

> Kabalabala, a man who lived along the Kabompo River, possessed charms with which he could turn himself into a lion. People who walked long distances would get tired and would rest along the road, where they would erect temporary shelters to spend the night. Especially those travellers returning from the towns to their villages would carry considerable possessions, purchased with urban wages and serving as gifts or items of exchange and use in the village. Kabalabala would come and chat with these people during the day, covertly making an inventory of their possessions. At night Kabalabala would transform himself into a lion, return to the travellers' camp, steal all their belongings and kill one or more members of the travelling group. Clothing, pots and all other goods would be taken from the travellers by Kabalabala, who would sell these items for money. This made travelling to and from town very dangerous, because Kabalabala could not be killed by spears, axes or

---

571   Barrett, 'Walking Home Majestically.'
572   Englund, 'The Village in the City', 151.
573   Comaroff and Comaroff, 'The Madman and the Migrant', explore the negative effects of
        labour migration.

guns. Travellers not only risked losing their belongings, but might die if attacked by Kabalabala.[574]

This narrative suggests that wealth is not merely economic but also social. Wealth is inherently risky and has to be translated into social relationships in order to become legitimate. This can be done by distributing wealth among kin, neighbours, and friends. Labour migration was a strategy for self-realisation, but it also entailed a loss of village labour force. Village kin benefitted from migrant remittances, but they would also make claims that a migrant could not meet, resulting in grudges, witchcraft accusations, and narratives such as *Kabalabala*. Wealth could thus be dangerous, as much as it was beneficial (see Chapter 5). The outcome of labour migration might be 'the creation of wealth that can grow over time', but migrants' wealth and success had to be translated into social status within the village community, expressed through self-realisation and social connectivity.[575]

Labour migration, thus, enabled wealth and success, being a pathway for self-realisation. Returning migrants who had accumulated 'considerable savings' might become 'Big Men' by deploying their savings to diversify agricultural livelihoods, engage in craft production, or trade.[576] But because self-realisation is an inherently social process that occurs in relation to others, labour migration has inevitably influenced rural communities as a whole. Colonial officials attributed material gain and improved living standards in the villages to migrants' engagement in the flourishing urban economy, suggesting the thoroughly intertwined nature of rural and urban fortunes. The 1948 Mwinilunga Annual Report stated:

> Wages have been substantially increased, especially on the Mines and Railways (...) the African standard of living both in town and country has risen appreciably. A man and his family are better clothed and better nourished than they were even three years ago.[577]

Officials further noted that returning labour migrants made a definite impact on village life: 'The return to the villages of people who have been working

---

574 Compilation from several interviews, especially Minas Kantumoya Kasolu Kachacha, 27 July 2010, Kanongesha, and Fred Mpenji, 3 August 2010, Kanongesha. For comparable cases of vampires on the Copperbelt; see White, *Speaking with Vampires*.
575 Cohen and Sirkeci, *Cultures of Migration*, 31.
576 (NAZ) SEC2/966, M.A. Hinds, Mwinilunga District Tour Report, 22 September 1958.
577 (NAZ) SEC2/155, Western Province Annual Report, 1948.

for numerous years on the Copperbelt, was most marked'. Yet officials equally feared that this influence would merely encourage further migration, or that migrants' stories 'might be detrimental to efforts at stimulation of the production of an economic crop'.[578] Labour migration might thus influence village societies either positively or negatively. Yet, importantly, the relationship between rural and urban areas did not have to be conflicting, but was symbiotic.

Labour migration and the social connectivity to which it gave rise created a variety of rural-urban ties. Whereas some migrants chose to uphold tight links with their kin in the village, others severed connections and sought urban wealth and influence.[579] A survey held among labour migrants from Mwinilunga in 1952 illustrates this diversity. Whereas some migrants retained houses in Mwinilunga, others did not. Colonial officials assumed that the absence of a house and a field would make the return of migrant labourers less likely:

> Where 12 adult males had residence in the village 4 others were away at work yet had houses in the village ready for their return, and another 3 were away at work having no house or garden in the village and maintaining contact only by mail or other means.[580]

The survey illustrates the flexible, precarious yet definite nature of rural-urban links created by migrant labourers during periods of employment in town:

> A very considerable number of those who go away to work maintain contact by letter, but have no house or garden in the village. Most of those who go away, remain away for a number of years, but nearly always return eventually. The majority of men go away to the line at some stage during their lives (...) Those men who stay away longest nearly always have a valuable contribution to make to rural life on their return.[581]

This suggests that labour migrants viewed urban residence through the prism of rural aspirations. Consequently, it becomes crucial to look at social connectivity and at aims for self-realisation in order to understand the dynamics of labour migration from Mwinilunga District. Labour migration was not transformative, but proved constitutive of rural life, as Englund has depicted:

---

578   (NAZ) SEC2/957, A. Stockwell-Jones, Mwinilunga District Tour Report, 30 January 1949.
579   Turner, *Schism and Continuity*, 133–35.
580   (NAZ) SEC2/960, K.J. Forder, Mwinilunga District Tour Report, 23 September 1952.
581   (NAZ) SEC2/135, R.C. Dening, Mwinilunga District Annual Report, 1952.

The rural (...) is the key ideological domain in which migrants anchor their understandings of their aspirations and dilemmas. The domain of the rural, both as the object of moral imagination and as a geographical site, is constantly re-made in relation to what migrants achieve and fail to achieve during their stays in town.[582]

Not all migrants returned to Mwinilunga. Some found opportunities in town more attractive or were driven away from their village due to quarrels or witch-craft accusations. Others, perhaps, settled in villages where they had kin or friends or in the *boma* where employment opportunities, trade avenues, and social amenities were more favourable than in the villages.[583] Even so, labour migration should be seen as a strategy that connected rural and urban areas, rather than dividing them. Although some migrants severed ties to rural areas, most sought to enhance social standing by cultivating both rural and urban linkages. Instead of leading to rural impoverishment, labour migration en-hanced opportunities within rural areas by offering a means for self-realisation.

2.4   *Conclusion*

By looking at labour migration from Mwinilunga during the twentieth century, it has been argued that examining trajectories of labour migration through the lens of self-realisation advances understanding of labour migration in the broader Central African region. First of all, viewing labour migration as a strat-egy for self-realisation places this form of mobility within its full societal con-text. Labour migration is not just propelled by an economic rationale or politi-cal necessity, but builds on sociocultural dispositions, which are crucial to a proper understanding of the dynamics of mobility.[584] Secondly, a focus on self-realisation enables the bridging of the discursive rural-urban divide.[585] Even if some migrants did eventually sever ties with rural areas, urban residence was fundamentally driven by rural realities. It therefore becomes crucial to look at rural-urban connections.[586] Thirdly, this approach permits an understanding of the relative attractions of urban versus rural areas. Rather than resulting from rural poverty, labour migration is part of aspirations for the 'good life', which might be located in either rural or urban areas.[587] Most importantly,

---

582   Englund, 'The Village in the City', 153.
583   Turner, *Schism and Continuity*; Turner and Turner, 'Money Economy.'
584   See: Englund, 'The Village in the City'; Andersson, 'Informal Moves.'
585   See: Andersson, 'Administrators' Knowledge'; Geschiere and Gugler, 'The Urban-Rural Connection.'
586   Englund, 'The Village in the City'; Ferguson, *Expectations of Modernity.*
587   Bakewell, 'Keeping Them in Their Place.'

this approach does not stress the transformative aspects of labour migration, but suggests that the practice might have been constitutive of the locality of Mwinilunga. A focus on self-realisation challenges the 'modernist narrative', which proposes sharp ruptures and stages of labour migration.[588] A focus on self-realisation provides an alternative perspective that places labour migration within the broader context of mobility and social connectivity.

Labour migration emerged from within the culture of mobility in Mwinilunga. It was a means of coping with circumstances within the village and straddling the rural-urban divide. Labour migration built on pre-existing customs, aspirations, and morals that fused into a hybrid work ethic and guided workers' entrance into the labour market. The practice stemmed from established notions of work and movement, but provided access to new opportunities as well. Within Mwinilunga, labour migration functioned as a strategy to realise aspirations, develop relationships, and enhance status. Although labour migration formed a powerful alternative to local livelihood strategies, such as agricultural production or hunting, various strategies were not mutually exclusive. Moreover, there were considerable variations in workers' careers, some planning to retire in rural areas, others choosing to remain in town indefinitely: 'similar socio-cultural dispositions regulating (...) migrants' behaviour (...) may give rise to different urban [and rural] trajectories', as there are many alternative trajectories 'whereby positions of high status can be attained'.[589] In order to understand the dynamics of labour migration, it is imperative to look at case studies of migrants' life histories and at specific areas. Life histories of migrants from Mwinilunga highlight variety, flexibility, and agency. In Mwinilunga, a mobile work force negotiated work contracts according to their own preferences, using mobility as a tool for tax evasion or to avoid recruitment. Individual strategies were underpinned by a relative judgement of opportunities and risks, costs, and benefits in rural and urban areas. The motivation to move to urban areas was rooted in rural realities and opportunities. In the 1930s, officials were still surprised 'to note in a District so close to the industrialised areas how very thoroughly most of those returned from work on the mines seemed to have been reabsorbed by their traditional environment'.[590] This appears less surprising if rural and urban areas are viewed as connected through the process of self-realisation. By partaking in rural-urban networks, migrants reconfigured ideas of locality, success, and personhood. Labour

---

588   Ferguson, *Expectations of Modernity.*
589   Andersson, 'Reinterpreting the Rural-Urban Connection', 105.
590   (NAZ) NWP1/2/2 Loc.4897, A.F.C. Campbell, Mwinilunga District Tour Report, 23 August 1937.

migration, thus, served to constitute the locality of Mwinilunga. In the end, 'the motive for migration was, perhaps (…) to seek alternative means of being local'.[591]

Mobility, in the form of population movement, trade, or labour migration, served to realise aspirations of secure and profitable livelihoods. Although agricultural production provided a stable livelihood for some in Mwinilunga, mobility constituted a complementary livelihood strategy. Even if mobility was a high-risk undertaking, it equally held the promise of high profits. Mobility provided access to markets, material gain, and social standing, and it therefore remained a persistently attractive strategy in the area of Mwinilunga. Continuity and change went hand in hand, as mobility built on historical roots and a flexible 'culture of mobility', but simultaneously adapted to changing social, economic, and political circumstances. Through mobility the inhabitants of Mwinilunga negotiated the global and the local, Zambia, Angola, and Congo. Moreover, mobility was an avenue for consumption. Both labour migration and cross-border trade were spurred by a desire to access items such as clothing, pots, pans, and guns. Objects of consumption were themselves mobile, only rarely being produced and consumed by a single person in a confined area. Consumer goods travelled through long-distance trade and international marketing, for instance. The relationship between production and consumption, the ways in which consumer goods and their circulation changed over time, and the meaning of goods in society are at the centre of the following chapter.

---

591   Ngwane, 'Christmas Time', 689.

PHOTO 9
A porter carrying his load, 1930s
COURTESY OF DENNIS BRUBACHER,
SAKEJI SCHOOL

PHOTO 10   Returned labour migrants, 1950s
COURTESY OF BETTY DENING

CHAPTER 4

Consumption: Goods, Wealth, and Meaning

So many have been led away by the wave of prosperity & materialism (...)
at present they are eager rather to gain the world – It's not to be surprised
at – to possess a bicycle & good clothes & a brick house is so much more
than their father even dreamed of.[1]

∴

Over the course of the twentieth century, dramatic changes in patterns of
consumption have occurred in Mwinilunga.[2] Around 1900, communities in
this area had still appeared relatively 'self-sufficient'. People had been able, at
least in theory, to produce most items required for daily subsistence within
the village or neighbourhood. Bark cloth and animal skins for clothing, clay
pots for cooking, housing material from the forest, and iron tools for agricultural production could all be procured locally.[3] The volume and importance of
imported goods increased significantly as the twentieth century progressed,
though.[4] Mass-manufactured, store-bought items replaced local alternatives,
particularly after 1940.[5] Goods such as enamel plates and cups, candles, cloth,
bicycles, and much more, spread widely even in remote villages. Although
the pre-colonial long-distance trade had precipitated these changes and had
introduced goods from overseas many centuries earlier, it was only after the inception of colonial rule that the outward manifestation of this consumer shift

---

1 (EOS) H. Julyan Hoyte, 19 November 1947.
2 See Ross, Hinfelaar, and Peša, *The Objects of Life*; and compare to Trentmann, ed., *The Oxford Handbook of the History of Consumption*.
3 Von Oppen, *Terms of Trade*; Miller, *Way of Death*.
4 David M. Gordon, 'Wearing Cloth, Wielding Guns: Consumption, Trade, and Politics in the South Central African Interior During the Nineteenth Century', in Ross, Hinfelaar, and Peša, *The Objects of Life*, 17–40; Karen T. Hansen, *Salaula: The World of Secondhand Clothing and Zambia* (Chicago: University of Chicago Press, 2000).
5 Timothy Burke, *Lifebuoy Men, Lux Women: Commodification, Consumption and Cleanliness in Modern Zimbabwe* (Durham: Duke University Press, 1996); Margaret J. Hay, 'Material Culture and the Shaping of Consumer Society in Colonial Western Kenya', *Working Papers in African Studies* (Boston University, 1994).

became fully and unmistakably apparent.[6] What had once been luxury items for the elite, used as markers of identity and status because of their scarcity, became widely diffused, accepted, and generally expected items in all layers of society and everyday life.[7]

In the 1950s, the District Commissioner Mwinilunga indeed observed that marked shifts in patterns of consumption had occurred: 'dresses, clothes were better, there were more bicycles, more Kimberley brick houses, lamps, suitcases, blankets etc. all seemed to have improved'.[8] More generally, the acquisition of consumer goods was linked to notions of 'improvement'.[9] In official discourse and public consciousness consumption was assigned positive qualities and an expansive dynamic, 'more money creating fresh wants'.[10] Officials in the area believed that consumption would entail involvement with the market economy, as individuals would be obliged to earn money in order to purchase desired items from emergent village stores. Money would become a necessity, supplanting modes of exchange based on barter. In this sense, consumption would serve a 'civilising mission' and lead to 'development'.[11] Nevertheless, 'materialism' and 'riches' admittedly had dubious and potentially dangerous flip sides, causing the dissipation of communal social bonds and initiating a trend towards individualism.[12] Competitive consumptive display was particularly condemned by missionaries, who stated that 'the inroads of so-called civilisation have brought materialism and the deification of riches which are hardening the hearts of many'.[13]

Looking beyond the outward appearance of consumption, this chapter focuses on the socially embedded and contested process of how the meaning and value of goods has been constructed over time.[14] No matter how complete

---

6   Von Oppen, *Terms of Trade*; Gordon, 'Wearing Cloth'; Miller, *Way of Death*.

7   Gordon, 'Wearing Cloth'; Gordon, 'The Abolition of the Slave Trade', 915–38; Prestholdt, *Domesticating the World*.

8   (NAZ) SEC2/966, R.J. Short, Mwinilunga District Tour Report, July 1958.

9   See: Frank Trentmann, 'Beyond Consumerism: New Historical Perspectives on Consumption', *Journal of Contemporary History* 39, No. 3 (2004): 373–401; Frank Trentmann, 'Crossing Divides: Consumption and Globalization in History', *Journal of Consumer Culture* 9, No. 2 (2009): 187–220; Daniel Miller, 'Consumption and Commodities', *Annual Review of Anthropology* 24 (1995): 141–61.

10   (NAZ) SEC2/131 Vol.1, Kasempa Province Annual Report, 31 December 1929.

11   Burke, *Lifebuoy Men*, 84–85; Comaroff and Comaroff, *Of Revelation and Revolution*, 166–217.

12   Jonathan Parry and Marc Bloch, eds., *Money and the Morality of Exchange* (Cambridge: Cambridge University Press, 1989), 4; Barber, 'Money, Self-Realization and the Person', 205.

13   (EOS) W. Singleton Fisher, n.d.

14   See: Arjun Appadurai, ed., *The Social Life of Things: Commodities in Cultural Perspective* (Cambridge: Cambridge University Press, 1986); Mary Douglas and Baron C. Isherwood,

the 'consumer revolution' might seem, it was slow, complex, and at times contradictory.[15] Unravelling the meaning and value of goods can be a first step
towards understanding their social impact. Both changes and continuities in
patterns of consumption during the nineteenth and twentieth century will be
dealt with. Next to the functional motives behind consumer shifts, the labour
input required for the acquisition of consumer goods has to be taken into consideration. By looking at a number of examples, namely changes in ironworking, clothing, and housing, the links between consumption, trade, production,
and social relationships will be examined. Although consumer habits underwent fundamental change, there are equally long-term threads weaving past
and present patterns of consumption together, particularly with regard to concepts of 'wealth in people' and 'self-realisation'.[16]

1   From Locally Produced to Store-Bought Goods: Exchange and the
         Creation of Value

Exchange and trade occupy a prominent place in historiographical debates
on African consumption.[17] These debates generally assume that modes of
exchange and networks of trade have developed consecutively, along a linear course.[18] By means of increasingly complex and long-distance trade networks, an imminent transition from small-scale and relatively self-sufficient
communities to market integration, commercialisation, and globalisation
would be set in motion.[19] Modes of exchange, in tandem, would progress from

The World of Goods: Towards an Anthropology of Consumption (London: Routledge, 1979);
        Guyer, 'Wealth in People and Self-Realization', 243–65; Hansen, Salaula; Burke, Lifebuoy
        Men; Prestholdt, Domesticating the World.

15   Robert Ross, Marja Hinfelaar, and Iva Peša, 'Introduction: Material Culture and Consump-
        tion Patterns: A Southern African Revolution', in Ross, Hinfelaar, and Peša, The Objects of
        Life, 1–13.

16   Guyer, 'Wealth in People and Self-Realization'; Jane I. Guyer, 'Wealth in People, Wealth in
        Things – Introduction', Journal of African History 36, No. 1 (1995): 83–90; De Boeck, 'Do-
        mesticating Diamonds and Dollars', 777–810.

17   See: Gray and Birmingham, Pre-colonial African Trade; Jeremy Prestholdt, 'Africa and the
        Global Lives of Things', in Trentmann, The Oxford Handbook of the History of Consump-
        tion, 85–107.

18   For a critique, see Cooper, 'What is the Concept of Globalization Good for?', 189–213.

19   Vansina, 'Long-distance Trade Routes', 375–90, suggests a tripartite division between local
        trade from village to village, trade over longer distances, and direct long-distance trade;
        Gray and Birmingham, Pre-colonial African Trade, suggest a distinction between subsis-
        tence-oriented and market-oriented trade. Certain debates on globalisation assume that

non-monetary gift exchange and barter to capitalist commodity exchange.[20] For the area of Mwinilunga, such clearly demarcated stages of trade do not seem to apply. Far from being successive stages, 'subsistence' and 'market production' coincided.[21] Even today, barter and monetised exchange exist side by side, whereas village trade is complemented by imported trade items from across the globe. This diversity of trade enhanced rather than undermined economic activity.[22]

Notwithstanding apparent trade diversity, officials in Mwinilunga persistently complained about 'self-sufficiency' and 'subsistence', lamenting the lack of 'market integration' of the area.[23] In the 1920s, one District Commissioner deplored that 'it could not be other than depressing to a political economist to see a community that exports nothing and buys little or nothing that is imported'.[24] Reports from the 1970s were only moderately more positive: 'Most of the people are still subsistence farmers, growing enough only for their consumption requirements, and only selling a little which enables them to purchase basic household utensils'.[25] Through taxation, cash crop production, salaried labour, and consumption, the colonial administration made attempts to integrate the population of Mwinilunga into the market economy.[26] In doing so, officials presupposed an ultimately inevitable transition from subsistence to market incorporation.[27] Looking at pre-colonial precedents of exchange, trade, and market interaction with a focus on consumption challenges such binary discourses of subsistence and market incorporation. People in Mwinilunga had longstanding interactions with objects, trade, and markets, enabling them to assign meaning and value to consumer goods, and to appropriate and

'local' or 'bounded' units have increasingly become connected to 'the rest of the world' through the flow of people, goods, and ideas.

20   Parry and Bloch, *Money and the Morality of Exchange*, 8–12; Jane I. Guyer, ed., *Money Matters: Instability, Values and Social Payments in the Modern History of West African Communities* (Portsmouth: Heinemann, 1995), 1–6.

21   Von Oppen, *Terms of Trade*; Pritchett, *Lunda-Ndembu*; Crehan, 'Mukunashi', 83.

22   Sara S. Berry, 'Stable Prices, Unstable Values: Some Thoughts on Monetization and the Meaning of Transactions in West African Economies', in Guyer, *Money Matters*, 309.

23   This is based on a wide reading of archival sources (NAZ); see Pritchett, *Lunda-Ndembu*.

24   (NAZ) KSE6/1/4, F.V. Bruce-Miller, Mwinilunga District Annual Report, 31 March 1922.

25   (NAZ) MRD1/8/27 Loc.4272, North-Western Province Development Committee, 20 March 1970.

26   Timothy Burke, 'Unexpected Subversions: Modern Colonialism, Globalization, and Commodity Culture', in Trentmann, *The Oxford Handbook of the History of Consumption*, 470–72; Comaroff and Comaroff, *Of Revelation and Revolution*, 166–68.

27   See: Thomas, 'Modernity's Failings', 727–40; Cooper, 'What is the Concept of Globalization Good for?'

domesticate them in locally specific ways.[28] Such interactions set the stage for colonial and post-colonial consumer behaviour and demonstrate how the meaning and value of goods has been socially constructed.

1.1   *Production and Exchange: The Foundations of Trade*
Throughout the pre-colonial period most goods required for daily subsistence could, in principle, be procured or produced within the confines of the village or its direct surroundings.[29] This ability to locally access and make a wide range of products was due to extraordinary skill and knowledge, emanating from years of habitation in the specific environment of Mwinilunga.[30] Continual innovation, adaptation, and borrowing gave rise to a multiplicity of crafts. This entrepreneurial spirit resulted in the weaving of a range of mats that have become renowned far beyond Mwinilunga. Examples are *chisesa* (mat of split palm or bamboo), *chisalu* or *chikongolu* (mat for drying or enclosing), *chikanga* (bed mat), and *chisasa* (worn-out mat), all made either from bamboo, grass, reed, or palm fibres.[31] The proliferation of so many types of mats went beyond the requisites of subsistence or utility value, and therefore suggests productive differentiation, craftsmanship, and exchange value.[32] Rather than implying primitive isolation – as travellers and officials have suggested – self-sufficiency in Mwinilunga was a rarely obtained ideal carrying connotations of strength, autonomy, and wealth.[33] This notion of self-sufficiency is captured by the Lunda verb *dikilakesha*, which is based on the verb *kula*, meaning to grow, to grow up to maturity, to be an adult. Self-sufficiency required the careful composition of skills, strategies, and resources within the individual, household or village unit.[34]

---

28   Von Oppen, *Terms of Trade*; Prestholdt, *Domesticating the World*.

29   Miller, *Way of Death*, 48: 'Most western central Africans personally produced a much higher percentage of what they consumed than do modern people, and their cultural assumptions made it appear easier to fabricate what they desired for themselves than to acquire it from others, although that sometimes required extending the concept of the "self" to include assemblages of the kinspeople and dependents necessary to accomplish the tasks at hand ... axioms of production for use by oneself and one's own must have profoundly influenced the ways that people generally thought about goods.'

30   Von Oppen, *Terms of Trade*. See: Vansina, *Paths in the Rainforests*; Guyer and Eno Belinga, 'Wealth in People as Wealth in Knowledge', 91–120.

31   This view is based on numerous interviews, for example Lukaki Salukenga and Lutaya, 6 August 2010, Kanongesha. See Fisher, *Lunda-Ndembu Dictionary*.

32   Crehan, 'Mukunashi', 88.

33   De Boeck, 'Domesticating Diamonds and Dollars', 795–96.

34   See: Guyer and Eno Belinga, 'Wealth in People as Wealth in Knowledge'; Guyer, 'Wealth in People and Self-Realization.'

To give examples of the variety of local production, some women wove baskets (to carry and store crops and fish or to sift meal), or produced plates and cups from calabashes, whereas blacksmiths produced hunting spears and fishing hooks.[35] A sense of this vibrant workmanship was captured in the 1950s when a crafts show boasted numerous types of mats, baskets, pots, stools, spoons, spears, bows and arrows, walking sticks, drums, combs and brushes, next to tables, chairs, cupboards, doors, window frames, and needlework.[36] In spite of the presence of store-bought alternatives, local production retained its attractions throughout the twentieth century, going beyond factors of functionality, availability, or price. Yet even if most goods could indeed be produced locally, and notwithstanding the ingenuity of artisans, neither the process of production nor access to finished goods was by any means unproblematic.[37] To enable and regulate access to scarce goods, relationships of exchange and trade developed. These encompassed the straightforward exchange of goods between neighbouring villages, but could also comprise complex and long-distance trade networks.[38] Due to various factors, trade was indispensable in the area of Mwinilunga.

Firstly, natural resources were and are spread unevenly across the landscape, problematising issues of access.[39] Not all parts of the district can easily access the *wumba* soils from which clay cooking pots are made, for instance, as this soil is only found next to certain rivers.[40] Furthermore, salt proved difficult to obtain. Whereas high-quality saltpans were and are available across the border in Angola and in adjacent Kasempa, in the area of Mwinilunga vegetal salt (*mungwa wamusengu, mungwa webanda* or *mukeli*) was relied on.[41] Although inferior to marine or rock salt, it would be used to season vegetables in the absence of alternatives.[42] Exchange and trade – connecting local,

---

35   See: Von Oppen, *Terms of Trade*; Pritchett, *Lunda-Ndembu.*

36   (NAZ) Box 5A Shelf No. 9, Mwinilunga District Show, 15 June 1956.

37   Studies of local crafts are scarce; see exceptions on ironworking: Kriger, *Pride of Men*; Eugenia W. Herbert, *Iron, Gender, and Power: Rituals of Transformation in African Societies* (Bloomington: Indiana University Press, 1993).

38   See: Vansina, *Paths in the Rainforests*; Von Oppen, *Terms of Trade.*

39   Vansina, *Paths in the Rainforests*; Miller, *Way of Death*; Herbert, *Iron, Gender, and Power.*

40   This view is based on numerous interviews, for example Levu Mongu, 17 May 2010, Nyakaseya.

41   This view is based on numerous interviews, for example Mandosa Kabanda, 2 August 2010, Kanongesha; *Lunda-Ndembu Dictionary.*

42   Miller, *Way of Death,* 56–57. Vegetal salt would be obtained by burning certain types of grass, which grow in silted river marshes. After sifting the ashes and mixing them with water, vegetal salt can be used to season vegetables, yet, due to its taste and quality, informants considered this type of salt unsuitable to season valuable game meat. In the

regional, and international actors – balanced out scarcity and abundance, allowing the tapping of alternatives to local resources.[43] Trade spread salt through the area, enabling villages far removed from saltpans access to this scarce resource. Livingstone, for example, mentioned traders carrying salt as a medium of exchange in the 1850s.[44] Adapting to changing circumstances, this trade carried on well into the colonial period, as the District Commissioner explained in 1935:

> Salt is gathered in the Kasempa salt pans by Mwinilunga natives and car-ried here for sale at 1 ½ d per lb. Some take small presents of salt to Chief Kasempa, some barter fish for salt, while others just gather their salt and return, meeting with no hindrance (...) Missions to the North can import very cheaply from Angola where the salt is of better quality.[45]

This example suggests that distinct types of goods were exchanged for one an-other (fish for salt, salt for money) over long distances, subject to relationships of power and interdependence (as the payment of tribute to Chief Kasempa implies), and that this exchange created determinants of value and routes of trade, which proved remarkably enduring.[46] Trade occurred between neigh-bouring villages and over longer distances, involving the exchange of bulky foodstuffs as well as scarce luxuries. Making a virtue out of environmental necessity, trade was actively sought rather than reluctantly acceded to. Fur-thermore, trade stimulated the creation of sociopolitical and economic ties with the wider region, as trading partners exchanged ideas and skills along with goods.[47] In this sense, as Vansina argues, 'trade has been a major avenue for stimulating innovation and diffusion, because ideas always accompany trade'.[48]

Secondly, the production of goods required labour input, particularly giv-en prevailing technological bottlenecks. Securing adequate labour supplies

---

nineteenth and twentieth centuries, trade salt remained highly valued, as described in the 1930s: 'Salt was a very precious commodity, and a little of it in a screw of paper would make an old Lunda woman happy for days ... Salt is very precious and every grain that I inadvertently dropped was eagerly licked up by the small children.' Burr, *Kalene Memo-ries*, 93, 110.
43   Vansina, *Paths in the Rainforests*; Von Oppen, *Terms of Trade*.
44   Schapera, *Livingstone's African Journal*, 121.
45   (NAZ) SEC2/133, N.S. Price, Mwinilunga District Annual Report, 31 December 1935.
46   Von Oppen, *Terms of Trade*; Gordon, 'Wearing Cloth.'
47   See: Miller, *Way of Death*; Von Oppen, *Terms of Trade*.
48   Vansina, *Paths in the Rainforests*, 94.

necessitated elaborate planning to accommodate all productive activities (agriculture, crafts, construction, etc.).[49] To construct a wattle-and-daub house, for example, preparations would start early in the dry season. Appropriate poles and thatching grass would then be gathered and left to dry, but the final structure would only be completed once the rains commenced, four to five months later.[50] Because of its scarcity, the allocation of labour was subject to relationships of power, involving hierarchies of gender, age, and status.[51] House construction is gendered, as men are responsible for erecting houses and women can lay claims on this.[52] The failure to erect a proper house is a legitimate reason for a woman to request divorce from her husband.[53] Revealing age as well as gender hierarchies, a girl's parents could request their son-in-law to construct a house for them as part of the bride service arrangements during betrothal. Similarly, a chief could call on his subjects to erect a house for him.[54] This is a symbol of power and authority, a mark of 'singularity', which sets the chief apart from the rest of the population, as not even headmen can claim assistance in house construction.[55] Because human labour is a scarce and finite resource, the quintessential expression of power is to acquire access to and control over labour resources, to build wealth in people.[56] This control, if successful, would result in the increased production of goods (iron tools, game, and houses are but some examples), but it equally caused dependency.[57] No one person can possibly produce all goods single-handedly, whether for want of physical strength, knowledge, or time. This gives rise to divisions of labour, power hierarchies, and trade.[58] Because hunters traded game meat for iron spears produced by blacksmiths, social relationships, political alliances, and networks of trade resulted. Household self-sufficiency, although perhaps a professed goal, was never more than an ideal.[59]

---

49   Miller, *Way of Death,* 40; Austin, 'Resources, Techniques and Strategies', 587–624.

50   Turner, *Schism and Continuity*, 36.

51   Pritchett, *Lunda-Ndembu.*

52   Ibidem, 181–82.

53   This view is based on numerous interviews, for example Nsombi, 30 July 2010, Kanongesha.

54   This view is based on numerous interviews; see Mulumbi Datuuma II, 'Customs of the Lunda Ndembu.'

55   Igor Kopytoff, 'The Cultural Biography of Things: Commoditization as Process', in *The Social Life of Things,* ed., Appadurai, 73.

56   Miller, *Way of Death*; Guyer, 'Wealth in People and Self-realization'; De Boeck, 'Domesticating Diamonds and Dollars.'

57   Gordon, 'Wearing Cloth.'

58   Vansina, *Paths in the Rainforests.*

59   Crehan, 'Mukunashi.'

Thirdly, the production of consumer goods required knowledge and expertise.[60] Examples from neighbouring areas mention closed, hierarchical, and esoteric associations, organised along lines of gender or kinship, which monopolised access to knowledge of a specialist craft, such as ironworking.[61] What is perhaps remarkable about Lunda social organisation is that, generally speaking, access to knowledge is unrestricted and full specialisation remains rare.[62] Nevertheless, access to knowledge would be segregated according to gender, age, or heredity. Whereas women specialised in pottery, men focused on ironworking. Furthermore, certain lineages dominated specific occupations, and specialised hunting guilds did exist, most notably the *wuyanga* cult for gun-hunters.[63] Yet even if knowledge was guarded by rules, taboos, or birth, barriers remained highly permeable. In theory, access to knowledge is open to all based on personal capacity and interest.[64] Any woman showing proclivity to do so could weave mats or make pots, although in practice very few did. Limited demand, competition, access to resources, labour, and knowledge all restricted the number of craftsmen and women in a village.[65] Furthermore, artisans overwhelmingly diversified their livelihoods, continuing to produce their own food, hunt, or fish next to manufacturing hoes or baskets. Dependency on a single source of livelihood was deemed risky, unwise, and ultimately unsustainable.[66] Nevertheless, even partial craft specialisation evoked the necessity of exchange and trade. Not all villages possessed potters, and therefore pots had to be obtained from distant locations where production was acclaimed, in exchange for chickens, cassava meal, or hoes. Such patterns of trade necessarily obfuscate notions of 'subsistence' or 'self-sufficiency'.[67] Natural resource allocation, access to labour, and specialist knowledge all encouraged exchange and trade beyond the boundaries of the individual, household, or village level.[68]

Exchange and trade have established socioeconomic and political relationships, and hierarchies of power between Mwinilunga and the broader region.[69]

---

60   Guyer and Eno Belinga, 'Wealth in People as Wealth in Knowledge', 109, 117.
61   Herbert, *Iron, Gender, and Power*, 26–27.
62   Pritchett, *Lunda-Ndembu*; Von Oppen, *Terms of Trade*.
63   Turner, *Schism and Continuity*, 30.
64   Pritchett, *Lunda-Ndembu*; Guyer and Eno Belinga, 'Wealth in People as Wealth in Knowledge', 93.
65   Crehan, 'Mukunashi', 88.
66   Crehan, 'Mukunashi', 89; see John K. Thornton, 'Pre-colonial African Industry and the Atlantic Trade, 1500–1800', *African Economic History* 19 (1990/91): 1–19.
67   Crehan, 'Mukunashi'; Prestholdt, *Domesticating the World*.
68   Vansina, *Paths in the Rainforests*; Von Oppen, *Terms of Trade*.
69   Von Oppen, *Terms of Trade*; Gordon, 'Wearing Cloth.'

During the pre-colonial period both the barter of bulk goods, such as the exchange of sorghum for fish or game meat between neighbouring villages, and access to scarce luxury goods through long-distance trade, proved important.[70] An example of the range and complexity of trade networks is provided by the description of markets in Musumba, the Lunda capital to which Mwinilunga was linked through allegiance, tribute, and trade.[71] In the 1880s the Portuguese explorers Capelo and Ivens described these markets as follows:

> At a short distance from the *mu-sumba* are established vast markets, true bazaars containing straight lanes or streets where flour of various kinds, peanuts, palm-oil, fresh and dried meat, millet, salt, tobacco, palm wine, sorghum, and other articles are displayed, and are bartered for merchandise, such as blue and red baize, cottons, printed calico, large white and small red beads, powder, arms and bracelets.[72]

Local, regional, and long-distance trade networks were clearly interrelated. Foodstuffs produced locally were gathered at regional centres, where goods supplied through the long-distance trade could be obtained. These goods were then distributed through networks of tribute, allegiance, and trade to all corners of the Lunda polity, including Mwinilunga.[73] Production and consumption were linked and transcended the local level in both supply and demand. Local and long-distance trade were further linked through caravans. Caravans travelled long distances at a slow speed, carrying imported trade goods such as guns and cloth, and stopping at villages along the way to exchange these goods for locally produced food, ivory, beeswax, or rubber. In this sense, caravans functioned as large mobile markets.[74] The long-distance trade, significantly, provided access to a wide range of imported goods.[75] Some of these were categorically similar to items that had been produced locally – manufactured cloth could be used as a substitute for bark cloth or skins.[76] Other goods, however, were unknown and evoked change. Guns fundamentally differed from

70   Miller, *Way of Death*; Von Oppen, *Terms of Trade*; Gordon, 'The Abolition of the Slave Trade.'
71   See: Bustin, *Lunda Under Belgian Rule*; Hoover, 'The Seduction of Ruwej.'
72   Capelo and Ivens, *De Benguela as terras de Iaca*, 315. Quoted in Turner, *Schism and Continuity*, 4–5.
73   See Chapter 1.
74   See: Rockel, *Carriers of Culture*; Von Oppen, *Terms of Trade*.
75   Gordon, 'Wearing Cloth.'
76   Prestholdt, 'Africa and the Global Lives of Things', 90.

spears and thereby altered the practice of hunting.[77] Imports included cloth, beads, guns and gunpowder, liquor, and a whole range of other items.[78] Due to their seemingly unintelligible demand, some of these items were denounced as 'trinkets' by European traders.[79] By the turn of the twentieth century, an official in Mwinilunga described that 'the custom is for a black trader to appear twice a year to purchase rubber and ivory. If he does not appear the village becomes uneasy – the ladies impatient for their new clothes, and gentlemen half wild for tobacco'.[80] How can this demand for imports, which has been portrayed dramatically by Pritchett as the 'unquenchable African thirst for foreign goods',[81] be explained?

1.2   *Goods, Value, and Meaning: Wealth in People and Self-Realisation*

Through their interaction with goods, people in Mwinilunga have assigned meaning to objects, thereby creating and contesting their value. The value of goods largely informs their demand and thus helps explain patterns of exchange. Going beyond functional or economic aspects, consumption is inherently social, involving interpersonal relationships and hierarchies of power.[82] As Appadurai usefully points out:

> Economic exchange creates value. Value is embodied in commodities that are exchanged. Focusing on the things that are exchanged, rather than simply on the forms or functions of exchange, makes it possible to argue that what creates the link between exchange and value is *politics*, construed broadly.[83]

Goods are given meaning and value through use and exchange, and are therefore cultural, as Douglas and Isherwood underline:

> Consumption is the very arena in which culture is fought over and licked into shape (...) Instead of supposing that goods are primarily needed for

77   Macola, 'Reassessing the Significance of Firearms', 301–21.
78   Stanley B. Alpern, 'What Africans Got for Their Slaves: A Master List of European Trade Goods', *History in Africa* 22 (1995): 5–43.
79   Jeremy Prestholdt, 'On the Global Repercussions of East African Consumerism', *The American Historical Review* 109, No. 3 (2004): 761; Miller, *Way of Death*, 73.
80   Steel, 'Zambezi-Congo Watershed', 187.
81   Pritchett, *Lunda-Ndembu*, 208.
82   See: Prestholdt, *Domesticating the World*; Burke, *Lifebuoy Men*; Ross, Hinfelaar, and Peša, *The Objects of Life*.
83   Appadurai, *The Social Life of Things*, 3, 57.

subsistence plus competitive display, let us assume that they are needed
for making visible and stable the categories of culture (...) This approach
to goods, emphasizing their double role in providing subsistence and in
drawing the lines of social relationships, is (...) the way to a proper understanding of why people need goods (...) consumption activity is the joint
production, with fellow consumers, of a universe of values. Consumption
uses goods to make firm and visible a particular set of judgments in the
fluid processes of classifying persons and events.[84]

Such views focus on consumption as a social process, involving interpersonal
relationships, competition, and hierarchies of power. In this sense, goods are
best understood as markers of social relationships and media of power and
control.[85]

For Central Africa, particularly for the pre-colonial period, Miller and Guyer
have proposed 'wealth in people' as a concept for understanding the relationships between value, meaning, goods, and people.[86] The notion of 'wealth in
people' explores how, in Miller's words, 'control of necessary and scarce material goods mediates authority over people and, conversely, how those with
power and authority use their power to channel access to material wealth'.[87]
Entangled in webs of meaning and power, people and goods were mutually
constitutive, as one could be used to gain access to and control over the other.
Miller explains how:

> Economic wealth and political power and authority were frequently in-
> distinguishable in Africa, where capital was people. A wealthy man in-
> creased productivity by organizing and controlling people (...) the prime
> economic resource remained human labor put to work in the fields and
> (...) control of people thus opened the road to wealth.[88]

Throughout the nineteenth and twentieth century, people and human labour
remained highly valued in various African societies as factors of production
and wealth. Vansina equally asserted that, 'for all that wealth was sought by
traders, wealth for its own sake did not acquire followers (...) Wealth remained

---

84   Douglas and Isherwood, *The World of Goods,* 57, 59, 60, 67.
85   See: Jean M. Allman, ed., *Fashioning Africa: Power and the Politics of Dress* (Bloomington:
      Indiana University Press, 2001); Burke, 'Unexpected Subversions'; Prestholdt, 'Africa and
      the Global Lives of Things.'
86   See Guyer, 'Wealth in People and Self-Realization.'
87   Miller, *Way of Death,* 41.
88   Ibidem, 43, 45.

what it had always been: a crucial avenue to authority and power'.[89] Understanding this relationship between people, goods, and value can help explain
the driving forces behind patterns of consumption in Mwinilunga.

In the area of Mwinilunga, a hierarchical model of wealth in people possibly
applied to the period of slave raiding at the end of the nineteenth century.[90]
During this period, large villages were established under strong headmen who
dispensed goods to followers in order to gain their allegiance. Village heads
provided protection from hostile attack and acted as gatekeepers, bringing
in and controlling the distribution of imported goods.[91] Through goods, 'Big
Men' sought to attract followers and build hierarchies of power, dependency,
and debt. By controlling imports and limiting competition, village heads cemented relations of dominance and subservience. Access to imported cloth
and beads served to attract the allegiance of wives, children, and slaves, for
example. In turn, this boosted the prestige and productive capacities of village heads, enabling them to attract even more followers and create a cycle
of commodities-dependents-commodities.[92] Thus, 'power had to do with the
control of imported goods'.[93] This situation was short-lived and fragile, though,
being challenged at the beginning of the twentieth century.[94] As the District
Commissioner of Mwinilunga explained in 1908:

> The accumulation of wealth and property or stock invited murder and
> the gathering together of large communities invited attack from more
> powerful communities, neighbours on the west (...) armed with muskets
> and large supplies of powder, freely obtained in exchange for the fruits of
> their expeditions, whether slaves, rubber or ivory.[95]

Consequently, large stockaded villages once again dissipated into small household settlements, where competition rather than monopolistic control predominated.[96] Processes of accumulation and the hierarchical control of goods,
therefore, do not fully reflect the variety of patterns of consumption and power
relations in Mwinilunga in the nineteenth and twentieth century.[97]

---

89   Vansina, *Paths in the Rainforests*, 237.
90   See Gordon, 'The Abolition of the Slave Trade.'
91   See: Prestholdt, 'Africa and the Global Lives of Things', 87; Gordon, 'Wearing Cloth', 25–34.
92   Miller, *Way of Death*; Gordon, 'Wearing Cloth.'
93   Ross, Hinfelaar, and Peša, *The Objects of Life*, 4.
94   Gordon, 'Wearing Cloth', 34–38.
95   (NAZ) KSE6/1/1, G.A. MacGregor, Balunda District Annual Report, 1908–9.
96   Guyer, 'Wealth in People and Self-Realization'; Gordon, 'Wearing Cloth.'
97   Von Oppen, *Terms of Trade;* Pritchett, *Lunda-Ndembu*.

Notions of wealth in people as 'self-realisation' appear more applicable to small villages where a competitive spirit prevails and headmen have been described not as powerful rulers but as *primus inter pares*.[98] Rather than solely aiming to accumulate a large following, self-realisation could take many personalised forms, as Guyer, Barber, and De Boeck explain.[99] This approach emphasises fluidity, by suggesting, as Guyer does, 'a *multiplicity* of control and access mechanisms, at many levels, that makes definitive order – of either the goods, or the people, or the principles of operation – virtually impossible. All control, however apparently effective, was partial, provisional and ephemeral'.[100] Self-realisation acknowledges the intrinsic value of people, stressing the goal of making oneself a respected member of society.[101] By realising the full potential of individual personality, one attracted the esteem and loyalty of others. As De Boeck argues, the achievement of personhood could never be a purely individual goal but was instead connected to:

> A growing sense of insertion into and responsibility for the lives of other members of one's kin group (...) The elder ideally forms the middle of the relationships that are being knotted around him and of which he becomes the constituting focal point and nexus (...) [this involves] social responsibility, highlighting the elder's capacity to weave the social network and give a tangible form to ties of reciprocity and solidarity.[102]

In Mwinilunga, self-realisation could be achieved through a diversity of strategies, such as agricultural production, hunting or labour migration, but it also found expression through consumption.[103]

Social responsibility, individual personhood, and wealth could all be demonstrated through the acquisition of goods. The influx of imported goods in Mwinilunga, which accelerated greatly over the course of the twentieth century, did not constitute a qualitative shift in ideas of wealth in people, but did provide additional options for self-realisation.[104] Material wealth, in the form of clothing, bicycles, or housing, continues to be invested in social relationships

---

98   Turner, *Schism and Continuity*; Guyer, 'Wealth in People and Self-Realization'; De Boeck, 'Domesticating Diamonds and Dollars.'

99   Barber, 'Money, Self-Realization and the Person.'

100   Guyer, 'Wealth in People and Self-Realization', 252.

101   Guyer, 'Wealth in People and Self-Realization'; De Boeck, 'Domesticating Diamonds and Dollars.'

102   De Boeck, 'Domesticating Diamonds and Dollars', 797.

103   Andersson, 'Reinterpreting the Rural-Urban Connection', 82–112.

104   Guyer, 'Wealth in People and Self-Realization.'

and serves to build alliances even at present, thereby underlining the enduring importance of connections between people, goods, and wealth.[105] Due to the wide range of available consumer goods in the twentieth century, individual personhood gained a competitive element, which had profound consequences for productive and social relationships.[106] The meaning and value of goods (conveying status, hierarchy, and power) was constituted through interpersonal relationships; goods embodied and contested social hierarchies. Three examples, ironworking, clothing, and housing, illustrate how this played out in Mwinilunga.

2   Ironworking: Smelters, Smiths, and Craftsmanship

Ironworking is a long-established craft in Mwinilunga.[107] The development of metallurgical skills probably dates back to the earlier half of the first millennium A.D.[108] Although its initial spread was slow and haphazard, in the long run ironworking knowledge constituted a 'technological breakthrough', as Vansina has shown.[109] Access to iron ore and the production of iron artefacts proved to be of vital importance, as iron tools contributed to the development of agricultural production, hunting, and fishing, but equally influenced settlement patterns and social organisation in the area.[110] Several localities in Mwinilunga boast deposits of iron ore, although these vary in quality, accessibility, and workability.[111] In the vicinity of these sites, ironworkers have historically engaged in both smelting and smithing activities. The items that these craftsmen produced, such as knives, spears, arrowheads, hoes, and axes, were indispensable to production and survival, but could also serve as a medium of exchange in the long-distance trade or be deployed as symbols of political power, prestige and beauty. Iron items, especially *mubulu* bracelets that symbolise betrothal

---

105   See the contributions to Ross, Hinfelaar, and Peša, *The Objects of Life.*
106   Guyer, 'Wealth in People and Self-Realization'; Gordon, 'Wearing Cloth'; Hansen, *Salaula.*
107   Von Oppen, *Terms of Trade,* 105, argues that metallurgy was probably developed around 500 A.D. as part of 'a set of rather revolutionary productive innovations.'
108   Jan Vansina, 'Linguistic Evidence for the Introduction of Ironworking into Bantu-speaking Africa', *History in Africa* 33 (2006): 321–61; Vansina, *How Societies Are Born,* 60–67, tentatively dates the beginning of the Iron Age in West Central Africa to the 4th century A.D. See Kriger, *Pride of Men,* 34–41. Copper smelting at nearby Kansanshi has been dated to the 5th–7th centuries A.D.
109   Vansina, *Paths in the Rainforests,* 58, 60.
110   Kriger, *Pride of Men;* Herbert, *Iron, Gender, and Power.*
111   In the 1850s, Livingstone described such a site, Schapera, *Livingstone's African Journal,* 239.

and fertility, were used as bodily adornment, whereas standardised iron bars served as currency.[112] Notwithstanding the vibrancy and value of metallurgy, this section examines why throughout the twentieth century locally produced iron items were increasingly replaced by industrially manufactured and imported ironware.[113]

2.1   The Practice of Ironworking in Mwinilunga

The importance of the metallurgical craft, as well as the extraordinary knowledge and expertise involved, were acknowledged by the Mwinilunga District Commissioner in 1910:

> In several localities where rich ore or iron stone is to be found the smelting of the ore and working of the pig iron, which is of an extremely tough nature, into hoes, axes, spears and arrow points, is carried on by a few natives who seem to acquire a reputation for this work which is handed down from generation to generation.[114]

Despite its high value, only several decades later had iron production all but died out in the area of Mwinilunga. Reasons for this decline should not only be sought in competition from mass-produced iron tools but also in the organisation of the metallurgical craft itself. Access to raw materials, labour input, and expertise proved problematic even before the advent of imported axes and hoes.[115]

For one, iron ore deposits are not distributed uniformly over the area of Mwinilunga. Deposits are concentrated along rivers and streams with clayey soil types, but are unavailable in other areas.[116] Moreover, large amounts of hardwood are required for smelting purposes. This resource, similarly to iron ore, is not universally accessible. Smelting (the extraction of workable bloom from iron ore, whilst discarding residue slag) necessitates extremely high

---

112   Iron was increasingly replaced by cheaper, more readily accessible, and easier to mould brass as the raw material for *mubulu* bracelets over the course of the twentieth century.

113   Compare with: Candice L. Goucher, 'Iron is Iron 'Til It Rust: Trade and Ecology in the Decline of West African Iron Smelting', *Journal of African History* 22, No. 2 (1981): 179–89; Wyatt MacGaffey, 'The Blacksmiths of Tamale: The Dynamics of Space and Time in a Ghanaian Industry', *Africa* 79, No. 2 (2009): 169–85; Kriger, *Pride of Men*, Epilogue; Thornton, 'Precolonial African Industry', 8–9.

114   (NAZ) KSE6/1/1, C.S. Bellis, Lunda District Annual Report, 31 March 1910.

115   Herbert, *Iron, Gender, and Power.*

116   Some deposits of iron ore would be of very low quality or so tough that they would prove difficult to work.

temperatures, which can only be achieved by making use of ample amounts of the right types of charcoal. This is such a drain on forest resources that in some parts of the district hardwood has become scarce and difficult to obtain.[117] Smelting, furthermore, required extensive preparations. A furnace had to be constructed (most commonly at the foot of a large anthill), supplies of wood had to be gathered, and rituals had to be observed. Not only did a ceremony precede the inauguration of the furnace, but metallurgists had to adhere to strict sexual and food taboos as well.[118] Smelting extended over several days, or even weeks, if preparations are taken into consideration. From dawn until dusk, groups of up to twenty men would be employed full time, pumping bellows to generate the heat necessary to smelt iron. After smelting, the bloom iron would again be transformed into useful products through labour intensive smithing. All this contributed to the high value and limited availability of iron utensils in the pre-colonial period.[119]

Apart from access to natural resources and labour input, the individual skills of the smelter and smith were crucial to ironworking success. Metallurgical knowledge was difficult to obtain.[120] Knowledge of ironworking remained confined to a select group of men, mastered only after years of diligent apprenticeship. Although smelters and smiths most probably never constituted a separate or strictly demarcated class of the population, craftsmen did enjoy high levels of respect.[121] Master ironworkers were widely known in the region, and informants today hold great pride in their descent from these famous men, or even boast merely having witnessed the act of smelting during their lifetime.[122] This adds credence to Guyer's claim that 'there was potential for self-valuation, for partial authorship, in the competitive validation of the work contributions of young men to iron-smelting'.[123] Metallurgy could be a means for men to make a name for themselves, to create personal as well as material value and power, a means of self-realisation. Both the knowledge and the

---

117   Goucher, 'Iron is Iron'; Kriger, *Pride of Men*.

118   These views are based on numerous interviews, for example Headman Kachacha, 27 July 2010, Kanongesha.

119   Kriger, *Pride of Men*; Herbert, *Iron, Gender, and Power*.

120   In this respect, smelting was more difficult than smithing.

121   Access to the ironworking craft was not restricted by kinship or heredity in any strict sense. Although certain lineages dominated ironworking, apprenticeship was open to both patrilineal and matrilineal descendants, and even to outsiders. See: Kriger, *Pride of Men*; Herbert, *Iron, Gender, and Power*.

122   This view is based on numerous interviews, for example Kenneth Kalota, July 2010, Kanongesha. Metallurgy was a strictly male enterprise; women would be kept from even witnessing the smelt.

123   Guyer, 'Wealth in People and Self-Realization', 254.

practice of ironworking were ritually embedded, as metallurgists abided by strict rules and taboos. This further elevated the status of ironworking and the value of its output.[124]

Ironworking was thus a labour intensive and specialist craft, producing items that were valuable, scarce, and in persistently high demand. It probably even holds true that demand structurally outstripped supply before the twentieth century, thereby giving rise to an elaborate long-distance trade in iron items.[125] Iron tools were required not only for clearing the land but also for constructing houses, cooking, and cultivating. Yet even though iron smelting and blacksmithing were in many ways indispensable to village life and subsistence, iron tools were neither abundant nor easily accessible. In the 1920s, it was reported that one village containing 24 adult women possessed only 3 hoes.[126] Although this case might have been exceptional, knives, hoes, and axes were highly valued and could be bartered for goods such as livestock, agricultural produce, or even for items imported through the long-distance trade. At the outset of the twentieth century, the Mwinilunga District Commissioner remarked that iron articles 'are usually bartered for calico, powder or caps, the buyer having previously bartered rubber with the Portuguese traders for these goods'.[127] Products of metallurgy were part of networks of exchange, barter, and sale, occasionally involving trade over long distances, interwoven with local supply and demand.[128]

2.2   Mass-Manufactured Iron Tools: Competition or Opportunity?

Smelters and blacksmiths faced competition from mass-manufactured iron tools and scrap metal, once these became widely available at the turn of the twentieth century, especially because the local production of iron tools was a labour intensive and intricate process, and output was consequently restricted.[129] Whether imported from overseas or produced in the burgeoning urban centres of the region, alternative sources of iron posed challenges to established ironworkers. Competition caused the decline of local smelting activity during the first half of the twentieth century and furthermore compelled

---

124   Kriger, *Pride of Men*; Herbert, *Iron, Gender, and Power*; Vansina, *Paths in the Rainforests*, 60.

125   Kriger, *Pride of Men*, 66–69.

126   (NAZ) KSE6/1/4, F.V. Bruce-Miller, Mwinilunga Sub-District Annual Report, 31 March 1921.

127   (NAZ) KSE6/1/1, C.S. Bellis, Lunda District Annual Report, 31 March 1910.

128   Herbert, *Iron, Gender, and Power*; Vansina, *Paths in the Rainforests*, 60.

129   See Shehu T. Yusuf, 'Stealing from the Railways: Blacksmiths, Colonialism and Innovation in Northern Nigeria', in *Transforming Innovations in Africa: Explorative Studies on Appropriation in African Societies*, eds., Jan-Bart Gewald, André Leliveld, and Iva Peša (Leiden: Brill, 2012), 275–95.

the smithing craft to either transform its activities or anticipate a similar decline.[130] By the end of the 1920s, the outlook of metallurgists appeared bleak, as District Commissioner Bruce-Miller remarked:

> The old blacksmiths (...) are gradually dying off, or getting too old to work and the younger generations do not appear anxious to learn the trade, so it can only be a matter of a few years when nothing but imported hoes and axes will be seen in the villages.[131]

In another report, Bruce-Miller provided a different, and more revealing, explanation for the decline of the metallurgical craft:

> The reason for this pathetic decay in local industries is not difficult to see: scrap iron can be picked up at any of the Mines and the less energetic present day native is thus saved the arduous toil of extracting his ore from the iron stone rock; while indifferent German ware can be purchased at any of the appropriate stores.[132]

Factors such as knowledge, skill, and apprenticeship of metallurgists, as well as labour and price differentials played a role in the decline of local ironworking. However, these factors cannot fully account for why industrially manufactured iron goods came to supplant established local production. Especially if it is considered that consumers deemed local products to be of better quality ('stronger') and more serviceable than imports; the rapid spread of mass-produced iron tools appears paradoxical.[133]

Narratives explaining the decline of local crafts by reference solely to external stimuli and unfavourable (international) terms of trade or pricing mechanisms should be balanced by taking local factors and dynamics, such as labour supply, raw materials distribution, and ironworking knowledge into account.[134] Items are embedded in social relationships, hierarchies of power, and processes of meaning making, all of which need to be considered when assessing

---

130   See MacGaffey, 'The Blacksmiths of Tamale.'
131   (NAZ) KSE6/1/5, F.V. Bruce-Miller, Mwinilunga Sub-District Annual Report, 1927.
132   (NAZ) KSE6/1/6, F.V. Bruce-Miller, Mwinilunga Sub-District Annual Report, 31 December 1928.
133   Kriger, *Pride of Men,* Epilogue; Confirmed by interviews in Mwinilunga.
134   Ralph A. Austen and Daniel Headrick, 'The Role of Technology in the African Past', *African Studies Review* 26, No. 3/4 (1983): 163–84; Thornton, 'Precolonial African Industry'; Burke, *Lifebuoy Men,* 202–03.

shifts in consumer behaviour.[135] Before the twentieth century ironworking knowledge had been confined to a select number of men, who enjoyed great prestige due to their expertise and control of output. These individuals held power and had opportunities for self-realisation through the creation of valuable goods. Their singular personalities and skills enabled them to build large followings and amass wealth in goods as well as people.[136] Smelters and smiths were 'Big Men' *par excellence*, because 'knowledge was particularly highly valued and complexly organized', as Guyer and Eno Belinga have argued.[137] Nevertheless, their position remained tenuous and contested, especially because output was rarely high enough to meet demand. The attractions of imported iron goods have to be seen in this light. These goods could compete with locally produced items because hoes, axes, knives, and spears were essential to the productive life of all members of society and hence to the self-realisation of hunters, agricultural producers, and carpenters. Access to iron tools, which had previously remained restricted – as men had to enter into ties of dependency with smelters to acquire spears, whereas women could obtain hoes only after marriage – was opened up through channels of mass supply.[138]

In the long run, competition eroded the privileged position that smelters and smiths had enjoyed. High consumer demand and abundant market supply dissipated the frail monopoly power of local smelters who could no longer control output. The path was thereby paved for self-realisation of a different type, not through metallurgical skill but through other productive activities that made use of iron tools.[139] Cultivating large fields, erecting houses, and riding bicycles, all facilitated by access to industrial iron, served to build alternative forms of wealth, in goods, people, and knowledge. Although smiths remained important, as their activities were indispensable for mending broken tools and for various other services, the balance of power had shifted.[140] With a degree of sarcasm, by the late 1940s, the Mwinilunga District Commissioner observed that 'in this age of progress, people cannot be bothered to toil at creating a useful object when a mass produced article can be bought at the local stores'.[141]

Issues of labour scarcity, price mechanisms, competition, and the viability of local crafts can be illustrated by looking at attempts by the colonial government

---

135   Burke, *Lifebuoy Men*; Prestholdt, *Domesticating the World*; Hansen, *Salaula*.
136   Kriger, *Pride of Men*.
137   Guyer and Eno Belinga, 'Wealth in People as Wealth in Knowledge', 93.
138   See Guyer, 'Wealth in People and Self-Realization.'
139   Compare to: Gordon, 'Wearing Cloth'; Prestholdt, 'Africa and the Global Lives of Things.'
140   MacGaffey, 'The Blacksmiths of Tamale.'
141   (NAZ) SEC2/957, R.N. Lines, Mwinilunga District Tour Report, 29 July 1949.

to revive the blacksmith craft in the 1920s and 1930s.[142] At the start of the twentieth century, officials had observed that demand for iron tools structurally outstripped supply in Mwinilunga. In an endeavour to correct this imbalance, officials tried to stimulate local metallurgy. Such attempts aimed to enhance local money-earning opportunities, to provide men with an alternative to labour migration, and to encourage agricultural production through the provision of affordable hoes and axes. In 1921, the Mwinilunga District Commissioner explained that:

> Two years ago it was extremely difficult to find one of the coming generation apprenticed to this [blacksmithing] craft, and our efforts to save the industry seemed doomed to failure until the price of the imported article increased to such an extent that it seemed a favourable opportunity to renew our attack. The smiths were told early in April last that I was willing to purchase at local rates every hoe and axe made in the sub-District and that all articles bought would be resold at the same price to either natives or Europeans – i.e. no commission would be charged or profit made (...) the smiths began to think that after all it might be worth their while to start working at their trade in real earnest (...) even if it is impossible to work up a small export trade, it is highly desirable that enough Alunda hoes should be made, at a reasonable price, to supply the local demand.[143]

Yet in order to stimulate metallurgy, the administration had to offer high prices, creating a *de facto* subsidised ironworking craft. Although this proved untenable in the long run, a temporary rise in output did result from such policies, as the 1926 annual report documents:

> A moderately successful effort was made to revive the almost dead blacksmiths industry. The output from these smithies gradually increased until the smiths were selling upwards of 1000 hoes and axes per annum with the local Native Commissioner's aid; i.e. in addition to those sold in their villages.[144]

---

142   Burke, 'Unexpected Subversions', explains contradictory colonial policies towards African consumption.
143   (NAZ) KSE6/1/4, F.V. Bruce-Miller, Mwinilunga Sub-District Annual Report, 31 March 1921.
144   (NAZ) KSE6/1/5, F.V. Bruce-Miller, Mwinilunga Sub-District Annual Report, 31 March 1926.

In the 1920s, prices for locally produced iron tools ranged from 1/- to 2/6 for hoes, whereas axe heads were sold for 1/- to 1/6 each, allowing for a small profit to the artisan. Officials overwhelmingly stressed price differentials of imported versus locally produced iron tools as a factor explaining output, competition, and patterns of consumption.[145] District Commissioner Bruce-Miller attributed the temporary rise in output of locally produced hoes and axes in the 1920s, following inducements by colonial officials, squarely to pricing:

> They [blacksmiths] will, however, make a few dozen [hoes] each month when they know the Native Commissioner is willing to pay cash for all they bring along. The imported article is expensive (owing to the distance from railhead). The Alunda are poor and improvident and often quite unable to pay the price asked by the storekeeper for his hoes: the store-keeper in his turn is not keen on handling the native made article, there is no profit on them – the Alunda know their value too well.[146]

Even if they could be produced in sufficient quantities, local hoes and axes proved too expensive to be sold outside of the district, due to prohibitive costs of transport and marketing. Nevertheless, this purely economic rationale has to be questioned, as both production and consumption should be understood within their broader socioeconomic, political, and cultural context.[147]

The attractions of store-bought hoes and axes lay in their availability and favourable price, but factors such as utility or form equally played a role. The 1921 annual report acknowledged that 'hoes were being imported by the store-keepers, of a smoother surface than those manufactured locally, with the result that they were readily purchased by the natives'.[148] Over the course of the twentieth century, imported hoes and axes gradually became more plentiful and affordable in Mwinilunga. Not only did the price of mass-manufactured iron tools decrease but local purchasing power also increased as a result of salaried employment and the sale of agricultural produce.[149] In a 1997 reflection, former Member of Parliament Peter Matoka attributed the decline of the local ironworking craft to externally induced 'underdevelopment',[150] resulting from debilitating colonial policies: 'Developing technologies such as iron smelting,

---

145   Burke, 'Unexpected Subversions', describes the colonial focus on price differentials of consumer goods.
146   (NAZ) KSE6/1/5, F.V. Bruce-Miller, Mwinilunga Sub-District Annual Report, 31 March 1926.
147   Appadurai, *The Social Life of Things*; Prestholdt, *Domesticating the World*.
148   (NAZ) KSE6/1/4, F.V. Bruce-Miller, Mwinilunga Sub-District Annual Report, 31 March 1921.
149   See Burke, *Lifebuoy Men*, 106–08, for a discussion about the 'creation of an African market.'
150   Burke, 'Unexpected Subversions', 471; Burke, *Lifebuoy Men*, 84–85; see Hansen, *Salaula*.

gunsmith, cloth weaving, salt preparation, hoe and axe making were discouraged over the years in favour of factory made items from Europe for which
markets had to be developed'.[151]

Nevertheless, the long-term economic consequences of the replacement of
locally produced iron tools by mass-manufactured items remain ambiguous.[152]
For local metallurgists the transition was mostly negative. Previously smelters and smiths had been a relatively privileged and affluent segment of the
population. Ironworking had provided income-earning opportunities within
the district, mitigating the need to seek alternative employment to pay taxes or
to satisfy monetary requirements. In the 1920s officials noted that 'blacksmiths
can readily earn money for their tax – and more – if they wish. The others
have to go afield'.[153] Yet over the course of the twentieth century, their income
dwindled. Still, some blacksmiths were able to successfully transform their enterprises and adapt their activities to changing circumstances.[154] In the 1950s,
the Mwinilunga District Commissioner could report that:

> A small iron industry still flourishes in this district (spears, axes, hoes and
> knives are made). Annual production: 50 hoes sold at 4/- for large size,
> 3/- for small size; 30 axes sold at 2/- each; 60 hunting knives at 1/- each; 50
> spearheads at 3/- each; annually £23 handed down as family business.[155]

Whereas some metallurgists resorted to mending broken hoes and axes, creating a recycling business that reduced the need to purchase tools from the stores,
others engaged in new activities, such as gun, bicycle, or motorcar repairs. As
Mwinilunga is far removed from the main areas of industrial production and
supply, repairmen and other craftsmen are in high demand and enjoy much
esteem.[156] The existing knowledge and expertise of craftsmen could thus, to
a certain extent, be transformed and adapted to meet changing conditions.[157]

The negative view of decline or underdevelopment of ironworking can be
qualified by linking the availability of imported iron tools to other spheres of

151   (NAZ) HM77/PP/2, P.W. Matoka, Review of Zambia's 33 Years of Independence, 8 Novem-
      ber 1997.
152   Herbert, *Iron, Gender, and Power*; Kriger, *Pride of Men*.
153   (NAZ) KSE6/2/2, F.V. Bruce-Miller, Mwinilunga Sub-District Quarterly Report, 31 Decem-
      ber 1921.
154   MacGaffey, 'The Blacksmiths of Tamale'; Yusuf, 'Stealing from the Railways.'
155   (NAZ) SEC2/963, R.S. Thompson, Mwinilunga District Tour Report, 16 June 1955.
156   Pritchett, *Lunda-Ndembu*.
157   Kriger, *Pride of Men*, Epilogue; Burke, *Lifebuoy Men*, 205.

production.[158] Colonial officials related the supply of iron hoes and axes to agricultural output. In 1927, the District Commissioner observed that 'in the cultivating season there is a great demand for these articles [hoes and axes], and a
shrinkage in the supply results in a diminution in the acreage cultivated'.[159] In
this connection, the ready availability of mass-produced iron tools positively
influenced agriculture by facilitating the cultivation of fields.[160] Whereas previously there had been a scarcity of iron tools, industrial production made supply more abundant, if still expensive. In the 1920s, officials further established
the connection between metallurgy and agricultural production, in an attempt
to spur both:

> With an increased number of cheap hoes and axes available cultivation
> improved so much that it is now possible to purchase nearly all the meal
> we require locally (…) it is hoped that now the smiths efforts are slacken-
> ing the acreage cultivated will not shrink in sympathy (…) the lethargic
> smiths (…) [should] store hoes for the demand they know arises each
> year during the cultivating season.[161]

Metallurgy influenced productive activities beyond agriculture. Access to a
bicycle enabled the marketing of agricultural produce at distant markets, by
facilitating travel and mobility. Furthermore, iron tools are indispensable to
the craft of carpentry, which developed in Mwinilunga due to missionary education and occupational training.[162] In these and other ways, access to iron
was directly connected to productive activities, which in turn served to build
status and wealth.

The widespread availability of imported iron tools provided a means to challenge the authority of smelters and smiths. Due to their knowledge and expertise, these individuals had been able to amass wealth in people. Imported iron
tools, however, provided new avenues for self-realisation by enabling the composition of singular personalities through fishing, agriculture, or hunting.[163]
Competition and the diversification of sources of supply enabled a different
balance of power in the area, jeopardising the position of smelters, but opening up alternative opportunities. Even so, blacksmiths adapted and perse-
vered in their enterprises. Innovative individuals continue to repair bicycles,

158   Miller, 'Consumption and Commodities', 144.
159   (NAZ) KSE6/1/5, F.V. Bruce-Miller, Mwinilunga Sub-District Annual Report, 1927.
160   Allan, *The African Husbandman*.
161   (NAZ) KSE6/1/5, F.V. Bruce-Miller, Mwinilunga Sub-District Annual Report, 31 March 1926.
162   Peša, 'Buying Pineapples, Selling Cloth', 262–63, 279–80.
163   Guyer, 'Wealth in People and Self-Realization', 252–53.

construct door bolts, and manufacture fishhooks from iron.[164] Yet, unmistakably, in the twentieth century, supply and competition broadened the previously more exclusive hold on power and resources held by smelters and smiths.[165] The rapid influx of iron played a role in the transition from locally produced to store-bought utensils, but so did issues of price, labour, natural resources, and knowledge. The result has not been a simple replacement of 'old' by 'new', or a complete decline of previous artisanal activity. Rather, a complex consumer landscape has emerged. Whereas previously metallurgical knowledge had been a key 'resource' as well as a 'means of production',[166] with the advent of mass-manufactured iron tools, value came to lie in the skill of composition, as Guyer explains: 'The value of objects and the work that produces them was part of this larger process through which people achieved "reality", a singular composition of multiple dimensions'.[167] Diversity, proliferation, and compositional skills, rather than monopolistic control, came to prevail over the course of the twentieth century. Being able to exploit opportunities through access to iron tools, individuals still remained primarily interested in building wealth in knowledge, goods, and people.[168] By hosting agricultural work parties or constructing large houses, the deployment of iron tools served to attain prestige and wealth. Even if a transition from locally produced to store-bought goods occurred, this transition did not signal a major rupture in underlying notions of wealth and social relationships. The outward appearance of goods changed, but iron tools could still be used to build personhood, express status, attract a large following, and thereby enhance productive and reproductive capacities. Iron tools continue to be fundamentally connected to notions of wealth in people, and this explains their persistent value.[169]

3   Cloth, Clothing, and Culture

Similarly to metallurgy, a clothing transition from locally produced to mass-manufactured and store-bought garments has occurred in Mwinilunga. Over the course of the nineteenth and twentieth century, bark cloth and animal skins were largely replaced by industrially manufactured cloth.[170] Clothing is a

---

164   See Pritchett, *Friends for Life.*
165   Guyer, 'Wealth in People and Self-Realization', 258–59.
166   Guyer and Eno Belinga, 'Wealth in People as Wealth in Knowledge', 117.
167   Guyer, 'Wealth in People and Self-Realization', 253.
168   De Boeck, 'Domesticating Diamonds and Dollars.'
169   Vansina, *Paths in the Rainforests,* 237; Guyer, 'Wealth in People and Self-Realization.'
170   Gordon, 'Wearing Cloth', 25–29; Hansen, *Salaula,* 24–39.

particularly interesting item in the study of consumption, because of the way in which it mediates between the individual and society. Clothing dresses the body for social display and thereby engages in processes of meaning-making, struggles over power, and hierarchy.[171] As Hendrickson asserts, clothing 'being personal, is susceptible to individual manipulation. Being public, it has social import'.[172] Clothing can be both an expression and an agent of social change, by constructing or challenging social identities, conveying class, gender, and generational distinctions and aspirations.[173] Godfrey Wilson, during his 1930s fieldwork in the urban area of Broken Hill (Kabwe), aptly depicted the relevance of clothing. Due to the labour migration connecting the two areas, his observations can feasibly be extrapolated to Mwinilunga. Mineworkers in Broken Hill spent 51.4% of all cash earnings on clothing:

> The desire for clothes is the normal conscious motive that brings men to town, and "nakedness" is the usual answer to the question "what made you leave the country?" (...) Every African man of whatever social group tries to dress smartly for strolling round the town, or for visiting in his spare time, and loves to astonish the world with a new jacket, or a new pair of trousers of distinguished appearance. Women behave in the same way; and they judge husbands and lovers largely according to the amounts of money which they are given by them to spend on clothes. Clothes are discussed unceasingly (...) they are tended lovingly and carefully housed in boxes at night. It is largely by accumulating clothes that men save. Clothes (...) are the chief medium in which obligations to country relatives are fulfilled. The Africans of Broken Hill are not a cattle people, nor a goat people, nor a fishing people, nor a tree cutting people, they are a dressed people (...) clothes symbolize their claim to civilized status.[174]

Evidently, clothing did not merely function as body covering but was also an item of display, a means of conveying social status, a negotiating tool in gender

---

171   Hansen, *Salaula*, 6–12; Karen T. Hansen, 'Second-hand Clothing Encounters in Zambia: Global Discourses, Western Commodities, and Local Histories', *Africa* 69, No. 3 (1999): 343–65; Allman, *Fashioning Africa*, 2–6.

172   Hildi Hendrickson, ed., *Clothing and Difference: Embodied Identities in Colonial and Post-Colonial Africa* (Durham: Duke University Press, 1996), 2.

173   Phyllis M. Martin, 'Contesting Clothes in Colonial Brazzaville', *Journal of African History* 35, No. 3 (1994): 401–26, especially 420; Robert J. Ross, *Clothing: A Global History* (Cambridge: Polity Press, 2008).

174   Wilson, *The Economics of Detribalization*, 18.

relations, and a medium to fulfil social obligations.[175] By paying particular attention to changes in production, style, and status, this section examines the history, meaning, and importance of clothing in Mwinilunga. Clothing served to build social relationships, but it could equally challenge existing hierarchies of power, allowing, as Hansen argues, 'the expression of variety, individuality, and uniqueness'.[176] By highlighting the changing functions and meanings of clothing in the social life of Mwinilunga, the cultural biography of clothing can be traced.[177]

During the seventeenth century, imported manufactured cloth had started to trickle in to the area of Mwinilunga through the long-distance trade.[178] In the eighteenth century, textiles constituted 55% to 80% of all imports to Central Africa.[179] Yet the circulation of textiles only really increased in the second half of the nineteenth century, when, as Gordon points out, 'an industrial commodity replaced a mercantile one'.[180] Due to increased supply, imported cloth was transformed from a luxury item for elite use to a quotidian item for public use, imbued with multiple layers of meaning. In Mwinilunga, clothing became an item of mass consumption through a gradual process that would only be completed in the twentieth century. For Zambia more generally, Hansen noted how: 'A rare thing had become a necessity that people craved'.[181] As was remarked by Silva Porto in 1880, imported garments had captured local fancy and had been highly valued for quite a while: 'The gold of these areas is cloth, and cloth fascinates the savages'.[182] Although Silva Porto's account suggests eccentricity, an association did indeed exist between 'power and material wealth', as Central Africans possessed, in Martin's words, a 'well-informed knowledge of the symbolic importance of dress and the association of style, finery, wealth and power'. Far from simply copying European dress styles or accepting imports without discrimination, people in Mwinilunga 'appropriated foreign items in a purposeful manner derived from their pre-existing cultural

---

175   See: Allman, *Fashioning Africa;* Hansen, *Salaula;* Hendrickson, *Clothing and Difference;* Ross, *Clothing.*
176   Hansen, 'Second-hand Clothing Encounters', 346.
177   Kopytoff, 'The Cultural Biography of Things', 66–67.
178   Compare to: Prestholdt, *Domesticating the World.*
179   Von Oppen, *Terms of Trade,* 224; Miller, *Way of Death,* 74–75n3.
180   Gordon, 'Wearing Cloth', 27.
181   Hansen, *Salaula,* 26.
182   Von Oppen, *Terms of Trade,* 223; Quoting A.F.F. da Silva Porto (1885), *Viagens e apontamentos de um Portuense em Africa* (Coimbra, 1986), 606.

perceptions'.[183] In order to understand local interactions with imported clothing, established patterns of dress first have to be examined.

3.1   Bark Cloth and Animal Skins: The Meaning and Value of Clothing

Prior to the advent of mass-manufactured imported garments, bark cloth and animal skins had provided covering, protection, warmth, and clothing to the inhabitants of Mwinilunga. Although bark cloth and animal skins were worn by men and women in public and private settings, subtle differences distinguished the two.[184] Whereas bark cloth was most frequently associated with quotidian and domestic spheres, with women and children, garments made out of skins were associated with luxury and status, with chiefs, hunters, and prominent men, with political and economic power.[185] In the 1870s, Cameron noted the gender division of dress: 'The clothing of the men consisted of skin aprons, whilst the women contented themselves with wearing a few shreds of bark cloth'.[186] Further distinctions could be made. The skins of small animals that held little prestige, such as duiker (*nkayi*) or impala (*mupaala*), were used to carry newborn babies in. Contrastingly, leopard skins (*chisumpa*) were a chiefly prerogative connoting wealth and power, circulated through networks of tribute that linked Mwinilunga to the central Lunda court.[187] Although bark cloth and skins had benefits (protecting the body against the elements, expressing identity, and portraying social status) some qualifications did apply. Access to raw materials proved problematic, as the *musamba*, *mupuchi*, and *katochi* trees from which bark cloth is obtained are spread sparsely over the area. Moreover, the production of bark cloth is a labour intensive process. Trees are cut down; the bark is stripped from the tree, soaked, and then beaten until soft.[188] Animal skins, similarly, were difficult to procure. Access to animal

---

183   Martin, 'Contesting Clothes', 405.

184   These views are based on numerous interviews, for example Chief Kanongesha's mother, 12 August 2010, Kanongesha. Detailed descriptions of the use of bark cloth or animal skins as clothing are rare. See: Von Oppen, *Terms of Trade*; Miller, *Way of Death*.

185   Von Oppen, *Terms of Trade*, 225, suggests the opposite, that bark cloth was highly labour intensive and prestigious, more so than skins. It might be that the relative prestige of bark cloth and skins shifted over time. Similarly to skins, bark cloth is imbued with ritual meaning and importance, being used in initiation and healing ceremonies, as well as in the annual *Chisemwa ChaLunda* celebration.

186   Cameron, *Across Africa*, 403.

187   This view is based on numerous interviews; Mulumbi Datuuma II, 'Customs of the Lunda Ndembu'; (NAZ) NWP1/2/23, R.C. Dening, Comments on H. Vaux's Report; (NAZ) SEC2/402, H. Vaux, Report on the Sailunga Kindred, 1936.

188   Von Oppen, *Terms of Trade*, 225.

skins depended either on hunting skills or on ties of kinship, clientage, and trade with hunters in areas where game was scarce.[189]

Due to the temperate climate of Mwinilunga, clothing needs remained minimal.[190] Elders recall dressing in a loincloth (*mwinda*), which was still common among women and children during the first half of the twentieth century.[191] A narrow piece of cloth or skin was strapped between the legs to cover the pubic area, leaving the chest and legs bare. Livingstone described this in the 1850s:

> The women as usual were nearly naked in front, and a little piece of cloth, about a foot long by 6 inches and less in breadth, was usually thrust between the thighs when near us. The covering behind (a skin of some small antelope) was much broader and longer than that in front – a curious perversion of the feelings of decency.[192]

Even if there was generally adequate clothing for adults, additional requirements (such as cloth to carry babies in, clothing for small children, or blankets to provide warmth during the cold season) could only be met with difficulty.[193] In the absence of blankets, for example, people would burn fires inside their huts to prevent feeling cold. Livingstone provides evidence of the scarcity of cloth in the 1850s:

> The women here shew that cloth is very scarce, for instead of a cloth in which to suspend their children a belt of about 1 ½ inch[es] is made of bark and slung from the shoulder to the opposite side. The child is placed in this as a partial support against the side of the mother. (...) I suppose that the chief clothing of the parents is the fire at night.[194]

The quantity of imported cloth was particularly advantageous in this respect, even if supply increased only gradually.[195] Foreign trade made affordable clothing accessible in previously unimaginable quantities and this explains part of the eagerness to obtain imported mass-manufactured cloth.[196]

---

189   See Chapter 2.
190   See: Von Oppen, *Terms of Trade*, 224; Miller, *Way of Death*, 79–81.
191   This view is based on numerous interviews, for example Nakineli, 14 April 2010, Ikelenge; *Lunda-Ndembu Dictionary*.
192   Schapera, *Livingstone's African Journal*, 36.
193   See Gordon, 'Wearing Cloth', 26–27.
194   Schapera, *Livingstone's African Journal*, 228.
195   Von Oppen, *Terms of Trade*, 226.
196   Prestholdt, 'On the Global Repercussions.'

3.2   *From Imported Goods to Objects of Desire: The Spread and*
        Attractions of Manufactured Clothing

At the beginning of the twentieth century, European travellers, traders, missionaries, and colonial officials were the principal suppliers of imported cloth to Mwinilunga. Nonetheless, to dispense cloth in the villages they frequently had to rely on African intermediaries.[197] Europeans supposed a 'universal' demand among the local population for 'superior' imported cloth, which in their eyes expressed a higher degree of 'civilisation' and 'modernity' than bark cloth or skins conveyed.[198] Travellers, such as Livingstone, commented on the 'craving for cloth' among the Lunda:[199]

> Clothing is much more eagerly enquired after by all than beads or other ornaments (...) Cotton cloth is in great demand. Men and women come running after us with fowls, meal, &c, which we would gladly purchase had we the means, and when they find we have no cloth they turn back disappointed.[200]

There was equally some attention for the more ambiguous effects of the influx of imported cloth into Mwinilunga. Although colonial officials actively promoted the spread of cloth in the area, they foresaw that heightened demand might have problematic consequences. In 1913, one official complained, for example, that the purchase of cloth would thwart attempts at monetisation:

> The desire of bought calicoes etc. is inordinately developed amongst these people, and almost as soon as they handle cash they wish to turn it into calico, which at the beginning will make it extremely difficult to obtain their cash before it reaches the store.[201]

Traders, missionaries, and administrators differently envisaged the purpose and effects of clothing on African societies. Within broader imperial and colonial projects, dress was part of a 'civilising mission'.[202] Clothing, however, was not

---

197   Hansen, *Salaula*, 24–29.
198   See: Burke, *Lifebuoy Men*, 84–86; Leander Schneider, 'The Maasai's New Clothes: A Developmentalist Modernity and Its Exclusions', *Africa Today* 53, No. 1 (2006): 101–31; Hansen, *Salaula*; Thomas, 'Modernity's Failings', 727–40; Ross, *Clothing*, 83–84; Comaroff and Comaroff, *Of Revelation and Revolution*, 218–73.
199   Burke, 'Unexpected Subversions', 475, refers to 'the allure of the foreign.'
200   Schapera, *Livingstone's African Journal*, 69, 102.
201   (NAZ) KSE 6/2/1, J.M. Pound, Lunda District Quarterly Report, June 1913.
202   Hansen, *Salaula*, 27; Ross, *Clothing*, Chapter 7; Comaroff and Comaroff, *Of Revelation and Revolution*, 218–73.

merely an issue of culture and morals, of dressing 'properly' or 'decently', but was connected to economic interests. In an attempt to entrench industrious behaviour and involvement with the market economy, colonial officials used clothing as an aid. By insisting on dressing in imported apparel, which could only be purchased in European trading stores with cash, the colonial adminis-tration tried to propel individuals into salaried labour or cash crop production to earn money over and above their tax requirements.[203] Even after indepen-dence, clothing discourses continued to be firmly grounded in ideologies of 'improvement' and 'development'.[204] Such views poorly reflected the meaning and value of cloth and clothing in Mwinilunga. Everyday clothing practices often differed from and subverted official discourses. Consumers appropriated manufactured garments in unexpected and locally specific ways, reimagining and refashioning them in their circulation, based on 'existing relationships to global commodity flows', as Prestholdt has explained.[205] Therefore, paying at-tention to how imported cloth and clothing has been incorporated and given meaning in Mwinilunga reveals changes in material culture and values, but equally sheds light on the engagement of local actors with missions, markets, and states.[206] Function and taste were important when composing apparel, but clothing choices were equally enmeshed in social, cultural, economic, and political processes. In order to grasp the changing meaning and value of cloth-ing, the societal context has to be understood. Ross stresses that 'since clothing is inescapably a demonstration of identity, wearing clothes – or for that matter not doing so – is inevitably a political act, in the widest possible sense of that word'.[207]

Local dress preferences in Mwinilunga have been formulated ever since the earliest interactions with imported cloth.[208] Such preferences changed over time, in accordance with concepts of style. To their despair, European traders and officials could exert little influence over such changes in fashion.[209] In the opening decades of the twentieth century, for example, road workers would

203   Burke, *Lifebuoy Men*, 66–70, 84; Comaroff and Comaroff, *Of Revelation and Revolution*, on missionaries.
204   Schneider, 'The Maasai's New Clothes', 107.
205   Prestholdt, 'Africa and the Global Lives of Things', 89; Burke, 'Unexpected Subversions', 471.
206   Hansen, 'Second-hand Clothing Encounters'; Prestholdt, *Domesticating the World.*
207   Ross, *Clothing*, 12; Allman, *Fashioning Africa.*
208   See: Martin, 'Contesting Clothes'; Prestholdt, 'On the Global Repercussions.'
209   Prestholdt, *Domesticating the World,* Chapter 3.

request wages exclusively in calico of a particular type (blue, white, etc.) and officials had little choice but to answer such demands.[210] Expressing independent tastes in pursuit of their clothes, the inhabitants of Mwinilunga at times frustrated the economic interests and hegemony of colonial rule itself. In 1910, officials complained that by crossing borders and trading with the Portuguese in Angola, people 'obtain all the calico they require to settle their numerous disputes, or cases amongst themselves, and of the particular sort they like, from the Portuguese traders and are therefore quite independent of this station in this respect'.[211] Although Europeans largely dominated the supply of cloth, the terms of its use and appropriation proved unexpected and distinctly ordained by the specific context of Mwinilunga.[212]

Cloth gained meaning through socioeconomic and political negotiations. Social relationships shaped the circulation, acceptance, and use of imported cloth.[213] Due to its limited supply in Mwinilunga prior to 1850, imported cloth was a highly valued luxury commodity. Its distribution was confined to political elites (mainly chiefs and headmen) who would hand out small pieces of cloth to kin and dependents, circulating cloth through gifts and channels of tribute.[214] Cloth, as a status symbol, strengthened the prestige of those with access to it and enabled the expansion of ties of allegiance and dependency. In this sense, dress was imbued with social meaning, being used as a marker of status, an expression of wealth, hierarchy, and power.[215] Travellers, such as Cameron, juxtaposed descriptions of a 'dirty and wild-looking' population with the apparel of their headman who 'was dressed for the occasion in a coloured shirt, felt hat, and a long petticoat made of coloured pocket-handkerchiefs'.[216] In the 1930s, one missionary described her encounter with Chief Kakoma as follows: 'He was dressed in many yards of trade cloth billowing all around him, and on top of all a weird and wonderful coat of some military uniform of ancient design'.[217] Notwithstanding the overt exoticisation of such descriptions, they do provide an insight into the local meaning and use of clothing. In Mwinilunga,

---

210 (NAZ) KSE6/5/1, C.S. Bellis, Balunda District Monthly Report, September 1909: Workers demanded to be paid in only blue calico that month.
211 (NAZ) KSE6/5/1, C.S. Bellis, Balunda District Monthly Report, September 1910.
212 Prestholdt, 'On the Global Repercussions'; Hansen, *Salaula.*
213 Allman, *Fashioning Africa.*
214 Gordon, 'Wearing Cloth', 25.
215 See Miller, *Way of Death,* 81.
216 Cameron, *Across Africa,* 403, 413.
217 Burr, *Kalene Memories,* 117.

cloth was used to establish social relationships, to assert status, build hierarchies of power, and create dependency.[218]

Even the economic importance of cloth was entwined with social relationships. Particularly in the nineteenth and the first half of the twentieth century, cloth was used as a medium of exchange and at times as a standardised currency.[219] Various measuring units derived from the human body were used, notably short (*chibeli, chitambala*), one yard (*chitenda*), two yards (*chilala, luvunga, mudjoka*), and narrow-width cloth (*mukwamba*).[220] Cloth was a central commodity in trade relations, especially in the long-distance caravan trade. Cloth could be obtained in exchange for ivory, rubber, beeswax, and slaves.[221] The high value of cloth, consequently, mediated social relationships. As a unit of payment, cloth figured in initiation ceremonies, bridewealth, and funeral payments, as remuneration for the services of witchdoctors and healers, or cloth payment would be imposed as a fine in judicial disputes.[222] Court cases provide evidence of such uses of cloth. In one case in 1915, cloth was used to cover funerary expenses:

> Mapupu himself came to me to claim goods in compensation for his son Chindora's death, saying that since my sister had killed him, being a witch, I her brother must pay (...) I paid him 8 yards calico, one short flintlock gun, one blanket and one string of beads, and he accepted these.[223]

Cloth was occasionally even used to redeem individuals from slavery, implying that cloth and human lives – wealth in goods and wealth in people – were directly interchangeable.[224] A court case from 1915 suggests this:

> I went to Swana Chirombo with two guns and some calico to release Kalukeki's child Lusenga from slavery (...) I asked Katoyi to release Lusenga and gave him two pieces of calico (4 yds. and 2 yds.) and a brass anklet, and told him I would find other goods to give him.[225]

---

218 Martin, 'Contesting Clothes.'
219 See: Gordon, 'Wearing Cloth', 28; Von Oppen, *Terms of Trade.*
220 A yard was defined as the length from the tip of the fingers to the middle of the chest; whereas two yards was the distance from fingertip to fingertip of outstretched arms. See Miller, *Way of Death*, 69; *Lunda-Ndembu Dictionary*; these lengths of cloth differ somewhat from the list compiled by C.M.N. White and cited in Von Oppen, *Terms of Trade.*
221 See: Gordon, 'Wearing Cloth'; Miller, *Way of Death*; Von Oppen, *Terms of Trade.*
222 Turner, *Schism and Continuity*; Turner and Turner, 'Money Economy', 19–37, provide examples.
223 (NAZ) KSE3/2/2/2 Rex v. Mapupu, 9 January 1915.
224 See: Gordon, 'Wearing Cloth'; Miller, *Way of Death*, 81.
225 (NAZ) KSE3/2/2/2, Rex v. Katoyi, 25 July 1915.

Further signifying the links between economic value and social relationships, cloth was a regular constituent of bridewealth. In a 1917 example, a man
gave his 'mother-in-law 5 pieces of calico (3 pieces of 4 yards each & one piece
of 8 yards & one of 2 yards) also some brass wire (3/-) and a plate'.[226] In 1912, a
colonial official suggested that this social function of cloth was perhaps even
more important than its utility as dress: 'For years the people have said "What,
we Wandembo, pay tax, we have no money, and are not strong, we don't even
wear calico". Incidentally forgetting to say that they have hundreds of yards to
pay off some affair'.[227] In Mwinilunga cloth was thus used as a store of wealth,
being kept as an insurance stock with which to fulfil social obligations and
payments. In this sense, cloth acted as a medium to establish and maintain
social relationships, building wealth in goods as well as people.[228] The social
importance of cloth did not cancel out its use value as garment. Rather, the two
reinforced each other.

Cloth retained its use as a unit of payment throughout the colonial period.[229] Because British currency was far from universal in Mwinilunga in the
opening decades of the twentieth century, cloth was used as an alternative.
Food or other goods could be purchased with cloth and labour was regularly
paid in cloth.[230] Official reports, for example in 1909, reflect such practices:

> After leaving calico in liberal payment for necessary food taken from the
> gardens, I [D.C.] eventually returned to Mwinilunga (...) I distributed as
> much calico as possible to the women and children. They showed confi-
> dence by returning again and again to Camp to sell a handful of beans or
> a little meal (...) I paid off the defaulting carriers of a day, and gave a piece
> of cloth to each man brought in.[231]

Both intentionally and unintentionally, colonial rule reinforced the importance of cloth. Agricultural producers, wage labourers, and mission workers
were all remunerated in cloth. In this manner, the colonial administration encouraged the spread and use of cloth in all layers of society in Mwinilunga.[232]

---

226   (NAZ) KSE3/1/2/1. Mashau of Shimbi v. Nyaikwatelu, 4 August 1917.
227   (NAZ) KSE6/2/1, T.M. Lawman, Lunda District Quarterly Report, 14 October 1912.
228   Gordon, 'Wearing Cloth'; Martin, 'Contesting Clothes'; Miller, *Way of Death*.
229   See: Hansen, *Salaula;* Comaroff and Comaroff, *Of Revelation and Revolution;* Prestholdt,
      'Africa and the Global Lives of Things.'
230   Fisher and Hoyte, *Ndotolu.*
231   (NAZ) BS2/199 IN2/1/3, G.A. MacGregor, Balunda Sub-District Monthly Report, January
      1909.
232   Hansen, *Salaula,* 24–39.

Yet in spite of the initial use of cloth as a unit of barter and payment, officials – especially after 1920 – sought to advocate monetisation, in the form of British currency. Using cash instead of cloth proved problematic, though, as the 1911 annual report attests:

> The introduction of cash is a great thing and avoids much bother in keeping calico etc., but at the same time, in a place like this where calico cannot be bought or if at all, only at a high price, money will always be taken less willingly than cloth: natives here have a stupid habit of coming in some way with a small load of food for sale, say 20 or 25 lbs. One cannot give them much cash for this and with calico at 1/- a yard (the price today at store) they do not receive much benefit by selling, from their point of view. I have landed calico for my own use at 6d a yard but this does not allow of any profit to a trader.[233]

Notwithstanding objections by officials, cloth continued to be a unit of payment for labour (blankets were often part of road labourers' wages) or a unit of barter when selling crops to missionaries (a basket of cassava could be exchanged for a length of cloth), throughout much of the twentieth century.[234]

Over the course of the twentieth century, cloth transitioned from a luxury good for the elite to a common and everyday item of use.[235] The value of cloth was occasionally even standardised, if not fixed, as an example from 1908 shows:

> Wages are from 5/- to 7/- per month and are invariably paid in calico valued at 6d per yard (...) No goat is to be purchased under from 10 yards to 16 yards of calico (...) Fowls are far from plentiful and are valued at from 1 to 2 yards of calico each (...) Calico (common white or blue) is valued at 6d per yard by all natives.[236]

Going beyond its utilitarian value, cloth held great significance. Its use as a medium of exchange, a unit of payment and a mediator in social relationships enhanced the desirability and importance of cloth. Cloth therefore spread rapidly and broadly once supply became more plentiful under colonial rule.[237]

---

233 (NAZ) KSE6/1/2, J.M.C. Pound, Lunda Sub-District Annual Report, 1911–12.
234 This view is based on numerous interviews, Mandamu Sapotu, 10 March 2010, Ikelenge.
235 Hansen, *Salaula*; Gordon, 'Wearing Cloth.'
236 (NAZ) KSE6/1/1, G.A. MacGregor, Balunda District Annual Report, 1908–9.
237 It is important to stress, as Hansen and Burke do, that the supply of cloth under colonialism (especially before 1945) remained limited, and that supply could not fully meet

Even if there were continuities with previous uses of clothing, this transition had profound consequences for the meaning and value of cloth.

Access to imported cloth, purchased mainly in European trading stores, was by no means universal in the opening decades of the twentieth century.[238] Due to economic hardship and unfavourable terms of trade in the 1920s and 1930s, officials noted that people who had once worn imported cloth had gone back to bark cloth and animal skins, signifying the recent and reversible nature of the clothing transition: 'The high prices still asked by the stores for calico and blankets naturally causes a good deal of dissatisfaction among the natives – a large proportion of whom are reverting to skins and bark cloth to cover their nakedness'.[239] Nevertheless, as the twentieth century progressed, cloth was increasingly defined as one of the 'articles that have become necessities'.[240] What was regarded as a necessity was of course culturally defined and contested; yet the spread of clothing through Mwinilunga District was by all means general and popular. Despite the marked price increases in trading stores between 1914 and 1921, clothing sales continued unabatedly.[241]

	Price in 1914	Price in 1921
White calico	1/- a yard	2/6 to 3/- a yard
Blue or striped calico	1/- a yard	2/6 a yard
Shirts	3/- each	7/- each
Blankets	4/3 each	8/6 each

Prices paid for agricultural produce did not rise in proportion, making it necessary to produce and sell more crops to obtain the same amount of cloth; nonetheless clothing consumption did not contract. The value of clothing is clearly illustrated by a survey from the 1950s conducted by Turner, which concluded that on average men spent £5 17s 4d a year on clothing, out of a total income of £14 10s 4d. Approximately 40% of all male income was spent on clothing, and for those aged between 40 and 60 this percentage was even higher. This pattern differed but slightly for women, who on average spent 33% of their income on clothing, £1 15s 3d out of a total income of £5 5s 6d a year. No

demand. Nevertheless, when compared to the nineteenth century the supply of cloth in the twentieth century had increased greatly.

238   Hansen, *Salaula*.
239   (NAZ) KSE6/1/4, F.V. Bruce-Miller, Mwinilunga Sub-District Annual Report, 31 March 1924.
240   (NAZ) NWP1/2/78 Loc.4913, E.L. Button, Mwinilunga District Annual Report, 1959.
241   (NAZ) KSE 6/1/4, F.V. Bruce-Miller, Mwinilunga Sub-District Annual Report, 31 March 1921.

other item of expenditure approximated the significance of clothing. Taxation, household utensils, and other store-bought goods were but minor expenses in comparison to store-bought garments.[242] Placing these patterns of clothing consumption, taste, and appearance in the context of agricultural production, labour migration, and social relationships helps explain the central position of clothing in Mwinilunga.

3.3   *Clothing, Production, and Social Relationships*

The economic repercussions of clothing had been debated by European travellers, traders, and officials ever since the introduction of mass-manufactured garments into Mwinilunga.[243] In the 1850s, Livingstone acclaimed the wonders of commerce, as 'the prints of Manchester are by means of it brought to the centre of Africa'.[244] These views perceived the general spread of clothing as beneficial, as this would spur participation in the market economy. The need to earn cash with which to purchase dress would propel individuals to work, either as wage labourers or as cash crop producers. Industrial mass manufacture thus made it possible to tap into the lucrative African market, thereby contributing to economic growth and supporting the broader aims of imperialism.[245] Yet only after the 1940s, when clothing consumption really universalised and spread through the district, was the full potential of the consumer market realised.[246] Due to booming copper production, labour migration, and high producer prices on the world market, consumptive aspirations in Mwinilunga appeared virtually unrestrained. Labour migrants would return to their villages loaded with trousers, dresses, and shirts, rather than a single blanket, as had been the case in the 1920s. Policies of 'development' further promoted the acquisition of consumer goods after independence. Only once this favourable climate gave way to a worldwide economic recession towards the end of the 1970s did clothing consumption become problematised once more.[247]

Colonial officials supposed a direct relationship between consumption and production. The 1913 annual report, for example, remarked that 'the Lunda people are extremely fond of calico, and later on they will be found to improve in physique and will turn out a good working population'.[248] Similarly, officials were convinced that the demand for cloth would lead to increased agricultural

---

242   Turner and Turner, 'Money Economy', 30.
243   Prestholdt, *Domesticating the World*; Hansen, *Salaula*.
244   Schapera, *Livingstone's African Journal*, 32.
245   Burke, *Lifebuoy Men*, Chapter 3; Prestholdt, *Domesticating the World*, Chapter 3; Hansen, 'Second-hand Clothing Encounters', 352–54.
246   Burke, *Lifebuoy Men*; Hansen, *Salaula*.
247   Hansen, *Salaula*, 24–39.
248   (NAZ) KSE6/2/1, J.M. Pound, Lunda District Quarterly Report, 31 December 1913.

production, as a report from 1950 suggests: 'People are very interested to grow crops because when they take their crops to the traders they get much money and cloth'.[249] This relationship was two-way: increased production enabled access to consumer goods, such as clothing, but moreover, the prospect of consumption acted as a stimulus for enhanced productive activities. Within this logic, some officials linked consumption to 'development', as a desire for clothing might spur individuals to make larger fields or engage in salaried employment in urban areas.[250] Government officials, in their attempts to propagate industrious behaviour and a transition from 'subsistence' to 'market' production, eagerly promoted consumption as a tool to boost productive activities.[251]

Labour migration particularly articulated the links between clothing and productive activities.[252] In 1930, the missionary Alfred Digby Fisher observed that 'the people in this district are away a great deal working for the white men in the towns, where they earn good money and so for the most part are well clothed'.[253] Clothes were not only regarded as a reward for salaried employment, they even acted as an enticement for men and women to leave their homes to earn income with which to buy the latest fashion.[254] Makajina Kahilu made the long trip from Angola via Mwinilunga to Johannesburg, largely on foot, in pursuit of a nice suit. After having made several stops on the Zambian Copperbelt, in Livingstone and Zimbabwe, he proceeded to Johannesburg where the 'latest fashion' was found. He only returned to settle in Mwinilunga once he had obtained two black suits and other consumer goods, such as a saucepan radio.[255] Even if Makajina's case was exceptional in the paramount importance attached to clothing, it certainly depicts a broader trend. Other migrants would spend their first wages on clothing, or they sent clothes home as remittances to maintain ties with kin.[256] Production and consumption were thoroughly intertwined, not only in the minds of officials but above all in the daily lives of the consuming public. The purchase of fashionable clothing required a cash income. Yet those with access to the latest fashion, in turn,

249 (NAZ) NWP1/2/21 Loc.4901, Agricultural Report Chief Kanongeshya Area, 8 February 1950.
250 Ross, Hinfelaar, and Peša, *The Objects of Life*, Introduction. Perhaps consumption caused something akin to an 'industrious revolution': Jan de Vries, *The Industrious Revolution: Consumer Behavior and the Household Economy, 1650 To The Present* (Cambridge: Cambridge University Press, 2008), 10, 72.
251 Burke, 'Unexpected Subversions.'
252 See Barrett, 'Walking Home Majestically,' 93–113.
253 (EOS) Alfred Digby Fisher, December 1930.
254 The Rhodes Livingstone Institute researchers have described this process with eloquence.
255 Interview with Makajina Kahilu, 8 March 2010, Ikelenge.
256 Wilson, *The Economics of Detribalization*.

attracted the admiration of others, building personal status, value, and wealth. Within the framework of wealth in people, clothing consumption furthered aspirations for self-realisation, as Prestholdt has argued: 'By representing aspirations publicly, new consumer imports were tools in the constitution of personhood and strategies of distinction'.[257] Clothing served to build, maintain, or challenge social relationships. Through its ability to convey status, hierarchy, and power, clothing was distinctly social and political.[258]

Clothing served as a public statement of personal worth, wealth, and status. Prior to the twentieth century, imported cloth had still entered the area in relatively small quantities through a limited number of channels, enabling the control of this supply by a small group of powerful individuals. The political elite of chiefs, headmen, and traders directed the import of cloth, a good that conveyed prestige and commanded respect to the owner.[259] Cloth was used as a status symbol, the distribution of which attracted followers, dependents, and wives.[260] Within the context of wealth in people, 'Big Men' acted as gatekeepers, monopolising imports and thereby building and maintaining social and political hierarchies.[261] A cycle was created whereby goods were used to gain human allegiance, which in turn served to increase productivity and obtain more goods (cloth-people-more cloth).[262] Through the labour power of their dependents, which facilitated the acquisition of ivory, rubber, and beeswax, chiefs and headmen gained access to cloth and other imported goods of the long-distance trade. By dispensing cloth to their dependents, chiefs and headmen augmented their productive activities, generating means to obtain even more cloth.[263] The slave trade was the apex of this cycle of goods and people. In the 1950s one District Commissioner revealingly recalled that:

> Not so long ago (...) lengths of cloth could only be obtained by barter with the Yimbundu [Ovimbundu] tribe, who brought their goods from Angola. The price paid for lengths of cloth was human: five lengths for a boy slave, and ten for a girl.[264]

---

257   Prestholdt, 'Africa and the Global Lives of Things', 96.
258   Martin, 'Contesting Clothes'; Ross, *Clothing*.
259   Gordon, 'Wearing Cloth', 25–26; Miller, *Way of Death*, 81.
260   Guyer, 'Wealth in People and Self-Realization', 258–59.
261   Prestholdt, 'Africa and the Global Lives of Things', 87.
262   Miller, *Way of Death*; Ross, Hinfelaar, and Peša, *The Objects of Life*, 4.
263   Miller, *Way of Death*, 71–73; Gordon, 'The Abolition of the Slave Trade.'
264   (NAZ) SEC2/962 P.L.N. Hannaford, Mwinilunga District Tour Report, April 1954.

Once the supply of cloth increased in the twentieth century, this gatekeeper mechanism of control was challenged and eventually undermined. People aspiring to build an alternative base of power started to amass and distribute imports to challenge established figures of authority.[265] As described by Prestholdt, aspirants 'destabilized structures of authority in novel ways by enhancing their prestige through access to imported goods'.[266] Cloth became accessible to a variety of individuals through multiple channels of supply, enabling younger wage labourers to contest the authority of elders. Although access to mass-manufactured cloth challenged the power of established 'Big Men', it enabled others to build up their own authority.[267] In this sense, access to cloth functioned as a means for self-realisation. Throughout this period, people continued to use the power of cloth to gain respect and human allegiance.[268]

3.4   Clothing, Culture, and Self-Realisation

Rather than being used in ways ordained by its European suppliers, cloth in Mwinilunga was reinterpreted and given new meanings.[269] Cloth functioned as a means of distinction, expressing status and evoking admiration. Through cloth, people built wealth, demonstrated power, and realised personhood.[270] Instead of being simply cumulative, wealth acquisition was compositional and self-realisation could be achieved in multiple manners, indicating, as Guyer argues, 'the competitive and constantly innovative process of valorization along multiple routes', making effective control or hierarchy impossible.[271] Whilst in the nineteenth century cloth was mainly a means of control over people, in the twentieth century cloth continued to be a marker of prestige and wealth. Because clothing expressed personal power and value, wearing fashionable clothes was a means for building personhood and status, attracting the admiration and allegiance of other people.[272] According to Guyer's principle of self-realisation, 'the assets were not things at all, but the singular persons who harnessed sources and controlled fates'.[273] Cloth not only boosted the prestige of the owner but was also handed out to kin, and served to build and

---

265   Gordon, 'Wearing Cloth', 25, 33.
266   Prestholdt, 'Africa and the Global Lives of Things', 97.
267   Guyer and Eno Belinga, 'Wealth in People as Wealth in Knowledge', 119–20.
268   See also Hansen, Salaula.
269   Burke, 'Unexpected Subversions', 481; Prestholdt, 'On the Global Repercussions.'
270   Martin, 'Contesting Clothes'; Gordon, 'Wearing Cloth.'
271   Guyer, 'Wealth in People and Self-Realization', 246, 253.
272   See: Hansen, Salaula; Hansen, 'Second-hand Clothing Encounters', 344.
273   Guyer, 'Wealth in People and Self-Realization', 257.

strengthen social relationships. Migrant labourers would thus carry cloth for their relatives while on leave, remit cloth from town, or stock clothes as a store of wealth. Returning migrants were viewed with admiration, mainly because of their fashionable clothes.[274] Cloth enabled a labourer to marry the wife of his choice, or it provided remuneration for work parties. Because these work parties assisted the host with the construction of a new house, or with the cultivation of a large field, cloth had the potential of being productive in an economic sense, as well as enhancing social relations and prestige.[275] Marital relationships built on the exchange of cloth, as a husband would be expected to provide his wife with new cloth on a regular basis (once a year is the norm today). Failure to fulfil this obligation justified claims of neglect and could even lead to divorce.[276] In a 1918 court case, a man whose wife had requested divorce defended himself by stating: 'I have given her clothes and treated her properly'.[277] In order to build and maintain social relationships, it was necessary not only to have access to cloth but also more importantly to distribute it. A respectable man had to provide cloth for his household.[278] On the other hand, a man hoarding cloth solely for his own use, while his wife and children walked around in rags, would be strongly condemned.[279] Wearing a nice suit was not only a personal but also a fundamentally social act.

Clothing became an object of popular desire during the twentieth century. The proverb '*vwala musamba, ihina dakala kutonda*' – 'wear bark cloth, cotton cloth is hard to find', reflects the difficulty of obtaining cloth.[280] Still, clothing became widely available during the colonial period, and within several decades a marked shift in patterns of consumption could be observed. Whereas in the 1930s a missionary still remarked that 'most of the women wear a long cloth knotted around the arm pits. When they have enough money they get a blouse and skirt',[281] by the 1960s, it was common to possess a spare set of clothing, as well as two blankets.[282] Especially from the 1940s onwards, a variety of fabrics, designs, and qualities of cloth, tailored clothing, and ready-to-wear garments

274   Barrett, 'Walking Home Majestically'; Wilson, *The Economics of Detribalization*.
275   Turner and Turner, 'Money Economy.'
276   This view is based on numerous interviews, for example Julian Chiyezhi, 2008, Mwinilunga; see Chapter 5.
277   (NAZ) KSE3/1/2/1, Kambai of Kanyika v. Nyansamba of Muloa, 25 June 1918.
278   See: Parpart, 'Where Is Your Mother?', 241–71; Powdermaker, *Copper Town*.
279   See the reference to the song Kabwengenenge below.
280   Proverb recited by Justin Kambidimba, September 2010, Ntambu.
281   (NAZ) HM8FI4/2/1, Singleton Fisher, Missionary Work Among the African People – Life at Kalene Hill, n.d. [1930?].
282   (NAZ) LGH5/4/2 Loc.3615, Mwinilunga Security Scheme 1963: Assessment of Common Goods in the District.

became commonly accessible. Changes in attire from the colonial and early post-colonial period are still vividly recalled and discussed at present. During the opening decades of the twentieth century, various types of cloth circulated. The most common varieties were *kanyiki* (blue calico), *mutoma* (white calico), and *sapato* (khaki coloured calico), worn by both men and women.[283] White cloth was considered the most prestigious of these, being reserved for chiefs, headmen, and their wives. In later periods, different types of cloth, under a variety of names, spread throughout the area. This complicated the distinction of quality or value, but nevertheless, consumers expressed clear preferences. Zimbabwean cloth, *chiwankie*, was considered inferior to Congolese varieties of cloth, such as *tumbela* or *katende*, which were less stiff and kept their colour better than cheaper alternatives. *Muzukila* was an affordable cloth worn by the masses, whereas varieties such as *pindalo* conveyed wealth, making a person *mbongu* (a boaster, a person who is very rich).[284] Styles were also highly gendered. Whereas initially both men and women would wear the same type of cloth, wrapped around the lower part of their body or knotted under one armpit, styles were increasingly differentiated by gender once cloth became more plentiful. Women continued to wear cloth throughout the twentieth century, though of different varieties. Affluent women would wear two or three pieces of cloth, one wrapped around the lower part of the body, one around the chest, and one as headgear. Furthermore, women would wear tailored *chitenge* or *chikwembi* (printed cotton cloth) dresses, or ready-made blouses and skirts. Men, on the other hand, would wear shorts and blouses (*kahuma*, jacket; *chikovwelu*, shirt; *mupila*, vest; *kaputula*, shorts). After independence, long trousers became the standard for men, as it was no longer considered respectable to wear shorts.[285] Appropriate footwear would complete the apparel. Lunda men had made shoes out of animal skins, or in exceptional cases out of tree bark, and these would be worn by hunters when they went into the bush. Nevertheless, footwear had not been an item of widespread use in the nineteenth or early twentieth century. Road workers and migrant labourers remembered wearing rubber shoes made of used car tyres to protect their feet. From the 1930s onwards, canvas shoes became accessible to men and women. Later still, returning migrant labourers introduced leather shoes. Footwear, an

---

283   These types of cloth are also mentioned by Gordon, 'Wearing Cloth'; Von Oppen, *Terms of Trade*; Prestholdt, *Domesticating the World*.

284   This is based on numerous interviews, for example Mandosa Kabanda, 2 August 2010, Kanongesha.

285   Such shifts have equally been described by Hansen, *Salaula;* Interview with Christina Kalumbu, 13 May 2010, Nyakaseya.

item that had once been regarded as superfluous, was transformed into a necessity and a marker of status.[286]

Cloth was able to convey value and hierarchy, thus enabling status distinctions.[287] That is why chiefs so fervently discussed the form and colour of their uniforms, suggesting in the 1960s: 'A dark blue or black suit with golden buttons and gold braid down the seams of the trousers. The decorations should be different for Chiefs, Senior Chiefs and Paramount Chiefs'.[288] Similarly, the colonial administration in Mwinilunga linked clothing to notions of social distinction, wealth, and 'civilisation',[289] as a report from 1933 shows: 'The appearance of the natives in this area very definitely suggests poverty; few of the natives can boast of anything more pretentious than loin cloths made of skin and bark cloth'.[290] But even in popular consciousness, clothing served as a visible marker of wealth. By the 1950s, an old woman wearing rags and walking around barefoot was considered destitute. Whether this was because she lacked the strength to cultivate her own garden or because she had lost her husband and had no sons who could provide for her, absence of clothing was a visible marker of poverty. Poverty, thus, was not only a lack of material possessions but also a lack of social relationships. A woman without a husband and children lacked 'wealth in people'. More frequently, clothing served as a positive marker of wealth and power. A prosperous female pineapple farmer might well use her profits to buy clothes for herself and her children, visualising her achievements and social status. The envy her clothing attracted from less affluent neighbours merely underlined her personal success. Furthermore, she could use cloth as a payment to attract other women for work parties, enabling her to increase production and attain self-realisation.[291] As a personal medium that visualised social relationships, clothes mediated wealth in people and self-realisation. Clothing served various functions, not only marking status distinctions but also consolidating interpersonal relationships.

Influenced by the rise of nationalism in the 1950s, clothing was used by chiefs, headmen, and politicians to assert equality or even to claim superiority vis-à-vis colonial officials (see Photo 11).[292] As Burke suggests, clothing

---

286   Pritchett, *Friends for Life*, describes the same.
287   Compare to: Martin, 'Contesting Clothes.'
288   (NAZ) LGH5/2/8 Loc.3613, North-Western Province Resident Secretaries Conference, 20 October 1969.
289   Schneider, 'The Maasai's New Clothes', 110.
290   (NAZ) SEC2/953, G.S. Jones, Mwinilunga District Tour Report, 27 February 1933.
291   Interview with Nanci Kamafumbu, 19 April 2010, Ikelenge.
292   See Ross, *Clothing*, Chapter 9.

consumption might be 'a tool for achieving legitimacy and parity within global modernity'.[293] Under colonial rule officials and missionaries had attempted to keep Africans in their place by delineating racial and class boundaries through dress.[294] Yet such attempts did not go unchallenged. Wearing the right apparel served to assert decency, or even 'civilisation' and 'modernity'.[295] A discussion, initiated by several chiefs from Mwinilunga in the Provincial Council, evidences such aspirations: 'Africans desirous of living a decent life, get their requirements from European stores, I do not think any of us here today is wearing clothing bought in an African store'.[296] Nevertheless, clothing was more than a simple emulation or 'mimicry' of whites.[297] As Ross argues, people 'wore European clothes as an attempt to make clear that they were as good as anyone in the world, and certainly the equals of those who were perceived as looking down at the wearer of the suit'.[298] Clothing was used to assert social and political status in locally specific ways. After independence, the importance of clothing did not subside. Government officials designated clothing 'improvement' as one of the main markers of 'development'.[299] In reports and public statements, it was decreed that 'no person should ever really dress in rags in Zambia nor indeed go barefooted'.[300] By the 1970s, it was even stated that 'the principle task of any government like ours in a developing country is, as quickly as possible to provide (...) better clothing'.[301] Clothing became a marker of 'development' and 'modernity',[302] as Schneider has explained, securing 'membership as respectable equals (...) in the nation'.[303]

To the present day, the importance of clothing remains paramount. A popular song, *Kabwengenenge* (2007), depicts a man who does not like to cultivate his fields. Due to his poverty the man is unable to buy cloth for his wife, which causes her to steal the *chitenge* (printed cotton cloth) of her neighbour. This shames her to such an extent that she subsequently sneaks around the village, using shortcuts so that nobody can see her. Nevertheless, the neighbour discovers the theft and claims the *chitenge* back, leaving the woman nude and

293   Burke, 'Unexpected Subversions', 476.
294   See Burke, *Lifebuoy Men,* 99.
295   See: Schneider, 'The Maasai's New Clothes'; Allman, *Fashioning Africa.*
296   (NAZ) North-Western Province African Provincial Council, May 1958.
297   James Ferguson, 'Of Mimicry and Membership: Africans and the "New World Society"', *Cultural Anthropology* 17, No. 4 (2002): 551–69.
298   Ross, *Clothing,* 170.
299   Hansen, *Salaula,* 38.
300   (NAZ) Second National Convention on Rural Development, 12 December 1969.
301   (NAZ) A New Strategy for Rural Development in Zambia, 1974.
302   Schneider, 'The Maasai's New Clothes', 116.
303   Ibidem, 124.

embarrassed.[304] This song connects the themes of production and consumption, underlining the importance of cloth, as well as its links to social distinction, status, wealth, and work. The moral of the song is that a husband should work hard to provide his wife with a decent garment, because without cloth a woman is poor and unworthy. Cloth did not gain such enduring importance as an item of utility alone. The use and meaning of cloth changed over time, but its significance was based on the interrelations between clothing, social relationships, power, and status. Clothing practices and preferences can only be understood by looking at clothing, people, and wealth in all their complexity.

4   Grass, Mud, and Bricks: Housing, Community, and Permanence

Even more than metallurgy or clothing, housing is a locus of consumption where the individual meets a wider collective.[305] Inhabited by individuals, nuclear families or extended kin-based entities, dwellings are integrated into larger units of settlement, such as farms, villages, or towns.[306] As Lewinson asserts, housing expresses social negotiations between men and women, between chiefs, the government, and their subjects: 'Within the domestic realm and the social worlds of its residents, individuals enact state- or civically-generated definitions of the family, perform daily acts of sustenance, and act on deeply held beliefs of "the good life."'[307] Architectural styles in Mwinilunga are connected to social relationships and notions of wealth. Housing mediates the personal or domestic sphere and broader issues of culture, ideology, society, and economy, as Gabrilopoulos, Mather, and Apentiik explain:

> The built environment constitutes a carefully contrived stage on which social action occurs. Dwellings in particular are a universal aspect of material culture that cross-culturally define the domestic domain, often serve as a setting for corporate economic activity and solidarity, and provide an affirmation of cultural values.[308]

---

304   Kabwengenenge, Kanongesha Band, 2007. This song was translated and explained by Julian Chiyezhi, September–October 2008, Mwinilunga.

305   Miller, 'Consumption and Commodities', 155.

306   Kay, *Social Aspects of Village Regrouping*.

307   Anne S. Lewinson, 'Domestic Realms, Social Bonds, and Class: Ideologies and Indigenizing Modernity in Dar es Salaam, Tanzania', *Canadian Journal of African Studies* 40, No. 3 (2006): 463–64.

308   Nick Gabrilopoulos, Charle Mather, and Caesar R. Apentiik, 'Lineage Organisation of the Tallensi Compound: The Social Logic of Domestic Space in Northern Ghana', *Africa* 72, No. 2 (2002): 222.

Turner has explored the sociocultural and political importance with which housing was imbued in the area of Mwinilunga in the 1950s. He depicted the 'spatial separation of adjacent genealogical generations' within the village, which acted as a hierarchical ordering mechanism for power relations, the 'visible end-result of a number of social tendencies'.[309] An inherently social expression, housing in Mwinilunga was connected to broader issues of socio-economic and political power, holding complex meaning for its occupants.

Housing is pivotal in daily life and social well-being. Therefore it is essential to study, as Myers proposes, the 'sociocultural precepts of building form', in order to illustrate how an 'indigenous micro-planning system served as the spatial embodiment of the popular consciousness', closely connected to issues of wealth and power.[310] This section examines the tension between discourse and practice, between colonial/post-colonial government doctrine and housing construction in Mwinilunga. In official discourse issues of housing have been connected to debates on permanent residence, agricultural productivity, and ultimately to issues of 'modernity'.[311] Such a link between housing, health, social welfare, and material well-being is suggested by an official statement from the 1980s:

> Housing is a basic human necessity which plays an important part in maintaining good health habits and social stability of a nation. It provides the necessary physical environment in which the family develops and such physical environment plays a decisive role in raising the general level of the standard of living of the people.[312]

Housing was afforded particular prominence in UNIP campaigns and policies after independence. It was decreed that 'No person should really fail to have a decent two- or three-roomed Kimberley brick house'.[313] This mode of reasoning was a continuation of colonial rhetoric. Colonial/post-colonial officials viewed the transition from grass housing to wattle and daub, and later sundried or burnt brick housing, roofed with iron sheets instead of grass, not

---

309   Victor W. Turner, 'The Spatial Separation of Generations in Ndembu Village Structure', *Africa* 25, No. 2 (1955): 121–37.

310   Garth A. Myers, 'Sticks and Stones: Colonialism and Zanzibari Housing', *Africa* 67, No. 2 (1997): 253.

311   See Comaroff and Comaroff, *Of Revelation and Revolution*, 274–322.

312   (NAZ) Department of Community Development, North-Western Province, 1980.

313   (UNIPA) Kimberley brick is a term used for sundried mud brick structures.

only as positive and desirable, but ultimately as inevitable.[314] The underlying assumption was that transitions in building style would be accompanied by a trend towards permanent residence (as opposed to frequent shifting), as well as improved methods of agricultural production and increased material prosperity.[315] The colonial and post-colonial state viewed housing and building control as 'spatial strategies aimed at social control'.[316] Ultimately, Lewinson asserts: 'Colonial regimes articulated power and a vision of modernity through architecture that materialized the regulating, authoritative nature of bureaucracy and the state'.[317] In the case of Mwinilunga shifts in housing patterns were complex, at times contradictory or reversible, but above all they were not determined by government pressure or economic incentives alone.[318] Official visions were contested through daily practices. Struggles over housing expressed a mixture of socioeconomic and political factors, cultural and ideological values. Housing held complex local meaning.[319] As Myers explains, more often than not, government officials 'misunderstood (...) customs and the contradictory dynamics within them as practised', and therefore attempts at control, planning and authority regularly proved 'ineffective in shaping space to control', or 'remaking spatiality'.[320] Relating housing to social relationships and meaning making helps explain changes in housing styles in Mwinilunga.

4.1   Grass, Mud, and the Meaning of Housing
Early colonial officials voiced recurrent complaints about the 'impermanence' of Lunda housing.[321] In the nineteenth century settlements in Mwinilunga had indeed been small and had shifted their location frequently.[322] Travelling through the area in the 1870s Cameron described how his party:

> ... passed many small hamlets consisting only of a few huts in the centre of a patch of cleared and cultivated ground (...) The huts were all small, and while some were circular with conical roofs and walls of stakes, with

---

314   Kay, *Social Aspects of Village Regrouping*, 23–32; Von Oppen, 'The Village as Territory', 57–61.
315   Von Oppen, 'The Village as Territory'; Moore and Vaughan, *Cutting Down Trees*. See Comaroff and Comaroff, *Of Revelation and Revolution*, 274–78.
316   Myers, 'Sticks and Stones', 252.
317   Lewinson, 'Domestic Realms, Social Bonds, and Class', 466.
318   Pritchett, *Lunda-Ndembu*, Chapter 3.
319   Turner, 'The Spatial Separation.'
320   Myers, 'Sticks and Stones', 252–53.
321   Compare to: Moore and Vaughan, *Cutting Down Trees*.
322   Kay, *Social Aspects of Village Regrouping*, 5–9; Turner, *Schism and Continuity*, 2–3.

the interstices filled in with grass, others were oblong with sloping roofs and were lined with mats.[323]

Houses could be constructed in a number of ways, but grass or wattle-and-daub structures were most common. These were conical, round, or square, possessing sloping grass thatched roofs.[324] To some extent, architectural style did depend on permanence of residence. When founding a settlement in a new location, residents would start by building a grass *nkunka* (see Photo 12).[325] As temporary dwellings that would be destructed on departure, *nkunka* were built near the fields during harvest time or in the bush during hunting expeditions. Equally, *nkunka* would be constructed for ritual purposes. They housed boys and girls during initiation ceremonies, patients during healing rituals, or they functioned as seclusion huts for menstruating women. In most cases, they would be abandoned within a single season. Generally, *nkunka* would be replaced after several months by fortified wattle-and-daub housing, which could be inhabited for years if repaired regularly.[326] Only in exceptional circumstances would *nkunka* be inhabited for more than one or two years.[327]

Housing, however, was not only connected to permanence, but equally to status and hierarchies of power based on gender and age. Turner described that 'older men are the first to move into permanent mud houses when a new village is being built, while the sisters' sons, who are working for their uncles, are still quartered in the grass houses'.[328] Some elder widows might be housed in *nkunka* permanently, because they lacked access to male labour to procure poles for wattle-and-daub constructions. Especially the access to and mobilisation of labour for house construction reflects social power relations and hierarchies. House construction is labour intensive, and therefore access to extra-household labour for tasks such as woodcutting or roofing becomes desirable. Furthermore, house construction is gendered, depending on male labour for heavy work. Access to male labour could be negotiated through marriage (women commanding the labour of their husbands), age (elders commanding the labour of juniors), and status hierarchies (chiefs commanding the labour

---

323   Cameron, *Across Africa*, 404–05.
324   These views are based on numerous interviews and a reading of archival sources (NAZ).
325   See Chapter 1 for *nkunka* (conical grass structure).
326   According to informants wattle-and-daub houses would be inhabited for four to five years before shifting.
327   See Turner, *Schism and Continuity*.
328   Turner, 'The Spatial Separation', 130, refers to Merran McCulloch, *The Southern Lunda and Related Peoples (Northern Rhodesia, Belgian Congo, Angola)* (London, 1951), 40.

of subjects).[329] Housing is thus thoroughly social, expressing hierarchies of gender, age, wealth, and social status.

Furthermore, the design of a village was connected to ritual power.[330] As has been described by Livingstone, religious meaning permeated the space of the village:

> They are idolators, near every village an Idol is seen, a block of wood with a rough human head carved on it, or a lion made of clay and two shells for eyes standing in a little shed. The people when unsuccessful in any enterprise, or sick, beat a drum before them all night (...) In the deep dark forests near their villages we always met with idols and places of prayer (...) the worshipper – either male or female – comes alone and prays to the gods (Barimo) or spirits of departed relatives, and when an answer to the petition seems granted, meal or other food is sprinkled on the spot as a thankoffering.[331]

The spirits of ancestors, who are buried on the outskirts of a village, connect village residents to the land. These ancestral connections are a prerequisite for village well-being, fertility, and prosperity, although ancestors can influence village affairs benevolently and malevolently.[332] Because death is interpreted as a bad omen, especially if it involves the headman or prominent elders, a village tends to shift its location after the occurrence of several deaths.[333] Going beyond matters of architecture, housing is imbued with ritual, socioeconomic, and political meaning.

Colonial observers have all too often condemned the impermanence of Lunda housing, connecting this to issues of 'laziness', lack of hygiene, or even 'primitivity'.[334] Nevertheless, impermanence had its own logic. Both grass and wattle-and-daub houses were constructed from locally procured materials. Poles and thatching grass, from specific hardwood trees and reeds, were difficult to access as they tended to be dispersed over the landscape. Grass and

---

329   Pritchett, *Lunda-Ndembu*, Chapter 2; Turner, *Schism and Continuity*.
330   Turner, *Schism and Continuity*.
331   David Chamberlain, ed., *Some Letters from Livingstone, 1840–72* (Oxford: Oxford University Press, 1940), 219, 249–50.
332   Turner, *Schism and Continuity*, 173.
333   This view is based on numerous interviews for example Zakewa Kahangu, 26 April 2010, Nyakaseya, a reading of archival sources (NAZ) and is reflected in Turner, *Schism and Continuity*, 263–65.
334   Kay, *Social Aspects of Village Regrouping*, 9–12; Compare to: Moore and Vaughan, *Cutting Down Trees*; Comaroff and Comaroff, *Of Revelation and Revolution*.

especially wattle-and-daub houses were, nonetheless, remarkably strong and durable, if properly constructed.[335] These structures provided shelter and comfort, offered protection against wild animals, and they could withstand the vagaries of the long rainy season in Mwinilunga.[336] Yet if house construction needed to be completed rapidly, inferior alternatives to established building practices would be resorted to. Due to constraints of time, labour, or natural resources, houses were sometimes put together in a haphazard way, making frequent modifications, repairs, and rethatching necessary. White ants might attack the poles, or rain and humidity would affect roofing.[337] All these factors encouraged the frequent relocation of settlements.

Impermanence was informed by considerations other than architecture, though. The search for hunting, fishing, or cultivating grounds, disputes within a village, war and enemy attack, or death and improvidence were all reasons for a household or village to relocate. Generally, villages would shift their location in intervals from one to twenty years.[338] This mobility was coupled with, and facilitated by, the small size of villages. In the 1950s, Turner noted that population increase seemed 'to have led to an increase in the number of villages rather than in the size of individual villages'.[339] Turner attributed the small size of villages to ecological factors (the carrying capacity of land for agricultural production and an occupational focus on hunting) as well as the fissile nature of virilocal marriage in a matrilineal descent system.[340] This tendency towards small and mobile villages was temporarily offset at the end of the nineteenth century, due to slave raids and ensuing insecurity. Centralisation of population and authority resulted, as people sought security in numbers and founded large settlements headed by elders who exercised an exceptional level of authority.[341] Such settlements were surrounded by a stockade, which had earlier served to keep away wild animals, such as lions and hyenas.[342] Due to the labour required to erect a stockade, these settlements most probably remained in the same place for a longer period, signalling increased permanence of residence. 'Big Men' acted as gatekeepers, as a large village conveyed status

---

335   Von Oppen, *Terms of Trade*.
336   Pritchett, *Lunda-Ndembu*.
337   This view is based on numerous interviews.
338   Pritchett, *Lunda-Ndembu*, 91; (NAZ) SEC2/955, R.C. Dening, Mwinilunga District Tour Report, 1947; (NAZ) NWP1/2/17, F.M.N. Heath, Mwinilunga District Travelling Report, 1948.
339   Turner, 'The Spatial Separation', 122.
340   Turner, *Schism and Continuity*.
341   Kay, *Social Aspects of Village Regrouping*, 3; Gordon, 'The Abolition of the Slave Trade.'
342   This view is based on interviews, for example Headman Chinkonja, 13 August 2010, Kanongesha.

and power. Through the authority of the village head, wealth in people was built and strengthened.[343] A large village was a sign of respect and status for village heads, whose ultimate aim was to give their name to such a village.[344] Nevertheless, at the beginning of the twentieth century these concentrated and more permanent villages had started to split up once more. This was not only due to the cessation of slave raiding but also due to changes following the inception of colonial rule.[345] In both discourse and practice, colonial rule profoundly influenced housing and building forms.

4.2   *Promoting 'Improved' Housing: Attempts at Housing Reform*

Colonial observers denounced the impermanent housing styles in Mwinilunga as crude or even 'primitive', propagating permanent brick houses instead.[346] In a project of social engineering, as Scott describes, the colonial state set out 'to reduce the chaotic, disorderly, constantly changing social reality beneath it', attempting 'to create a terrain and a population with precisely those standardized characteristics that will be easiest to monitor, count, assess, and manage'.[347] That is why existing settlements in Mwinilunga were described in derogatory terms as collections of 'wretched huts and dirty villages'.[348] Even if both grass and wattle and daub structures were condemned, *nkunka* were particularly detested. Officials, instead, promoted the sedentarisation of settlements and patterns of cultivation. In this connection, *nkunka* appeared 'illegible and resistant to the narrow purposes of the state'.[349] Colonial officials even convicted people in court for building and living in *nkunka*, as a 1928 example shows:

> I found the two accused living in "nkunkas", their wives were there – also their fowls and their possessions (...) I arrested them for living in the forest & building nkunka without permission – and took them to their village (...) I quite see that it is necessary for natives to protect their crops – but this is no excuse to desert their huts in the village & leave them for months in a filthy condition & allow grass to grow in them – which shows they must have been away for a long time.[350]

---

343   See: Gordon, 'Wearing Cloth'; Miller, *Way of Death*.
344   Turner, *Schism and Continuity*, 104–05.
345   Pritchett, *Lunda-Ndembu*, Chapter 1.
346   Kay, *Social Aspects of Village Regrouping*, 12.
347   Scott, *Seeing Like a State*, 81–82.
348   (NAZ) KSE6/1/2, F.V. Bruce-Miller, Lunda Sub-District Annual Report, 1913–14.
349   Scott, *Seeing Like a State*, 224.
350   (NAZ) KSE3/2/2/7, Rex v. Shiwimbi, 17 January 1928.

Although discussions among officials centred on the outward appearance of housing, the logic behind colonial spatial planning 'was at once aesthetic, scientific, and practical', as Scott explains.[351] Rather than mere architecture, issues of control, order, and authority were at stake. Housing 'improvement' was cast in a discourse of development and civilisation, encompassing hygiene and livelihood security.[352] In promoting 'improved' and 'permanent' housing the underlying aim was to make villages sedentary and 'legible', amenable to government control.[353] Such attempts had a powerful aesthetic dimension, as 'the visual aesthetics of how a proper village should look combined elements of administrative regularity, tidiness, and legibility', linked to a particular representation of order.[354] Sedentarisation and permanent housing, officials believed, would result in a disciplined and productive population, replacing the unruly mass of shifting cultivators that had proved so difficult to control. In sum, permanent settlement would facilitate tax collection, spur agricultural production, salaried labour, and ultimately create governable subjects.[355]

Officials did recognise that people in Mwinilunga had specific reasons for shifting their settlements every so often, but nevertheless they continued to insist on permanence and administrative control, as a 1916 report shows:

> Some villages are well kept and have quite well built huts, whereas others are just collections of grass shelters which the builders would be at no great loss to leave (...) all are of very nomadic habits and although in many cases they have built good huts to live in and have made decent villages they are only too ready and anxious to shift their habitat. They have their own native reasons for shifting which to them are good enough but from an official point of view not adequate. Three years seems long for them to reside on one spot when having had a number of deaths in the village and having played out the surrounding land by their wretched method of kachai [finger millet] cultivation they crave to move and start lopping off timber in a new area and building again.[356]

Even if officials linked improved housing to increased permanence of residence, the connection between the two proved far from straightforward.[357]

---

351 Scott, *Seeing Like a State*, 140.

352 Schneider, 'The Maasai's New Clothes'; Scott, *Seeing Like a State*, 188.

353 See Moore and Vaughan, *Cutting Down Trees*.

354 Scott, *Seeing Like a State*, 237.

355 Moore and Vaughan, *Cutting Down Trees*; Scott, *Seeing like a State*; Comaroff and Comaroff, *Of Revelation and Revolution*.

356 (NAZ) KSE6/2/1, F.V. Bruce-Miller, Lunda District Quarterly Report, 30 September 1916.

357 Moore and Vaughan, *Cutting Down Trees*; Turner, *Schism and Continuity*.

A well-built house might be abandoned once residents moved to another site, in the same fashion as a less permanent house would be. Deep-rooted dispositions for shifting settlements worked against the construction of brick houses.[358] Nonetheless, the colonial administration persistently asserted the desirability of building more permanent houses, preferably in brick, even if such attempts met with resistance from Mwinilunga's population. A 1915 report remarked:

> With a few, very few, exceptions there was a marked improvement in the appearance of the villages. They are *beginning* to look more prosperous. Having collected the scattered family groups I have been busy persuading them to build a better type hut (...) In some cases I have met rebuffs; take Nyachikanda for example: When asking this gentleman why he lives in such a miserable hut when the majority of his people had built themselves respectable houses, he said: 'If I live in my present hovel of grass and leaves; shall I someday die?' 'If I build a hut of wattle and daub; shall I someday die?' On receiving an answer to both these questions in the affirmative he naively said: 'Why then would I worry to build a good hut!'[359]

Whilst the efficacy of government campaigns might have remained questionable initially, by the end of the 1940s a housing transition from mud to brick appeared to be in full swing. A 1947 tour report explained in detail:

> The general outline [of a village] is an open circular layout, which in some cases has been turned consciously into a square (...) Huts or houses fall into three categories: (1) Small wattle and daub huts, approximately 7' x 10' (...) These are not by any means temporary dwellings, found only in new villages, but some villages of many years standing are still entirely composed of them. (2) Medium sized huts, normally wattle and daub and often two-roomed approximately 11' x 17' in size – Most of the huts in established villages are of this type (...) a commendable effort is being made to build this type of hut in Kimberley brick in several villages (...) it appears that exhortation and incessant visits are having some effect. (3) Comparatively large Kimberley brick houses, of three rooms or more, of good construction (...) Besides the Chief, the only other Kimberley brick dwelling of four rooms belonged to a wealthy villager in an outlying area (...) It appears to be beyond the physical capacity of the normal householder to construct anything larger than the medium sized two room

---

358   Turner, 'The Spatial Separation.'
359   (NAZ) KSE6/2/1, F.V. Bruce-Miller, Lunda District Quarterly Report, 30 September 1915.

hut. For larger construction extra labourers are required, and that means money, which the ordinary villager has not got.[360]

The transition from grass or wattle-and-daub housing to brick housing and the implications of this trend turned out to be all but straightforward.

The construction of sundried brick houses required a considerable investment of time, labour, and capital. Despite the general scarcity of labour and capital in Mwinilunga, one official in 1963 still remarked that 'the standard of house building in this District is amongst the highest in the Territory'.[361] By the 1950s a transition to brick housing could be observed throughout the district, connected to aspirations of self-realisation, as this tour report shows:

> The general tendency to replace pole and dagga houses with Kimberley brick structures which has been noted in the past two years, is becoming increasingly pronounced in all areas. It appears that to own a well-built Kimberley brick house gives one almost as much added "face" as owning a bicycle does.[362]

This shift towards sundried brick houses was clearly reflected in the 1963 census. By then, 50.5% of all houses in the North-Western Province were constructed in brick, whereas 49.5% remained wattle and daub.[363] Although constructing a large brick house enhanced the status of the owner, it was equally a considerable expense (see Photo 13). Making bricks, whether sundried or burnt, involved a long process. Brick housing required store-bought materials (glass for windows, doorframes, metal accessories, etc.), access to (extra-household) labour and capital.[364] Moreover, brick houses were not necessarily more permanent than well-built wattle-and-daub houses. Sundried bricks could be attacked by white ants, whereas roofing still had to be repaired regularly, especially if it was made of grass. Nevertheless, government officials invariably connected brick housing to notions of permanence and 'civilisation'. A 1958 report remarked that 'we all know that there is a growing demand for better houses, as our country becomes more civilised. The standard of housing in an area establishes in the minds of visitors the degree of civilisation in that area'.[365] Even if constructing a brick house involved a considerable

---

360 (BOD) Richard Cranmer Dening Papers, Mwinilunga District Tour Report No.6, 1947.
361 (NAZ) NWP1/2/105 Loc.4920, H.T. Bayldon, North-Western Province Annual Report, 1963.
362 (NAZ) NWP1/2/33, K. Duff-White, Mwinilunga District Tour Report, 5 October 1950.
363 (NAZ) CO3/1/36, Final Report of the May/June 1963 Census of Africans.
364 Pritchett, Lunda-Ndembu, Chapter 3.
365 (NAZ) North-Western Province, African Provincial Council, May 1958.

expense of time, labour, and material resources, brick housing gained popularity throughout Mwinilunga because of the connections between housing, status, wealth, and self-realisation.[366] The meaning of brick housing, however, did not conform to colonial expectations regarding permanence, civilisation, and development. Brick housing was, instead, part of sociocultural dispositions, relationships of power and hierarchy specific to the locality of Mwinilunga.[367]

Although brick housing exhibited status and power within the community, resources and wealth were required to construct a brick house. Both productive resources and social power had to be mobilised to realise housing consumption. Labour migration, for example, served to meet the expenses of constructing a brick house.[368] Returning migrant labourers might spend their savings on iron sheet roofing, or they would commission a work party to construct a house upon return from town. This made some labour migrants 'Big Men' who enjoyed respect and status in the village, as Andersson remarks for the case of Zimbabwe: 'a brick-built house plastered with cement and roofed with asbestos or iron sheets reflects urban success'.[369] Furthermore, advancing aims of self-realisation, earnings from cash crop agriculture were sometimes invested in house construction. Because housing carried an element of prestige, pineapple farmers would invest their profits in the construction of large brick houses.[370] Status and prestige were inherently social and therefore one pineapple farmer constructed a brick house with ten rooms. Signalling that he was able to take care of his family, the owner of this large, well-built brick house gained standing in his community.[371] The word for house, *itala*, is derived from the verb *tala*, to look at or to attract the regard of others.[372] Personal achievement thus gained public expression through housing. That is why Chief London Ikelenge built a two-storey sundried brick house in the 1950s. Chief Ikelenge used his resources to build a large house, which enabled him not only to display his prestige and power but also to accommodate extended family and host guests.[373] Housing, beyond serving as an expression of personhood and self-realisation, enhanced wealth in people by anchoring social

---

366   Pritchett, *Lunda-Ndembu*, Chapter 3.
367   Myers, 'Sticks and Stones.'
368   This view is based on numerous interviews, for example Safukah Kazomba, 28 April 2010, Nyakaseya.
369   Andersson, 'Reinterpreting the Rural-Urban Connection', 99.
370   Peša, 'Buying Pineapples', 277–78.
371   Interview with Ngomi Kamafumbu, 8 March 2010, Ikelenge.
372   Fisher, *Lunda-Ndembu Dictionary.*
373   Interview with Yiness Ikelenge, 10 April 2010, Ikelenge; (NAZ) KSE4/1, Mwinilunga District Notebooks.

relationships. The construction of a large house could attract the settlement of extended kin and even strangers, thereby enhancing the labour, resources, and power of the house owner.[374] This social dynamic informed the construction of brick houses in Mwinilunga.

The specific local meaning of housing was contested and could easily be misinterpreted, though. With a sense of puzzlement, a colonial official in 1955 remarked that 'size rather than quality still remains the African's ideal, however, no doubt from motives of prestige; and a large tumble down house is preferred to a small sound one'.[375] Brick housing conferred more prestige than wattle-and-daub constructions, but a large wattle-and-daub house could still form the centrepiece of a prosperous village and boost the status of its owner.[376] The meaning of housing was equally connected to chiefly authority. In discussions with colonial officials, chiefs suggested that respectable housing was a requisite if chiefs wanted to gain recognition from and exert influence over the population. Especially because of the material wealth of labour migrants and emergent agricultural producers, chiefs sought to assert equality with – or preferably superiority over – their subjects in matters of housing. If they failed to do so, the legitimacy of their power risked being questioned. In 1960 the Provincial Commissioner tried to explain this:

> It is quite impossible for a Chief to maintain his position and influence among the emergent and sophisticated Africans if he is confined to a hovel. With these people prestige is largely derived from visible material wealth and a large house has a very considerable influence in this direction. The general trend is for improved housing and a higher standard of living.[377]

Housing, inextricably connected to status and authority, was thus inherently social and relational. Wealth in goods was connected to wealth in people, as chiefs in Mwinilunga sought to assert their authority and gain respect among their following through material wealth in housing. Some chiefs lacked the material resources or capacity to do so, and they would make claims on government officials to erect houses for them. This issue was discussed in the House of Chiefs in 1965:

---

374   Turner, *Schism and Continuity.*
375   (NAZ) NWP1/2/78 Loc.4913, F.R.G. Phillips, Mwinilunga District Annual Report, 1955.
376   Turner, *Schism and Continuity.*
377   (NAZ) NWP1/3/2 Loc.4921, Provincial Commissioner Solwezi, 6 May 1960.

> The government should build houses for Chiefs (...) The Chiefs them-
> selves were not able to do so, as they did not have the means (...) Many
> Chiefs lived in poor houses with the result that their standard of living
> was low.[378]

Housing could not be separated from authority, power, and wealth in people.
Yet the colonial and post-colonial government insisted on the construction of
large and permanent houses for quite different reasons.

Both the colonial and the post-colonial government propagated housing
'improvement', as it was universally presented, as a means to achieve permanent settlement and increased (agricultural) productivity. Colonial policies
aiming to eradicate shifting cultivation (slash-and-burn *chitemene* agriculture)
were closely related to issues of order, control, and agricultural productivity.[379]
Because, as Scott explains, 'shifting cultivation is an exceptionally complex
and hence quite illegible form of agriculture', the state aimed 'to replace this
illegible and potentially seditious space with permanent settlements and permanent (preferably monocropped) fields'.[380] Failing to recognise the inherent
logic of shifting fields and settlements in a fragile environment – the 'disorderly order' of a practice which could yield high returns – colonial officials
advocated fixed settlements with permanent houses as 'superior' alternatives
instead.[381] Official discourse established a strong connection between agricultural production, permanent settlement, and housing. In the 1940s, officials
in Mwinilunga asserted that 'the progressive trend towards Kimberley brick
houses was most noticeable. If shifting cultivation is remedied over the course
of years, then more substantial houses will inevitably follow'.[382] According to
such reasoning, the trend towards permanent housing would inevitably entail
higher agricultural productivity. In the 1950s, officials noticed that 'mud and
wattle houses are dying out rapidly with the general raising of the standard of
living brought about, to a certain extent, by agricultural development'.[383] Similar discourses were replicated by the post-colonial state. In schemes such as
Intensive Development Zones, 'model villages' were meant to function as centres for 'development'.[384] Moreover, a strong connection between improved

378   (NAZ) LGH5/4/12 Loc.3618, House of Chiefs, 12 July 1965.
379   Moore and Vaughan, *Cutting Down Trees;* Comaroff and Comaroff, *Of Revelation and Revo-*
       lution; Kay, *Social Aspects of Village Regrouping.*
380   Scott, *Seeing Like a State,* 282.
381   Myers, 'Sticks and Stones.'
382   (NAZ) SEC2/956, F.M.N. Heath, Mwinilunga District Tour Report, 18 July 1948.
383   (NAZ) SEC2/962, R.S. Thompson, Mwinilunga District Tour Report, 20 August 1954.
384   Crehan and Von Oppen, *Planners and History.*

housing and 'modern life' was established after independence. Government discourse put housing forward as the hallmark of 'development', a fundamental right of citizens.[385] Under Kaunda's administration, several loan schemes were set up, which connected housing to social welfare. In 1964, the Mwinilunga Rural Council explained:

> The Ministry of Housing and Social Welfare was prepared to give out money to people in the rural areas to enable them to build better houses in model villages. The villages they had were not the villages needed in future. If people lived in these villages the Government would build schools, dispensaries, post offices, recreation centres.[386]

Officials envisaged that permanent houses in model villages would bring about nothing less than a personality change – creating a superior type of individual who would earn money, produce for the market, send children to school, and so on.[387]

One of the first priorities brought forward in Mwinilunga during political mobilisation from 1950 onwards was housing. The construction of permanent houses was among the independent government's most successful schemes, as a report from 1965 acknowledged:

> The group housing scheme proved to be most significant in the activities of the department and met with an encouraging response from local communities in all provinces (...) in all cases, communities willingly contributed communal labour and available local resources.[388]

By the 1970s, officials even described the transition to brick housing in terms of a 'revolution': 'The desire of the people to build permanent structures (...) has indeed become real in this Province (...) There is a complete rural village housing revolution.'[389] During this period, official discourse established the connection between housing, permanence and productivity more clearly than ever. A 1972 pamphlet illustrates this:

---

385   See Ferguson, *Expectations of Modernity.*
386   (NAZ) LGH5/1/3 Loc.3604, Mwinilunga Rural Council, 29 December 1964.
387   Moore and Vaughan, *Cutting Down Trees,* 114–21; Crehan and Von Oppen, *Planners and History.*
388   (NAZ) Department of Community Development, 1965.
389   (NAZ) North-Western Province Department of Community Development, 1973.

We now know for certain that our communities are stable enough in the
rural areas; they do not move their villages any time they feel to do so as
was the case in the not too distant past, hence the need for permanent
houses (...) Unless the rural areas are developed to a certain standard, we
shall continue to have the present problem of rural population flocking
to urban areas. One of the most important ways to stop this is to improve
rural houses (...) It follows, therefore, that in such villages productivity in
whatever venture by villagers, is higher than in certain disorganised villages with poor types of houses.[390]

Yet as housing held multiple socioeconomic, ritual, and political meanings in
Mwinilunga, housing practices regularly clashed with official discourses and
intentions.[391] The equivocal meanings residents read into housing only rarely
conformed to government policies. To the exasperation of government officials, no clear-cut connection between housing and permanence or agricultural productivity could be established.[392] Especially the appearance of farms in
the 1940s and 1950s was a nuisance to officials, who were puzzled by continuing 'impermanence'.[393] The 1940 land tenure report illustrates this:

Even the building of Kimberley brick houses has failed to compete with
Lunda instability, and one can see whole villages of abandoned Kimberley brick houses whose occupants have split up and moved on. The
present strong tendency for individuals in this area to break away from
villages and set up their own "farms" or individual settlements is an illustration of this. For a progressive individual living in a village has no
assurance that he can stay there permanently.[394]

Because officials failed to comprehend the social logic and meaning of housing, their policies to eradicate the impermanence of settlements met with little
success.[395] Contrary to government regulations, individuals continued to shift
their settlements throughout the twentieth century.

Although the transition from grass and wattle-and-daub housing to brick
housing did indeed accelerate from the 1950s onwards, the meaning attached

---

390   (NAZ) National Literacy Gazette, 1972.
391   Turner, *Schism and Continuity.*
392   Pritchett, *Lunda-Ndembu,* Chapter 3.
393   Turner, *Schism and Continuity,* 42–43.
394   (NAZ) LGH5/5/11 Loc.3621, C.M.N. White, Mwinilunga District Land Tenure report
      No. 7, 1940.
395   Compare to: Myers, 'Sticks and Stones.'

to housing was not ordained by government policy. Housing was and remained a fundamentally social act, establishing a connection between the individual and the village community.[396] Housing was imbued with deeply rooted ritual, cultural, and social meanings, conveying status, hierarchy, and power. Through housing, wealth in people was given physical expression. Even if individuals no longer always live in large kin-based settlements, housing can still express interpersonal ties, and that is why housing carries so much prestige in Mwinilunga. More important than its appearance, housing holds social meaning, and this has remained imperative throughout the transition from grass and mud to brick housing.[397] The construction of a well-built brick house went beyond ostentation. The fundamental aim of house construction, both past and present, is for the owner of the house to become the focal point of a large and prosperous village. As Turner states, the 'prestige attached to living in a long-established village' was considerable, exactly because of high rates of village fission.[398] Powerful individuals sought to give their names to such a village, so that their memory would endure in the afterlife. Turner explains: 'When a village has become unquestionably established as a persistent social unit, the personal name of an outstanding headman tends to petrify into a title which is inherited by his successors'.[399] Similarly, Piot remarks that through housing a 'man is able to achieve a certain sense of immortality, to produce something which endures beyond his lifetime, to inscribe his name in a lasting, more permanent, way in the social life of his community'.[400] The rationale behind, and the desired end-result of investment in housing, was to attract kin and dependents, to build a large homestead. Despite changes in outward appearance, housing remained connected to wealth in people.

Deviating from official intentions, the construction of brick houses in Mwinilunga did not automatically result in economic growth or in the emergence of nuclear families.[401] Housing was invested with prior socioeconomic, cultural, and ideological meaning, rather than being a clean slate onto which government officials could write their modernising discourses. By contesting official intentions, house owners negotiated their environment.[402] Housing is an ultimate means of self-realisation, as a house owner becomes the centre of

---

396 Turner, *Schism and Continuity*.
397 Turner, 'The Spatial Separation.'
398 Turner, *Schism and Continuity*, 104.
399 Ibidem, 105.
400 Charles Piot, 'Of Persons and Things: Some Reflections on African Spheres of Exchange', *Man* 26, No. 3 (1991): 417.
401 Compare with Moore and Vaughan, *Cutting Down Trees*.
402 Myers, 'Sticks and Stones.'

a group of kin and dependents. Constructing a large house is therefore an act of social adulthood, entailing rights as well as obligations, potential as well as risks.[403] Material wealth was consolidated in housing and with this wealth house owners attracted a large following, building wealth in people. The labour power that house owners thereby attracted might serve to expand (agricultural) production and create more wealth in future, setting a dynamic of growth in motion. Nevertheless, although brick houses did increasingly spread through the district, the habit of building in brick did not simply remedy shifting cultivation or create 'modern' individuals as officials had intended.[404] In sum, housing needs to be understood within a social and relational logic, as a house stands in relation to other houses in a village. Housing appears, thus, as an expression of meaning, prestige, and a tool for self-realisation, serving to build wealth in people.

5   Goods, People, and Wealth: Rationales of Consumption

What the previous examples have suggested is that in order to access consumer goods (either locally produced or mass-manufactured and store-bought) it was necessary to mobilise resources. These resources changed over time. Land, political authority, and forms of currency could all be deployed to gain access to goods.[405] Yet human labour remained the chief productive resource, constituting the fundamental continuity in patterns of consumption in the area of Mwinilunga.[406] One accessed wealth through people by means of their labour, knowledge, and skills, as De Boeck has also argued: 'Wealth in money and things is just one aspect of a wider reality that also includes wealth in people'.[407] The desired end-result of consumption – which can be defined, following Hahn, as 'the articulation of the individual's social identity, and also a matter of social agency'[408] – found expression through people, social relationships, and status.[409] The connection between human labour power, consumption, and

---

403   De Boeck, 'Domesticating Diamonds and Dollars'; Pritchett, *Lunda-Ndembu,* Chapter 3.

404   Moore and Vaughan, *Cutting Down Trees.*

405   Sara S. Berry, 'Social Institutions and Access to Resources', *Africa* 59, No. 1 (1989): 41–55.

406   This goes beyond the 'labour theory of value', encompassing social relationships and wealth in people. See: Parry and Bloch, *Money and the Morality of Exchange,* 4; Miller, *Way of Death,* 40–41.

407   De Boeck, 'Borderland Breccia.'

408   Hans P. Hahn, ed., *Consumption in Africa: Anthropological Approaches* (Berlin: LIT Verlag, 2008), 10.

409   Guyer, 'Wealth in People and Self-Realization'; Miller, *Way of Death.*

wealth is particularly apparent in the case of local ironworking, as the production of iron tools depended on the labour and expertise of smelters and
smiths, but spears and axes could subsequently be used to generate material
wealth and wealth in people.[410] Labour remained indispensable even when
goods were purchased in village stores through the mediation of cash. In order
to earn money, an individual had to resort to salaried employment or cash crop
production, both highly labour intensive enterprises.[411] Ties to other people
were valued and fostered, as it was almost impossible to generate wealth in
isolation. In Mwinilunga, wealth continues to be defined as people. As Piot
explains, 'ultimate value is placed on relationships', and therefore 'the conver-
sion of things into relationships is a first and unquestioned principle of social
life'.[412] Forms of currency mediated the connections between wealth, people,
and goods. Examining the role of currencies in Mwinilunga further elucidates
the functions of exchange and the meaning of wealth.

To facilitate exchange, various forms of currency circulated in Mwinilunga
in the nineteenth and twentieth century. Cloth, iron bars, beads, and other
items co-existed as a medium of exchange, standardised to various extents.[413]
In the opening decades of the twentieth century the colonial administration
sought to supplant this multiplicity of currencies with a single general purpose currency, the British pound sterling. Scholars have attributed profound
and far-reaching consequences, both positive and negative, to this monetary
'revolution'.[414] On the one hand, money has been seen as destructive of kinship
ties, promoting 'the growth of individualism and the destruction of solidary
communities'.[415] On the other hand, more positively, 'monetization is assumed
to act as a catalyst to economic growth and structural change. By permitting (or
compelling) people to participate in supra-local circuits of exchange, monetization promotes specialization and exchange and, hence, economic growth'.[416]
Money had disruptive and constructive potential in the area of Mwinilunga,
contributing to the development of local notions of accumulation, expenditure,

---

410   Kriger, *Pride of Men*; Guyer, 'Wealth in People and Self-Realization', 254.
411   Turner, *Schism and Continuity.*
412   Piot, 'Of Persons and Things', 417.
413   See: Von Oppen, *Terms of Trade;* Miller, *Way of Death*; Gordon, 'The Abolition of the Slave
      Trade.'
414   Paul Bohannan, 'The Impact of Money on an African Subsistence Economy', *The Journal
      of Economic History* 19, No. 4 (1959): 491–503; James L.A. Webb Jr., 'Toward the Compara-
      tive Study of Money: A Reconsideration of West African Currencies and Neo-Classical
      Monetary Concepts', *The International Journal of African Historical Studies* 15, No. 3 (1982):
      455–66; Comaroff and Comaroff, *Of Revelation and Revolution,* 166–217.
415   Parry and Bloch, *Money and the Morality of Exchange,* 4, refer to Simmel and Marx.
416   Berry, 'Stable Prices, Unstable Values', 300.

and wealth.[417] Money, however, was not an autonomous or depersonalised force, but proved significant exactly because it was embedded in social relationships.[418] As Parry and Bloch explain, the symbolism and meaning of money 'relates to culturally constructed notions of production, consumption, circulation and exchange'.[419] In the 1950s, Turner described the tendency towards monetisation with a sense of astonishment, noting:

> ... the extent to which money economy was replacing the traditional economy of barter and exchange. Marriage payments, for instance, formerly made in cloths, guns or small livestock, are now made in cash. Hoe- and axe-blades, once exchanged by blacksmiths for meat and vegetable produce, are now sold by them for money. Kin nowadays give each other presents of money as well as of fowls and cassava meal. Doctors and herbalists are paid in cash instead of in goods. Money economy, in fact, is penetrating into all the pores of social life.[420]

This account highlights the intertwined nature of money and social relationships.[421] Money was used in social payments, for bridewealth or funeral expenses, for gifts, and it even served as a payment for witchdoctors.[422] Tracing the process of monetisation reveals the sources and social meanings of wealth, underlining the connection between monetary wealth and wealth in people.

At the start of the twentieth century, European observers exoticised Lunda use of money, due to a difference in values and attitudes. Colonial officials assumed that Africans, supposedly accustomed only to barter and 'simple' exchange, would be unable to deal with British currency.[423] A 1914 report stated this in particularly blunt terms:

> To give an example with what a backward tribe we have to deal: When I was on tour recently along the Portuguese Border a headman brought to me a small basket of yams. I gave him a shilling. He looked at it suspiciously for some time, then asked: "What is this – a nose ornament?"!! It was explained that money was much sought after by his more enlightened

---

417   De Boeck, 'Domesticating Diamonds and Dollars.'
418   Comaroff and Comaroff, *Of Revelation and Revolution*, 174–75.
419   Parry and Bloch, *Money and the Morality of Exchange*, 1.
420   Turner and Turner, 'Money Economy', 19.
421   De Boeck, 'Domesticating Diamonds and Dollars.'
422   See Turner, *Schism and Continuity.*
423   Compare: Comaroff and Comaroff, *Of Revelation and Revolution.*

brothers; he refused to believe it and asked for salt in exchange for his yams.[424]

Forms of exchange in the area of Mwinilunga had been complex and market-oriented long before the advent of colonial rule.[425] Numerous currencies, which could be standardised but were not fixed, existed side by side. In the 1850s, Livingstone had noted, for instance, that 'The native traders generally carry salt and a few pieces of cloth, a few beads, and cartouches with iron balls'.[426] Various items functioned as a medium of exchange. Beads could be used to obtain salt, salt and beads were used to settle affairs, whereas slaves could be redeemed with guns, cloth, or beads.[427] In case of a death, as this 1928 court statement testifies, a man might give his wife's relatives 'a pair of shorts, 8 yards of cloth and a cup, as compensation for the death of this woman'.[428] Colonial officials in the opening decade of the twentieth century remarked that 'beads are very popular amongst these people, and the smallest spoonful of beads obtains wonderful value in meal'.[429] Items such as beads, shells, salt, and cloth, as well as guns and iron bars, fulfilled the monetary functions of standard of measurement, store of value, medium of exchange, and means of payment.[430] Miller and Von Oppen have argued that it was exactly the co-existence of various forms of currency that enabled such high levels of economic activity during the pre-colonial period of long-distance trade.[431] The fluidity and negotiability of multiple forms of currency facilitated widespread exchange among all layers of society, promoting entrepreneurship and trade. The availability of multiple currencies spread the risks of expressing wealth in terms of a single currency. Sensitive to value fluctuations, single currencies moreover proved prone to attempts at monopoly control by political elites or the state.[432] In this context, multiple currencies, the diversification of income earning opportunities, and the variety of means of access to wealth in Mwinilunga appeared particularly sound.

Under colonial rule, attempts were made to impose a single standardised currency to replace previous multiplicity. Officials assumed that monetisation

---

424   (NAZ) KSE6/2/1, F.V. Bruce-Miller, Lunda District Quarterly Report, 30 September 1914.
425   Von Oppen, *Terms of Trade*.
426   Schapera, *Livingstone's African Journal*, 121.
427   (NAZ) KSE3/1/2/1, Msangi v. Chingbwambu, 7 July 1912.
428   (NAZ) KSE3/2/2/7, Rex v. Nyaluhana, 8 June 1928.
429   (NAZ) KSE6/6/1, Captain Stennett, Balunda District Tour Report, 20 August 1909.
430   Webb Jr., 'Toward the Comparative Study of Money', 457; Von Oppen, *Terms of Trade*.
431   Miller, *Way of Death*; Von Oppen, *Terms of Trade*.
432   Berry, 'Stable Prices, Unstable Values', 302, 309.

would facilitate market interaction and promote economic growth.[433] Yet despite benevolent rhetoric, British currency did not catch on immediately. In 1911, the Mwinilunga District Commissioner complained that 'cash is not yet in general use either for purchasing or payment of labour and in many instances is refused'.[434] Staunchly convinced of the inherent superiority of British currency, colonial officials had no doubt that cash would eventually be accepted, though: 'When they [Lunda] have reaped the benefit of the stores and traded a little the idea of cash will not appear to them so dreadful'.[435] The use of British currency, far from being all-purpose, initially remained highly restricted, limited to the payment of taxes or the purchase of consumer goods.[436] By 1960, officials still remarked that 'the economic necessity of obtaining the basics of existence does not arise and the only incentive for a local African to work is to pay his tax or to purchase a particular article which he requires'.[437] Over time, monetary spending did increase and cash gained a variety of uses. A survey conducted in the 1940s concluded that 'the average villager appears to spend from 15/- to £3-0-0d per annum on consumer goods'.[438] Linking monetisation to 'development', colonial officials asserted that trading activities, especially the marketing of agricultural produce, would 'provide the African with ready cash in his pocket for the purchase of consumer goods (...) bringing about a general raising of the social standards of the people'.[439] Yet the connection between monetisation and economic development proved anything but direct. District reports repeatedly lamented that rather than productively investing their earnings, individuals would engage in 'conspicuous consumption', spending money immediately and allegedly 'irrationally'.[440] In the 1940s, officials complained that 'natives are still unable to forego the lure of ready cash in spite of the threat of hunger or famine'.[441] Money was even said to be 'a necessity to the welfare of man nowadays'.[442] Money became widespread because it provided

---

433   Comaroff and Comaroff, *Of Revelation and Revolution*; Parry and Bloch, *Money and the Morality of Exchange*.
434   (NAZ) KSE6/1/1, G.A. MacGregor, Lunda District Annual Report, 31 March 1911.
435   (NAZ) KSE6/6/1, J.M. Pound, Balunda District Tour Report, 30 September 1910.
436   Compare to Guyer, *Money Matters*.
437   (NAZ) NWP1/2/90 Loc.4916, Labour in Mwinilunga, Reports and Returns, 1961.
438   (NAZ) SEC2/955, F.M.N. Heath, Mwinilunga District Tour Report, 16 November 1947.
439   (NAZ) NWP1/2/65 Loc.4910, R.S. Thompson, Mwinilunga District Tour Report, 19 November 1954.
440   See Martin Prowse, 'Becoming a Bwana and Burley Tobacco in the Central Region of Malawi', *Journal of Modern African Studies* 47, No. 4 (2009): 575–602, for the rationale behind conspicuous consumption.
441   (NAZ) SEC2/957, Mr. Sanford, Comment, 1940.
442   (NAZ) North-Western Province African Provincial Council, June 1954.

access to store-bought goods, such as soap, paraffin, matches, candles, cooking oil, salt, sugar, clothing, and blankets. Still, the desirability of money and store-bought goods can only be understood by looking at the social logics of consumption.[443] Wealth cannot simply be equated to money, as notions of wealth are informed by a specific sociocultural and political context.[444] Notions of wealth in Mwinilunga link consumption to social relationships, hierarchies of status, and aspirations of self-realisation.[445]

The connections between money, consumer goods, and social relationships have been much discussed by social scientists and historians.[446] Money enables access to consumer goods in a market economy. In Mwinilunga, productive activities such as cash crop agriculture or labour migration generated material wealth, making cloth and brick houses quotidian items of consumption rather than luxury goods.[447] Economic theory has, furthermore, connected monetisation and consumption to processes of individualisation and the destruction of social solidarity.[448] Turner argued similarly in the 1950s:

> Wherever our kind of Western individualism crops up in Central Africa (…) men plunge into the struggle to earn and save cash for the new goods and prestige symbols that money can buy. To save money they must break the corporate kinship nexus; for in the old order of society, that which a man acquires, he must share out among his kin and neighbours. He cannot both save and distribute money. Thus, the crucial value attached to corporateness is rejected, and with it go many other values and obligations; frankness between group members, comradeship in adversity, mutual generosity and reciprocity (…) As one Ndembu put it to me, 'For Europeans, things are more important than people, for us, people are more important than things'. But Africans are rapidly becoming more 'Europeanized' in this sense.[449]

The predicted trend towards individualisation was not clear-cut, though. Rather, connections between consumer goods, wealth, and people proved complex and enduring.

---

443   Ross, Hinfelaar, and Peša, *The Objects of Life.*
444   James Ferguson, 'The Cultural Topography of Wealth: Commodity Paths and the Structure of Property in Rural Lesotho', *American Anthropologist* 94, No. 1 (1992): 55–73.
445   De Boeck, 'Domesticating Diamonds and Dollars.'
446   Piot, 'Of Persons and Things'; Jonathan Friedman, 'Consuming Desires: Strategies of Selfhood and Appropriation', *Cultural Anthropology* 6, No. 2 (1991): 154–63.
447   Burke, *Lifebuoy Men.*
448   Parry and Bloch, *Money and the Morality of Exchange.*
449   Turner, *The Drums of Affliction,* 22–23.

Berry has argued that material wealth in many cases continued 'to be used to gain control over people, as well as vice versa, and exchange remains closely tied to the definition of social identities'.[450] In Mwinilunga, similarly, money was used to realise and strengthen social relationships.[451] A 1913 account suggests that money would regularly be converted into both consumer goods and personal allegiances: 'Mulepa was more pleased with 3 cigarettes than with the 10/- apparently! I don't blame him, money to him – except with great pawns – only means payment of hut tax or calico for his wives'.[452] Through money, wealth in people was enacted, as the purchase and distribution of cloth attracted allegiance and served to build a large and prosperous household, in turn enhancing labour power and productive resources.[453] Inherently social, money proved distinctly enabling, as Barber stresses: 'Money is what *constitutes* social relationships and indeed social being (...) [money] is conceived of as constitutive of individual self-realization (...) money is inseparable from the social regard and the social bonds that support the successful individual'.[454] Rather than being flaunted, money was used in productive ways. Money served to build social personhood and prestige, attract a large following and thereby enhance productive and reproductive capacities.[455] People in Mwinilunga deployed money in socially meaningful and productive ways, as the District Commissioner noted in 1959: 'One Ishimo, a trader and an active man, has in fact opted to use his money and energy within the framework of his home village, and is running for the headmanship'.[456] In a relational setting, wealthy individuals used money to gain political power and further their assets. Even after independence and in the sphere of formal politics, money continued to be used to attract allegiance. Within a neo-patrimonial logic, government funds were handed out to win support and votes for the ruling party.[457] Whereas loans would exclusively be given out to UNIP members, they would be denied to ANC supporters.[458] The connection between money and social relationships, between wealth and self-realisation thus appeared compelling.

---

450   Berry, 'Stable Prices, Unstable Values', 305.
451   Barber, 'Money, Self-Realization and the Person.'
452   (BOD) Mss Afr S 776, Theodore Williams Diary, 23 January 1913.
453   Gordon, 'Wearing Cloth.'
454   Barber, 'Money, Self-Realization and the Person', 207.
455   De Boeck, 'Domesticating Diamonds and Dollars.'
456   (NAZ) SEC2/966, W.D. Grant, Mwinilunga District Tour Report, 21 April 1959.
457   See: Melle Leenstra, *Beyond the Façade: Instrumentalisation of the Zambian Health Sector* (Leiden: African Studies Centre, 2012); Ross, Hinfelaar, and Peša, *The Objects of Life*, 8–9.
458   (NAZ) LGH5/2/7 Loc.3612, J. Chindefu to H. Kikombe, 23 February 1966; see also Chapter 3 Section 1.

Self-realisation was a long-established goal in the area of Mwinilunga, involving the development of personhood, the promotion of social status, and interactions between wealth and people.[459] Individuals could obtain social recognition and prestige through a multitude of channels, for example through hunting, ironworking, labour migration, or by becoming a headman of a large prosperous village. Social adulthood was a process.[460] Through a number of steps, involving continuous hard work and participation in the life of the broader community, well-being and prestige would increase. Wealth was connected to notions of fertility, procreation, and social relationships, as De Boeck explains:

> In Luunda land new sources and forms of material wealth, introduced from the outside in the form of new commodities as well as money, have always been incorporated into a wider notion of fecundity in terms of physical health and social and physical reproduction (in relation to agriculture, hunting and reproductive sexuality).[461]

Wealth was social, rather than purely material. A wealthy man not only possessed much cloth but above all had many children. *Chikoli*, a ritual to promote prosperity, good health, and strength, centred on the *katochi* tree, which symbolised 'many children' due to its numerous roots.[462] Contrastingly, barrenness was perhaps the most severe form of social destitution.[463] Wealth and social relationships were connected in terms of life-giving reciprocity. In order to become a wealthy 'Big Man' a person had to share with his kin, neighbours, and friends. Being selfish or self-centred (denoted by the verbs *dikokweja* and *dikokela* or the noun *chifwa*) involved avoiding others, evoking a state of isolation that might even cause death (*kokweja*, attract others by kindness; *kokela*, draw towards, attract; *fwa*, die, be broken). Contrastingly, a person with *kashinshi* (reliability, responsibility, trustworthiness) and *kavumbi* (good manners, courtesy, self-respect) would be highly valued, exactly because these personal

---

459   See: De Boeck, 'Domesticating Diamonds and Dollars'; De Boeck, 'Borderland Breccia.'
460   Guyer, 'Wealth in People and Self-Realization'; see Turner, *Schism and Continuity.*
461   De Boeck, 'Domesticating Diamonds and Dollars', 784.
462   This view is based on interviews, for example Maladi, 16 May 2010, Nyakaseya; Fisher, *Lunda-Ndembu Dictionary.*
463   See Turner, *Drums of Affliction,* for fertility rituals aimed to prevent barrenness, such as *nkula* and *wubwangu*. Turner, 'The Spatial Separation', 136, describes how a man's 'reputation as a sorcerer appears to have been assisted by the fact that although he married eight times (and was divorced five times and widowed once) he had no children.'

attributes were inherently social, relational, and reciprocal.[464] The selfish accumulation of wealth was associated with blockage and sorcery, because goods
had to flow through social relationships. One wealthy pineapple farmer, for example, was attacked by an *ilomba* (mythical snake, familiar spirit connected to
witchcraft), because he failed to share his profit among kin. He faced hardship,
misfortune, and bad luck, because he had built a large house for his nuclear
family in isolation from others.[465] Individuals engaging in selfish accumulation thus risk being ostracised, because in Mwinilunga wealth is understood as
social, marked by solidarity and reciprocity.[466]

Neither goods nor money created wealth in and of themselves, though.
Rather, goods and money were a means to become a person. One could generate wealth and realise one's full potential only by becoming the centrepiece of
a community of friends, kin, or of a village.[467] A fundamentally social process,
this provided prospects of prosperity and good luck, but equally entailed responsibilities, as De Boeck explains:

> The more one becomes the focus of the social life of the kin group, the
> more one is given respect, but the more, also, one becomes responsible
> for the redistribution and sharing of the goods that circulate in the kin
> group.[468]

To be respected (*kalemesha*, respectfulness; *lemesha*, to glorify, esteem, honour) involved a heavy duty and hard work (*lema*, to be heavy, important, valuable). Yet hard work paid, because it enabled the expansion of productive and
reproductive capacities, through access to the labour power of dependents.[469]
Although not necessarily falling within a capitalist logic, this did usher an
expansive dynamic of goods and people. Goods, which increasingly became
available and affordable through emergent village stores (see Map 2), served
to gain allegiance, which in turn expanded productive capacities and thereby

---

464   This view is based on numerous interviews, for example Justin Kambidimba, Septem-
      ber 2010, Ntambu; Fisher, *Lunda-Ndembu Dictionary*; Turner, *Schism and Continuity*; De
      Boeck, 'Domesticating Diamonds and Dollars.'
465   Interview with Aaron Chikewa, 27 April 2010, Nyakaseya; his current short height is at-
      tributed to witchcraft.
466   See Chapter 5, also Edith Turner, *Experiencing Ritual: A New Interpretation of African
      Healing* (Philadephia: University of Pennsylvania Press, 1992); W. Singleton Fisher, 'Black
      Magic Feuds', *African Studies* (1949): 20–22; Frank Melland, *In Witch-Bound Africa: An Ac-
      count of the Primitive Kaonde Tribe And Their Beliefs* (London, 1967).
467   Turner, *Schism and Continuity*; Pritchett, *Friends for Life.*
468   De Boeck, 'Domesticating Diamonds and Dollars', 794.
469   Pritchett, *Lunda-Ndembu*; De Boeck, 'Domesticating Diamonds and Dollars.'

further enhanced access to goods.[470] The attraction of goods can be explained by reference to their social capacity to convey distinction, status, hierarchy, and ultimately power. This also explains the motivation to acquire goods by engaging in productive activities, or consumptive production.[471] Power relations, hierarchies, and the meaning of goods did change over time, though. For much of the pre-colonial period the consumption of luxury goods was still largely confined to the top of the political hierarchy, as the limited supply of imported goods was controlled by headmen and traders. Similarly, the production of iron tools was limited by access to natural resources and the labour power of blacksmiths, making iron goods scarce and limiting their circulation. Under colonial rule and especially after independence, consumer goods increasingly started to defy pre-existing boundaries, as industrial manufacturing and trade enabled access to a greatly enlarged flow of goods. This access broadened the potential avenues for self-realisation, beyond the control of headmen, hunters, or ironworkers. Power could be accessed through a multiplicity of channels and could be derived from a multiplicity of sources, but wealth and power continued to be thoroughly vested in people and social relationships.[472]

In this setting, consumption revolved around the human factor. Consumption did not lead to a complete dependence on the market.[473] Although consumer goods were indeed predominantly accessed through the market, their value was expressed in personal and relational, rather than strictly monetary terms. Goods proved meaningful because they could advance goals of self-realisation, further personhood, and enable the composition of singular personalities.[474] Far from promoting an individualising tendency, money, and wealth were thoroughly related to people, as Berry explains:

> Creating allegiances may no longer have been the primary purpose of holding material wealth, but remained a necessary condition for acquiring and controlling it. Accordingly, wealth continued to be invested in building allegiances and maintaining the social relationships and institutions that sustain them.[475]

---

470   Miller, *Way of Death;* Gordon, 'Wearing Cloth.'
471   Piot, 'Of Persons and Things', 411, Quoting Chris A. Gregory, *Gifts and Commodities* (Chicago: University of Chicago Press, 1982).
472   See: Gordon, 'Wearing Cloth'; Guyer, 'Wealth in People and Self-Realization'; De Boeck, 'Domesticating Diamonds and Dollars.'
473   Parry and Bloch, *Money and the Morality of Exchange,* 1–7.
474   De Boeck, 'Domesticating Diamonds and Dollars'; Guyer, 'Wealth in People and Self-Realization.'
475   Berry, 'Stable Prices, Unstable Values', 307.

Although there has been a transition from locally produced to mass-manufactured store-bought goods over the course of the nineteenth and twentieth century in Mwinilunga, this transition has not necessarily caused a radical transformation of society.[476] The underlying motive for the acquisition of goods was and continued to be the social and relational potential of objects. Even if it has been realised in historically diverse ways, the goal of building wealth in people through consumption has endured in Mwinilunga.

6   Conclusion

Although a transition from locally produced to store-bought goods has occurred in Mwinilunga, this transition did not signal a major rupture in notions of wealth or social relationships. The outward appearance of goods did change, but this did not signify a 'consumer revolution', as objects continued to be used to forge interpersonal relationships, for purposes of prestige and to express hierarchy. Through broadened access to goods during the twentieth century, avenues for self-realisation were opened up and diversified, but the ultimate goal remained to become the head of a large and prosperous household. Goods did not primarily hold meaning in themselves, but were valued because of their potential to forge ties with other people. Goods served to build personhood, express status and hierarchy, attract a large following, and thereby enhance productive and reproductive capacities. The continuity in patterns of consumption in Mwinilunga lies in this connection between goods, wealth, and people, between money, consumption, and social relationships.

Within modernist narratives, consumption, money, and the market economy have been afforded profound transformative potential. According to such views, through access to consumer goods, individuals would automatically be turned into profit-oriented 'modern' consumers.[477] In the area of Mwinilunga, the outward appearance of consumer goods indeed underwent major change. Nonetheless, goods, whether imported or locally produced, were appropriated and invested with meaning in the local setting. Although consumption was boosted by processes of globalisation, homogenisation did not ensue.[478] The production of meaning continued to be a specifically local process. As Prestholdt explains, consumer goods possess plasticity, being 'reimagined and

---

476   See contributions to: Ross, Hinfelaar, and Peša, *The Objects of Life*.
477   See: Parry and Bloch, *Money and the Morality of Exchange*; Comaroff and Comaroff, *Of Revelation and Revolution*.
478   Burke, 'Unexpected Subversions', 481.

refashioned in their circulation'.[479] In Mwinilunga, goods hold social meaning and are used as a means of self-realisation within the framework of wealth in people. Goods have been appropriated as a means to gain access to people, and although the external manifestation of consumer goods has changed, the underlying motives for consumption have remained far more constant. Premised on the value of social relationships, consumers in Mwinilunga have developed unique patterns of consumption. In the next chapter, the dynamics of settlement patterns and social change will be further explored.

---

479   Prestholdt, 'Africa and the Global Lives of Things', 89.

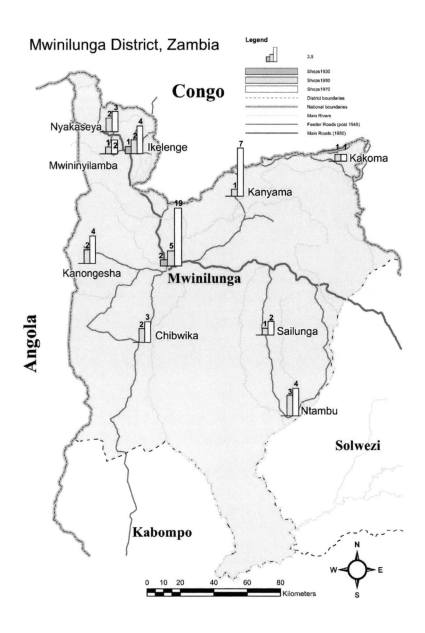

MAP 2   Trading stores in Mwinilunga District
           MAP DRAWN WITH THE ASSISTANCE OF ERIC DULLAERT

PHOTO 11   Chief Ikelenge in his car, 1950s
NATIONAL ARCHIVES OF ZAMBIA, MWINILUNGA DISTRICT NOTEBOOKS

PHOTO 12   *Nkunka*, 1950s
NATIONAL ARCHIVES OF ZAMBIA, MWINILUNGA DISTRICT NOTEBOOKS

PHOTO 13   A trader's Kimberley brick house in Mwinilunga Town, 1950s
NATIONAL ARCHIVES OF ZAMBIA, MWINILUNGA DISTRICT NOTEBOOKS

CHAPTER 5

Settlements and Social Change: Continuity and Change in Village Life

Mukala wasema yawantu, mukala diyi amaama yawantu – The village gives birth to the people, therefore the village is the mother of the people[1]

∙ ∙ ∙

Tunga kwisanga, wumonanga ihungu; tunga kwitu, wutiyanga nyiswalu – If you build in the bush, you see trouble; if you build in the jungle to hide from trouble, you hear rustling (Living in a village can cause problems, but it is better than living alone; you cannot find peace by running away from trouble)[2]

∙∙
∙

In the 1950s, Turner witnessed conflict and village fission in Mwinilunga, which he described as 'the spectacle of corporate groups of kin disintegrating and the emergence of smaller residential units based on the elementary family'.[3] He assumed that colonial rule, coupled with factors such as labour migration, cash crop production, education, and the spread of Christianity would cause erosive social change in village life.[4] Together with a host of missionaries and colonial officials, Turner predicted that these processes of change would lead to a transition from solidarity and communalism to individualism, competitiveness, and a nucleation of the family.[5] Most notably, under the influence of

---

1   Interview with Kenneth Kalota, July and August 2010, Kanongesha.
2   (BOD) R.C. Dening Papers, Uncatalogued, Lunda Proverbs.
3   Turner, *Schism and Continuity*, 43.
4   Turner, *Schism and Continuity*; Turner, *The Drums of Affliction*. Turner's work tied into RLI concerns with social change. More generally, see Bates, 'Capital, Kinship, and Conflict', 151–64.
5   For critiques, see Neil Price and Neil Thomas, 'Continuity and Change in the Gwembe Tonga Family and Their Relevance to Demography's Nucleation Thesis', *Africa* 69, No. 4 (1999):

© KONINKLIJKE BRILL NV, LEIDEN, 2019 | DOI:10.1163/9789004408968_007

capitalism large stable villages would disintegrate into smaller units ('farms'), where nuclear families would prevail over extended kin-based associations.[6] Can such views indeed be endorsed when viewed in a longer-term historical perspective? Over the course of the twentieth century, village organisation and social relationships in Mwinilunga changed profoundly. Due to processes of social change categories of kinship, age, and gender were questioned, authority was redefined, and tradition was negotiated.[7] Change, however, did not simply lead to a demise of previous practices. Crucially, far from disintegrating, people continue to live in villages, and they still attach importance to kinship relations and communality.[8] Long-standing beliefs concerning the authority of chieftainship, prestige, and the value of village life have remained significant even as they have incorporated new elements and meanings.[9] By closely examining village residence and social relationships, continuity and change will be at the heart of this chapter. How did social change influence relationships between people, especially relating to kinship and authority?

Despite profound socioeconomic and political change in Mwinilunga over the course of the twentieth century, it is the question whether this has led to deep changes in the social order. Rather than succumbing to village breakup and crisis, kinship structures and their attendant ideologies have been flexible enough to accommodate changes.[10] This chapter views village settlement patterns in Mwinilunga from a historical perspective, to understand whether the emergence of the 'farm' was indeed an expression of village breakup and societal fission, or whether there might have been longer-term continuities behind such settlement patterns.[11] Did social change necessarily sever communal ties, or could change heighten the need to invest in personal relationships as a means to gain influence and wealth?[12] Did modes of thought, patterns of conduct, and interpersonal association experience rupture, or did they creatively adjust, retaining significance even under changed circumstances?

510–34; De Boeck, 'Domesticating Diamonds and Dollars', 777–810; Berry, *No Condition is Permanent*.

6   Turner, *Schism and Continuity*; this view is reflected in colonial reports (NAZ).
7   Pritchett, *Lunda-Ndembu*.
8   See Von Oppen, 'Bounding Villages.'
9   Edith Turner, 'Zambia's Kankanga Dances: The Changing Life of Ritual', *Performing Arts Journal* 10, No. 3 (1987): 57–71; Turner, *Experiencing Ritual.*
10   Wilson and Wilson, *The Analysis of Social Change.*
11   Pritchett, *Lunda-Ndembu*, Chapter 3.
12   Berry, *No Condition Is Permanent.*

1   Villages and Farms: Settlement Patterns and Social Organisation

Only by unpacking the discourses through which the appearance of farms in
Mwinilunga has been represented, can a fuller understanding of processes of
social change be obtained. Building on previous chapters, this section places
narratives by colonial and post-colonial government officials, missionaries,
and anthropologists on settlement change in a longer-term historical perspective in order to elucidate continuity and change in social relationships and village organisation. According to a surprisingly thorough, yet deeply romantic
view, pre-colonial African societies once belonged to a harmonious and ho-
mogenous 'culture'.[13] Turner described the 'traditional village' in Mwinilunga
in such stereotypical terms, suggesting a village setting marked by egalitarian-
ism, solidarity, and strong kinship bonds: 'The traditional village was a circle
of pole-and-mud huts typically containing a core of matrilineally related kin
under the leadership of a member of the senior genealogical generation chosen by the villagers'.[14] The most striking change Turner observed during his
fieldwork in the 1950s was the breakup of these large and stable villages into
so-called 'farms':

> In the last few years profound changes have occurred in the residential
> structure in this area: the most noteworthy has been the breakdown of
> traditional villages into small units headed by younger men who partici-
> pate in the encroaching cash economy (...) The *ifwami* or 'farm' consists
> of one or more Kimberley-brick houses bordered by a few mud huts and
> it is occupied by the farm head, his elementary family and a small fringe
> of kin and unrelated persons.[15]

Turner, in accordance with colonial officials and missionaries, causally linked
the process of village breakup to the dissipation of ties between extended
matrilineal kin and weakening village authority. The penetration of the cash
economy, wage labour, and agricultural market production would inevitably
result in a trend towards individualisation and the emergence of nuclear families.[16] Was the appearance of farms really so new, and did it indeed prompt
changes in social organisation?

---

13   De Boeck, 'Domesticating Diamonds and Dollars', 800; Crehan, 'Tribes and the People
      Who Read Books', 203–18.
14   Turner, *Schism and Continuity,* 10, 189.
15   Ibidem, 10.
16   Turner and Turner, 'Money economy', 19–37; Turner, *Schism and Continuity,* 43.

As previous chapters have already suggested, pre-colonial Lunda villages were neither stable nor necessarily large.[17] Even if there had been some large villages, surrounding chiefly courts or along rivers and on fertile plains, most villages in the area of Mwinilunga remained small, dispersed, and they would shift regularly.[18] Around 1870, Cameron described in his travel report how: 'The winding road passed many small hamlets consisting only of a few huts in the centre of a patch of cleared and cultivated ground'.[19] Although large villages were a symbol of power, signifying that the village head was the leader of a prosperous household (a 'Big Man'), this ideal was rarely achieved.[20] The emergence and persistence of a large village was always a precarious construct, depending, according to Turner, 'on such factors as the ability of the headman to keep his following together, the maintenance of reasonably good relations between the men of the matrilineal core and their brothers-in-law, and the biological accidents of fertility and freedom from disease'.[21] Given ill-defined and malleable rules of succession, most Lunda elders could make claims to become a village head. The status and authority that came with such a title caused competition over positions of village leadership. As Livingstone observed in the 1850s, this resulted in the proliferation of small settlements: 'People are scattered over the country, each in his own little village. This arrangement pleases the Africans vastly, and any one who expects to have a village gives himself airs in consequence'.[22] Low population density and the fragile environmental setting of Mwinilunga further prevented strong centralised forms of authority, favouring the small size and mobile nature of villages instead.[23]

Early colonial reports corroborate the small size and lack of stability of villages in Mwinilunga. In the opening decades of the twentieth century, District Commissioner Bruce-Miller regularly recorded villages 'from one to four huts', as 'every man wants to be his own headman'.[24] Resembling Turner's description of a 'farm', another official in 1932 reported that 'several natives were

17   Turner, *Schism and Continuity*, 40–42; Turner does acknowledge that Lunda villages might never have been very large, but nevertheless he argues that the appearance of 'farms' is a new phenomenon. See Gordon, 'The Abolition of the Slave Trade', 915–38.
18   See Von Oppen, *Terms of Trade*.
19   Cameron, *Across Africa*, 404.
20   Pritchett, *Lunda-Ndembu*, Chapter 3; Turner, *Schism and Continuity*; Kate Crehan, 'Of Chickens and Guinea Fowl: Living Matriliny in North-Western Zambia in the 1980s', *Critique of Anthropology* 17, No. 211 (1997): 225.
21   Turner, *Schism and Continuity*, 76.
22   Schapera, *Livingstone's African Journal*, 248.
23   Schecter, 'History and Historiography.'
24   (NAZ) KSE 6/2/1, F.V. Bruce-Miller, Mwinilunga Sub-District Quarterly Report, 31 December 1914.

discovered to be living singly in the bush away from their villages'.[25] Village authority in this setting appeared to be fragile, open to continuous contestation. Colonial officials repeatedly received complaints from headmen because 'their followings are leaving them, and making small family villages in the bush', prompting Bruce-Miller to remark that 'the tendency of the natives to form small family communities and build some distance away from their chief or headman is more marked in this sub-district than in any I know'.[26] Such reports linked the propensity to establish small settlements to competition over authority and power, as 'the ambition of the Alunda is to collect a dozen natives around him and then request that he may be recognised as a headman'.[27] In the light of these examples, the establishment of small settlements seems to have been inherent to Lunda social organisation.[28] The trend towards village breakup, which Turner described in the 1950s, thus, appears far from new.

Even if colonial observers described the occurrence of farms as preponderant in the 1950s, small settlements had long historical precedents in the area of Mwinilunga.[29] As Turner himself suggested, farms probably resembled pre-colonial settlement patterns.[30] More than farms were, the large village established under colonial legislative pressure in the opening decades of the twentieth century was an anomaly.[31] Notwithstanding administrative attempts, such as the ten-taxpayer rule, to encourage the establishment of large villages, small settlements continued to predominate, as a 1940s report laments:

> Before the arrival of the Europeans in this corner of the Territory the Lunda were accustomed to live in small family settlements of often only three or four men with their wives and families. The Government however has always encouraged larger villages but they have never been popular here: big villages would lead to factions and quarrelling.[32]

Village breakup into farms was, thus, cyclical rather than progressive. Large and long-established villages held much prestige, creating, in Turner's words,

---

25   (NAZ) SEC2/952, C.H. Hazell, Mwinilunga District Tour Report, 23 August 1932.
26   (NAZ) KSE6/2/1, F.V. Bruce-Miller, Mwinilunga Sub-District Quarterly Report, 31 March 1914.
27   (NAZ) KSE6/6/2, G. Hughes-Chamberlain, Mwinilunga Sub-District Tour Report, 12 November 1926.
28   Kay, *Social Aspects of Village Regrouping in Zambia.*
29   Von Oppen, *Terms of Trade*; Kay, *Social Aspects of Village Regrouping.*
30   Turner, *Schism and Continuity*, 41: 'the present small size of villages represents partly a return to an ancient type.'
31   Pritchett, *Lunda-Ndembu*; Crehan, *The Fractured Community*; Moore and Vaughan, *Cutting Down Trees.*
32   (NAZ) SEC2/955, H.B. Waugh, Mwinilunga District Tour Report, 11 October 1940.

'a certain amount of moral pressure' among residents 'not to secede from it and "kill the village"'.[33] Yet irrespective of their stature, large villages lacked stability. All too often conflicts would arise, leading to village fission and the formation of new settlements, which observers in the 1950s called farms.[34] This cycle of village growth, breakup, and regeneration was an ongoing historical process. Even if curbed temporarily by the emergence of large stockaded villages during slave raiding, or by colonial and post-colonial legislative pressure, village fission was never eradicated.[35] In the area of Mwinilunga, far from being stable units, villages were sites of struggle for influence and power.

Small settlements, rather than being attempts to escape from village authority, constituted the nuclei from which larger villages could eventually grow up. That is why farm heads aspired to attract kin and dependents to their settlements, to build wealth in people and political authority. Even in the 1980s, Pritchett described that young men, instead of going to the village of their maternal uncle and waiting for succession there, would generally 'prefer to start their own villages and then invite relatives to join them at the point when they can most profitably use additional labor'.[36] A large village remained an ideal within the framework of wealth in people, but interpersonal and inter-village rivalry fostered the appearance of small settlements. Over time, some farms developed into large villages, although tension, competition, and fission prevented this in many cases.[37] Throughout the twentieth century there was a continual process of village build-up and breakup, giving rise to a large number of small villages rather than a select number of larger ones. This process should not be attributed solely to the erosive forces of capitalism or colonialism, as contemporary observers have mostly done, but was instead an intrinsic feature of village organisation in Mwinilunga.[38]

Complaining about village instability, colonial officials in the 1940s and 1950s connected the appearance of farms to the weakening authority of village heads. In 1940 District Commissioner Waugh noted that 'there seems to be a growing tendency for villages to split up and chiefs seem inclined to favour this as more villages, however small, give them greater prestige than a few large ones'.[39] Other officials linked the dwindling authority of village heads to intergenerational struggles, claiming that 'many of the younger generation' felt the

---

33   Turner, *Schism and Continuity*, 104.
34   Turner, *Schism and Continuity*; Pritchett, *Lunda-Ndembu*.
35   Gordon, 'The Abolition of the Slave Trade'; Kay, *Social Aspects of Village Regrouping*.
36   Pritchett, *Lunda-Ndembu*, 196.
37   See Pritchett, *Lunda-Ndembu*, Chapter 3.
38   Kay, *Social Aspects of Village Regrouping*; Jaeger, *Settlement Patterns and Rural Development*.
39   (NAZ) SEC2/955, H.B. Waugh, Mwinilunga District Tour Report, 11 October 1940.

urge to 'break away from their headmen and village discipline'.[40] In a 1950s tour report, it was lamented that 'many old headmen are little more than immobile receptacles of old custom and it is inevitable that the average villager, often an ex-line [of rail] worker, loses patience with them'.[41] Officials subsequently connected village authority and generational struggle to the encroaching cash economy, as in this report from the 1950s:

> Cash wealth has tended to fall into the hands of the younger and more active men rather than those of the older headmen. The former have de- veloped ambitions to found villages of their own and the result has been the multiple fission of older villages into a number of "farms".[42]

According to such reasoning, younger men who had earned monetary wealth would aspire to become the head of a prosperous village settlement, achieving the status of 'Big Man'.[43] Because not all men could realise their aspirations within existing villages, some would be enticed to move away and establish their own settlements elsewhere. Attributing the occurrence of farms to such quarrels over influence and power, one report from the 1950s concluded that 'if people lived in close proximity to each other friction was bound to ensue'.[44] Most frequently, contemporary observers blamed factors related to capitalism for the appearance of farms in Mwinilunga.[45]

Colonial officials repeatedly attributed the appearance of farms to transfor- mative socioeconomic processes such as the spread of the cash economy, la- bour migration, or the sale of agricultural produce. Turner described that 'most true farms are situated beside the motor roads, for the typical farm-head is a man who has earned money, often on the line-of-rail, and who intends to earn more locally'.[46] According to such views, the establishment of farms was driv- en by the entrepreneurial spirit of individuals aspiring to accumulate money and build wealth through farming or trade.[47] In 1950, a tour report mentioned one such exemplary case:

> There is one man who has shown himself to be possessed of an unusu- al amount of initiative (...) having established himself as a trader, he

---

40   (NAZ) NWP1/2/78 Loc.4913, F.R.G. Phillips, North-Western Province Annual Report, 1957.
41   (NAZ) NWP1/2/33, D. Clough, Mwinilunga District Tour Report, 1950.
42   (NAZ) NWP1/12/18 Loc.4951, T.M. Lawman to P.C. Solwezi, 12 August 1953.
43   Compare to: Moore and Vaughan, *Cutting Down Trees*.
44   (NAZ) SEC2/963, R.S. Thompson, Mwinilunga District Tour Report, July 1955.
45   Kay, *Social Aspects of Village Regrouping*.
46   Turner, *Schism and Continuity*, 36.
47   Moore and Vaughan, *Cutting Down Trees*.

recently built a good standard Kimberley house, and cut a passable motor road to enable lorries to fetch away cassava meal.[48]

This man had built his house at a considerable distance from the main village in order to expand commercial agricultural production. In such instances,
colonial officials positively assessed the appearance of farms. Allegedly, living
on a farm would enhance individual entrepreneurship, which had previously
been restrained by the communal claims and redistributive expectations prevalent in larger villages. The establishment of farms, according to such reasoning, was an attempt to avoid the burdensome obligations of sharing with kin.[49]
In a 1950s report, District Commissioner Dening justified the appearance of
farms. Due to the individualism spurred by the expansive tendencies of the
money economy, Dening asserted that a man might legitimately claim that:

> It was not worth his while to work hard to produce a plentiful supply of
> food for sale, or to maintain big flocks, since the inept and the idle in the
> village, as well as the sick and the old, would claim a share in his wealth
> as of right. People were therefore, given permission to live by themselves
> in 'farms' (...) There is no doubt that it has resulted in very great progress
> in rural conditions in the District, and has created a situation in which by
> propaganda and pressure the people can be driven to better themselves.[50]

Whereas large villages were associated with communal obligations, which
would lower productivity and profit, colonial officials connected farms to
higher productivity and economic development, as another report from the
1950s suggests: 'an enterprising man living by himself is not "sponged on" by
his relatives, to quite the same extent as would be the case if he were living
among them'.[51]

Other narratives connected farms to changes in patterns of kinship affiliation, entailing a shift from settlements based on extended matrilineal kinship
to an increasing focus on nuclear families and a trend towards individualism.
Turner asserted that this was a linear and largely inevitable development:
'Farm heads were disencumbering themselves of many of the obligations of
kinship, and retaining for their own use and for the use of their elementary
families money they earned as wages and by the sale of cash-crops or surplus

48   (NAZ) SEC2/958, K. Duff White, Mwinilunga District Tour Report, 12 November 1950.
49   Kay, *Social Aspects of Village Regrouping*.
50   (BOD) R.C. Dening Papers, Mwinilunga District Tour Report, No. 5, 1954.
51   (NAZ) SEC2/959, K.J. Forder, Mwinilunga District Tour Report, 5 November 1951.

subsistence crops'.[52] Similar to the observations made by colonial officials and missionaries, Turner argued that in time farms would come to supplant 'villages', as nuclear families would pursue their individualised economic interests in defiance of the grasping claims of extended kin and the 'traditional authority' of headmen and chiefs.[53] This trend did not materialise. The remainder of this chapter will attempt to explain why this was not the case by exploring the dynamics of accumulation and sharing, competition, and co-operation, as well as patterns of authority within the village (see Photo 14). In Mwinilunga, large villages continued to be an ideal, a means of building wealth in people, of gaining authority and power. Competition and individual entrepreneurship could indeed lead to the establishment of small settlements, yet this was a recurrent process rather than a linear trend brought about by external forces of colonialism or capitalism.[54] Over time, small villages grew and became larger villages, as living in villages continued to be an essential element of life and a structuring principle of everyday experience in Mwinilunga.[55]

The village has proven to be remarkably enduring. In the 1980s, Pritchett set out to restudy Turner's work, concluding that, rather than disintegrating, 'the village continues to be a fundamental location for the formulation of individual identity, a necessary element in productive strategies, and a key ingredient in individual plans for the afterlife'.[56] Although the size of individual villages had diminished somewhat, Pritchett advanced that villages had always been 'fluid, ever-changing units offering individuals a variety of residential options'.[57] By 2010, some villages, especially chiefly or administrative centres, had grown remarkably. Mwinilunga town had a population of about 14,500, but many other centres such as Ikelenge or Nyakaseya possessed villages of more than one hundred inhabitants. This section has sought to outline several dominant narratives through which the appearance of farms in Mwinilunga has been explained (such as references to capitalism, individualisation, or challenges to village authority). When placed in a historical context, these narratives lack causal power. Villages changed continuously, being reconfigured in reaction to social change. How can the persistence of the village be explained within an environment of flux, fission, and social change? By looking at examples of the social organisation of village life, an answer to this question will be sought.

---

52   Turner, *Schism and Continuity*, 133.
53   Ibidem.
54   Pritchett, *Lunda-Ndembu*, Chapter 3.
55   Von Oppen, 'The Village as Territory', 57–75.
56   Pritchett, *Lunda-Ndembu*, 108.
57   Ibidem, 103.

2   Chiefs, Headmen, and Authority: Governing Village Life

As the previous section has shown, processes of village breakup and the establishment of farms have commonly been associated with the weak/weakening
authority of village heads. In the 1950s, official reports described how young
ambitious men sought to disencumber themselves from the authority of headmen and chiefs by establishing their own settlements.[58] Exploring the historical development of village authority, patterns of chieftaincy and headmanship
counter such views. The trend towards individualisation and the demise of
'traditional authority', which Turner identified, was not straightforward.[59] Village authority had never been stable. Instead, intravillage competition worked
against the establishment of large settlements.[60] Nonetheless, the position of
headmen and chiefs was a highly desirable one. Village heads mediated between the village population and the outside world, gaining status and respect
within conceptualisations of wealth in people.[61] Examining the foundations of
authority in Mwinilunga provides insight into the daily governance of village
life and village cohesion over time.

   Despite numerous changes in the nineteenth and twentieth century, chiefs
and headmen in the area of Mwinilunga have transformed but maintained
their position.[62] Their continued influence is based on a number of ritual, socioeconomic, and political pillars, which have enabled village heads to act as
effective intermediaries between local, regional, national, and international
actors and forces.[63] For one, chiefs and headmen have mediated their position vis-à-vis other headmen and chiefs within the Lunda polity. From the
time of their departure from Musumba, chiefs in Mwinilunga have maintained contact with other Lunda chiefs, such as Senior Chief Musokantanda,

---

58   Turner, *Schism and Continuity*, 43.
59   Wazha G. Morapedi, 'Demise or Resilience? Customary Law and Chieftaincy in Twenty-
      first Century Botswana', *Journal of Contemporary African Studies* 28, No. 2 (2010): 215–30.
60   Von Oppen, *Terms of Trade*, 345–49.
61   Turner, *Schism and Continuity*; Pritchett, *Lunda-Ndembu*; Crehan, 'Of Chickens and Guin-
      ea Fowl.'
62   On the resurgence of chieftaincy, see Mahmood Mamdani, *Citizen and Subject: Contem-
      porary Africa and the Legacy of Late Colonialism* (Princeton: Princeton University Press,
      1996); A.A. Costa, 'Chieftaincy and Civilisation: African Structures of Government and
      Colonial Administration in South Africa', *African Studies* 59, No. 1 (2000): 13–43; Barba-
      ra Oomen, '"We Must Now Go Back to Our History": Retraditionalisation in a Northern
      Province Chieftaincy', *African Studies* 59, No. 1 (2000): 71–95; Janine Ubink, 'Traditional
      Authority Revisited: Popular Perceptions of Chiefs and Chieftaincy in Peri-Urban Kumasi,
      Ghana', *Journal of Legal Pluralism* 55 (2007): 124.
63   For the concept of mediation, see Ubink, 'Traditional Authority Revisited', 125–28.

Ishinde, or Kazembe, as well as with Paramount Chief Mwantiamvwa. This has forged enduring links between Mwinilunga, Angola, Congo, and other parts of Zambia.[64] Through trade and tribute, intermarriage and ceremonies, ties have been upheld between different parts of the Lunda polity.[65] Allegiance has been materialised through hierarchical flows of tribute, from individuals through village heads to chiefs, ultimately connected to Mwantiamvwa and his court.[66] Due to boundary demarcation and other regulations, this system of tribute was largely discontinued under colonial rule, yet occasional gifts between subordinates and superiors continued to be exchanged during formal visits, cementing regional ties within the Lunda polity.[67] Nonetheless, colonial officials asserted that connections between Lunda chiefs seemed to be weakening as the twentieth century progressed. In 1940, colonial official and ethnographer C.M.N. White observed that 'relations with (...) Mwachiamvwa appear to be breaking up in many ways quite rapidly'.[68] Yet expectations that ties within the Lunda polity would be severed turned out to be ill founded. In a 1955 tour report, it was admitted that 'great respect continues to be shown to Chief Mwatiamvwa across the Congo border by all Lunda/Ndembu'.[69] In 2010, when Paramount Chief Mwantiamvwa was scheduled to attend the *Chisemwa ChaLunda* ceremony hosted by Senior Chief Kanongesha, the announcement instantly attracted crowds of spectators from Angola, Congo, and the Zambian Copperbelt.[70] The Lunda connection was more than symbolic, influencing trade, identity, as well as the formulation of political claims and allegiances (see Chapter 3 Section 1).[71] Through Lunda ties, headmen and chiefs persistently underlined connections between the local, regional, and international level, boosting their power as intermediaries.

Chiefs and headmen, furthermore, proved imperative in negotiating involvement with the colonial and post-colonial state.[72] Chiefs depended on the state for official recognition and the payment of their subsidies, but the

---

64   Pritchett, *Friends for Life*; Bustin, *Lunda Under Belgian Rule*.

65   Hoover, 'The Seduction of Ruwej'; Schecter, 'History and Historiography.'

66   (NAZ) SEC2/402, Harry Vaux Report on Sailunga Kindred, 1936.

67   Bustin, *Lunda Under Belgian Rule*; Bakewell, 'Refugees Repatriating.'

68   (NAZ) SEC2/955, C.M.N. White, Mwinilunga District Tour Report, 20 April 1940.

69   (NAZ) SEC2/963, P.L.N. Hannaford, Mwinilunga District Tour Report, 17 March 1955.

70   Observations from Kanongesha area, July 2010.

71   Pritchett, *Friends for Life*; Bakewell, 'Refugees Repatriating'; Bustin, *Lunda Under Belgian Rule*.

72   Mamdani, *Citizen and Subject*; Samuel N. Chipungu, 'African Leadership Under Indirect Rule in Colonial Zambia', in *Guardians in Their Time: Experiences of Zambians Under Colonial Rule, 1890–1964*, ed., Samuel N. Chipungu (London: Macmillan, 1992), 50–73.

state depended on chiefs in various ways as well.[73] The collection of taxes or the recruitment of labour, for example, was premised on the collaboration of headmen and chiefs.[74] The colonial government regularly gave chiefs quotas to supply a number of labourers for road construction work. Similarly, when recruiting labourers for the mines, the co-operation of chiefs and headmen was indispensable to persuade men to go to work.[75] As the main representatives of state policies within a local setting, chiefs became central actors in the administration of law and order.[76] Nevertheless, chiefs did not simply comply with government policies, as one official grudgingly admitted in 1910: 'The truth is that, even where they might, these chiefs and headmen will not assist the Administration if such assistance in any way affects their own people'.[77] Chiefs and headmen would hide tax defaulters, disguise poachers, or deliberately fail to meet recruitment quotas.[78] A 1936 report concluded that, as mediators between the population and the government, chiefs and headmen 'perform, in reality, the day to day administration'.[79] Even after independence, this remained the case. As the 1965 annual report sets out, the government relied on chiefs to assist in 'calls to the people for voluntary effort, selfhelp schemes, emergency school building and fund raising for a new University', arguing that 'the success of these projects depends very largely on the mobility and influence of a Chief'.[80]

Chiefs and headmen often played a role as mediators of trade, underlining their vital position in village affairs.[81] Within the pre-colonial long-distance trade, chiefs and headmen regularly functioned as middlemen between traders and the village community. They would establish contacts with traders, exact tribute, fees, and goods from them, and secure favourable terms of trade.[82] In order to smooth commercial transactions, caravan leaders had to donate copious gifts to village heads, without whose consent trade relations were bound to fail.[83] Revealing his own lack of power, Livingstone desperately described how one chief:

---

73   Spear, 'Neo-Traditionalism', 3–27.
74   Pritchett, *Lunda-Ndembu*, 40–41.
75   (NAZ) KSE6/1/3, F.V. Bruce-Miller, Mwinilunga Sub-District Annual Report, 31 March 1918.
76   Chanock, *Law, Custom and Social Order*; Berry, 'Hegemony on a Shoestring', 327–55.
77   (NAZ) KSE6/5/1, J.M. Pound, Balunda District Monthly Report, October 1910.
78   See: Pritchett, *Friends for Life*; Bakewell, 'Refugees Repatriating.'
79   (NAZ) SEC2/402, Harry Vaux Report on Sailunga Kindred, 1936.
80   (UNIPA) UNIP5/3/1/13, Annual Report North-Western Province, 1965.
81   See: Gordon, 'The Abolition of the Slave Trade'; Von Oppen, *Terms of Trade*.
82   Compare with: Rockel, *Carriers of Culture*; Prestholdt, 'On the Global Repercussions', 755–81.
83   Pritchett, *Lunda-Ndembu*. Chapter 6: based on my own reading of pre-colonial travel accounts.

... made a demand of either a tusk, beads, a man, copper armlets, a shell, or we should not be permitted to enter his august presence. No one was admitted without something of the sort, and as the country belonged to him we should not pass through, unless we came down handsomely.[84]

In the nineteenth century, some village heads and chiefs grew wealthy by amassing cloth, firearms, and beads, which they distributed among subjects to secure their allegiance. By gaining influence as trade intermediaries, village heads could become 'Big Men' within frameworks of wealth in people.[85] The slave trade was the dramatic apex of this exchange of goods for human allegiance.[86] Years later, colonial officials sarcastically described how the predecessors of current chiefs were the ones 'who grew rich by the simple means of selling their people into slavery'.[87] Further testifying to their economic and political leadership, chiefs and headmen could guarantee debts or could be held responsible for the payment of fines for their subjects. If a person had a case with somebody from another village, but was unable to pay the fine, he or she would rely on the goodwill of the village head to fulfil the payment.[88] The authority of village heads, thus, comprised not only rights but also responsibilities. Throughout the twentieth century, village heads continued to play a pivotal role in mediating the economic lives of their villages.[89]

Another enduring aspect of the economic importance of chiefs and headmen in Mwinilunga was their connection to the land, from which they derived a degree of their authority to rule.[90] Land rights, granted in usufruct, were allocated by chiefs to headmen and then to household heads.[91] When land tenure reforms were discussed in the 1950s, officials could not simply circumvent the authority of chiefs over the land: 'As all Chiefs hold the land of the Chieftainship in trust for their descendants they are unable to give, dispose of or sell any of their land outright'.[92] Chiefs and headmen derived great power and prestige

84   Schapera, *Livingstone's African Journal*, 98.

85   Gordon, 'The Abolition of the Slave Trade'; Miller, *Way of Death*.

86   Piot, 'Of Slaves and the Gift', 31–49.

87   (NAZ) SEC2/953, N.S. Price, Mwinilunga District Tour Report, 29 September 1957.

88   Gordon, 'The Abolition of the Slave Trade'; Miller, *Way of Death*.

89   Von Oppen, *Terms of Trade;* Pritchett, *Lunda-Ndembu.*

90   Vansina, *How Societies Are Born*; Schecter, 'History and Historiography.'

91   See: Elizabeth Colson, 'The Impact of the Colonial Period on the Definition of Land Rights', in *Colonialism in Africa, 1870–1960, Volume 3*, ed., Victor W. Turner (Cambridge: Cambridge University Press, 1971); Parker Shipton and Mitzi Goheen, 'Introduction: Understanding African Land-holding: Power, Wealth, and Meaning', *Africa* 62, No. 3 (1997): 307–25.

92   (NAZ) NWP1/12/18 Loc.4951, District Commissioner Mwinilunga to Provincial Commissioner Solwezi, 4 November 1954.

from their control over land, as officials lamented: 'The influence of Chiefs is such that few, if any, rural Africans would be bold enough to make any suggestion of a freehold title if they still wished to retain the protection and assistance of the Chiefs in domestic affairs'.[93] Even if after independence land officially became vested in the president, leasehold or freehold tenure continues to remain the exception in Mwinilunga to this day.[94] Access to and control over land afforded village heads unique economic prominence, enabling them to exert influence over the activities that take place on the land.[95] Some chiefs successfully encouraged economic activity in their area, for example. In 1955, a report commended that Chief Ntambu 'encourages the growth of many varieties of produce', developing agricultural market production.[96] Official reports from the 1950s underlined that 'the encouragement to develop agriculture rests (...) principally with the Chief (...) the advancement of an area depends upon the Chief being one step ahead of his people'.[97] The relationship between chiefs, village heads, and the land proved a lasting source of influence over village affairs. Major economic stakeholders, such as Chinese mining companies who appeared in Chief Chibwika's area in 2009, were required to pass through the chief and obtain his formal approval before commencing mining activities.[98] Due to such complex economic, political, and social mediation on local, regional, national, and international levels, village heads were able to secure a persistently important position.[99] Yet exactly because of their influence, the position of village head was fiercely contested, giving rise to village fission and the small size of settlements.[100]

Prior to colonial attempts to establish administrative hierarchies, the titles of village heads and chiefs never appear to have been fixed or well defined.[101]

---

93   (NAZ) NWP1/12/18 Loc. 4951, R.S. Thompson to Provincial Commissioner Solwezi, 17 December 1954.

94   Pritchett, *Lunda-Ndembu.*

95   Compare to: Moore and Vaughan, *Cutting Down Trees;* Walima T. Kalusa, *Kalonga Gawa Undi x: A Biography of an African Chief and Nationalist* (Lusaka: Lembani Trust, 2010).

96   (NAZ) SEC2/963, P.L.N. Hannaford, Mwinilunga District Tour Report, 26 May 1955.

97   (NAZ) NWP1/12/18 Loc.4951, District Commissioner Mwinilunga to Provincial Commissioner Solwezi, 4 November 1954.

98   Based on observations in Kanongesha, July 2010; Rohit Negi, 'The Micropolitics of Mining and Development in Zambia: Insights from the Northwestern Province', *African Studies Quarterly* 12, No. 2 (2010/11): 27–44.

99   Ubink, 'Traditional Authority Revisited', 125–28; Spear, 'Neo-traditionalism'; Pierre Englebert, 'Patterns and Theories of Traditional Resurgence in Tropical Africa', *Mondes en développement* 30, No. 118 (2002): 51–64.

100 Turner, *Schism and Continuity*; Crehan, 'Of Chickens and Guinea Fowl.'

101 Schecter, 'History and Historiography'; Pritchett, *Lunda-Ndembu*, 37–38; Vansina, *How Societies Are Born.*

The title *mwanta* (chief) is a generic term, which can signify master, headman, employer, or can be used by a woman to call her husband. Only when reference to a *lukanu* (royal bracelet) is added, *mwanta walukanu*, does it become clear that a chief is meant.[102] This suggests that chieftaincy in the area of Mwinilunga was a fluid and contested category. The position of chief was not clearly demarcated from that of a village head, but instead depended on individual merit, performance, and claims of historical precedence.[103] Succession to the title of chief or headman was open to competition, as a report on the Sailunga chieftaincy from 1936 documents: 'at one time all the Hierarchy were Heads of Extended Families (...) [The Chief] may be succeeded by any of his titular children, which means that in theory anyone (...) may be chosen provided age and deportment permit'.[104] Even if there were rules of succession, these could be manipulated to a large extent, giving rise to contestation and an opening up of the chance of assuming village leadership.[105] The Mwinilunga District Notebooks explain the official procedure for succession to the position of headman:

> Succession usually runs in the male line; all things being equal the eldest son succeeds – next come the younger sons – then the sons of a brother – failing these the sons of a sister. To these rules I have come across a good many exceptions. If popular, a headman's nephew will often be chosen to succeed, even when the headman has several eligible sons.[106]

Open to ambitious men (and women in exceptional cases), the position of village head was highly coveted throughout Mwinilunga. This resulted in fierce competition over positions of village leadership.[107]

The position of a village head was based on achievement rather than ascription. Authority depended on the ability to mediate social, economic, and political influences between the village and the outside world. Some village heads achieved great power and influence over the village population. Nonetheless, the balance of power always remained fragile, and the authority of village heads was continuously questioned. Malleable rules of succession and low population densities spurred ambitious young men to move away from large villages and establish their own settlements elsewhere. In 1956, White

---

102   Turner, *Schism and Continuity*, 323–24; Schecter, 'History and Historiography'; Confirmed by interviews.
103   Crehan, 'Of Chickens and Guinea Fowl'; Von Oppen, *Terms of Trade*, 345–70.
104   (NAZ) SEC2/402, Harry Vaux Report on Sailunga Kindred, 1936.
105   Turner, *Schism and Continuity*, 87–90; Schecter, 'History and Historiography.'
106   (NAZ) KSE4/1, Mwinilunga District Notebooks, 141.
107   Pritchett, *Lunda-Ndembu*, 94–95.

described that 'in a Lunda village nephews get tired of the perpetuation of the authority of the generation above them, and break away to form separate villages'.[108] This tendency had been noted by Bruce-Miller in the 1920s, as he recorded that 'every man wants to be his own headman' and consequently 'the ambition of the Alunda is to collect a dozen natives around him and then request that he may be recognised as a headman'.[109] This competition over positions of village leadership was not necessarily an expression of village break-up or the demise of authority. Rather, it was a recurrent tendency through which new village nuclei were established, which could grow to become full-fledged villages.[110] Due to such competition, colonial officials remarked that 'internecine disputes, and mutual distrust between every village and its every neighbour make combination [of small villages into larger ones] most remote, if not utterly impossible'.[111] Establishing a new village and becoming the village head of a settlement was a route to prominence and power in Mwinilunga, but this could fail, nonetheless, and the village might remain small or even disappear over time.[112] This dynamic will be elaborated on by examining the changes colonial and post-colonial rule brought to village authority.

2.1   Village Leadership in a Historical Perspective

The origins of chieftaincy in Mwinilunga date back at least to the Lunda settlement of the Upper Zambezi around 1740 (see Chapter 1).[113] Although the power of chiefs has been profoundly affected by colonial and post-colonial policies, chiefs continue to be important in mediating local, national, and international forces.[114] In present-day Mwinilunga, there has even been a resurgence of 'traditional ceremonies', such as *Chisemwa ChaLunda* hosted by Senior Chief Kanongesha. Many observers have questioned the viability of the institution of

---

108   (NAZ) LGH5/5/11 Loc. 3621, C.M.N. White, Land Tenure Report North-Western Province, 1956.
109   (NAZ) KSE6/6/2, F.V. Bruce-Miller, Mwinilunga Sub-District Tour Report, 14 February 1926.
110   Pritchett, *Lunda-Ndembu*, Chapter 3.
111   (NAZ) HC1/2/43 BS2/251 Loc. 130, G.A. MacGregor, Balunda Monthly Report, January 1909.
112   Kathryn M. de Luna, 'Affect and Society in Precolonial Africa', *International Journal of African Historical Studies* 46, No. 1 (2013): 123–50; Vansina, *Paths in the Rainforests*, 69, 99.
113   Schecter, 'History and Historiography'; Vansina, *How Societies Are Born*. '*Anyanta ejima adi na nyichidi yawu, na nshimbi yawu, na yisemwa yawu, ilanga chisemwa yawantu yawaLunda chidi chimu hohu*' – 'All chiefs have their own ways, their own laws, their own traditions, but the tradition of the Lunda people is only one', Interview with Jesman Sambaulu, 10 August 2010, Kanongesha.
114   Ubink, 'Traditional Authority Revisited'; Englebert, 'Patterns and Theories of Traditional Resurgence.'

chieftainship, associated with small-scale and bounded social units, especially when challenged by nation-states and processes of globalisation.[115] The surprising resilience of chieftaincy in Mwinilunga thus needs to be explained.

Notwithstanding their potential importance on the village level, it is doubtful whether chiefs and headmen in the area of Mwinilunga ever held positions of overwhelming regional political or military power.[116] Turner, for example, soberly asserted that:

> High spatial mobility contributed powerfully to the considerable political autonomy of the village (...) with the continual movement of villages from site to site, and with the frequency of village fission, it became extremely difficult for (...) headmen to exert political authority over the inhabitants of their areas.[117]

In a similar manner, early colonial officials complained that 'there is no powerful Chief in this division (...) These men have but little power, nor do they seem anxious to be made powerful'.[118] Another report from the 1950s remarked upon the limited powers of chiefs and village heads, comparing them to *'primus inter pares'*, whose 'administrative, judicial and economic control did not extend beyond (...) [their] own immediate area'.[119] Rather than using force, village heads would give guidance to their communities by relying on ritual power and moral justification.[120] Chiefs' 'symbolic significance as epitomising Lunda tribal identity' further legitimised and strengthened their rule.[121] Within notions of wealth in people, the position of headmen and chiefs was highly aspirational.[122] Turner explained that people 'saw success in life as measured by the number of followers a man could acquire', and consequently men aimed 'to obtain influence, and subsequently office, in traditional villages'.[123] Despite general aspirations to become the leader of a prosperous village, patterns of succession to the title of headman frustrated the ambitions of enterprising men, who

---

115 Morapedi, 'Demise or Resilience?', 216; Mamdani, *Citizen and Subject*; Costa, 'Chieftaincy and Civilisation'; Oomen, 'We Must Now Go Back to Our History.'
116 Schecter, 'History and Historiography'; Vansina, *How Societies Are Born*, 258.
117 Turner, *Schism and Continuity*, 6, 15.
118 (NAZ) KSE6/1/3, F.V. Bruce-Miller, Mwinilunga Sub-District Annual Report, 31 March 1915.
119 (NAZ) NWP1/12/18 Loc. 4951, T.M. Lawman to Provincial Commissioner Solwezi, 12 August 1953.
120 Turner, *Schism and Continuity*, 318–21; Schecter, 'History and Historiography', 5–6; Hoover, 'The Seduction of Ruwej', 103.
121 (NAZ) NWP1/2/83 Loc. 4914, Land Tenure Report, North-Western Province, 1947.
122 De Luna, 'Affect and Society'; Vansina, *How Societies Are Born*.
123 Turner, *Schism and Continuity*, 134–35.

might instead choose to move away and establish their own village.[124] Turner describes this structural competition within villages, as impatience to succeed to the office of headman led some to 'hive off from the village' and 'found new settlements', because if a man 'wishes to enjoy a long period of leadership, he may well prefer to give up his chance of succeeding to office in a long-established village, despite the greater prestige of such an office, than to wait until he is old'.[125] Such competition encouraged the small size of village settlements.

In the second half of the nineteenth century, the position of chiefs and headmen changed, as the long-distance trade enabled some rulers to amass wealth, while slave raiding caused insecurity and warfare among others.[126] As a consequence of raids and warfare, villages with more than one hundred inhabitants sprang up. These large villages, epitomising wealth in people, were ruled by strong village heads ('Big Men'), who were able to organise unified action in case of attack. In this setting, chiefs and headmen commanded unprecedented authority over village affairs, deciding over matters of life and death.[127] This form of governance proved short-lived, though, as an early colonial recollection testifies:

> The people concentrated in large villages heavily stockaded and porticullised but spread out into temporary hamlets during interludes of peace (...) The compact strategic concentrations made necessary by the threat of slave raids, have been superseded by scattered hamlets, where complicated machinery of administration is not required.[128]

Small villages, loose patterns of authority and constant competition were temporarily offset by the threats of slave raids and the need to congregate into larger and more formally organised villages.[129] At the start of the twentieth century, large villages broke up into smaller units once again. Soon thereafter, the authority of village heads was profoundly affected by colonial rule.

2.2 Colonial Adaptation: Authority, Recognition, and Village Fission

In the light of colonial concerns to reduce expenditure, the policy of indirect rule 'with its co-option of local authority figures as an extremely cheap lower

---

124   Vansina, *Paths in the Rainforests*, 69, 73–82, 99.
125   Turner, *Schism and Continuity*, 88–89.
126   Gordon, 'The Abolition of the Slave Trade'; Miller, *Way of Death*.
127   Gordon, 'The Abolition of the Slave Trade.'
128   (NAZ) SEC2/402, Harry Vaux Report on Sailunga Kindred, 1936.
129   Von Oppen, *Terms of Trade*.

tier of colonial administration', appeared attractive.[130] British colonialism formally claimed to uphold the position of headmen, chiefs, and customary rules,
yet it brought about profound changes in forms of governance, according to
some even 'inventing tradition'.[131] The colonial administration sought to rule
through chiefs and headmen, using their existing authority and keeping established forms of governance in place. At the same time, chiefs and headmen
were given new tasks under colonial legislation.[132] Chiefs were held responsible for judicial, legislative, executive, and administrative tasks, amounting
to a complex and contradictory fusion of authority.[133] The judicial role of the
chief changed under colonialism, as Chief Ikelenge summarised:

> Chiefs did not in the past hold court. We all know that the Chief's role in
> so far as courts were concerned was that of an adviser who counselled
> with his subjects whose duty it was to try cases. This practice was re-
> versed by the Colonial Government which required Chiefs to hold court
> as part of the functions for which they were paid.[134]

In some respects, the colonial administration strategically boosted the position of chiefs and headmen by assigning administrative tasks to them.[135] Colonial officials noted that 'there is no doubt that under our influence the Chiefs
themselves have taken up more and more of an executive position'.[136] Next to
judicial tasks, the collection of taxes, the compilation of census, the maintenance of law and order, the enforcement of forestry, game, and agricultural
legislation, and much more became the responsibility of chiefs and, to a lesser
extent, headmen as well.[137]

Existing rivalries between headmen and chiefs were merely heightened as a
result of their new responsibilities and formalised status in the administrative
hierarchy. Because chiefs received a salary and colonial rule aimed to minimise
expenses, debates arose over who was – and who was not – to be recognised as

---

130   Crehan, 'Tribes and the People Who Read Books', 205; Berry, 'Hegemony on a Shoestring';
      Spear, 'Neo-traditionalism.'
131   Chanock, *Law, Custom and Social Order*; Mamdani, *Citizen and Subject*; Hobsbawm and
      Ranger, *The Invention of Tradition.*
132   Chipungu, 'African Leadership Under Indirect Rule.'
133   Pritchett, *Lunda-Ndembu*, 40–42; Turner, *Schism and Continuity*, 10–18.
134   (NAZ) LGH5/4/12 Loc. 3618, House of Chiefs Minutes, 9 December 1965.
135   Berry, 'Hegemony on a Shoestring.'
136   (NAZ) NWP1/12/23, R.C. Dening Comments on Harry Vaux's Report, 31 May 1954.
137   Pritchett, *Lunda-Ndembu*, 40–42.

a chief or headman.[138] From 1931 onwards, 'Government Staffs of Office' were awarded to a limited number of titleholders, creating a formal hierarchy. Due to the scarcity of government funds, the number of salaried chiefs was limited to nine under the Lunda-Ndembo Native Authority. Sailunga (Lunda) and Kanongesha (Ndembo) were awarded the title of Senior Chief, whereas Kanyama, Kakoma, and Ntambu (Lunda) and Nyakaseya, Ikelenge, Mwininyilamba, and Chibwika (Ndembo) were appointed as chiefs.[139] During the pre-colonial period, the distinction between headmen, chiefs, and senior chiefs had been more difficult to make, or had perhaps not existed at all.[140] According to Chief Ikelenge there was 'no seniority amongst the chiefs when they first came to this country. At present there is none – they sit on equal mats before Kanongeshya'.[141] Under colonial rule, however, chiefly recognition and hierarchy were formalised, giving rise to quarrels over authority and recognition. Because many people could claim an influential position due to malleable rules of succession, 'the competition for any traditionally acknowledged headmanship, with its potential of succeeding to the salaried position of Native Authority chief', became fierce.[142] When deciding which chiefs to recognise, colonial government considered the personality of a chief (whether he/she was likely to do good work) and population size (whether an area's population was big enough to warrant chieftainship).[143] Factors such as population density, facilities (schools, missions, roads, and levels of agricultural production), as well as the character and co-operation of a chief, all played a role. Quite different from pre-colonial qualifications for chiefly authority (lineage, age, and rhetorical ability), colonial rule introduced new markers of success.[144]

There are numerous headmen in Mwinilunga District today who claim to have been chiefs in the past – although some can substantiate their claims more convincingly than others.[145] One example of a chief who was deposed under colonial rule is Ntambu-Sachitolu.[146] Because Ntambu-Sachitolu

---

138 Crehan, 'Tribes and the People Who Read Books.'
139 This is based on a reading of archival sources, (NAZ); see Pritchett, Lunda-Ndembu; Turner, Schism and Continuity.
140 Schecter, 'History and Historiography'; Turner, Schism and Continuity.
141 (NAZ) SEC2/222, Provincial Commissioner North-Western Province to Chief Secretary Lusaka, 13 December 1945.
142 Pritchett, Lunda-Ndembu, 42.
143 (NAZ) NWP1/3/2 Loc. 4921, H.T. Bayldon, North-Western Province, 24 August 1961.
144 Von Oppen, 'The Village as Territory.'
145 This view is based on numerous interviews, for example Headman Mwinilunga, 31 October 2010, Mwinilunga; see Schecter, 'History and Historiography.'
146 Turner, Schism and Continuity, 12–13; Confirmed by a reading of archival sources (NAZ) and interviews.

refused to co-operate with the collection of taxes, his staff of office was taken away by officials in the 1920s.[147] This act had far-reaching consequences for his authority and for the villages in his area:

> We the children of Ntambo are very sorrowful that the Chieftainship is no longer recognised; he was our father very powerful and respected (...) Now he has no government recognition his people are scattering and we feel like orphans without a father [sic].[148]

Whereas Ntambu-Sachitolu tried to contest his deposition in the 1940s, other chiefs declined to recognise his claims, fearing their own standing in the competitive colonial environment: 'All the Chiefs were agreed that at no time had Ntambo any valid claim to chieftainship nor any right to territory or population'.[149] Lack of colonial recognition could thus result in the small size of villages and in the dispersal of population, as chiefly authority faded. Yet even some recognised chiefs complained that their authority was jeopardised due to colonial rule. Chief Sailunga, for example, claimed that 'he was losing his power and that the headmen never now come to visit him'.[150]

In some instances, colonial recognition could boost the position of chiefs and draw population to their areas. A case in point is Chief Ikelenge, who was subordinate to Chief Kanongesha yet managed to gain power due to his co-operative stance towards the government and due to the large mission that was established in his area.[151] Consequently, Chief Ikelenge's area became the nucleus of a concentrated, large, and prosperous population. In the competitive political climate of the 1960s, ANC members condemned Chief Ikelenge for being 'a "Mission and government stooge"', pleading to Chief Kanongesha that 'the government is grooming Chief Ikelenge to take over the senior Chieftainship'.[152] Due to government loyalty, Ikelenge's chiefdom became the hub of agricultural investment and schemes of post-colonial development,

---

147   This view is based on numerous interviews, for example with Ex-Chief Ntambu-Lukonkesha, 11 August 2010, Kanongesha, as well as a reading of archival sources (NAZ). The exact date of Ntambu-Sachitolu's deposition is not recorded in the archives, but it was somewhere in the 1920s.

148   (NAZ) SEC2/304, James Ntambo to Legislative Council Lusaka, 9 February 1946.

149   (NAZ) SEC2/304, Provincial Commissioner North-Western Province to Chief Secretary Lusaka, 30 April 1946.

150   (NAZ) KSE6/5/1, C.S. Bellis, Balunda District Monthly Report, July 1910.

151   This view is based on: observations; interviews; a reading of archival sources (NAZ); Fisher and Hoyte, *Ndotolu*.

152   (NAZ) LGH5/4/5, Lunda-Ndembo Native Authority Minutes, 6 May 1961.

attracting even more population to the area.[153] The attitude of chiefs, thus, considerably influenced population density and settlement patterns in an area, leading either to village dispersal or to the concentration and growth of settlements.

Headmen would only be recognised by the colonial administration if their villages contained a minimum of ten taxpaying men.[154] Nevertheless, villages with ten taxpaying men never became the rule, evidenced by the small number of registered villages in official censuses.[155] Colonial officials repeatedly complained that chiefs and headmen could not live up to their expectations, as District Commissioner MacGregor's denunciation in 1908 clearly shows: 'the small headmen who crow from the dung heaps of their villages are but idle fellows and not to be taken too seriously'.[156] Despite official encouragement to form large and stable villages, the contrary appeared to be occurring, as villages split up into small settlements.[157] Officials attributed this to the weak authority of village heads, as this 1940 account testifies: 'There are now very few headmen who are respected enough to lead the people to perform their ordinary village duties and labours', and consequently 'there seems to be a tendency for villages to split up'.[158] The demise of the authority of village heads was blamed partially on inter-generational struggles. Headmen were described as operating within 'the old tight, custom bound village circle'.[159] The personality of a headman could further contribute to the tendency, noticed by the District Commissioner in 1956, of 'many of the younger generation to break away from their headmen and village discipline' in order to found their own settlements.[160] Within the previously described competitive atmosphere over authority and recognition in Mwinilunga, the establishment of small settlements is not surprising. Throughout the nineteenth and twentieth centuries, competition and fission had been inherent to Lunda villages and village breakup rather than cohesion appeared to be the norm.[161] Colonial rule merely enhanced existing competition between village heads, by imposing new administrative tasks but recognising only a limited number of official positions. Even if this

---

153   This view is based on observations and interviews, for example Yiness Ikelenge, 10 April 2010, Ikelenge; also a reading of archival sources (UNIPA).
154   Pritchett, *Lunda-Ndembu*; Moore and Vaughan, *Cutting Down Trees*.
155   Turner, *Schism and Continuity*, 34, 37.
156   (NAZ) KSE6/5/1, G.A. MacGregor, Balunda District Monthly Report, 1 November 1908.
157   Turner, *Schism and Continuity*.
158   (NAZ) SEC2/955, H.B. Waugh, Mwinilunga District Tour Report, 11 October 1940.
159   (NAZ) NWP1/2/33, D. Clough, Mwinilunga District Tour Report, 1950.
160   (NAZ) NWP1/2/78 Loc. 4913, F.R.G. Phillips, North-Western Province Annual Report, 1956.
161   Kay, *Social Aspects of Village Regrouping*; Turner, *Schism and Continuity*.

put additional pressure on the remaining headmen and chiefs, chiefly rule and the authority of headmen adapted to changing circumstances.[162] Contradictions and conflicts did not merely result in small villages, as a number of large villages headed by strong headmen or chiefs did arise. Influenced by nation building in independent Zambia, the position of headmen and chiefs was further altered.

2.3   *Village Leadership and the Zambian Nation-State*

After independence, chieftaincy played an ambiguous role within the Zambian nation-state. Even as the Zambian government created a 'House of Chiefs' as a complementary body to parliament, the role of chiefs remained advisory.[163] Yet in a 1965 discussion of the North-Western Provincial Development committee, government officials wanted to reassure chiefs:

> ... that they have a significant role to play even in the changed circumstances of the administration. It is also important that Chiefs are identified as far as possible with the development of the country and the people, and do not feel that they are being by-passed or brushed aside.[164]

The influence and power of chiefs was confined, for example, by policies that vested land in the president. Chiefs in Mwinilunga consequently complained, as official policies affected the relationship between chiefs and the population: 'Many Chiefs feel that they have little part to play in the day to day running of their areas and that they are ignored and unwanted by their own people'.[165] A 1966 newspaper article suggested that the government could deliberately limit the independent powers of chiefs, in an attempt to centralise authority:

> President Kaunda today warned Chiefs here [in Mwinilunga] that if they flouted Government authority and tried to exercise their own in its place they would be dismissed instantly (...) The President told the Chiefs the Government would not be obstructed in its present role of building up the country.[166]

---

162   Crehan, 'Of Chickens and Guinea Fowl'; Von Oppen, 'The Village as Territory.'
163   Wim M.J. Van Binsbergen, 'Chiefs and the State in Independent Zambia: Exploring the Zambian National Press', *Journal of Legal Pluralism and Unofficial Law* 25/6 (1987): 139–201; Englebert, 'Patterns and Theories of Traditional Resurgence.'
164   (NAZ) LGH5/2/5 Loc. 3612, North-Western Provincial Development Committee, May 1965.
165   (NAZ) LGH5/2/7 Loc. 3612, Mwinilunga District Quarterly Newsletter, May 1967.
166   (NAZ) Times of Zambia, 24 June 1966.

Nation building aspirations occasionally threatened chiefs and village heads, particularly if they did not co-operate with government aims.[167] In such a context, it might have been expected that villages would disintegrate into small units, as the authority of village heads was challenged by a more hegemonic nation-state. Nevertheless, this did not occur. In the 1980s, Pritchett described that men would 'still dream of arriving at old age as the headman of a large village'.[168] Long after independence, chiefs and headmen have retained their positions and influence, as Crehan describes: 'it was still headmen who were the key players in local political life and the de facto power of headmen (...) depended to a significant extent on their ability to build up their villages by getting kin to settle with them'.[169] The authority of village heads depended on attracting followers and building wealth in people, mediating between the village and a broader national and international setting. Since the 1990s it even appears that chiefs and headmen have been experiencing a 'resurgence' of their authority. Chiefs managed to reinvent their position and assert their continued authority, for example by instituting 'traditional ceremonies', such as *Chisemwa ChaLunda*.[170]

The prediction that village authority would weaken over time, as expressed by Turner and colonial officials in the 1940s and 1950s, has not proven true. The occurrence of small settlements or farms cannot be linked directly to the diminishing power of village heads, as their position has long been precarious and contested. Competition between village heads indeed fostered the establishment of small settlements, yet the personal qualities of a headman or chief equally enabled the establishment of large, prosperous settlements.[171] The role of the village head reveals the tension between individual aspirations and communalism, village cohesion and fission. Turner described the personality of the 'ideal' village headman, the leader of a large village, as follows:

> The good headman is the good fellow, the man who 'laughs with everyone', who is hospitable, self-respecting, helpful and democratic (...) His field of friendly co-activity is not circumscribed by narrow minimal lineage relations; it extends outwards to include everyone of the village, regardless of their precise degree of relationship to him. The headman in

---

167 Larmer, *Rethinking African Politics*.
168 Pritchett, *Lunda-Ndembu*, 194.
169 Crehan, 'Of Chickens and Guinea Fowl', 225.
170 Ubink, 'Traditional Authority Revisited'; Englebert, 'Patterns and Theories of Traditional Resurgence.'
171 Vansina, *Paths in the Rainforests*, 73–82.

his person should typify and exemplify the most general norms governing social interaction within the village.[172]

Few individuals could meet these exacting standards. Because of tensions between individualism and communalism, large villages only rarely appeared or
split up after some time, as both Turner and Pritchett noted: 'Because few men
possess or develop the personality ideally required for headmen new settlements often fail to become established'.[173] In Mwinilunga, tension and competition within the village were recurrent. They did not cause the progressive
disintegration of villages into the smaller units that Turner had predicted. No
matter how precarious the balance, due to the skills of social, economic, and
political mediation, the position of village heads has remained established
throughout the twentieth century. Ultimately, the most important form of mediation was that over people. Chiefs and headmen aimed to become 'Big Men'
with a large following, yet due to competitive tendencies the following of a
village head rarely remained stable for long. The position of village heads was
reconfigured in reaction to government policies and social change, yet village
heads persistently asserted their importance at the interstices of individual,
village, regional, and national/international authority.[174] Headmen and chiefs
mediated over people in a continually shifting setting, and this constituted
the basis of their authority, the long-term thread in their rule. This tension between individualism and communalism not only manifested itself in the position of village heads but also permeated many other aspects of village life.

3   Continuity and Change in Village Life

In the 1950s, Turner predicted pervasive change in the social fabric of village
life in Mwinilunga. In a later publication, he identified that 'there was clearly "a
wind of change," economic, political, social, religious, legal, and so on, sweeping the whole of central Africa and originating *outside* all village societies'.[175]
According to Turner, these changes were epitomised by the appearance of the
farm, where nuclear families rather than extended kinship affiliations and individual profit accumulation rather than communal sharing would prevail.
Yet despite profound social change, villages have continued to exist, whereas

---

172   Turner, *Schism and Continuity*, 202.
173   Turner, *Schism and Continuity*, 203; Pritchett, *Lunda-Ndembu*, 191.
174   See Kalusa, *Kalonga Gawa Undi X*.
175   Turner, *Dramas, Fields, and Metaphors*, 31–32.

categories of kinship, age, and gender, and patterns of authority have retained their significance, even whilst transforming and incorporating change. The changes that Turner, as well as colonial officials and missionaries, foresaw at the time appear less clear-cut or unidirectional when viewed within a long-term historical perspective. Several examples bring out the continued salience of village life, kinship relations, and reciprocity.

3.1   Accumulation, Wealth, and Personhood

Observers persistently linked the appearance of farms in Mwinilunga in the 1940s and 1950s to patterns of individualisation and a nucleation of the family.[176] Turner attributed village breakup to a trend towards individual accumulation, whilst disregarding relationships of reciprocity among extended kin.[177] Colonial officials, missionaries, and anthropologists alike proposed that, in Bates' words, 'capital has a profound impact upon the structure of kinship systems at the local level'.[178] Contemporary colonial officials in Mwinilunga greeted individualism with a degree of scepticism, for although it might contribute to economic entrepreneurship and development (exemplified by the 'progressive farmer'), it could equally hinder the orderly functioning of village society (causing heightened accusations of witchcraft, for example).[179] Such observations relied on binary oppositions between communalism and individualism, household reciprocity versus self-interested accumulation, and kinship obligations versus a nucleation of the family.[180] Turner argued that the 'cash economy tends to destroy ties of corporate kinship *within* villages'.[181] Nevertheless, straightforward trends towards individualisation and accumulation need to be questioned.[182] If individualisation and family nucleation materialised, this

176   Turner, *Schism and Continuity*, 43; Turner and Turner, 'Money Economy'; Price and Thomas, 'Continuity and Change in the Gwembe Tonga Family.'
177   Turner, *Schism and Continuity*; see: Bates, 'Capital, Kinship and Conflict'; Kate Crehan, 'Women and Development in North Western Zambia: From Producer to Housewife', *Review of African Political Economy* 27/8 (1983): 51–66.
178   Bates, 'Capital, Kinship, and Conflict', 151.
179   This view is based on a reading of archival sources (NAZ); see also Edith Turner, 'Philip Kabwita, Ghost Doctor: The Ndembu in 1985', *The Drama Review* 30, No. 4 (1986): 12–35; Karen E. Fields, 'Political Contingencies of Witchcraft in Colonial Central Africa: Culture and the State in Marxist Theory', *Canadian Journal of African Studies* 16, No. 3 (1982): 567–93.
180   Price and Thomas, 'Continuity and Change in the Gwembe Tonga Family'; De Boeck, 'Domesticating Diamonds and Dollars', 800; Bates, 'Capital, Kinship and Conflict.'
181   Turner, *Schism and Continuity*, 51.
182   See: Berry, *No Condition Is Permanent*; De Boeck, 'Domesticating Diamonds and Dollars'; Price and Thomas, 'Continuity and Change in the Gwembe Tonga Family.'

would have far-reaching and indeed transformative effects on patterns of so-cial relationships, gender, kinship, and village residence.[183] By paying attention to historical contestation and negotiation within the village, family, and house-hold, a view that is quite different from family nucleation or individualisation arises.[184] This suggests that 'changes in the family and kinship structure in response to local social and economic transformation can be equated not with nuclearisation [or individualisation] but with the emergence of a modified form of family and kinship'.[185] The tensions between accumulation and reci-procity will be brought out through several examples. It will be proposed that there was an inherent competitiveness in Lunda villages, yet that this did not necessarily disrupt patterns of reciprocity or co-operation.[186] Rather than di-minishing due to the money economy, kinship relations retained importance, constituting the essence of self-realisation and personhood, and underpinning residence in villages.[187]

As part of a more general trend from communalism to individualisation, Turner predicted that commercialisation (through agricultural marketing or labour migration) would strain reciprocity and promote individual ac-cumulation.[188] Yet, in a context of social change, and economic or political insecurity, social ties could on the contrary be a 'safety network'.[189] In Mwini-lunga, wealth in people was a desired goal, and a 'Big Man' would, according to Pritchett, '*diisha antu yakudya*, feed the people, that is, spend wealth on social prestige, transform *maheta* (things) into *kavumbi* (respect)'.[190] Becom-ing a 'Big Man' involved a 'balance of acquisitiveness and self-aggrandisement with sharing, avoidance of greed, generosity, and restraint'.[191] Even if sharing involved responsibilities, it could accrue benefits, creating a web of ties within the community. Englund has aptly described how wealth is always social. One could only become a 'Big Man' through the support of others, which involved responsibility for their well-being. There might be:

---

183 Price and Thomas, 'Continuity and Change in the Gwembe Tonga Family'; Kay, *Social As-pects of Village Regrouping*; Moore and Vaughan, *Cutting Down Trees.*

184 Price and Thomas, 'Continuity and Change in the Gwembe Tonga Family.'

185 Ibidem, 512.

186 Pritchett, *Lunda-Ndembu*; Von Oppen, *Terms of Trade.*

187 Berry, *No Condition Is Permanent*; Guyer, 'Wealth in People and Self-Realization', 243–65.

188 Turner, *Schism and Continuity*, 24; compare with Moore and Vaughan, *Cutting Down Trees.*

189 Berry, *No Condition Is Permanent.*

190 Pritchett, *Lunda-Ndembu*, 131.

191 John Hamer, 'Commensality, Process and the Moral Order: An Example from Southern Ethiopia', *Africa* 64, No. 1 (1994): 130.

... self-interested actors whose concern is to protect, and possibly increase, personal wealth. Yet wealth (...) becomes wealth only when it mobilises others (...) Wealth which is individual and private, mobilising no one but the person him- or herself, constitutes its proprietor as the inversion of moral being.[192]

An individual could not attain wealth single-handedly, but depended on others for their labour, skills, and for building personal prestige and power. Self-realisation was dependent on social relationships, which constituted social and moral personhood.[193] A focus on wealth in people and self-realisation emphasises the multiple forms of interdependence within village communities. Communalism has not withered away, as it continues to be a way to constitute and express social relationships, upon which wealth, influence, and power are based.[194] Influence and power, personhood and status, continued to depend on people in the area of Mwinilunga.

Ideas about wealth in people, self-realisation, and legitimate wealth can be illustrated by looking at witchcraft. The notion of *maheta* (wealth, riches, property) implies not only material possessions but also fertility in the broadest sense of the word, including offspring, agricultural produce, meat, and fish.[195] Fertility is highly valued within the ideology of wealth in people in Mwinilunga. Norms of solidarity, reciprocity, and fertility, according to De Boeck, 'characterize the cultural order of life in the village'. This cultural order is 'defined by life-giving reciprocity between hunter and family, husband and wife, between living and dead, and between the generations'.[196] This is why social relationships are vital to the constitution of moral personhood. Underlining the notion of wealth in people, social relationships are valued as major assets. Rather than being self-generating, wealth (*maheta*) has to be actively produced or even captured (*heta* to gain, possess, own).[197] Norms stipulate what is considered to be 'legitimate accumulation' of wealth, versus illegitimate 'self-interested profit-making'; yet norms are continuously breached, and these breaches

---

192   Harri Englund, 'The Self in Self-interest: Land, Labour and Temporalities in Malawi's Agrarian Change', *Africa* 69, No. 1 (1999): 151.
193   De Boeck, 'Domesticating Diamonds and Dollars'; Englund, 'The Self in Self-interest.'
194   Hamer, 'Commensality, Process and the Moral Order'; De Boeck, 'When Hunger Goes Around the Land.'
195   Fisher, *Lunda-Ndembu Dictionary*; De Boeck, 'Domesticating Diamonds and Dollars.'
196   De Boeck, 'Domesticating Diamonds and Dollars', 789.
197   De Boeck, 'Borderland Breccia.'

find expression in idioms of witchcraft.[198] Witchcraft accusations might occur when a person has accumulated wealth and power, but has failed to share
this adequately with kin and neighbours. Such individuals risk being accused
of or attacked by malignant witchcraft.[199] One woman explained the death of
her brother through reference to witchcraft. Because he had bought several
motorcars and had started a successful trading business, others felt jealous and
plotted to kill him through witchcraft, because he had not shared his riches
among his kin.[200] Witchcraft has been associated negatively with social levelling mechanisms, discouraging entrepreneurship, and favouring an attitude of
'getting things from others for nothing'.[201] Allegedly, as Fisher states, nobody
would want to 'put his head above the parapet', because 'he will be bewitched
because he thinks he is better than his fellows'.[202] Nevertheless, witchcraft
should not necessarily be associated with the limitation of wealth or levelling
processes. Norms of reciprocity within the village were not universally shared
or uncontested, but were rather debated through idioms of witchcraft.[203] In
the case of chiefs or successful hunters, witchcraft might enhance individual
accumulation, enabling the building of wealth and power. Witchcraft was neither a sign of individualisation and self-interested accumulation, nor a social
levelling mechanism espousing communal solidarity. Instead, witchcraft could
be a discourse about the constitution of moral personhood, the ideal being a
person who is 'courageous, firm and brave, who has self-restraint and shows
perseverance, strong will, character, courage, and a sense of responsibility'.[204]
Accumulation of wealth and power itself was not critiqued through witchcraft,
but pathways of accumulation could be questioned. In Mwinilunga, moral personhood was conceived as thoroughly social and relational, and therefore a

---

198   Harri Englund, 'Witchcraft, Modernity and the Person: The Morality of Accumulation in
      Central Malawi', *Critique of Anthropology* 16, No. 3 (1996): 257–79; George C. Bond and
      Diane Ciekawy, eds., *Witchcraft Dialogues: Anthropological and Philosophical Exchanges*
      (Athens: Ohio University Press, 2001).
199   Cyprian F. Fisiy and Peter Geschiere, 'Sorcery, Witchcraft and Accumulation: Regional
      Variations in South and West Cameroon', *Critique of Anthropology* 11, No. 3 (1991): 251–78;
      Englund, 'Witchcraft, Modernity and the Person', 271–72; Fields, 'Political Contingencies
      of Witchcraft.'
200   Anonymous interview, March 2010, Ikelenge.
201   (NAZ) MCD1/3/29, North-Western Province, African Provincial Council, June 1955.
202   Interview with Paul Fisher, 27 September 2008, Hillwood Farm. On witchcraft and social
      levelling, see Henrietta L. Moore and Todd Sanders, eds., *Magical Interpretations, Material
      Realities: Modernity, Witchcraft and the Occult In Postcolonial Africa* (London: Psychology
      Press, 2001).
203   Elizabeth Colson, 'The Father as Witch', *Africa* 70, No. 3 (2000): 333–58; Englund, 'Witch-
      craft, Modernity and the Person.'
204   De Boeck, 'Domesticating Diamonds and Dollars', 794.

person who achieved wealth without making his or her constitutive relationships visible would be suspected of witchcraft.[205]

Looking at marriage further illustrates the importance of interpersonal relationships and extended kinship in villages in Mwinilunga. Being more than
a link between two individuals, marriage among the Lunda creates a bond between kin groups.[206] Obtaining a marriage partner from a different village is
therefore a political act, as Turner explains: 'Any link between villages might be
the precursor of further links of kinship and affinity within and between vici-
nages and chiefdoms in the loose, decentralized polity'.[207] Because marriage is
so intimately connected to procreation and fertility, marriage continues to be
socially expected throughout Mwinilunga.[208] The additional labour power of
children is highly valued. In this sparsely populated district where general labour scarcity prevails, fertility is a tool to build a loyal following and to become
a respected member of society (see Photo 15). The envisaged outcome of the
marriage bond is childbirth, which expands and strengthens the kin group, and
creates enduring bonds between dispersed households. Within the context of
wealth in people, the route to success in Mwinilunga is premised on a large and
prosperous household, following, and village, and therefore 'Big Men' and 'Big
Women' desire offspring.[209] Thus the proverb *iyala walema wudi namumbanda*
('an important man has a wife').[210] On the other hand, unmarried, widowed,
or childless men and women risk social ostracism.[211] Claims to children and
their labour were fiercely contested, particularly between fathers and mothers'
brothers in this matrilineal society where virilocal residence upon marriage
is the norm.[212] Marriage revolved around labour, created social networks, and
acted as a visible marker of social relationships, embodying wealth in people.[213] Marriage ties were malleable, and rights conferred by marriage were
contestable. But it is exactly herein that their strength, adaptability, and enduring importance lies. Marriage was essentially a social bond in which spouses

---

205   Englund, 'Witchcraft, Modernity and the Person'; Fisiy and Geschiere, 'Sorcery, Witchcraft
       and Accumulation.'
206   Pritchett, *Lunda-Ndembu*; Crehan, 'Of Chickens and Guinea Fowl.'
207   Turner, *Drums of Affliction*, 264.
208   Turner, *Schism and Continuity*; Pritchett, *Lunda-Ndembu*; De Boeck, 'When Hunger Goes
       Around the Land.'
209   Turner, *Schism and Continuity*; Pritchett, *Lunda-Ndembu*.
210   Proverb recorded by Gibby Kamuhuza, May 2010, Ikelenge.
211   Turner, 'The spatial separation', 121–37.
212   Turner, *Schism and Continuity*.
213   Barbara Cooper, 'Women's Worth and Wedding Gift Exchange in Maradi, Niger, 1907–89',
       Journal of African History 36, No. 1 (1995): 121.

laid claim to each other's labour and offspring. Rather than leading to individualisation or nucleation of the family, marriage underlined the importance of
the extended family and strong bonds of kinship.[214] Spouses and their kin laid
claim to the labour and offspring of the other spouse, creating enduring but
contested bonds. Claims and expectations did change over time, and negotiations over rights and property occurred, yet the marriage bond underlined the
importance of the concept of wealth in people, relationships of kinship, and
marital interdependence.[215]

3.2   *Individualisation, Kinship, and Wealth in People*
Turner anticipated that cash crop production and wealth generated through
labour migration would cause associations between extended kin to dissolve
into nuclear families, propelling increasing individualisation: 'economic individualism both in production and consumption seems to be the keynote of
the new cash economy. This individualism is snapping the traditional ties of
extended kinship and breaking up corporate residential groupings such as
the village'.[216] Gough, in accordance with other anthropologists, has similarly suggested that matrilineal kinship would be vulnerable under conditions
of increased wealth, social differentiation, and inequality: 'under economic
changes brought about by contact with Western industrial nations, matrilineal descent groups gradually disintegrate. In their place, the elementary family
eventually emerges as the key kinship group with respect to residence, economic cooperation, legal responsibility, and socialization'.[217] Kinship, descent,
and affiliation were inexorably linked to 'goods, claims, obligations, positions,
and statuses', being inherently social and part of power struggles in society.[218]
Despite profound changes, ties of extended kinship remain of paramount importance in Mwinilunga.[219] Kinship continued to provide 'the basic threads

---

214   Berry, *No Condition Is Permanent*; Price and Thomas, 'Continuity and Change in the
       Gwembe Tonga Family.'
215   De Boeck, 'Domesticating Diamonds and Dollars.'
216   Turner and Turner, 'Money Economy', 36.
217   Kathleen Gough, 'The Modern Disintegration of Matrilineal Descent Groups', in *Matrilin-
       eal Kinship,* eds., David M. Schneider and Kathleen Gough (Berkeley: University of Cali-
       fornia Press, 1961), 631; Mary Douglas, 'Is Matriliny Doomed in Africa?', in *Man in Africa,*
       eds., Mary Douglas and Phyllis M. Kaberry (London: Tavistock, 1969): 121–33; Pauline E.
       Peters, 'Revisiting the Puzzle of Matriliny in South-Central Africa', *Critique of Anthropol-
       ogy* 17, No. 2 (1997): 126–27.
218   Vansina, *How Societies Are Born,* 93.
219   See: Price and Thomas, 'Continuity and Change in the Gwembe Tonga Family'; Berry, *No
       Condition Is Permanent.*

out of which social life was woven'.[220] Ties of kinship proved important in a social, economic, and political sense. A Lunda saying goes that 'to be without social linkages is akin to being lost in the deep forest'.[221] How could ties of kinship and social relationships adapt to changing circumstances?

Ties of kinship constituted a source of influence and power, making a person famous (*mpuhu*), a 'Big Man' within the framework of wealth in people.[222] In case of political contestations, members of kin were one's following and source of support, as Turner explains:

> When a man wishes to succeed to office or to found a village of his own, he looks for the backing of his own children in these ventures, as well as to his uterine kin. A man's major unit of political support is the circle of his closest kin (…) In addition to his own and his sisters' children, these kin include his brothers and their children. Such a group contains the nucleus of a new generation, the junior adjacent genealogical generation over which he and his siblings exercise authority and control.[223]

Exactly because of village fission and high levels of mobility, a wide range of interpersonal relationships was created and upheld in the area of Mwinilunga: 'the continual flow of visits between matrilineal kin, however far apart in space, serves to maintain their connection'.[224] Fluid ties of kinship constituted an asset within a competitive environment, as a person could gain influence and power by attracting the allegiance of distant kin and establishing a large settlement. Up to the present, it remains the ideal to become the headman of a large and prosperous village, and for this the support of kin is indispensable, as Pritchett describes: 'The essence of life is to become both *mukwakuheta* (one who possesses many things) and *mukwakwashi* (one who helps many people). Such individuals are adorned with praise and surrounded by followers anxious to do their bidding'.[225]

The continued salience of kinship is illustrated by looking at strategies for self-realisation.[226] Within a Lunda village, those who have a name (*akweti*

---

220   Crehan, 'Of Chickens and Guinea Fowl', 214.
221   Pritchett, *Lunda-Ndembu*, 84.
222   De Boeck, 'Domesticating Diamonds and Dollars'; Pritchett, *Lunda-Ndembu*, 113; Pritchett, *Friends for Life*, 225.
223   Turner, *Schism and Continuity*, 108.
224   Ibidem, 87.
225   Pritchett, *Friends for Life*, 107.
226   Guyer, 'Wealth in People and Self-Realization'; De Boeck, 'Domesticating Diamonds and Dollars.'

majina) are distinguished from those who lack a name (*abula majina*).[227] Whether through hunting, cultivation, labour migration, or ritual eminence, individuals sought to establish a name for themselves. Yet establishing a name for oneself could never be a solitary act. Rather, it involved profound social engagement, which underlined the importance of kinship bonds.[228] Growing towards personhood involved both 'the realization of one's individual self-identity, autonomy and responsibility' and 'a gradual body-centred insertion (...) into the lives of other individuals'. This process implied social responsibility, as De Boeck explains:

> The more one becomes the focus of the social life of the kin group, the more one is given respect, but the more, also, one becomes responsible for the redistribution and sharing of the goods that circulate in the kin group.[229]

A person was not only expected to develop individual personhood but also to foster social relationships by becoming a 'Big Man' or a 'Big Woman', a *mukwakwashi*, one who takes care of others and is thereby able to build a large and prosperous household and village.[230] Prominent individuals derived respect and influence from neighbours, kin, and following, but were also expected to reciprocate this support by occupying an exemplary position, as colonial reports underlined: 'The higher the status of a villager, the more he is bound theoretically to fulfil his communal obligations as an example to the public'.[231] Ties of kinship were inherently flexible and negotiable. Individuals could claim allegiance to either the maternal or the paternal side of their family, whereas the residence of children was continually contested in Mwinilunga.[232] Exactly because of this ambiguity, ties of kinship were a resource in times of stress, providing support and protection, as Berry has noted:

> If access to resources and opportunities depends on one's ability to negotiate, people may be more interested in keeping options open than cutting

---

227 This issue was raised in numerous interviews, for example Jackson Jinguluka, May 2010, Nyakaseya; (NAZ) SEC2/402, Harry Vaux Report on Sailunga Kindred.
228 Turner, *Schism and Continuity*; De Boeck, 'Domesticating Diamonds and Dollars'; Pritchett, *Friends for Life,* 107, 109.
229 De Boeck, 'Domesticating Diamonds and Dollars', 794.
230 Turner, *Schism and Continuity*; De Boeck, 'Domesticating Diamonds and Dollars'; Pritchett, *Lunda-Ndembu*, 131; Pritchett, *Friends for Life,* 227.
231 (NAZ) SEC2/402, Harry Vaux Report on Sailunga Kindred, 1936.
232 Crehan, 'Of Chickens and Guinea Fowl'; Turner, *Schism and Continuity.*

them off, and in strengthening their ability to participate in and influence negotiations rather than acquiring exclusive control over resources
and severing connections which are not immediately profitable.[233]

Although interpersonal ties could be liabilities as well as assets, power and
prestige continued to depend on social relationships, as Pritchett underlined:
'People do not just do things for you because you have prestige; rather, you
have prestige because people do things for you'.[234]

The persistence of extended kinship bonds in Mwinilunga was occasionally viewed as a nuisance by outside observers.[235] Wealthy individuals complained about being 'sponged upon' by their less fortunate relatives. As a result,
migrant labourers experienced difficulties, as Member of Parliament Peter Matoka outlined: 'The tradition of extended families was working against town
dwellers. Relatives flocked to stay with their townfolk. Even where there was
no chance of being employed uncles, cousins, sisters, and aunts found their
way to towns'.[236] Nevertheless, kinship was more often an asset than a burden.
In the 1950s, Turner described several cases of enterprising individuals who
continued to value kinship affiliation, because they:

> ... saw success in life as measured by the number of followers a man
> could acquire, and not by the insignia of conspicuous wealth that could
> be purchased by money (...) [They] continued to work in their gardens,
> to gossip and discuss cases in the village *chota*, to participate in ritual as
> cult-members and patients, to exercise their traditional rights and fulfil
> obligations as kin (...) they felt that the royal road to eminence within the
> village way of life now lay through the acquisition of cash. Possessions of
> cash gave them large houses, bride-wealth for several wives who might
> give them children and enable them to offer hospitality, and the means
> of retaining their children and giving them a good education. They want-
> ed money to better their position within the traditional system, not as a
> means of loosening their ties with it.[237]

Even if they participated actively in the money economy, these men clearly
valued wealth in people. Simultaneously, Turner described the rise of a new

233   Berry, *No Condition Is Permanent,* 14.
234   Pritchett, *Lunda-Ndembu,* 131.
235   Ibidem.
236   (NAZ) HM77/PP/2, Peter Matoka, Review of Zambia's 33 Years of Independence, 8 Novem-
      ber 1997.
237   Turner, *Schism and Continuity,* 134.

type of man, of the younger generation, who pursued money and wealth for its own sake, feeling 'embarrassed by the demands of their kin for presents in cash or kind' and wishing to 'separate themselves from the village sphere and village way of life'.[238] According to Turner the second pattern would come to predominate in the long run, giving rise to individualisation and the establishment of farms. This prediction did not prove to be true.[239]

Given the overwhelming importance of social ties in the area of Mwinilunga, the establishment of farms cannot be attributed to a straightforward process of individualisation. Farms, rather than being the result of village disintegration, constituted the nuclei from which new, larger villages could grow. In this sense, kinship was redefined and gained new significance in farms. Acquiring a large following and establishing a prosperous village continued to be a widely held ideal, and to achieve this goal kinship support proved indispensable.[240] By fostering kinship bonds, people in Mwinilunga gained access to productive resources (labour, crops, and money) and advanced their social standing. Through participation in social life, according to Berry, individuals could 'gain respect and create obligations', which served 'to reaffirm or advance their status within their families and communities and their ability to draw on the resources or support of the group in negotiating their own claims to productive resources'.[241] That is why no village in Mwinilunga today is composed exclusively of nuclear families; instead, nephews, nieces, and other extended kin reside in a village to gain access to education, medical facilities, or markets.[242] Relationships between extended kin continue to be used as resources to maximise opportunities, enabling trade relationships over long distances, or facilitating the reception of a labour migrant in town.[243] The UNIP government after independence actively promoted aspects of community cohesion, self-help, co-operative production, and communal labour.[244] As has been described for the Gwembe Tonga in Southern Zambia: 'Many family and kinship systems, in changing social and economic contexts, do not nucleate but adapt and reconstruct; in a number of cases extended kin bonds strengthen under pressure from "modernising" forces'.[245] Rather than becoming obsolete in times

---

238   Ibidem, 135.
239   Pritchett, *Lunda-Ndembu,* Chapter 3; see Moore and Vaughan, *Cutting Down Trees.*
240   Pritchett, *Lunda-Ndembu,* 142, 194.
241   Berry, *No Condition Is Permanent,* 160.
242   Based on my observations; see Pritchett, *Lunda-Ndembu.*
243   See: Von Oppen, *Terms of Trade*; Pritchett, *Friends for Life.*
244   (NAZ) Department of Community Development, Annual Report 1964.
245   Price and Thomas, 'Continuity and Change in the Gwembe Tonga Family', 528–29.

of stress and social change, bonds of kinship in Mwinilunga were reaffirmed, underlining the salience of village residence and concepts of wealth in people.

3.3   *Social Change in Mwinilunga*

This chapter has provided examples of how individuals appropriate change by 'following the rules yet creating new forms at the same time'.[246] Through 'a deeply rooted habitus, a past, a bedrock of moral matrixes' the present is renegotiated and invested with meaning.[247] Rather than resulting in a disintegration of the social fabric, in Mwinilunga change propelled the continual negotiation and redefinition of existing categories and social relationships. Thus, 'long-term continuity and active creation are in fact compatible'.[248] Cultural categories and social relationships were not fixed but contested, being sites of struggle. As this chapter has argued, social relationships were subject to definite but gradual change. Although prominent individuals could uphold the moral premises and communal norms of the village, they could equally deviate from these norms and establish new patterns, for example by displaying exceptional hunting skill, by achieving status through an initiation ceremony, or through witchcraft. Such exceptional individuals caused change in society and in patterns of belief, yet, change built upon established norms and a preexisting order.[249] Norms did not remain fixed, but were continually contested and reconfigured. Individuals 'reinvent older notions, mentalities, practices, and moralities' within the changing circumstances of their daily lives.[250]

Continuity and change thus coincided in villages throughout Mwinilunga. Existing social structures changed continuously, yet in such a manner that a discursive continuity could still be upheld. Although norms, moralities, and patterns of social relationships were contested, they formed the foundation from which action took off. Whilst there was continuous change, change was gradual. Rather than constituting a sharp breach with past practices, change was domesticated and familiarised: 'We can thus speak of both the continuity of tradition *and* its transformation as part of a single unending process of renovation, innovation and transformation'.[251] *Chisemwa*, tradition, could change and endure. Enterprising individuals, who sought to make a name for themselves by establishing a large and prosperous household or by exhibiting rhetorical ability in the village palaver hut, might deviate from social norms

---

246   Feierman, *Peasant Intellectuals*, 13.
247   De Boeck, 'Domesticating Diamonds and Dollars', 806.
248   Feierman, *Peasant Intellectuals*, 3, 21.
249   Ibidem, 28.
250   De Boeck, 'Domesticating Diamonds and Dollars', 801; Feierman, *Peasant Intellectuals*.
251   Spear, *Mountain Farmers*, 238–39.

and thereby establish their own rules, creating a precedent for others to follow. Traditions changed, whilst remaining intact, providing 'individuals with a
rich corpus of pre-established (traditional) forms *and* with the opportunity to
"swing free" in creative endeavours that inevitably transform those forms'.[252]

4   Conclusion

Beyond a doubt, villages in the area of Mwinilunga today look different and are
organised in a different way than those at the start of the twentieth century. Yet
despite profound social change, villages persist and have not disintegrated as
Turner predicted in the 1950s. Villages and the social relationships that form
the core of village life have changed over the course of the twentieth century,
but this change did not follow a clear, preconceived, or linear course. Change
was the outcome of active and purposive production/reproduction. Change
could result in the rearticulating of existing discourses or the reconfiguration
of previous practices rather than in the emergence of wholly new forms.
    Linear transitions from communalism to individualism, from extended
kinship to family nucleation, or from sharing to accumulation did not materialise. Binary oppositions were more discursive than real, as competition and
contestation had long been part of village life. The establishment of 'farms',
which Turner observed, was not a sign of individualisation, but matched
long-established trends of inter-village competition and underlined aspects
of wealth in people. Wealth in people was what underpinned the continued
importance of social relationships. A *mukwakuheta* (rich person) could not
become powerful without simultaneously being considered a *mukwakwashi*
(one who helps others). Although capitalism exacerbated existing rivalries
within villages, this did not evoke radical change in social relationships, which
remained pivoted around webs of interdependence and personal allegiance.
Becoming a 'Big Man' involved investing in the village rather than distancing
oneself from it. This explains the persistence of village residence and the paramount importance of social relationships.

---

252   Richard Handler and Jocelyn Linnekin, 'Tradition, Genuine or Spurious', *The Journal of
      American Folklore* 97, No. 385 (1984): 287.

PHOTO 14   A chief drinking beer in the village, 1950s
            NATIONAL ARCHIVES OF ZAMBIA, MWINILUNGA DISTRICT NOTEBOOKS

PHOTO 15   Women welcoming the District Commissioner, 1950s
            NATIONAL ARCHIVES OF ZAMBIA, MWINILUNGA DISTRICT NOTEBOOKS

Conclusion

When industrial mining enterprises commenced in Lumwana in 2008, plans were made for prospecting throughout Mwinilunga District. Journalists, policy makers, and academics instantly heralded an 'epochal divide', predicting that Mwinilunga would become part of Zambia's 'New Copperbelt'.[1] Through mining, the district would be lifted out of poverty, and this would have a profound influence, not only on the economy but also on modes of thought, as Negi describes: 'the development of an entirely new town by the Lumwana company in what was until very recently "bush" has led to new "expectations of modernity" in the region'.[2] Much like colonialism or capitalism previously, mining was expected to propel profound and transformative change. This book has argued against such narratives of linear and externally generated social change. As the example of recent copper mining shows, narratives of linear social change are clearly not obsolete relics, as they continue to be actively reproduced.[3] Undoubtedly, the opening of mines will have a profound impact on the area, yet it remains the question whether change will follow a linear course and whether social transformation will necessarily result.[4] The dominant narrative within which social change in Mwinilunga has hitherto been described is one of transformative and linear change. This book has sought to move away from and beyond this narrative, arguing that such a narrative obscures rather than illuminates the course of history. Instead of paying attention to ruptures or discontinuity, this book has placed emphasis on long-term trends, local negotiation, and gradual change, in order to understand how the process of social change

---

1   A remark about an 'epochal divide' due to the mining boom in Zambia's North-Western Province was made by Margaret O'Callaghan, at the 'Narratives of Nationhood' Conference in Lusaka, Zambia, in September 2012. She referred back to the Rhodes-Livingstone Institute scholars, most notably Godfrey Wilson, yet such views are equally expressed in much recent journalism.

2   Rohit Negi, 'The Mining Boom, Capital, and Chiefs in the "New Copperbelt"', in *Zambia, Mining, and Neoliberalism: Boom and Bust on the Globalized Copperbelt,* eds., Alastair Fraser and Miles Larmer (New York: Palgrave Macmillan, 2010), 209.

3   Ferguson, *Expectations of Modernity*, 16.

4   James Van Alstine, 'Community and Company Capacity: The Challenge of Resource-Led Development in Zambia's "New Copperbelt"', *Community Development Journal* 48, No. 3 (2013): 360–76; Rita Kesselring, 'The Electricity Crisis in Zambia: Blackouts and Social Stratification in New Mining Towns', *Energy Research & Social Science* 30 (2017): 94–102; Marja Hinfelaar and Jessica Achberger, 'The Politics of Natural Resource Extraction in Zambia', in Anthony Bebbington, et al., *Governing Extractive Industries: Politics, Histories, Ideas* (Oxford: Oxford University Press, 2018).

© KONINKLIJKE BRILL NV, LEIDEN, 2019 | DOI:10.1163/9789004408968_008

(exemplified by issues of production, mobility, consumption, and social relationships) has been negotiated in the area of Mwinilunga between 1870 and 1970. By questioning narratives of linear change, this book has not suggested that change did not occur in Mwinilunga. On the contrary, continuous and at times profound change has been locally negotiated and appropriated within existing frameworks of thought, action, and historical consciousness.[5] Moore and Vaughan have stressed that no matter how '"new" a situation may be, it will have to be appropriated to a certain extent in terms of a set of practices and discourses that are already known'.[6] It is the tension between continuity and change that has been at the heart of this work.

Each thematic chapter of this book has set out and tested one hypothesis about the course of social change in Mwinilunga. These hypotheses have been formulated within the metanarrative of social change, which has prevailed among officials, scholars, and the local population for much of the twentieth century. Challenging trends of capitalist penetration, state integration, or family nucleation, events in Mwinilunga appear to have taken a different course. Predictions of linear transitions from subsistence to market production, from self-sufficiency to consumerism, from immobility to mobility, or from kinship to individualisation have proven far from straightforward.[7] Categories were messy from the outset, and simple narratives fail to capture the ambiguous course of historical practice. Rather than analysing change through ideas of 'development' or 'modernisation', the course of history in Mwinilunga can be better understood by adopting terms such as the 'foundations of production', 'culture of mobility', 'self-realisation', or 'wealth in people'. These terms point towards long-term trends and continuities, thereby arguing that change was domesticated within existing patterns of thought, action, and daily life.[8] Change was incremental, building on existing foundations rather than transforming these.[9] This book has asserted that people in Mwinilunga showed a distinct ability to incorporate change continuously, yet that they did so in a way that accorded with existing methods of production, ideology, and interpersonal relationships, thereby projecting an image of continuity towards the outside world.[10]

---

5   Pritchett, *Lunda-Ndembu*; see also Spear, *Mountain Farmers*.
6   Moore and Vaughan, *Cutting Down Trees*, 233.
7   See: Thomas, 'Modernity's Failings', 727–40; Cooper, 'What is the Concept of Globalization Good for?', 189–213.
8   For a similar argument, see Prestholdt, *Domesticating the World*.
9   Feierman, *Peasant Intellectuals*.
10   Pritchett, *Lunda-Ndembu*; Spear, *Mountain Farmers*; Feierman, *Peasant Intellectuals*.

This book has sought various roads through Mwinilunga, as roads 'carry us back and forth between the sweeping narratives of globalisation, and the specific, tangible materialities of particular times and places'.[11] The inhabitants of Mwinilunga moved incessantly. In the 1950s, there was a trend of movement towards the roadside, yet this movement did not entail a straightforward step towards 'development' or 'modernity', as contemporary observers expected. Turner's predictions of village disintegration, individualisation, and capitalist penetration did not hold true.[12] Rather, people in Mwinilunga continued to live in villages, to attach importance to ties of extended kinship, and to produce cassava next to cash crops. This evidenced an ability to incorporate change within existing frameworks and historical practice. Instead of being driven by external forces, individuals were able to reconfigure influences of colonialism and capitalism so that these would fit into familiar conceptualisations and ways of doing.[13] Individuals moved towards the roadside to take advantage of opportunities, but this did not necessarily involve abandoning existing forms of social organisation, patterns of livelihood procurement, or modes of thought. The movement towards the roadside was not a step towards government control or market involvement. Instead, forms of village residence, social organisation, and tradition retained importance and served to negotiate, appropriate, and domesticate change. Social change did not follow the course predicted by officials, experts, or scholars, but became incorporated into flexible and changing patterns of historical practice.[14]

This study of Mwinilunga has argued for the local specificity of social change. Social change cannot be adequately understood within universal frameworks. Carefully located case studies are necessary to 'accurately describe *African historical trajectories* and contemporary realities, rather than simply forcing these to conform to theoretical templates carved from Western history'.[15] Perhaps exactly because of its location on the margins of the state and major markets, people in Mwinilunga were able to more freely negotiate change.[16] The case of Mwinilunga illustrates the impact of 'large forces', such as colonialism, capitalism, or globalisation, by stressing their internally negotiated, rather

---

11   Dimitris Dalakoglou and Penny Harvey, 'Roads and Anthropology: Ethnographic Perspectives on Space, Time and (Im)Mobility', *Mobilities* 7, No. 4 (2012): 459. See also Beck, Klaeger, and Stasik, *The Making of the African Road*.
12   Turner, *Schism and Continuity*.
13   See parallels in Spear, *Mountain Farmers*.
14   Pritchett, *Lunda-Ndembu*.
15   Crehan, *The Fractured Community*, 229.
16   Cooper, 'What is the Concept of Globalization Good for?'; compare with: Piot, *Remotely Global.*

than external or transformative nature. Idiosyncrasies and anomalies can be illustrative of the working of markets, states, and capital.[17] Through a specific case, Crehan argues, 'on the one hand, we can begin to understand something of the role of overarching global relationships in creating local heterogeneity; and, on the other, also begin to rethink some of those broad narratives'.[18] Markets, state policies, and development schemes could not operate through 'one size fits all' measures. Rather, the outcome of interactions depended on agency and local specificity. However small a case might appear, 'it is in the intimate context of lives lived (...) that larger processes and policies have their effects, and indeed, to a certain extent, their origins'.[19]

The chapters of this book have placed historical practice at the centre of analysis. In Mwinilunga historical practices have been continuously and creatively reworked, and they are therefore essential to an understanding of processes of social change. This book has juxtaposed historical practice to narratives of social change. The two have been studied in conjunction, as they stand in a dialectical relationship: 'hegemonic accounts are, to however small a degree, shaped by the concrete conditions that they attempt to explain'.[20] Descriptions of historical practice 'are formulated in terms of existing discourses, and they take shape in the light of previous histories; as such, they are grafted onto a version of the past to be remade in the present'.[21] Social change, far from being external or transformative, was locally negotiated in accordance with forms of historical practice, which underwent continuous but gradual change. Forms of gradually changing historical practice generated a sense of long-term continuity in Mwinilunga District.

Village life, social organisation, and idioms of tradition retained their salience, whilst continuously incorporating change. Struggles within society over new forms of wealth generated through labour migration could lead to contestations of categories of gender, age, and social hierarchy. Even if such contestations evoked a negotiation and rearticulation of existing categories, these categories were not necessarily transformed; in some cases they could be revitalised. Labour migration and mass-manufactured consumer goods, such as bicycles, radios, or cloth, could lead to new tensions and power relationships, which were nevertheless channelled through familiar patterns of action, thought, and social organisation. Concepts of 'wealth in people' and

---

17   See: Thomas, 'Modernity's Failings'; Cooper, 'What is the Concept of Globalization Good for?'
18   Crehan, *The Fractured Community*, 233.
19   Moore and Vaughan, *Cutting Down Trees*, 232.
20   Crehan, *The Fractured Community*, 226.
21   Moore and Vaughan, *Cutting Down Trees*, 233.

'self-realisation' lay at the basis of labour migration and motivated the acquisition of consumer goods and their social usage. Consumption revolved around the human factor and did not lead to an axiomatic dependence on the market. Contrary to expectations, market involvement in Mwinilunga proved fluctuating rather than progressive. The desire to generate a stable basis of subsistence often figured more prominently in producer deliberations than objectives of profit-maximisation. The foundations of production, which encompass repertoires, values, and rationales, are therefore imperative to an understanding of market involvement or non-involvement in Mwinilunga. Capitalist models of market integration fail to explain why the shift of settlements towards the roadside did not automatically lead to market production or scientific methods of farming.[22] Alternative concepts and frameworks are thus called for, and these have been proposed in the chapters of this work.

The case study of Mwinilunga has sought to contribute to three general debates in Zambian and Central African historiography, namely those on labour migration, capitalism, and kinship. This book has primarily argued that local specificity should be substituted for universal claims about the course of history. Labour migration, rather than being analysed within a 'modernist narrative', can be better understood by looking at life histories and at the variety of migrant trajectories.[23] In the area of Mwinilunga, labour migration built on a culture of mobility, which shaped both the incentives and objectives of migration. Rather than fitting into fixed stages of migration, leading to either rural prosperity or breakdown, labour migration had a variety of possible outcomes, depending on individual trajectories, aims for self-realisation, and the specificity of the local setting.[24] Capitalism should equally be approached with local specificity.[25] Capitalist penetration did not lead to either development or underdevelopment, but had a variety of effects, being negotiated through a foundation of production and through notions of wealth in people and self-realisation. Kinship, likewise, should not be viewed within a framework of breakdown or individualisation, as kinship proved flexible and adaptive to change, retaining importance over time.[26] Dominant narratives, advanced by officials, policy-makers or academics, suggest linear and transformative processes of social change. Yet such representations obscure historical practice, which is ambiguous, diffuse, and gradually changing.[27] In order to understand

---

22   See the previous chapters, especially Chapters 2 and 4.
23   Ferguson, *Expectations of Modernity*; Andersson, 'Informal Moves', 375–97.
24   See Andersson, 'Re-interpreting the Rural-Urban Connection', 82–112.
25   See Crehan, *The Fractured Community*.
26   See: Moore and Vaughan, *Cutting Down Trees*; Berry, *No Condition Is Permanent*.
27   See Moore and Vaughan, *Cutting Down Trees*.

processes of social change it is necessary to adopt an analytical framework that more closely reflects the course of historical practice.

Even as this work has applied a broad-ranging thematic approach, a number of topics have been left largely untouched. Much more could be explored with regard to themes of religion or formal politics. Turner's seminal studies laid the basis for our understanding of religion and ritual in Mwinilunga District, whereas Pritchett and Kalusa have built on and expanded Turner's work.[28] Historical research into religious subjects would most definitely prove valuable. The topic of formal politics, as opposed to the everyday micro-politics explored in Chapter 5, are addressed in a separate article.[29] Many themes touched upon throughout this work deserve further elaboration, notably the role of initiation ceremonies and changes in marriage patterns. Overall, it has been argued that changes within the spheres of production, mobility, consumption, and social relationships did not occur at the same pace, but cut across each other. Social, economic, and political change did not concur within a 'total social field'.[30] In order to reach conclusions about the nature, pace, and direction of social change, an attempt has been made to counterpoise linear narratives of social change with the historical and local specificity of Mwinilunga District. Yet there remains much scope for future research, which might refine or challenge the line of argument proposed here.

The locality of Mwinilunga has been embedded within a broader regional and historical context. The case of Mwinilunga holds comparative potential, generating insight into broader trends, and historical developments. Nonetheless, the specificity of historical events, personal experiences and processes of social change in Mwinilunga District have to be stressed. Although certain aspects of the general argument can be extrapolated to other areas or settings, suggesting for example the feeble nature of colonial rule in the opening decades of the twentieth century in Central Africa or the inadequacy of prevailing periodisation into pre-colonial, colonial, or post-colonial periods, this book makes no claims of general applicability. The account provided here might not apply to Zambia's Southern or Northern Province. This book has merely argued that linear narratives – adopting ideas of 'development' or 'modernity', and postulating a clear direction of historical change – should be nuanced

---

28   Turner, *Schism and Continuity*; Pritchett, *Lunda-Ndembu*; Kalusa, 'Disease and the Remaking of Missionary Medicine'.

29   This article focuses on the interaction between national and local politics, by analysing the rivalry between UNIP and ANC from the 1950s to the 1970s: Peša, 'We Have Killed This Animal Together.'

30   See the Introduction for the RLI discussion on the 'total social field'.

by accounts of local specificity.[31] Broad generalisations need to be reassessed through specific case studies, for only then can historical understanding be advanced.

Current practices in the area of Mwinilunga have constantly adapted to changing circumstances and a complex setting, involving local, regional, national and international factors and actors. Over the course of the twentieth century, village organisation and social relationships have changed profoundly. Influenced by social change, categories of kinship, age, and gender have been questioned, authority has been redefined, and tradition has been negotiated. Yet change did not lead to a demise of previous practices, which in most cases proved flexible and resilient. Tradition has changed and adapted, yet it has retained its salience and it has provided the inhabitants of Mwinilunga District with the power to domesticate and make sense of change.[32] In this sense, tradition offers, as Schoenbrun states, 'to modern people a reservoir, a shared past, which they might draw on to face problems in the present'.[33] Due to the incorporation of change, past practices continued to be significant, and that is why people in Mwinilunga still avow that they have kept hold of their traditions. In 'tradition' the inhabitants of Mwinilunga District oppose themselves to the 'modernist narrative', proposed by RLI scholars and replicated in much later historiography.[34] In such an understanding of a flexible tradition lies the key to solving the paradox between continuity and change. A tradition that incorporates change yet retains its form and importance over time enables a different understanding of the process of social change in Mwinilunga.

---

31   See: Ferguson, *Expectations of Modernity*; Crehan, *The Fractured Community*; Moore and Vaughan, *Cutting Down Trees*.
32   Vansina, *Paths in the Rainforests*.
33   David L. Schoenbrun, *A Green Place, a Good Place: Agrarian Change, Gender and Social Identity in the Great Lakes Region to the 15th Century* (Portsmouth: Heinemann, 1998), 3.
34   Ferguson, *Expectations of Modernity*; Pritchett, *Lunda-Ndembu*.

Sources

I: Archival Sources

National Archives of Zambia (NAZ), Lusaka, Zambia

British South Africa Company Papers

A1/1/12 Loc. 3975	Slave Trading North Western Rhodesia, 1909–1910.
A1/2/17 Loc. 3979	BSA2 Boundary Commission, 1911.
A2/1/1 Loc. 3980	Barotse Representative Indunas – Kasempa, 1907–1908.
A2/1/4 Loc. 3981	BSA 2 Tax Evasion.
A3/7/1 Loc. 3985	North Western Rhodesia Correspondence Boundaries General, 1909–1911.
A3/28/2 Loc. 3996	Rubber Legislation, 1903–1909.
A5/1/5 Loc. 4002	Land Department Annual Report, 1908–1910.
A5/2/1 Loc. 4003	Balunda District Annual Report, 1908–1909.
A5/2/9 Loc. 4005	Lunda District Annual Report, 1910–1911.
BS2/199 IN2/1/3	Balunda District Monthly Reports.
HC1/2/43 Loc. 130	MacGregor's Conduct.

Manuscripts, Diaries, and Personal Papers

HM6/CO3/3/1	Edward Arden Copeman Papers.
HM6/CO3/4/1	Edward Arden Copeman Papers.
HM6/CO3/4/3–4	Edward Arden Copeman Papers.
HM8/FI2/6/1/1	Walter and Anna Fisher Correspondences and Diaries, Folios 1485–1857.
HM8/FI2/6/2	Eileen Darling Correspondences.
HM8/FI4/2/1	Singleton Fisher Papers.
HM17/MI5/1	Frederick Vernon Bruce-Miller Papers.
HM17/MI5/2	Frederick Vernon Bruce-Miller Papers.
HM70/9	NRANC Newsletters, 1953–1957.
HM77/PP/1	Peter Matoka Papers.
HM77/PP/2	Peter Matoka Papers.
HM84/PP/1	Andrew Sardanis Papers.

District Notebooks and Reports

KDD4/1/1	Kasempa District Inspection of Mwinilunga District, 1925–1929.
KDD5/1	Kasempa District Notebooks.
KDE8/1/1	Barotseland Annual Reports, 1906–1907.
KSE	Files Mwinilunga Sub-District, 1908–1929.

KSE1/1/1	Mwinilunga Sub-District Correspondence Recruitment of Labour, 1914–1917.
KSE1/2/1	Mwinilunga Sub-District Correspondence Native Authorities, 1929–1930.
KSE1/3/1	Mwinilunga Sub-District Correspondence Roads and Routes, 1916–1923.
KSE3/1/2/1	North Western Rhodesia, Native Cases Civil.
KSE3/2/1/1	Mwinilunga Sub-District Magistrate's Court Criminal Records, 1922–1923.
KSE3/2/2/1	Mwinilunga Sub-District Magistrate's Court Criminal Records, 1909–1911.
KSE3/2/2/2	Mwinilunga Sub-District Native Commissioner and Assistant Magistrate Court Criminal Cases 1915.
KSE3/2/2/7	Mwinilunga Sub-District Criminal Cases, 1928–1929.
KSE4/1	Mwinilunga District Notebooks.
KSE5/1	Mwinilunga Sub-District, Native Commissioner's Court Register, 1914–1919.
KSE5/4/1+2	Mwinilunga Sub-District, Tax Register, 1925–1929.
KSE6/1/1	Mwinilunga Sub-District Annual Reports, 1908–1911.
KSE6/1/2	Mwinilunga Sub-District Annual Reports, 1911–1914.
KSE6/1/3	Mwinilunga Sub-District Annual Reports, 1914–1920.
KSE6/1/4	Mwinilunga Sub-District Annual Reports, 1920–1925.
KSE6/1/5	Mwinilunga Sub-District Annual Reports, 1925–1927.
KSE6/1/6	Mwinilunga Sub-District Annual Reports, 1928–1929.
KSE6/2/1	Mwinilunga Sub-District Half Yearly and Quarterly Reports, 1911–1917.
KSE6/2/2	Mwinilunga Sub-District Half Yearly and Quarterly Reports, 1918–1929.
KSE6/3/1	Mwinilunga Sub-District Report Indaba, 1916.
KSE6/3/2	Mwinilunga Sub-District Report Indaba, 1927–1929.
KSE6/4/1	Mwinilunga Sub-District Reports Lunda Tribe, 1917.
KSE6/5/1	Mwinilunga Sub-District Monthly Reports, 1908–1910.
KSE6/6/1	Mwinilunga Sub-District Tour Reports, 1909–1910.
KSE6/6/2	Mwinilunga Sub-District Tour Reports, 1924–1929.

Secretariat Files

SEC2/41	Development of Mwinilunga – Benguela Railway, 1937.
SEC2/46	Redistribution of Districts Western Province.
SEC2/64	Kasempa Quarterly Reports.
SEC2/131	Kasempa Province Annual Reports, 1929–1930.
SEC2/133	Mwinilunga District Annual Reports, 1935–1937.
SEC2/135	North Western Province Annual Reports, 1951–1952.

SEC2/136	North Western Province Annual Report, 1953.
SEC2/137	North Western Province Annual Reports, 1954–1955.
SEC2/151	Western Province Annual Report, 1937.
SEC2/153	Western and Kaonde-Lunda Provinces Annual Report, 1939.
SEC2/154	Western Province Annual Report, 1947.
SEC2/155	Western Province Annual Report, 1948.
SEC2/156	Western Province Annual Report, 1949.
SEC2/157	Western Province District and Provincial Organisation Annual Reports, 1950–1951.
SEC2/177	Western Province District Commissioners' Conferences, 1936–1939.
SEC2/185	Kaonde-Lunda Province District Commissioners' Conferences, 1946–1956.
SEC2/193	Kaonde-Lunda Province Newsletters, 1941–1946.
SEC2/222	Native Government Re-Organisation Kaonde-Lunda Province.
SEC2/230	Kaonde-Lunda Province Regional Councils, 1944–1947.
SEC2/257	Native Industries – Restrictions on the Sale of Foodstuffs, 1934–1947.
SEC2/258	Industries and Trade – Agriculture – General Development and Improvement, 1931–1944.
SEC2/279	Kaonde-Lunda Province: Five Year Development Plan, 1943.
SEC2/304	Chiefs and Headmen Recognition Kaonde-Lunda Province.
SEC2/326	Native Land Tenure, 1947–1948.
SEC2/336	Peasant Farm Blocks: Experimental Schemes, 1947–1948.
SEC2/346	Native Tax Ordinance, 1938.
SEC2/402	Proposal for Sailunga Native Administration.
SEC2/952	Mwinilunga District Tour Reports, 1932–1933.
SEC2/953	Mwinilunga District Tour Reports, 1933–1939.
SEC2/954	Mwinilunga District Tour Reports, 1939–1940.
SEC2/955	Mwinilunga District Tour Reports, 1940–1948.
SEC2/956	Mwinilunga District Tour Reports, 1948.
SEC2/957	Mwinilunga District Tour Reports, 1949.
SEC2/958	Mwinilunga District Tour Reports, 1950–1951.
SEC2/959	Mwinilunga District Tour Reports, 1951.
SEC2/960	Mwinilunga District Tour Reports, 1952.
SEC2/961	Mwinilunga District Tour Reports, 1953.
SEC2/962	Mwinilunga District Tour Reports, 1954.
SEC2/963	Mwinilunga District Tour Reports, 1955.
SEC2/964	Photographs as Attachments to Tour Reports.
SEC2/965	Mwinilunga District Tour Reports, 1956.
SEC2/966	Mwinilunga District Tour Reports, 1958.
SEC2/967	Mwinilunga District Tour Reports, 1959.
SEC2/968	Mwinilunga District Tour Reports, 1960.

SEC2/1126	Native Newspapers, 1930–1936.
SEC2/1127	Native Newspapers, 1936.
SEC3/192	Provincial Roads Advisory Committee, Kaonde-Lunda Province.
SEC3/289	Anglo-Belgian Boundary Commission Vol. I.
SEC3/290	Anglo-Belgian Boundary Commission, 1928–1929.
SEC3/291	Anglo-Belgian Boundary Commission Vol. II.
SEC3/320	Native Reserves – Land Commission Mwinilunga District.
SEC5/136	Development Area Schools, North Western Province.
SEC5/153	District Commissioners Conference Western Province.
SEC5/214	Land Policy North Western Province.
SEC5/217	Land North Western Province, Native Trust Land.
SEC5/242	Misconduct of Chiefs, Chief Chibwika.
SEC5/320	Native Courts North Western Province.
SEC5/364	Native Trust Land North Western Province, Fisher's Farm.
SEC5/420	Provincial and District Organisation North Western Province.
SEC5/431	Provincial Native Treasury Funds North Western Province.
SEC6/422	Western Province Solwezi Reports Game Ranger.
SEC6/894	Mwinilunga Boma Water Supply, 1959.

North Western Province Reports and Papers

NWP1/1/7	Loc.4887 Development Team Minutes, 1950–1952.
NWP1/1/15	Loc.4889 District Development Teams, 1952–1954.
NWP1/1/25	Loc.4892 Development Team Minutes, 1954.
NWP1/2/2	Loc.4897 Mwinilunga District Travelling Reports, 1934–1939.
NWP1/2/7	Loc.4898 Mwinilunga District Travelling Reports, Native Case: Tax & Labour, 1937–1940.
NWP1/2/10	Loc.4898 Mwinilunga District Travelling Reports, 1939.
NWP1/2/12	Loc.4899 Mwinilunga District Travelling Reports, 1940–1946.
NWP1/2/17	Mwinilunga District Travelling Reports, 1946–1949.
NWP1/2/21	Loc.4901 Mwinilunga District, Agricultural Instructors Reports, 1949–1950.
NWP1/2/26	Loc.4901 Mwinilunga District Travelling Reports, 1949.
NWP1/2/29	Angola – Reports and General, 1950.
NWP1/2/33	Mwinilunga District Tour Reports, 1950.
NWP1/2/37	Loc.4903 Mwinilunga District Annual Report, 1950.
NWP1/2/38	Loc.4903 Tour Reports by African Staff.
NWP1/2/40	Mwinilunga District Tour Reports, 1950–1952.
NWP1/2/43	Loc.4905 North Western Province Annual Reports by Departmental Officers, 1951–1953.

NWP1/2/51   North Western Province Tours by Ministers and Heads of
                 Departments, 1956–1958.
NWP1/2/52   Mwinilunga District Annual Report, 1952.
NWP1/2/57   Loc.4908 Mwinilunga District Tour Reports, 1953.
NWP1/2/63   Loc.4910 Mwinilunga District Tour Reports, 1954.
NWP1/2/65   Loc.4910 Mwinilunga District Tour Reports 1954 Overflow.
NWP1/2/68   Loc.4911 North Western Province Departmental Annual Reports,
                 1954–1955.
NWP1/2/75   Loc.4913 Mwinilunga District Tour Reports, 1955.
NWP1/2/78   Loc.4913 North Western Province Annual Reports, 1955–1961.
NWP1/2/83   Loc.4914 North Western Province Departmental Annual Reports,
                 1956–1958.
NWP1/2/90   Loc.4916 Reports and Returns: Labour in Mwinilunga District,
                 1955–1961.
NWP1/2/101   Loc.4919 Northern Rhodesia Annual Reports 1960s.
NWP1/2/102   Loc.4919 North Western Province Annual Reports, 1960–1962.
NWP1/2/105   Loc.4920 North Western Province Annual Report, 1963.
NWP1/3/2   Loc.4921 Native Authority and Chief's Policy.
NWP1/10/2   Loc.4941 Chiefs and Headmen.
NWP1/12/1   Loc.4947 Native Affairs General.
NWP1/12/18   Loc.4951 African Land Tenure General.
NWP1/12/23   Sailunga Kindred Native Administration Harry Vaux.

Magisterial Papers and Reports

MAG1/10/1   Loc.76 North Western Province Agricultural Development,
                 1946–1960.
MAG1/18/6   North Western Province Tour Reports, Ministry of Agriculture,
                 1959–1965.
MAG1/20/4   Cassava, 1960–1968.
MAG2/2/25   Loc.114 North Western Province, Provincial Team Minutes,
                 1953–1958.
MAG2/2/45   Loc.118 North Western Province, Provincial Team Minutes,
                 1958–1961.
MAG2/3/41   Provincial Young Farmers Club Council Minutes.
MAG2/5/9   Loc.131 Native Agriculture – North Western Province Tour Reports,
                 1939–1940.
MAG2/5/91   Loc.144 North Western Province Tours Agriculture, 1964–1971.
MAG2/9/3   Loc.170 Ecological Survey Reports.
MAG2/9/4   Loc.170 J.N. Clothier Ecological Survey Report, 1932–1933.

MAG2/9/6   Loc.170 Ecological Survey General.
MAG2/9/9   Loc.170 Ecological Survey General.
MAG2/9/11   Loc.171 Economic Survey and Agricultural Statistics.
MAG2/17/86   Loc.199 Pineapples.
MAG2/18/3   Stock Taking North Western Province.
MAG2/21/86   North Western Province General.
MAG4/3/24   Agricultural Productivity Committee North Western Province,
                1968

Ministry of Community Development

MCD1/3/12   North Western Province, Native Treasury Committee.
MCD1/3/13   Loc. 4440 Provincial Team Minutes North Western Province.
MCD1/3/21   Area Team Minutes, Mwinilunga, North Western Province.
MCD1/3/29   Rural Development, Provincial Team Minutes North Western
                Province.

Ministry of Commerce and Industry

MCI2/2/18   Norton Company Limited.
MCI2/2/27   Pioneer Stores Limited.

Ministry of Land and Works

ML1/16/6   Loc.4575 Beeswax and Honey Co-Operatives.
MLW1/1/21   Loc.5693 Provincial Team Minutes, North Western Province,
                1964.
MRD1/8/27   Loc. 4272 Regional Development Committee, North Western
                Province, 1969–1970.

Ministry of Local Government and Housing

LGH1/17/1   Loc.3498 Ministry of Agriculture Correspondence.
LGH1/18/97   Provincial Team North Western Province.
LGH5/1/3   Loc.3604 Minutes of the Mwinilunga Rural Council.
LGH5/1/8   Loc.3605 Provincial Local Government Service Board, North
                Western Province.
LGH5/1/10   Loc.3608 Mwinilunga Rural Council, 1967–1972.
LGH5/2/1   Provincial Four-Year Development Plan, North Western Province,
                1956.
LGH5/2/2   Loc.3611 District Commissioners Conferences, North Western
                Province.
LGH5/2/4   Loc.3611 Mwinilunga Areas and Boundaries.

LGH5/2/5	Loc.3612 North Western Province Rural Economic Development, 1960–1968.
LGH5/2/7	Loc.3612 North Western Province Development, 1964–1968.
LGH5/2/8	Loc.3613 Resident Secretaries Conferences.
LGH5/2/9	Loc.3613 The National Convention Committee, 1967.
LGH5/3/2	Loc.3614 Mwinilunga Rural Council, Rules and Orders.
LGH5/4/2	Loc.3615 Internal Security Scheme, Mwinilunga.
LGH5/4/5	Loc.3616 Mwinilunga District Chiefs.
LGH5/4/12	Loc.3618 House of Chiefs.
LGH5/5/5	Loc.3620 Tours by the Governor.
LGH5/5/6	Health, Taxation, Miscellaneous.
LGH5/5/7	Loc.3621 Women's Work, North Western Province.
LGH5/5/8	Mwinilunga District Development Plan, 1956.
LGH5/5/11	Loc.3621 African Land Tenure.
LGH5/5/12	Agriculture General, 1968–1970.
LGH5/5/14	Loc.3619 Tours by Governor, 1957.

Cabinet Office

| CO3/1/36 | Census of Population, 1963–1967. |
| CO4/1/3 | National Development Plans North Western Province, 1965–1967. |

Library, Government Publications, and Reports

Northern Rhodesia – Agriculture Annual Reports, 1913–1920.

Northern Rhodesia – Agriculture Annual Reports, 1920–1934.

Northern Rhodesia – Agriculture Annual Reports, 1935–1956.

Mwinilunga District Show June 15th 1956.

African Provincial Council, North Western Province, 1954–1958.

Ministry of Agriculture, Monthly Economic Bulletin, 1966–1970.

Annual Report of the Ministry of Agriculture, 1964–1965.

Agricultural Marketing Committee, 1965–68.

First National Development Plan, 1966–70.

Department of Co-Operatives Annual Report 1969.

Report of the Second National Convention on Rural Development, 1969.

A New Strategy for Rural Development in Zambia, 1970.

Department of Marketing Annual Report, 1970–1977.

R.C. Kamanga Address to the District Governor's Workshop, 1971.

Pineapple Production Questions and Answers, Radio Farm Forum, 1973.

Programme for the Nation, Rural Development Seminar, 1974.

Yearbook of the Ministry of Rural Development, 1975.

Quarterly Agricultural Statistical Bulletin, 1975.
Department of Community Development, Annual Reports, 1968–1980.

    Newspapers
Mutende   1936, 1937, 1941, 1942, 1943, 1944, 1945, 1947, 1948, 1949, 1950.
Times of Zambia 1966.

United National Independence Party Archives (UNIPA), Lusaka, Zambia

    African National Congress (ANC)
ANC2/1   Arrangements of Visits and Tours, 1954–1962.
ANC2/4   ANC Statistical Records, General, 1959.
ANC2/7   Correspondences North Western Province, 1960–1965.
ANC2/11   ANC Reports, 1961–1963.
ANC2/18   General Correspondence, 1956–1963.
ANC3/7   Chiefs and Tribal History, 1954–1961.
ANC3/8   Native Authority Rules and Orders, Anti-ANC, 1954–1961.
ANC3/10   Education and Schools, 1953–1959.
ANC3/20   Federal Scheme, 1952–1958.
ANC3/21   General Correspondence, 1957–1962.
ANC3/24   Government Anti-Congress Propaganda, 1953–1961.
ANC3/26   New Branches Registration, 1957–1962.
ANC3/30   ANC Correspondence with Government, 1960–1961.
ANC4/4   Annual General Conference, 1956–1964.
ANC4/9   Minutes, 1962–1969.
ANC5/18   Correspondence on Labour, 1953–1961.
ANC5/19   Minutes, 1956–1969.
ANC7/14   Minutes and Circulars, 1968–1972.
ANC7/15   Correspondence, 1964–1970.
ANC7/23   Independence Constitution, 1964.
ANC7/24   Local Government Elections, 1964–1972.
ANC7/30   Correspondence, 1965–1972.
ANC7/32   General, 1960–1972.
ANC7/34   Correspondence, 1964–1972.
ANC7/45   Minutes, 1962–1969.
ANC7/88   Zambezi River Transport, 1962–1967.
ANC9/51   Registers from Provinces, 1962–1964.

    United National Independence Party (UNIP)
UNIP1/1/2   1961–1963: National Council Minutes.
UNIP1/1/6   1963–1967: National Council Minutes.

UNIP1/1/7	1964–1965: National Council Minutes.
UNIP1/1/8	1964–1967: National Council Minutes.
UNIP1/1/9	1965–1966: National Council Minutes.
UNIP1/1/10	1965–1971: National Council Minutes.
UNIP1/1/11	1967: First National Convention Zambia.
UNIP1/1/15	1969–1971: National Council Minutes.
UNIP1/1/18	1967–1972: National Council Minutes.
UNIP1/2/5	1969: National Council, North Western Province Report.
UNIP1/2/12	1973–1974: National Council and Province Reports.
UNIP1/2/13	1975: National Council, North Western Province Report.
UNIP1/2/21	1977: National Council, North Western Province Report.
UNIP1/2/30	1978: National Council and Province Reports.
UNIP1/2/31	1974: National Council, Annual Report.
UNIP1/2/33	1974: National Council, Reports from Provinces.
UNIP1/2/35	1974–1975: National Council, Reports.
UNIP1/2/39	1978: National Council, Provincial Reports.
UNIP1/2/42	1979: National Council, Annual Reports.
UNIP1/3/23	1979: Blue Print for Economic Development.
UNIP5/3/1/T/8	1967–1969: Mwinilunga District Transport.
UNIP5/3/1/1	1961–1963: UNIP Regional Headquarters Solwezi-Mwinilunga Correspondence.
UNIP5/3/1/5	1962: UNIP Regional Headquarters North Western Province Registers.
UNIP5/3/1/8	1962–1963: UNIP Regional Headquarters Solwezi-Mwinilunga Correspondence.
UNIP5/3/1/13	1962–1965: UNIP Regional Headquarters Solwezi-Mwinilunga Correspondence.
UNIP5/3/1/17	1963: UNIP Regional Headquarters Mwinilunga Correspondence.
UNIP5/3/1/20	1963–1966: UNIP Regional Headquarters Correspondence Mwinilunga.
UNIP5/3/1/26	1964–1966: UNIP Regional Headquarters Correspondence Mwinilunga.
UNIP5/3/1/28	1966: UNIP National Headquarters Mwinilunga Correspondence.
UNIP5/3/1/30	1966–1969: UNIP National Headquarters Mwinilunga Correspondence.
UNIP5/3/1/40	1967–1969: UNIP Regional Headquarters Mwinilunga Correspondence.
UNIP5/3/1/48	1969–1973: UNIP Regional Headquarters Mwinilunga Correspondence.
UNIP5/3/1/52	1970–1973: UNIP Regional Headquarters Mwinilunga Correspondence.

UNIP5/3/1/57   1964–1970: Chief's Correspondences with UNIP, Mwinilunga.

UNIP5/3/1/60   1977: Provincial Political Committee North Western Province
                 Minutes.

UNIP5/3/1/62   1962: Regional Headquarters Solwezi-Mwinilunga
                 Correspondence.

UNIP5/3/2/1/1   1964–1969: District Secretaries North Western Province
                 Independence Celebrations.

UNIP5/3/2/1/2   1969–1973: District Governor Mwinilunga.

UNIP5/3/2/1/10   1977: District Governor Mwinilunga.

UNIP5/3/2/2/1   1965–1966: Correspondence Resident Minister North Western
                 Province.

UNIP5/3/2/2/2   1967–1969: Minister of State Correspondence North Western
                 Province.

UNIP5/3/2/2/3   1967–1969: Minister of State Correspondence North Western
                 Province.

UNIP5/3/2/2/4   1969–1973: Minister of State Correspondence North Western
                 Province.

UNIP5/3/2/2/5   1970–1972: Cabinet Minister Minutes North Western Province.

UNIP5/3/2/2/6   1972–1973: Cabinet Minister Minutes North Western Province.

UNIP5/3/2/2/7   1973–1977: Minister of State Minutes North Western Province.

UNIP5/3/2/2/8   1973: Minister of State Correspondence North Western
                 Province.

UNIP5/3/2/2/9   1978: Cabinet Minister Report North Western Province.

UNIP5/3/2/4/1   1972: Provincial Development Committee North Western
                 Province.

UNIP5/3/2/4/2   1977–1978: Provincial Development Committee North Western
                 Province.

UNIP5/3/2/5/1   1962: Elections Correspondence North Western Province.

UNIP5/3/2/6/2   1963: Elections Correspondence North Western Province.

UNIP5/3/2/6/2   1974–1984: District Councils North Western Province.

UNIP5/9/24   1974–1976: Provincial Administration Tour Reports, Local &
                 Foreign Tours by MCC.

UNIP5/9/26   1975: Provincial Administration Tour Reports, North Western
                 Province.

UNIP5/9/28   1975–1976: Provincial Administration Tour Reports, North Western
                 Province.

UNIP7/5/13   1976–1977: Ministry of Finance Correspondence.

UNIP7/10/1   UNIP Policy on Economy and Agriculture.

UNIP7/10/10   1968: National Agricultural Marketing Act.

UNIP7/25/3   1963: Proposed Feasibility Scheme for Poultry Projects, Northern
                 Rhodesia.

UNIP7/25/5	1965: Co-Operatives Correspondence.
UNIP8/1/66	1974–1976: Rural Development Committee Reports.
UNIP8/1/107	1976–1980: Central Committee, Visits and Tours within Zambia.
UNIP8/3/30	1975: Third National Development Plan.
UNIP8/3/43	1976–1978: Central Committee, Correspondence from Provinces.
UNIP8/3/44	1976–1978: Economics & Finance Committee.
UNIP8/5/2	1974: The Role of the Rural Development Committee, Minutes.
UNIP8/5/5	1974–1975: MCC Rural Development Committee, Memoranda.
UNIP8/5/17	1978–1980: Rural Development Committee Reports.
UNIP8/5/18	1975–1981: Rural Development Committee.
UNIP8/5/20	1976: Provincial Meetings Rural Development.
UNIP8/5/21	1976: Tour Reports Rural Development.
UNIP8/5/22	1976–1977: Rural Development Committee Minutes.
UNIP8/7/3	1974: Achievements to Social and Cultural Committee Resolutions.
UNIP8/9/7	1969: Central Committee Provinces, North Western Province Report.
UNIP8/9/8	1975: Central Committee Provinces, Reports and Meetings, North Western Province.
UNIP8/9/27	1976: Central Committee Provinces, MCC North Western Province Correspondence.
UNIP8/9/36	1980: Central Committee Provinces, MCC North Western Province.
UNIP8/9/46	1978: Central Committee Provinces, North Western Province Minutes.
UNIP8/11/26	1977: Co-Operative Movement.
UNIP8/12/2	1978: Central Committee Decentralisation, Report Seminars North Western Province.
UNIP10/1/25	1964–1966: Youth League Solwezi-Mwinilunga.
UNIP11/1/1	1961–1963: Women's League Solwezi-Mwinilunga.
UNIP11/1/69	1968: Women's League Mwinilunga.
UNIP12/1/34	1968–1969: Zambia African Traders Union.
UNIP15/1/15	1969: Census of Population.

Zambia Consolidated Copper Mines Archives (ZCCM), Ndola, Zambia

Northern Rhodesia African National Trade Unions, Rations	100.20.24, Loc.1.8.5B.
Second Report on Urban African Budget Survey, 1960	Loc. 1.9.2C.
Post-Retirement Plans of the Mine Labour Force	Loc. 3.1.5B.
African Housing	300.40.12, Loc. 11.6.7A.
African Housing, 1964–1965	300.40.14, Loc. 11.6.7A.

Local Employees Housing, 1965	300.40.15, Loc. 11.6.7B.
Commission of Enquiry, Housing and Social Services, 1966	300.40B.1, Loc. 11.6.7B.
Roan/Mpatamatu Management Board, 1968–1970	300.74.2.5, Loc. 11.6.7C.
Roan/Mpatamatu Management Board, 1973	300.74.2.7, Loc. 11.6.7C.
Mpatamatu Township Management Board, 1962–1964	300.74.2, Loc. 11.6.7C.
African Feeding, Malnutrition	205.11.1, Loc. 12.8.9F.
African Labour – Compound Manager's Committee General	202.14, Loc. 14.2.9B.
African Education – Luanshya Schools, 1930–1955	203.3.1, Loc. 15.1.7B.
African Education General – 1953–1956	203.3.1, Loc. 15.1.7B.
African Welfare – Luanshya	203.5, Loc. 15.1.7B.
African Welfare – Beer Halls and Canteens	203.6, Loc. 15.1.7B.
First Report on Urban African Budget Survey, 1960	Loc.17.2.5A.
The Structure of the Labour Force in the Copper Mining Industry	Loc.18.4.7E.
Conditions of Service, 1967–71	2.6C.1, Loc. 22.8.5C.

Personal Files, Nchanga Mine, Chingola, Lunda Workers from Mwinilunga, 18 Files

Rhodes House (BOD), Oxford, United Kingdom
Mss Afr. S 776 Theodore Williams Diaries 1912–1914.
Mss Afr. S 777 Theodore Williams Diaries 1913–1914.
Mss Afr. S 778 Theodore Williams Diaries 1915–1921.
Mss Afr. S 779 Theodore Williams Correspondences 1912–1914.
Mss Afr. S 780 Theodore Williams Correspondences 1915–1918.
Richard Cranmer Dening, Personal Papers, Uncatalogued, 15 Boxes.

Echoes of Service (EOS), John Rylands Library, Manchester, United Kingdom
Personal Files
Grace O. Adlington.
N.S. and O.R. Arnot.
Samuel and Jean Arnot.
Winifred D. Arnot.
Sydney Walter Buckland.
A.R. Chapman.
H. Cunningham and J. Cunningham.
Harry J.T. Faulkner and Ada Faulkner.
Wilfrid W. Revington Fisher and Georgina Fisher.
W. Singleton Fisher and M. Kitty Fisher.
A. Charles Fisher.
Alfred Digby Fisher.
Walter Fisher and Anna Fisher.

Walter ffolliott Fisher and Ethelynne Downing Fisher.

Annie E. Fulton.

Peggy E. Gilmour.

Adelaide Hobbs.

H. Julyan Hoyte.

Ruth Hurrell.

Laura M. Jacobs.

David W.S. Kaye and Roseannah Kaye.

Hilda Kelly.

Agnes A. Laird.

Catherine Anderson McGregor.

Elsie Burr-Milligan.

Charles Rowland Nightingale and Evelyn A. Nightingale.

Thomas Rea.

Agnes Lind Riddell.

Gordon Suckling and Peggy Suckling.

Echoes of Service Magazine, An Illustrated Record of Labour in the Lord's Name in Many Lands, 1906–1915, No. 593–814

Public Records Office (PRO), Kew, United Kingdom

AY 4/2786 Beeswax: Trade evaluation UK markets – Northern Rhodesia Office of the Chief Conservator of Forests.

CO 1015/1168 The Conduct of European Surveyors in the Mwinilunga District of Northern Rhodesia.

CO 1018/54 Western Province, Northern Rhodesia.

DO 35/385/5 Benguela Railway – Railway Connection to Kansanshi Copper Mine in N. Rhodesia, 12 June 1931.

FO 371/24063 Anglo-Portuguese Boundary Demarcation 1934.

OD 6/653 Air Photography and Topographical Survey N. Rhodesia.

II: Secondary Sources: Books and Articles

'The Barotse Boundary Award'. *The Geographical Journal* 26, No. 2 (1905): 201–04.

Abraham, Garth. "'Lines upon Maps": Africa and the Sanctity of African Boundaries'. *African Journal of International and Comparative Law* 15, No. 1 (2007): 61–84.

Achberger, Jessica. *Negotiating for Development: Zambian Economic Development in the Cold War.* Forthcoming.

Adas, Michael. *Machines as the Measure of Men: Science, Technology, and Ideologies of Western Dominance.* Ithaca: Cornell University Press, 1989.

Adenaike, Carolyn K., and Jan Vansina, eds. *In Pursuit of History: Fieldwork in Africa*. Portsmouth: Heinemann, 1996.

Allan, William. *The African Husbandman*. Münster: LIT Verlag, 1965.

Allina-Pisano, Eric. 'Borderlands, Boundaries, and the Contours of Colonial Rule: African Labor in Manica District, Mozambique, c. 1904–1908'. *The International Journal of African Historical Studies* 36, No. 1 (2003): 59–82.

Allman, Jean M., ed. *Fashioning Africa: Power and the Politics of Dress*. Bloomington: Indiana University Press, 2004.

Alpern, Stanley B. 'What Africans Got for Their Slaves: A Master List of European Trade Goods'. *History in Africa* 22 (1995): 5–43.

Amin, Samir. 'Underdevelopment and Dependence in Black Africa: Historical Origin'. *Journal of Peace Research* 9, No. 105 (1972): 105–19.

Andersson, Jens A. 'Re-interpreting the Rural-Urban Connection: Migration Practices and Sociocultural Dispositions of Buhera Workers in Harare'. *Africa* 71, No. 1 (2001): 82–112.

Andersson, Jens A. 'Administrators' Knowledge and State Control in Colonial Zimbabwe: The Invention of the Rural-Urban Divide in Buhera District, 1912–80'. *Journal of African History* 43, No. 1 (2002): 119–43.

Andersson, Jens A. 'Informal Moves, Informal Markets: International Migrants and Traders from Mzimba, Malawi'. *African Affairs* 105, No. 420 (2006): 375–97.

Appadurai, Arjun. 'Introduction: Commodities and the Politics of Value'. In *The Social Life of Things: Commodities in Cultural Perspective,* edited by Arjun Appadurai, 3–63. Cambridge: Cambridge University Press, 1986.

Appadurai, Arjun. *Modernity at Large: Cultural Dimensions of Globalization*. Minneapolis: University of Minnesota Press, 2003.

Arnot, Frederick S. *Garenganze, or, Seven Year's Pioneer Mission Work in Central Africa*. London: Paternoster, 1969.

Arnot, Frederick S. *Missionary Travels in Central Africa*. Bath: Echoes of Service, 1987.

Arrighi, Giovanni. 'Labour Supplies in Historical Perspective: A Study of Proletarianization of the African Peasantry in Rhodesia'. *The Journal of Development Studies* 6, No. 3 (1969/70): 197–234.

Atkins, Keletso E. '"Kafir Time": Preindustrial Temporal Concepts and Labour Discipline in Nineteenth-Century Colonial Natal'. *Journal of African History* 29, No. 2 (1988): 229–44.

Austen, Ralph A., and Daniel Headrick. 'The role of Technology in the African Past'. *African Studies Review* 26, No. 3/4 (1983): 163–84.

Austin, Gareth. 'Reciprocal Comparison and African History: Tackling Conceptual Eurocentrism in the Study of Africa's Economic Past'. *African Studies Review* 50, No. 3 (2007): 1–28.

Austin, Gareth. 'Resources, Techniques and Strategies South of the Sahara: Revising the Factor Endowments Perspective on African Economic Development, 1500–2000'. *Economic History Review* 61, No. 3 (2008): 587–624.

Bakewell, Oliver. 'Refugees Repatriating or Migrating Villagers: A Study of Movement from North West Zambia to Angola'. Unpublished PhD Thesis, University of Bath, 1999.

Bakewell, Oliver. 'Repatriation and Self-Settled Refugees in Zambia: Bringing Solutions to the Wrong Problems'. *Journal of Refugee Studies* 13, No. 4 (2000): 356–73.

Bakewell, Oliver. 'Repatriation: Angolan Refugees or Migrating Villagers?' in *Refugees and the Transformation of Society: Agency, Policies, Ethics and Politics,* edited by Philomena Essed, Georg Frerks and Joke Schrijvers, 31–41. New York: Berghahn, 2004.

Bakewell, Oliver. 'The Meaning and Use of Identity Papers: Handheld and Heartfelt Nationality in the Borderlands of North-West Zambia'. *International Migration Institute Working Paper 5,* University of Oxford, 2007.

Bakewell, Oliver. '"Keeping Them in Their Place": The Ambivalent Relationship Between Development and Migration in Africa'. *Third World Quarterly* 29, No. 7 (2008): 1341–58.

Barber, Karin. 'Money, Self-Realization and the Person in Yoruba Texts'. in *Money Matters: Instability, Values and Social Payments in the Modern History of West African Communities,* edited by Jane I. Guyer, 205–24. Portsmouth: Heinemann, 1995.

Barrett, Michael. 'The Social Significance of Crossing State Borders: Home, Mobility and Life Paths in the Angolan-Zambian Borderland'. in *Struggles for Home: Violence, Hope and the Movement of People,* edited by Stef Jansen and Staffan Löfving, 85–107. New York: Berghahn, 2009.

Barrett, Michael. '"Walking Home Majestically": Consumption and the Enactment of Social Status Among Labour Migrants from Barotseland, 1935–1965'. In *The Objects of Life in Central Africa: The History of Consumption and Social Change, 1840–1980,* edited by Robert Ross, Marja Hinfelaar and Iva Peša, 93–113. Leiden: Brill, 2013.

Bates, Robert H. 'Some Conventional Orthodoxies in the Study of Agrarian Change'. *World Politics* 36, No. 2 (1984): 234–54.

Bates, Robert H. 'Capital, Kinship, and Conflict: The Structuring Influence of Capital in Kinship Societies'. *Canadian Journal of African Studies* 24, No. 2 (1990): 151–64.

Beck, Kurt, Gabriel Klaeger and Michael Stasik, eds. *The Making of the African Road* (Leiden: Brill, 2017).

Beinart, William. *The Political Economy of Pondoland, 1860–1930.* Cambridge: Cambridge University Press, 1982.

Beinart, William, and Peter Coates. *Historical Connections: Environment and History, The Taming of Nature in the USA and South Africa.* London: Routledge, 1995.

Beinart, William. 'African History and Environmental History'. *African Affairs* 99, No. 395 (2000): 269–302.

Beinart, William, Karen Brown and Daniel Gilfoyle. 'Experts and Expertise in Colonial Africa Reconsidered: Science and the Interpenetration of Knowledge'. *African Affairs* 108, No. 432 (2009): 413–33.

Bennett, Jane. *Vibrant Matter: A Political Ecology of Things.* Durham: Duke University Press, 2010.

Berman, Bruce J., and John M. Lonsdale. *Unhappy Valley: Conflict in Kenya and Africa.* Athens: Ohio University Press, 1992.

Berry, Sara S. 'The Food Crisis and Agrarian Change in Africa: A Review Essay'. *African Studies Review* 27, No. 2 (1984): 59–112.

Berry, Sara S. 'Social Institutions and Access to Resources'. *Africa* 59, No. 1 (1989): 41–55.

Berry, Sara S. 'Hegemony on a Shoestring: Indirect Rule and Access to Agricultural Land'. *Africa* 62, No. 3 (1992): 327–55.

Berry, Sara S. *No Condition Is Permanent: The Social Dynamics of Agrarian Change in Sub-Saharan Africa.* Madison: University of Wisconsin Press, 1993.

Berry, Sara S. 'Stable Prices, Unstable Values: Some Thoughts on Monetization and the Meaning of Transactions in West African Economies'. In *Money Matters: Instability, Values and Social Payments in the Modern History of West African Communities,* edited by Jane I. Guyer, 299–313. Portsmouth: Heinemann, 1995.

Binsbergen, Wim M.J. 'Chiefs and the State in Independent Zambia: Exploring the Zambian National Press'. *Journal of Legal Pluralism and Unofficial Law* 25/6 (1987): 139–201.

Birmingham, David. *Frontline Nationalism in Angola and Mozambique.* London: Africa Research, 1992.

Bohannan, Paul. 'The Impact of Money on an African Subsistence Economy'. *Journal of Economic History* 19, No. 4 (1959): 491–503.

Bohannan, Paul J., and George Dalton, eds. *Markets in Africa.* Evanston: Northwestern University Press, 1962.

Bond, George C., and Diane Ciekawy, eds. *Witchcraft Dialogues: Anthropological and Philosophical Exchanges.* Athens: Ohio University Press, 2001.

Bonneuil, Christophe. 'Development as Experiment: Science and State Building in Late Colonial and Postcolonial Africa, 1930–1970'. *Osiris* 2, No. 15 (2000): 2–81.

Boone, Catherine. *Political Topographies of the African State: Territorial Authority and Institutional Choice.* Cambridge: Cambridge University Press, 2003.

Booth, William J. 'On the Idea of the Moral Economy'. *The American Political Science Review* 88, No. 3 (1994): 653–67.

Bowman, Andrew. 'Ecology to Technocracy: Scientists, Surveys and Power in the Agricultural Development of Late-Colonial Zambia'. *Journal of Southern African Studies* 37, No. 1 (2011): 135–53.

Bowman, Andrew. 'Mass Production or Production by the Masses? Tractors, Cooperatives, and the Politics of Rural Development in Post-Independence Zambia'. *Journal of African History* 52, No. 2 (2011): 201–21.

Brewer, John. 'Microhistory and the Histories of Everyday Life'. *Cultural and Social History* 7, No. 1 (2010): 87–109.

Burke, Timothy. *Lifebuoy Men, Lux Women: Commodification, Consumption and Cleanliness in Modern Zimbabwe.* Durham: Duke University Press, 1996.

Burke, Timothy. 'Unexpected Subversions'. In *The Oxford Handbook of the History of Consumption,* edited by Frank Trentmann, 467–84. Oxford: Oxford University Press, 2012.

Burr, Elsie. *Kalene Memories: Annals of the Old Hill.* London: Pickering & Inglis, 1956.

Burton, Andrew, "The Eye of the Authority': 'Native' Taxation, Colonial Governance and Resistance in Inter-War Tanganyika'. *Journal of Eastern African Studies* 2, No. 1 (2008): 74–94.

Bush, Barbara, and Josephine Maltby. 'Taxation in West Africa: Transforming the Colonial Subject into the "Governable Person"'. *Critical Perspectives on Accounting* 15 (2004): 5–34.

Bustin, Edouard. *Lunda Under Belgian Rule: The Politics of Ethnicity.* Lawrence: Harvard University Press, 1975.

Cameron, Verney L. *Across Africa.* New York: Harper & Brothers, 1885.

Capelo, Hermenegildo C.B, and Roberto Ivens. *De Benguela às terras de Iaca – Descrição de uma viagem na África central e occidental, 1887–1890 Vol. 1.* Coimbra, 1996.

Carswell, Grace. 'Food Crops as Cash Crops: The Case of Colonial Kigezi, Uganda'. *Journal of Agrarian Change* 3, No. 4 (2003): 521–51.

Carswell, Grace. 'Multiple Historical Geographies: Responses and Resistance to Colonial Conservation Schemes in East Africa'. *Journal of Historical Geography* 32 (2006): 398–421.

Carswell, Grace. *Cultivating Success in Uganda: Kigezi Farmers & Colonial Policies.* Oxford: James Currey, 2007.

Chabatama, Chewe M. 'Peasant Farming, The State, and Food Security in the North-Western Province of Zambia, 1902–1964'. Unpublished PhD Thesis, University of Toronto, 1999.

Chamberlain, David, ed. *Some Letters from Livingstone, 1840–72.* Oxford: Oxford University Press, 1940.

Chanock, Martin L. *Law, Custom and Social Order: The Colonial Experience in Malawi and Zambia.* Cambridge: Cambridge University Press, 1985.

Chauncey, George. 'The Locus of Reproduction: Women's Labour in the Zambian Copperbelt, 1927–1953'. *Journal of Southern African Studies* 7, No. 2 (1980/81): 135–64.

Chipungu, Samuel N., ed. *Guardians in Their Time: Experiences of Zambians Under Colonial Rule 1890–1964.* London: Macmillan, 1992.

Cocks, Paul M. 'Applied Anthropology or the Anthropology of Modernity?: Max Gluckman's Vision of Southern African Society, 1939–1947'. *Journal of Southern African Studies* 38, No. 3 (2012): 649–65.

Cohen, Jeffrey H., and Ibrahim Sirkeci. *Cultures of Migration: The Global Nature of Contemporary Mobility.* Austin: University of Texas Press, 2011.

Colson, Elizabeth. *Social Organization of the Gwembe Tonga.* Manchester: Manchester University Press, 1960.

Colson, Elizabeth. 'The Impact of the Colonial Period on the Definition of Land Rights'. In *Colonialism in Africa 1870–1960, Vol. 3, Profiles of Change: African Society and Colonial Rule,* edited by Victor W. Turner, 193–215. Cambridge: Cambridge University Press, 1971.

Colson, Elizabeth. 'The Father as Witch'. *Africa* 70, No. 3 (2000): 333–58.

Comaroff, John, and Jean Comaroff. 'The Madman and the Migrant: Work and Labor in the Historical Consciousness of a South African People'. *American Ethnologist* 14, No. 2 (1987): 191–209.

Comaroff, John, and Jean Comaroff. *Ethnography and the Historical Imagination.* Boulder: Westview Press, 1992.

Comaroff, John, and Jean Comaroff. *Of Revelation and Revolution: The Dialectics of Modernity on a South African Frontier, Volume Two.* Chicago: University of Chicago Press, 1997.

Cooper, Barbara. 'Women's Worth and Wedding Gift Exchange in Maradi, Niger, 1907–89'. *Journal of African History* 36, No. 1 (1995): 121–40.

Cooper, Barbara M. 'Oral Sources and the Challenge of African History'. In *Writing African History,* edited by John E. Philips, 191–215. Rochester: University of Rochester Press, 2005.

Cooper, Frederick. 'Africa and the World Economy'. *African Studies Review* 24, No. 2/3 (1981): 1–86.

Cooper, Frederick, ed. *Struggle for the City: Migrant Labor, Capital, and the State in Urban Africa.* New York: Sage, 1983.

Cooper, Frederick. 'Africa's Pasts and Africa's Historians'. *Canadian Journal of African Studies* 34, No. 2 (2000): 298–336.

Cooper, Frederick. 'What is the Concept of Globalization Good for? An African Historian's Perspective'. *African Affairs* 100, No. 399 (2001): 189–213.

Copeman, Edward A. 'The Violence of Kasanza'. *The Northern Rhodesia Journal* 1, No. 5 (1952): 64–67.

Costa, A.A. 'Chieftaincy and Civilisation: African Structures of Government and Colonial Administration in South Africa'. *African Studies* 59, No. 1 (2000): 13–43.

Crehan, Kate. 'Mukunashi: An Exploration of Some Effects of the Penetration of Capital in North-Western Zambia'. *Journal of Southern African Studies* 8, No. 1 (1981/82): 82–93.

Crehan, Kate. 'Women and Development in North Western Zambia from Producer to Housewife'. *Review of African Political Economy* 27/8 (1983): 51–66.

Crehan, Kate, and Achim von Oppen. 'Understandings of "Development": An Arena of Struggle: The Story of a Development Project in Zambia'. *Sociologia Ruralis* 28, No. 2 (1988): 113–45.

Crehan, Kate, and Achim von Oppen, eds. *Planners and History: Negotiating 'Development' in Rural Zambia.* Lusaka: Multimedia Publications, 1994.

Crehan, Kate. *The Fractured Community: Landscapes of Power and Gender in Rural Zambia.* Berkeley: University of California Press, 1997.

Crehan, Kate. 'Of Chickens and Guinea Fowl: Living Matriliny in North-Western Zambia in the 1980s'. *Critique of Anthropology* 17, No. 2 (1997): 211–27.

Crehan, Kate. '"Tribes" and the People Who Read Books: Managing History in Colonial Zambia'. *Journal of Southern African Studies* 23, No. 2 (1998): 203–18.

Cronon, William. 'A Place for Stories: Nature, History, and Narrative'. *Journal of American History* 78, No. 4 (1992): 1347–76.

Crosby, Alfred W. Jr. *The Columbian Exchange: Biological and Cultural Consequences of 1492.* Westport: Praeger, 1972.

Cullather, Nick. 'Miracles of Modernization: The Green Revolution and the Apotheosis of Technology'. *Diplomatic History* 28, No. 2 (2004): 227–54.

Cullather, Nick. 'Development? It's History'. *Diplomatic History* 24, No. 4 (2000): 641–53.

Dalakoglou, Dimitris, and Penny Harvey. 'Roads and Anthropology: Ethnographic Perspectives on Space, Time and (Im)mobility'. *Mobilities* 7, No. 4 (2012): 459–65.

Davies, Mary E. 'The Locality of Chieftainship: Chiefly Authority in Colonial Malawi, 1932–1974'. Unpublished PhD Thesis, Leiden University, 2014.

De Boeck, Filip. '"When Hunger Goes Around the Land": Hunger and Food Among the Aluund of Zaire'. *Man* 29, No. 2 (1994): 257–82.

De Boeck, Filip. 'Domesticating Diamonds and Dollars: Identity, Expenditure and Sharing in Southwestern Zaire (1984–1997)'. *Development and Change* 29, No. 4 (1998): 777–810.

De Boeck, Filip. 'Borderland Breccia: The Mutant Hero in the Historical Imagination of a Central-African Diamond Frontier'. *Journal of Colonialism and Colonial History* 1, No. 2 (2000).

De, Bruijn, Mirjam E., Rijk A. van Dijk, and Dick Foeken, eds. *Mobile Africa: Changing Patterns of Movement in Africa and Beyond.* Leiden: Brill, 2001.

De Haan, Arjan. 'Livelihoods and Poverty: The Role of Migration – a Critical Review of the Migration Literature'. *The Journal of Development Studies* 36, No. 2 (1999): 1–47.

De Heusch, Luc. 'What Shall We Do with the Drunken King?' *Africa* 45, No. 4 (1975): 363–72.

de Luna, Kathryn M. 'Affect and Society in Precolonial Africa'. *International Journal of African Historical Studies* 46, No. 1 (2013): 123–50.

De Vries, Jan. *The Industrious Revolution: Consumer Behavior and the Household Economy, 1650 to the Present.* Cambridge: Cambridge University Press, 2008.

Doevenspeck, Martin. 'Constructing the Border from Below: Narratives from the Congolese-Rwandan State Boundary'. *Political Geography* 30 (2011): 129–42.

Donaldson, John W. 'Pillars and Perspective: Demarcation of the Belgian Congo-Northern Rhodesia Boundary'. *Journal of Historical Geography* 34 (2008): 471–93.

Donge, Jan-Kees van. 'Understanding Rural Zambia Today: The Relevance of the Rhodes-Livingstone Institute'. *Africa* 55, No. 1 (1985): 60–76.

Doorne, J.H. van. 'Situational Analysis: Its Potential and Limitations for Anthropological Research on Social Change in Africa'. *Cahiers d'études africaines* 21, No. 84 (1981): 479–506.

Douglas, Mary. 'Is Matriliny Doomed in Africa?' in *Man in Africa,* edited by Mary Douglas and Phyllis M. Kaberry, 121–33. London: Tavistock, 1969.

Douglas, Mary, and Baron Isherwood. *The World of Goods: Towards an Anthropology of Consumption.* London: Routledge, 1979.

Doyle, Shane D. *Crisis and Decline in Bunyoro: Population and Environment in Western Uganda 1860–1955.* Athens: Ohio University Press, 2006.

Duysters, Leon. 'Histoire des Aluunda'. *Problèmes d'Afrique Centrale* 12, No. 40 (1958): 75–98.

Eisenstadt, Shmuel N. *Tradition, Change, and Modernity.* London: John Wiley & Sons, 1972.

Ellis, Stephen. 'Writing Histories of Contemporary Africa'. *Journal of African History* 43, No. 1 (2002): 1–26.

Engerman, David C., and Corinna R. Unger. 'Introduction: Towards a Global History of Modernization'. *Diplomatic History* 33, No. 3 (2009): 375–85.

Englebert, Pierre. 'Patterns and Theories of Traditional Resurgence in Tropical Africa'. *Mondes en développement* 30, No. 118 (2002): 51–64.

Englund, Harri. 'Witchcraft, Modernity and the Person: The Morality of Accumulation in Central Malawi'. *Critique of Anthropology* 16, No. 3 (1996): 257–79.

Englund, Harri. 'The Self in Self-Interest: Land, Labour and Temporalities in Malawi's Agrarian Change'. *Africa* 69, No. 1 (1999): 139–59.

Englund, Harri, and James Leach. 'Ethnography and the Meta-Narratives of Modernity'. *Current Anthropology* 41, No. 2 (2000): 225–48.

Englund, Harri. 'The Village in the City, the City in the Village: Migrants in Lilongwe'. *Journal of Southern African Studies* 28, No. 1 (2002): 137–54.

Epstein, Arnold L. *Politics in an Urban African Community.* Manchester: Manchester University Press, 1958.

Epstein, Arnold L. 'Urbanization and Social Change in Africa'. *Current Anthropology* 8, No. 4 (1967): 275–95.

Falola, Toyin. 'Mission and Colonial Documents'. In *Writing African History,* edited by John E. Philips, 266–84. Rochester: University of Rochester Press, 2005.

Feierman, Steven. *Peasant Intellectuals: Anthropology and History in Tanzania*. Madison: University of Wisconsin Press, 1990.

Feierman, Steven. 'African Histories and the Dissolution of World History'. In *Africa and the Disciplines: The Contributions of Research in Africa to the Social Sciences and Humanities*, edited by Valentin Y. Mudimbe, Jean F. O'Barr, and Robert H. Bates, 167–212. Chicago: University of Chicago Press, 1993.

Ferguson, James. 'The Bovine Mystique: Power, Property and Livestock in Rural Lesotho'. *Man* 20, No. 4 (1985): 647–74.

Ferguson, James. *The Anti-Politics Machine: 'Development', Depoliticization, and Bureaucratic Power in Lesotho*. Minneapolis: University of Minnesota Press, 1990.

Ferguson, James. 'Mobile Workers, Modernist Narratives: A Critique of the Historiography of Transition on the Zambian Copperbelt, Part One & Two'. *Journal of Southern African Studies* 16, No. 3–4 (1990): 385–412 and 603–21.

Ferguson, James. 'The Country and the City on the Copperbelt'. *Cultural Anthropology* 7, No. 1 (1992): 80–92.

Ferguson, James. 'The Cultural Topography of Wealth: Commodity Paths and the Structure of Property in Rural Lesotho'. *American Anthropologist* 94, No. 1 (1992): 55–73.

Ferguson, James. *Expectations of Modernity: Myths and Meanings of Urban Life on the Zambian Copperbelt*. Berkeley: University of California Press, 1999.

Ferguson, James. 'Of Mimicry and Membership: Africans and the "New World Society"'. *Cultural Anthropology* 17, No. 4 (2002): 551–69.

Fetter, Bruce, ed. *Demography from Scanty Evidence: Central Africa in the Colonial Era*. Boulder: Lynne Rienner Publishers, 1990.

Fields, Karen E. 'Political Contingencies of Witchcraft in Colonial Central Africa: Culture and the State in Marxist Theory'. *Canadian Journal of African Studies* 16, No. 3 (1982): 567–93.

Fisher, M.K. *Lunda-Ndembu Dictionary*. Rev. edn., Ikelenge: Lunda-Ndembu Publications, 1984.

Fisher, W. Singleton. 'Burning the Bush for Game'. *African Studies* 7, No. 1 (1948): 36–38.

Fisher, W. Singleton. 'Black Magic Feuds'. *African Studies* (1949): 20–22.

Fisher, W. Singleton, and Julyan Hoyte. *Ndotolu: The Life Stories of Walter and Anna Fisher of Central Africa*. Rev. edn., Ikelenge: Lunda-Ndembu Publications, 1992.

Fisiy, Cipryan F., and Peter Geschiere. 'Sorcery, Witchcraft and Accumulation: Regional Variations in South and West Cameroon'. *Critique of Anthropology* 11, No. 3 (1991): 251–78.

Flint, Lawrence S. 'State Building in Central Southern Africa: Citizenship and Subjectivity in Barotseland and Caprivi'. *The International Journal of African Historical Studies* 36, No. 2 (2003): 393–428.

Flynn, Donna K. '"We Are the Border": Identity, Exchange, and the State Along the Benin-Nigeria Border'. *American Ethnologist* 24, No. 2 (1997): 311–30.

Fourshey, Cymone C. "'The Remedy for Hunger Is Bending the Back": Maize and British Agricultural Policy in Southwestern Tanzania 1920–1960'. *The International Journal of African Historical Studies* 41, No. 2 (2008): 223–61.

Freund, Paul J., and Katele Kalumba. 'Spontaneously Settled Refugees in Northwestern Province, Zambia'. *International Migration Review* 20, No. 2 (1986): 299–312.

Friedman, Jonathan. 'Consuming Desires: Strategies of Selfhood and Appropriation'. *Cultural Anthropology* 6, No. 2 (1991): 154–63.

Gabel, Creighton. 'Terminal Food-Collectors and Agricultural Initiative in East and Southern Africa'. *The International Journal of African Historical Studies* 7, No. 1 (1974): 56–68.

Gabrilopoulos, Nick, Charle Mather, and Caesar R. Apentiik. 'Lineage Organisation of the Tallensi Compound: The Social Logic of Domestic Space in Northern Ghana'. *Africa* 72, No. 2 (2002): 221–44.

Gann, Louis H. *The Birth of a Plural Society: The Development of Northern Rhodesia Under the British South Africa Company, 1894–1914.* Manchester: Manchester University Press, 1958.

Geschiere, Peter. 'Working Groups or Wage Labour? Cash-Crops, Reciprocity and Money Among the Maka of Southeastern Cameroon'. *Development and Change* 26, No. 3 (1995): 503–23.

Geschiere, Peter, and Josef Gugler. 'The Urban-Rural Connection: Changing Issues of Belonging and Identification'. *Africa* 68, No. 3 (1998): 309–19.

Gewald, Jan-Bart. 'Researching and Writing in the Twilight of an Imagined Conquest: Anthropology in Northern Rhodesia 1930–1960'. *History and Anthropology* 18, No. 4 (2007): 459–87.

Gewald, Jan-Bart, Marja Hinfelaar, and Giacomo Macola, eds. *One Zambia, Many Histories: Towards a History of Post-Colonial Zambia.* Leiden: Brill, 2008.

Gewald, Jan-Bart. 'People, Mines and Cars: Towards a Revision of Zambian History, 1890–1930'. In *The Speed of Change: Motor Vehicles and People in Africa 1890–2000,* edited by Jan-Bart Gewald, Sabine Luning, and Klaas van Walraven, 21–47. Leiden: Brill, 2009.

Gewald, Jan-Bart. *Forged in the Great War: People, Transport, and Labour, The Establishment of Colonial Rule in Zambia, 1890–1920.* Leiden: African Studies Centre Leiden, 2015.

Gibbons, Alfred St.H. *Africa from South to North Through Marotseland.* New York: John Lane, 1904.

Gluckman, Max. *Analysis of a Social Situation in Modern Zululand.* Rhodes-Livingstone Papers No.28. Lusaka, 1958.

Gluckman, Max. 'Tribalism in Modern British Central Africa'. *Cahiers d'études africaines* 1, No. 1 (1960): 55–70.

Gluckman, Max. *Politics, Law and Ritual in Tribal Society*. New Brunswick: Transaction Publishers, 1965.

Goody, Jack. *Cooking, Cuisine and Class: A Study in Comparative Sociology*. Cambridge: Cambridge University Press, 1982.

Gordon, David M. 'Rites of Rebellion: Recent Anthropology from Zambia'. *African Studies* 62, No. 1 (2003): 125–39.

Gordon, David M. 'The Abolition of the Slave Trade and the Transformation of the South-Central African Interior During the Nineteenth Century'. *The William and Mary Quarterly* 66, No. 4 (2009): 915–38.

Gordon, David M. *Invisible Agents: Spirits in a Central African History*. Athens: Ohio University Press, 2012.

Gordon, David M. 'Wearing Cloth, Wielding Guns: Consumption, Trade, and Politics in the South Central African Interior During the Nineteenth Century'. In *The Objects of Life in Central Africa: The History of Consumption and Social Change, 1840–1980*, edited by Robert Ross, Marja Hinfelaar, and Iva Peša, 17–40. Leiden: Brill, 2013.

Goucher, Candice L. 'Iron Is Iron 'Til It Rust: Trade and Ecology in the Decline of West African Iron Smelting'. *Journal of African History* 22, No. 2 (1981): 179–89.

Gould, Jeremy. 'On the Genealogy of the Post-Colonial State: Lugard and Kaunda on Cooperatives and Authority in Rural Zambia'. In *Improved Natural Resource Management: The Role of Formal Organisations and Informal Networks and Institutions*, edited by Henrik Marcussen, 232–57. Roskilde: Roskilde University, 1996.

Grant, William D. *Zambia Then and Now: Colonial Rulers and Their African Successors*. London: Routledge, 2008.

Gray, Christopher J. *Colonial Rule and Crisis in Equatorial Africa: Southern Gabon, ca. 1850–1940*. Rochester: University of Rochester Press, 2002.

Gray, Richard, and David Birmingham, eds. *Pre-Colonial African Trade: Essays on Trade in Central and Eastern Africa Before 1900*. Oxford: Oxford University Press, 1970.

Green, Erik. 'A Lasting Story: Conservation and Agricultural Extension Services in Colonial Malawi'. *Journal of African History* 50, No. 2 (2009): 247–67.

Guene, Enid. *Copper, Borders and Nation-Building: The Katangese Factor in Zambian Political and Economic History*. Leiden: African Studies Centre, 2017.

Guyer, Jane I. 'Naturalism in Models of African Production'. *Man* 19, No. 3 (1984): 371–88.

Guyer, Jane I. 'Wealth in People and Self-Realization in Equatorial Africa'. *Man* 28, No. 2 (1993): 243–65.

Guyer, Jane I., ed. *Money Matters: Instability, Values and Social Payments in the Modern History of West African Communities*. Portsmouth: Heinemann, 1995.

Guyer, Jane I. 'Wealth in People, Wealth in Things – Introduction'. *Journal of African History* 36, No. 1 (1995): 83–90.

Guyer, Jane I., and Samuel M. Eno Belinga. 'Wealth in People as Wealth in Knowledge: Accumulation and Composition in Equatorial Africa'. *Journal of African History* 36, No. 1 (1995): 91–120.

Haggblade, Steven, and Ballard Zulu. 'The Recent Cassava Surge in Zambia and Malawi'. *Successes in African Agriculture*, Conference in Pretoria, 1–3 December 2003.

Hahn, Hans P., and Georg Klute, eds. *Cultures of Migration: African Perspectives*. Münster: LIT Verlag, 2007.

Hahn, Hans P., ed. *Consumption in Africa: Anthropological Approaches*. Berlin: LIT Verlag, 2008.

Hall, Richard S. *Zambia*. London: Pall Mall Press, 1965.

Hamer, John. 'Commensality, Process and the Moral Order: An Example from Southern Ethiopia'. *Africa* 64, No. 1 (1994): 126–44.

Handler, Richard, and Jocelyn Linnekin. 'Tradition, Genuine or Spurious'. *The Journal of American Folklore* 97, No. 385 (1984): 273–90.

Hansen, Art. 'Once the Running Stops: The Social and Economic Incorporation of Angolan Refugees into Zambian Border Villages'. Unpublished PhD Thesis, Cornell University, 1977.

Hansen, Art. 'Once the Running Stops: Assimilation of Angolan Refugees into Zambian Border Villages'. *Disasters* 3, No. 4 (1979): 369–74.

Hansen, Art. 'Refugee Dynamics: Angolans in Zambia 1966 to 1972'. *International Migration Review* 15, No. 1/2 (1981): 175–94.

Hansen, Art, and Della E. MacMillan, eds. *Food in Sub-Saharan Africa*. Boulder: Lynne Riener Publishers, 1986.

Hansen, Karen T. *Keeping House in Lusaka*. Columbia: Columbia University Press, 1997.

Hansen, Karen T. 'Second-Hand Clothing Encounters in Zambia: Global Discourses, Western Commodities, and Local Histories'. *Africa* 69, No. 3 (1999): 343–65.

Hansen, Karen T. *Salaula: The World of Secondhand Clothing and Zambia*. Chicago: University of Chicago Press, 2000.

Harries, Patrick. *Work, Culture, and Identity: Migrant Laborers in Mozambique and South Africa, c. 1860–1910*. Portsmouth: Heinemann, 1994.

Harries, Patrick. 'Imagery, Symbolism and Tradition in a South African Bantustan: Mangosuthu Buthelezi, Inkhata, and Zulu history'. *History and Theory* 32, No. 4 (1993): 105–25.

Hay, Margaret J. 'Material Culture and the Shaping of Consumer Society in Colonial Western Kenya'. *Working Papers in African Studies,* Boston University, 1994.

Heisler, Helmuth. *Urbanisation and the Government of Migration: The Inter-Relation of Urban and Rural Life in Zambia*. New York: St. Martin's Press, 1974.

Hellen, J.A. *Rural Economic Development in Zambia, 1890–1964*. München: Weltforum Verlag, 1968.

Hendrickson, Hildi, ed. *Clothing and Difference: Embodied Identities in Colonial and Post-Colonial Africa.* Durham: Duke University Press, 1996.

Henige, David. 'Oral Tradition as a Means of Reconstructing the Past'. In *Writing African History,* edited by John E. Philips, 169–90. Rochester: University of Rochester Press, 2005.

Herbert, Eugenia W. *Iron, Gender, and Power: Rituals of Transformation in African Societies.* Bloomington: Indiana University Press, 1993.

Herbst, Jeffrey I. *States and Power in Africa: Comparative Lessons in Authority and Control.* Princeton: Princeton University Press, 2000.

Heywood, Linda M. 'Slavery and Forced Labor in the Changing Political Economy of Central Angola, 1850–1949'. In *The End of Slavery in Africa,* edited by Suzanne M. Miers and Richard L. Roberts, 415–35. Madison: University of Wisconsin Press, 1988.

Higginson, John. 'Disputing the Machines: Scientific Management and the Transformation of the Work Routine at the Union-Miniere du Haut Katanga, 1918–1930'. *African Economic History* 17 (1988): 1–21.

Higginson, John. *A Working Class in the Making: Belgian Colonial Labour Policy, Private Enterprise, and the African Mineworker, 1907–1951.* Madison: University of Wisconsin Press, 1989.

Hinfelaar, Marja, and Giacomo Macola, eds. *A First Guide to Non-Governmental Archives in Zambia.* Lusaka: National Archives of Zambia, 2004.

Hinfelaar, Marja. 'The Politics of Natural Resource Extraction in Zambia'. In *Governing Extractive Industries: Politics, Histories, Ideas,* Anthony Bebbington, et al. Oxford: Oxford University Press, 2018.

Hobsbawm, Eric, and Terence Ranger, eds. *The Invention of Tradition.* Cambridge: Cambridge University Press, 1983.

Hobsbawm, Eric. *The Age of Empire 1875–1914.* London: Abacus, 1987.

Hodge, Joseph M. *Triumph of the Expert: Agrarian Doctrines of Development and the Legacies of British Colonialism.* Athens: Ohio University Press, 2007.

Hodge, Joseph M. 'Writing the History of Development (Part 1: The First Wave)'. *Humanity: An International Journal of Human Rights, Humanitarianism, and Development* 6, No. 3 (2015): 429–63.

Hodge, Joseph M. 'Writing the History of Development (Part 2: Longer, Deeper, Wider)'. *Humanity: An International Journal of Human Rights, Humanitarianism, and Development* 7, No. 1 (2016): 125–74.

Hogendoorn, J.S., and K.M. Scott. 'The East African Groundnut Scheme: Lessons of a Large-Scale Agricultural Failure'. *African Economic History* 10 (1981): 81–115.

Hoover, Jeffrey J. 'The Seduction of Ruwej: Reconstructing Ruund History (The Nuclear Lunda: Zaïre, Angola, Zambia)'. Unpublished PhD Thesis, Yale University, 1978.

Hopkins, Anthony G. 'The New Economic History of Africa'. *Journal of African History* 50, No. 2 (2009): 155–77.

Hoppers, Wim H.M.L. *Education in A Rural Society: Primary Pupils and School Leavers in Mwinilunga, Zambia.* The Hague, 1981.

Howard, Allen M. 'Nodes, Networks, Landscapes, and Regions: Reading the Social History of Tropical Africa 1700s–1920'. In *The Spatial Factor in African History: The Relationship Between the Social, Material, and Perceptual,* edited by Allen M. Howard and Richard M. Shain, 103–30. Leiden: Brill, 2005.

Hughes, Matthew. 'Fighting for White Rule in Africa: The Central African Federation, Katanga, and the Congo Crisis, 1958–1965'. *The International History Review* 25, No. 3 (2003): 592–615.

Hyden, Goran. *Beyond Ujamaa in Tanzania: Underdevelopment and an Uncaptured Peasantry.* Berkeley: University of California Press, 1980.

Iliffe, John. *Africans: The History of a Continent.* Cambridge: Cambridge University Press, 1995.

Ingold, Tim. *The Perception of the Environment: Essays on Livelihood, Dwelling and Skill.* London: Routledge, 2000.

Isaacman, Allen. 'Peasants and Rural Social Protest in Africa'. *African Studies Review* 33, No. 2 (1990): 1–120.

Jackman, Mary E. *Recent Population Movements in Zambia: Some Aspects of the 1969 Census.* Manchester: Manchester University Press, 1973.

Jaeger, Dick. *Settlement Patterns and Rural Development: A Human-Geographical Study of the Kaonde, Kasempa District, Zambia.* Amsterdam: Royal Tropical Institute, 1981.

Jamal, Vali, and John Weeks. 'The Vanishing Rural-Urban Gap in Sub-Saharan Africa'. *International Labour Review* 127, No. 3 (1988): 271–92.

Johnson, D.S., ed. *Handbook to the North-Western Province.* Lusaka: Government Printer, 1980.

Jones, William O. *Manioc in Africa.* Stanford: Stanford University Press, 1959.

Jules-Rosette, Bennetta. 'Decentering Ethnography: Victor Turner's Vision of Anthropology'. *Journal of Religion in Africa* 24, No. 2 (1994): 160–81.

Kakoma, Ben C. 'Colonial Administration in Northern Rhodesia: A Case Study of Colonial Policy in the Mwinilunga District of Zambia, 1901–1939'. MA Thesis, University of Auckland, 1971.

Kalusa, Walima T. 'Disease and the Remaking of Missionary Medicine in Colonial Northwestern Zambia: A Case Study of Mwinilunga District, 1902–1964'. Unpublished PhD Thesis, Johns Hopkins University, 2003.

Kalusa, Walima T. 'Language, Medical Auxiliaries, and the Re-Interpretation of Missionary Medicine in Colonial Mwinilunga, Zambia, 1922–51'. *Journal of Eastern African Studies* 1, No. 1 (2007): 57–78.

Kalusa, Walima T. *Kalonga Gawa Undi X: A Biography of an African Chief and Nationalist.* Lusaka: Lembani Trust, 2010.

Kalusa, Walima T., and Megan Vaughan. *Death, Belief and Politics in Central African History*. Lusaka: Lembani Trust, 2013.

Kaufmann, Jeffrey C. 'The Sediment of Nomadism'. *History in Africa* 36 (2009): 235–64.

Kay, George. *Social Aspects of Village Regrouping in Zambia*. Hull: University of Hull, 1967.

Kennes, Erik, and Miles Larmer. *The Katangese Gendarmes and War in Central Africa: Fighting Their Way Home*. Bloomington: Indiana University Press, 2016.

Kesselring, Rita. 'The Electricity Crisis in Zambia: Blackouts and Social Stratification in New Mining Towns'. *Energy Research & Social Science* 30 (2017): 94–102.

Kesselring, Rita. 'At an Extractive Pace: Conflicting Temporalities in a Resettlement Process in Solwezi, Zambia'. *The Extractive Industries and Society* 5, No. 2 (2018): 237–44.

Keverne, Gloria. *A Man Cannot Cry: The Towering Saga of Passion, Violence and Love*. London: Tudor Communications, 1985.

Klein, Martin A. 'The Slave Trade and Decentralized Societies'. *Journal of African History* 42 (2001): 49–65.

Kodesh, Neil. 'Renovating Tradition: The Discourse of Succession in Colonial Buganda'. *The International Journal of African Historical Studies* 34, No. 3 (2001): 511–41.

Konings, Piet J.J. 'Chieftaincy, Labour Control and Capitalist Development in Cameroon'. *Journal of Legal Pluralism and Unofficial Law* 37/8 (1996): 329–46.

Kopytoff, Igor. 'The Cultural Biography of Things: Commoditization as Process'. In *The Social Life of Things: Commodities in Cultural Perspective,* edited by Arjun Appadurai, 64–94. Cambridge: Cambridge University Press, 1986.

Kopytoff, Igor. 'The Internal African Frontier: The Making of African Political Culture'. In *The African Frontier: The Reproduction of Traditional African Societies,* edited by Igor Kopytoff. Bloomington: Indiana University Press, 1987.

Kratz, Corinne A. "'We've Always Done It Like This ... Except for a Few Details": "Tradition" and "Innovation" in Okiek Ceremonies'. *Comparative Studies in Society and History* 35, No. 1 (1993): 30–65.

Kreike, Emmanuel. 'De-Globalisation and Deforestation in Colonial Africa: Closed Markets, The Cattle Complex, and Environmental Change in North-Central Namibia, 1890–1990'. *Journal of Southern African Studies* 35, No. 1 (2009): 81–98.

Kriger, Colleen E. *Pride of Men: Ironworking in Nineteenth Century West Central Africa*. Portsmouth: Heinemann, 1999.

Kuper, Adam. *Wives for Cattle: Bridewealth and Marriage in Southern Africa*. London: Routledge, 1982.

Kuper, Adam. *Anthropology & Anthropologists: The Modern British School*. 3rd edn., London: Routledge, 1996.

Lander, Richard P. 'The British South Africa Company: An Essay on Its Commercial History'. *Heritage of Zimbabwe* 11 (1992): 1–40.

Larmer, Miles, and Giacomo Macola, 'The Origins, Context, and Political Significance of the Mushala Rebellion Against the Zambian One-Party State'. *The International Journal of African Historical Studies* 40, No. 3 (2007): 471–96.

Larmer, Miles. *Rethinking African Politics: A History of Opposition in Zambia.* Farnham: Ashgate, 2011.

Larmer, Miles. 'At the Crossroads: Mining and Political Change on the Katangese-Zambian Copperbelt'. *Oxford Handbooks Online* (2016): DOI: 10.1093/oxfordhb/9780199935369.013.20

Leenstra, Melle. *Beyond the Façade: Instrumentalisation of the Zambian Health Sector.* Leiden: African Studies Centre, 2012.

Lemarchand, René. 'African Peasantries, Reciprocity and the Market: The Economy of Affection Reconsidered'. *Cahiers d'études africaines* 29, No. 113 (1989): 33–67.

Lewinson, Anne S. 'Domestic Realms, Social Bonds, and Class: Ideologies and Indigenizing Modernity in Dar es Salaam, Tanzania'. *Canadian Journal of African Studies* 40, No. 3 (2006): 462–95.

Lindsay, Lisa A. 'Biography in African History'. *History in Africa* 44 (2017): 11–26.

Long, Norman. *Social Change and the Individual: A Study of the Social and Religious Responses to Innovation in a Zambian Rural Community.* Manchester: Manchester University Press, 1968.

Lovejoy, Paul E. 'The Business of Slaving: Pawnship in Western Africa, c.1600–1810'. *Journal of African History* 42 (2001): 67–89.

Low, D.A., and John Lonsdale. 'Introduction'. In *Oxford History of East Africa, Vol. 3,* edited by D.A. Low and Alison Smith, 1–63. Oxford: Oxford University Press, 1976.

Lucassen, Jan, and Leo Lucassen. 'The Mobility Transition Revisited, 1500–1900: What the Case of Europe Can Offer to Global History'. *Journal of Global History* 4, No. 3 (2009): 347–77.

Luchembe, Chipasha. 'Ethnic Stereotypes, Violence and Labour in Early Colonial Zambia, 1889–1924'. In *Guardians in Their Time: Experiences of Zambians Under Colonial Rule, 1890–1964,* edited by Samuel N. Chipungu, 30–49. London: Macmillan, 1992.

Lukanty, J., and Adrian P. Wood. 'Agricultural Policy in the Colonial Period'. In *The Dynamics of Agricultural Policy and Reform in Zambia,* edited by Adrian P. Wood, et al., 3–18. Ames: Iowa State Press, 1990.

MacGaffey, Janet. *The Real Economy of Zaire: The Contribution of Smuggling and Other Unofficial Activities to National Wealth.* Oxford: James Currey, 1991.

MacGaffey, Wyatt. 'Changing Representations in Central African History'. *Journal of African History* 46, No. 2 (2005): 189–207.

MacGaffey, Wyatt. 'Kongo Slavery Remembered by Themselves: Texts from 1915'. *International Journal of African Historical Studies* 41, No. 1 (2008): 55–76.

MacGaffey, Wyatt. 'The Blacksmiths of Tamale: The Dynamics of Space and Time in a Ghanaian Industry'. *Africa* 79, No. 2 (2009): 169–85.

MacKenzie, John M. *The Empire of Nature: Hunting, Conservation and British Imperialism.* Manchester: Manchester University Press, 1988.

Macmillan, Hugh. 'The Historiography of Transition on the Zambian Copperbelt: Another View'. *Journal of Southern African Studies* 19, No. 4 (1993): 681–712.

Macmillan, Hugh. 'Return to the Malungwana Drift – Max Gluckman, the Zulu Nation and the Common Society'. *African Affairs* 94, No. 374 (1995): 39–65.

Macola, Giacomo. *The Kingdom of Kazembe: History and Politics in North-Eastern Zambia and Katanga to 1950.* Münster: LIT Verlag, 2002.

Macola, Giacomo. 'Reassessing the Significance of Firearms in Central Africa: The Case of North-Western Zambia to the 1920s'. *Journal of African History* 51, No. 3 (2010): 301–21.

Macola, Giacomo. *Liberal Nationalism in Central Africa: A Biography of Harry Mwaanga Nkumbula.* New York: Palgrave Macmillan, 2010.

Macola, Giacomo. *The Gun in Central Africa: A History of Technology and Politics.* Athens: Ohio University Press, 2016.

Macpherson, Fergus. *Anatomy of a Conquest: The British Occupation of Zambia, 1884–1924.* Harlow: Longman, 1981.

Makambe, E.P. 'The Mobilisation of African Labour Across the Zambezi for the Zimbabwean Colonial Market Before the Chibaro Era, 1898–1903'. *African Studies* 51, No. 2 (1992): 277–94.

Mamdani, Mahmood. *Citizen and Subject: Contemporary Africa and the Legacy of Late Colonialism.* Princeton: Princeton University Press, 1996.

Mandala, Elias. *The End of Chidyerano: A History of Food and Everyday Life in Malawi, 1860–2004.* Portsmouth: Heinemann, 2005.

Marks, Stuart A. *Large Mammals and a Brave People: Subsistence Hunters in Zambia.* London: Routledge, 2005.

Martin, Phyllis M. 'Contesting Clothes in Colonial Brazzaville'. *Journal of African History* 35, No. 3 (1994): 401–26.

Mbembe, Achille. 'At the Edge of the World: Boundaries, Territoriality and Sovereignty in Africa'. *Public Culture* 12, No. 1 (2000): 259–84.

McCann, James C. 'Agriculture and African History'. *Journal of African History* 32, No. 3 (1991): 507–13.

McCann, James C. *People of the Plow: An Agricultural History of Ethiopia, 1800–1900.* Madison: University of Wisconsin Press, 1995.

McCann, James C. *Green Land, Brown Land, Black Land: An Environmental History of Africa, 1800–1990.* Portsmouth: Heinemann, 1999.

McCann, James C. *Maize and Grace: Africa's Encounter with a New World Crop, 1500–2000.* New Haven: Harvard University Press, 2005.

McCann, James C. *Stirring the Pot: A History of African Cuisine*. Athens: Ohio University Press, 2009.

McCracken, John. 'Experts and Expertise in Colonial Malawi'. *African Affairs* 81, No. 322 (1982): 101–16.

McCulloch, Merran. *The Southern Lunda and Related Peoples (Northern Rhodesia, Belgian Congo, Angola)*. London, 1951.

Melland, Frank H. *In Witch-Bound Africa: An Account of the Primitive Kaonde Tribe and Their Beliefs*. London, 1967.

Mendes Ferrão, José E. *The Adventure of Plants and the Portuguese Discoveries*. n.p., 1994.

Miller, Daniel. 'Consumption and Commodities'. *Annual Review of Anthropology* 24 (1995): 141–61.

Miller, Joseph C. 'Cokwe Trade and Conquest in the Nineteenth Century'. In *Pre-Colonial African Trade: Essays on Trade in Central and Eastern Africa before 1900*, edited by Richard Gray and David Birmingham, 175–201. Oxford: Oxford University Press, 1970.

Miller, Joseph C. *Way of Death: Merchant Capitalism and the Angolan Slave Trade 1730–1830*. Madison: University of Wisconsin Press, 1988.

Miller, Joseph C. 'History and Africa/Africa and History'. *The American Historical Review* 104, No. 1 (1999): 1–32.

Minter, William. *Apartheid's Contras: An Inquiry into the Roots of War in Angola and Mozambique*. London: Zed Books, 1994.

Miracle, Marvin P. *Agriculture in the Congo Basin: Tradition and Change in African Rural Economies*. Madison: University of Wisconsin Press, 1967.

Mitchell, J. Clyde. *The Kalela Dance: Aspects of Social Relationships Among Urban Africans in Northern Rhodesia*. Manchester: Manchester University Press, 1956.

Mitchell, J. Clyde, and Arnold L. Epstein. 'Occupational Prestige and Social Status Among Urban Africans in Northern Rhodesia'. *Africa* 29, No. 1 (1959): 22–40.

Mitchell, J. Clyde. 'The Causes of Labour Migration'. *Inter-African Labour Institute Bulletin* 6, No. 1 (1959): 12–47.

Mitchell, J. Clyde, ed. *Social Networks in Urban Situations: Analyses of Personal Relationships in Central African Towns*. Manchester: Manchester University Press, 1969.

Money, Duncan J. 'The World of European Labour on the Zambian Copperbelt, 1940–1945'. *International Review of Social History* 60, No. 2 (2015): 225–55.

Moore, Henrietta L., and Megan Vaughan. *Cutting Down Trees: Gender, Nutrition, and Agricultural Change in the Northern Province of Zambia 1890–1990*. Portsmouth: Heinemann, 1994.

Moore, Henrietta L., and Todd Sanders, eds. *Magical Interpretations, Material Realities: Modernity, Witchcraft and the Occult in Postcolonial Africa*. London: Psychology Press, 2001.

Moorsom, Toby. '"Black Settlers": Hybridity, Neoliberalism and Ecosystemic Change Among Tonga Farmers of Southern Zambia, 1964–2008'. Unpublished PhD Thesis, Queen's University at Kingston, 2016.

Morapedi, Wazha G. 'Demise or Resilience? Customary Law and Chieftaincy in Twenty-First Century Botswana'. *Journal of Contemporary African Studies* 28, No. 2 (2010): 215–30.

Mudimbe, Valentin Y. *The Invention of Africa: Gnosis, Philosophy and the Order of Knowledge.* Bloomington: Indiana University Press, 1988.

Mulford, David C. *Zambia: The Politics of Independence, 1957–1964.* Oxford: Oxford University Press, 1967.

Mulumbi Datuuma II. 'Customs of the Lunda-Ndembu, Volume I, The Kanong'esha Chieftainship Succession in Zambia'. Unpublished manuscript, Mwinilunga, 2010.

Musambachime, Mwelwa C. 'Escape from Tyranny: Flights Across the Rhodesia-Congo Boundary'. *Transafrican Journal of History* 18 (1989): 147–59.

Mususa, Patience N. 'There Used To Be Order: Life on the Copperbelt After the Privatisation of the Zambia Consolidated Copper Mines'. Unplublished PhD Thesis, University of Cape Town, 2014.

Mvusi, Thandekile R.M. 'The "Politics of Trypanosomiasis" Revisited: Labour Mobilization and Labour Migration in Colonial Zambia: The Robert Williams Company in Lubemba, 1901–1911'. *Transafrican Journal of History* 23 (1994): 43–68.

Myers, Garth A. 'Sticks and Stones: Colonialism and Zanzibari Housing'. *Africa* 67, No. 2 (1997): 252–72.

Negi, Rohit. 'The Mining Boom, Capital, and Chiefs in the "New Copperbelt"'. In *Zambia, Mining, and Neoliberalism: Boom and Bust on the Globalized Copperbelt,* edited by Alastair Fraser and Miles Larmer, 209–36. New York: Palgrave Macmillan, 2010.

Negi, Rohit. 'The Micropolitics of Mining and Development in Zambia: Insights from the Northwestern Province'. *African Studies Quarterly* 12, No. 2 (2010/11): 27–44.

Negi, Rohit. '"Solwezi *Mabanga*": Ambivalent Developments on Zambia's New Mining Frontier'. *Journal of Southern African Studies* 40, No. 5 (2014): 999–1013.

Newman, David, and Anssi Paasi. 'Fences and Neighbours in the Postmodern World: Boundary Narratives in Political Geography'. *Progress in Human Geography* 22, No. 2 (1998): 186–207.

Ngwane, Zolani. '"Christmas Time" and the Struggles for the Household in the Countryside: Rethinking the Cultural Geography of Migrant Labour in South Africa'. *Journal of Southern African Studies* 29, No. 3 (2003): 681–99.

Nugent, Paul, and A.I. Asiwaju, eds. *African Boundaries: Barriers, Conduits and Opportunities.* London: Cassell/Pinter, 1996.

Nweke, Felix I., Dunstan S.C. Spencer, and John K. Lynam. *The Cassava Transformation: Africa's Best-Kept Secret.* East Lansing: Michigan State University Press, 2002.

Obadare, Ebenezer, and Wale Adebanwi. 'Transnational Resource Flow and the Paradoxes of Belonging: Redirecting the Debate on Transnationalism, Remittances, State and Citizenship in Africa'. *Review of African Political Economy* 36, No. 122 (2009): 499–517.

Ohadike, Patrick O. *Demographic Perspectives in Zambia: Rural-Urban Growth and Social Change.* Manchester: Manchester University Press, 1981.

O'Laughlin, Bridget. 'Proletarianisation, Agency and Changing Rural Livelihoods: Forced Labour and Resistance in Colonial Mozambique'. *Journal of Southern African Studies* 28, No. 3 (2002): 511–30.

Oliver, Roland, and John D. Fage. *A Short History of Africa.* London: Penguin Books, 1962.

Onslow, Sue, ed. *Cold War in Southern Africa: White Power, Black Liberation.* London: Routledge, 2009.

Oomen, Barbara. '"We Must Now Go Back to Our History": Retraditionalisation in a Northern Province Chieftaincy'. *African Studies* 59, No. 1 (2000): 71–95.

Palmer, Robin H., and Neil Parsons, eds. *The Roots of Rural Poverty in Central and Southern Africa.* Berkeley: University of California Press, 1977.

Palmer, Robin H. 'Land Tenure Insecurity on the Zambian Copperbelt, 1998: Anyone Going Back to the Land?' *Social Dynamics* 26, No. 2 (2000): 154–70.

Palomera, Jaime, and Theodora Vetta. 'Moral Economy: Rethinking a Radical Concept'. *Anthropological Theory* 16, No. 4 (2016): 413–32.

Papstein, Robert J. 'The Upper Zambezi: A History of the Luvale People, 1000–1900'. Unpublished PhD Thesis, University of California, 1978.

Parpart, Jane L. '"Where Is Your Mother?" Gender, Urban Marriage, and Colonial Discourse on the Zambian Copperbelt, 1924–1945'. *The International Journal of African Historical Studies* 27, No. 2 (1994): 241–71.

Parry, Jonathan, and Marc Bloch, eds. *Money and the Morality of Exchange.* Cambridge: Cambridge University Press, 1989.

Peša, Iva. 'Cinderella's Cassava: A Historical Study of Agricultural Adaptation in Mwinilunga District From Pre-colonial Times to Independence'. Mphil Thesis, Leiden University, 2009.

Peša, I., '"Cassava Is Our Chief": Negotiating Identity, Markets and the State Through Cassava in Mwinilunga, Zambia'. in *Transforming Innovations in Africa: Explorative Studies on Appropriation in African Societies,* edited by Jan-Bart Gewald, André Leliveld, and Iva Peša, 169–90. Leiden: Brill, 2012.

Peša, Iva. 'Buying Pineapples, Selling Cloth: Traders and Trading Stores in Mwinilunga District, 1940–1970'. In *The Objects of Life in Central Africa: The History of Consumption and Social Change, 1840–1980,* edited by Robert Ross, Marja Hinfelaar, and Iva Peša, 259–80. Leiden: Brill, 2013.

Peša, Iva. 'Wealth, Success and Personhood: Trajectories of Labour Migration from Mwinilunga District, 1930s-1970s'. *Zambia Social Science Journal* 4, No. 1 (2013).

Peša, Iva. '"We Have Killed This Animal Together, May I Also Have a Share?": Local-National Political Dynamics in Mwinilunga District, Zambia, 1950s-1970s'. *Journal of Southern African Studies* 40, No. 5 (2014): 925–41.

Peša, Iva. 'Between Success and Failure: The Mwinilunga Pineapple Canning Factory in the 1960s and 1970s'. In *Magnifying Perspectives: Contributions to History, a Festschrift for Robert Ross,* edited by Iva Peša and Jan-Bart Gewald, 285–307. Leiden: African Studies Centre, 2017.

Peters, Pauline E. 'Revisiting the Puzzle of Matriliny in South-Central Africa'. *Critique of Anthropology* 17, No. 2 (1997): 125–46.

Phiri, Bizeck J. *A Political History of Zambia: From Colonial Rule to the Third Republic 1890–2001.* Trenton: Africa World Press, 2006.

Piot, Charles. 'Of Persons and Things: Some Reflections on African Spheres of Exchange'. *Man* 26, No. 3 (1991): 405–24.

Piot, Charles. 'Of Slaves and the Gift: Kabre Sale of Kin During the Era of the Slave Trade'. *Journal of African History* 37 (1996): 31–49.

Piot, Charles. *Remotely Global: Village Modernity in West Africa.* Chicago: University of Chicago Press, 1999.

Plange, Nii-K. 'Opportunity Cost and Labour Migration: A Misinterpretation of Proletarianisation in Northern Ghana'. *The Journal of Modern African Studies* 17, No. 4 (1979): 655–76.

Polanyi, Karl, Conrad M. Arensberg, and Harry W. Pearson, eds. *Trade and Market in the Early Empires: Economies in History and Theory.* Glencoe: The Free Press, 1957.

Ponte, Stefano. 'Trapped in Decline? Reassessing Agrarian Change and Economic Diversification on the Uluguru Mountains, Tanzania'. *The Journal of Modern African Studies* 39, No. 1 (2001): 81–100.

Popkin, Samuel L. *The Rational Peasant: The Political Economy of Rural Society in Vietnam.* Berkeley: University of California Press, 1979.

Posner, Daniel N. 'The Political Salience of Cultural Difference: Why Chewas and Tumbukas Are Allies in Zambia and Adversaries in Malawi'. *American Political Science Review* 98, No. 4 (2004): 529–45.

Pottier, Johan. *Migrants No More: Settlement and Survival in Mambwe Villages, Zambia.* Manchester: Manchester University Press, 1988.

Potts, Deborah. 'Shall We Go Home? Increasing Urban Poverty in African Cities and Migration Processes'. *The Geographical Journal* 161, No. 3 (1995): 245–64.

Potts, Deborah. 'Worker-Peasants and Farmer-Housewives in Africa: The Debate About 'Committed' Farmers, Access to Land and Agricultural Production'. *Journal of Southern African Studies* 26, No. 4 (2000): 807–32.

Potts, Deborah. 'Counter-Urbanization on the Zambian Copperbelt? Interpretations and Implications'. *Urban Studies* 42, No. 4 (2005): 583–609.

Powdermaker, Hortense. *Copper Town: Changing Africa: The Human Situation on the Rhodesian Copperbelt.* New York: Harper and Row, 1962.

Prestholdt, Jeremy. 'On the Global Repercussions of East African Consumerism'. *The American Historical Review* 109, No. 3 (2004): 755–81.

Prestholdt, Jeremy. *Domesticating the World: African Consumerism and the Genealogies of Globalization.* Berkeley: University of California Press, 2008.

Prestholdt, Jeremy. 'Africa and the Global Lives of Things'. In *The Oxford Handbook of the History of Consumption*, edited by Frank Trentmann, 85–107. Oxford: Oxford University Press, 2012.

Price, Neil, and Neil Thomas. 'Continuity and Change in the Gwembe Tonga Family and Their Relevance to Demography's Nucleation Thesis'. *Africa* 69, No. 4 (1999): 510–34.

Pritchett, James A. *The Lunda-Ndembu: Style, Change and Social Transformation in South Central Africa.* Madison: University of Wisconsin Press, 2001.

Pritchett, James A. *Friends for Life, Friends for Death: Cohorts and Consciousness Among the Lunda-Ndembu.* Charlottesville: University Press of Virginia, 2007.

Prowse, Martin. 'Becoming a Bwana and Burley Tobacco in the Central Region of Malawi'. *Journal of Modern African Studies* 47, No. 4 (2009): 575–602.

Raeymakers, Timothy. 'The Silent Encroachment of the Frontier: A Politics of Trans-border Trade in the Semliki Valley (Congo-Uganda)'. *Political Geography* 28 (2009): 55–65.

Ranger, Terence. 'Growing from the Roots: Reflections on Peasant Research in Central and Southern Africa'. *Journal of Southern African Studies* 5, No. 1 (1978/79): 99–133.

Reefe, Thomas Q. 'Traditions of Genesis and the Luba Diaspora'. *History in Africa* 4 (1977): 183–206.

Reid, Richard. 'Past and Presentism: The "Precolonial" and the Foreshortening of African History'. *Journal of African History* 52, No. 2 (2011): 135–55.

Richards, Audrey I. *Land, Labour and Diet in Northern Rhodesia.* London: Royal African Institute, 1939.

Richards, Paul. *Indigenous Agricultural Revolution: Ecology and Food Production in West Africa.* Boulder: Westview, 1985.

Roberts, Andrew D. *A History of Zambia.* New York: Holmes & Meier, 1976.

Roberts, Andrew D. 'Notes towards a Financial History of Copper Mining in Northern Rhodesia'. *Canadian Journal of African Studies* 16, No. 2 (1982): 347–59.

Rockell, Stephen J. *Carriers of Culture: Labor on the Road in Nineteenth Century East Africa.* Portsmouth: Heinemann, 2006.

Roitman, Janet L. 'The Politics of Informal Markets in Sub-Saharan Africa'. *The Journal of Modern African Studies* 28, No. 4 (1990): 671–96.

Ross, Robert J. *Clothing: A Global History.* Cambridge: Polity Press, 2008.

Ross, Robert, Marja Hinfelaar, and Iva Peša, eds. *The Objects of Life in Central Africa: The History of Consumption and Social Change, 1840–1980.* Leiden: Brill, 2013.

Rostow, Walt W. *The Stages of Economic Growth: A Non-Communist Manifesto.* Cambridge: Cambridge University Press, 1960.

Rubbers, Benjamin. *Le paternalisme en question: Les anciens ouvriers de la Gécamines face à la libéralisation du secteur minier katangais (RD Congo).* Paris: L'Harmattan, 2013.

Sack, Robert D. *Human Territoriality: Its Theory and History.* Cambridge: Cambridge University Press, 1986.

Sardanis, Andrew. *Africa, Another Side of the Coin: Northern Rhodesia's Final Years and Zambia's Nationhood.* London: I.B. Tauris, 2003.

Schapera, Isaac, ed. *Livingstone's Missionary Correspondence 1841–1856.* London: Chatto and Windus, 1961.

Schapera, Isaac, ed. *Livingstone's African Journal 1853–56.* London: Chatto and Windus, 1963.

Schecter, Robert E. 'History and Historiography on a Frontier of Lunda Expansion: The Origins and Early Development of the Kanongesha'. Unpublished PhD Thesis, University of Wisconsin Madison, 1976.

Schecter, Robert E. 'A Propos the Drunken King: Cosmology and History'. In *The African Past Speaks: Essays on Oral Tradition and History,* edited by Joseph C. Miller, 108–25. Hamden: Dawson and Sons, 1980.

Schneider, David M., and Kathleen Gough, eds. *Matrilineal Kinship.* Berkeley: University of California Press, 1961.

Schneider, Leander. 'The Maasai's New Clothes: A Developmentalist Modernity and Its Exclusions'. *Africa Today* 53, No. 1 (2006): 101–31.

Schoenbrun, David L. *A Green Place, a Good Place: Agrarian Change, Gender and Social Identity in the Great Lakes Region to the 15th Century.* Portsmouth: Heinemann, 1998.

Schoenbrun, David L. 'Conjuring the Modern in Africa: Durability and Rupture in Histories of Public Healing Between the Great Lakes of East Africa'. *The American Historical Review* 111, No. 5 (2006): 1403–39.

Schumaker, Lyn. *Africanizing Anthropology: Fieldwork, Networks, and the Making of Cultural Knowledge in Central Africa.* Durham: Duke University Press, 2001.

Scott, James C. *The Moral Economy of the Peasant: Rebellion and Subsistence in South-East Asia.* New Haven: Yale University Press, 1976.

Scott, James C. *Weapons of the Weak: Everyday Forms of Peasant Resistance.* New Haven: Yale University Press, 1985.

Scott, James C. *Seeing like a State: How Certain Schemes to Improve the Human Condition Have Failed.* New Haven: Yale University Press, 1998.

Scott, James C. *The Art of Not Being Governed: An Anarchist History of Upland Southeast Asia*. New Haven: Yale University Press, 2009.

Shipton, Parker, and Mitzi Goheen. 'Introduction: Understanding African Land-Holding: Power, Wealth, and Meaning'. *Africa* 62, No. 3 (1992): 307–25.

Short, Robin. *African Sunset*. London: Johnson, 1973.

Siegel, Brian. 'The "Wild" and "Lazy" Lamba as Ethnic Stereotype on the Central African Copperbelt'. In *The Creation of Tribalism in Southern Africa,* edited by Leroy Vail, 350–71. Berkeley: University of California Press, 1989.

Silberfein, Marilyn, ed. *Rural Settlement Structure and African Development.* Boulder: Westview Press, 1997.

Simone, AbdouMaliq, and Abelghani Abouhani, eds. *Urban Africa: Changing Contours of Survival in the City.* London: Zed Books, 2005.

Slinn, Peter. 'Commercial Concessions and Politics During the Colonial Period: The Role of the British South Africa Company in Northern Rhodesia 1890–1964'. *African Affairs* 70, No. 281 (1971): 365–84.

Spear, Thomas T. *Mountain Farmers: Moral Economies of Land and Agricultural Development in Arusha and Meru*. Oxford: James Currey, 1997.

Spear, Thomas T. 'Neo-Traditionalism and the Limits of Invention in British Colonial Africa'. *Journal of African History* 44, No. 1 (2003): 3–27.

Spring, Anita, and Art Hansen. *Women's Agricultural Work in Rural Zambia: From Valuation to Subordination*. Gainesville: Waltham, 1979.

Spring, Anita, and Art Hansen. 'The Underside of Development: Agricultural Development and Women in Zambia'. *Agriculture and Human Values* 2, No. 1 (1985): 60–67.

Steel, E.A. 'Zambezi-Congo Watershed'. *The Geographical Journal* 50, No. 3 (1917): 180–93.

Stoler, Ann L. *Along the Archival Grain: Epistemic Anxieties and Colonial Common Sense.* Princeton: Princeton University Press, 2009.

Sunseri, Thaddeus. 'Labour Migration in Colonial Tanzania and the Hegemony of South African Historiography', *African Affairs* 95, No. 381 (1996): 581–98.

Taaffe, Edward J., Richard L. Morrill, and Peter B. Gould. 'Transport Expansion in Underdeveloped Countries: A Comparative Analysis', *Geographical Review* 53, No. 4 (1963): 503–29.

Thomas, Lynn M. 'Modernity's Failings, Political Claims, and Intermediate Concepts', *The American Historical Review* 116, No. 3 (2011): 727–40.

Thompson, Edward P. 'The Moral Economy of the English Crowd in the Eighteenth Century'. *Past and Present* 50 (1971): 76–136.

Thornton, John. 'Precolonial African Industry and the Atlantic Trade, 1500–1800'. *African Economic History* 19 (1990/1): 1–19.

Thornton, John. 'European Documents and African History'. In *Writing African History*, edited by John E. Philips, 254–65. Rochester: University of Rochester Press, 2005.

Tilley, Helen. 'African Environments & Environmental Sciences: The African Research Survey, Ecological Paradigms & British Colonial Development, 1920–40'. In *Social History & African Environments*, edited by William Beinart and JoAnn McGregor, 109–30. Athens: Ohio University Press, 2003.

Tosh, John. 'The Cash-Crop Revolution in Tropical Africa: An Agricultural Reappraisal'. *African Affairs* 79, No. 314 (1980): 79–94.

Trapnell, Colin G., and J. Neil Clothier. *The Soils, Vegetation, and Agricultural Systems of Northwestern Rhodesia: Report of the Ecological Survey.* 2nd edn., Lusaka: Government Printer, 1957.

Trentmann, Frank. 'Beyond Consumerism: New Historical Perspectives on Consumption'. *Journal of Contemporary History* 39, No. 3 (2004): 373–401.

Trentmann, Frank. 'Crossing Divides: Consumption and Globalization in History'. *Journal of Consumer Culture* 9, No. 2 (2009): 187–220.

Trentmann, Frank, ed. *The Oxford Handbook of the History of Consumption.* Oxford: Oxford University Press, 2012.

Tsing, Anna L. 'From the Margins'. *Cultural Anthropology* 9, No. 3 (1994): 279–97.

Tuck, Michael W. '"The Rupee Disease": Taxation, Authority, and Social Conditions in Early Colonial Uganda'. *International Journal of African Historical Studies* 39, No. 2 (2006): 221–45.

Tuck, Michael W. 'Woodland Commodities, Global Trade, and Local Struggles: The Beeswax Trade in British Tanzania'. *Journal of Eastern African Studies* 3, No. 2 (2009): 259–74.

Turkon, David. 'Modernity, Tradition and the Demystification of Cattle in Lesotho'. *African Studies* 62, No. 2 (2003): 147–69.

Turner, Edith. 'Philip Kabwita, Ghost Doctor: The Ndembu in 1985'. *The Drama Review* 30, No. 4 (1986): 12–35.

Turner, Edith. 'Zambia's Kankanga Dances: The Changing Life of Ritual'. *Performing Arts Journal* 10, No. 3 (1987): 57–71.

Turner, Edith. *Experiencing Ritual: A New Interpretation of African Healing.* Philadelphia: University of Pennsylvania Press, 1992.

Turner, Victor W. 'The Spatial Separation of Generations in Ndembu Village Structure'. *Africa* 25, No. 2 (1955): 121–37.

Turner, Victor W., and Edith L.B. Turner. 'Money Economy Among the Mwinilunga Ndembu: A Study of Some Individual Cash Budgets'. *Rhodes-Livingstone Journal* 18 (1955): 19–37.

Turner, Victor W. 'A Lunda Love Story and Its Consequences'. *Rhodes Livingstone Journal* 19 (1955): 1–26.

Turner, Victor W. *Schism and Continuity in an African Society: A Study of Ndembu Village Life*. Manchester: Manchester University Press, 1957.

Turner, Victor W. 'Themes in the Symbolism of Ndembu Hunting Ritual'. *Anthropological Quarterly* 35, No. 2 (1962): 37–57.

Turner, Victor W. *The Drums of Affliction: A Study of Religious Processes Among the Ndembu of Zambia*. Oxford: Clarendon Press, 1968.

Turner, Victor W. *The Ritual Process: Structure and Anti-Structure*. New Brunswick: Transaction Publishers, 1969.

Turner, Victor W. *The Forest of Symbols: Aspects of Ndembu Ritual*. Ithaca: Cornell University Press, 1970.

Turner, Victor W. 'Lunda Rites and Ceremonies'. *The Occasional Papers of the Rhodes-Livingstone Museum* 1974, 335–88.

Turner, Victor W. *Dramas, Fields, and Metaphors: Symbolic Action in Human Society*. Ithaca: Cornell University Press, 1974.

Turner, Victor W. *On the Edge of the Bush: Anthropology as Experience*. Tucson: University of Arizona Press, 1985.

Ubink, Janine. 'Traditional Authority Revisited: Popular Perceptions of Chiefs and Chieftaincy In Peri-Urban Kumasi, Ghana'. *Journal of Legal Pluralism* 55 (2007): 123–61.

Urry, John. *Mobilities*. Cambridge: Polity, 2007.

Vail, Leroy, ed. *The Creation of Tribalism in Southern Africa*. Berkeley: University of California Press, 1989.

Van Alstine, James. 'Community and Company Capacity: The Challenge of Resource-led Development in Zambia's "New Copperbelt"'. *Community Development Journal* 48, No. 3 (2013): 360–76.

Van Binsbergen, Wim M.J. 'Globalization and Virtuality: Analytical Problems Posed by the Contemporary Transformation of African Societies'. *Development and Change* 29, No. 4 (1998): 873–903.

Van Binsbergen, Wim M.J. 'Manchester as the Birth Place of Modern Agency Research: The Manchester School Explained from the Perspective of Evans-Pritchard's Book "The Nuer"'. In *Strength Beyond Structure: Social and Historical Trajectories of Agency in Africa,* edited by Mirjam De Bruijn, Rijk Van Dijk, and Jan-Bart Gewald, 16–61. Leiden: Brill, 2007.

Van Binsbergen, Wim M.J. *Tears of Rain: Ethnicity and History in Central Western Zambia*. London: Routledge, 1992.

Vansina, Jan. 'Long-distance Trade-Routes in Central Africa'. *Journal of African History* 3, No. 3 (1962): 375–90.

Vansina, Jan. *Les anciens royaumes de la savane: Les états des savanes méridionales de l'Afrique central des origines á l'occupation coloniale*. Kinshasa: Université Lovanium Léopoldville, 1965.

Vansina, Jan. *Paths in the Rainforests: Toward a History of Political Tradition in Equato-rial Africa.* Madison: University of Wisconsin Press, 1990.

Vansina, Jan. 'Histoire du manioc en Afrique centrale avant 1850'. *Paideuma* 43 (1997): 255–79.

Vansina, Jan. *How Societies Are Born: Governance in West Central Africa.* Charlottesville: The University of Virginia Press, 2004.

Vansina, Jan. 'Linguistic Evidence for the Introduction of Ironworking into Bantu-Speaking Africa'. *History in Africa* 33 (2006): 321–61.

Vansina, Jan. *Being Colonized: The Kuba Experience in Rural Congo, 1880–1960.* Madison: University of Wisconsin Press, 2010.

Van Teeffelen, T. 'The Manchester School in Africa and Israel: A Critique'. *Dialectical Anthropology* 3, No. 1 (1978): 67–83.

Van Velsen, Jaap. 'Labour Migration as a Positive Factor in the Continuity of Tonga Tribal Society'. In *Social Change in Modern Africa,* edited by Aidan Southall, 230–41. Oxford: Oxford University Press, 1961.

Vellut, Jean-Luc. 'Notes sur le Lunda et la frontière luso-africaine (1700–1900)'. *Études d'histoire africaine* 3 (1972): 61–166.

Vellut, Jean-Luc. 'Diversification de l'économie de la cueillette: Miel et cire dans les sociétés da la forêt claire d'Afrique centrale (c. 1750–1950)'. *African Economic History* 7 (1979): 93–112.

Vellut, Jean-Luc. 'Mining in the Belgian Congo'. In *History of Central Africa II,* edited by David Birmingham and Phyllis M. Martin, 126–62. London: Longman, 1998.

Vellut, Jean-Luc. 'Angola-Congo. L'invention de la frontière du Lunda (1889–1893)'. *Africana Studia* 9 (2006): 159–84.

Vickery, Kenneth P. 'Saving Settlers: Maize Control in Northern Rhodesia'. *Journal of Southern African Studies* 11, No. 2 (1985): 212–34.

Vickery, Kenneth P. *Black and White in Southern Zambia: The Tonga Plateau Economy and British Imperialism, 1890–1939.* New York: Greenwood Publishing, 1986.

Von Onselen, Charles. *Chibaro: African Mine Labour in Southern Rhodesia, 1900–1933.* Pluto Press, 1976.

Von Oppen, Achim. '"Endogene agrarrevolution" im vorkolonialen Afrika?: Eine fall-studie'. *Paideuma* 38 (1992): 269–96.

Von Oppen, Achim. *Terms of Trade and Terms of Trust: The History and Contexts of Pre-Colonial Market Production Around the Upper Zambezi and Kasai.* Münster: LIT Verlag, 1994.

Von Oppen, Achim. 'Cassava, "The Lazy Man's Food"? Indigenous Agricultural Innova-tion and Dietary Change in Northwestern Zambia (ca. 1650–1970)'. In *Changing Food Habits: Case Studies from Africa, South America and Europe,* edited by Carola Lentz, 43–72. London: Routledge, 1999.

Von Oppen, Achim. 'Cinderella Province: Discourses of Locality and Nation State in a Zambian Periphery (1950s to 1990s)'. *Sociologus* 52 (2002): 11–46.

Von Oppen, Achim. 'Bounding Villages: The Enclosure of Locality in Central Africa, 1890s to 1990s'. Habilitationsgeschrift, Humboldt University of Berlin, 2003.

Von Oppen, Achim. 'A Place in the World: Markers of the Local Along the Upper Zambezi'. In *Between Resistance and Expansion: Explorations of Local Vitality in Africa*, edited by Peter Probst and Gerd Spittler, 175–92. Münster: LIT Verlag, 2004.

Von Oppen, Achim. 'The Village as Territory: Enclosing Locality in Northwest Zambia, 1950s to 1990s'. *Journal of African History* 47, No. 1 (2006): 57–75.

Waters, Tony. 'A Cultural Analysis of the Economy of Affection and the Uncaptured Peasantry in Tanzania'. *The Journal of Modern African Studies* 30, No. 1 (1992): 163–75.

Waters, Tony. 'The Persistence of Subsistence and the Limits to Development Studies: The Challenge of Tanzania'. *Africa* 70, No. 4 (2000): 614–52.

Watson, William. *Tribal Cohesion in a Money Economy: A Study of the Mambwe People of Northern Rhodesia*. Manchester: Manchester University Press, 1958.

Webb Jr., J.L.A. 'Toward the Comparative Study of Money: A Reconsideration of West African Currencies and Neo-Classical Monetary Concepts'. *The International Journal of African Historical Studies* 15, No. 3 (1982): 455–66.

Wele, Patrick M. *Kaunda and Mushala Rebellion: The Untold Story*. Lusaka: Multimedia Publications, 1987.

Wele, Patrick M. *Zambia's Most Famous Dissidents: From Mushala to Luchembe*. Solwezi, 1995.

Werbner, Richard P. 'The Manchester School in South-Central Africa'. *Annual Review of Anthropology* 13 (1984): 157–85.

White, C.M.N. 'Notes on the Circumcision Rites of the Balovale Tribes'. *African Studies* 12, No. 2 (1953): 41–56.

White, C.M.N. 'Clan, Chieftainship, and Slavery in Luvale Political Organization'. *Africa* 27, No. 1 (1957): 59–75.

White, Landeg. *Magomero: Portrait of an African Village*. Cambridge: Cambridge University Press, 1987.

White, Luise. *Speaking with Vampires: Rumor and History in Colonial Africa*. Berkeley: University of California Press, 2000.

Wilson, Godfrey, and Monica H. Wilson. *The Analysis of Social Change: Based on Observations in Central Africa*. Cambridge: Cambridge University Press, 1945.

Wilson, Godfrey. *The Economics of Detribalization in Northern Rhodesia I & II*. Rhodes-Livingstone Papers, No. 5–6. Manchester: Manchester University Press, 1942; reprinted 1968.

Wilson, Monica H. 'Zig-zag Change'. *Africa* 46, No. 4 (1976): 399–409.

Wood, Adrian P., et al., ed. *The Dynamics of Agricultural Policy and Reform in Zambia*. Basingstoke: Macmillan, 1990.

Yusuf, Shehu T. 'Stealing from the Railways: Blacksmiths, Colonialism and Innovation in Northern Nigeria'. In *Transforming Innovations in Africa: Explorative Studies on Appropriation in African Societies,* edited by Jan-Bart Gewald, André Leliveld, and Iva Peša, 275–95. Leiden: Brill, 2012.

III: Oral Sources: Interviews

Mwinilunga (2008)

Julian Chiyezhi, 5 September 2008, Mwinilunga.

Katoka, 5 September 2008, Mwinilunga.

Ethel Muvila, 5 September 2008, Mwinilunga.

Samugole, 6 September 2008, Mwinilunga.

Kawangu, 6 September 2008, Mwinilunga.

Ian Ntambu, 7 September 2008, Mwinilunga.

Solomon Kanswata, 8 September 2008 and 18 October 2008, Mwinilunga.

Kamwana, 18 October 2008, Mwinilunga.

Chitambala, 12 December 2008, Mwinilunga.

Mapulanga, 12 December 2008, Mwinilunga.

Mwangala, 8 September 2008, Mwinilunga.

Alfred Lupinda, 12 December 2008, Mwinilunga.

Luvua, 30 September 30 2008, Mwinilunga.

Ambrose Musanda, 1 October 2008, Mwinilunga.

Paul Chitadi, 8 September 2008, Kampemba.

Damson Kazeya, 9 September 2008, Kampemba.

Brian Kandamba, 9 September 2008, Kampemba.

Boaz Chitokola, 10 September 2008, Kampemba.

Kanongesha (2008)

John J. Chiyuka, 10 September 2008, Kanongesha.

Chief Kanongesha's mother and uncle, 11 September 2008, Kanongesha.

Daimon Sambongi, 11 September 2008, Kanongesha.

Spoon Kapanga, Headman of Wenga village, 12 September 2008, Kanongesha.

Headman Kazovu and Headman Kashiku, 12 September 2008, Kanongesha.

Maimbo and Katongo, 13 September 2008, Kanongesha.

Ikelenge (2008)

Mutale and Mbewe, 15 September 2008, Ikelenge.

Chieftainess Ikelenge, 16 September 2008, Ikelenge.

Headman Samahina and his wife, 16 September 2008, Ikelenge.

Margaret Mulopa, Harry Ventina and Larson Samahina, 16 September 2008, Ikelenge.

John Kapaypi, 16 September 2008, Ikelenge.

Benson Kema, 17 September 2008, Ikelenge.

M. Keshala, 17 September 2008, Ikelenge.

Headman Felix Ntemba, 17 September 2008, Ikelenge.

Konsul Chinyama, 17 September 2008, Ikelenge.

Paul Soneka, 17 September 2008, Ikelenge.

Morris Chipoya, 18 September 2008, Ikelenge.

Headman Chimbila and Skin Chimbila, 18 September 2008, Ikelenge.

Martin Muzeya, 19 September 2008, Ikelenge.

Fordson Deyau, 19 September 2008, Ikelenge.

Judy Mudimina, 19 September 2008, Ikelenge.

Alfonsina Kusaloka, 19 September 2008, Ikelenge.

Argret Otela, 19 September 2008, Ikelenge.

Florence Mukona, 22 September 2008, Ikelenge.

Venus Kalusa, 22 September 2008, Ikelenge.

Edson Pondala, 22 September 2008, Ikelenge.

Headman Frank Chipoya, 22 September 2008, Ikelenge.

Nyakaseya (2008)

Zaza, 23 September 2008, Nyakaseya.

Aaron Chiyuma, 23 September 2008, Nyakaseya.

Paddy Samakai, 23 September 2008, Nyakaseya.

Sawita, 24 September 2008, Nyakaseya.

William Zavwiyi, 24 September 2008, Nyakaseya.

Frank Kafolesha, 24 September 2008, Nyakaseya.

Gibson, 25 September 2008, Nyakaseya.

Ngelekwa Kapenda, 25 September 2008, Nyakaseya.

Paul Lemba, 25 September 2008, Nyakaseya.

Paul Poidevin, Headmaster Sakeji School, 20 September 2008, Hillwood Farm.

Mel Ferguson, 26 September 2008, Hillwood Farm.

Esther and Hilda, Hillwood farm orphanage, 28 September 2008, Hillwood Farm.

Paul Fisher, 27 September 2008, Hillwood Farm.

Chibwika (2008)

Phiri, Kalusa and Kayama, 2 October 2008, Chibwika.

Chief Chibwika, 2 October 2008, Chibwika.

Headman Kadoka, 2 October 2008, Chibwika.

Headman Kasapatu, 2 October 2008, Chibwika.

Benwa, 2 October 2008, Chibwika.

Elias Kalenga, 3 October 2008, Chibwika.

Muhemba, 4 October 2008, Chibwika.

Kamiji, 4 October 2008, Chibwika.

Samanjombi, Chief Chibwika's brother, 4 October 2008, Chibwika.

Maria Samanjombi, Chief Chibwika's sister, 4 October 2008, Chibwika.

Godfrey, 4 October 2008, Chibwika.

Chiyesu, 5 October 2008, Chibwika.

Mangalasa, 5 October 2008, Chibwika.

Bibiana, 5 October 2008, Chibwika.

Agnes Kasweulu, 6 October 2008, Chibwika.

Ntambu (2008)

Chinshe, 13 October 2008, Ntambu.

Masamba, 8 October 2008, Ntambu.

Helford Masamba, 9 October 2008, Ntambu.

Han Manyingu, 9 October 2008, Ntambu.

Benja Sampoko, 9 October 2008, Ntambu.

Yesta Muyutu and her mother, 9 October 2008, Ntambu.

Kasonda, 10 October 2008, Ntambu.

Harrison Makina, 10 October 2008, Ntambu.

Andrew Kambowa, 10 October 2008, Ntambu.

Paul Mapende, 10 October 2008, Ntambu.

Harrison Zimba, 10 October 2008, Ntambu.

Lorence Floranga, 10 October 2008, Ntambu.

Royman Chimanasa, 11 October 2008, Ntambu.

Venus Makariki, 11 October 2008, Ntambu.

Jonas Luvey, 11 October 2008, Ntambu.

Tedson Kanjima, 12 October 2008, Ntambu.

Alfonsina Chingangu, 15 October 2008, Ntambu.

Charles Walanga, 15 October 2008, Ntambu.

Benwell, 16 October 2008, Ntambu.

Kanyama (2008)

Ngambi, 9 December 2008, Kanyama.

Headman Kakeza, 9 December 2008, Kanyama.

Godfrey Masambwisha, 9 December 2008, Kanyama.

Chief Kanyama, 9 December 2008, Kanyama.

Grace Mulusa, 10 December 2008, Kanyama.

Headman Noah Ipoza, 10 December 2008, Kanyama.

Lukwesa Kajimoto, 10 December 2008, Kanyama.

Lusaka (2010)
Andrew Sardanis, 14 December 2009, Lusaka.
Peter Matoka, 9 January 2010, Lusaka.
Metheryn Katoka, 10 January 2010, Lusaka.
Wilson Nswana Kanyembo, 16 January 2010, Lusaka.
Ada Ikombu, 17 January 2010, Lusaka.
Brighton Matoka, 18 January 2010, Lusaka.
Kabwiku, 19 January 2010, Lusaka.
Philip Lemba, 27 January 2010, Lusaka.
Fesa Kaumba, 28 January 2010, Lusaka.
Leonard Kantumoya, 29 January 2010, Lusaka.

Copperbelt (2010)
Mama Mapesa, 2 February 2010, Ndola.
Georgina, 4 February 2010, Ndola.
Lucy and Gladys, 6 February 2010, Kalulushi.
Sambaulu, 10 February 2010, Ndola.
Everyn, 13 February 2010, Kakolo, Kitwe.
Jane Chibote, 14 February 2010, Kalulushi.
Pastor Jacob, 14 February 2010, Chibuluma.
Setty Chitukutuku, 17 February 2010, Kitwe.
Chiyengi, 17 February 2010, Kitwe.
Lilian Chiyesu, 25 February 2010, Ndola.
William Ngangu, 26 February 2010, Ndola.

Ikelenge (2010)
Makajina Kahilu, 8 March 2010, Ikelenge.
Goodwell Masomba and Fibby Chinjambo, 8 March 2010, Ikelenge.
Ngomi Kamafumbu, 8 March 2010, Ikelenge.
Mandamu Sapotu, 10 March 2010, Ikelenge.
Anyes Samukoko, 10 March 2010, Ikelenge.
Lontina Chilengi, 10 March 2010, Ikelenge.
Peter Machai, 10 March 2010, Ikelenge.
Yines Solwezi, 10 March 2010, Ikelenge.
Fesa, 11 March 2010, Ikelenge.
Rose Matafwali, 13 March 2010, Ikelenge.
Kona Ilunga, 15 March 2010, Ikelenge.
Thomas Makondo, 15 March 2010, Ikelenge.
Ilunga, 16 March 2010, Ikelenge.
John Kapayipi, 17 March 2010, Ikelenge.
Larson Samahina and his wife, 17 March 2010, Ikelenge.

Joshua Kapiya, 18 March 2010, Ikelenge.

Elyss Chinjamba, 18 March 2010, Ikelenge.

Alick Nfweta, 19 March 2010, Ikelenge.

Kambolokonyi Chingonyu, 19 March 2010, Ikelenge.

Saipilinga Kahongo, 22 March 2010, Ikelenge.

Alick Ndumba, 23 March 2010, Ikelenge.

Kephas Sakwimba, 24 March & 9 April 2010, Ikelenge.

John Kakoma, 2 April 2010, Ikelenge.

Fred Chisenga Tambo, 6 April 2010, Ikelenge.

Beth Kanungulu, 6 April 2010, Ikelenge.

Alfonsina, 7 April 2010, Ikelenge.

Rosina Sakandula, 8 April 2010, Ikelenge.

William Chiyanzu, 9 April 2010, Ikelenge.

Yiness Ikelenge, 10 April 2010, Ikelenge.

Wilson Kasochi Kabanda, 12 April 2010, Ikelenge.

Sahandu Fwalice, James Kinga and Damson Chihamba, 13 April 2010.

Nakineli, 14 April 2010, Ikelenge.

Josephine Sokawuta, 15 April 2010, Ikelenge.

Jackson Samakai, 16 April 2010, Ikelenge.

Louis Kasongu, 17 April 2010, Ikelenge.

Ngomi and Nanci Kamafumbu, 19 April 2010, Ikelenge.

Donas Katanda, 19 April 2010, Ikelenge.

Moris Sakakomba, 20 April 2010, Ikelenge.

Sokawuta, 22 & 23 April 2010, Ikelenge.

Benwa Lukama, 23 April 2010, Ikelenge.

Shame Kamundongu, 24 April 2010, Ikelenge.

Nyakaseya (2010)

Zakewa Kahangu, 26 April 2010, Nyakaseya.

Aaron Chikewa, 27 April 2010, Nyakaseya.

Wombeki, 27 April, 11 May & 24 May 2010, Nyakaseya.

Samuel Nshindwa, 28 April 2010, Nyakaseya.

Sefukah Kazomba, 28 April 2010, Nyakaseya.

Marciana and Suzana, 29 April 2010, Nyakaseya.

Fanwel, Reece Samakai and Andele Maciana, 30 April & 5 May 2010, Nyakaseya.

Pierre Shimishi, 1 May 2010, Nyakaseya.

Bernard, 3 May 2010, Nyakaseya.

Goldwel Mushindi, 3 May 2010, Nyakaseya.

Mandama, Nyota Chingaji, Evelina Chidimi and Donia Mahongo, 4 May 2010, Nyamu-
    weji, Nyakaseya.

William Zavwiji, 5 May 2010, Nyakaseya.

Suze Savita, 7 May 2010, Nyakaseya.

Chilaudi Chiyanzu, 7 May 2010, Nyakaseya.

Zabetha Nkemba, 8 May 2010, Nyakaseya.

Mischek Alfons Maseka, 11 May 2010, Nyakaseya.

Mushipi Musungumuki, 12 May 2010, Nyakaseya.

Paulina Kahemba, 12 May 2010, Nyakaseya.

Christina Kalumbu, 13 May 2010, Nyakaseya.

Venus Petrol Kayombo, 15 May 2010, Nyakaseya.

Maladi Mukomena Ntanda, 16 May 2010, Nyakaseya.

Levu Mongu, 17 May 2010, Nyakaseya.

Mazondu Sanyikosa, 17 May 2010, Nyakaseya.

Paul Maseka, 18 May 2010, Nyakaseya.

Group Interview, Kayuka Village, 19 May 2010, Nyakaseya.

Smata Chimbimbi Muchayila, 19 May 2010, Nyakaseya.

Kabanda, 22 May 2010, Nyakaseya.

Kanongesha (2010)

Spoon Kapanga, 26 July 2010, Kanongesha.

Headman Kazovu, 26 July 2010, Kanongesha.

Headman Kachacha, 27 & 31 July 2010, Kanongesha.

Margaret Kachai, 27 July 2010, Kanongesha.

Mamfwela Moris, 28 July 2010, Kanongesha.

Kasongu Mapulanga, 29 July & 17 August 2010, Kanongesha.

Ridgeway, 30 July 2010, Kanongesha.

Nsombi, 30 July 2010, Kanongesha.

Mandosa Kabanda, 2 August 2010, Kanongesha.

Fred Mpenji, 3 August 2010, Kanongesha.

Shimishi, 4 August 2010, Kanongesha.

Brother Joe Weisling, 4 August 2010, Kanongesha.

Lukaki Salukenga and Lutaya, 6 August 2010, Kanongesha.

Robert Sakawumba, 6 August 2010, Kanongesha.

Mandosa, 10 August 2010, Kanongesha.

Jesman Sambaulu, 10 August 2010, Kanongesha.

Ntambu Lukonkesha, 11 August 2010, Kanongesha.

Chief Kanongesha's mother, 12 August 2010, Kanongesha.

Headman Chinkonja, 13 August 2010, Kanongesha.

Windson Mbimbi, 14 August & 6 September 2010, Kanongesha.

Amon Sawila, 7 September 2010, Kanongesha.

Juda Sapetulu, 8 September 2010, Kanongesha.

Chief Kanongesha from Angola, 10 September 2010, Kanongesha.

Suckling, Representative of Chief Chibwika, 14 September 2010, Kanongesha.

Ntambu (*2010*)

Peter Ndumba, 27 September 2010, Ntambu.

Enia, 28 September 2010, Ntambu.

Amon Kakisa, 28 September 2010, Ntambu.

Thomas, 29 September 2010, Ntambu.

Martin Kahangu, 30 September 2010, Ntambu.

Kasonda, 1 October 2010, Ntambu.

Andrew Kambowa, 2 October 2010, Ntambu.

Headman Mpurumba and Kamena, 4 October 2010, Ntambu.

James Kasonga, 4 October 2010, Ntambu.

Mukosayi Mujunga, 5 October 2010, Ntambu.

Kadansonu Mukeya, 7 October 2010, Ntambu.

Doris Kandumba, 9 October 2010, Ntambu.

Tepson Kandungu, 11 October 2010, Ntambu.

Fascen Ndoji, 12 October 2010, Ntambu.

Bigwan Masondi, 13 October 2010, Ntambu.

Steven Chikwili, 14 October 2010, Ntambu.

Headman Kayongi, 15 October 2010, Ntambu.

Elias Kapokosu, 15 October 2010, Ntambu.

Peter Luberenga, 18 October 2010, Ntambu.

Bandwell Mulandu, 20 October 2010, Ntambu.

Karekanya Katanvwa, 21 October 2010, Ntambu.

Justin Kambidimba, 22 October 2010, Ntambu.

Mwinilunga (*2010*)

Group Interview, Kakuula Machai, 29 March 2010, Mwinilunga.

Group Interview, Kampemba, 30 March 2010, Mwinilunga.

Ntanga, 4 March & 27 October 2010, Mwinilunga.

Julius Musesa, 28 October 2010, Mwinilunga.

Filip Chiyangi Kayawu, 29 October 2010, Mwinilunga.

Jacob Chiyengi, 29 October 2010, Mwinilunga.

Headman Mwinilunga, 31 October 2010, Mwinilunga.

Beston Mapulanga, 1 November 2010, Mwinilunga.

Chief Mukangala, 3 November 2010, Mwinilunga.

Miscellaneous

Betty Dening, 1 July 2011, United Kingdom.

Index

African National Congress   85–88, 194–97,
   322, 351
agriculture   95–162
   beans   58, 78, 81, 89, 101–02, 121, 125, 158,
      161, 243, 289
   cash crops   33, 78, 83, 90, 103, 105, 111–14,
      124–28, 151, 157–60, 206
   see cassava
   foundations of production   39, 98–109,
      112–14, 123, 137, 144, 150, 157–62, 373
   fruit   4, 112, 114, 116–17, 151–55
   groundnuts   36, 58, 81, 89, 158–59
   input   9, 111, 121–23, 127, 149, 158, 245, 247
   intercropping   99, 102
   loan schemes   87–89, 109, 122–23, 139,
      195, 322
   see maize
   marketing of agricultural produce   9,
      79–80, 88–91, 96, 104–15, 119, 121–29,
      141–44, 147–61, 180, 239, 245–47, 320
   see millet, pineapples
   rice   79, 81, 89–90, 100, 121, 127, 158–59
   slash-and-burn (chitemene)   101, 109, 117,
      312
   see sorghum
   subsistence   9, 39, 95–98, 102–108, 114,
      118–19, 121–28, 130, 135–37, 144–45,
      150–51, 158–62, 256, 259–60, 264, 293,
      370, 373
   sweet potatoes   55, 102, 114
   vegetables   89, 102, 152
ancestors   45, 50, 304
Angola   1–2, 9, 30, 46, 55, 58–59, 65, 67–68,
      72, 74, 78, 80–81, 85, 87–91, 118, 121,
      136–37, 143–47, 151–52, 168–69, 171–81,
      185–99, 208–09, 244, 254, 261–62, 287,
      294, 341
   civil war   180–81, 185, 197
   refugees   9, 190–94
animal husbandry see livestock
animal skins   47–48, 55, 134, 265, 280,
      283–85, 291, 297
archives
   Echoes of Service   34, 388–89
   National Archives of Zambia   34, 377–84

Public Records Office   34, 389
Rhodes House library   34, 388
United National Independence Party   34,
      384–87
Zambia Consolidated Copper Mines   34,
      387–88

Barotseland   134
barter   55, 78, 104–05, 257–59, 262, 265, 273,
      290, 294, 318
beads   47, 55–60, 146, 235, 265–68, 285, 288,
      317, 319, 343
beer   117, 146, 155
beeswax   56, 58–59, 61–62, 96, 145–51, 157,
      161, 210, 265, 288, 294
Bemba   195, 215, 220
Berlin Conference   65–66
bicycle   78–80, 235, 248, 256–57, 269, 275,
      279, 309, 372
'Big Man'   232, 249, 323, 334, 337, 357,
      362–63, 367
boundary   172–99
   chiefly   74, 87, 220, 341
   demarcation   48, 64, 76, 81, 171–76, 216,
      341
   international   29, 68, 85, 89, 135–37, 147,
      166, 176–79, 181–99, 207–08, 217–18, 254,
      261, 287
Brethren, Plymouth   34, 152, 244, 290, 351
bridewealth   57, 235, 288–89, 318
British South Africa Company   66, 70
Broken Hill (Kabwe)   218, 281
Bruce-Miller, F.V.   173, 274, 277, 334–35, 346

Cameron, Verney Lovett   56n76, 59, 283, 287,
      302, 334
Capelo, Hermenegildo and Roberto
      Ivens   46–47, 265
capitalism   26–30, 78, 83–84, 103, 106–07, 171,
      229, 332, 337, 339, 367, 371, 373
capitao   149, 219
cash economy   5, 16, 103, 237, 333, 337, 356,
      361
cassava   8–9, 55, 68, 78, 81–82, 89, 96,
      99–100, 102, 114–28, 144, 155, 157–63, 176,

182–83, 239, 241, 247–48, 290,
    318, 338, 371
cattle   79, 138–40, 142–43, 181, 227, 247
census   66, 71, 110, 171, 207, 222n384,
    243–44, 309, 352
charms   63, 136, 218, 249
Chibinda Ilunga   129
chiefs
    Chibwika   57, 344, 350
    Ikelenge   37, 49, 152, 155, 310, 329, 339,
        349–51
    Kakoma   287, 350
    Kanongesha   37, 43, 48–49, 51, 63, 74,
        86–87, 94, 169, 172, 341, 346, 350–51
    Kanyama   350
    Mukangala   50
    Mwinimilamba   49, 50n43, 75–76
    Ntambu   37, 344, 350
    Ntambu Sachitolu   75, 350–51
    Nyakaseya   37, 49, 62, 75, 155, 226, 339,
        350
    Sailunga   48n28, 55, 62, 345, 350–51
chieftaincy   43, 45–57, 63–65, 74–75, 77, 80,
    84–87, 90, 129, 135, 143, 169–72, 189, 192,
    195, 197, 209, 216, 263, 283, 287, 294,
    298–99, 311–12, 335–36, 339, 340–55
Chingola   2, 225–26
Chinyama   46
Chisemwa ChaLunda   43, 341, 346, 354
Chokwe   48, 61–62
Cinderella Province   77, 79, 188
climate, of Mwinilunga   99–102, 122, 284
Clothier, J. Neil   100n24, 145
clothing   7, 55, 57–60, 146, 154, 176, 182, 256,
    265–68, 280–300, 319, 322–23, 343, 372
    see animal skins
    bark cloth   256, 265, 280, 283, 285, 291,
        296, 298
    calico   47, 56–57, 60, 176–78, 182, 235, 265,
        273, 285, 287–92, 297, 322
    store-bought cloth (*chitenge*)   297, 299
colonial occupation, of Mwinilunga   10–11,
    65–70, 206–08
Columbian exchange   118, 121
Congo   30, 45–46, 57, 67–68, 70–72, 78,
    80–81, 87, 136–37, 140–41, 143–44, 157,
    168–69, 172–99, 205, 207–10, 214, 217–20,
    244, 341
co-operatives   88, 148–49, 365

Copperbelt   25, 77–78, 80–81, 87–88, 117, 122,
    139–41, 144, 153–54, 157, 183, 187, 189,
    197, 210, 217–29, 233–34, 242, 251, 369
craft production   250, 260–61, 264, 270–79
    baskets   261, 264
    iron tools *see* metallurgy
    mats   54, 260–61, 264
    pots   148, 235, 254, 256, 261–62, 264
    specialisation   54–55, 264

dambo   100, 139
Dening, R.C.   338, 388
detribalisation   7, 167, 201
development schemes
    Intensive Development Zones   89, 109,
        112, 312
    peasant farming scheme   111–12
District Commissioners *see* Frederick Vernon
    Bruce-Miller, Richard Cranmer Den-
    ing, William Grant, George Alexander
    MacGregor, N.S. Price, Robin Short,
    H.B. Waugh, Theodore Williams

education   78, 85, 88–90, 113, 192, 244–45,
    279, 313, 342, 350, 365
Élisabethville (Lubumbashi)   191, 218, 224
ethnicity   43n3, 179, 186, 189, 194
everyday history   32, 339

Ferguson, James   14–15, 18, 20, 161–62
fertility   271, 304, 323, 358, 360
firearms   47, 55, 58–62, 72, 85, 118, 129–30,
    134, 136, 143, 169, 176–78, 191, 265–66,
    318–19, 343
Fisher, Alfred Digby   293
Fisher, ffolliott   147
Fisher, Singleton   377, 388
Fisher, Walter   69, 377, 388
fishing   52, 55, 78, 95, 98, 100–02, 170, 261, 305
    fishponds   78, 88
foraging   52, 71, 98, 102, 114–16, 128
forestry   2, 79, 100, 116, 146, 349

game *see also* hunting
    meat   47, 55, 135–37, 142–44, 176, 185, 265
    presence of   52, 100, 129–37, 143–44, 161
gender   16, 38, 53, 60, 133, 154, 223, 238,
    241–43, 261, 263–64, 273–75, 281,
    283–85, 297, 303–04, 332, 360

generation   16, 29, 84, 229, 274–76, 281, 301,
        333, 336–37, 346, 352, 358, 362, 365
Gibbons, Alfred St. Hill   51n46, 56n76, 62–63,
        134, 146
Gluckman, Max   13–14
Grant, William   99
guns *see* firearms
        gunpowder   55, 71, 136, 178, 180, 208n289,
        266

headman   4–5, 45, 51, 53–57, 63–65, 71,
        74–77, 80, 84, 90, 132, 192, 216, 268–69,
        287, 294, 298, 304, 315, 322–23, 325,
        334–39, 340–55, 362
Hillwood Farm   80, 138n250
honey   4, 55, 101, 115–17, 145–150
household   7, 102, 104, 112, 160, 242–43, 263,
        296, 322, 326, 334, 360, 363, 366
housing   300–315
        grass (*nkunka*)   4, 72, 303, 306, 329
        Kimberley (sundried) brick   7, 81–82,
        227, 248, 257, 301, 308–12, 314–16, 330,
        333, 338
        wattle and daub   263, 301, 303–06,
        308–09, 311–12, 314
hunting   48, 52, 58, 62, 95, 98–102, 109, 114,
        116, 128–37, 142–44, 160–62, 170, 219, 232,
        263–64, 284, 303, 305, 359, 366
        guilds   129n194, 264
        legislation   71, 85, 129–37, 143, 161, 185,
        349

Ikelenge, London   310
independence of Zambia   2, 24, 85–91, 112,
        185, 194–97, 230, 301, 344, 353–54, 365
Indian Ocean   55
indirect rule   74, 348–49
infrastructure   1–3, 5, 29, 79, 150, 188, 206,
        247
        railway   1–2, 43, 80, 180, 183, 186, 218, 277
        Benguela railway   1–2, 79–80, 147, 185
        line-of-rail   183, 186–187, 197, 231, 235,
        337
        roads   1–6, 8, 72, 78–80, 82–84, 88, 90, 118,
        153, 155, 195, 218, 334, 337–38, 371
initiation ceremony   38, 101, 170, 288, 303,
        366, 374
iron ore, deposits   101, 270–71

Ishinde   49, 341
ivory   47–48, 56, 58–59, 61–62, 72, 80, 134,
        146, 176–77, 265–68, 288, 294

Japau, Ronald John   86–87, 196–97
Jimbe   2, 80
Johannesburg   146–47, 218, 293

Kabompo River   55, 249
Kalahari sands   52, 100, 119
Kalusa, Walima   23–24, 374
Kambove   60, 218
Kanongesha, Ndembi   87
Kansanshi   2, 81, 153, 220
Kaonde   70
Kasempa   25, 130, 227, 261–62
Katanga   181, 183–84, 189, 192, 196–97, 220
Kaunda, Kenneth   85, 88, 195, 313, 353
Kazembe   46, 341
Kazembe Mutanda   49
kinship   5, 8, 14, 16, 28–29, 41, 46, 50–51, 53,
        179, 186–87, 194, 212, 317, 321, 332–33,
        338, 355–57, 360–66, 371, 373
        extended kinship   7–8, 29, 33, 41, 112,
        310–11, 332–33, 338–39, 356, 360–61,
        364–67
        family nucleation   6–7, 29, 33, 41, 112, 324,
        331–32, 338–39, 355–57, 361, 365
        individualisation   6–8, 12, 28–29, 33, 41,
        84, 132, 223, 257, 317, 321, 333, 338–40,
        355–59, 361, 365, 367, 371
Kipushi   220–21
Kitwe   224–25
knowledge (expertise)   65, 95, 97–99, 107–
        08, 147, 217, 233, 260, 263–64, 270–72,
        274–75, 278–80, 282, 316–17
Kolwezi   191, 218, 224, 227

labour migration   40, 71, 81, 126, 166, 201–53
        ethnic stereotyping   206, 212–15
        length of service   214
        pass laws   40, 71, 166, 171, 208n289, 219
        remittances   203, 236, 243, 246–50, 293
        rural decay   40, 81n220, 168, 199, 201,
        236–39, 244–46
        statistics (ratios)   126, 221–222, 239,
        243–44
        work ethic   204–05, 207, 213–14, 217, 253

labour recruitment   212–17, 221, 253, 342
  desertion   205–06, 213
  intermediaries   216, 340
land   28, 45, 50, 52–53, 82–83, 99, 102, 109,
    116–17, 120, 127, 140, 193, 237, 304, 343
  land tenure   343–44, 353
legitimate trade   61, 198
licence, hunting   71, 135–37
life history   14, 26, 36, 40, 221, 224–27, 253,
    373
livestock   54, 111, 114, 132, 138–44, 180–82, 210,
    273, 318 *see also* cattle
  chickens   141, 143, 181–82, 227, 264
  goats   138, 140–41, 143, 181–82, 290
  pigs   138, 140
  poultry   139–40, 180
  sheep   138, 140–41, 143, 181–82
Livingstone, David   51, 56n76, 58, 146, 151,
    262, 284–85, 292, 304, 319, 334, 342–43
Lualaba River   46, 57–58
Luanda   55
Luba   48, 129
Lueji   129
Lumwana   2, 242, 369
Lunda-Ndembu   48, 350
Lunda polity   45–51, 54–56, 59, 62, 86, 129,
    169–70, 172, 174–76, 189, 195–98, 265,
    340–41
Lusaka   29, 75, 151n327, 187, 197, 222, 233
Luvale   55, 61, 63n112

MacGregor, George Alexander   67–68, 96,
    179, 352
Macpherson, Fergus   22, 65
maize   8–9, 55, 58, 81, 89, 100–102, 114–15, 117,
    121–23, 127–29, 158, 183, 193
Mangangu, Rhodes   86
marginality   29, 77, 79, 85, 87, 91, 157, 178,
    187–90, 192, 195–99
marketing boards   88–89, 121–23
  Agricultural Rural Marketing Board
    123
marriage   28, 47, 51, 53, 170, 172, 198, 235,
    303, 305, 318, 360–61, 374 *see also*
    bridewealth
Matoka, Peter   87, 222, 277–78, 364
matriliny   16, 28, 45, 49, 52–53, 305, 333–34,
    338, 360–62

Mbwela   49–51, 91
medical facilities   23, 78, 85, 88, 90, 113, 195,
    365
messengers   66, 69, 213, 216, 242
metallurgy   270–79
  axes   169, 210, 247, 270–79, 317–18
  blacksmiths   169, 261, 263, 273–79, 318,
    325
  hoes   169, 210, 247, 264, 270–79, 318
  smelting   270–80, 317
millet   81, 102, 114–20, 123n165, 128–29, 161,
    241, 265, 307
mining   2, 80–82, 159, 166, 181, 218, 344,
    369
missions   34, 134n220, 152, 157, 210, 233,
    244, 257, 279, 285–86, 289–90, 293,
    351
  Kalene Hill (*see also*: Plymouth Brethren)
    80, 152, 226, 244
  Lwawu (Catholic)   225
mobility, importance of   29, 54, 129,
    165–254
  culture of mobility   167–68, 171–72, 176,
    187, 199, 201, 203, 211, 213, 218, 228, 243,
    253–54, 370
monetisation   29, 183–84, 271, 285, 290, 316,
    317–21
  British currency   147, 210, 289–90
  cloth currency   288–89, 317
moral economy   106–07
motorcar   79–80, 155–56, 180, 278, 329, 359
Mushala, Adamson   198
Musokantanda   46, 49, 55, 340
Musonoi   218
Musumba   45–47, 49, 56, 62, 63, 265, 340
Mutshatsha   80, 183, 186, 218
Mwantianvwa, Lunda Paramount Chief
    45–49, 59, 86

nationalism   86, 194–98, 298
Nchanga (Chingola)   2, 221, 225–26
Ndola   183, 218, 226
Nkumbula, Harry Mwaanga   85
Nyanja   195

oral history   10, 22, 34–36
oral tradition   34–35, 49, 51
Ovimbundu   55, 60, 129n194, 152, 176, 294

Pax Britannica   5, 120, 166

pineapples   2, 88–89, 106, 125–27, 151–57, 159, 161, 185, 188, 226, 245, 248, 298, 310, 324
  pineapple-canning factory G.M. Rucom   88–89, 153–56

portage   59, 62, 66, 69, 78, 203, 206 *see also* caravan trade

Price, N.S.   175

Pritchett, James Anthony   3, 10, 22, 29, 119, 266, 336, 339, 354–55, 357, 362, 364, 374

proletarianisation   26, 167, 201, 237

religion   21, 374
  Christianity   331
  indigenous *see* ritual

Rhodes Livingstone Institute, *see* Max Gluckman, Audrey Richards, Victor Turner, Godfrey and Monica Wilson   3, 12–18, 24–25, 28–29, 77n193, 81n220, 103n37, 166, 201, 375

Rhodes, Mangangu   86

Richards, Audrey   15, 26n149

ritual   15n85, 16–17, 21, 28, 38, 45–47, 50, 54, 74, 101, 104–05, 129–30, 140–41, 170n39, 272–73, 303–04, 314–15, 323, 347, 363–64, 374

road construction   2, 4–5, 78–83, 88–90, 195, 334, 337–38
  labour   71, 208, 210–11, 221, 240, 286, 290, 297, 342

rubber   56, 58, 61–62, 71–72, 148, 176–80, 207–08, 266, 268, 273, 288

rural-urban connection   64–90, 236–52 *see also* labour migration

Ruwe   218

salt   47–48, 55–56, 58–59, 65, 146, 261–62, 265, 319, 321

Samahina   152

schools *see* education

sedentarisation   40, 137, 140–41, 143, 162, 165, 173, 306–07

self-realisation   26, 168, 170, 188, 199, 201–03, 224, 231–36, 242–53, 258, 268–69, 272, 275, 294–95, 298, 309–10, 321–27, 357–58, 370, 373

settlement patterns   300–15, 333–39
  concentration   4, 52, 62–63, 72, 89–90, 112–13, 134n220, 208, 306, 348, 351–52

farm   83–84, 300, 314, 332–40, 354–56, 365, 367

roadside village   3, 5–6, 8, 30, 82–84, 90, 113, 371, 373

shifting   4, 52–53, 72n169, 82, 101, 109, 120, 137, 140, 143, 302, 307–08, 312

stockade   3–4, 62–64, 268, 305, 336, 348

shifting cultivation *see* agriculture

Short, Robin   142

Silva Porto, António da   282

slavery   57–64, 319
  slave raiding   3–4, 48, 61–64, 120, 171, 268, 305–06, 336, 348
  slave trade   48, 56–61, 72, 146, 176–77, 288, 294, 343

social change
  metanarrative of   3, 5–41, 43–44, 77n193, 165–66, 201–02, 223, 227–28, 331–33, 339, 355, 357, 366–67, 369–75

Solwezi   80, 153, 193, 219, 242

sorghum   81, 102, 114–20, 128, 161, 241, 265

South Africa   70, 205, 210

Southern Rhodesia (Zimbabwe)   70, 205, 210

spatial approach (locality)   3, 29–32, 40, 168, 187, 196, 201, 237, 245, 253–54, 374

taxation   10–11, 47, 66, 68–73, 75–76, 81, 110, 141, 166, 173, 180–82, 184, 190–92, 205–12, 217, 229, 237, 278, 320, 335, 342, 351–52
  hut tax   68–69, 180, 205, 207, 322
  tax default   70–71, 209, 219, 243–44, 289
  tax evasion   10–11, 68–71, 75–76, 180–81, 190–92, 205–12, 247

Tonga   195, 365

trade   47, 54–64, 72, 78, 80, 101, 104–05, 118–19, 121, 145–61, 176–90, 198, 226–27, 243, 248, 252, 254, 258–66, 284–88, 293–94, 319–20, 337–38, 342–43, 365
  caravan   55–62, 64, 78, 80, 96, 104, 118–19, 161, 179, 203, 265, 288, 342
  cross-border   54–64, 72, 76, 85, 141–42, 145–61, 168–69, 176–88, 284–88
  long-distance   8, 47, 54–62, 64–65, 78, 118, 121, 151, 172, 176–79, 190, 203, 258, 265, 273, 282, 288, 294, 319, 342, 348

traders
  African   5, 54–64, 78, 80, 146, 178, 226, 319, 337–38

INDEX										429

European   54–65, 149, 183
intermediaries   55–60, 342–43
Portuguese   55–64, 72, 147, 185, 207, 273
trading store   80, 83, 90, 145–61, 176–88, 258–66, 290
tradition   8–11, 16–18, 20–21, 43–44, 128, 161–62, 333, 339, 346, 349, 354, 364, 366–67, 375
Trapnell, Colin Graham   100n24, 145–46
tribute, payment of   45, 47–48, 55–57, 174, 176, 262, 265, 283, 287, 341–42
tsetse fly   79, 90, 132, 138, 143
Tshombe, Moïse   86, 189
Turner, Victor   3, 5–6, 10, 15–17, 28, 30, 40–41, 43–44, 53, 78, 83–84, 95, 131–32, 144, 232, 237, 244, 248, 291, 301, 303, 305, 315, 318, 321, 331–40, 347–48, 354–57, 360–65, 367, 374

Union Minière du Haut Katanga   220
United National Independence Party   34, 85–90, 92, 153, 187, 194–98, 301, 322, 365

Vansina, Jan   35, 37, 262, 267, 270

village fission   15, 315, 331–32, 336–37, 339, 344, 347, 352, 354, 362
Von Oppen, Achim   24, 31, 86n243, 119, 283n185, 319

Waugh, H.B.   336
wealth in people   40, 61, 64, 232, 258, 263, 266–69, 279–80, 288, 294, 298, 306, 310–12, 315–18, 322, 326–27, 336, 339–40, 343, 347–48, 354, 357–58, 360–62, 364, 366–67, 370, 372–73
White, C.M.N.   341, 345–46
Williams, Theodore   1, 68, 207, 209
Wilson, Godfrey and Monica   13n69, 15, 281, 369n1
witchcraft   63, 132–33, 141, 156, 170, 250, 252, 324, 356, 358–60, 366
work party   105n46, 310

Zambezi River   99, 173
Upper Zambezi   49, 51, 59n91, 118–19, 129, 169, 346
Zambezi District   142, 193
Zambia   1–2, 13, 21–29, 46, 87–90, 121, 141, 144, 157, 184–85, 187–88, 197–99, 220, 222, 233, 254, 299, 341, 353, 369, 373–74